THE

SACRED BOOKS OF THE HINDUS

EXTRA VOL. 4

AMS PRESS
NEW YORK

The Sacred Books of the Hindus
Translated by various Sanskrit Scholars
AND
Edited by Major B. D. Basu, I. M. S. (Retired)
Extra Volume 4

THE Aitareya Brahmanam of the Rigveda,

CONTAINING THE

EARLIEST SPECULATIONS OF THE BRAHMANS ON THE MEANING OF THE SACRIFICIAL PRAYERS,

AND ON

THE ORIGIN, PERFORMANCE AND SENSE OF THE

RITES OF THE VEDIC RELIGION

EDITED, TRANSLATED AND EXPLAINED, WITH PREFACE, INTRODUCTORY ESSAY, AND A MAP OF THE SACRIFICIAL COMPOUND AT THE SOMA SACRIFICE

BY

MARTIN HAUG, Ph. D.,

Superintendent of Sanscrit Studies in the Poona College, &c., &c.

REPRINTED AND PUBLISHED BY
SUDHINDRA NATH VASU, M. B., AT THE PANINI OFFICE,
BAHADURGANJ, ALLAHABAD.
1922.

Library of Congress Cataloging in Publication Data

Brahmanas. Aitareyabrāhmaṇa. English.
The Aitareya Brahmanam of the Rigveda.

Original ed., a reprint of Haugh's translation of 1863, minus the Sanskrit text, issued as extra v. 4 of The Sacred books of the Hindus.

Includes Sāyaṇa's commentary, the Mādhavīyavedārthaprakāśa.

I. Sāyana, son of Māyana, d. 1387. Mādhavīyavedārthaprakāśa. English. 1974. II. Haug, Martin, 1827-1876, tr. III. Title. IV. Series: The Sacred books of the Hindus, extra v. 4.

BL1119.5.A36E54 294'.12 73-3830
ISBN 0-404-57848-9

Reprinted from the edition of 1922, Allahabad
First AMS edition published, 1974
Manufactured in the United States of America

International Standard Book Number:
Complete Set: 0-404-57800-4
Extra Volume 4: 0-404-57848-9

AMS Press, INC.
New York, N.Y. 10003

THE
Aitareya Brahmanam of the Rigveda,

CONTAINING THE

EARLIEST SPECULATIONS OF THE BRAHMANS ON THE MEANING OF THE SACRIFICIAL PRAYERS,

AND ON

THE ORIGIN, PERFORMANCE AND SENSE OF THE

RITES OF THE VEDIC RELIGION

EDITED, TRANSLATED AND EXPLAINED, WITH PREFACE, INTRODUCTORY ESSAY, AND A MAP OF THE SACRIFICIAL COMPOUND AT THE SOMA SACRIFICE

BY

MARTIN HAUG, Ph. D.,

Superintendent of Sanscrit Studies in the Poona College, &c., &c.

REPRINTED AND PUBLISHED BY

SUDHINDRA NATH VASU, M. B., AT THE PANINI OFFICE,

BAHADURGANJ, ALLAHABAD.

1922.

FOREWARD
BY
THE EDITOR.

Dr. Martin Haug's translation of the Aitareya Brâhmaṇa has been out of print for a long time, and so it has been reprinted as an extra volume in the series of the Sacred Books of the Hindus. To facilitate references to the original edition, paging of that edition has been given in Square brackets, thus [ ]. It has not been considered necessary to reprint the Sanskrit text, as better editions of that text are now available.

Extracts from Professor Max Müller's review of this work are reproduced below :—

The Aitareya-brâhmaṇa, containing the earliest speculations of the Brahmaṇs on the meaning of their sacrificial prayers, and the purport of their ancient religious rites, is a work which could be properly edited nowhere but in India. It is only a small work of about two hundred pages, but it presupposes so thorough a familiarity with all the externals of the religion of the Brahmaṇs, the various offices of their priests, the times and seasons of their sacred rites, the form of their innumerable sacrificial utensils, and the preparation of their offerings, that no amount of Sanskrit scholarship, such as can be gained in England, would have been sufficient to unravel the intricate speculations concerning the matters which form the bulk of tho Aitareya-brâhmaṇa.........

The ancient Indian ceremonial, however, is one of the most artificial and complicated forms of worship that can well be imagined ; and though its details are, no doubt, most minutely described in the Brâhmaṇas and the Sûtras, yet, without having seen the actual site on which the sacrifices are offered, the altars constructed for the occasion, the instruments employed by different priests—the *tout-ensemble*, in fact, of the sacred rites—the reader seems to deal with words, but with words only, and is unable to reproduce in his imagination the acts and facts which were intended to be conveyed by them.........

Dr. Haug succeeded, however, at last in procuring the assistance of a real Doctor of Divinity, who had not only performed the minor Vedic sacrifices, such as the full and new moon offerings, but had officiated at some of the great Soma sacrifices, now very rarely to be seen in any part of India. He was induced, we are sorry to say, by very mercenary considerations, to perform the principal ceremonies in a secluded part of Dr. Haug's premises. This lasted five days, and the same assistance was afterwards rendered by the same worthy and some of his brethren whenever Dr. Haug was in any doubt as to the proper meaning of the ceremonial treatises which give the outlines of the Vedic sacrifices. Dr. Haug was actually allowed to taste that sacred beverage, the Soma, which gives health, wealth, wisdom, inspiration, nay immortality, to those who receive it from the hands of a twice-born priest.........

After having gone through all these ordeals. Dr. Haug may well say that his explanations of sacrificial terms, as given in the notes, can be relied upon as certain ; that they proceed from what he himself witnessed, and what he was able to learn from men who had inherited the kowledge from the most ancient times.........

In the preface to his edition of the Aitareya-brâhmaṇa, Dr. Haug has thrown out some new ideas on the chronology of Vedic literature which deserve careful consideration. Beginning with the hymns of the Rig-veda, he admits, indeed, that there are in that collection ancient and modern hymns, but he doubts whether it will be possible to draw a sharp line between what has been called the Chhandas period, representing the free growth of sacred poetry, and the Mantra period, during which the ancient hymns were supposed to have been collected and new ones added, chiefly intended for sacrificial purposes. Dr. Haug maintains that some hymns of a decidedly sacrificial character should be ascribed to the earliest period of Vedic poetry. He takes, for instance, the hymns describing the horse-sacrifice, and he concludes from the fact that seven priests only are mentioned in it by name, and that none of them belongs to the class of the Udgâtars (singers) and Brahmans (superintendents), that this hymn was written before the estabiishment of these two classes of priests. As these priests are mentioned in other Vedic hymns, he concludes that the hymn describing the horse-sacrifice is of a very early date. Dr. Haug strengthens his case by a reference to the Zoroastrian ceremonial, in which, as he says, the chanters and superintendents are entirely unknown, whereas the other two classes, the Hotars (reciters) and Adhvaryus (assistants) are mentioned by the same names as Zaotar and Rathwiskare. The establishment of the two new classes of priests would, therefore, seem to have taken place in India after the Zoroastrians had separated from the Brahmans ; and Dr. Haug would ascribe the Vedic hymns in which no more than two classes of priests are mentioned to a period preceding, others in which the other two classes of priests are mentioned to a period succeeding, that ancient schism......

According to Dr. Haug, the period during which the Vedic hymns were composed extends from 1400 to 2000 B. C. The oldest hymns, hewever, and the sacrificial formulas he would place between 2000 and 2400 B. C. This period, corresponding to what has been called the Chhandas and Mantra poriods, would be succeeded by the Brâhmaṇa period, and Dr. Haug would place the bulk of the Brâhmaṇas, all written in prose, between 1400 and 1200 B. C. He does not attribute much weight to the distinction made by the Brâhmaṇs themselves between revealed and profane literature, and would place the Sûtras almost contemporaneous with the Brâhmaṇas. The only fixed point from which he starts in his chronological arrangement is the date implied by the position of the solstitial points mentioned in a little treatise, the Jyotiṣa, a date which has been accurately fixed by the Rev. R. Main at 1186 B. C.* Dr. Haug fully admits that such an observation was an absolute necessity for the Brahmans in regulating their calendar :......

This argument of Dr. Haug's seems correct as far as the date of the establishment of the ceremonial is concerned, and it is curious that several scholars who have lately written on the origin of the Vedic calendar, and the possibility of its foreign origin, should not have perceived the intimate relation between that calendar and the whole ceremonial system of the Brahmans. Dr. Haug is, no doubt, perfectly right when he claims the invention of the Naksatras, or the Lunar Zodiac of the Brahmans, if we may so call it, for India ; he may be right also when he assigns the twelfth century as the earliest date for the origin of that simple astronomical system on which the calendar of the Vedic festivals is founded. He calls the theories of others, who have lately tried to claim the first discovery of the Nakṣatras for China, Babylon, or some other Asiatic country, absurd, and takes no notice of the sanguine expectations of certain scholars, who imagine they will soon have discovered the very means of the Indian Nakṣatras in Babylonian inscriptions. But does it follow that, because the ceremonial presupposes an observation of the solstitial points in about the twelfth century, therefore the theological works in which that ceremonial is explained, commented upon, and furnished with all kinds of mysterious meanings, were composed at that early date ? We see no stringency whatever in this argument of Dr, Haug's, and we think it will be necessary to look for other anchors by which to fix the drifting wrecks of Vedic literature..........

However intertsing the Brâhmanas may be to students of Indian literature, they are of small interest to the general reader. The greater portion of them is simply twaddle, and what is worse, theological twaddle. No person who is not acquainted beforehand with the place which the Brâhmaṇas fill in the history of the Indian mind, could read more than ten pages without being disgusted. To the historian, however, and to the philosopher, they are of infinite importance—to the former as a real link between the ancient and modern literature of India ; to the latter as a most important phase in the growth of human mind, in its passage from health to disease.

* See preface to the fourth volume of my edition of the Rigveda.

PREFACE.

The present work is the first edition, and first translation of one of the most important works of the Brâhmaṇa literature.......................

The editing of the text and the translation of the numerous stories contained in the work was a comparatively easy task, and might have been carried out as well in Europe by any respectable Sanscrit scholar in possession of the necessary materials obtainable there. But the case stands different with the translation of the technical parts of the work and principally the numerous explanatory notes which are indispensable for an actual understanding of the book. Though Sâyaṇa's excellent Commentary, which I have used throughout, is a great help for making out the proper meaning of many an obscure word, or phrase, it is not sufficient for obtaining a complete insight into the real meaning of many terms and passages occurring in the work. Besides, a good many passages in the Commentary itself, though they may convey a correct meaning, are hardly intelligible to European Sanscrit scholars who have no access to oral sources of information. The difficulties mainly lie in the large number of technical terms of the sacrificial art, which occur in all Brâhmaṇas, and are, to those uninitiated into the mysteries of this certainly ancient craft, for the most part unintelligible. It is, therefore, not surprising that no Sanscrit scholar as yet ever attempted the translation of the whole of a Brâhmaṇa; for the attempt would, in many essential points, have proved a failure.

What might be expected in the explanation of sacrificial terms from scholars unaided by oral information, may be learnt from the three volumes hitherto published of the great Sanscrit Dictionary, compiled by Bœhtlingk and Roth. The explanations of these terms there given (as well as those of many words of the Samhitâ) are nothing but guesses, having no other foundation than the individual opinion of a scholar who never made himself familiar with the sacrificial art, even as far as it would be possible in Europe, by a careful study of the commentaries on the Sûtras and Brâhmaṇas, and who appears to have thought his own conjectures to be superior to the opinions of the greatest divines of Hindustan, who were especially trained for the sacrificial profession from times immemorial. These defects of a work which is in other respects a monument of gignatic toil and labour, and on account of its containing numerous references and quotations extremely useful to the small number of Sanscrit scholars who are able to make independent researches, have been already repeatedly pointed out by Professor Theodor Goldstücker, one of the most accurate Sanscrit scholars in Europe. Although his remarks excited the wrath principally of some savants at Berlin, who had tried to praise up the work as a masterpiece of perfection and ingenuity almost unparalleled in the history of lexicography, they are, nevertheless, though in some points too severe, not quite so undeserved and unjust, as the defenders of the Dictionary made them to appear. Goldstücker justly does not only find fault with its explanation of ritual terms, but with the meanings given to many words in the saṁhitâ. Though I am far from defending even the greater majority of Sâyaṇa's explanations of the more difficult words and sentences of the Saṁhitâ, it would have been at any rate advisable for the compilers of a Sanscrit Dictionary, which includes the Vedic words, to give Sâyaṇa's explanations along with their own. Even granted that all Sâyaṇa's explanations are only either guesses of his own, or of the great Bhaṭṭâchâryas* before him, whose labours he principally used, they nevertheless deserve all attention as the opinions and observations of men who had a much deeper knowledge of the Sanscrit language in general, and the rites of the Vedic religion, than any European scholar has ever attained to. It is quite erroneous to presuppose, as the editors of the Dictionary appear to do, that Sâyaṇa himself made the majority of explanations in his Commentary. All Pandits who have any knowledge of the subject unanimously assert that he used a good many predecessors, and that comparatively few explanations are entirely his own. The so-called Kâuśika Bhâṣya is said to be more ancient than that of Sâyaṇa, and also the Râvana Bhâṣya. Both are said to be still extant, but I have not yet been able to obtain copies of them.

Seeing the great difficulties, nay impossibility, of attaining to anything like a real understanding of the sacrificial art from all the numerous books I had collected, I made the greatest efforts to obtain oral informa-

* This is the name of those Hindu scholars who not only learn, as the Bhaṭṭas do, one of the Vedas completely by heart, but who study the meaning of each verse and word, so as to be able to give orally the explanation of any passage required. The number of this class of scholars who represent the Doctors of Hindu theology, is now very small. In this part of India, though there are many hundreds of parrotlike repeaters of the sacred texts, there is not a single one to be found. Some (three or four) are said to be at Benares. They are highly respected, and, as incarnations of Bṛihaspati—the Pandit of the Gods, at certain occasions regularly worshipped.

tion from some of those few Brâhmaṇs who are known by the name of Śrotriyas, or Śrautis, and who alone are the preservers of the sacrificial mysteries as they descended from the remotest times. The task was no easy one, and no European scholar in this country before me even succeeded in it. This is not to be wondered at; for the proper knowledge of the ritual is everywhere in India now rapidly dying out, and in many parts, chiefly in those under British rule, it has already died out. Besides, the communication of these mysteries to foreigners is regarded by old devout Brâhmaṇs (and they alone have the knowledge) as such a monstrous profanation of their sacred creed, and fraught with the most serious consequences to their position, that they can only, after long efforts, and under payment of very handsome sums, be prevailed upon to give information. Notwithstanding, at length I succeeded in procuring the assistance of a Śrauti, who not only had performed the small sacrifices, such as the Darśapûrnamâsa Iṣṭi, but who had even officiated as one of the Hotars, or Udgâtars, at several Soma sacrifices, which are now very rarely brought. In order to obtain a thorough understanding of the whole course of an Iṣṭi, and a Soma sacrifice, I induced him (about 18 months ago) to show me in some secluded place in my premises, the principal ceremonies. After the place had been properly arranged, and the necessary implements brought to the spot, the performance began. I noted carefully everything I saw during about five days, and always asked for explanation if I did not properly comprehend it. I was always referred to the Sûtras and the Prayogas or pocket books of the sacrificial priest, so that no deception could take place. All information was conveyed to me by means of the Marathi language, of which I had by that time already acquired a sufficient knowledge for carrying on any conversation. In this way I obtained some sort of rough knowledge of the principal ceremonies (for they were generally only partially, in order to save time, and rapidly performed), which I completed afterwards by oral instruction, derived from the same and some other sacrificial priests, and Agnihotris, who had the sacrificial operations performed on themselves and in their behalf. Thus I was enabled to understand the various Sûtras, and consequently the technicalities of the Brâhmaṇas. Therefore the explanations of sacrificial terms, as given in the notes, can be relied upon as certain; for they are neither guesses of my own, nor of any other Hindu or European scholar, but proceed from what I have myself witnessed, and been taught by the only men who have inherited the knowledge from the most ancient times. My notes are therefore, for the most part, independent of Sâyaṇa, for I had almost as good sources as he himself had. He, however, does not appear to have troubled himself much with a minute study of the actual operations of the sacrificial priests, but derived all his knowledge almost entirely from the Sûtras only.

It had been easy for me to swell by accumulation of notes the work to double the size which it is now; but I confined myself to give only what was necessary...

MARTIN HAUG.

Poona, 22nd November 1863.

CONTENTS.

FIFTH BOOK.

SIXTH BOOK.

SEVENTH BOOK.

EIGHTH BOOK.

INTRODUCTION.

I.

On the Mantras, Brâhmaṇas, and Sûtras, and their mutual relationship. Probable origin and age of the Mantras, and Brâhmaṇas.

The Veda, or Scripture of the Brâhmans, consists, according to the opinion of the most eminent divines of Hindustan, of two principal parts, *viz.*, *Mantra* and *Brâhmaṇam*. All that is regarded as revelation must be brought under these two heads. What of the revealed word is no Mantra, that is a Brâhmaṇam; and what is no Brâhmaṇam, must be a Mantra. This is the line of argument followed by the Brâhmanic theologians. But this does neither make clear what a Mantra is, nor what we have to understand by a Brâhmaṇam. Both terms are technical, and their full bearing, and characteristic difference from one another, is to be comprehended only from a careful study of those works which bear either of these titles. The Brâhmanical divines have, of course, not failed to give definitions of both, and shown what topics fall under the head of either. But, as Sâyaṇa (in his preface to his Commentary on the Aitareya Brâhmaṇam) justly remarks, all definitions of either term which were attempted, are unsatisfactory.

[2] We have here nothing to do with the theological definitions of these two terms; we are only concerned with their meaning, from a literary point of view. And this we can state without reference to Brâhmanic authorities.

Each of the four Vedas (Rik, Yajus, Sâman, and Atharvan) has a Mantra, as well as a Brâhmaṇa portion. The difference between both may be briefly stated as follows: That part which contains the sacred prayers, the invocations of the different deities, the sacred verses for chanting at the sacrifices, the sacrificial formulas, blessings and curses, pronounced by priests is called *mantra*,[1] *i.e.*, the produce of thinking. This word is of a very early date; for we find it in the Zend-Avesta in the form of *manthra* also. Its meaning there is that of a sacred prayer, or formula, to which a magical effect was ascribed, just as to the Vedic mantras. Zoroaster is called a *manthran*, *i.e.*, a speaker of mantras, and one of the earliest names of the Scriptures of the Parsis, is *manthra śpenta*, *i.e.*, the holy prayer (now corrupted to *mansar spent*).

[1] See more about it in Goldstücker, "Pâṇini, his Place in Sanscrit Literature," page 68.

This fact clearly shows, that the term *mantra* in its proper meaning was already known at that early period of Aryan history when the ancestors of the Brâhmaṇs and those of the Parsis (the ancient Iranians) lived as brother tribes peacefully together. This time was anterior to the combats of [3] the Devas and Asuras, which are so frequently mentioned in the Brâhmaṇas, the former representing the Hindus, the latter the Iranians.[2]

At this time the whole sacred knowledge was, no doubt, comprised by the térm *mantra*. The Brâhmaṇam was unknown ; and there is actually nowhere in the whole Zend-Avesta a word to be found which conveys the same or a similar meaning which has been attached to the word " Brâhmaṇam " in the Indian Literature.

The Brâhmaṇam always presupposes the Mantra ; for without the latter it would have no meaning, nay, its very existence would be impossible. By " Brâhmaṇam" we have always to understand that part of the Veda (Brâhmaṇical revelation) which contains speculations on the meaning of the mantras, gives precepts for their application, relates stories of their origin in connection with that of sacrificial rites, and explains the secret meaning of the latter. It is, to say it in short, a kind of primitive theology and philosophy of the Brahmans. The objects for these theological, philosophical, grammatical, etymological, and metrical speculations were the Maṅtras, and the sacrifices, principally the great ones, for the performance of which the Brahmans were actually trained, a custom which has obtained almost up to the present day in some parts of India (such as Mahârâṣṭra).

[4] Etymologically the word is derived from *brahmán*[3] which properly

---

[2] See my Essays on the Sacred Language, Writings, and Religion of the Parsis, pp. 225-29.

[3] *Brahmán* is derived from *Brahma*. This is an abstract noun, in the neuter gender, of a root *bṛih* (original from *barh*), to which the two meanings " to raise," and " to grow" are given by the Indian grammarians. The latter thought both meanings so irreconcilable that they substituted two roots *bṛih*. But there is certainly no necessity for that. What grows, becomes bigger, and higher and thus " rising in height," is a necessary consequence of growth. It is, however, very doubtful whether the root *bṛih* without a preposition (such as *ud*) can convey the meaning " to raise." The meaning " to grow" is at any rate the original one. Thus derived *brahma* means originally " growth." That this was the *original* sense of the word, can be proved from other reasons also. *Brahma* is the same word in every respect, as the *bareśma* of the Zend-Avesta, the ' *h* ' of Sanscrit, being changed according to the phonetical laws of the Zend grammar, into a sibilant. This means a bunch of twigs tied together by a reed which is used up to the present day by the Parsi priests when performing the Homa ceremony. The Brahmans use at all their sacrifices a bunch of kuśa grass which is also tied together. They call it *Veda* (see Aśv., śr. 8. 1, 11 *vedam patnyâi praddya*

signifies the Brahma priest who must [5] know all Vedas, and understand the whole course and meannig of the sacrifice. He is supposed to be a perfect master of divinity, and has in this capacity to direct and superintend the sacrificial ceremonies. The most eminent of this class of priests laid down rules for the proper performance of sacrificial rites, explained them, and defended their own opinions, on such topics against those of their antagonists; moreover, they delighted in speculations on matters of a more universal character, on this life, and that life, on the best means of securing wealth, progeny, fame, heaven, &c., on mind, soul, salvation, the Supreme Being; the dictum of such a Brahma priest who passed as a great authority, was called a *Brâhmaṇam.*

---

vâchayet, *i.e.*, after having handed over to the wife of the sacrificer that bunch of kuśa grass which is called Veda, he should make her repeat this mantra, &c). *Veda* is a synonymous word for *brahma*; for the latter term is often explained by *veda* (so does Kaiyata in his notes on Patañjali's explanation of Pâṇini's Sûtra 6, 3, 86, in the Mahâbhâṣya), and thus identified with the designation of the whole body of sacred knowledge of the Brahmans. In the Nighaṇṭavas, the ancient collection of Vedic words, *brahma* occurs twice, once as a name for "food" (2, 7), and another time as that for "wealth." Both these meanings, principally the former, can easily be connected with that of "growth." They appear to be founded on passages of the Brâhmaṇas, where it is said that the Brahma is food. In the Saṁhitâ, however, these meanings are never to be met with; but from this circumstance it certainly does not follow that they never existed. The meaning attached to the word in the Saṁhitâ appears to be that of "sacred hymn chant." Sâyaṇa explains it often by *stotra*, *i.e.* the performance of the Sâma chanters (see his commentary on Rigveda, 7, 22, 9) or by *stotrâṇi haviṁṣicha* (7, 23, 1), *i.e.* chants and offerings. This meaning is, however, not the original one, and does even in the Saṁhitâ hardly express its proper sense. It cannot be an equivalent either for *mantra* or *sâman* or *stotram*, or *havis*, and if it appear to be used in one of these senses, it means their common source; for the hymn, repeated by the Hotar, as well as the chant of the Sâma singers and the oblations given to the fire by the Adhvaryu, are all equally made sacred by means of their participation in the *brahma*. Such expressions as, "to make the brahma," "to stir up the brahma," (*brahma jinvati*) throw some light on its nature. They show (as one may clearly see from such passages as Taittirîya Brâhmaṇam 1, 1) that it was regarded as a latent power, like electricity, which was to be stirred up at the time of the performance of a ceremony. The apparatus were the sacred vessels, or the hymns, or chants. So, at a certain ceremony at the morning libation of the Soma feast, the Adhvaryu and Pratipasthâtâr put the two Grahas (Soma cups), called Śukra and Manthi (see Ait. Br. 3, 1) together, and address them in the following way, "Put, ye two (Grahas)! together the Brahma; may ye stir it up for me," &c., (Taittir. Br. 1, 1). This evidently means, that these two Grahas are put together for the purpose of eliciting the Brahma-power, and all the other powers, dependent upon it, such as the *Kṣattram*, &c. The presence of the *brahma* at every sacrifice is necessary; for it is the invisible link connecting the ceremony performed with the fruits wished for, such as sovereignty, leadership, cattle, food, &c.

It is, as we have seen, symbolically represented by a bunch of kuśa grass, which is always wandering from one person to another, as long as the sacrifice lasts. It expresses

[6] Strictly speaking, only the rule regarding the performance of a particular rite,[4] or the authoritative opinion on a certain point of speculative theology went by this name, and we have accordingly in the works called Brâhmaṇas, nothing more or less than collections of the dicta of those Brahma priests on the topics mentioned. Afterwards the term Brâhmaṇam, which originally signified only a single dictum, was applied to the whole collection.

In a still more comprehensive sense we have to understand by "Brâhmaṇa," a whole kind of literature, including the so-called Araṇyakas and Upaniṣads.

Each Veda has a Brâhmaṇam, or collectiou of the dicta of Brahma priests, of its own. But they also show in style, expression, line of argument, and object and tendency of their speculations, such a close affinity, and even identity, that the common origin of all Brâhmaṇas is indisputable. They owe mainly their origin to those Brahmans who constituted themselves into regular sacrificial congregations, in order to perform the so-called *Sattras* or sacrificial sessions, some of which could last for many years. The legendary history of India knows of such sessions which are said to have lasted for one hundred, and even one thousand years.[5] Though these reports [7] are extravagant, they undoubtedly show that there was a time in Hindustan when large bodies of Brahmans spent almost their whole lives in sacrificing. This time is to be sought for at a very early period of Indian history; for the Brâhmaṇas with their frequent allusions and references to the Sattras of the Ṛiṣis on the banks of the Sarasvatî, and those held by the half-mythical Añgiras, and by the Adityas (a class of gods), or even by the cows, trees, snakes, &c., presuppose their existence from times immemorial. Likewise we find in the Mahâbhârata frequent mention made of these sacrificial sessions which constitute one of the characteristic features of the earliest Brahmanic settlements in the northwest of Hindustan. It is chiefly at these Sattras that we have to look for the development and refinement of the sacrificial art, and the establishment of certain rules regarding the performance of sacrificial ceremonies.

---

the productive power in nature, which manifests itself in the growth of plants, and all other creatures. The sacrificer wishes by means of the mystical process of the sacrifice to get hold of it; for only then he is sure of obtaining anything he might wish for.

4 So are, for instance, the rules given for the repetition of the *Dûrohaṇam* (4, 19) quoted as a "Brâhmaṇam" (in 6, 25). See also 8, 2.

5 See Mahâbhârata 3, 105,13, where a Sattra, *Iṣṭâkṛita* by name, is mentioned as lasting for one thousand years.

When the Brâhmaṇas were brought into that form, in which we possess them now, not only the whole *kalpa* (*i.e.* the way of performing the sacrificial ceremonies) was settled, save some minor points, but even the symbolical and mystical meaning of the majority of rites. It took, no doubt, many centuries before the almost endless number of rites and ceremonies, and their bewildering complications could form themselves into such a regular system of sacrificial rules, as we find already exhibited in the Brâhmaṇas. For the Sûtras which belong to each class of Brâhmaṇas generally contain nothing novel, **[8]** no innovation in the sacrificial art; they supply only the *external* form to a system which is already complete in the Brâhmaṇas, and serve as text-books to the sacrificial priests. And even in their arrangement they follow often their Brâhmaṇas to which they belong. So for instance the fourth, fifth, and sixth Adhyayas of the Aśvalâyana Sûtras, which treat of the Agniṣṭoma, Soma sacrifice, and its modifications, Ukthya, Ṣolaśî, and Atirâtra, closely correspond to the three first books, and the two first chapters of the fourth, of the Aitareya Brâhmaṇam; and the seventh and eighth Adhyâya of those Sûtras treat exactly of the same subjects, as the three last chapters of the fourth book, and the fifth and sixth books of our Brâhmaṇam, *viz.*, on the various parts of the Sattras, or sacrificial sessions, and the numerous recitations required for their performance. In many passages, the Aitareya Brâhmaṇam and the Aśvalâyana Sûtras even literally agree. The latter could, from their very nature as a "string of rules" for the guidance of the sacrificial priests, dispense with almost all the numerous speculations of the meaning and effect of certain verses and rites, and all points of controversy in which some of the Brâhmaṇas abound; but as regards the actual performance of rites, what mantras were required at certain occasions, and in what way they were to be repeated, the Sûtras must give much more detail and be far more complete than the Brâhmaṇas. From this nature of both classes of works, and the relation in which they stand to one **[9]** another, it would not be difficult to show, that both might have originated at the same time. Pâṇini distinguishes between old and new Brâhmaṇas as well as between old and new Kalpa works (Sûtras). The strict distinction between a Brâhmaṇa and Sûtra period is, on a closer inquiry, hardly tenable. The Brâhmaṇas were only more complete collections of the same traditional stock which was in existence on the sacrificial art and its meaning than the Sûtras, which were compiled for practical purposes only.

We may safely conclude from the complicated nature and the multitude of the Brahminical sacrifices which were already developed and almost complete at the time of the composition of the Vedic hymns, not only at that of the Brâhmaṇas, that the compilation of sacrificial manuals containing all the rules for the actual performance of the duties of a certain class of priests (such as the Hotṛis or repeaters of the Ṛik verses, the Udgâtṛis, the chanters of the Ṛik verses, and the Adhvaryuṣ, the manual labourers and sacred cooks), was quite necessary at a very early time, certainly not posterior to the collection of the Mantras and the dicta of the Brahma priests into separate works.

The Sûtras contain many special rules which will be in vain sought for in the Brâhmaṇas, but which are there simply presupposed. So we do not find, for instance, the description of the Darśapurṇama iṣṭhi (the New and Full Moon sacrifice), or that of the Châturmâsya-iṣṭi, in the Aitareya Brâhmaṇam, though their names are occasionally mentioned, but [10] we find them in the Aśvalâyana Sûtras. The recital of the Sâmidhenî verses (required when kindling the fire at the commencement of any sacrificial rite) is briefly mentioned in the Brâhmaṇas, but minutely described in the Sûtras (1, 2). That they were left out in the Brâhmaṇam cannot be accounted for by assuming that their exposition was alien to the purpose of its author, or that they were unknown to him, but only by believing, that they were regarded as too trivial matters, too commonly known to deserve any special notice on his part. Certain modifications in repeating mantras (required at the great Soma sacrifices), such as the Dûrohaṇâm, the Nyûṅkha, the peculiar construction and repetition of the Ṣoḷaśí and Vâlkhilya Śastras, &c., are in the Brâhmaṇam almost as minutely and accurately described, aś we find them in the Sûtras (compare, for instance, Ait. Br. 4, 19 with Asv. Śr. S. 8, 2). This clearly shows that the authors of the Brâhmaṇas knew as well all the details of the sacrificial art as the compilers of the Sûtras. The circumstance that many such things, as the recital of the Sâmidhenî verses, &c., were left out in the Brâhmaṇam, though they are neither very simple to comprehend, nor were they unknown, entitles us to assume that they were taught in separate treatises, which could be nothing else than works like the present Sûtras.

The Sûtras which we possess at present are, no doubt, posterior to the Brâhmaṇas to which they belong ; but there is every reason to believe that there were Sûtras more ancient, and simple in their [11] style, which served the authors of the present ones as sources of information, and these works may have been co-eval with the majority of our Brâhmaṇas.

Although we cannot discover any material difference between the Brâhmaṇas and the Sûtras so as to regard the latter as developing and systematizing the ideas contained in the former, as is the case with the Vedânta philosophy in reference to the Upaniṣads, yet there exists one between the Brâhmaṇas, and the Mantras and hymns. This difference is, however, not very great, and can be accounted for partially from other causes than that of age. Already the hymns presuppose a settled ritual, and contain many speculative ideas similar to those of the Brâhmaṇas.

Some scholars hold that the occurrence of sacrificial terms, or of philosophical and mystical ideas, are suggestive of the late date of the hymn in which they are found. But these circumstances do by no means afford any sure test as to the relative age of the Vedic hymns. One has even drawn a strict line of distinction between a Mantra and Chhandas period, assigning to the former all the sacrificial hymns, to the latter those expressive of religious and devotional feelings in general, without any reference to sacrificial rites. But I have grave doubts whether this distinction will prove tenable on further inquiries, chiefly if this question as to the age of a certain hymn is made entirely to depend upon what period (the Mantra or Chhandas period) it might belong to. There are sacrificial hymns which, to judge from their style and their general ideas, must [12] be as ancient as any which have been assigned to the Chhandas period.

I may instance here the hymn required at the horse-sacrifice (Ṛigveda, 1, 162) and the Nâbhânediṣṭha Sûkta (10, 61 ; on its origin see Ait. Br. 5, 14). The former is assigned by Max Müller [6] to the Mantra period (between 1000-800) on no other ground but because of its containing technical terms of the sacrificial art. But this reason is certainly not sufficient to make it late. On the contrary, its rather unpolished style, its poor imagery, its beginning with the invocation of the most ancient triad of Indian gods, *Mitra*, *Varuṇa*, and *Aryaman*, the very names of which deities are even to be met with in kindred nations, such as the Iranians and Greeks, the mentioṇing of several sacrificial priests by obsolete and uncommon names,—all these circumstances combined tend to show, that it is rather one of the earliest than one of the latest productions of Vedic poetry. We find in it the sacrificial art, if compared with its description in the Brâmaṇas, in its infancy, yet containing all the germs of the latter system. Because of almost all incidents attendant upon a sacrifice being mentioned in this hymn, it affords us the best means for investigating into the extent

---

[6] History of Ancient Sanscrit Literature, page 558.

and development of the sacrificial art at the time of its composition. Let us point out some of the most remarkable facts which may be elicited from it.

[13] In the fifth verse the names of the performing priests are mentioned. They are only six in number, *viz. Hotar*, *Adhvaryu*, *Avayâj*, *Agnimindha*, *Grâvagrâbha*, and *Śaṁstar*. Four of these names are quite uncommon or obsolete. Avayâj is the Pratiprasthâtar, Agnimindha (the fire-kindler), the Agnídhra, Grâvagrâbha the Grâvastut, and Śaṁstar the Maitrâvaruṇa of the Brâhmaṇas. The small number of priests at the horse-sacrifice (*aśvamedha*), which was at later times, as we may learn from descriptions given of it in the epic poems, the greatest, most complicated and costly which the Brahmans used to perform, must surprise, principally if we consider, that the Agniṣṭoma, which was the most simple Soma sacrifice, required for its performance already at the time of the Brâhmaṇas, and even anterior to it, sixteen officiating priests.

There can be no doubt that in the most ancient times a comparatively small number of priests was sufficient for the performance of a simple animal or Soma sacrifice. The two most ancient offices were those of the Hotar and Adhvaryu; they were known already when the ancient Iranians separated from the ancestors of the Hindus; for we easily recognise them by the names *Zota* and *Rathwi* (now corrupted to Raspi) in the Zend-Avesta.

The Pratiprasthâtar appears to have been an assistant of the Adhvaryu from a very remote time; for we find the two Aśvins called the two Adhvaryus (Ait. Br. I, 18), by which expression we can only understand the Adhvaryu and [14] his constant assistant the Pratiprasthâtar. That there was a plurality of Adhvaryus already at the time of the Ṛiṣis, we may learn from several passages of the Saṁhitâ of the Ṛigveda (2, 37, 2; 8, 2, 4).

The fourth priest here mentioned is the Agnîdhra; for by the term *Agnimindha* we can only understand him. His office appears to be very old and he is once mentioned by his very name *Agnîdhra* in a Vedic song (2, 36, 4). Besides, we meet with the well-known formula which he has, as the protector of the sacrifice, to repeat as often as the Adhvaryu commences a set of oblations accompanied by the Anuvâkyâ and Yâjyâ mantras of the Hotar. This is *astu śrauṣaṭ* (1, 139, 1), which he has to repeat when the Adhvaryu calls upon him to do so, by the formula *ô śrâvaya.*[7] Before he repeats it, he takes a wooden sword, called

[7] This formula is repeated just before the commencement of the so-called Prayâjas. Aśval. Śr. S. 1, 4, gives the following rules; *Adhvaryur âśrâvayati pratyâśrâvayed*

sphya[8] into his hand, and ties round it twelve stalks of kuśa grass, called *idhmasannahanâni* (what is tied round the wood), making three knots (*trisandhana*). He must hold it up as long as the principal offerings last, from [15] the time of the beginning of the Prayâjas till the Sviṣṭakrit is over. The purpose of this act as explained by the Śrotrîyas (sacrificial priests) of the present day is to keep the Rakṣasas and evil spirits away from the sacrifice. Now the whole ceremony, along with the formulas used, resembles so closely what is recorded in the Zend-Avesta of the angel *Śraosha* (now called *Seroṣh*), that we can fairly conclude that the office, or at any rate, the duties, of the Agnîdhra priests were already known to the Aryas before the Iranians separated from the Indians. Serosh, as may be seen from the Serosh Yasht (Yaśna 57), holds in his hand a sword (*śnaithis*) in order to fight against the Devas, and to keep them away from the creation of Ormazd. He first spread the sacred grass or twigs; he first repeated (*fraśrâvayat*) the sacred prayers. His very name of *Śraosha* reminds of the call *śrauṣaṭ*. One of the duties of the Agnîdhra, or Agnît, was to kindle the fire. Such an office is known also to the Parsi ritual. It is that of the *Atarevakṣo, i. e.* who feeds the fire, a name often applied to the Rathwi, in which we have recognised the Adhvaryu.

The fifth priest is the *Grâvagrâbha*, a name no further mentioned in other Vedic books. Sâyaṇa identifies him with the Grâvastut[9] of the ceremonial of the Brâhmaṇas. The office of the latter is to repeat the Pâvamânya verses when the Soma juice is being prepared. But the name *Grâvagrâbha* [16] implies more, for it means, one who holds, or seizes the Grâvaṇas[10] (Soma squeezing stones). This is done by the Adhvaryu himself. In ancient times the Soma juice was very likely extracted by that priest who had to repeat the mantras for the purification of the Soma juice, that is, by the Grâvastut. Such a priest who was engaged in the preparation of the Soma (Homa) juice is also known in the Zend-Avesta.

âgnidhraḥ, i. e. the Adhvaryu calls, *ŏ śrâvaya*, to which the Agnidhra responds by *astu śrauṣaṭ*. Both formulas are mentioned or alluded to in two Sûtras of Pâṇini (8, 2, 91-92), who teaches that the first vowel in *śrâuṣaṭ*, and the first and second in *ŏ śravaya* are to be pronounced in the *pluta* way, *i.e.* with three moras. Regarding *śrâuṣaṭ* Aśval. gives the same rule (*astu śrâuṣaṭ iti aukaram plâvayan*); but the pronunciation of *ŏ śrâvaya* he does not particularly mention.

[8] Other interpretations have been given of this word by European scholars. But being myself in possession of a sphya, and having seen its use at the sacrifice, I can prove beyond any doubt, that it is a wooden sword.

[9] On his office, see 6, 1-2, pp. 379-80.

[10] See the note on the preparation of the *Soma* 7, 32 pp. 488-90.

His name there is *havanan*,[11] *i.e.* one who makes or prepares the *havana*=*savana* "libation."

The sixth priest mentioned in the Aśvamedha hymn is the *Śaṁstar*, *i.e.* the repeater of Śastras. This is no doubt the Maitrâvaruṇa of the later ritual, who is several times mentioned by the name of *Praśâstar* in other passages of the Saṁhitâ (1, 94, 6) and in the Brâhmaṇas. Sâyaṇa takes the same view.

Besides the names of the officiating priests, we have to examine some of the technical terms of the sacrificial art. In the 15th verse we find **[17]** the expressions, *iṣṭam, vitam, abhigûrtam, vaṣaṭkṛitam*, which all refer to the repetition of the Yâjyâ mantra by the Hotar when the Adhvaryu is ready to throw the offering into the fire. *Iṣṭam* is the technical term for pronouncing the Yâjyâ mantra itself; *abhigârtam*, which is the same as *âgûrtam*, signifies the formula *ye yajâmahe* (generally called *âgur*) which always precedes the Yâjyâ verse; *vaṣaṭkṛitam* is the pronunciation of the formula *vâuṣaṭ* at the end of the Yâjyâ verse; *vîtam* refers to the formula *Agne vîhi*, which follows the *vaṣaṭkâra*, and is itself followed by another *vaṣaṭkâra* (the so-called Anuvaṣṭkâra).

Let us now sum up the evidence furnished by this sacrificial hymn as bearing upon the history of the sacrificial art in its relationship to the mass of other Vedic songs on the one, and to the Brâhmaṇas on the other, side.

In examining the names of the officiating priests, we can here discover only two classes instead of the four, known to other Vedic hymns, and principally to the Brâhmaṇas. We have only Adhvaryus and Hotṛis, but no Brahma priests, and no Udgâtṛis (chanters). Without the two latter classes no solemn sacrifice at which Soma was used could be performed even at a time far anterior to the Brâhmaṇas. There is no doubt, the introduction of each of these two classes marks a new epoch in the history of the sacrificial art, just as the separation of the offices of Adh-

[11] See Viśparad 3, 1. The term *havana* occurs in the Gâthâs for Homa (Yaśna, 10). That it means the same as the Vedic *savana* with which it is identical follows unmistakably from the context. A *fratarem havanem* and an *uparem havanem*, that is, a first and second libation, are even distinguished (Yaśna 10, 2 ed. Westergaard). The *fratarem havanem* is the *prâtaḥ savanam*, *i.e.* morning libation of the ritual books; the *uparem*, *i. e.* latter, following, corresponds to the *mâdhyandina savanam*. The Parsi priests prepare up to the present day actually the Homa juice *twice* when performing the Homa ceremony. The first preparation takes place before the *Zota* (the Hotar of the Brahmans) appears; the second commences at the beginning of the proper ceremony, and is finished along with it. The Zota drinks the Homa which was prepared first by the Raspi (Adhvaryu); that one prepared during the ceremony is thrown into a well as a kind of offering.

varyu and Hotar in the ante-Vedic times, indicates the first step in the development of the art of sacrificing. At that early time when the [18] Iranians left their Indian brethren on account of a bitter religious contest, which is known in the Brâhmaṇas as the struggle between the Devas and Asuras, already the offices of an Adhvaryu and Hotar were distinct, as we may learn from the Zend-Avesta, which exhibits the religion of the Asuras (Ahura religion, its professors calling themselves *ahurotkêshô*=*asura-dîkṣâ*, *i.e.* initiated into the Asura rites).

But the offices of Udgâtrîs and that of the Brahma priests were not known to the Aryas at that time; they were introduced subsequently, after the separation. In many Vedic hymns we find, however, the duties principally of the former class (the chanters) mentioned. They are often juxtaposed with those of the Hotars. The term for the performance of the Hotṛi-priests is *śaṁs*, to praise, recite; that for that of the Udgâtṛîs *stu* or *gâi* to sing (see, for instance, Ṛigveda Saṁh (8, 1, 1; 6, 62, 5; 6, 69, 2-3); besides the technical names *uktha*=*Śastra* and *Stoma*, *sâma*, are frequently to be met with (see 8, 1, 15; 3, 3, 6; 6, 3; 16, 9; 14, 11; 6, 24, 7, &c.). Now the absence of all such terms, indicatory of the functions of the Udgâtṛîs (chanters) in the Aśvamedha hymn is certainly remarkable. Their not occuring might, perhaps, be accounted for by the supposition that the chanters were not required at the horse sacrifice. It is true, several smaller sacrifices, such as the Darśapûrnamâsa, the Châturmâsya Iṣṭis and the animal sacrifice (if performed apart without forming part of a Soma sacrifice) are performed without any chanting; [19] but for Soma sacrifices of whatever description, the chanters are as indispensable as the Hotars. That the Aśvamedha was connected with a Soma sacrifice[12] already at the time of the composition of the hymn in question, undoubtedly follows from the office of *Grâvagrâbha* being mentioned in it; for this priest is only required for the extracting of the Soma juice, and has nothing whatever to do with any other sacrificial rite. The mentioning of the Śaṁstar (Maitrâvruṇa) is another indication that the Aśvamedha already at that early time was accompanied by a Soma sacrifice. For one of the principal duties of the Maitrâvaruṇa, who may be called the first assistant of the Hotar, is to repeat Śastras, which are only required at Soma sacrifices as the necessary accompaniments of all chants.

Besides the Udgâtris, we miss the class of the Brahma priests, *viz.* Brahmâ, Brâhmaṇâchaṁsî, and Subrahmaṇyâ, whose services are required

[12] According to Aśval. Śr. Sûtras (10, 8) there are three Soma days (*satyani*, required for the horse sacrifice.

at all great sacrifices. The Brahmâ cannot, even at small sacrifices, such as the Darśapûrṇamâsa Iṣṭi, be dispensed with. The Brâhmaṇâchaṁsî aud Subrahmaṇyâ are at Soma sacrifices as indispensable as the Maitrâvaruṇa; the first has to repeat also Śastras for the chants, the latter to invite every day Indra to the Soma feast (see the note to 6, 3, pp. 382-84).

The introduction of the Brahmâ priest marks no doubt a new era in the history of the sacrificial art; **[20]** for to judge from the nature of his duties as superintendent of the sacrifical ceremonies, he was only necessary at a time when the sacrifice had become already very complicated, and was liable to many mistakes. The origin of the office dates earlier than the Brâhmaṇas. Unmistakeable traces of it are to be found already in the Saṁhitâ of the Ṛigveda. In one passage 1, 10, 1, the Brahmâ priests (*brahmâṇas*) are juxtaposed with the Hotṛis (*arkinaḥ*) and Udgâtṛis (*gâyatriṇaḥ*). They are there said to "raise Indra just as (one raises) a reed." Similarly we find together *gâyata*, chant, *śaṁsata*, praise, and *brahma kṛiṇuta* make the Brahma (8, 32, 17). In 10, 91, 10 the Brahmâ is mentioned along with other priests also, such as the Potar, Neṣṭar, &c. The little work done by the Brahmâ priests, or rather their idleness, is mentioned, 8, 92, 30, "do not be as lazy as a Brahmâ priest" (*mo ṣu brahmeva tandrayur bhuvaḥ*). That the Brahmâ priests were thus reproached may clearly be seen from Ait. Brâhm. 5, 34. The Brahmâ priest is the speaker or expounder of religious matters (10, 71, 11; 117, 8), in which capacity they became the authors of the Brâhmaṇas. That the Brahmâ was expected to know all secret things, may be inferred from several passages (10, 85, 3; 16; 35; 36). Bṛihaspati, the teacher of the gods, is also called *brahmâ* (10, 143, 3), and Agni is honoured with the same name (7, 7, 5), as well as his pious worshippers of old, the so-called Aṅgirasaḥ (7, 42, 1). Sometimes the name signifies the Brahman as distinguished from the Kṣattriyas *brahmaṇi râjani vâ* (1, 108, 7).

[21] It is certainly remarkable, that none of the Brahmâ priests is to be found among the priests enumerated in the Aśvamedha hymn, and we may safely conclude, that their offices were not known at that time. The word *brahma* (neuter) itself occurs in it (in the seventeenth verse), "If any one, in order to make thee sit, did thee harm by kicking thee with his heels, or striking thee with a whip violently so that thou didst snort, I cause all to go off from thee by means of the Brahma, just as I make flow (the drops of melted butter) by means of a Sruch (sacrificial spoon) over the piece which is among the ready-made offerings (*adhvareṣu*). Brahma has here very likely its original meaning, "the sacrificial grass" or a certain bunch of it (see the note on pages 4, 5 of this Introduction). For the meaning "prayer," which is here given to it by Sâyaṇa, does not suit the simile. In order to understand it fully, one has to bear in mind that the Adhvaryu after having cooked and made ready any offering (Purodâśa or flesh, or Charu, &c.) generally pours from a Sruch some drops of melted butter over it. Now the *brahma* by means of which the priest is to soothe all injury which the sacrificial horse may have received from kicking or striking, is compared with this Sruch; the drops of melted butter are then the several stalks of the bunch of the sacrificial grass, required at all sacrifices and their taking out, and throwing away (as is done at all sacrifices, see note 8 to page 79), is compared to the flowing of the drops from the sacrificial spoon.

Not only is the number of priests less, but the **[22]** ceremonies are also more simple. It appears from verse 15th, that there was no Puronuvâkyâ or introductory mantra required, but the Yâjyâ alone was sufficient. The latter consisted already of the same parts as in the Brâhmaṇas, *viz.* the Agur, the Yâjyâ mantra, the Vaṣaṭkâra and Anuvaṣaṭkâra (see note 32 to page 95, page 126, and note 11 to page 133-34). The Agúr or the introductory formula, *ye yajâmahe, i.e.*, "what (gods are), those we worship by sacrificing," is very ancient, and seems to go back even beyond the properly so-called Vedic times; for we meet it even with the same name already in the Zend-Avesta (see note 11 to page 134); even a large number of the Parsi prayer formulas commence with it up to this day, *viz. yazâmaidê.* The Vaṣaṭkâra or the call *vâuṣaṭ,* and the Anuvaṣaṭkâra, or the second call *vâuṣaṭ* preceded by *Agni vihi, i. e.,* "Agni eat (the food)," must be also very old, though we do not find any trace of them in the Parsi ritual, which circumstance can be, however, easily accounted for. The first call *vâuṣaṭ* being required in the very moment of the offering being thrown into the fire, and the second at once after it, there was no occasion for them at the Zoroastrian sacrifices; for the priests are not allowed to throw flesh, or Homa, or even cakes into the fire; they have only to show their offerings to the sacred element. In the Saṁhitâ itself, the Vaṣaṭkâra is frequently mentioned, and in hymns which show by no means a modern origin (see 1, 14, 8; 120, 4; 21, 5; 7, 14, 3; 15, 6; 99, 7, &c); some of them apparently allude to the **[23]** Anuvaṣaṭkâra, (so, for instance, 7, 156, *semâm vetu vaṣaṭkṛitim,* 'may he eat this piece' offered by the call *vauṣat! vi* (in *vîhi*) being one of the characteristic terms of the *Anuvaṣaṭára*).

From all we have seen as yet it clearly follows that the Aśvamedha hymn is by no means a late, but a very early, production of Vedic poetry, and that consequently a strict distinction between a Chhandas and Mantra period, making the former by about two hundred years older than the latter, is hardly admissible.

The same result is to be gained from a more close examination of other pre-eminetly sacrificial hymns, which all would fall under the Mantra period. There being here no occasion to investigate into all hymns of that character, I will only here make some remarks on the Nâbhânediṣṭha hymns (10, 61-62). Their history is given in the Ait. Brâhm. itself (5, 14). They are traced to Manu, the progenitor of the human race, who gave them to his son, Nâbhânediṣṭha. He should communicate them to the Aṅgiras, for enabling them to perform successfully the ceremonies of the sixth day (in the Ṣaḷaha, see note 9 to page 279), and receive all their property as a sacrificial reward.

This whole story appears to have no other foundation, [13] but the two hymns themselves, principally the [24] latter. The first is very difficult to understand, the second is on the the whole simple. Both are by tradition ascribed to Nâbhânediṣṭha, the son of Manu, whose existence is very doubtful. They differ so much in style, that they cannont have the same author. Several traits of the legend, however, are to be found in them. The refrain of the first four verses of 10, 62 which is addressed to the Aṅgiras, "receive the son of Manu," re-occurs in the legend ; also the gift of a thousand. In a verse of the former (10, 61, 18) the word *nâbhânediṣṭha* occurs, but it does not mean there a human, but some divine, being. I give the 18th and 19th verses in translation.

(18) "His relative, the wealthy Nâbhânediṣṭha who, directing his thoughts towards thee, speaks on looking forward (as follows) 'this our navel is the highest ; as often as required I was behind him (the Nâbhânediṣṭha on earth).' "

(19) "This is my navel, here is what resides with me ; these gods are mine ; I am everything. Those who are first born, and those who are born for a second time (by reproduction),—the cow milked that (seed) from the truth, (and) they are born." [14]

---

[13] It is to be found also with little difference in the Taittiriya Saṁhitâ 3, 1, 9, 4-6. Instead of the two Suktas (hymns) Manu there is said to have given his son a Brâhmaṇam on a certain rite concerning the share of Rudra in the Soma libation, to help the Aṅgiras to heaven. The "sixth day" is not mentioned in it. The man in a "blackish dress" of the Aitareya Br. is here called *Rudra.*

[14] The explanation given by Sâyaṇa of these difficult verses is very artificial. He tries to get out of the hymn everywhere the story told of Nâbhânediṣṭha in the Ait. Br. 5, 14.

From these two verses as well as from several others in it (principally 2 and 5-8 describing Prajâpati's illicit intercourse with his [25] daughter, see Ait. Br. 3, 33), we may clearly perceive that Nâbhânedişṭha and the hymn in question refer to generation. This view is fully corroborated by the application of it at the sacrifice, as expounded by the Brâhmaṇam, and as even pre-supposed in the hymn itself.

We know from various passages of the Brâhmaṇas, that one of the principal acts of the sacrificial priests was to make a new body to the sacrificer, and produce him anew by mantras, and various rites, by making him mystically undergo the same process to which he owed his natural life. So, for instance, the whole Pravargya ceremony (see note 1 to pages 41-43), the Ajya and Pra-uga Śastras (see Ait. Br. 2, 35-38; 3, 2) of the morning libation, and the so-called Śilpa Śastras (6, 27-31) of the Hotṛi-priests are intended for this purpose. Of the latter the two Nâbhânedişṭha hymns form the two first parts, representing the seed effused, and its transformation to an embryo in its rudest state (see 6, 27). Nâbhânedişṭha is the sperm when effused; after having undergone some change in the womb, it is called Narâśaṁsa.[15] That the hymn originally had such a mystical sense, is evident from the two first verses:

[26] (1) "May this awful Brahma, which he (Prajâpati) thus skilfully pronounced in words at the congregation, at the assembly, fill the seven Hotars on the day of cooking (the sacrificial food), when his (the sarificer's) parents (and other) liberal men (the priests) are making (his body)."

(2) "He established (as place) for the reception of his gift the altar (*vedi*), destroying and ejecting the enemy with his weapons. (After having thus made the place safe) he then hastily under a very loud cry poured forth his sperm in one continuous (stream)."

The meaning of these two verses can only be the following: the poet who was no doubt a sacrificial priest himself wishes, that the hymn which he regards as a revelation from Prajâpati, who repeated it at the great sacrificial session which he is so frequently said to have held, may fill the seven Hotṛi-priests when they, with the same liberality as Prajâpati

---

[15] This idea must be very old; for we find an unmistakeable trace of it in the Zoroastrian tradition. So we read in the Bundehesh (page 80 in Westergaard's edition of the Pehlevi text) that the angel Nerioseng (*nerioseng yazd=narâśaṁsa yajata* in Sanscrit) intercepted the three particles of sperm which Zoroaster is said to have once lost, and out of which the three great prophets, *Oshadar* (*bâmi*), *Oshadar mâh*, and *Sosiosh* are expected to spring at the end of the world. Nerioseng clothed the said sperms with lustre and strength (*rosnas Zor*), and handed them over to *Anâhit* (the Persian Venus) to look at them. They are guarded against the attacks of the Devas (the Indian gods) by 999,999 Frohars (a kind of angels).

(when he poured forth his sperm) are like parents making by their hymns the new celestial body to the sacrificer. The place for reception of the seed poured out mystically in prayer by the Hotars, is the altar; for standing near it (and even touching it with their feet) they repeat the mantras. The reason that they have to regard the Vedi as the safe receptacle of the seed, is to be sought for in the antecedent of Prajâpati, who prepared it for the purpose, defending [27] it against the attacks of enemies. After having made it safe, he poured out his seed whence then all creatures sprang (see Ait. Br. 3, 34).

Nâbhânediṣṭha is, according to the verses above quoted, the heavenly guardian of all germs of generation; all gods, men, beasts, &c., come from him. His assistance is required when the sacrificial priests are producing the new celestial body of the sacrificer. He looks down from heaven at his relative, that is, the seeds containing the germ of new life poured out mystically by the Hotars in their prayers. His navel is the centre of all births in the universe; as being nearest ('nearest to the navel' is the literal meaning of *nâbhânediṣṭha*), he is the guardian of all seeds. Every seed on earth has only effect as far as he participates in it. We have here the Zoroastrian idea of the Fravashis (Frohars) who are the prototypes of all things existing.[16] The word *nâbhânediṣṭha* must be very old; for we find it several times in the form *nabânazdista* in the Zend Avesta. It is an epithet of the Fravashis (Yaśna, 1, 18. Yashts 13, 156), and signifies the lineal descendants in future generations[17] (Vend. 4, 5-10 Westergaard).

[28] Although the Nâbhânediṣṭha hymn (10, 61) is purely sacrificial, and composed at a time when the Ṛiṣis already indulged in speculations on the mystical meaning of sacrificial rites, no trace can be found, to show that it is a modern composition. The circumstance, that it is already in the Aitareya Brâhmaṇam traced to Manu, the progenitor of the human race, shows, that its origin is entirely lost in the depths of antiquity. The mentioning of *Kakṣîvan* in verse 16, and the occurrence of the "seven Hotars" (in the 1st verse) are no proofs of a late origin. For

---

[16] See my Essays on the Sacred Language, Writings and Religion of the Parsis, page 186.

[17] This is the sense of *narâm nabânâzdistanâm*, in the fourth Frargard of the Vendidâd. In the passage in question, the punishment consequent on the breach of a promise is said to extend to so and so many *narâm nabânazdistanâm*, literally, men who are nearest the navel of the offender, that is, his lineal descendants. The Pehlevi translation gives in its notes about the same meaning to it. So it has for instance to 4, 5 the note: 300 *sanat bîm dâresn* "for three hundred years there will be danger (for the *nabânazdistas*)." This is also the opinion of many Dasturs.

Kakṣîvan appears as a celebrated Ṛiṣi, who was distinguished as a great chanter and Soma drinker in many other passages, principally in the first book (see Ṛigveda Saṁh. 1, 18, 1-2 ; 51, 13 ; 116, 7 ; 117, 6 ; 4, 26, 1), who enjoyed the special favour of the Aśvins. He is to the majority of the Vedic Ṛiṣis whose hymns are kept, a personage of as remote an antiquity as *Kâvya*, *Uśanâs*, the *Añgiras*, &c. The "seven Hotars"[18] occur several times besides (3, 29, 14 ; 8, 49, 16), most of them with their very names, *viz.*, Potar, Neṣṭar, Agnîd, Praśâstar, &c., (1, 15, 2-5 ; 9 ; 1, 94, 6 ; 10, 91, 10).

The second Nâbhânediṣṭha hymn is certainly later than the first, and contains the germs of the later legend on Nâbhânediṣṭha. The reason that it was also referred to him, is certainly to be sought **[29]** for in the 4th verse, where is said, "This one (*i.e.* I) speaks through the navel,[19] (*nâbhâ*), hails you in your residence ; hear, O sons of the gods, ye Ṛiṣis (to my speech)." The song is addressed to the Añgiras, who are requested to receive the poet. The gift of thousand is also mentioned.

Let us, after this discussion regarding the antiquity of the Aśvamedha and Nâbhânediṣṭha hymns, return to the general question on the relationship between the pre-eminently sacrificial mantras and the other production of Vedic poetry.

If we look at the history of poetry with other nations, we nowhere find profane songs precede religious poetry. The latter owes its origin entirely to the practical worship of beings of a higher order, and must, as every art does, go through many phases before it can arrive at any state of perfection and refinement. Now, in the collection of the hymns of the Ṛigveda, we find the religious poetry already so highly developed, the language so polished, the metres already so artificially composed, as to justify the assumption, that the songs which have reached our time, are not the earliest productions of the poetical genius, and the devout mind of the ancient Indians. Generations of poets and many family **[30]** schools in which sacred poetry was regularly taught, just as the art of the bards and scalds with the Celtic and Scandinavian nations, must have preceded that period to which we owe the present

[18] They are, according to the Brâhmaṇas (see Ait. Br. 6, 10-12), Hotar, Maitrâvaruṇa, Brâhmaṇâchhaṁsi, Achhâvâka, Potar, Neṣṭar, and Agnîdhra.

[19] This expression appears to be strange. It implies a very ancient idea, which must have been current with the Iranians and Indians alike. The navel was regarded as the seat of an internal light, by means of which the seers received what they called revelation. It is up to the present day a belief of the Parsi priests, that the Dasturs or High-priests have a fire in their navel, by means of which they can see things which are hidden. This reminds us of some phenomena in modern somnambulism.

collection. If an old song was replaced by a new one, which appeared more beautiful and finished, the former was, in most cases, irrecoverably lost. Old and new poets are frequently mentioned in the hymns of the Ṛigveda; but the more modern Ṛiṣis of the Vedic period appear not to have regarded the productions of their predecessors with any particular reverence which might have induced them to keep their early relics.

Now the question arises, are the finished and polished hymns of the Ṛigveda with their artificial metres the most ancient relics of the whole religious literature of the Brâhmans, or are still more ancient pieces in the other Vedic writings to be found? It is hardly credible, that the Brahmanical priests employed at their sacrifices in the earliest times hymns similar to those which were used when the ritual became settled. The first sacrifices were no doubt simple offerings performed without much ceremonial. A few appropriate solemn words, indicating the giver, the nature of the offering, the diety to which as well as the purpose for which it was offered, and addresses to the objects that were offered, were sufficient. All this could be embodied in the sacrificial formulas known in later times principally by the name of *Yajus*, whilst the older one appears to have been *Yâja* (preserved in *pra-yâja*, *anu-yâja*, &c). The invocation of the deity by different names, **[31]** and its invitation to enjoy the meal prepared, may be equally old. It was justly regarded only as a kind of Yajus, and called *Nigada*[20] or *Nivid*. The latter term was principally applied to the enumeration of the titles, qualities, &c., of a particular deity, accompanied with an invitation. At the most ancient times it appears that all sacrificial formulas were spoken by the Hotar alone; the Adhvaryu was only his assistant, who arranged the sacrificial compound, provided the implements, and performed all manual labour. It was only at the time when regular metrical verses and hymns were introduced into the ritual, that a part of the duties of the Hotar devolved on the Adhvaryu. There are, in the present ritual, traces to be found, that the Hotar actually must have performed part of the duties of the Adhvaryu.

According to the ritual which appears to have been in force for the last three thousand years without undergoing any considerable change, it is one of the principal duties of the Adhvaryu to give orders

[20] See Madhusûdana's Prasthânabheda in Weber's *Indische Studien*, i. page 14, and the Bhâgavata Purâṇa 12, 6, 52 (in the Bombay edition) where the *yajurgaṇa*, *i. e.* the series of Yajus mantras is called *nigada*. Madhusûdana comprises by this name, as it appears, principally the Praiṣas or orders by the Adhvaryu to the other priests to do their respective duties.

(*praiṣa*) to most of the officiating priests, to perform their respective duties. Now at several occasions, especilly at the more solemn sacrifices, the order is to be given either by the Hotar himself, or his principal assistant, the Maitrâvaruṇa. So, for instance, the order to the slaughterers of the sacrificial animal, **[32]** which is known by the name of Adhrigu-Praiṣa-mantra (see Ait. Br. 2, 6-7) is given by the Hotar himself, though the formulas of which it is composed have all characteristics of what was termed in the ritual *Yajus*, and consequently assigned to the Adhvaryu. At the Soma sacrifice all orders to the Hotar to repeat the Yâjyâ mantra, before the libations are thrown into the fire, are to be given by the Maitrâvaruṇa, and not by the Adhvaryu. The formulas by which the gods are called to appear, the address to the fire when it is kindled are repeated by the Hotar, not by the Adhvaryu, though they cannot be termed *rik*, the repetition of which alone was in later times regarded as incumbent upon the Hotar. The later rule, "The Hotar performs his duties with the Ṛigveda" (in the introductory chapter to the Hiraṇyakeśi and Âpastamba Śrâuta Sutras) is therefore not quite correct. The Hotar himself even sacrifices on certain occasions what is, according to the later ritual, to be done by the Adhvaryu alone, or, when the offering is given as penance, by the Brahmâ. So, for instance, he sacrifices melted butter before repeating the Aśvina Śastra (see the note to 4, 7, page 268), which is, as far as its principal parts are concerned, certainly very ancient.

Now, if we compare the sacrificial formulas as contained in the Yajurveda, and principally the so-called Nigadas, and Nivids, preserved in the Brâhmaṇas and Sûtras with the bulk of the Ṛigveda hymns, we come to the conclusion, that the former are more ancient, and served the Ṛiṣis as a kind of **[33]** sacred text, just as passages of the Bible suggest ideas to religious poets among Christians. That Vedic poets were perfectly acquainted with several of such formulas and addresses which are still extant, can be proved beyond any doubt.

Reserving a more detailed treatment of this important question to a future occasion, I here instance only some of the most striking proofs.

One reference to the Nivid inserted in the Vaiśvadeva hymn at the Vaiśvadeva Śastra, and my remarks on it (see pages 212-13), the reader will find, that the great Ṛiṣi Viśvâmitra who with some of his sons are the poets of many hymns which we now possess (as, for instance, of the whole third Maṇḍala), knew this ancient sacrificial formula very well; for one of its sentences setting forth the number of deities is alluded to by him.

Certain stereotyped formulas which occur in every Nivid, to whatever deity it might be addressed, occur in hymns and even commence them. I instance the hymn *predam brahma* (8, 37), which is certainly an allusion to the sentence which occurs in all Nivids, *predam brahma predam kṣattram* (see note 25 on page 189.) That the coincidence is no mere chance follows from some other characteristic Nivid terms made use of in the hymn in question; compare *âvitha pra sunvataḥ* with *predam sunvantam yajamânam avatu* in all Nivids, and *kṣattriya tvaṃ avasi* with *predam kṣattram* (*avatu*).

The Subrahmaṇyâ formulas, which is generally called a Nigadâ (see on it the note to 6, 3 on pages 383-84) **[34]** is unmistakably alluded to in the hymn, 1, 51, principally in the first and thirteenth verses. In both, Indra is called *meṣa*, a ram, and *vṛiṣaṇaś vasya menâ*.

The call of the *Agnîdhra*, *astu śrâuṣaṭ* as well as the Agur addressed to the Hotar, *hotâ yakṣat*, were known to the Ṛiṣis, as we learn from 1, 139, 1. 10.

The so-called Ṛituyâjas which are extant in a particular collection of sacrificial formulas, called *praiṣa sûkta* or *praiṣâdhyaya*, occur even with their very words in several hymns, such as 1, 15; 2, 37. (On the Rituyâjas, see note 35 on pages 135-36).

The so-called Aprî hymns are nothing but a poetical development of the more ancient Prayâjas, and Anuyâjas (compare the notes 12 on page 18; 14 on pages 81-82; and 25 on page 110.)

Many hymns were directly composed not only for sacrificial purposes in general, but even for particular rites. This is principally the case with several hymns of Viśvâmitra. So, for instance, the whole of hymn 3, 8 *añjanti tvâm adhvare* (see about it, Ait. Br. 2, 2) refers only to the anointing, erecting, and decorating, of the sacrificial post; 3, 21 is evidently made for addressing the drops of melted butter which drip from the omentum, over which they were poured (see Ait. Br. 2, 12); 3 52, celebrates the offering of the Purodâśa consisting of fried grains, pap, &c., which belongs to each Soma libation (see Ait. Br. 2, 23.)

The first ten hymns of the first book of the Ṛigveda Saṁhitâ contain, as it appears, the Soma ritual **[35]** of Madhuchhandâs, the son of Viśvâmitra. It provides, however, only for two libations, *viz.*, the morning and midday. The first hymn has exactly the nature of an Ajya hymn, which forms the principal part of the first Śastra, the so-called Ajya. The second and third hymns contain the Pra-uga Śastra, which is the second at the morning libation, in all its particulars. The following seven hymns (4-10) all celebrate Indra and it appears from some remarks in the Ait. Br. (3, 20, page 192), that in ancient times the midday libation belonged exclusively to Indra. The ritual for the evening libation is of so peculiar a nature, and so complicated, that we must ascribe to it quite a different origin than to the two other libations.

The hymns 12-23 appear to contain a more comprehensive ritual of the Kaṇva family, which is ancient. The 12th hymn (the first in this collection) is addressed to the Agni of the ancestors, the *pravara*, who must be invoked at the commencement of every sacrifice; it contains three parts of the later ritual—(*a*) the *pravara*, (*b*) the invocation of Agni by the Nigada, and (*c*) the request to Agni to bring the gods (the so-called *devâvahanam*). The 13th is an aprî Sûkta containing the Prayâjas, which accompany the very first offerings at every sacrifice.

These three hymns were, it appears, appropriate to a simple Isṭi, as it precedes every greater sacrifice. The following hymns refer to the Soma sacrifice. The 15th is a Ṛituyâja hymn; the Ṛituyâjas always precede the Ajya Śastra. The hymns from **[36]** 16-19 contain a ritual for the midday libation, and in 20-22 we find the principal deities of the Śastras of the evening libation.

The hymns from 44-50 in the first book by Praskaṇva, the son of Kaṇva, contain, if the Indra hymn (51) is also reckoned, all the principal deities, and metres of the Aśvina Śastra, the former even in their proper order, *viz.*, Agni, Uṣâs, the Aśvins, Sûrya, Indra (see Ait. Br. 4, 7-11).

These instances, which could be easily greatly enlarged, will, I think, suffice to show that the ritual of the Brâhmaṇas in its main features was almost complete at the time when the principal Ṛishis, such as the Kaṇvas, Viśvâmitra, Vasiṣṭha, &c., lived.

I must lay particular stress on the Nivids which I believe to be more ancient than almost all the hymns contained in the Ṛigveda. The principal ones (nine in number) are all to be found in the notes to my translation of the 3rd Pañchikâ (book). That no attention has been paid as yet to these important documents by the few Vedic scholars in Europe, is principally owing to the circumstance of their not having been known to them. It being now generally believed, that the earliest relics of Vedic literature are to be found only in the Ṛigveda Saṁhitâ, it is of course incumbent on me to state briefly the reasons why I refer the so-called Nivid to a still more remote antiquity.

The word *nivid* frequently occurs in the hymns, and even with the epithet *pûrva* or *pûrvya*, old **[37]** (see 1, 89, 3; 96, 2; 2, 36, 6.) The

Marutvatîya Nivid[21] is, as it appears, even referred to by Vâmadeva (4, 18, 7, compared with note 25, on page 189); the repetition of the Nivids is juxtaposed with the performance of the chanters, and the recital of the Śastras (6, 67, 10). The Brâhmaṇam regards the Nivids, particularly that one addressed to Agni, as those words of Prajâpati, by means of which he created all beings (see Ait. Br. 2, 33-34). That such an idea, which entirely coincides with the Zoroastrian of Ahuramazda (Ormazd) having created the world through the *yathâ-ahû-vairyô* prayer (see the 19th chapter of the Yaśna), must be more ancient than the Brâhmaṇas, we learn from a hymn of the old Ṛisi Kutsa, who is already in many Vedic songs looked upon as a sage of the remote past. He says (1, 96, 2) that Agni created by means of the "first Nivid" the creatures of the Manus (see page 143). In 1, 89, 3-4, an old Nivid appears to be quoted. For the words which follow the sentence, "we call them with the old Nivid," bear quite the stamp of such a piece.

Many Nivids, even the majority of them, are certainly lost. But the few pieces of this kind of religious literature which are still extant, are sufficient to show that they must be very ancient, and are not to be regarded as fabrications of the sacrificial priests at the times when the Brâhmaṇas were composed. **[38]** Their style is, in the main, just the same in which the hymns are composed, and far more ancient than that of the Brâhmaṇas. They contain, in short sentences, the principal names, epithets, and feats of the deity invoked. They have no regular metre, but a kind of rhythmus; or even a parallelismus membrorum as the ancient Hebrew poetry.

The circumstance that in the ritual such a paramount importance is attached to such half poetical, half prose pieces as the Nivids are (see particularly Ait. Br. 2, 33; 3, 10-11), clearly tends to prove, that they must have been regarded as very efficacious. This could be hardly accounted for at a time when beautiful and finished songs were forthcoming in abundance to serve the same purpose, had they not been very ancient, and their employment been sanctioned by the example of the most ancient Ṛiṣis.

We have already seen, that several of those Nivid formulas which we have now were known to some Vedic poets. I will give here a few more instances. The hymn to the Marutas by Viśvâmitra (3, 47) is evidently based on the Marutvatîya Nivids (see them on page 189); the

[21] When the word *nivid* appears often in the plural, then the several pâdas, of which the Nivid consists, are to be understood.

verse to Savitar (3, 54, 11) alludes to Savitṛi Nivids (see them on page 208); the hymn to Dyâvâpṛithivî (1, 160) is a poetical imitation of the Dyâvâpṛithivî Nivids (page 209); the Ṛibhu hymn (4, 33) resembles very much the Ribhu Nivids (page 210), &c.

Another proof of the high antiquity of the Nivids is furnished by the Zend-Avesta. The many prayer **[39]** formulas in the Yaśna which commence with *nivaê-ahayêmi, i.e.*, I invite, are exactly of the same nature as the Nivids.

The Nivids along with many so-called Yajus formulas which are preserved in the Yajurveda, the Nigadas, such as the Subrâhmaṇyâ and the so-called Japa formulas (such as Ait. Br. 2, 38), which are muttered with a low voice only, are doubtless the most ancient pieces of Vedic poetry. The Ṛiṣis tried their poetical talent first in the composition of Yâjyâs or verses recited at the occasion of an offering being thrown into the fire. Thence we meet so many verses requesting the deity to accept the offering, and taste it. These Yâjyâs were extended into little songs, which, on account of their finished form, were called *sûktam, i.e.* well, beautifully spoken. The principal ideas for the Yâjyâs were furnished by the sacrificial formulas in which the Yajurveda abounds, and those of the hymns were suggested by the Nigadas and Nivids. There can be hardly any doubt, that the oldest hymns which we possess, are purely sacrificial, and made only for sacrificial purposes. Those which express more general ideas, or philosophical thoughts, or confessions of sins, such as many of those addressed to Varuṇa, are comparatively late.

In order to illustrate that the development of the sacrificial and religious poetry of the ancient Brahmans took such a course as here described, I may adduce the similar one which we find with the Hebrews. The sacrificial ritual of Moses, as laid **[40]** down in the Leviticus, knows no rythmical sentences nor hymns which accompanied the oblations offered to Jehovah. It describes only such manual labour, as found with the Brahmans its place in the Yajurveda, and mentions but very few and simple formulas which the officiating priest appears to have spoken when throwing the offering into the fire of the altar. They differed, according to the occasion, but very little. The principal formula was ניחח ליהוה אשה ריח "a fire offering of pleasant smell for Jehovah," which exactly corresponds with the Vedic *ágnaye, indráya*, &c. *svâhâ!* [22] *i.e.* a good offering to Agni, Indra, &c. If it was the solemn holocaustum, then the word עלה, *i.e.*

[22] The term *svâhâ* is to be traced to the root *dhâ*, to put, with *â*, to put in, into, and stands for *svâdhâ* (*su*+*âdhâ*). It means the gift which is thrown into the fire.

holocaustum, was used in addition (Leviticus 1, 9-13); if it was the so-called *zebakh shlâmîm* or sacrifice for continued welfare, the word לחם food, bread, was added (Levit. 3, 11); if it was a penance, the words אשם הוא (Levit. 7, 5), "this is a penance," were required. When the priest absolved a sacrificer who brought an offering as a penance, he appears to have used a formula also, which is preserved in the so-frequently occuring sentence: רנכז עליר מחטאתר אשר חטא רנסלח לז (Lev. iv, 25, 31: v. 6, 10.) "and he (the priest) shall annul the sin which he has committed, so that he will be pardoned." [23]

[41] If we compare these formulas with the psalms, which were composed and used for the worship of Jehovah, then we find exactly the same difference between both, as we discover between the Yajus formulas, Nivids, &c., and the finished hymns of the Rigveda Saṁhitâ. In the same way as there is a considerable interval of time between the establishment of the Mosaic ritual and the composition of the psalms, we are completely justified in supposing that a similar space of time intervened between the Brahmanical ritual with its sacrifical formulas, and the composition of the majority of the Vedic hymns. Between Moses and David there is an interval of five hundred years, and if we assume a similar one between the simple Yajus formulas, and such finished hymns as those addressed to Varuṇa which M. Müller ascribes to his Chhandas period, we shall not be in the wrong.

Another proof that the purely sacrificial poetry is more ancient than either profane songs or hymns of a more general religious character, is furnished by the *Shi-king* or Book of Odes of the Chinese. Of its four divisions, *viz. kûo-fung, i.e.* popular songs of the different territories of ancient China, *ta-ya* and *siao ya, i.e.* imperial songs, to be used with music at the imperial festivals, and *sung, i.e.* hymns in honour of deceased emperors, and vassal kings, the latter, which are of a purely sacrificial character, are the most ancient pieces. The three last odes in this fourth division go back as far as the commencement of the *Shang* dynasty, which ascended the dragon seat in **[42]** the year 1766 B.C., whilst almost all other pieces in the collection are composed from the earlier part of the reign of the Chou dynasty down almost to Confucius' time (from 1120 B.C. till about 600 B.C.)

If we consider that the difference of time between the purely sacrificial and non-sacrificial hymns of the Chinese thus amounts to about

[23] The priest appears to have addressed these words to the sinner who was to be absolved in this manner, "I annul the sin which thou hast committed, and thou shalt be pardoned."

1,000 years, we would not be very wrong in presuming similar intervals to exist between the different hymns of the Ṛigveda. Ṛiṣis like Kâvya, Uśanâs, Kakṣivat, Hiraṇyastûpa, to whom several hymns are traced, were for the Kaṇvas, Viśvâmitra, Vasiṣṭha, &c., as ancient personages, as the emperors Tang (1765 B.C.) and Wuwang (1120 B.C.) to Confacious (born 551 B. C.)

On account of the utter want of Indian chronology for the Vedic and post-Vedic times, it will be of course for ever impossible to fix exactly the age of the several hymns of the Ṛigveda, as can be done with most of the psalms and many of the odes of the Shi-king. But happily we possess at least one astronomical date which furnishes at any rate the external proof of the high antiquity of Vedic literature, which considerably tends to strengthen the internal evidence of the same fact. I here mean the well known passage in the Jyotiṣam, or Vedic calendar, about the position of the solstitial points. The position there given carries us back to the year 1181 according to Archdeacon Pratt's, and to 1186 **[43]** B.C. according to the Rev. R. Main's calculations.[24] The questions on the age of this little treatise and the origin of the Nakṣatra [25] system, about which **[44]** there has been of late so much wrangling among the few Sanscrit scholars of Europe and America, are of

---

[24] See the Journal of the Asiatic Society of Bengal of the year 1862 pages 49-50. Max Müller's Preface to the 4th Volume of his edition of the Ṛigveda Saṁhitâ, page Lxxxv.

[25] There can be hardly any doubt, that the Nakṣatra system of the Indians, Chinese, Persians and Arabs is of a common origin, but it is very difficult to determine with what nation it originated. The original number was twenty-eight. I do not intend fully to discuss here the important question, but I wish only to direct attention to the circumstance overlooked as yet by all the writers on the subject, that the terms which the Indians, Arabs, and Chinese use for expressing the idea "constellation" have in all the three languages, Sanscrit, Chinese, and Arabic, precisely the same meaning, viz. a place where to pass the night, a station. This is certainly no mere chance, but can only be accounted for by the supposition, that the framers of the Nakṣatra system regarded the several Nakṣatras as heavenly stations, or night quarters, where the travelling moon was believed to put on his journey through the heavens. Let us examine these terms.

The Chinese expression for *Nakṣatra* is *Siu* (spelt by Morrison *suh* and *sew*, by Medhurst *sew* with the third or departing tone). The character representing it which is to be found under the 40th radical, strokes 8 (see Morrison's Chinese Dictionary, Vol. 1 page 847) is composed of three signs, *viz.* that for a *roof*, that for *man*, and that for a *hundred.* Its original meaning therefore is "a place where a hundred men find shelter, a station or night quarters for a company of soldiers." The word is, as is the case with most of the Chinese words, used as a substantive, adjective, and verb.

As a substantive it denotes "a resting place to pass the night at" with a road-house (*lu shih*), *i.e.* an inn, or a halting place in general; such places were situated at the distance of every thirty Li. Thence it is metaphorically employed to express the

[45] minor importance compared with the fact and the age of the observation itself. That an astronomical observation was taken by the

---

station on the heavens where the travelling moon is supposed to put up. In this sense the Chinese speak of *ölh shih pâ siu* "the twenty-eight halting places" (on the heavens).

As an objective it means *past, former, i. e.* the night-quarters which were just left.

In the sense of a verb, but never in that of a substantive, we find it frequently used in two of the so-called See-shu or four Classical books of the Chinese, *viz.* the *Lun-yu* (the Confucian Analects) and in *Meng-tse.*

In order to show the use of this important word in the Classical writings, I here quote some instances :

(a) intrans, *to pass the night, to stop over night,* Lun-yu 14, 41 ; *tse lu siu yu Shih-man, i.e.* Tse-lu (one of the most ardent and zealous disciples of Confucius) passed the night at Shih-man ; 18. 7. 3 ibidem ; *chih Tse-lu siu, i.e.* he detained Tse-lu to pass the night (with him). Meng-tse 2, 2, 11, 1 ; *Meng-tse k'iu Tsi sia yu Chaw, i. e.* Meng-tse after having left Tsi, passed the night at Chow ; 2, 2, 12, 4, ibidem : *yu san siu ölh hĕu chùh Chow, yu yu sin i wei suh, i. e.* When I, after having stopped for three nights left Chow, I thought in my mind my departure to be speedy still.

(b) trans. *to make pass the night, to keep over night.* Lun-yu 10, 8, 8 : *tse yu kung pü siu já,* when he (Confucius) sacrificed at the Duke's (assisted the Duke in sacrificing) he did not keep the (sacrificial) flesh over night. In this sense it is several times metaphorically used ; so Lun-yu 12. 2, 2 : *Tse-lu wu siu no, i.e.* Tse-lu never kept a promise over night (he carried it out at one, before he went to rest).

(c) *to have taken up his quarters, to be at rest.* Lun-yu 7, 26 : *yih pü shê siu,* he (Confucius) shot, but not with an arrow and string at (animals) which were at rest (asleep).

The Arabic word for the Nakshatras is منزل *manzil* phur. منازل *menázil,* "a place where to put up, qurters," from the root نزل, to make a journey, to put up at a place as a guest.

This name for the constellations must be very ancient with the Semitic nations, for we find it already in the Old Testament (Book of the Kings ii. 23, 5) in the form מדלרח *mazzaloth* ; it has no proper etymology in Hebrew (for the root נדל *nazal,* to which alone it could be traced, means *to flow*), and is apparently introduced as a foreign word from some other Semitic nation, probably the Babylonians. The Jewish commentators had no clear conception of the proper meaning of the word ; they take it to mean *star* in general, and then the twelve signs of the Zodiac. But from the context of the passage in the Book of the Kings, just quoted, where it stands together with the *moon and the whole host of the heavens* (" for the moon and the mazzaloth and the whole host of the heaven") it undoubtedly follows, that its meaning cannot be " star" in general, which idea is expressed by the " whole host of the heavens," but something particular in the heavens connected with the moon. The use of the same word in Arabic for expressing the idea of constellation, heavenly mansions of the moon, proves beyond any doubt, that the *mazzaloth* mean the same.

Now the Sanscrit word *nakṣatra* has originally no other meaning than either *siu* or *manzil* have. The arrangement of the meaning of this word which is made in Boehtlingk and Roth's Sanscrit Dictionary is insufficient and treated with the same superficiality as the majority of the more difficult Vedic words in that much-lauded work. They make it to mean *star* in general (sidus), the *stars,* and then *constellation, station of the moon.* But the very formation of the word by means of the suffix *atrá*

Brahmans as early as the 12th century before Christ is proved beyond any doubt by the date to be elicited from the observation itself. If astronomical calculations of past events are of any worth, we must accept as settled the date of the position of the solstitial [46] points as recorded in the Jyotisam. To believe that such an observation was imported from some foreign country, Babylon or China, could be absurd, for there is nothing in it to show, that it cannot have been made in the north-western part of India, or a closely adjacent country. A regulation of the calendar by such observations was an absolute necessity for the Brahmans; for the proper time of commencing and ending their sacrifices, principally the so-called Sattras or sacrificial sessions, could not be known without an accurate knowledge of the time of the sun's northern and southern progress. The knowledge of the calendar forms such an essential part of the ritual, that many important conditions of the latter cannot be carried out without the former. The sacrifices are allowed to commence only at certain lucky constellations, and in certain months. So, for instance, as a rule, no great sacrifice can commence during the sun's southern progress (*dakṣiṇâyana*); for this is regarded up to the present day as an unlucky period by the

---

indicates, that something particular must be attached to its meaning; compare *patatra* a wing, literally a means for flying, *vadhatra* a weapon, literally a means for striking, *yajatram* the keeping of a sacrificial fire, literally the means or place for sacrificing; *amatra*, a drinking vessel, literally a place to which a thing goes which holds it. According to all analogy we can derive the word only from *nakṣ*, which is a purely Vedic root, and means to "arrive at." Thus *nakṣatra* etymologically means, either the means by which one arrives, or the place where one arrives, a station. This expresses most adequately the idea attached by the Indians to the Nakṣatras as mansions for the travelling moon. But even if we waive this derivation, and make it a compound of *nak* (instead of *naktá*, see Ṛigveda 7, 71, 1) and *satra=sattra*, a session for the night, night quarters, we arrive at the same meaning. The latter derivation is, I think, even preferable to the former. The meanings of the word are to be classed as follows: (1) *station*, qurters where to pass the night. In this sense it is out of use; (2) especially the *stations on the heavens* where the travelling moon is supposed to put up, the twenty-eight constellations; (3) metonymiclly *stars* in general, *the starry sphere* (Rigveda 7, 86, 1: *nakṣatram paprathachcha bhûma*, he spread the starry sphere, and the earth). The latter use is pre-eminently poetical, as poets always can use *pars pro toto*. The *nakṣatras* as stations of the moon were perfectly known to the Ṛiṣis, as every one can convince himself from the many passages in the Taitirîya Brâhmaṇam, and the Atharvaveda. That these books are throughout much later than the songs of the Ṛigveda is just what I have strong reasons to doubt. The arrangement of the meanings of *nakṣatra* as given here entirely coincides with all we know of the history of either the word *siu* in Chinese, or *manzil*, *mazzaloth* in the semitic languages. The Chinese, especially poets, used the word *siu* in the sense of *star* or *stars* in general, and so did the Rabbîs in the Mishnah and the Talmud, according to the testimony of Juda ben Karish (see Gesenii Thesaurus Linguæ Hebrææ, et Chaldææ ii. page 869).

Brahmans, in which even to die is belived to be a misfortune. The great sacrifices take place generally in spring, in the months *Chaitra* and *Vaiśâkha* (April and May). The sattras which lasted for one year were, as one may learn from a careful perusal of the 4th book of the Aitareya Brâhmaṇam, nothing but an imitation of the sun's yearly course. They were divided into two distinct parts, each consisting of six months of thirty days each ; in the midst of both was the *Viṣuvan, i.e.* equator or central day, cutting the **[47]** whole Sattra into two halves. The ceremonies were in both the halves exactly the same ; but they were in the latter half performed in an inverted order. This represents the increase of the days in the northern, and their decrease in the southern progress ; for both increase and decrease take place exactly in the same proportions.

In consideration that these Sattras were already at the time of the compilation of the Brâhmaṇas an old institution, we certainly can find nothing surprising in the circumstance, that the Indian astronomers made the observation above-mentioned so early as the 12th century B.C. For the Sattras are certainly as early as, if not earlier than, this time. Sattras lasting for sixty years appear even to have been known already to the authors of the Brâhmaṇas (see page 287).

Now that observation proves two things beyond doubt : (1) That the Indians had made already such a considerable progress in astronomical science, early in the 12th century, as to enable them to take such observations; (2) That by that time the whole ritual in its main features as laid down in the Brâhmaṇas was complete.

We do not hesitate therefore to assign the composition of the bulk of the Brâhmaṇas to the years 1400-1200 B.C.; for the Saṁhitâ we require a period of *at least* 500-600 years, with an interval of about two hundred years between the end of the proper Brâhmaṇa period. Thus we obtain for the bulk of the Saṁhitâ the space from 1400-2000; the oldest hymns and **[48]** sacrificial formulas may be a few hundred years more ancient still, so that we would fix the very commencement of Vedic Literature between 2400-2000 B. C. If we consider the completely authenticated antiquity of several of the sacred books of the Chinese, such as the original documents, of which the Shu-king, or Book of History, is composed, and the antiquity of the sacrificial songs of the Shi-king, which all carry us back to 1700-2200 B.C., it will certainly not be surprising that we assign a similar antiquity to the most ancient parts of the Vedas. For there is nowhere any reason to show, that the Vedas must be less ancient than the earliest parts of the sacred books of the Chinese, but there is on the contrary much ground to believe, that they can fully lay claim to the same antiquity. Already at the time of the composition of the Brâhmaṇas, which as we have seen, cannot be later than about 1200 B. C., the three principal Vedas, *i.e.* their respective Saṁhitâs, were believed to have proceeded directly from the mouth of Prajâpati, the lord of the creatures, who occupies in the early Vedic mythology the same place which is, in the later writings, held by Brahmadeva. This could not have been the case, had they not been very ancient. In a similar way, the Chinese ascribe the ground text of their most ancient and most sacred book, the *Y-king*, *i.e.* Book of Changes, to a kind of revelation too, which was made to *Fuhi*, the Adam of the Chinese, by a Dragon horse, called *Lung-ma*.

Speculations on the nature of the sacrificial rites, **[49]** and cognate topics of a mystical character which form the proper sphere of the Brâhmaṇas, commenced already during the Saṁhitâ period, as one may learn from such hymns as Ṛigveda 1, 95, and the so called Vâmana Sûkta 1, 164. Even at the time of the composition of the present Brâhmaṇas, there existed already some time-hallowed sayings, which resemble in every respect those dicta of the Brahmâ priests, of which the bulk of the Brâhmaṇas consists. I instance here the *Brahmodyam* (Ait. Br. 5, 25), which was used already at that time at the conclusion of the tenth day's performance of the Dvâdaśâha sacrifice. It is, therefore, very difficult to draw a strict line of separation between the period during which the hymns were composed, and that one which brought forward the speculations known by the name of Brâhmaṇas. On a more close comparison of the mystical parts of the Saṁhitâ with the Brâhmaṇas, one must come to the conclusion, that the latter were commenced already during the period of the former.

Let us say a few words on the division made of the contents of the Brâhmaṇas by the Indian divines and philosophers. According to the introductory chapters to the Hiraṇyâkeśi (and Apastamba Sûtras) the Brâhmaṇas contain the following topics:—

(1) *Karmavidhânam*, or *vidhi*, *i.e.* rules on the performance of particular rites. To this class all those sentences in the Brâhmaṇas are referred which contain an order expressed in the potential mood, such as *yajeta*, he ought to sacrifice; *śaṁset*, he ought **[50]** to repeat (such and such a verse); *kuryât*, he ought to proceed (in such or such a way), &c. This is the principal part of the Brâhmaṇas, and has for the Brahmans

about the same significance as in the Talmudic Literature the *halakah* has for the Jews; it is simply authoritative.

(2) *Arthavâda*. This term comprises the numerous explanatory remarks on the meaning of mantras and particular rites, the reasons why a certain rite must be performed in a certain way. This is the speculative part, and is on account of its containing the germs of all Hindu philosophy, and even of grammar, of the greatest importance. There is nowhere anything like an approach to a regular system perceptible, but only occasional remarks bearing on philosophical and grammatical topics. For the history of grammar, the fifth Pañchikâ of the Aitareya Brâhmaṇam is of a particular interest. We learn from it, that at that time not only numerous attempts were made to explain the meaning of words by etymology, but that the Brahmans even had already commenced to analyse the forms of speech by making distinctions between singular and plural, present, past, and future tenses, &c. The idea of *mukti* or final absorption in the Supreme Being, as taught in the later Vedânta philosophy, is even with most of its particulars spoken out in several of those explanatory remarks. I allude here to the frequently occurring terms, *sayujyatâ* junction, *sarupata* identity of form, *salokatâ* identity of place, which mark in the later times different stages of the final beatitude. **[51]** The principal tendency of this part is, to show the close connection of the visible and invisible worlds, between things on earth, and their counterparts or prototypes in heaven. Pantheistic ideas pervade all the Brâhmaṇas, and are already traceable in hymns of the Saṁhitâ.

(3) *Nindâ*, censure. This refers principally to the controversial remarks contained in all Brâhmaṇas. There was amongst these ancient divines and metaphysicians often difference of opinion as to the performance of a certain rite, or the choice of a particular mantra, or their meaning. One criticised the practice of the other, and condemned its application often in the strongest terms. The censure is generally introduced by the expression, "but this opinion is not to be attended to." The sacrificers are often cautioned from adopting such a malpractice, by the assertion that if a priest would proceed in such or such a way, the sacrificer would lose his life, be burned by the sacrificial fire, &c.

(4) *Śaṁsâ*, *i. e.* praise, recommendation. This part comprises principally those phrases which express that the performance of such or such a rite with the proper knowledge, produces the effect desired. They almost invariably contain the expression, *ya evam veda*, *i.e.* who has such a

knowledge. The extreme frequency of this phrase in the Brâhmaṇas, and Upaniṣads, is probably the reason, that the whole sacred knowledge was comprised afterwards only by the general term *veda*. Originally [52] it appears to have applied to Brâhmaṇa like sentences and explanations only.

(5) *Purâkalpa, i. e.* performance of sacrificial rites in former times. Under this head come the numerous stories of the fights of the Devas and Asuras, to which the origin of many rites is attributed, as also all legends on the sacrifices performed by the gods. This very interesting part forms the historical (or rather legendary) background of the whole sacrificial art. All rites were traced to the gods as their originators, or even to Prajâpati, the Supreme Being, the Lord of creatures. We can derive one important historical fact from the legends on the fight between the Devas and Asuras, *viz.*, that the religious contest between the ancient Indians (represented by the Devas) and the Iranians (represented by the Asuras, contained in the name Ahuramazda = Ormazd) took place long before the time of the composition of the Brâhmaṇas, that is, before the 12th century B.C. This is another proof corroborative of the high antiquity ascribed by Grecian writers to Zarathustra (Zoroaster), the prophet of the Asura nation (Iranians), who did manfully battle against idolatry and the worship of the Devas, branded by him as "devils." That contest which must have been lasting for many years appeared to the writers of the Brâhmaṇas as old as the feats of King Arthur appear to English writers of the nineteenth century.

(6) *Parakṛiti, i.e.* the achievement or feat of another. This head comprises the stories of certain performances of renowned Śrotriyas, or sacrificial [53] priests, of gifts presented by kings to Brahmans, the successes they achieved. The last book of the Aitareya particularly is full of this class of topics.

These six heads are often, however, brought only under two principal ones, *viz.*, *vidhi* and *arthavâda*. The latter then comprises all that is not injunction, that is, all topics from 2 to 6. This philosophical division exactly corresponds to the division of the contents of the Talmud by the Jewish Rabbis into two principal parts, *viz* : *halakah, i.e.* rule of conduct, which is as authoritative as the *thorah* (law of Moses), and *haggadah, i.e.* story, parable, and in fact everything illustrative of the former.

II.

The Aitareya Brâhmaṇam in particular.

The Aitareya Brâhmaṇam is one of the collections of the sayings of ancient Brahmâ priests (divines and philosophers), illustrative and explanatory of the duties of the so-called Hotṛi-priests. The latter performing the principal part of their duties by means of the mantras, termed *ṛik*, and contained in the so-called Ṛigveda Saṁhitâ, the Aitareya is therefore one of the Brâhmaṇas belonging to the Ṛigveda. There must have been, as we may learn from Pâṇini and Patañjali's Mahâbhâṣya, a much larger number of Brâhmaṇas belonging to each Veda; and even Sâyaṇa, who lived only about four hundred years ago, was acquainted with more than we have now. To the Ṛigveda we know at present besides **[54]** the Aitareya, only the Kâuṣîtaki Brâhmaṇam, which is also called Sâñkhâyana. Both appear to have been known to the grammarian Pâṇini,[1] as one may gather from the rule (v. 1, 62) which he gives regarding the formation of names of Brâhmaṇas consisting of thirty and forty Adhyâyas; for the Kauṣîtaki actually consists of thirty and the Aitareya of forty Adhyâyas, which were afterwards divided into eight Pañchikâs, each of which comprises five Adhyâyas.

The name "Aitareya" is by Indian tradition traced to *Itarâ*. Sâyaṇa tells regarding the origin of the name and of the Brâhmaṇa itself, in his introduction to the Aitareya Brâhmaṇam, the following story, on the authority of the *saṁpradâya-vidaḥ*, *i.e.* men versed in traditional stories. An ancient Ṛiṣi had among his many wives one who was called *Itarâ.* She had a son *Mahidâsa* by name, who is mentioned in the Aitareya Araṇyaka as Mahidâsa Aitareya. The Ṛiṣi perferred the sons of his other wives to Mahidâsa, and went even so far as to insult him once by placing all his other children in his lap to his exclusion. His mother, grieved at this ill-treatment of her son, prayed to her family deity (*kuladevatâ*), the Earth (*bhûmi*), who appeared in her celestial form in the midst of the assembly, placed him on a throne (*siṁhâsana*), and gave him as a token of honour for his surpassing all other children in learning a boon **[55]** (*vara*) which had the appearance of a Brâhmaṇa. After having received this gift, a Brâhmaṇam consisting of forty Adhyâyas, which commenced with the words, *agnir vâi devânâm avamo* (the first sentence of the Aitareya), and ended with *stṛiṇute stṛiṇute* (the two last words of the Aitareya), came forth through the mind of Mahdiâsa.

---

[1] The attention of Sanscrit scholars was first directed by Professor Weber at Berlir to this circumstance.

Afterwards the Brâhmaṇam, commencing with *atha mahâvratam* (the beginning words of the first Aitareya Araṇyaka) and ending with *âchârya âchârya* (the two last words of the third Araṇyaka)[2] was also revealed in the shape of the vow of an hermit[3] (*âranyakavratarûpam*).

The Aitareya Brâhmaṇam, as well as the Kâuṣitaki, do not treat of all the sacrifices and sacrificial rites which are mentioned and described in the books of Yajurveda, which may be (principally the Sûtras) regarded as the proper sacrificial encyclopediæ. They were, however, perfectly well known to the authors of these Brâhmaṇas, as we may learn from the fact, that the names of several sacrifices, such as Vâjapeya, Aptoryâma (see 3, 41) are mentioned without the description of the rituals belonging to them. Several things concerning **[56]** the Hotṛis whose duties principally are treated at every Soma sacrifice are left out. So the ceremony of choosing the sacrificial priests (*ṛitvig-varaṇam*) by the sacrificer, iacluding the Hotars, is left out, as Sâyaṇa has already observed. But every *Hâutra-prayoga*, *i.e.* practical hand-book for the Hotṛi-priests (for each sacrifice there are separate *prayogas* for each set of priests required), commences with it; the topic is generally treated in the Sûtras belonging to the Yajurveda; the principal mantras required at that occasion are to be found in the first chapter of the Tâṇdya Brâhmaṇam of the Sâmaveda. The dialogue used at this occasion is interesting, and throws some light on the nature and character of some sacrifices; therefore I give here some account of it.

The person who wishes to perform the Agniṣṭoma sacrifice, for instance, sends a delegate called *Somapravâka* to all Śrotriyas (sacrificial priests) whose services he wishes to engage for his forthcoming Soma sacrifice, to ask whether they would be willing to officiate at this occasion. The dialogue between the Somapravâka and the Hotar is as follows: S. "There will be a Soma sacrifice of such and such one; you are respectfully requested to act as Hotar at it." H. "What sacrifice is it?" S. "The *Jyotiṣṭoma-Agniṣṭoma-Soma* sacrifice." H. "What priests (*ṛitvijaḥ*) will officiate?', S. "Viṣṇu, Mitra,[4]" &c. H. "What is the reward for

[2] This remark throws some light on the relationship in which the five treatises, of which the present Aitareya Araṇyaka consists, and each of which bears the name *âraṇyaka*, stand to one another. Only the three first Araṇyakas were according to this notice regarded as a divine revelation to the Aitareya Ṛiṣi; the two others are then later additions, and did not form originally part of the Aitareya Araṇyaka.

[3] According to Brahminical ideas, a vow, a curse, a blessing, &c., can assume a visible form and so bocome manifest to the mental eyes of men.

[4] The priests represent the gods.

the priests?" S. "One hundred and twelve cows." [57] If the priests have accepted the invitation, then the sacrificer has actually to appoint them to their respective offices. This is the *varaṇam* or selection (of the priests).

The sacrificer first mentions the gods who are to act as his priests, "Agni (the fire) is my Hotar, Aditya (the sun) my Adhvaryu, the Moon my Brahmâ, Parjanya (the god of rain) my Udgâtar, the Sky (*âkâśa*) is my Sadasya (superintendent), the waters are my Hotrâśaṁsis (all the minor Hotṛi-priests); the rays my Chamasa Adhvaryus (cup-bearers). These divine priests I choose (for my sacrifice)." After having thus appointed the gods, who are to act as his divine priests, he now proceeds to appoint the "human" (*mânuṣa*) priests, This is at the Agniṣṭoma done with the following formula, "I (the name) of such and such a Gotra, will bring the Jyotiṣṭoma sacrifice by means of its Agniṣṭoma part, with the Rathantara-Pṛiṣṭha, four Stomas (the nine, fifteen, seventeen and twenty-one-fold), for which ten things, cows and so on are required, and for which as fee one hundred and twelve cows must be given. At this sacrifice be thou my Hotar.". The Hotar then accepts the appoin ment by the following formula: "May the great thing thou spokest of (unto me), the splendour thou spokest of, the glory thou spokest of, the Stoma thou spokest of, the way of performance thou spokest of, the enjoyment thou spokest of, the satisfaction thou spokest of; may all that thou spokest of come to me; may it enter me; may I have enjoyment through it. Agni is thy Hotar. He is [58] thy (divine) Hotar. I am thy (human) Hotar.' All priests are appointed in the same way, and by the same formulas.

After this disgression let us discuss the contents of the Aitareya Brâhmaṇam. It treats in its eight books, or forty chapters, each of which is subdivided into a certain number of *kaṇḍikâs, i.e.* small sections, paragraphs, as we have seen, almost exclusively of the duties of the seven Hotṛi-priests at the great Soma sacrifices, and the different royal inauguration ceremonies. All minor sacrifices and Iṣṭis, although they require the services of a Hotar, are excluded. The Hotṛi-priests are to be divided into three distinct classes: (1) The *Hotar*, the chief of all Hotṛi-priests. (2) The *Hotrakas, i.e.*, the little Hotras; these are, Maitrâvaruṇa (Praśâstar) Brâhmaṇâchhaṁsî, and Achhâvâka. (3) The *Hotrâśaṁsinaḥ, i.e.* the repeaters of the Hotṛi verses; they are, Potar, Neṣṭar, and Agnîdhra.

The first thirteen chapters (the two first books, and the three first chapters (of the third) treat of the duties of the chief Hotar at the Agniṣṭoma Soma sacrifices only; for this is the model (*prakṛiti*) of all Soma sacrifices which last for one day only (the so-called *aikâhikas*); all other Soma sacrifices of the same duration are mere modifications (*vikṛiti*) of it. It is regarded as an integral part of the Jyotiṣṭoma, and said to consist of the following seven sacrifices: (1) Agniṣṭoma, (2) Atyagniṣṭoma, (3) Ukthya, (4) Śoḷaśi, (5) Atirâtra, (6) Vâjapeya, (7) Aptoryâma Aśv. Śr. S. 6, 11). In many places, however, the **[59]** term Jyotiṣṭoma is equivalent to Agniṣṭoma. The Aitareya does not know these seven parts, as belonging together, but simply remarks, that they follow the Agniṣṭoma as their *prakṛiti* (3, 41). The Atyagniṣṭoma is not even mentioned in it at all.

All the duties of the Hotar at the Agniṣṭoma are mentioned almost in the exact order in which they are required. It lasts generally for five days. The ceremonies are then divided as follows:

First day.—Preliminary ceremonies, such as the election of the priests giving them presents (*madhuparka*), the Dîkṣanîya Iṣṭi, and the Dîkṣâ itself.

Second day.—The Prâyaṇîya or opening Iṣṭi; the buying of the Soma; the Atithya Iṣṭi, Pravargya, and Upasad twice (once in the forenoon, and once in the afternoon).

Third day.—Pravargya and Upasad twice again.

Fourth day.—Agnipraṇayanam, Agni-Soma-praṇayanam, Havirdhâna praṇayanam. The animal sacrifice.

Fifth day.—The squeezing, offering and drinking of the Soma juice at the three great Libations, *viz.* the morning, midday, and evening Libations. The concluding Iṣṭi (*udayanîya*). Ablution (*avabhrita*).

The ceremonies of the four first days are only introductory, but absolutely necessary; for without them no one is allowed to sacrifice and drink the Soma juice. The Soma ceremony is the holiest rite in the whole Brahmanical service, just as the Homa ceremony of the Parsi priests is regarded by them as **[60]** the most sacred performance. No Parsi priest is allowed to perform it, if he does not very frequently undergo the great purification ceremony, called the Barashnom of nine nights. In the same way every Brahman has, as often as he brings a Soma sacrifi'ce to undergo the Dîkṣâ (see 1, 3; 4, 26.) One such ceremony is even not considered sufficient. For the sacrifice has besides the Dîkṣâ to undergo the Pravargya, which is a similar preparation for the great Soma day. Even the animal sacrifice must precede the solemn Soma fiestival; for it is of minor importance. The animal is instead of the sacrificer himself.

The animal when sacrificed in the fire, goes to the gods, and so does the sacrificer in the shape of the animal (see page 80 of the translation). The animal sacrifice is vicarious. Being thus received among the gods, the sacrificer is deemed worthy to enjoy the divine beverage, the Soma, and participate in the heavenly king, who is Soma. The drinking of the Soma juice makes him a new man; though a new celestial body had been prepared for him at the Pravargya ceremony, the enjoyment of the Soma-beverage transforms him again; for the nectar of the gods flows for the first time in his veins, purifying and sanctifying him. This last birth to the complete enjoyment of all divine rights is symbolically indicated in rites of the morning libation (see 32, 35; 38; 3, 2).

The principal features of this Agniṣṭoma sacrifice must be very ancient. For we discover them almost complete with the Parsis. They also do not prepare [61] the corresponding Homa (Soma) juice alone, but it must always be accompanied with other offerings. The Puroḍâśa of the Brahmans, which always belongs to a Soma libation, is represented by the Dârûn (holy bread), the animal offering indicated by the ring of hair (*varaśa*) taken from an ox, to be placed on the same table with the Homa. The Homa shoots are treated in the same way, when brought to the spot, as the Brahmans treat them. The Parsi priest sprinkles them with water,[5] which is exactly the *âpyâyana* ceremony of the Brahmans. He must go round the fire with the Homa just as the Brahmans carry the Soma round the sacrificial compound (see 1, 14). The ceremonies of preparing and drinking both the Homa and Soma juice are quite similar.[6] The water required for it must be consecrated, which exactly corresponds to the Vasatîvarîs and Ekadhanâs of the Brahmanical Soma service (2, 20). The Zota of the Parsis drinks his cup filled with Homa in three turns, so does the Hotar also from the Graha. After the libation has been poured from the Grahas into the fire, and drunk by the Hotar, the Stotras are chanted, and then the Śastras belonging to them recited. In a similar way the Zota priest repeats, shortly after having enjoyed the Homa, the *Gâthâs* of Zarathustra Spitama (Zoroaster), which [62] are metrical compositions, and represent the Śastras of the Brahmanical Soma service. He must repeat five such Gâthâs, just as there are five Śastras, at the morning

[5]The mantra repeated at that occasion is Yaśna 10, 1, "May the water-drops (sprinkled over the Homa) fall to the destruction of the Devas, and Devis."

[6]Compare notes 8 on page 118, 5 on page 131, 14 on page 137, and my Essays on the Sacred Language, &c., of the Parsis, pages 132-33, 167.

and midday libations, and at the Ukthya Soma sacrifice at the evening libations also.

These are only a few of the points of comparison which I could easily enlarge; but they will be sufficient to show, that the Agniṣṭoma Soma sacrifice was originally the same ceremony as the Homa rite of the Parsi priests. The opinions of both the Brahmans and Parsis on the effect of the drinking of the Soma (Homa) juice are besides exactly the same. The Brahmans believe that it leads to heaven; so do the Parsi Priests. They say, that Homa is a plant, and a great angel. Any one who has drunk the Homa juice becomes united with this angel, and after his death an inhabitant of paradise. For the juice which is in the body of the priest who has drunk him, goes to heaven, and connects him mystically with the angel.

With particular care are the the so-called Śastras or recitations of the Hotṛi priests treated in the Aitareya Brâhmaṇam. The fifth chapter of the second, and the three first chapters of the third book are entirely taken up with the exposition of the Shastras of the Hotar at the morning, midday, and evening libations. As the reader may learn from a perusal principally of the third book, the Śastras always belong to Stotras or performances by the Sâma singers, *viz*: the Udgâtar or chief singer, the Prastotar who chants the prelude, and the Pratihartar **[63]** who chants the response. Their recitations must be very ancient, as we have seen; for they are by the name *uktha* (exactly corresponding to *ukhdhem* in the Zend language) frequently mentioned in the Saṁhitâ. A closer examination of them will throw much light on the history of the composition of the Vedic hymns. As ancient as the Śastras are the Stomas, the exposition of which forms one of the topics of the Sâmaveda Brâhmaṇas (see note 18 on page 237-38). The word *stoma* is in the form *stoma* also known in the Zend-Avesta. The Parsi priests understand by it a particular sacrificial ceremony of minor importance, which consists in consecrating a meal (meat is at this occasion indispensable) in the honour of an angel or a deceased person, to be enjoyed afterwards by the whole party assembled. That the idea of "sacrificial rite" was attached also by the Brahmans to the word, clearly follows from the terms, *Agniṣṭoma* and *Jyotiṣṭoma*. The musical performance which was originally alone called a Stoma, formed a necessary part of certain sacrifices, and was then, as *pars pro toto*, applied to the whole rite.

The universal character of the Agniṣṭoma and its meaning is treated especially in the fourth chapter of the third book. In its last chapter, and in the two first of the fourth, the principal modifications of the Agniṣṭoma are mentioned, and briefly described, *viz.*, the Ukthya, Śoḷaśi, and Atirâtra, along with the Aśvina Śastra.

The Atirâtra sacrifice introduces, however, the **[64]** Sattras or sacrificial sessions, the principal rules for the Hotṛi performances of which are laid down in the third chapter of the fourth book. They are applicable for Sattras which last for a whole year. The two last chapters of the fourth, and the first four chapters of the fifth book describe very minutely the duties of the Hotar during the ten principal days of the Dvâdaśâha which may be performed as a Sattra, or as a Ahîna (a Soma sacrifice lasting for more than one, and less than thirteen days).

The last chapter of the fifth book is taken up with miscellaneous matter, such as the penances required of an Agnihotri when he becomes guilty of some fault, or if some misfortune should befal him regarding his duties towards his sacred fires, and the question, whether the Agnihotram (daily burnt offering) is to be offered before or after sunrise ; it further treats of the duties of the Brahmâ priest, how he has to perform the penances for mistakes committed by any one of the performing priests.

The whole sixth book treats, after some remarks on the offices of the Grâvastut and Subrahmaṇyâ, almost exclusively of the duties of the six minor Hotṛi-priests, principally at the great Soma sacrifices, which last for one week at least, or for a series of weeks (*Ṣaḷaha*) We find in it descriptions of the so-called Śilpa Śastras, or "skilful (rather very artificial) recitations" of the minor Hotars. These Śastras, principally the Vâlakhilyas, the Vṛiṣâkapi, Evayâmarut, and the so-called Kuntâpa hymns, are no doubt the latest additions, looking like **[65]** decorations, to the ritual of the Hotṛi-priests. The whole book has the appearance of a suppliment to the fourth and fifth.

The seventh and eighth books treat principally of the sacrifices of the Kṣattriyas and the relationship in which the princes stand to the Brahmans. They are, from an historical point of view, the most important part of the whole Brâhmaṇam.

The seventh book describes first the division of the sacrificial animal into thirty-six single pieces, and their distribution among the officiating priests, the sacrificer, his wife, and other persons connected with the performance of the sacrifice.

Then follows a chapter of penances for neglects on the part of an Agnihotri, or mishaps which might befal him. This is a continuation of the fifth chapter in the fifth book.

In the third chapter we are introduced to the rites of the princely inauguration ceremonies connected with a sacrifice, by the story of *Śunaśḥepa*. On account of its containing Ṛik verses, as well as Gâthâs (stanzas) it was to be told to the king on the day of its inauguration by the Hotar. The story is highly interesting; for it proves beyond doubt the existence of human sacrifices among the ancient Brahmans, and shows that they were in a half savage state; for we find here a Brahman selling his son to a prince to be immolated.

Now three kinds of such inauguratory sacrifices for the king, called *Râjasûyas*, are described, *viz.* **[66]** *Abhiṣeka*, *Punarabhiṣeka*, and *Mahâbhiṣeka*. The principal part of all these ceremonies consists in the sprinkling of holy water over the head of the kings, which is called *abhiṣeka*. It corresponds to the ceremony of anointing the kings with the Jews. It is of particular interest to observe that the Brahmans at this occasion did not allow the king to drink the proper Soma juice, but that he had to drink instead of it, a beverage prepared from the roots and leaves of several trees. The enjoyment of the Soma juice was a privilege reserved by the Brahmans to themselves alone. The king was, properly speaking, even not entitled to bring a sacrifice at all. It was only for the sake of the most extravagant gifts which the shrewd Brahmans extorted from kings for their offices, that they allowed him to bring a sacrifice. But before he could do so, he was to be made first a Brahman himself; at the conclusion of the ceremony he had, however, to resign his Brahmanship, and return to his former caste.

The last chapter of the Brâhmaṇam is taken up with the appointment by the king of a duly qualified Brahman to the office of a house-priest, who is called *purohita*, *i.e.*, president, superintendent. The word, as well as the office, must be very ancient; for we find it not only in the Saṁhitâ of the Ṛigveda, but even in the Zend-Avesta. It is, as to etymology, the same word as *paradhâta*,[7] which is generally **[67]** the epithet of one of the most ancient Iranian heroes, of *Haoshyaṇha* (see Yashts 5, 20; 9, 3; 15, 7; 17, 24 ed. Westergaard) the Hosheng of the Shâhnâmah. The later Iranian legends, as preserved in the Shâhnâmah, made of the *paradhâtas* a whole dynasty of kings, which they call *Peshdadians* (the modern Persian corruption of the primitive *paradhâta*) who then precede the *Kayanians* (the Kavis of the Vedas). This shows that the institution of

---

The word *purohita* is composed of *puras* before, and *hita* placed (from the root *dhâ*); so *paradhâta* also; *parâ* is the Zend form of *purâ* before, which is equivalent to *puras*, and *dhâta* is the Zend participle of the root *dhâ*.

a Purohita, who was not only a mere house-priest, but a political functionary, goes back to that early period of history when the Iranians and Indians lived peacefully together as one nation, The Paradhâtas of the Iranian kings appear however not to have been as successful in making the Shahs of Iran their slaves, as the Indian Purohitas were in enslaving the Indian Râjas in the bonds of a spiritual threldom. How far the Brahmans must have succeeded in carrying out their design of a spiritual supremacy over the royal caste, every reader may learn from this last chapter, and convince himself at the same time that hierarchical rule was known in the world more than a thousand years before the foundation of the Sea of St. Peter.

The ceremonial part of the last book is much enlivened by short stories of kings who were said to have performed the "great inauguration ceremony," and of course attained to supreme rule over the whole earth (that is to say, of three or four Indian principalities). It is an imitation of the ceremony by which the gods are said to have installed Indra to the sovereignty over them. The whole concludes [68] with the description of a magical performance (they are callen *kṛityâ*) by means of which a king can destroy secretly all his enemies.

After this summary statement of the contents of the Aitareya Brâhmaṇam, the question arises whether the work in its present form is the composition of one author or of several. Although there is, as we have seen, a certain plan perceptible, in the arrangement of the subject matter, we may easily distinguish some repetitions, discrepancies, and interpolations, which are hardly explicable if the book had only one author. So we find the Ajya hymn at the morning libaticn twice explained in 2, 40 and 41, but with slight differences; the origin of the formula, *agnir deveddhaḥ* is mentioned twice 2, 33 and 39, but in the former passage it is called Nivid, whilst in the latter the name "Puroruk" is given to it. The four last kaṇḍikâs in the second book 38-41 appear to be a kind of appendix taken from some other source. The piece 5, 27 is identical with 7, 3; 6, 5 and 17 treat in the main of the same topic, the relation between Stotriya and Anurûpa at the Ahîna sacrifices. There are several repititions in the 8th book; so the 13th kaṇḍikâ is identical with the 18th and the 14th with the 19th. The 10th and 11th kaṇḍikâs in the seventh book are evidently interpolations, interrupting the context, and exhibiting a different style. The latter is very remarkable on account of its mentioning two other Vedic Śâkhâs by their names, viz. *Paingya* and *Kâuşîtaki*; it appears to have appertained to an old treatise on astronomy.

[69] The style of the Brâhmaṇam is on the whole uniform. There are certain phrases which constantly re-occur in the work, as for instance, "what is at the sacrifice appropriate, that is successful, when the verse (which is repeated) alludes to the ceremony which is being performed;" "(he who should observe a Hotar do so contrary to the precept) should tell him[a] that the sacrificer would die; thus it always happens;" "This is done for production (*prajâtyâi*)," &c. The language is, of course, like that of all Brâhmaṇas, more recent than that of the Saṁhitâ; but it is, however, not the classical Sanscrit. Purely Vedic forms occur, such as the infinitive forms in *tos*, *e. g. karttos, arttos, roddhos, mathitos* (see 1, 10; 2, 20) generally dependent on *îśvara*, *i.e.* able, who has the power, (*îśvaraḥ karttoḥ* he has the power to do; *îśvaro roddhoḥ*, he has the power to obstruct, &c.), *satartavâi* (from *śtṛi*); *stomebhir* instead of *stomáir* (4, 15), &c.

The bulk of the work appears to have proceeded from one author; some additions were made afterwards. As regards the materials which our author, whom we may (with Sâyaṇa in various places of his commentary) call the Aitareya Ṛiṣi, that is, the Ṛiṣi of the Aitareya Śâkhâ of the Ṛigveda, used for the compilation of his work, we can principally distinguish four kinds, *viz.* (1) *Sacred texts* and *formulas*, such as the Adhrigu Praiṣa mantra (2, 6, 7), the Nivid (2, 34), &c., [70] which are, as we have seen, more ancient than the majority of the hymns; 2) *Gâthâ*, *i. e.* stanzas, principally impromptus on sacrificial things, and topics of a more wordly nature, and *Itihâsas*, *i.e.* stories; (3) *Rules on the performance of the duties of the Hotṛipriests*; (4) *Theological expositions* of the meaning of mantras, sacred rites, &c., according to the teaching of the most eminent Brahmâ priests who preceded our author.

These materials were worked together by him, but not without many additions of his own, and with the view to present to the followers of his Śâkhâ a kind of encyclopediæ of theological learning, and a supplement to their Veda. The theology of his Śâkhâ being founded on the hymns of the Ṛiṣis, and the latter being repeated by the Hotṛipriests only at the sacrifices, he confined himself for the most part to the speculations of the Hotṛis and their duties. The aim of our author was like that of all other Brâhmaṇa compilers, a double one, viz. to

[a] The phrase is always elliptical; it is only *ya enam bruyât*, if any one should tell him; but the meaning of the whole phrase is only that one which is here (and in the translation) given.

serve practical as well as theoretical ends. From a practical point of view it was to be a guide to the repeaters of the mantras of the Ṛigveda in some of their most important performances; but as regards the theoretical one, the author intenned to instruct them on the real ends of their profession, viz. to make the sacrificer, by means of the mystical power ascribed to the mantras, either attain to anything he might wish for, or if the Hotar should from some reason or other choose to do so, to deprive him through the same power of his property, children, and [71]life. The Hotṛis could learn from such a book how great their power was as the preservers of the sacred Ṛik verses. Every one who wished to perform a sacrifice as the only means for obtaining the favour of the gods, was entirely given up to the hands of the Hotṛi-priests, who could do with him what they pleased.

The mantras referred to are, for the most part, to be found in the Ṛigveda Saṁhitâ which we have at present. There are, however, several quoted, which are not to be met with in it, whence we must conclude, that the Saṁhitâ of the Aitareyins belonged to a Śâkhâ different from that one (the Śâkala Śâkhâ) which is at present only known to us. Aśvalâyana, in his Śrâuta Sûtras, which are, as we have seen, founded on the Aitareya Brâhmaṇam, generally supplies the text of those mantras which are wanting in the Saṁhitâ. Several of them are in the Atharvaveda Saṁhitâ, but they generally show different readings. In comparing both, those in the Aśvalâyana Sûtras, and those in the Atharvaveda Saṁhitâ, we find that, if there is any difference, the text of the Atharva is then always incorrect. It is remarkable that we do not only discover some relationship between the supposed Śâkhâ of the Aitareyins and the Atharvaveda Saṁhitâ, but also between the Aitareya and Gopatha Brâhmaṇam. Whole kaṇdikâs of the Aitareya, such as those on the Vaṣatkâra (3, 7-8) on Atirâtra (4, 5) are almost literally to be found in the Gopatha Brâhmaṇam of the Atharvaveda.

The author's own additions consisted principally [72] in critical remarks, recommending certain practices, and rejecting others, statement of reasons, why a particular rite must be performed in a particular way, and explanations of apparent anomalies in the ritual. The author does never, however, speak in the first person; for the whole he has the appearance of a tradition having descended from him. He is referred to only in the third person by the words, *taddha smâha*, "this he told." The theologians whose opinions are either accepted or rejected, are generally mentioned in the third person plural by the words "they say." Now and then they are called *mahâvadâḥ*, *i.e.* the speakers of great things. But their real name appears to have been *Brahmavâdins*, *i. e.* the speakers on Brahma (theologians, divines), which term we frequently meet in the Taittiriya Veda (Black Yajurveda.)

The work was, like the other Brâhmaṇas, no doubt, like the Saṁhitâ, orally handed down. Some external mark is still visible. At the end of each Adhyâya the last word, or phrase, is put twice. The same fact we observe in all other Brâhmaṇas as well as in the Sûtras. This was evidently a mark for the repeater as well as the hearer by which to recognise the end of a chapter, each of which formed a little treatise for itself.

Regarding the repetition of the Brâhmaṇam we have to remark, that it is done in a very slow tone, but quite monotonously, whilst the Brâhmaṇas of the Yajurveda are recited with the proper accents, like the Saṁhitâs. Of very frequent occurrence in it is the *pluti i.e.* the lengthening of a vowel to **[73]** three moras marked by ३. This Pluti is used in three cases, (1) to ask a question, (2) to deliberate or consider whether a thing should be done or not, and (3) to give some emphasis to a certain word. In the two first cases it expresses exactly the idea of our sign of interrogation, in the latter that of our underlining or italicising of certain important words.

Let us make before we conclude some remarks on the principal sacrificial and theological ideas (as far as they have not been touched already) which pervade the Aitareya Brâhmaṇam.

The sacrifice is regarded as the means for obtaining power over this and the other world, over visible as well as invisible beings, animate as well as inanimate creatures. Who knows its proper application, and has it duly performed, is in fact looked upon as the real master of the world; for any desire he may entertain, if it be even the most ambitious, can be gratified, any object he has in view can be obtained by means of it. The *Yajña* (sacrifice) taken as a whole is conceived to be a kind of machinery. in which every piece must tally with the other, or a sort of large chain in which no link is allowed to be wanting, or a staircase, by which one may ascend to heaven, or as a personage, endowed with all the characteristics of a human body. It exists from eternity, and proceeded from the Supreme Being (Prajâpati or Brahma) along with the *Traividyâ*, *i. e.* the three-fold sacred science (the Ṛik verses, the Sâmans or chants, and the Yajus or sacrificial formulas). The creation of the world **[74]** itself was even regarded as the fruit of sacrifice performed by the

Supreme Being. The Yajña exists as an invisible thing at all times, it is like the latent power of electricity in an electrifying machine, requiring only the operation of a suitable apparatus in order to be elicited. It is supposed to extend, when unrolled, from the Ahavanîya or sacrificial fire into which all oblations are thrown, to heaven, forming thus a bridge or ladder, by means of which the sacrificer can communicate with the world of gods and spirits, and even ascend when alive to their abodes. The term for beginning the sacrificial operations is "to spread the sacrifice;" this means that the invisible thing, representing the ideal sacrifice which was lying dormant, as it were, is set into motion, in consequence of which its several parts or limbs are unfolding themselves, and thus the whole becomes extended. This ideal sacrifice stands in the closest relationship with all the sacrificial implements, the sacrificial place, and all the sacred verses and words spoken during its actual performance. The sacrifice being often represented as a kind of being with a body like that of men, certain ceremonies form his head, others his neck, otbers his eye, &c. The most important thing at a sacrifice is that all its several parts should tally together, and that consequently there should neither anything be in excess, nor deficient in it. This agreeing of the several parts of the sacrifice constitutes its *rûpa i. e.* form. The proper form is obtained, when the mantras which are repeated are in **[75]** strictest accordance with the ceremony for which they are repeated, or (if the sacrifice lasts for several or many days) when they have the characteristics of the respective days. If the form is vitiated, the whole sacrifice is lost. Mistakes being, on account of the so extremely complicated ritual, unavoidable, the sacrificial being was to be attended by a physician in the person of the Brahma priest (5, 34). Each mistake must be made good by a *prâyaśchitta, i.e.* penance, or propitiatory offering.

The power and significance of the Hotri-priests at a sacrifice consists in their being the masters of the sacred word, which is frequently personified by *Vâch i.e.* Speech, who is indentical with Sarasvatî, the goddess of learning in the latter Hindu Pantheon. Speech has, according to the opinion of the earliest Hindu divines, the power of vivifying and killing. The sacred words pronounced by the Hotar effect, by dint of the innate power of Vâch, the spiritual birth of the sacrificer, form his body, raise him up to heaven, connect him with the prototypes of those things which he wishes to obtain (such as children, cattle, &c.) and make him attain to his full life term, which is a hundred years; but they are at the same time a weapon by means of which the sacrificer's enemies, or he himself (if the Hotar have any evil designs against him) can be killed, and all evil consequences of sin (this is termed *pâpman*) be destroyed. The power and effect of Speech as regards the obtaining of any particular thing wished for, mainly lies in the form in which it is uttered. Thence [76] the great importance of the metres, and the choice of words and terms. Each metre is the invisible master of something obtainable in this world; it is, as it were, its exponent, and ideal. This great significance of the metrical speech is derived from the number of syllables of which it consists; for each thing has, (just as in the Pythogorean system) a certain numerical proportion. The Gâyatrî metre, which cansists of three times eight syllables, is the most sacred, and is the proper metre for Agni, the god of fire, and chaplain of the gods. It expresses the idea of Brahma; therefore the sacrificer must use it when he wishes for anything closely connected with the Brahma, such as acquirement of sacred knowledge, and the thorough understanding of all problems of theology. The Triṣṭubh, which consists of four times eleven syllables, expresses the idea of strength, and royal power; thence it is the proper metre by which Indra, the king of the gods, is to be invoked. Any one wishing to obtain strength and royal power, principally a Kṣattriya, must use it. A variety of it the Uṣṇih metre of twenty-eight syllables, is to be employed by a sacrificer who aspires for longevity, for twenty-eight is the symbol of life. The Jagatî, a metre of forty-eight syllable, expresses the idea of cattle. Any one who wishes for wealth in cattle, must use it. The same idea (or that of the sacrifice) is expressed by the Paṅkti metre (five times eight syllables). The Bṛihatî, which consists of thirty-six syllables, is to be used when a sacrificer is aspiring to fame and renown for this metre is the exponent [77] of those ideas. The Anuṣṭubh metre, of thirty-two, syllables, is the symbol of the celestial world; thence a candidate for a place in heaven has to use it. The Virâj of thirty syllables, is food and satisfaction; thence one who wishes for plenty of food, must employ it.

The words contained in these different metrical forms must always be appropriate to the occasion. If the oblation is given to Agni, the verse repeated must contain his name, or an allusion to it; were it to contain the name of Indra, or one of his characteristics, the offering would be thrown away. Every act, even the most trifling one, is at the sacrificial performance accompanied with mantras, and always such a verse is to be chosen as contains (or is made to contain by interpretation) an allusion to it. This will all be clear to the reader on reference, for instance, to 2, 2, where the mantras connected with every particular act of the ceremony of anointing and erecting the sacrificial post is given.

Of almost equal importance with the metres are the so-called Stomas, based also on numerical proportions. Each Stoma contains a certain number of verses, chanted according to one and the same tune. The number is very often obtained only by frequent repetition of the same triplet of verses (see about the particulars of the Stomas note 18 on pages 237-38 of the translation). Each has, just as the metres, its peculiar symbolical meaning. The Trivṛit (nine-fold) stoma, is, for instance, the symbol of Brahma, and the theological wisdom, and has Agni, the house-priest of the gods, for its deity: the Pañchadaśa (fifteen-fold) is the [78] symbol of royal power and thence appropriate to Indra, and the Kṣatriyas: the Saptadaśa (seventeen-fold) is the exponent of wealth in cattle; thence a Vaiśya should use it, or any other sacrificer who wishes to obtain wealth: the Ekaviṁśa-(twenty-one-fold) is the symbol of generation: thence it is principally to be used at the third libation, many rites of which refer to the propagation of progeny. The other Stomas, such as the *Triṇava* (twenty-seven fold), *Trayastriṁs'a* (thirty-three-fold), &c., have a similarly symbolical meaning.

Besides the Stomas, the so-called Pṛiṣṭhas (the name of certain Sâmans and their combinations) are a necessary requisite at all the Soma sacrifices. They form the centre of all the ceremonies, and the principal one of them is always regarded as the womb (*yoni*) of the sacrificial being. They are generally only used at the midday libation. The two principal Pṛiṣṭhas are the Rathantara and Bṛihat Sâmans (*abhitvâ sûva nonuma*, and *tvâmiddhi havâmahe*). They can be used singly, or along with one of their kindred (see notes 29 on page 193, 14 on page 282, and 4, 28). The name Pṛiṣṭha means "back," for they are regarded on the whole as the back of the sacrifice.

All these things, metres (*chhandas*), Stomas and Pṛiṣṭhas, are believed to be as eternal and divine, as the words themselves they contain. The earliest Hindu divines did not only believe in a primitive revelation of the words of the sacred texts, but even in that of the various forms, which might be used for their repetition or chanting. These forms along with their contents, [79] the everlasting Veda words, are symbols expressive of things of the invisible world, and in several respects comparable to the Platonic ideas. They are in the hands of the sacrificial priests the instruments for accomplishing anything they might wish for in behalf of the sacrificer. But a great deal depends upon the way of using those spiritual instruments. It is a matter of importance whether a mantra is repeated without stopping, or pâda by pâda (quarter by quarter), or half verse by half verse. The four feet (pâdas), of which many metres are composed, represent the four feet of animals. The repetition of such a verse, half verse by half verse, that is, with two stops only, represents the sacrificer who as a human being, has two legs. By thus combining the ideas of four and two-footed beings, the sacrificer is mystically placed amidst cattle, and obtains them, in future, in the largest quantity. Another important point is, whether the mantra is repeated *upâṁśu*, *i.e.* with an almost inaudible voice, or *tûṣṇîm*, *i.e.* silently, or with a low and slow voice (*mandrasvara*), or with a middle tone (*madhyama*), or very loud (*uttama*). (See 3, 44).

Among the large number of the sacred words, there are always some which have a destructive quality, and must, therefore, be used with great caution. In order to protect the sacrificer, as well as himself, from the dangerous effects of such words, the repeater must, by means of certain other words, or formulas, deprive them of their destructive power, and thus propitiate them. This is generally called *śânti* **[80]** (propitiation, appeasing). Such dangerous words are for instance, *vâuṣaṭ* (see 3, 8) and *rudra*, the name of Śiva, the god of destruction (3, 34).

The sacrificer, who is the object of all these mystical operations on the part (of the priests) by means of their mantras, chants, and manual labour, is not allowed to remain inactive, but he himself has to repeat certain mantras, expressive of his desires. When, for instance, the Hotar is performing the mystical operation of placing him among cattle, he must say, "May I become rich in cattle!" When the same priest makes a firm standing place (a *pratiṣṭhâ*) for him, he must say, "May I go to my place!" Thus he obtains the fulfilment of any desire which might be obtainable by means of a particular verse or mode of repeating, or chant, or performance of a particular rite, when he repeats the appropriate formula at the right time and occasion. For what he himself speaks, connects him with the ideals of his wishes, which are brought within his grasp by the priest.

The objects sacrificed for are manifold, viz. offspring, cattle, wealth, fame, theological learning, skill for performance of sacrifices, and heaven. For gaining heaven a Soma sacrifice is indispensable. For the sacred Soma juice has, according to the opinions of the ancient Hindu theologians, pre-eminently the power of uniting the sacrificer on this earth with the celestial king Soma, and make him thus one of his subjects, and consequently an associate of the gods, and an inhabitant of the celestial world.

THE
AITAREYA BRAHMANAM OF THE RIGVEDA.
FIRST BOOK

FIRST CHAPTER (ADHYAYA).

(The Dîkṣaṇîya Iṣṭi, with the Initiatory Rites.)

1.

Agni, among the gods, has the lowest,[1] *Viṣṇu* the highest, place; between them stand all the other deities.

[1] Sâyaṇa, whom M. Müller follows in his translation of the first six chapters of the first book, as given in his "History of Ancient Saṃskṛit Literature" (pages 390-405), explains the words *avama* and *parama* by "first" and "last." To prove this meaning to be the true one, Sâyaṇa adduces the mantra (1,4. Aśval. Śr. S. 4, 2), *agnir mukham prathamo devatânâm samgatânâm uttamo Viṣṇur âsît*, *i.e.*, *Agni* was the first of the deities assembled, (and) *Viṣṇu* the last. In the Kauṣîtaki-Brâhmaṇam (7, 1) Agni is called *avarârdhya* (instead of *avama*), and Viṣṇu *parârdhya* (instead of *parama*), *i.e.*, belonging to the lower and higher halves (or forming the lower and higher halves). That the meaning "first" cannot be reasonably given to the word *avama*, one may learn from some passages of the Rigveda Saṃhitâ, where *avama* and *parama* are not applied to denote rank and dignity, but only to mark place and locality. See Rigveda 1, 108, 9, 10: *avamasyâm pṛithivyâm, madhyamasyâm, paramasyâm uta*, *i.e.*, in the lowest place, the middle (place), and the highest (place). *Agni*, the fire, has, among the gods, the lowest place; for he resides with man on the earth; while the other gods are either in the air, or in the sky. *Viṣṇu* occupies, of all gods, the highest place; for he represents (in the Rigveda) the sun in its daily and yearly course. In its daily course it reaches the highest point in the sky, when passing the zenith on the horizon; thence *Viṣṇu* is called the "highest" of the gods. Sâyaṇa understands "first" and "last" in reference to the respective order of deities in the twelve liturgies (*Śâstra*) of the Soma day at the *Agniṣṭoma* sacrifice. For, says he, "The first of these liturgies, the so-called *Ajya-Śâstra* (see 2, 31), belongs to Agni, and in the last out of the twelve, in the so-called *Agnamâruta Śâstra* (see 3, 32-38), there is one verse addressed to Viṣṇu. But this argument, advanced by Sâyaṇa, proves nothing for his opinion that "Agni is the first, and Viṣṇu [2] the last deity;" for these twelve liturgies belong to the fifth day of the Agniṣṭoma sacrifice, whilst the *Dîkṣaṇîya-iṣṭi*, in connection with which ceremony the Brâhmaṇam makes the remark

[2] They offer [2] the Agni-Viṣṇu rice-cake (*Purodâśa*) [3] which belongs to the *Dîkṣaṇîya iṣṭi* (and put its [3] several parts) on eleven potsherds

---

" *agnir vai devânâm avamo,*" &c., forms part of the first day. The ceremonies of the first and those of the fifth day have no connection with one another.

Equally inconclusive are two other arguments brought forward by Sâyaṇa. The one is, that in all the constituent parts of the *Jyotiṣṭoma* sacrifice, of which the *Agniṣṭoma* is the opening, the first place is assigned to Agni, and the last to Viṣṇu, and that the last *Stotra* (performance of the Sâma singers), and the last *Śâstra* (performance of the Hotṛi-priests), in the last part of that great cycle of sacrifices (the Jyotiṣṭoma), known by the name of *Aptoryâma*, are devoted to Viṣṇu. The other argument is, that Agni is worshipped in the first, or *Dîkṣaṇîya iṣṭi*, and that the *Vâjasaneyins* (the followers of the so-called White Yajurveda) use, instead of the last Iṣṭi (the *avasânîyâ*), the *Pûrṇâhuti* to Viṣṇu.

Both arguments prove only, that the ceremonies commenced with the deity who is on earth, that is, Agni, and ended with that one who occupies the highest place in heaven. Though, from a liturgical point of view, Sâyaṇa's opinion might be correct, yet he does not state any reason why the first place in certain invocations is assigned to Agni, and the last to Viṣṇu. But the translation "lowest and highest," as given here, does not only account for the liturgical arrangement, but states the proper reason of such an order besides. That these terms are really applicable to both respective deities, Agni and Viṣṇu, and that the words *avama* and *parama* actually convey such meaning, has been shown above.

[2] The term of the original is, *nirvapanti* (from *vap*, to strew, to sow). This expression, which very frequently occurs in liturgical writings of all kinds, means, originally, "to take some handfuls of dry substances (such as grains) from the heap in which they are collected, and put them into separate vessel." It is used in a similar sense of liquids also. Sâyaṇa restricts the meaning of this common sacrificial term somewhat too much. He says, that it means "to take four handfuls of rice from the whole load which is on the cart, and throw them into the winnowing basket (*Śûrpa*)." In this passage, he further adds, the term means the bringing of that offering the preparation of which begins with this act of taking four handfuls from the whole load. Sâyaṇa discusses the meaning of the form "*nirvapanti*" which is in the present tense, and in the plural number. Referring to a parallel in the "Black Yajurveda," *agnâvaiṣṇavam ekâdaśakapâlam nirvâped dîkṣiṣyamâṇaḥ*, where the potential (*nirvapet*) is used instead of the present tense of (*nirvapanti*), and to a rule of Pâṇini (3, 4, 7,) [3] which teachers that the conjunctive (Let) can have the meaning of the potential, he takes it in the sense of a conjunctive, implying an order. The plural instead of the singular is accounted for the supposition, that in the Vedic language the numbers might be interchanged. But the whole explanation is artificial.

[3] The principal food of the gods at the so-called Iṣṭis is the *purodâśa*. I here give a short description of its preparation, which I myself have witnessed. The Adhvaryu takes rice which is husked and ground (*piṣṭa*), throws it into a vessel of copper (*madantî*), kneads it with water, and gives the whole mass a globular shape. He then places this dough on a piece of wood to the Âhavanîya fire (the fire into which the oblations are thrown), in order to cook it. After it is half cooked, he takes it off, gives it the shape of a tortoise, and places the whole on eleven potsherds (*kapâlas*). To complete cooking it, he takes Darbha grass, kindles it and puts it on the Purodâśa. After it is made ready, he pours melted butter over it and puts the ready dish in the so-called *Iḍâpâtra*, which is placed on the Vedi, where it remains till it is sacrificed.

(*kapâla*). They offer it (the rice-cake) really to all the deities of this (Iṣṭi) without foregoing any one.[4] For Agni is all the deities, and Viṣṇu is all the deities. For these two (divine) bodies, Agni and Viṣṇu, are the two ends[5] of the sacrifice. Thus when they portion out the Agni-Viṣṇu rice-cake, they indeed make at the end[6] (after the ceremony is over) prosper[7] (all) the gods of this (ceremony).

[4] Here they say: if there be eleven potsherds on which portions of the rice-cake are put, and (only) two deities, Agni and Viṣṇu, what arrangement is there for the two, or what division?

(The answer is) The rice-cake portions on eight potsherds belong to Agni; for the *Gâyatrî* verse consists of eight syllables, and the *Gâyatrî* is Agni's metre. The rice-cake portions on the three potsherds belong to Viṣṇu; for Viṣṇu (the sun) strode thrice through the universe.[8] This the arrangement (to be made) for them; this the division.

---

[4] *Anantarâyam*: literally, without any one between, without an interval, the chain of the gods being uninterrupted.

[5] *Antye.* Sâyaṇa opines that this adjective here is *ekaśeṣa*, *i.e.*, that out of two or more things to be expressed, only one has actually remained. It stands, as he thinks, instead of *âdyâ* and *antyâ*, just as *pitarâu* means "father and mother." (Pâṇini, 1, 2, 70.)

[6] *Antataḥ.* Sây. "at the beginning and end of the sacrifice." But I doubt whether the term implies the beginning also. In the phrase: *antataḥ pratitiṣṭati*, which so frequently occurs in the Ait. Brâhm., *antataḥ* means only "ultimately," at the end of a particular ceremony or rite.

[7] *Ṛidhnuvanti.* Sây. *paricharanti*, they worship. He had, in all probability, *Nighaṇṭ.* 3, 5, in view, where this meaning is given to *ṛidhnoti.* But that this word conveys the sense of "prospering" follows unmistakeably from a good many passages of the Saṁhitâ of Ṛigveda and Manu. (See the Saṁskṛit Dictionary by Böhtlingk and Roth. s. v. ऋधं and Westergaard's Radices Sanscritæ s. v. ऋध, page 182.) In this passage the meaning "to worship," as given by Sâyaṇa, is too vague, and appears not quite appropriate to the sense. On account of its governing the accusative, we must take it here in the sense of a transitive verb, although it is generally an intransitive one. The meaning which lies nearest, is, "to make prosperous." At the first glance it might appear somewhat curious, how men should make the gods prosperous by sacrificial offerings. But if one takes into consideration, that the Vedas, and particularly the sacrificial rites inculcated in them, presuppose a mutual relationship between men and gods, one depending on the support of the other, the expression will no longer be found strange. Men must present offerings to the gods to increase the power and strength of their divine protectors. They must, for instance, inebriate Indra with Soma, that he might gather strength for conquering the demons. The meaning "to satisfy, to please," which is given to the word "*ṛidhnuvanti*" of the passage in question in Böhtlingk's and Roth's Dictionary, is a mere guess, and wholly untenable, being supported by no Brahmaṇik authority.

[8] This refers to the verse in the Ṛigveda Saṁhitâ 1,22,17,18: *idam Viṣṇur vichakrame tredhâ nidadhe padam*, *i.e.*, Viṣṇu strode through the universe; he put down thrice his foot; and *triṇi padâ vichakrame*, he strode three steps. These three steps of Viṣṇu, who represents the sun, are: sunrise, zenith, and sunset.

He who might think himself to have no position (not to be highly respected by others) should portion out (for being offered) *Charu* * over which clarified [5] butter is poured. For on this earth no one has a firm footing who does not enjoy a certain (high) position.[10] The clarified butter (poured over this *Charu*) is the milk of the woman ; the husked rice grains (*taṇḍula* of which Charu consists) belong to the male ; both are a pair. Thus the Charu on account of its consisting of a pair (of female and male parts) blesses him with the production of progeny and cattle, for his propagation (in his descendants and their property). He who has such a knowledge propagates his progeny and cattle.

He who brings the New and Full Moon oblations, has already made a beginning with the sacrifice, and made also a beginning with (the sacrificial worship of the) deities. After having brought the New or Full Moon oblations, he may be inaugurated in consequence of the offering made at these (oblations) and the sacrificial grass (having been spread) at these (oblations, at the time of making them). This (might be regarded) as one Dikṣâ (initiatory rite).[11]

* *Charu* is boiled rice. It can be mixed with milk and butter ; but it is no essential part. It is synonymous with *odanam*, the common term for "boiled rice." Śatap. Brâh. 4, 12, 1. There were different varieties of this dish ; some being prepared with the addition of barley, or some other grains. See Taittîriya Saṁh. 1, 8, 10, 1.

[5] [10] *Pratitiṣṭati*, which is here put twice, has a double sense, *viz.*, the original meaning "to have a firm footing, standing," and a figurative one "to have rank, position. dignity." In the latter sense, the substantive *pratiṣṭhâ* is of frequent occurrence Dignity and position depend on the largeness of family, wealth in cattle, &c.

[11] The present followers of the Vedik religion, the so-called Agnihotris, who take upon themselves the performance of all the manifold sacrificial rites enjoined in the Vedas, begin their arduous career for gaining a place in heaven, after the sacred fires have been established, with the regular monthly performance of the *Darśa* and *Pûrṇimaiṣṭi* or the New and Full Moon sacrifices. Then they bring the *Châturmâsya-iṣṭi*, and after this rite they proceed to bring the *Agniṣṭoma*, the first and model of all Soma sacrifices. By the bringing of the New and Full Moon offerings, the Agnihotri is already initiated into the grand rites ; he is already an adept (*Dîkṣita*) in it. Some of the links of the *yajna* or sacrifice which is regarded as a chain extending from this earth to heaven, by means of which the successful performer reaches the celestial world, the seat of the gods, are already established by these offerings ; with the deities, whose associate the sacrificer wishes to become after his death, the intercourse is opened ; for they have already received food (*haviḥ*), prepared [6] according to the precepts of sacred cookery, at his hands, and they have been sitting on the sacred seat (*barhis*) prepared of the sacrificial grass (*Darbha*). Thence the performance of the Full and New Moon sacrifices is here called one Dîkṣâ, *i.e.*, one initiatory rite. But if the Agnihotri, who is performing a Soma sacrifice, is already initiated (*Dîkṣita*) by means of the rites just mentioned, how does he require at the opening of the *Agniṣṭoma* (Soma-sacrifice) the so-called *Dîkṣaṇîya Iṣṭi*, or "offering for becoming initiated" ? This question was mooted already in ancient times. Thence, says *Aśvaláyana* in his Śrauta sûtras (4, 1), that, some are of opinion, the Soma-sacrifice should be performed, in the case of the means required being forthcoming

[6] The Hotar must recite seventeen verses for the wooden sticks to be thrown into the fire[12] (to feed it). For *Prajâpati* (the Lord of all creatures) is seventeenfold; the months are twelve, and the seasons five, by putting *Hemanta* (winter) and *Śiśira* (between winter and spring) as one. So much is the year. The year is Prajâpati. He who has such a knowledge prospers by these verses (just mentioned) which reside in Prajâpati.

2.

[7] The sacrifice went away from the gods. They wished to seek after it by means of the *Iṣṭis*. The Iṣṭis are called Iṣṭis, because they wished (*ish*, to wish) to seek after it. They found it. He who has such a knowledge prospers after he has found the sacrifice. The name *âhutis, i.e.*, oblations, stands instead of *âhûti, i.e.*, invocation; with them the sacrificer calls the gods. This is (the reason) why they are called *âhutis*. They (the *âhutis*) are called *ûtis*; for by their means the gods come to the call of the sacrificer (*âyanti*, they come). Or they are the paths (and) ways; for they are the ways to heaven for the sacrificer.

There they say, as another priest (the *Adhvaryu*) offers (*juhoti*) the oblations, why do they call that one, who repeats the *Anvâkyâ* and *Yâjyâ* verses, a *Hotar*? (The answer is) Because he causes the deities to be brought near (*âvâhayahti*), according to their place, (by saying) "bring this one, bring that one."[13] This is the reason why he is called a Hotar

(the sacrifice is very expensive), after the Full and New Moon sacrifices have been brought; others opine the Soma sacrifice might be performed before the Full and New Moon sacrifices. No doubt, the Agniṣṭoma was in ancient times a sacrifice wholly independent of the *Darśa Pûrṇimâ-iṣṭis*. This clearly follows from the fact, that just such Iṣṭis, as constitute the Full and New Moon sacrifices, are placed at the beginning of the Agniṣṭoma to introduce it.

[12] These verses are called *Sâmidhenîs*. They are only eleven in number; but by repeating the first and last verses thrice, the number is brought to *fifteen*. They are mentioned in Âśval. Śr. S. 1, 2.; several are taken from Ṛigveda 3, 27, as the first (*pra vo vâjâ abhidyavo*) fourth (*samidhyamâna*) 13th, 14th, and 15th (*îlenyo*) verses. Besides these three, Âśv. mentions: *agna âyâhi vîtaye* 6, 16; 10, 12, three verses), *agnim dûtam vriṇîmahe* (1, 12, 1.), and *samiddho agna* (5, 28, 5, 6, two verses). They are repeated monotonously without observing the usual three accents. The number of the *sâmidhenîs* is generally stated at fifteen; but now and then, *seventeen* are mentioned, as in the case of the *Dîkṣaṇîya iṣṭi*. The two additional mantras are called *Dhâyyâ, i.e.*, verses to be repeated when an additional wooden stick, after the ceremony of kindling is over, is thrown into the fire, in order to feed it. They are mentioned in Sâyaṇa's commentary on the Ṛigveda Saṁhitâ, vol. II., page 762 (ed. M. Müller). S. Âśval. 4, 2, two Dhâyyâs at the *Dîkṣaṇîya iṣṭi*.

[7] [13] At every Iṣṭi, the Hotar calls the particular gods to whom rice-cake portions are to be presented, by their names to appear. At the Dîkṣaṇîya Iṣṭi, for instance, he says: *agna agnim âvaha, viṣṇum âvaha, i.e.*, Agni! bring hither Agni! bring hither Viṣṇu. The name of the deity who is called near, is only muttered, whilst *âvaha* is pronounced with a loud voice, the first syllable *â* being *pluta, i.e.*, containing three short *a*. See Âśv. Śr. S. 1, 3.

(from *âvah*, to bring near). He who has such a knowledge is called a Hotar.[14]

3.

[8] The priests make him whom they initiate (by means of the Díkşâ ceremony) to be an embryo again (*i.e.*, they produce him anew altogether). They sprinkle him with water; for water is seed. By having thus provided him with seed (for his new birth), they initiate him. They besmear him with fresh butter (*navanîta*). The butter for the gods is called *âjya*,[15] that for men *surabhi ghṛitam*, that for the manes *âyuta*, and that for the embryos *navanîta*. Therefore by anointing him with fresh butter, they make him thrive through his own portion.

They besmear his eyes with collyrium. For this anointment is lustre for both eyes. By having imparted lustre to him, they make him a *Dîkşita*.

They rub him clean with twenty-one handfuls of Darbha grass. By having thus made pure and clean they make him a Dîkşita.

They make him enter the place destined for the Dîkşita.[16] For this is the womb of the Dîkşita. [9] When they make him enter the place destined for the Dîkşita, then they make him thus enter his own womb. In this (place) he sits as in a secure abode,[17] and thence he

---

[14] These etymologies of *işţi*, *âhuti*, *ûti*, and *hotâ* are fanciful and erroneous. The real root of *işţi* is *yäj*, to sacrifice; that of *âhuti* is *hu*, to bring an offering; that of *ûti* is *av*, to protect, to assist; that of *hotâ* is *hvê*, to call. The technical meaning of an *işţi* is a series of oblations to differeut deities, consisting chiefly of *Purodâśa*. An *âhuti* or *ûti*, which appears to be an older name of the same idea (this meaning is quite omitted in the Sanscrit Dictionary by B. and R.), is an oblation offered to one deity. This oblation is generally accompanied by two mantras, the first being called the *Anûvâkya* or [8] *Puro-anuvâkya*, the second *Yâjyâ*. When the second is recited, the oblation is thrown into the fire by the Adhvaryu. The Hotar repeats only the mantras.

[15] To remind his readers of the difference existing between *âjya* and *ghṛita*, Sây. quotes an ancient versus memorialis (*Kârikâ*), *sarpir vilînam âjyam syât*; *ghanîbhûtam ghṛitam viduḥ*, *i.e.*, they call the butter, which is in a liquid condition, *âjyâ*, and that one which is hardened is called *ghṛita*. *Ayuta* is the butter when but slightly molten, and *surabhi* when well seasoned. According to the opinion of the *Taittirîyas*, says Sâyaṇa, the butter for the gods is called *ghṛita*, that for the manes *astu*, and that for men *nişpakva*. *Astu* is the same as *âyuta*, slightly molten, and *nispakvâ*, the same as *âjya*, entirely molten.

[16] *Dîkşita-vimita*. It is that place which is generally called *prâchîna vaṁsa* (or *prâg-vaṁśa*). This place is to represent the womb which the Dîkşita enters in the shape of an embryo to be born again. This is clearly enough stated in the Bráhmaṇa of another Śâkhâ, which Sâyaṇa quotes: तेन प्राचीनवंशप्रवेशेन स्वकीययोनिप्रवेशः संपाद्यते.

[9] [17] Sâyaṇa takes the three ablatives—*tasmâd*, *dhruvâd*, *yoner*, in the sense of locatives; but I think this interpretation not quite correct. The ablative is chosen on account of the verb *charati*, he walks, goes, indicating the point, *whence* he starts. The other verb *âste*, he sits, would require the locative. Therefore we should expect both

departs. Therefore the embryos are placed in the womb as a secure place, and thence they are brought forth (as fruit). Therefore the sun should neither rise nor set over him finding him in any other place than the spot assigned to the Dîkṣita; nor should they speak to him (if he should be compelled to leave his place). [18]

They cover him with a cloth. For this cloth is the caul (*ulba*) of the Dîkṣita (with which he is to be born, like a child); thus they cover him with the caul. Outside (this cloth) there is (put by them) the skin of a black antelope. For outside the caul, there is the placenta (*jarâyu*). Thus they cover him (symbolically by the skin of the antelope) with the placenta. He closes his hands. For with closed hands the embryo lies within (the womb); with closed hands the child is born. As he closes his hands, he thus holds the sacrifice, and all its deities in his two hands closed.

They allege as a reason (why the Dîkṣita should close together both his hands) that he who takes (among two who are sacrificing on the same place and at the same time) his Dîkṣâ (initiation) first, is not guilty (of the sin) of "confusion of libations" (*saṁsava*). [19] For his sacrifice and the deities are held **[10]** fast (in his hands); and (consequently) he does not suffer any loss like that which falls on him who performed his Dîkṣâ later.

After having put off the skin of the black antelope he descends to bathe.

Thence embryos are born after they are separated from the placenta. He descends to bathe with the cloth (which was put on him) on. Thence a child is born together with the caul.

4.

The Hotar ought to repeat for him who has not yet brought a sacrifice two *Puronuvâkyâ* verses, *tvam agne sapratha asi* (Ṛig-veda Saṁhitâ 5, 13, 4) for the first, and *Soma yâs te mayobhuvaḥ* (1, 91, 9) for the second portion of (the offering of) melted butter. (By reading the third pâda of the first verse *tvayâ yajnam* "through thee (thy favour) they

---

cases, locative and ablative. On account of conciseness, only the latter is chosen, but the former is then to be understood.

[18] For performing, for instance, the functions of nature.—*Sây.*

[19] If two or more people offer their Soma-libations at the same time, and at places which are not separated from one another, either by a **[10]** river, or by a mountain, then a '*saṁsava*" or confusion of libation is caused, which is regarded as a great sin. He, however, who has performed his Dîkṣâ first, and holds the gods between his hands, is not guilty of such a sin, and the gods will be with him.—*Sây.*

extend [20] the sacrifice," the Hotar extends thus the sacrifice for him (who has not yet brought a sacrifice).

For him who has brought a sacrifice before, the Hotar has to recite (two other mantras instead): *agniḥ pratnena manmanâ* (8, 44, 12) and *Soma gîrbhiṣ ṭvâ vayam* (1, 91, 11). For by the word *pratnam, i. e.*, former (which occurs in the first verse), he alludes to the former sacrifice. But the recital of these verses (for a man who has performed a sacrifice, and for one who has not done so) may be dispensed [11] with. Let the Hotar rather use the two verses which refer to the destruction of *Vṛitra* (*vârtraghna*), *viz.*, *Agnir vṛitrâṇi janghanat* (6, 16, 24), and, *tvam soma asi satpatiḥ* (1, 91, 5). Since he whom the sacrifice approaches, destroys Vṛitra (the demon whom Indra conquers), the two verses referring to the destruction of Vṛitra are to be used. [21]

The *Anuvâkyâ* for the Agni-Viṣṇu-offering is: *Agnir mukham prathamo devatânâm*, the *Yâjyâ*: *agniścha Viṣṇo tapa.* [22]) These two verses (addressed) to *Agni* and *Viṣṇu* are corresponding (appropriate) in their form. What is appropriate in its form, is successful in the sacrifice; that is to say, when the verse which is recited refers to the ceremony which is being performed.

(Now follows a general paraphrase of the contents of these two verses) *Agni* and *Viṣṇu* are among the gods, the "guardians of the *Dîkṣâ*" (that is to say), they rule over the Dîkṣâ. When they offer the Agni-

---

[20] *Vitanvate.* The sacrifice is regarded as a kind of chain which, when not used, lies rolled up; but which when being used, is, as the instrument for ascending to heaven, to be wound off. This winding off of the sacrificial chain is expressed by the term *vitan*, to extend. Connected with this term are the expressions *vitana* and *vaitânika.*

[11] [21] The verses mentioned here are the *Puronuvâkyâs*, *i.e.*, such ones as are to be recited before the proper *Anuvâkyâ* with its *Yâjyâ* is to be repeated. The *Puro-anuvâkyâs* are introductory to the *Anuvâkyâ* and *Yâjyâ.*

[22] Both verses are not to be found in the Śâkala Śâkhâ of the Ṛig-veda, but they are in Âśval Śaruta Sûtras 4, 2. I put them here in their entirety:

अग्निर्मुखं प्रथमो देवतानां संगतानामुत्तमो विष्णुरासीत् ।
यजमानाय परिगृह्य देवान् दीक्षयेदं हविरागच्छतं नः ॥
अग्निश्चविष्णो तप उत्तमं महो दीक्षापालाय वनतं हि शक्रा ।
विश्वैर्देवैर्यज्ञियैः संविदानौ दीक्षामस्मै यजमानाय धत्तम् ॥

[12] *i.e.*, "Among the deities assembled, Agni, being at the head, was the first, and Viṣṇu the last (god). Ye both, come to our offering with the Dîkṣâ, taking (with you all) the gods for the sacrificer! (*i.e.*, come to this offering, and grant the Dîkṣâ to the sacrificer). Agni and Viṣṇu! ye two strong (gods)! burn with a great heat to the utmost (of your power) for the preservation of the Dîkṣâ. Joined by all the gods who participate in the sacrifice, grant, ye two, Dikṣâ to this sacrificer." Agni and Viṣṇu, the one representing the fire, the other the sun, are here invoked to burn the sacrificer, by combination of their rays, clean, and to purify him from all gross material dross. The Dîkṣâ should be made as lasting as a mark caused by branding.

Viṣṇu oblation, then those two who rule over the Dîkṣâ become pleased, and grant Dîkṣâ, that is to say, the two makers of Dîkṣâ, they both make the sacrificer a *Dîkṣita*. These verses are in the *Triṣṭubh* metre, that the sacrificer might acquire the properties of the god Indra (vigour and strength).

5

[12] He who wishes for beauty and acquisition of sacred knowledge should use at the *Sviṣṭakrit*[23] two verses in the Gâyatrî metre as his *Saṁyâjyâs*. For the Gâyatrî is beauty and sacred knowledge. He who having such a knowledge uses two Gâyatrîs[24] (at the Sviṣṭakrit) becomes full of beauty and acquires sacred knowledge.

He who wishes for long life, should use two verses in the *Uṣṇih* metre; for Uṣṇih is life. He who having such a knowledge uses two Uṣṇihs[25] arrives at his full age (*i.e.*, 100 years).

He who desires heaven, should use two *Anuṣṭubhs*. There are sixty-four syllables in two Anuṣṭubhs.[26] Each of these three worlds (earth, air, and sky) contains twenty-one places, one rising above the **[13]** other (just as the steps of a ladder). By twenty-one steps he ascends to each of these worlds severally;[27] by taking the sixty-fourth step he stands firm in the celestial world. He who, having such a knowledge, uses two Anuṣṭubhs, gains a footing (in the celestial world).

He who desires wealth and glory, should use two *Bṛihatîs*. For among the metres the Bṛihati[28] is wealth and glory. He who, having such a knowledge, uses two Bṛihatîs, bestows upon himself wealth and glory.

He who loves the sacrifice should use two *Paṅktis*.[29] For the sacrifice is like a Paṅkti. It comes to him who having such a knowledge uses two Paṅktis.

He who desires strength should use two Triṣṭubhs.[30] Triṣṭubh is strength, vigour, and sharpness of senses. He who knowing this, uses two Triṣṭubhs, becomes vigorous, endowed with sharp senses and strong.

---

23 The *Sviṣṭakṛit* is that part of an offering which is given to all gods indiscriminately, after the principal deities of the respective Iṣṭi (in the *Dîkṣâṇiya Iṣṭi*, these deities are *Agni*, *Soma*, and *Agni-Viṣṇu*) have received their share. The two mantras required for the *Sviṣṭakṛit* are called *Saṁyâjyâ*. On account of the general nature of this offering, the choice of the mantras is not so much limited as is the case when the offering is to be given to one particular deity.

24 They are, *sa havyavâl amartyaḥ* (3, 11, 2), and *Agnir hotâ purohitaḥ* (3, 11, 1).

25 They are, *agne vâjasya gomataḥ* (1, 79, 4), and *sa idhâno vasuṣ haviḥ* (1, 79, 5).

26 *Tvam agne vasûn* (1, 45, 1. 2).

[13] 27 This makes on the whole 63 steps.

28 They are, *ena vo agniṃ* (7, 16, 1), and *udasya śochiḥ* (7, 16, 3).

29 *Agnim tam\manye* (5, 6, 1. 2).

30 *Dve virûpe charathaḥ* (1. 95, 1, 2).

He who desires cattle should use two *Jagatîs* (verses in the Jagatî metre).[31] Cattle are Jagatî-like. He who knowing this, uses two Jagatîs, becomes rich in cattle.

He who desires food (*annâdya*) should use two verses in the *Virâj* metre.[32] *Virâj* is food. Therefore he who has most of food, shines (*virâjati*) most on earth. This is the reason why it is called *virâj* (from *vi-râj*, to shine). He who knows this, shines **[14]** forth among his own people, (and) becomes the most influential man among his own people.

6.

The *Virâj* metre possesses five powers. Because of its consisting of three lines (*pâdas*), it is *Gâyatrî* and *Uṣṇiḥ* (which metres have three lines also). Because of its lines consisting of eleven syllables, it is Triṣṭubh (4 times 11 syllables=44). Because of its having thirty-three syllables, it is *Anuṣṭubh.* (If it be said, that the two Virâj verses in question, *i.e.*, *preddho agne* and *imo agne* have, the one only 29, and the other 32 syllables, instead of 33, it must be borne in mind that) metres do not change by (the want of) one syllable or two[33]. The fifth power is, that it is *Virâj.*

He who knowing this, uses (at the *Sviṣṭakṛit*) two Virâj verses, obtains the power of all metres, gains the power of all metres, gains union, uniformity, and (complete) unison with all the metres.[34]

Therefore two Virâj verses are certainly to be used, those (which begin with) *agne preddho* (7, 1, 3), and *imo agne* (7, 1, 18).

Dîkṣâ is right, Dîkṣâ is truth ; thence a Dîkṣita should only speak the truth.

Now they say, what man can speak all truth ? Gods (alone) are full of truth, (but) men are full of falsehood.

[15] He should make each address (to another) by the word, "*vichakṣaṇa,*" *i.e.*, "of penetrating eye." The eye (*chakṣus*) is *vichakṣaṇa*, for with it he sees distinctly (*vi-paśyati*). For the eye is established as truth among men. Therefore people say to a man who tells something, 'Hast thou seen it ?' (*i.e.*, is it really true ?) And if he says, "I saw it," then they believe

---

[31] They are, *janasya gopâ* (5, 11, 1, 2).

[32] They are, *preddho agne* (7, 1, 3), and *imo agne* (7, 1, 18).

[14] [33] In the first verse quoted, there are even 4 syllables less than required. The Brâhmaṇam is not very accurate in its metrical discussion. The Anuṣṭubh has 32 syllables.

[34] The meaning is, by using two Virâj verses which contain the principal metres, he obtains collectively all those boons which each of the several metres is capable of bestowing upon him who uses them. So the Gâyatrî, for instance, grants beauty and sacred knowledge, the Triṣṭubh strength, &c. (See above). The metres are regarded as deities. He who employes them becomes pervaded, as it were, by them, and participates in all their virtues and properties.

him. And if one sees a thing himself, one does not believe others, even if they were many. Therefore he should add (always) to his addresses (to others) the word *vichakṣaṇa*,[35] " of penetrating, sharp eyes." Then the speech uttered by him becomes full of truth.

SECOND CHAPTER.

Prâyaṇîya Iṣṭi.

7

The *Prâyaṇîya iṣṭi* has its name "*prâyaṇîya*"[1] from the fact that by its means the sacrificers approach heaven (from *pra-yâ*, going forward). The *prâyaṇîya* **[16]**ceremony is the air inhaled (*prâṇa*), whereas the *udayanîya*, *i.e.*, concluding ceremony (of the whole sacrifice) is the air exhaled. The Hotar (who is required at both ceremonies) is the common hold of both the airs (*samâna*). Both the air inhaled and exhaled are held together (in the same body). (The performance of both ceremonies, the *prâyaṇîya* and *udayanîya* are intended) for making the vital airs, and for obtaining a discriminating knowledge of their several parts (*prâṇa*, *udâna*, *&c.*)[2]

The sacrifice (the mystical sacrificial personage) went away from the gods. The gods were (consequently) unable to perform any further ceremony. They did not know where it had gone to. They said to Aditi : Let us know the sacrifice through thee ! Aditi said : Let it be so ; but I will choose a boon from you. They said : Choose ! Then she chose this boon : all sacrifices shall commence with me, and end with me. Thence there is at (the beginning of) the *prâyaṇîya iṣṭi* a Charu-offering for Aditi,

[15] [35]. This explanation of the term *vichakṣaṇa* refers to the offering of two parts of melted butter (See chapter 4, page 10), which are called *chakṣuṣî*, *i.e.*, two eyes. The sacrificer obtains in a symbolical way new eyes by their means to view all things in the right way. The *Dîkṣita* ought to use the term *vichakṣaṇa* after the name of the person who is addressed ; for instance, 'Devadatta *Vichakṣaṇa*, bring the cow.' According to Âpastamba, this term should be added only to the names of a Kṣatriya and Vaiśya addressed; in addressing a Brâhmaṇa, the expression *chanasita* should be used instead.—*Sây.*

[1] यत्प्रायणीय : The masculine is here used, instead of the feminine. कर्मविशेष : is, as Sây. justly remarks, to be supplied. The common name of this ceremony is *Prâyaṇiya iṣṭi.* The Brâhmaṇam here attempts at giving an explanation of the terms *prâyaṇiya* and *udayanîya.*

[16] [2] The Prâyaṇîya ceremony is here regarded as the proper commencement of the *yajna*; for the Dîkṣaṇîyâ iṣṭi is only introductory to it. The beginning is compared to the *prâṇa* and the end to the *udâna*, both which vital airs are held together by the *samâna.* The Brâhmaṇa mentions here only three *prâṇas* or vital airs. Two others, *vyâna* and *apâna*, are omitted. This mystical explanation can be only understood if one bears in mind that the *yajna* or sacrifice itself is regarded as a spiritual man who shares all properties of the natural man.

and the same offering is given to her as the boon chosen by her at the end (of the sacrifice). Then she chose this (other) boon. Through me you shall know the eastern direction, through Agni the southern, through Soma the western, and through Savitar the northern direction. The Hotar repeats the (Anuvâkyâ and) Yâjyâ-mantra for the *Pathyâ*.[3] **[17]** Therefore the sun rises in the east and sets in the west; for it follows in its course the *Pathyâ*. He repeats the (Anuvâkyâ and) Yâjyâ verse for Agni.[4]

That is done because cereals first ripen in southern countries [5] (for Agni is posted at the southern direction); for cereals are Agni's. He repeats the (*Anuvâkyâ* and) *Yâjyâ*[6] for Soma. That is done, because many rivers flow towards the west (to fall into the sea), and the waters are Soma's. He repeats the (*Anuvâkyâ* and) *Yâjyâ* [7] mantra for *Savitar*. That is done, because the wind (*pavamânaḥ*) blows most from the north between the northern and western directions; it thus blows moved by *Savitar*.[8]

He repeats the (*Anuvâkyâ* and) *Yâjyâ* [9] mantra **[18]** for Aditi, who is the upper region.[10] This is done, because the sky (*asâu*) wets the earth with rain (and) dries it up (which is done from above). He repeats (*Anuvâkyâ* and) *Yâjyâ* verses for five deities. The sacrifice is five-fold. All (five)

---

[3] The two verses addressed to *Pathyâ* are Rigveda 10, 63, 15, 16, *svastir naḥ pathyâsu* (see Nirukti 11, 45). These verses are mentioned in Âśval. Śr. Sû. 4, 3. The word *yajati* is an abbreviation [17] for *anvhâa yajaticha, i.e.*, he repeats the Anuvâkyâ (first) and Yâjyâ (second) mantra when an offering is given. Sây. notes from another Śâkhâ the passage: पथ्यां स्वस्ति यजति प्राचीमेव तया दिशं प्रजानाति। *i.e.*, he (the Hotar) recognises the eastern direction by repeating the Yâjyâ verse addressed to *Pathyâ Svasti, i.e.*, well-being when making a journey, safe passage. According to Sâyaṇa, *Pathyâ* is only another name of *Aditi*. She represents here the line which connects the point of sunrise with that of sunset.

[4] These are, *agne naya supathâ* 1, 189, 1, and *â devânâm api panthâm* 10, 2, 3.

[5] Sây. states that in the north of the Vindhyâ mountains chiefly barley and wheat are cultivated, which ripen in the months of *Mâgha* and *Phâlguna* (February and March), whilst in the countries south from the Vindhyâ (*i.e.*, in the Dekkhan) rice prevails, which ripens in the months of *Kârtika* and *Mârgaśirṣa* (November and December).

[6] They are: *tvam soma prachikitô manîṣâ*, 1, 91, 1, and *yâ te- dhâmâni divi* 1, 91, 4. See 1, 9. Âśv. Śr. S. 4, 3.

[7] They are: *â viśvadevam satpatim* 5, 82, 7, and *ya imâ viśvâ jâtâni* 5, 82, 9.

[8] Sây. explains *Savitar* as, प्रेरकादेवः a moving, inciting god.

[9] These are *sutrâmâṇam prithivîm* 10, 63, 10, and *mahîm û ṣû mâtaram*. Atharva Veda 7, 6, 2.

[18] [10] Sây. explains *uttamâ*, by *ûrdhvâ*, referring to a passage of the Taittirîya Veda: आदित्योर्ध्वं (प्रजानात्). There is no doubt, the word can mean the upper region, but one would not be quite wrong in translating here the word by "last." For Aditi is here the last deity invoked.

directions are (thus) established; [11] and the sacrifice becomes also established. It becomes established for such people (only) with whom there is a Hotar having this knowledge (to separate and mark the regions in this way).

8

He who wishes for beauty and acquirement of sacred knowledge, should turn towards the east when making the offerings for the *Prayâja* deities. [12] For the eastern direction is beauty and sacred knowledge. He who having this knowledge turns eastward (when making the Prayâjas) obtains beauty and sacred knowledge.

He who wishes for food, should turn towards the south when making the offerings for the Prayâja deities. For Agni (who is posted at the southern direction) is the eater of food, and master of food. He who having this knowledge goes towards the south (when making the Prayâjas) becomes an eater [19] of food, a master of food; he obtains nourishment along with offspring.

He who desires cattle, should go towards the west when making the Prayâja offerings. For cattle are the waters (which are in the western direction). He who having such a knowledge goes westwards becomes rich in cattle.

He who desires the drinking of the Soma, should go towards the north when making the Prayâja offerings. For the northern direction is the king Soma. He who having such a knowledge goes northwards (when making the Prayâjas) obtains the drinking of the Soma.

The upper direction (*ûrdhvâ*) leads to heaven. He who performs the Prayâja offerings when standing in the upper direction [13] becomes successful in all directions. For these (three) worlds are linked together. They being in such a condition shine for the welfare of him who has such a knowledge.

He repeats the Yâjyâ for the *Pathyâ*. [14] By doing so, he places

---

[11] The fifth direction is '*ûrdhvâ*,' above. "The directions are established," means the directions which were previously not to be distinguished from one another, are now separated and may be known.

[12] They are formulas addressed to the following deities: *samidh*, the wooden sticks thrown into the fire; *tanûnapât*, a name of Agni; *idâ*, the sacrificial food; *barhis*, the kuśa grass spread over the sacrificial ground; and *svâhâkâra*, the call *svâhâ*! at the end of *Yâjyâ* verses, See Âśva. Śr. S. 1, 5.

[13] That is, in the middle of the north and west of the Âhavanîya fire.

[14] This refers to the words: ये यजामहे (*i.e.*, we who worship) पथ्यां स्वस्तिं which are repeated by the Hotar, after the *Anuvâkyâ* is over, and before the commencement of the proper Yâjyâ verse. These words are introductory to the latter. Before all Yâjyâ verses (as is generally done), the words ये यजामहे with the name of the respective deity are to be found.—*Saptahâutra*.

speech (represented by *Pathyâ*) at the beginning of the sacrifice. The breath (coming out of the mouth and the nostrils) is Agni; the breath (being within the mouth and nostrils) is Soma. Savitar is to set into motion (the ceremonial machinery), and Aditi is to establish a firm footing. When he repeats a Yâjyâ to Pathyâ, then he carries the sacrifice on its path. Agni and Soma verily are the two eyes; Savitar serves for moving it, and Aditi for establishing a firm footing (to it). For through the **[20]** eye the gods got aware of the sacrifice. For what is not perceivable (elsewhere) is to be perceived by the eye. If any one even after having run astray gets aware (of any thing) by exerting his eye successively [15] (in consequence of the successive exertions of the faculty of seeing), then he (really) knows it. When the gods (were exerting their eyes repeatedly, and looking from one object to the other) they got sight of the sacrifice. Thus they got sight of it on this earth; on the earth (therefore) they acquired the implements (required for performing the sacrifice). On her (the earth) the sacrifice is spread; on her it is performed; on her the sacrificial implements are acquired. This earth is *Aditi*; therefore the last Yâjyâ verse repeated is addressed to her. This is done (in order to enable the sacrificer) to get aware of the sacrifice (the mystical sacrificial man) and to behold afterwards the celestial world.

9

They say, the gods should be provided with *Vaiśyas* [16] (agriculturists and herdsmen). For if **[21]** the gods are provided with them, men

---

[21] [15] *Anuṣṭyâ* is explained by Sây.: **केनापि प्रयत्नविशेषेण.** It no doubt, literally means, one standing by the other, one after the other. The substantive *anuṣṭhâna* is the most general word for performance of a religious ceremony, being a succession of several acts. The meaning given to the word in Böhtlingk and Roth's Saṁskṛit Dictionary (I. page 124) "with his own eyes," is nothing but a bad guess unsupported by any authority and contrary to etymology and usage. The phrase *anuṣṭyâ prajânâti* properly means, he gets aware of the chief object after having got sight of an intermediate one which alone leads to the first. The sacrificer whose principal object is to reach heaven, must first see the medium by means of which he can ascend to the celestial world. This is the sacrifice. Therefore he first sees the sacrifice and then he casts a glance at the celestial world. A traveller who has run astray, must first recognise the direction, and then he may find the way to his homely village.

[16] According to Sâyaṇa, the word *viśah* may convey two meanings: 1. a subject in general; 2, men of the Vaiśya caste. I prefer the latter meaning. The Vaiśyas are to provide gods and men with food and [21] wealth. They are here evidently regarded as the subjected population. The gods are, as Sây. states with reference to the creation theory of the Vâjasaneyins, divided into four castes, just as men. *Agni* and *Bṛihaspati* are the Brâhmaṇs among the gods; *Indra, Varuṇa, Soma, the Rudras, Parjanya, Yama Mṛityu* are the Kṣatriyas; *Gaṇeśa*, the *Vasus*, the *Rudras*, the *Âdityas*, *Viśvedevas* and *Marutas* are the Vaiśyas, and *Pûṣan* belongs to the Śûdra caste.

subsequently obtain them also. If all Vaiśyas (to furnish the necessary supplies) are in readiness, then the sacrifice is prepared. It is prepared for that family in the midst of which there is a Hotar who has this knowledge (and makes provision accordingly).

(The gods are provided for with Vaiśyas by the recital of the verse, *svastinaḥ pathyâsu* : [17] 10, 63, 15), "O Maruts! grant us in the desert tracks prosperity (by providing us with water); grant us prosperity (by abundance) in waters in a desolated region over which the sky shines! grant prosperity to the wombs of our women for producing children! grant prosperity to our wealth." For the Maruts are the Vaiśyas of the gods (their agriculturists). The Hotar puts them by (repeating) this (mantra) in readiness at the beginning of the sacrifice.

They say, the Hotar should (as *Anuvâkyâ* and *Yâjyâ* verses at the Prâyaṇîya iṣṭi) use mantras of all (principal) metres. For the gods conquered the celestial world by means of having used for their (*Anuvakyâ* and) *Yâjyâ* verses mantras of all metres. Likewise, the sacrificer who does the same gains the celestial world. (The two verses) *svasti naḥ pathyâsu* and *svastir iddhi prapathe* (10, 63, 15, 16),[17] which are addressed to *path yâsvasti*, *i.e.*, safe journey, are in the Triṣṭubh metre. The two verses addressed to Agni, *agne naya supathâ* (1, 189, 1), and *â devânâm api panthâm* (10, 2, 3), **[22]** are also in the Triṣṭubh metre. The two verses, addressed to Soma, *tvam amos prachikito manîṣâ* (1, 91, 1), and *yâ te dhâmâni divi* (1, 91, 4) are (also) in the Triṣṭubh metre. The two verses addressed to *Savitâ* : *â viśvadevam satpatim* (5, 82, 7), and *yâ imâ viśvâ* (5, 82, 9), are in the Gâyatrî metre. The two verses addressed to Aditi, *sutrâmâṇam pṛithivîm* (10, 63, 10), and *mahîm û ṣu mâtaram* (Atharv. 7, 6, 2), are in Jagatî metre.[18] These are all the (principal) metres : *Gâyatrî*, *Triṣṭubh*, and *Jagatî*. Those (other metres) follow them. For these (three kinds of metres) are, as it were, of the most frequent occurrence (*pratamâm*) at a sacrifice. He, therefore, who having such a knowledge gets repeated his Anuvâkyâ and Yâjyâ verses in these (three) metres, gets repeated them in all metres (obtains the particular advantage to be derived not only from the three metres mentioned, but from all other metres also).

---

[17] See the 3rd note above, page 16. The translation of the whole is given in the context.

[18] All the *Anuvâkyâ* and *Yâjyâ* verses required for the five deities (see 1, 7), of the *Prâyaṇîya iṣṭi* are here mentioned.

10

These verses used as Anuvâkyâs and Yâjyâs at this offering (the Prâyaṇîya Iṣṭi), contain the words, *pra*, forward, forth[19] *nî*,[20] to carry; *pathin*,[21] path; *svasti*,[22] welfare. The gods after having performed an Iṣṭi by means of these verses, gained the celestial world. Likewise, a sacrificer, after having done the same, gains the celestial world. Among these verses there is a pada (a foot, here the last quarter verse of 10, 63, 15): "O Maruts! grant prosperity in wealth." The Maruts are the Vaiśyas (the subjects) of the gods, and are domi-
[23] ciled in the air. (By these words just mentioned) the sacrificer who goes to heaven is to be announced to them (the Maruts). For they have the power of preventing him (from going up) or even of killing him. By the words, "O Maruts! grant prosperity," &c., the Hotar announces the sacrificer (his projected journey up to the celestial world) to the Vaiśyas (the subjects) of the gods. The Maruts then neither prevent nor kill him who goes to the celestial world. He who has such a knowledge, is allowed a safe passage up to the celestial world by them.

The two *Saṁyâjyâ* verses required for the *Sviṣṭakṛit* (of the *Prâyaṇîya-iṣṭi*) ought to be in the Virâj metre, which consists of thirty-three syllables. These are: *sed agnir agnîṁr* (7, 1, 14) and *sed agnir yo* (7, 1, 15). The gods after having used for their *Saṁyâjyâs* two verses in the *Virâj* metre, gained the celestial world. Likewise does that sacrificer gain heaven who uses also two verses in the Virâj metre (when performing the *Sviṣṭakṛit* of the *Prâyaṇîya iṣṭi*). They (each of them) contain thirty-three syllables. For there are thirty-three gods, *viz.*, eight *Vasus*, eleven *Rudras*, twelve *Âdityas*, (one) *Prajâpati*, and (one) *Vaṣaṭ-kâra*. In this way, the Hotar makes the gods participate at the very first beginning of the sacrifice in the (33) syllables of the mantra recited; for each syllable is (as it were) a plate [23] for the gods, by which the sacrificer makes (all) deities pleased and satiates them.

11

They say, at the Prâyaṇîya iṣṭi are (only) the *Prayâja* [24] offer-

---

[19] In the word *prapathe*, in *svastir iddhi prapathe* (10, 63, 16).

[20] In the word *naya*, in *Agne naya* (1, 189, 1).

[21] In the words *pathyâ* and *supathâ*.

[23] [22] In the verses 10, 63, 15, 16.

[23] The syllables of the mantras represent different plates of food presented to the gods. They can be the food of the gods only in a mystical sense.

[24] See page 18, note 12.

ings to be made, but not the *Anuyâ* [24] *jas*;[25] for the latter are, as it were, a blank, and (if performed) cause delay. But this (precept) should not be observed; at the said Iṣṭi both the Prayâja as well as the Anuyâja offerings should be made. For the Prayâjas are the vital airs, and the Anuyâjas are offspring. When he thus foregoes the Prayâjas, he foregoes the vital airs of the sacrificer (deprives him of his life), and when he foregoes the *Anuyâjas*, he foregoes the offspring of the sacrificer (deprives him of it). Thence Prayâjas as well as *Anuyâjas* are required (at the Prâyaṇîya *iṣṭi*).

He should not repeat the *Saṁyâja* mantras addressed to the ladies[26] (*patnîs*, of the gods); nor should he use the *Saṁsthita-Yajus*[27] formula. Only inasmuch as this is done (*i.e.*, if the Patnî-saṁyâjya and Saṁsthita-Yajus offerings are omitted), the sacrifice is complete.[28]

He should keep the remainder of the Prâyaṇîya-iṣṭ offering and (after the Soma sacrifice is over) mix it together, with the offering required for the *Udâyanîya* (concluding) *iṣṭi*, in order to make the sacrifice one continuous uninterrupted whole. (There [25] is also another way for connecting both Iṣṭis). In the same vessel, in which he portions out the rice for the Purodâśa of the Prâyaṇîya iṣṭi, he should portion out also the rice for the Purodâśa of the *Udâyanîya* iṣṭi. Inasmuch as this is done, the sacrifice becomes continuous, uninterrupted. They say, in doing this the sacrificers succeed in that (the other) world, but not in this one, They use the expression Prâyaṇîyam (on several occasions). For, on the several portions of rice being taken out for the Purodâśa (by the Adhvaryu), the sacrificers say this is *Prâyaṇîya* (*i.e.*, to go forth, to progress), and on the Purodâśa oblations being thrown (into the fire), they say again, this is *Prâyaṇîyam* (*i.e.*, to progress). In this way, the sacrificers go forth (*Prayanti*) from this world. But they say so from ignorance (and this objection is consequently not to be regarded.)

The Anuvâkyâ and Yâjyâ verses of both the Prâyaṇîya and *Udâyanîya* iṣṭis should interchange in this way, that the Anuvâkyâ verses of the

---

[24] [25] In the common Iṣṭis there are generally three *Anuyâjas*, or oblations of clarified butter, after the Sviṣṭakṛit ceremony is over. The deities are: *devam barhis* (the divine seat), *deva narâśaṁsa*, and *deva agni sviṣṭakṛit*. *See* Âśv. Śr. S. 1, 8. The present practice is to leave out the Anuyâjas at the Prâyaṇîya iṣṭi.

[26] These mantras, which are addressed to several deities, chiefly the wives of the gods, are called, *Patnî-saṁyâjâs*. These women are: *Râkâ*, *Sinîvâli* (full moon), and *Kuhû* and *Anumati* (new moon). In the Âśv. Śr. S. 1, 10 *Anumati* is omitted.

[27] The last Yajus like mantra which is recited by the Hotar at the close of the iṣṭi. See Âśv. Śr. S. 1, 11.

[28] The usual concluding ceremonies of the Iṣṭi are to be dispensed with at the Prâyaṇîya, in order to connect it with the other parts of the sacrifice.

Prâyaṇîya iṣṭi should be used as the Yâjyâ verses for the Udâyanîya, and the Yâjyâ verses of the Prâyaṇîya as Anuvâkyâs of the Udâyanîya. The Hotar shifts in this way (the Anuvâkyâs and Yâjyâs of both the Iṣṭis) for ensuring success (to the sacrificer) in both worlds, for obtaining a firm footing (for the sacrificer) in both worlds. The sacrificer (thus) succeeds in both worlds, and obtains a firm footing in both worlds. He who has this knowledge, obtains a firm footing (in both worlds). The Charu oblation which is given to Aditi at the Prâyaṇîa as well as at the Udâyanîya iṣṭi serves for holding the sacrifice (at both its ends) together, to tie the two knots of the sacrifice (at the beginning and at the end), in order to prevent it from slipping down. Some one (a theologian) has told : this **[26]** (tying of the two ends of the sacrifice) is exactly corresponding to that (act of common life to which it alludes), as (for instance) one ties two knots at both the ends of a rope (*tejaniḥ*), in order to prevent (the load which is tied up) from slipping down. In the same way, the priest ties the knots at both ends of the sacrifice (the sacrificial chain) by means of the Charu oblation given to Aditi at the Prâyaṇîya as well as at the Udâyanîya iṣṭi. Among those (deities required at both the Iṣṭis) they commence with *Pathyâ Svasti* (at the Prâyaṇta iṣṭi), and conclude (at the Udâyanîya iṣṭi) also with *Pathyâ Svasti.* (Thus) the sacrificers start safely from here, and end (their journey there, in the other world), they end safely, safely (their journey there, in the other world).

THIRD CHAPTER.

The Buying and Bringing of the Soma. The Producing of Fire by Friction. The Atithyâ Iṣṭi.

12.

The gods bought the king Soma in the eastern direction. Thence he is (generally) bought in the eastern direction. They bought him from the thirteenth month. Thence the thirteenth month is found unfit (for any religious work to be done in it) ; a seller of the Soma is (likewise) found unfit (for intercourse). For such a man is a defaulter. (When the Soma, after having been bought, was brought to men (the sacrificers), his powers and his faculty of making the senses sharp moved from their place and scattered everywhere.[1] They tried to collect and keep them [**27**] together with one verse. But they failed. They (tried to keep them together) with two, then with three, then with four, then with five, then with six, then

[1] *Diśo* is to be taken as an ablative depending on the verb *vyudasîdan*, literally, they were upset (and scattered) everywhere. The preposition *ut* in this verb mainly requires the ablative.

with seven verses ; but they did not succeed in keeping them together. (Finally) with eight verses they succeeded, and recovered them (in their entirety and completeness). (Therefore) what is held together and obtained, that is called *aṣṭau, i.e.* eight (from *aś* to reach, obtain). He who has this knowledge obtains anything he might wish for. Thence there are in those ceremonies (which follow the bringing of the Soma to the sacrificial compound), eight verses, each time recited, in order to collect and hold together the strength and those qualities (of the Soma plant) which give sharpness of senses.

13.

The Adhvaryu then says (to the Hotar) : repeat a mantra for the Soma who is bought and being brought (to the sacrificial compound). The Hotar repeats : *Bhadrâd abhi śreyaḥ prehi,*[2] *i.e.*, go from **[28]** happiness to still greater bliss. By the word *bhadra, i.e.*, happy, this world (the earth) is meant. That world is better (*śreyân*) than this world. Thus the Hotar makes the sacrificer go to the celestial world (which is to be understood by *śreyas, i.e,* better). (The second pada of the verse is): *bṛihaspatiḥ pura etâ astu, i.e.*, the (thy) guide be Bṛihaspati ! If the Hotar has made (by repeating this pada) the Brahma his (the sacrificer's) guide, (the sacrifice) being thus provided with the Brahma will not be damaged. (The third pada of the verse is :) *atha îm avasya vara â pṛithivya, i.e.*, stop him (Soma) on the surface of the earth. *Vara* means the place for sacrificing

---

[2] The mantra is from the *Taittirîya Saṁhitâ.* We find it also in the *Atharvaveda Saṁhitâ* (7, 8, 1.) with some deviations, which are found alike in the printed edition and in an old manuscript which is in my possession. The verse reads in the Aitarey. Brahm. and Taittir. Samh. as follows :—

भद्रादभि श्रेयः प्रेहि, बृहस्पतिः पुर एता ते अस्तु ।
अथेमवस्य वर आ पृथिव्या आरे शत्रून् कृणुहि सर्ववीर : ॥

Instead of अ there is अधि in the A. V., and instead of अथेमवस्य (अथ । ईम् । अवस्य) there is अथेममस्या (अथ । इमं अस्या) ; instead of the plur. शत्रून् we have the sing. शत्रुं, and instead of सर्ववीरा there is सर्ववीरं. There is no doubt that the readings of the Atharva Veda look like corrections of the less intelligible parts of the original mantra, which is correct only in the form in which we find it in the Ait. Br. and the Taitt. S. अभि is less correct than अधि. The redactor of the A. V. chose it on account of the so extremely frequent combination of अधि with an ablative which generally precedes (*see* the large number of instances quoted in B. and R.'s Saṁskrit Dictionary I. pp. 142, 143), whilst अभि never governs an ablative, but rather an accusative, and is in this passage to be connected with श्रेयः. The words : अथेममस्या are a bad substitute for अथेममस्य. The term *avasya* " make an end, do away with him " (the enemy) was entirely misunderstood by the redactor. *Asya* he makes *asyá* and refers it to पृथिव्या ! The nominative सर्ववीरः which refers only to the deity invoked is made an accusative and referred to शत्रून्, which then became a singular, शत्रुं.

to the gods (*devayajana*). (By these words) the Hotar makes him (the Soma) stop (and remain in that place). (The fourth pada is :) *âre śatrûn kriṇuhi sarvavîraḥ, i.e.*, endowed with all powers, drive far off the enemies ! (By reading these words) the Hotar turns out the enemy who does injury to the sacrificer, and his adversary, (and) consigns him to the lowest condition.

The Hotar then repeats the triplet : *soma yâs te mayobhuvaḥ* (1, 91, 9-11), which is addressed to Soma, and is in the Gâyatri metre. In this way the Hotar makes the king Soma flourishing when he is being brought (to the sacrificial compound) by means of his own deity (the verse being addressed to **[29]** Soma himself), and his own metre (his favourite metre being the Gâyatrî. [3]) (The Hotar repeats :) *sarve[4] nandanti yaśasâ* (10, 71, 10), *i.e.*, "all friends rejoice at the arrival of the friend crowned with fame for having remained victor in the learned discussion (*sabhâ*); for as their (of his friends) protector from defects, and giver of food, he is fit and ready for providing them with strength." [5] (Now follows the ex **[30]** planation) : *Yaśaḥ,*

---

[3] The Gâyatrî is said to have assumed the shape of a bird, and brought the Soma from heaven. Thence this metre is sacred to him.

[4] Sây. understands by "the friend," Soma, and by "the friends, who rejoice at the friend's arrival," the priests and the sacrificer. About the same meaning he gives to the verse in his commentary on the Rigveda Samhitâ. There he explains सखायः, friends, by समानज्ञानाः being equal in knowledge. सर्वे he refers to "all men of the assembly." यशसा he takes in the sense of an adjective यशस्विना. But it is very doubtful whether this verse had originally any reference to Soma. In the whole hymn (बृहस्पते प्रथमं वाचो अग्रं०) of which it forms the eleventh verse, there is nowhere any allusion made to Soma. According to the Anukramaṇî, the hymn is "seen" (composed) by Bṛihaspati, the son of Aṅgiras. But this appears to be very unlikely ; for Bṛihaspati himself is addressed in the vocative. Sây. gets over the difficulty by asserting that Bṛihaspati (the teacher of the Gods and the receptacle of all sacred knowledge) is addressing these words to himself, after having had revealed the meaning and bearing of the Veda, before he ventured upon communicating the revelation (to the Gods). To judge from the contents of the hymn, the author prays to Bṛihaspati who is the same with *Vâchaspati*, the god of eloquence and speech, to endow him with the power of giving utterance in the proper words to his feelings, of which only the best ones should be revealed (v. 1). There is an interesting simile to be met with in the 2nd verse : "when the wise made the speech through their mind, purifying it (through their thoughts), just as they purify barley juice (*saktu*) through a filterer (*titau*)." *Saktu* is a kind of beer prepared by pouring water over barley, and by filtering it after having allowed it to remain for some time in this state. The whole hymn, in which the name "brâhmaṇa" (as that of a caste) is several times mentioned, appears to refer to the might of speech and the great success to be derived from it when engaged in sacrificing.

[5] The priests live on the presents which are given to them by the sacrificers. Hence the Soma, who is indispensable for the sacrificer, and who is to be administered in the proper way by priests only, is ' their giver of food '

i.e., fame, glory, is the king Soma. At his being bought, every one rejoices, he who has to gain something (in the shape of Dakṣiṇâ, the sacrificial reward), as well as he who has not. The king Soma "is the friend who remains victor at the learned discussions of the Brâhmans." He is *kilbiṣasprit.*, "the protector from defects." For he protects him from defects who becomes liable to them. He (that priest) who excels all others (regarding the power of speech and recitation) becomes liable to defects (voice becoming hoarse or the hands flag). Thence they (the sacrificers) say (to the Hotar): "do not repeat (if thy intention is only to excel a rival in skill) the mantra (wrong), and likewise (to the Adhvaryu :) do not (in a state of confusion) perform the ceremony (wrong); may they now not do anything wrong, in too great a hurry!" He is "*pituṣaṇir*," *i. e.*, giver of food; *pitu* is food, and *pitu* is the sacrificial reward (*dakṣiṇâ*). The sacrificer gives, on account of a Soma sacrifice having been performed for him (to the priests), a reward. Thus he makes him (the Soma) "the giver of food" (for the priests.) The word *vâjiṇam* means sharpness of senses and (bodily) strength. He who has this knowledge will preserve up to the end of his life the unimpaired use of his senses and strength.

The Hotar repeats: *âgan deva* (4, 53, 7.), *i.e.*, May the divine mover Savitar come [6] with the *Ṛitus* (*i.e.*, seasons)! May he make prosperous our household, and bless us with children and nourishment! May he favour us (with gifts) at day and night (always)! **[31]** May he let us obtain children and wealth! "*âgan* means: he (the Soma) has come and is here by that time (after having been bought). The Ṛitus (seasons) are the royal brothers of the king Soma, just as men have brothers. (By repeating this first pada) the Hotar makes him (the Soma) come with them (his brothers, the Ṛitus). By the words: "may he make prosperous," &c., he asks for a blessing. (By repeating the third pada) "may he favour us at day and night," he asks for a blessing for him (the sacrificer) at day and night. (By the fourth pada :) "may he let us," &c., he (also) asks for a blessing.

The Hotar repeats: *yâ te dhâmâni haviṣâ* (1, 91, 19), *i. e.*, "may all thy qualities which they honour (with prayers and with oblations) become manifest at (this) sacrifice everywhere! Enter, O Soma! (our) houses (the sacrificial hall) as an increaser of property (of cows), as a protector (from

---

The Brâhmaṇa as well as Sâyaṇa refer the conjunctive *âgan* to *Soma* which is certainly not the case. In his commentary on the Saṁhitâ, he refers it justly to Savitar (see vol. III, page 236, ed. M. Müller). No doubt the verse was originally intended for Savitar and not for Soma. The whole hymn whence the verse is taken is devoted to Savitar.

evil), as one who gives good children and does not hurt them (in any way)."

The words *gayasphâna*, *pratarana*, *suvîraḥ* mean: be an increaser and protector of our cattle. *Duryâḥ* means the premises (of the sacrificer) which are afraid of the king Soma having arrived. When the Hotar repeats this (last pada of the verse), he does it with a view to propitiate him (Soma). If the Hotar has thus propitiated him (the Soma), he neither kills the children nor the cattle of the sacrificer.

The Hotar concludes with the verse, addressed to Varuṇa: *imâm dhiyam śikṣamâṇasya deva* (8, 42, 3), *i.e.*, "O divine Varuṇa, instruct the pupil in understanding, performance and skill. May we ascend **[32]** the ship for crossing safely all evil waters and land in safety (on the other shore)." Soma is in the power of the god Varuṇa, as long as he is tied up (in the cloth),[7] and goes to the places of the *Prâgvaṁśa*. When reciting this verse, he thus makes the Soma prosper by means of his own deity (for as liquor he is *Vâruṇî*), and his own metre.[8] The "pupil" (learner) is he who sacrifices, for he is learning. By the words "instruct in understanding, performance, and skill," he means, teach, O Varuṇa, strength (and) knowledge. The "ship" is the sacrifice. The ship is of "good passage." The black goat-skin is the "good passage," and speech the ship. By means of this verse the sacrificer thus ascends speech (as his ship) and sails in it up to the celestial world.

These eight verses which he repeats, are complete in form. What is complete in form, that is successful in the sacrifice, when the verse repeated alludes to the ceremony which is being performed.

Of these verses he repeats the first and last thrice; this makes twelve (in all). The year consists of twelve months, and Prajâpati is the year. He who has this knowledge succeeds by these verses which reside in Prajâpati. By repeating the first and last verses thrice, he ties the two end knots of the sacrifice for fastening and tightening it, in order to prevent it from slipping down.

14

One of the bullocks (which carry the cart on which the king Soma is seated) is to remain yoked, the other **[33]** to be

---

[7] The Soma stalks are to be tied up in a cloth, when they are brought to the sacrificial compound, the front part of which, including the Ahavanîya, Dakṣiṇâ and Gârhapatya fires is called, *Prâgvaṁśa* or *Prîchâna-vaṁśa*.

[8] This is Triṣṭubh. According to another Śâkhâ, as Sây. says, this metre (very likely in the shape of a bird, as the Gâyatrî is said to have assumed) went to heaven to abstract the Soma, and brought down the Dakṣiṇâ (sacrificial reward), and the internal concentration of the vital powers (the so-called *tapas*). See Ait. Brah. 3, 25.

unyoked. Then they should take down (from the cart) the king (Soma). Were they to take him down when both are let loose, they would bring him into the power of the manes (*pitaraḥ*). Would they do so, when both are still yoked (to the cart), the sacrificer could not keep what he is possessed of, nor increase it; should he have any children, they would be scattered (everywhere, and consequently be lost for him). The bullock which is let loose, represents the children who are in the house, that one which remains yoked, the actions (ceremonies, and worldly pursuits). Those sacrificers who take the Soma down, whilst one of the bullocks is yoked and the other let loose, avail themselves of both actions, of acquiring property, and keeping what they have acquired.

The Devas and Asuras were fighting in these worlds. They fought in the eastern direction; there the Asuras defeated the Devas. They then fought in the southern direction, the Asuras defeated the Devas again. They then fought in the western direction, the Asuras defeated the Devas again. They fought in the northern direction, the Asuras defeated the Devas again. They then fought in the north-eastern direction [9], there the Devas did not sustain defeat. This direction is *aparâjitâ*, *i.e.*, unconquerable. Thence one should do work in this (north-eastern) direction, and have it done there; for such one (alone) is able to clear off his debts. [10]

The Devas said, it is on account of our having no king, that the Asuras defeat us. Let us elect a king. **[34]** All consented. They elected Soma their king. Headed by the king Soma, they were victorious in all directions. He who brings the sacrifice is the king Soma. The Soma faces the eastern direction, when the priests put him (on the cart). By this means the sacrificer conquers the eastern direction. The priests turn the cart round in the southern direction. By this means he conquers the southern direction. They turn (the cart) towards the west; by this means he conquers the western direction. When the cart stands in the northern direction, they take (the Soma) off. By this means he conquers the northern direction. He who has this knowledge conquers all directions.

15

After the king Soma has arrived, the reception offering is prepared. For the king Soma comes to the premises of the sacrificer

---

[9] It is called *âiśânî*, *i.e.*, the direction of *iśânaḥ*, who is Śiva.

[10] According to the Brahmanical notions, every man born is a debtor. His creditors are the gods, Ṛiṣis, the Pitaras, and men. His debt towards the Pitaras or manes, is cleared off by begetting a son. As long as he has begot no son, he is debtor to the manes. To clear his debts towards the gods by offering sacrifies to them, he must have some property. Any act required for the acquisition of anything, should be done in the north-eastern direction.

(as a guest). Thence the offering for receiving him as a guest (*atithi*) is called *Atithya-iṣṭi*. Its Purodâśa is made ready in nine potsherds (*i. e.*, the rice ball, making up the Purodâśa is placed on nine potsherds). For there are nine vital airs (*prâṇâḥ*). (This offering is made) for making the vital airs (to the sacrifice) and for making them severally known. It belongs to Viṣṇu; for Viṣṇu is the sacrifice. By means of his own deity and his own metre[11] he makes the sacrifice successful. For all metres and Priṣṭhas,[12] **[35]** follow the king Soma, when he is bought (as his retinue). To all who follow a king (as his retinue) a reception is given.

When the king Soma has arrived, then they produce fire by friction. Agni being the animal of the gods, this rite of producing Agni (and throwing him into another fire) is equivalent to the slaughter of an ox or a cow which miscarries, which rite is always performed when a king or another man who deserves high honour[13] is to be received.

16.

The Adhvaryu (says to the Hotar): repeat mantras for Agni, who is being produced by friction.

The Hotar repeats a verse addressed to Savitar: *abhi tvâ deva Savitar* (1, 24, 3). They ask: why does he repeat a verse addressed to Savitar for the Agni, who is being produced? (The answer is:) Savitar rules over all productions. Produced[14] (themselves) by Savitar, they (are able) to produce Agni (by friction). Thence a verse addressed to Savitar is required.

He repeats a verse, addressed to *Dyâvâ-pṛithivî*: *mahî dyâuḥ pṛithivîcha na* (4, 56, 1.)

[36] They ask: why does he repeat a verse addressed to *Dyâvâ-pṛithivî* for Agni, who is being produced (by friction)? They answer: the gods

---

[11] The Anuvâkyâ mantra is, *idaṁ Viṣṇur vichakrame* (1, 22, 17) and the Yâjyâ, *tad asya priyam abhipâtho* (1, 154, 5), See *Âśval. Sr. S.* 4, 5. Of both verses Viṣṇu is the deity. The metre of the first verse is *Gâyatrî*, that of the second, *Triṣṭubh*. These two metres are regarded as the principal ones, comprising all the rest.

[12] A Priṣṭha is a combination of two verses of the Sâmaveda. Some of the principal Sâmans are in the Triṣṭubh or Gâyatrî metre. These two metres represent all others.

[13] The term is *arhat*, a word well-known chiefly to the students of Buddhism. Sâyaṇa explains it by "a great Brâhman," or a Brâhman (in general). That cows were killed at the time of receiving a most distinguished guest, is stated in the Smṛitis. But, as Sâyaṇa observes (which entirely agrees with the opinions held now-a-days), this custom belongs to former Yugas (periods of the world). Thence the word: *goghna*, *i e.*, cow-killer means in the more ancient Saṁskrit books "a guest": (See the commentators on Pâṇini 3, 4, 73); for the reception of a high guest was the death of the cow of the house.

[14] Sâyaṇa explains *prasûta* as "allowed, permitted." According to his opinion, the meaning of the sentence is, "having been permitted by Savitâ to perform this ceremony, they perform it." *Prasava* is then "the permission for performing ceremonies." But I doubt whether this opinion is correct.

caught him (once), when he was born, between heaven and earth (*dyâvâ-prithivî*); since that time he is kept there enclosed (by heaven and earth). Thence the Hotar repeats a verse addressed to *Dyâvâ-prithivî*.

He repeats a triplet of verses addressed to Agni in the Gâyatrî metre: *trâm Agne puṣkarâd adhi* (6, 16, 13), when Agni is being produced. Thus he makes him (Agni) prosper by his own deity (the verses are addressed to Agni) and his own metre (Gâyatrî). The words, *atharvâ niramanthata,* [15] *i.e.*, the fire-priest produced thee out (of the two wooden sticks by means of friction), are complete in form.

What is complete in form, (that is) when the verse which is repeated alludes to the ceremony which is being performed, that is successful in the sacrifice.

Should Agni not be born (the fire not be produced), or should it take a long time, then the *Rakṣogṇî* [16] verses, which are in the Gâyatrî metre are to be repeated: *Agne haṁsi nyatrinam* (10, 118). These (verses) are intended for destroying the Râkṣasas (the evil-doers). For the Râkṣasas have seized him, if he is not born, or if his birth is delayed.

When Agni is born after the recital of the first or the second (and so on) of these (Rakṣognî verses), then the Hotar has to repeat a verse appropriate to him, who has been born, by containing the term "born," *uta bruvantu jantava* (1, 74, 3.)

What is appropriate in the sacrifice, that is successful. He repeats: *â yaṁ hastena khâdinam* (6, 16, 40).

[37] In this verse occurs the term "*hasta*, hand;" for they rub him (out of two wooden sticks) by means of their hands. In it there further occurs: *śiśur-jâtaḥ*, *i.e.*, a child born; for, just as a child, he is first born. The word *na* (in *na bibhrati* of the verse) has with the gods the same meaning as *om* (yes) with these (men). He repeats, *pra devam devavîtaye* (6, 16, 41). This verse is appropriate for Agni when he is being thrown into the Ahavanîya fire (after having come out of the two wooden sticks). The half verse, *â sve yonâu niṣîdatu* (which are contained in this verse), *i. e*, he may sit in his own house, means, that Agni (the Ahavanîya fire) is Agni's (who was just born by friction) proper place.

In the verse: *jâtam jâtavedasi* (6, 16, 42), the one is *jâta* (the Agni produced by friction), the other *jâtavedâs* (the Ahavanîya fire). The words, *priyam śiśîtha atithim* mean, Agni (the new born) is the beloved guest of the (other) Agni (the Ahavanîya). By the words, *syona â grihapatim*, he, the priest, places him at ease (by putting him into his

---

[15] They occur in the first verse of the triplet mentioned.

[16] Verses calculated to kill the Râkṣas who are preventing Agni from being born.

proper place, the Ahavanîya fire). *Agninâgniḥ samidhyate* (1, 12, 6) is appropriate (when the new born Agni has been thrown into the Ahavanîya fire). In the verse: *tvam hyagne agninâ vipro vipreṇa santsatâ* (8, 43, 14), the one *vipra* (wise) means one Agni, and the other *vipra*, the other Agni; the one *san* (being, existing) means the one, the other *san* in (*satâ*) the other Agni. The words, *sakhâ sakyâ samidhyase* (at the end of the verse quoted) mean, this Agni is the friend of the (other) Agni.

In the verse: *tam marjayanta sukratum* (8, 73, 8), the words, *sveṣu kṣayeṣu*, mean, this Agni is the other Agni's own residence.

With the verse, *yajñena yajñam ayajanta* (1, 164, 50), he concludes. By means of the sacrifice (the ideal omnipresent sacrifice) the gods thus **[38]** performed (the actual, visible) sacrifice. By having sacrificed Agni through Agni (having thrown the new born Agni into the Ahavanîya fire), the gods went to heaven. (In the remaining part of the verse) "these (producing fire, &c.) were the first rites; the great ones (the sacrificers) reached that heaven in which those gods who formerly performed the same rites reside" (1, 164, 50), the metres are the *sâdhyâ devâs*, *i.e.*, the gods who (formerly) performed. They sacrificed Agni at the beginning by means of Agni, and went to heaven. There were the Âdityaṣ, and the Angiras. They sacrificed at the beginning Agni by means of Agni and went to heaven. The offering of the fire (Agni) is that offering which leads to heaven. Even if the performing priest is no proper Brâhman[17] (in the strictest sense), or even pronounced to be an ill-reputed man, this sacrifice nevertheless goes up to the gods, and becomes not polluted by contagion with a wicked man (as in this case the performing priest is). The oblation (of Agni in the Ahavanîya fire) of him who has this knowledge goes up to the gods; and does not become infected by contagion with a wicked man.

The verses he repeats are thirteen in number; they are complete in form. If the form is complete and the verse alludes to the ceremony which is being performed, then the sacrifice is successful. Of these **[39]** verses he repeats the first and the last thrice; this makes seventeen.

---

[17] The term in the original is, *abrâhmaṇokta*, *i.e.*, who is declared to be no proper Brâhman. According to Sây. there are in the Smṛitis six kinds of men mentioned who are, strictly speaking, not capable of the Brâhmanship, though they are Brâhmans by birth, *viz.*, the servant of a king, a merchant (seller and buyer); the *bahuyâjî*, he who performs many sacrifices (for the sake of gain only); the *aś râuta-yâjaka*, *i.e.*, he who being properly appointed for the performance of the great (Śrauta) sacrifices, performs only the less important domestic rites (*smârta-karmâṇi*); the *grâmayâjî*, *i.e.*, he who performs out of covetousness alone sacrifices for all inhabitants of a village or town qualified or disqualified; the *brahmabandhu*, *i. e.*, he who performs the daily religious duties neither before sunrise nor sunset.

For Prajâpati is seventeen-fold, comprising such a year as consists of twelve months and five seasons. Prajâpati is the year.

He who has such a knowledge prospers by these verses which reside in Prajâpati. By repeating thrice the first and last verses he ties both the knots of the sacrifice to fasten and tighten it, and prevent it from slipping down.

17

(*The Remaining Rites of the Atithi-iṣṭi,*[18] *after the Ceremony of Producing Fire by Friction is finished*).

The two Puro-anuvâkyâs for both portions of melted butter[19] (which are to be offered) are, *samidhâgnim duvasyata* (8, 44, 1), and *âpyâyasva sametu* (1, 91, 16.) These two verses are complete in form; for they contain an allusion to guests.[20] When the verse (which is repeated) alludes to the ceremony which is being performed, then the form is complete, and (consequently) the sacrifice successful. The verse (8, 44, 1) alluding to the guest (*atithi*) belongs to Agni, whilst the verse addressed to Soma (1,91, 16), does not contain the word "guest." If there were a verse addressed to Soma, containing the word "guest," such one should always be used. But notwithstanding (there being no such verse) the verse mentioned (1, 91, 16) refers to a guest, for it contains the term "being fattened;" for, when one feeds a guest **[40]** (well), then he grows fat, as it were. The Yâjyâ mantra for both, Agni and Soma, commences with *juṣâṇaḥ*.[21] The Anuvâkyâ and Yâjyâ mantras (for the principal offering consisting of *Purodâśa*) are *idaṁ Viṣṇur*[22] *vichakrame* (1, 22, 17) and *tad asya priyam abhi pâtho* (1, 154, 5). Both verses are addressed to Viṣṇu. Having repeated as Anuvâkyâ a verse with three padas, he uses as Yâjyâ one consisting of four padas; thus seven padas are obtained.

For the ceremony of receiving a guest (*âtithyam—atithi-iṣṭi*) is the head of the sacrifice. There are seven vital airs in the head. By this ceremony the Hotar thus puts the seven vital airs in the head (of the sacrificer).

The two Saṁyâjyâ mantras, required at the *Sviṣṭakṛit* are: *hotâram chitraratham* (10, 1, 5), and *pra prâyam agnir* (7, 8, 4). Both verses are

---

18 See the Taittirîya Saṁhitâ 1, 2, 10, and Sây.'s commentary on it, vol. i., pp. 370—384, ed. Cowell. Âśval. Śrâuta S. 4, 5.

19 These two parts are the so-called *chakṣusi*, *i.e.*, eyes of the Iṣṭi, which always precede the principal offering, consisting of *Purodâśa*.

20. In the words of the second pada of *samidhâgnim*, viz., *ghṛitaih bodhayata atithim*, refresh the guest with clarified butter drops!

21 *Juṣâṇo agnir âjyasya vetu*; *juṣâṇo Soma âjyasya vetu*: may Agni pleased, eat the melted butter, &c.

22 The Purodâśa is given to *Viṣṇu* who is the chief deity of this Iṣṭi.

complete in form ; for in both the word *atithi*[23], a guest (referring to Agni's reception as a guest) occurs. The success of the sacrifice depends on the completeness of the form, *i.e.*, that the mantra (which is repeated) alludes to the ceremony which is being performed. Both Saṁyâjyâs (used at the Sviṣṭakṛit-of the Atithi-iṣṭi) are in the Tṛiṣṭubh metre, for getting possession of Indra's powers (for Indra is Triṣṭubh). The ceremony ends here with the eating of the sacrificial food.[24] The gods having (once) rested **[41]** satisfied with the Atithya-iṣṭi ending by the eating of the sacrificial food (on the part of the sacrificer and the priests), this Iṣṭi is to end with the eating of the sacrificial food (no further ceremonies being required).

They offer only the *Prayâjas* [25] at this (Iṣṭi), but not the *Anuyâjas.* The Prayâjas, as well as the Anuyâjas are the vital airs. The airs which are in the head are the Prayâjas, whilst those in the lower parts of the body are the Anuyâjas. He who should offer the Anuyâjas at this (Iṣṭi) is just like a man who, after having cut off the vital airs residing in the lower parts of the body), wishes to put them in the head. That would be superfluity, [26] were all the vital airs, those of the head as well as those of the lower parts of the body, to be found at the same place (*viz.*, in the head). If they therefore offer at this (Iṣṭi) only the Prayâjas without Anuyâjas, then the wish which one entertains at the offering of the Anuyâjas becomes also fulfilled (for the offering of the Anuyâjas on this occasion would be a mistake).

FOURTH CHAPTER

(*The Pravargya Ceremony.*[1])

18.

The sacrifice went away from the gods (saying), I shall not be your food. The gods said : do not go ; thou alone shalt be our food. The gods then killed **[42]** it. When it had been taken asunder

[23] In the last pada of the first mantra there occur the words *agnim atithim janânâm*, and also in the last pada of the second the words *daivyo atithiḥ*, the heavenly guest.

[24] That is to say, the ceremonies, which in the usual course of the Iṣṭi follow the eating of the sacrificial food, such as the *Anuyâjas*, the *Sûktavâk*, *Śanyuvâk*, *Patnîsaṁyâja* and *Saṁsthita Japa*, are left out on the occasion of the *Atithya-iṣṭi.*

[25] They precede the principal offering, which consists of *Puroḍâśa.*

[26] This is a mistake in the sacrifice which is to be propitiated.

[1] The Pravargya ceremony lasts for three days, and is always performed twice a day, in the forenoon and afternoon. It precedes the animal and Soma sacrifices. For without having undergone it, no one is allowed to take part in the solemn Soma feast prepared for the gods. It is a preparatory rite, just as the Dîkṣâ, and is intended for providing the sacrificer with a heavenly body, with which alone he is permitted to enter the residence of the gods. That the gods do not receive mortals at their residence when

(cut into pieces) by them, it was found not to be sufficient (to satisfy their appetite). The gods said : this sacrifice after having been taken asunder, will certainly not be sufficient for us. Well, let us dress (and fill up) this sacrifice. After having dressed it, they said to the Aśvins, cure this sacrifice ; for the Aśvins are the two physicians of the gods, they are the two Adhvaryus [2] **[43]** (sacred cooks). Thence two Adhvaryu priests provide for all the implements required for the Pravargya vessel (gharma). After having done so, they say, "Brahma ![3] we shall perform the Pravargya ceremony. Hotar ! repeat the appropriate mantras!"

arriving in their very bodies, one may learn from the amusing story of the king *Triśanku*, as reported in the Râmâyaṇa (1, 57-60). For the performance of this important ceremony extensive preparations are to be made by the Adhvaryu and his assistant, the Pratiprasthâtar. All the vessels and implements required are brought to the spot and placed at the left side of the *Gârhapatya* fire. The chief implements are : an earthen vessel of peculiar form, called *Mahâvîra* or *gharma* (*i.e.*, heat, or heated substance, for it is to be heated), a seat (*âsandî*) to sit on, two wooden pieces for lifting the *Mahâvîra* pot (called *śapha*), two shovels for charcoal (*dhṛiṣṭi*), one very large wooden spoon (*Upaymanî*) from which the sacrificer drinks milk (this forms part of the ceremony), three fans (*dhavitra*), six shavings from the Udumbara tree as fuel, thirteen sticks, to be laid round the Mahâvîra vessel (*paridhi*), two metal blades, one of gold and one of silver (called *suvarṇarajatâu rukmâu*). A cow and a female sheep are to be kept in readiness. Two bunches of kuśa grass are prepared, and tied in the midst. They are called *Veda*, and resemble very much the *Baresma* (Barsom) of the Parsis, which is also tied together by means of a reed (*aiwyâonhanem*).

The Mahâvîra is first put on the Vedi. Then the Adhvaryu makes a circle of clay, in which afterwards the Mahâvîra is put. This ring is called *khara*, *i.e.*, ass, for earth is always carried on the back of donkeys to the sacrificial compound. After the priests have repeated the mantras required for propitiation (*śânti*) *namo vâche*, &c., the Mahâvîra is taken from the Vedi and placed in that earthen ring (*khara*). Wooden sticks are put around it along with burning coals, and also fire is put in the khara just below the Mahâvîra, in order to make it hot. The fire is blown by three little fans which serve as bellows. The silver blade is put below, the gold blade above the Mahâvîra. Whilst the empty vessel is being heated, the Hotar repeats the first series of mantras, called the *pûrva paṭala*. After the vessel has been made quite hot, it is lifted up by means of the two Śaphas. The cow then is called, tied by the Adhvaryu with a cord, and milked. The milk is put on the left side of the Vedi, and then under recital of the mantra, *â daśabhir*, poured into the Mahâvîra. Then the milk of a goat whose kid is dead is taken, and mixed with that of the cow in the vessel. After this has been done, the contents of the Mahâvîra are thrown into the Ahavanîya fire. The sacrificer drinks milk from a large wooden spoon (Upayamanî) which has been first smelled by the Adhvaryu. The second series of mantras, the so-called *uttara paṭala*, is repeated when the cow is milked and her milk poured into the Mahâvîra. The whole ceremony has been witnessed by me.

[2] *Viz.*, the properly so-called Adhvaryu with his constant assistant *Pratiprasthâtâ*.

[3] The Brahma priests, *i.e.*, the president of the sacrifice, is here informed, that the priests are going to perform the Pravargya ceremony. The Hotar receives at the same time orders to repeat the appropriate mantras. The intimation to the Brahma priest as well as the order to the Hotar are given by the *Adhvaryu* and the *Pratiprasthâtar*, called the two Adhvaryus.

19.

The Hotar begins with *brahma jajnânam prathamam* (Vâj. S. 13, 5. Âśval. Ś. S 4, 6). In this mantra *Brahma* is Brihaspati (the teacher of the gods); by means of *Brahma* (*i.e.*, the Brahmans) the Hotar thus cures the Pravargya man (the mystical personage, called "sacrifice" which had been torn to pieces by the gods). By repeating the mantra, *iyam pitre râṣṭrî* (Âśval. Ś. S. 4, 6), the Hotar puts speech in the Pravargya man; for by *râṣṭrî*, *i.e.*, queen, speech is to be understood.

The verse, *mahân mahî astabhâyad* (Aśval. Ś. S. 4, 6), is addressed to Brahmaṇaspati. Brahma is Bṛihaspati; by means of Brahma the priest thus cures the Pravargya man.

[44] The verse addressed to Savitar is, *abhi tyam devam savitâram* (Vâj. S. 4, 25. Âśval. Ś. S. 4, 6). Savitar is the vital air; thus the Hotar puts the vital air in this Pravargya man.

By the verse, *saṁsîdasva mahân asi* (1, 36, 9), they make him (the Pravargya man) sit down.[4]

The verse, *aṁjanti yam prathayanto* (5, 43, 7), is appropriate to the ceremony of anointing (the Pravargya vessel with melted butter). What is appropriate in the sacrifice, that is successful.

Of the following mantras, *patangam aktamasurasya* (10, 177, 1), *yo no sanutyu abhidâsad* (6, 5, 4), *bhavâ no agne sumanâ upetau* (3, 18, 1), the first as well as the second verse [5] are appropriate.

The five verses required for killing the Rakṣas, commence with, *kṛiṇuṣva pâjaḥ prasitim* (4, 4, 1-5).

Now follow four single verses: [6]

Pari tvâ girvaṇo gira (1, 10, 12);

Adhi dvayor adadhâ ukthyam (1, 83, 3);

Śukram te anyad yajatam (6, 58, 1);

Apaśyan gopâm anipadyamânam (10, 177, 3).

All these verses (if counted) number to twenty, one. This (sacrificial) man is twenty-one fold; for he has ten fingers on his hands and ten

---

[4] The Adhvaryus put the Pravargya vessel, the so-called *Mahâvîra*, in an earthen ring, called *Khara*.

[5] That is to say: of the three mantras mentioned, always that one which immediately follows them in the Saṁhitâ, is to be repeated along with them. For instance, of 10,177,1 (*patangam aktam*, &c.), is the 2nd verse, to be also repeated.

[6] *Ekapâtinyaḥ*. An *ekapâtinî* is such a mantra which is taken single, and not followed by any other verse which comes immediately after it in the Saṁhitâ. The term is here used to mark a distinction between: *dve*, *i.e.*, two verses and *paṁcha*, *i.e.*, five verses, which follow one another in the Saṁhitâ.

on his feet, and the soul is reckoned as the twenty-first. He (thus) prepares the soul as the twenty-first (part).

20.

[45] (Now follow) nine Pâvamânî-verses (dedicated to the purification of the Soma juice) beginning with, *srakve drapsasya dhamataḥ* (9, 73, 1). There are nine vital airs. By repeating these (verses), the Hotar puts the vital airs in him (the Pravargya man). (Now he repeats) *ayam venaś chodayat* [7] (10, 123, 1). (When repeating this mantra, the Hotar points, when pronouncing the word *ayam*, *i.e.*, this, to the navel). "This" (the navel) is meant by *venaś*; for some vital airs are circulating (*venanti*) above the navel, others below it. On account of this vital air (the life) taking its origin from the navel, *venas* (circulation, from *ven* to circulate) means "navel." By repeating this mantra, the Hotar puts life in this (Pravargya man).

(Now he repeats the (verses), *pavitram te vitatam* (9, 83, 1), *tapash pavitram vitatam* (9, 83, 2), and *viyat pavitram dhiṣanâ atanvata.* On account of their containing the word "*pavitram*" (pure), the vital airs are purified (when these mantras are recited over them). These are the vital airs of the lower part of the body presiding over the semen, urine, and excrements. (By repeating these three verses) he puts these vital airs in this (Pravargya man).

21.

(He now repeats) a hymn, addressed to *Brahmaṇaspati.* [8] *Gaṇânâm tvâ gaṇapatim havâmahe* (2, 23) Brahma is Bṛihaspati; by means of Brahma he thus cures him (the sacrificial man, who had been torn to pieces). The verses beginning with *prathaścha* **[46]** *yasya saprathaścha nâma* (10, 181, 1-3) are the three *Gharmatanu*[9] mantras; by repeating them the Hotar provides the Pravargya man with a body, and a form. (For in the fourth pada of the first of these verses), there is said: "Vasiṣṭha brought the Rathantara Sâma," and (in the last half verse of the second Gharma-tanu mantra is said), "Bharadvâja made the Bṛihat Sâma out of Agni." [10] By repeating these mantras, the Hotar provides the Pravargya man with the Rathantara and Bṛihat-Sâmans (required for its prosperity).

---

[7] According to *Sâyaṇa* this verse is taken from another *Sâkhâ.*

[8] In the ?rd pada of the first verse, the name "*brahmaṇaspati*" is mentioned.

[9] This means, those mantras the recital of which is calculated to give the new body, which is to be made in the Pravargya vessel (the Gharma), the proper shape.

[10] The Riṣi of the Rathantara Sâma: *abhi tvâ śûra nonumaḥ* (7, 32, 22.) is Vaśiṣṭha, and that of the Bṛihat Sâma: *tvâm iddhi havâmahe* (6, 46, 1.) is Bharadvâja.

(By repeating) three verses (of the hymn) *apaśyan tvâ manasâ chekitânam* (10, 183, 1), the Ṛiṣi of which is *Prajâvân*, the son of *Prajâpati* (the Lord of creatures), he provides him with offspring.[11]

(Now the Hotar repeats) nine verses in different metres, commencing with *kâ râdhad dhotrâ* (1, 120, 1-9).

(These different metres represent the difference in magnitude and expansion of the extremities of the belly of the sacrificial man). For the extremities of the (mystical) sacrificial body (to be restored by means of the Pravargya ceremony) vary as to magnitude and largeness; some are rather thin, others are rather big.

Thence are verses of various metres required (for the verses represent the extremities of the body). By means of these verses (the Ṛiṣi) *Kakṣîvân* [47] went to the beloved residence of the Aśvins. He conquered the highest heaven. He who has this knowledge goes up to the beloved house of the Aśvins, and conquers the highest heaven.

(Now he repeats) the hymn: *Abhâty agnir uṣasâm* (5, 76.) The words: *pîpivâṁsam aśvinâ gharmam achha* (the fourth pada of the first verse of the hymn mentioned) are appropriate[12] to the ceremony. What is appropriate at the sacrifice, that is successful. This hymn is in the Triṣṭubh metre, for Triṣṭubh is strength; by this means he puts strength in this (Pravargya man.)

He repeats the hymn: *grâvaṇeva tad id artham jarethe* (2, 39). In this hymn there being expressions like, *akśî iva* "as the eyes" (2, 39, 5), *karṇâviva* "as two ears," *nâsa iva* "as a nose" (2, 39, 6), he puts in this way, by enumerating the limbs of the body, the senses in this (Pravargya man.) This hymn is in the Triṣṭubh metre; for Triṣṭubh is strength. In this way he puts strength in this (Pravargya man.)

He repeats the hymn: *îḷe dyâvâprithivî* (1, 112). (The words in the second pada:) *gharmam surucham* are appropriate.[13] This hymn is in the Jagatî metre; cattle is of the same (Jagatî) nature. Thus he provides this (Pravargya man) with cattle. By the words: "what assistance you (Aśyinâ) have rendered such and such a one" (which occur in every verse of the hymn mentioned), he provides this (Pravargya man) with all those wishes (and their fulfilment) which the Aśvins in this hymn are said to have deemed proper to fulfil.

[48] In repeating this hymn, the priest thus makes this (Pravargya man) thrive by means of those desires (including their satisfaction).

---

[11] The Hotar when repeating the first of these verses, looks at the sacrificer, when repeating the second, at the sacrificer's wife, when the third, at himself.

[12] The word "*gharma*," which is a name of the Pravargya vessel, is mentioned in it.

[13] For the word "*gharma*" (the Pravargya vessel) is mentioned in it.

He repeats the *ruchitavatî, i.e.*, the verse whose characteristic the word "*ruch*," to shine, is: *arûruchad uṣasaḥ pṛiśnir* (9, 83, 3). In this way he provides this (Pravargya man) with splendour.

With the verse, *dyubhir aktubhiḥ paripâtam* (1, 112, 25), he concludes (the ceremony). (In repeating this verse, the words of which) *ariṣṭebhir pṛithivî uta dyâuh* (contain a prayer for prosperity) he makes thus this Pravargya man thrive, granting him all that is wished for (in the verse mentioned). Now is (completed) the first part of the mantra collection (required at the Pravargya ceremony).

22.

The second part of the mantra collection [14] (required at the Pravargya ceremony) is as follows :—

1, *Upahvaye sudughâm dhenum* (1, 164, 26).
2, *Hiṁkṛiṇvatî vasupatnî* (1, 164, 27).
3, *Abhi tvâ deva Savitaḥ* (1, 24, 3).
4, *Samî vatsann amâtṛibhiḥ* (9, 104, 2).
5, *Saṁvatsa iva mâtṛibhiḥ* (9, 105, 2).
6, *Yaste stanaḥ śaśayo* (1, 164, 49).
7, *Gaur amîmed anuvatsam* (1, 164, 28).
8, *Namased upasîdatam* (9, 11, 6).
9, *Saṁjânânâ upasîdan* (1, 72, 5).
10, *Adaśabhir* (8, 61, 8).
11, *Duhanti saptâikân* (8, 61, 7).
12, *Samiddho Agnir Aśvinâ* (*Âśval.* 4, 7).
[49] 13, *Samiddho Agnir vriṣaṇâ* (*Âśval.* 4, 7).
14, *Tadu prayakṣatamam* (1, 62, 6).
15, *Âtmanvam nabho duhyate* (9, 74, 4).
16, *Uttiṣtha Brahmaṇaspate* (1, 40, 1).
17, *Adhukṣat pipyuṣîm iṣam* (8, 61, 16).
18, *Upadrava payasâ* (*Âśval.* 4, 7).
19, *Asute siṁchata śriyam* 8, 61, 13).
20, *Anûnam aśvinor* (8, 9, 7).
21, *Samutye mahatîr apaḥ* (8, 7, 22).

These twenty-one verses are appropriate. What is appropriate at a sacrifice, that is successful.

---

[14] During the recital of the first part of the Pravargya mantras, the vessel had been made only hot; now milk, butter, &c., are to be poured into it. A cow is brought to the spot, which is to be milked by the Adhvaryu. To this ceremony the first mantra of the second part, "I call the cow yielding good milk," refers.

The Hotar, when standing behind (the others),[15] repeats *ud u ṣya devaḥ Savitâ hiraṇyayâ* (6, 71, 1). When going forward, he repeats, *praitu Brahmaṇaspati* (1, 40, 3.) When looking at the *Khara* (the earthen ring, in which the Pravargya vessel is placed), he repeats: *Gandharva itthâ* (9, 83, 4). When repeating *nâke suparṇam upa yat* (9, 85, 11), he takes his seat. By the two mantras, *tapto vâṁ gharmo nakṣati svahotâ* (Atharv. 7, 73, 5. Âśv. 4, 7), and *ubhâ pibatam* (1, 46, 15), the Hotar sacrifices to the forenoon (the deity of the forenoon). After the formula: Agni eat! he pronounces *Vauṣaṭ*! which is in lieu of the *Sviṣṭakṛit*.

By the mantras, *yad usriyâsu svâhutam* (Atharv. 7, 73, 4. Âśv. 4, 7.), and *asya pibatam Aśvinâ* (8, 5, 14), he sacrifices for the afternoon. After the formula, Agni eat! he pronounces *Vauṣaṭ*! which is in lieu of the Sviṣṭakṛit. They take, for making Sviṣṭakṛit, parts of three offerings, *viz.*, Soma juice (contained in the stalks), the things thrown into the Pravargya vessel (milk, butter, etc.), and hot wheys. When the Hotar (after having repeated the two mantras, above mentioned, along with the formula, [50] Agni eat!) pronounces the formula *Vauṣaṭ*! then thus the omission of "*Agni Sviṣṭakṛit*" is replaced.[16]

The Brahma priest mutters (makes *japa*), *âśâ dakṣiṇâsad* (Âśv. 4, 7.)

(After the offering has been given to the fire) the Hotar repeats the following (seven) verses: *svâhâkṛitaḥ śuchir deveṣu* (Atharv. 7, 73, 3. Âśv 4, 7.); *samudrâd ûrmîm udiyarti veno* (10, 123, 2); *drapsaḥ samudram abhi* (10, 123, 8); *sakhe sakhâyam* (4, 1, 3); *ûrdhva û ṣu ṇa* (1, 36, 13); *ûrdhvo naḥ pâhi* (1, 36, 14); *taṁ ghem itthâ* (8, 58, 17). These verses are appropriate. What is appropriate at the sacrifice, that is successful.

By the mantra, *pâvaka śoche tava* (3, 2, 6), the Hotar wants to eat. When eating it, he says: "Let us eat the (remainder of the) offering which has been offered, of the sweet offering which has been thrown into the most brightly blazing (*indratama*) fire! (Let us eat) of thee, O divine gharma (the contents of the Pravargya vessel) which art full of honey, full of sap, full of food, and quite hot (*aṅgirasvat*[17]). Praise to thee (O gharma!); do me no harm!"

When the Pravargya vessel is put down, then the Hotar repeats these two mantras, *śyeno na yonim sadanam* (9, 71, 6), and *âyasmin sapta Vâsavaḥ*

---

[15] He stands behind the other priests, when the Pravargya vessel is taken away.

[16] *Anantar-iti* means "what has not gone into" = what is omitted.

[17] The word certainly has here no reference to the Aṅgiras, the celebrated Ṛiṣis. One of the characteristics of the Gharma food is that it is very hot. This is expressed here. *Aṅgiras* had no doubt originally the same meaning as *aṅgâra*.

(Âśval. 4, 7). In whatever (part of the) day (forenoon or afternoon), they are about to take off (the Pravargya vessel from its place), he repeats the mantra, *havir havişmo mahi* (9, 83, 5). With the verse, *sûyávasâd bhagavatî* (1, 164, 40), he concludes (the ceremony).

[51] The Gharma (ceremony) represents the cohabitation of the gods. The *Gharma* vessel is the penis; the two handles (placed underneath, to lift it) are the two testicles, the *Upayamanî*[18] the thighs. The milk (in the vessel) is the seed. This seed (in the shape of milk) is poured into Agni as the womb of the gods for production. For Agni is the womb of the gods.

He who knowing this, sacrifices according to this rite (*yajñakratu*), is born (anew) from the womb of Agni and the offerings, and participates in the nature of the Ṛik, Yajus, and Sâman, the Veda[19] (sacred knowledge), the Brahma (sacred element), and immortality, and is absorbed in the deity.

23.

(*Upasad.*)

The Devas and Asuras were fighting in these worlds. The Asuras made these worlds fortified castles, just as the strongest and most powerful (kings) do. Thus they made the earth an iron castle, the air a silver, the sky a golden castle, Thus they made these worlds castles. The Devas said, these Asuras have made these worlds castles; let us thus make other worlds in opposition to these castles. They made out of the earth in opposition (to the iron castle of the Asuras) a sitting-room[20] (*sadas*), out [52] of the air a fire-place (*âgnîdhrîya*), and out of the sky two repositories for food (*havirdhâna*). Such they made these worlds in opposition to the castles (into which the three worlds had been transformed by the Asuras). The gods said, Let us perform the burnt offerings called Upasads[21] (*i.e.*, besieging). For, by means of an *upasad*, *i.e.*, besieging, they conquer a large (fortified) town. Thus they did. When they performed the first Upasad, they drove by it them (the Asuras) out from this world (the earth).

[18] A large wooden spoon, from which the sacrificer drinks milk.

[19] Sâyaṇa here understands by Veda the Atharvaveda, or all the Vedas collectively. Brahma is according to him *Hiraṇyagarbha* (the universal soul), and *amṛita* the supreme soul. But it is very doubtful whether these interpretations are right. By "Veda" certainly the Atharva Veda cannot be meant; for it was not recognized as a sacred book at the time of the composition of the Brâhmaṇas.

[20] A place near the so-called *Uttarâ Vedi* which is outside that one appropriated for the performance of the *Işţis*. The latter place is called *Prâchîna vaṁśa*. This *sadas* is the sitting-room for the king Soma, after his removal from the *Prâchîna vaṁśa*.

[21] There is observable throughout this chapter a pun between the two meanings of *upasad* "siege," and, a certain ceremony.

By the performance of the second, they drove them out of the air, and by the performance of the third, out of the sky. Thus they were driven out of these worlds. The Asuras driven out of these (three) worlds, repaired to the Ritus (seasons). The gods said, Let us perform the Upasads. Thus they did.

These Upasads being three, they performed each twice ; (thus) they became six. There are six Ṛitus (seasons); thus they drove them (the Asuras) out of the Ritus. The Asuras driven out of the Ṛitus, repaired to the months. The Devas said, Let us perform the Upasads. Thus they did. The Upasads being six, Let us perform each twice, that makes twelve. There are twelve months. They drove them out of the months. The Asuras driven out of the months repaired to the half-months. The Devas said, Let us perform the Upasads. Thus they did. The Upasads being twelve, they performed each twice : that makes twenty-four. There are twenty-four half-months. They turned them (the Asuras) out of the half-months. The Asuras, turned out of [53] the half-months, repaired to Day and Night (*ahorâtra*). The Devas said, Let us perform the Upasads. Thus they did. By means of the Upasad which they performed for the first part of the day, they turned them out of day, and by means of that which they performed for the second part of the day, they turned them out of night. Thus they disappeared from both day and night. Thence the first Upasad is to be performed during the first part of the day, and the second, during the second part. By doing so, the sacrificer leaves only so much space to his enemy (as there is between the junction of day and night.)

24.

The Upasads are the goddesses of victory (*jitayaḥ*). For, by means of them, the gods gained a complete victory, destroying all their enemies. He who has such a knowledge, gains a victory, destroying all his enemies. All the victories which the gods gained in these (three) worlds, or in the Ṛitus (seasons), or in the months, or the half-months, or in day and night, will he (also) gain who has such a knowledge.

(*The Tânûnaptram*[11] *ceremony*, or *solemn oath taken by the priests.*)

The Devas were afraid, surmising the Asuras might become aware of their being disunited, and seize [54] their reign. They marched out in

[11] The Tânûnaptram ceremony which is alluded to and commented on in this paragraph, is to take place immediately after the *Atithya iṣṭi* is finished, and not, as it might appear from this passage, after the Upasad. It is a solemn oath taken by the sacrificer and all the officiating priests pledging themselves mutually not to injure one another. It is chiefly considered as a safeguard for the sacrificer who is, as it were, entirely given up to the hands of the priests. They are believed to have the power of

several divisions and deliberated. Agni marched out with the Vasus, and deliberated. Indra did so with the Rudras; Varuṇa with the Âdityas; and Bṛihaspati with the Visve Devas. Thus all, having severally marched out, deliberated. They said, "Well, let us put these our dearest bodies [23] in the house of Varuṇa, the king, (*i.e.*, water); he among us who should, out of greediness, transgress this (oath, not to do anything which might injure the sacrificer), he shall no more be joined with them." [24]

[55] They put their bodies in the house of Varuṇa. This putting of their bodies in the house of Varuṇa, the king, became their *Tânûnaptram* (joining of bodies). Thence they say : none of those joined together by the *tânûnaptram* ceremony is to be injured. Thence the Asuras could not conquer their (the gods') empire (for they all had been made inviolable by this ceremony).

25.

The Atithya-iṣṭi is the very head of the sacrifice (the sacrificial

---

destroying him, or cheating him out of what he is sacrificing for, by not performing the ceremonies required in the proper, but in a wrong, way. This oath is taken in the following way : The Adhvaryu takes one of the large sacrificial spoons, called *Dhruvâ*, and puts melted butter in it. He then takes a vessel (*Kaṁsâ*, a goblet) into which, after having placed it on the Vedi, he puts by means of a *Sruva* the melted butter contained in the Dhruvâ. He puts five times the *Sruva* in the *Dhruvâ*, and each time after a piece of melted butter having been taken out, a *Yajus* (sacrificial formula) is repeated, *viz* : *âpataye tvâ gṛihṇâmi; paripataye tvâ gṛihṇâmi; tânûnaptre tvâ gṛihṇâmi ; śâkvarâya tvâ gṛihṇâmi ; sakmann oʼiṣṭhâya tvâ gṛihṇâmi* (see Black Yajurveda 1, 2, 10, 2. ; Vâjasaneya-Saṁh. 5, 5, where *gṛihṇâmi* and *tvâ* are only put once). All priests with the sacrificer now touch the vessel (Kaṁsâ) in which the âjya or melted butter thus taken out of the Dhruvâ had been put. They may touch, however, the *âjya* (melted butter) by means of a stalk of Kuśa grass. When touching the butter, they all repeat the formula : *anâdhṛiṣṭam asi*, &c. (Bl. Y. 1, 2, 10, 2.) "thou art inviolable." All the seven Hotars then put their hands in the madantî, a copper vessel, which is filled with water. This latter ceremony, only performed by the Hotars, is regarded as the symbolical deposition of the priests' own bodies in the " house of Varuṇa, " which is only a poetical expression for the copper vessel filled with water.

As to the name *tânûnaptram*, one is induced to refer it to *tanûnapât*, a name of Agni, by which he is invoked in the Prayâjas and which occurs along with others at this very ceremony. But I doubt whether the name *tânûnaptram* has here anything to do with Agni *tanûnapât*. The latter word means only one's own son, or one's own relative. By taking this solemn oath, the sacrificer and the officiating priests come as it werenotiʼ the closest contact with one another, bound by ties as strong as family ties. The term, therefore, means only : contracting of the closest relationship, brotherhood.

[23] Sây. understands by this expression " wife and children." But this interpretation is doubtful to me.

[24] This is the formula of the oath, which is very ancient in language, as the forms : *Saṁgacchatâi*, 3rd pers. sing., conjunct., middle voice, and, *bhavishâd*, conjunct. of the aorist, clearly prove.

personage); the Upasads are his neck. The two stalks of Kuśa grass (held by the Hotar) are of the same length; for head and neck are equal.

The gods made the Upasads as an arrow (the upasad ceremony served them as an arrow); Agni was its shaft, Soma its steel, Viṣṇu its point, and Varuṇa its feathers. The gods holding this arrow represented by the Ajya (at the Upasad ceremony) discharged it, and, breaking with it the castles of the Asuras, entered them. For these (deities, Agni and so on) are in the Ajya offering. At first he (the sacrificer) undergoes the religious ceremony of drinking (milk) coming from four nipples (of the cow),[25] for the arrow in the Upasads consists of four parts, *viz.*, shaft, steel, point, and feathers. He (subsequently) undergoes the religious ceremony of drinking what comes from three nipples. For the arrow in the Upasads consists of three parts, *viz.*, shaft, steel, and point. He undergoes the religious ceremony of drinking what comes from two nipples. For the arrow in the Upasads consists of two parts, *viz.*, shaft and point. He undergoes the religious ceremony of drinking what comes from one nipple (alone). For, in the Upasads, there is only "one" arrow mentioned (as **[56]** a unit). By means of one alone (*i.e.*, by co-operation of all its parts) effect is produced. The worlds which are above are extended[26] and those which are below, contracted. The priest (in performing this ceremony) commences by that number of nipples (four) which represents the larger worlds, and proceeds to those which represent the smaller ones.[27] (That is done) for conquering these worlds.

(*Now the Sâmidhêni verses for the forenoon and afternoon Upasad ceremonies are mentioned*).[28]

Upasadyâya mîḷhushe (7, 15, 1-3), *Imâm me Agne samidham* (2, 6, 1-3). Three Sâmidhêni verses are to be repeated each time (the first set in the forenoon and the second in the afternoon). They are complete in form. When the form is complete, and the verse which is recited alludes to the ceremony which is being performed, then the sacrifice is successful. For *Anuvâkyâs* and *Yâjyâs*, *Jaghnivatî* verses (such verses, as contain derivatives of the root *han* to kill) ought to be used. These are: *agnir vṛitrâṇi jaṁghanat* (6, 16, 34); *ya agra iva śaryahâ* (6, 16, 39);

---

[25] See Black Yajurveda, ed. Cowell, 1, p. 400.

[26] The highest world is *Satyaloka* which is the largest of all; *Dyuloka* is smaller; *Antarikṣa loka* and *Bhûrloka* are successively smaller still.

[27] That is to say, he milks on the first day four nipples, on the second three, and on the third two and one.

[28] After some preliminary remarks on the importance and signification of the Upasad ceremony, the author goes on to set forth the duties of the Hotar when performing the Upasad, which has all the characteristics of a common Iṣṭi.

tvaṁ somâsi satpatiḥ (1, 91, 5); *gayasphâno amivaha* (1, 91, 12.); *idam Viṣṇur vichakrame* (1, 22, 17.); *trîṇi padâ vichakrame* (1, 22, 8).[29] This is the order for the forenoon ceremony). For the afternoon ceremony he inverts the order of these verses (so as to make the Yâjyâ of [57] the forenoon Anuvâkyâ in the afternoon, and *vice versâ*). By means of these Upasads the Devas defeated (the Asuras), and, breaking down their castles, entered them.

In performing the Upasad ceremony he should use verses in the same metre (for all the Âhutis), not such ones as are in different metres. When the Hotar uses different metres, then he produces the king's evil on the necks (of the sacrificers). Thus the Hotar has it in his power to produce diseases. Thence the mantras (for the chief deities at the *Upasad iṣṭi*) should be always of the same metre, not of different metres.

Upâviḥ, the son of *Janaśrutâ*, said in a Brâhmaṇam about the Upasads, as follows: "From this reason (on account of the Upasads) the face of an ugly-looking Śrotriya makes upon the eye of an observer the distinct impression, as if it were very full, and he like a person who is in the habit of singing." He said so, for the Upasad offerings, consisting of melted butter, appear on the throat as a face put over it.)

26.

(*Neither Prayâjas nor Anuyâjas are to be used at the Upasad Iṣṭi*).

The Prayâjas as well as the Anuyâjas are the armour of the gods. (The Upasad iṣṭi) is to be performed without both, in order to sharpen the arrow for preventing it from recoiling.

The Hotar repeats the mantras (at this occasion) only after having overstepped (the boundary between the Vedi and Ahavanîya fire on all sides[30]), in order to supervene the sacrifice, and prevent it from going.

[58] They (the divines) say: it is, as it were, a cruel act, when they perform ceremony of (touching) the melted butter (the Tânûnapatram) near the king Soma.[31] The reason is, that Indra, using melted butter as his thunderbolt, killed Vṛitra. In order to compensate the king Soma for any injury he might have received from the performance of the Tânûnaptram ceremony in his presence) they sprinkle the king (Soma)

---

[29] The respective deities of these Anuvâkyâs and Yâjyâs are: *Agni*, *Soma*, and *Viṣṇu*.

[30] In most ceremonies he oversteps this boundary only towards the south. But at the Upasad ceremony it is done on all sides.

[31] The vessel, containing the Ajya which is to be touched by all the priests and the sacrificer, in order to bind them together by a solemn oath, is placed over the Soma plant which is lying on the Vedi. To put anything on the king Soma, is regarded as a cruel treatment which is to be atoned for. Soma is to be pacified by sprinkling with water, which ceremony is called *âpyâyanam*—*Soma prayoga*.

with water (whilst the following mantra is repeated): *aṁśur aṁśuṣṭe deva Soma* (Taitt. 1, 2, 11, 2). When they perform this ceremony near him (Soma), which is, as it were, a cruel treatment of him, then they (subsequently) make him (Soma) by this (sprinkling of water) fat (when lying) on her (the Vedi), and make him grow.

The king Soma is the fruit of heaven and earth. When repeating the words : *eṣṭa râyaḥ,* [32] &c., they (the Hotṛi priests) throw the two bundles of kuśa grass (held in their hands, in the southern corner of the Vedi), and put their right hands ever their left ones[33] (to cover the kuśa grass). By making a bow to "heaven and earth" (which are represented by those two bundles of kuśa grass) they make them both grow.

---

[59] FIFTH CHAPTER.

(The Ceremonies of carrying the Fire, Soma, and the Offerings from their Places in the Prâchîna-vaṁsa to the Uttarâ Vedi.)

27.

The king Soma lived among the Gandharvas. The Gods and Ṛiṣis deliberated, as to how the king might be induced to return to them. *Vâch* (the goddess of speech) said, the Gandharvas lust after women. I (therefore) shall transform myself into a woman, and then you sell me to them (in exchange for Soma).[1] The gods answered: "No ! how may we live without thee ? She said, sell me unto them ; if you should want me, I shall return to you." Thus they did. In the disguise of a big naked woman she was sold (by the gods to the Gandharvas) in exchange for Soma. In imitation (of this precedent) they drive away an immaculate cow of one year's age, being the price[2] at which they purchase the king Soma. She (this cow) may, however, be rebought[3] ; for Vâch (whom this cow, for which the Soma is bought, represents) returned to the gods. Thence the mantras (after Soma has been bought) are to be repeated with a low voice. After Soma has been bought, Vâch is with the Gandharvas ; but she retuns as soon as the ceremony of the Agnipraṇayana is performed.

---

[32] These words follow the mantra mentioned above : *aṁśur aṁśuṣṭe,* &c. (Taitt. Saṁh. 1, 2, 11, 1. ; but the text differs a little from that in our Brâhmaṇam).

[33] The term used is : *prastarenihnavate,* literally, he conceals the two bundles of kuśa grass. The concealment is done in the manner expressed in the translation, as I myself have witnessed it.

[1] This is the meaning of the verb *paṇ*, which appears to be related to the Latin *pignus*, pawn.

[2] Instead of giving a cow, the sacrificer pays the price of a cow in money to the Brahman who brings him the Soma. To sell Soma is regarded as very disreputable. The seller is not admitted to the sacrificial compound, nor invited to the great dinner which the sacrificer must give to Brahmans at the end of the sacrifice.

[3] As a rule, the cows given in Dakṣiṇa, cannot be rebought by the giver.

28.

[60] *The Agni-praṇayana*, i.e., *Ceremony of Carrying the Sacrificial Fire to the Altar destined for the Animal and Soma Sacrifices.*)

The Adhvaryu orders (the Hotar), when the sacrificial fire is to be carried (to the Uttarâ Vedi), to repeat mantras appropriate (to the ceremony).

(He repeats :) *pra devam devyâ* (10, 176, 2). If the sacrificer be a Brahman, he ought to repeat a verse in the Gâyatrî metre ; for the Brahman belongs to the Gâyatrî metre (has its nature). The Gâyatri is beauty and acquisition of sacred knowledge. (This metre) makes him the (sacrificer) thus prosper by means of the beauty and sacred knowledge (which is contained in it).

If the sacrificer be a Kṣattriya, he should repeat a Triṣṭubh, *viz.*— *imam mahe vidathyâya* (3, 54, 1). For the Kṣattriya belongs to the Triṣṭubh (has its nature). Triṣṭubh is strength, sharpness of senses and power. By repeating thus a Triṣṭubh, the Hotar makes him (the sacrificer of the Kṣattriya caste) prosper through the strength, sharpness of sense and power (contained in the Triṣṭubh). By the words of the second pada of the verse mentioned) : *śaśvatkritva îdyâya prajabhrur*, *i.e.*, "they brought to him who is to be praised always (Agni), the Hotar brings the sacrificer at the head of his (the sacrificer's) family. By the second half verse, *śrinotu no damyebhir*, *&c.*, *i.e.*, may Agni hear us with the hosts (the flames) posted in his house; may he, the imperishable, hear (us) with his hosts in heaven ! (the Hotar effects that). Agni shines in the house of the sacrificer till the end of his life (*i.e.*, he is always protected by him).

If the sacrificer be a Vaiśya, the Hotar should repeat a verse in the Jagatî metre, *viz* :—*ayam iha prathamo* **[61]** (4, 7, 1). For the Vaiśya belongs to the Jagatî: cattle is of the same (Jagatî) nature. Thus he makes him prosper by means of cattle (provides him with it). In its fourth pada *vaneṣu*, &c., the word *viśe* (Vaiśya) is mentioned. This is appropriate. What is appropriate, that is successful in the sacrifice.

When repeating the verse : *ayaṁ u ṣya pra devayur* (10, 176, 3), which is in the Anuṣṭubh metre, the Hotar sends forth speech (*i.e*, he repeats for the first time, this mantra, with a loud voice again, after having only inaudibly muttered some of the preceding ones). For the *Anuṣṭubh* metre is speech. By repeating (an Anuṣṭubh), he thus sends forth speech in speech. By the words *ayaṁ u ṣya* he expresses the following sentence : I who formerly was living among the Gandharvas have come.[4]

The author of the Brâhmaṇam tries to find in the words *ayaṁ u ṣya* of the mantra.

By the verse: *ayam agnir uruṣyati*, &c. (10, 176, 4) *i.e.*, "this Agni makes (us) fearless by dint of his immortal nature, as it were," the Hotar provides him (the sacrificer) with immortality. (The second half of this verse), *sahasaś chit sahîyân devo jîvâtave kṛitaḥ*, *i.e.*, "the god has been made very powerful by means of (his own) power, in order to preserve [62] (our) lives" signifies, that he (Agni) is the god who, by (our) repeating this verse, is made the preserver of (our) lives.

(The Hotar now repeats:) *iḷâyâs tvâ pade vayam*, &c. (3, 29, 4), *i.e.*, "we put thee, O Jâtavedas! (Agni) in the place of *Iḷâ*, in the centre (*nâbhi* of the *Uttarâ Vedi*)[5] on the earth to carry up (our) offerings." By *nâbhi* (lit. navel), the *nâbhi* of the *Uttarâ Vedi* is meant. *Nidhîmahi* (lit. we put down) means "they are about to put him (Agni) down." The term "*havyâya voḷhave*" means: he is about to carry up the sacrifice.

(The Hotar repeats:) *Agne viśvebhiḥ svanîka* (6, 15, 16). "O Agni, "with thy well-armed host (the flames), take first with all the gods thy "seat in the hole which is stuffed with wool; carry well the sacrificial "offering, seasoned with melted butter, and deposited in thee as in a nest, "for the sacrificer who is producing (the mystical sacrificial man) anew." (When repeating the first and second padas:) *agne viśvebhiḥ*, he makes him (Agni) with all the gods sit. (When repeating the third pada: *kulâyinam ghṛitavantam*, &c.) a bird's nest, as it were, consisting of sticks of fir-tree wood, an odoriferous gum (*guggul*), a braid of hair (*ûrṇâstukâh*), and a kind of fragrant grass,[6] is prepared (for Agni) at the sacrifice.

---

in question, an allusion to the fable reported in 1, 27, on the Vâch's (speech) residence among the Gandharvas. But this interpretation is wholly ungrammatical and childish. *Ayam*, the masculine of the demonstrative pronoun, is here, as Sâyaṇa explains, according to the Brâhmaṇam, taken as a feminine, in order to make it refer to *Vâch*, which word is feminine. The impossibility of such an explanation will be apparent to every reader. The verse in question refers to the ceremony of the *Agni-praṇayanam*, the carrying of the fire from the Ahavanîya fire to the Uttarâ Vedi; but its subject is Agni, and not Vâch. I translate it as follows: "This very Hotar (*i.e.*, Agni, whom the Hotar represents) "desirous of worshipping the gods, is carried (thither, to the Uttarâ Vedi) for the per-"formance of the sacrifice (animal and Soma offering). He (when being carried) appears "by himself as a fiery chariot (the sun) surrounded (by a large retinue of priests and "sacrificers)."

[5] The *Nâbhi* of the *Uttarâ Vedi* (the altar outside the *Prâchîna vaṁśa* or place for the Iṣṭis with the three fires) is a hole of a quadrangular form in the midst of this altar, filled with kuśa grass, &c. (see below) in which the fire brought from the Ahavanîya is deposited.

[6] The articles here mentioned, are put in the Nâbhi, or hole in the Uttarâ Vedi. They are regarded as forming the nest of Agni. As living in this nest like a bird, he is called *kulâyî*.

(When repeating the fourth pada :) *yajnam naya*, &c., he thus places the sacrifice (the sacrificial personage) straight on him (Agni).

[63] (The Hotar repeats) : *sîda hotaḥ sva u loke*, &c. (3, 29, 8), *i.e.*, "sit, O Hotar ! (Agni) in thy own place (the Nâbhi), being conspi-"cuous ; make sit the sacrifice in the hole of the well-made (nest). "Mayst thou, Agni, who art going to the gods with the offering, "repeat sacrificial verses addressed to the gods[7]. Mayst thou grant the "sacrificer a life with abundance."

By "Hotar" Agni is to be understood ; for he is the Hotar of the gods. "His own place" (*sva u loke*) is the Nâbhi of the Uttarâ Vedi. By the words : make sit, &c., the Hotar asks a blessing for the sacrificer ; for the "*yajña*" (sacrifice, mentioned in this verse) is the sacrificer. When repeating the second half of this verse : *devâvír*, &c., the Hotar provides the sacrificer with life ; for "*vayas*" (mentioned in this verse) is life.

(The Hotar repeats :) *ni hotâ hotṛiṣadane* (2, 9, 1), *i.e.*, "the Hotar of "great knowledge and skill, who is brightly shining, sat down on the "Hotṛi-seat (place for the Hotar), Agni, who deeply comprehends the "inviolable laws (of the sacrificial art), he, the most splendid (*vasiṣṭhaḥ*) "who bears a thousand burdens (*i.e.*, preserver of all) and has a flaming tongue." By *Hotar* is Agni to be understood ; *hotṛiṣadanam* is the *nâbhi* of the *uttarâ vedi*. By "he sat down" is expressed that he was put there. The term "*vasiṣṭha*" means, that Agni is the most shining (*vasu*) among the gods. The term "*sahasraṁbhara*" means, that they, though he (Agni) be only one, multiply him by using him at different occasions. He who has this knowledge, has a thousand-fold profit.

The Hotar concludes with the verse : *tvam dûtas tvam u naḥ* (2, 9, 2), *i. e.*, "thou art our messenger, our **[64]** protector behind (us) ; "thou the bringer of wealth, O strong one ! O Agni ! do not neglect the "bodies (members) in the spread of our families. The herdsman "with his light was awake." Agni is the herdsman (*gopa*) of the gods. He who knowing this, concludes (the ceremony of Agni-praṇayanam) with this verse (mentioned), has Agni everywhere round him as herdsman (watchman) for himself and the sacrificer, and secures thus welfare for the whole year.

He recites these eight verses (just enumerated), which are complete in form. What is complete in form, that is, when the mantra recited alludes to the ceremony which is being performed, that is successful in

[7] The verb *yaj* has here (as in many other cases) the meaning : to repeat the Yâjyâ-mantra.

the sacrifice. Of these eight verses he repeats the first and last thrice; that makes twelve. Twelve months make a year; the year is Prajâpati. He who has such a knowledge, prospers through these verses which reside in Prajâpati.

By repeating the first and last verses thrice, he ties the two ends of the sacrifice, in order to give it a hold and tighten it to prevent it from falling down.

29.

(*The Carrying of the Repositories*[8] *of Sacred Food to the Uttarâ Vedi*).

The Adhvaryu calls (upon the Hotar): repeat the mantras appropriate to the two repositories with sacred food (*havirdhâna*) being carried (to the Uttarâ Vedi).

He repeats: *yuje*[9] *vâm brahma*, &c. (10, 13, 1), "the Brahma is joined to the praises of you both." **[65]** For the two Havirdhânas, which are gods, were united with the Brahma. By reciting this verse he joins both these (Havirdhânas) with the Brahma, and having this latter (Brahma) power, he does not suffer any harm.

He repeats the triplet: *pretâm yajnasya śambhuva* (2, 41, 19-21), which is addressed to Heaven and Earth.

They ask: "Why does the Hotar repeat a triplet addressed to Heaven and Earth, when he is reciting mantras to the two Havirdhânas being removed (to the Uttarâ Vedi)?" (The answer is): Because Heaven and Earth are the two Havirdhânas of the gods. They are always repositories for offerings; for every offering is between them (Heaven and Earth).

The verse, *yame iva yatamâne yadaitam* (10, 13, 2), means: these two Havirdhânas, walk together, like twins, their arms stretched. (The second pada of this verse) *pra vâm bharan mânuṣâ devayantaḥ* means, that men bring both (these Havirdhânas) when worshipping god. (The third and fourth padas:) *âsîdatam u lokam*, &c., allude to Soma (by the name *Indu*). By repeating this (half verse), the priest prepares for the king Soma (a seat) to sit on (alluding to *âsîdatam*).

(He repeats:) *adhi dvayor adadhâ ukthyam vachaḥ* (1, 83, 3). This *ukthyam vachaḥ* is as a cover, forming the third piece (in addition to the two Havirdhânas) put over both.[10] For *ukthyam vachaḥ* is the

---

[8] The two Havirdhânas, are two carts, on which the Soma and the other offerings are put, and covered with a cover (*chhadiḥ*), for carrying all things from the Prâchîna-vamśa to the Uttarâ Vedi. The cover consists of grass. See Black Yajurveda, ed. Cowell i. p. 428.

[9] It is to be taken as third person of the Âtmanepadam, not as a first one.

[10] This is symbolically to be understood. The author calls the expression *ukthyam vachaḥ* a cover, to which opinion he, probably, was led by the frequency of the term:

sacrificial performance. By means of this (*ukthyam vachaḥ*) he thus makes the sacrifice successful.

[66] The term *yata*, *i.e.*, cruel, used in the second pada (*yatasruchâ*, 1, 83, 3), is propitiated in the following third pada by *asaṁyata*, *i.e.*, appeased, propitiated.[11] By the fourth pada, *bhadrâ śaktir*, &c., he asks for a blessing.

He repeats the Viśvarûpa verse[12]: *viśvâ rûpâṇi pratimuñchate* (5, 81, 2). He ought to repeat this verse when looking at the upper part (*rarâṭî*)[13] of the posts (between which the two Havirdhânas are put); for, on this part there every form is hung, white and black, as it were. He who having such a knowledge repeats this verse when [67] looking at the upper part of the posts, obtains for himself and the sacrificer every form.

With the verse, *pari tvâ girvaṇo gira* (1, 10, 12), he concludes. He should repeat this concluding verse at the time he might think both the Havirdhânas closed by hanging over them the bunch of Darbha[14] (between the two posts). He who knowing thus concludes with this verse, when the two Havirdhânas are thus closed, secures for himself

---

uktham vâchi, *i. e.*, "the Śâstra has been repeated" at the end of the recitations of the Hotṛi-priests at the Soma libations to denote that they are finished. The Hotar must stop after having recited the first half of the verse, *adhi dvayor*, as is said in the Âśval. Śrauta Sûtras, 4, 9, and indicated in the Saptahautra prayoga. The rule in Aśval., which is strictly observed by the Śrotriyas up to this day, runs as follows.—

अधि द्वयोरदधा उक्थ्यं वच इति अर्धर्चं आरमेद् व्यवस्ता चेद्रराटी विश्वारूपाणि प्रतिमुंचते व्यवस्तायां;

i.e., He should stop after having repeated half of the verse *adhi dvayor*, when the bunch of kuśa grass is not yet hung over the two posts. When this bunch is hung over, he recites (the second half of that verse, and) *viśvâ rûpâṇi*. The form *vyavasta* is contraction of *vyava-sita* (from the root *si*, to tie, bind).

[11] The interpretation which the writer of the Brâhmaṇa gives of this passage, is egregiously wrong. *Yata-sruk* can only mean "with the sacrificial spoon kept in his hand;" *asaṁyata* (instead of *asaṁyatasruk*) then stands in opposition to it, meaning: having laid it aside. The meaning "cruel" is given to *yata* by Sâyaṇa.

[12] So called from the beginning words: *viśvâ rûpâṇi*. It refers to the objects of senses becoming manifest again by sunrise. For Savitar the sun, brings forth "all forms."

[13] This translation is made according to oral information obtained from a Brahman who officiated as a Hotar. Sâyaṇa explains it as "a garland of Darbha." It is true, a bunch of Darbha grass, consisting of dry and green stalks, the first representing the white, the latter the dark, colour, is hung up at the upper part of the two posts (called *methi*) between which the two Havirdhânas are put. Therefore, when the priest looks at the upper part of this gate, he necessarily glances at the bunch of Darbha grass which must be hung there. The garland which is hung up, is designated by the name: *rarâṭam*, as appears from the Yajus, which is repeated by the Adhvaryu at that time: *viṣṇor rarâṭam asi*. See Taittirîya Saṃh. 1, 2, 13, 3, and Sâyaṇa's Commentary on it, vol. i. p. 429, ed. Cowell.

[14] The term in the original is *pariśrita*, which literally means surrounded.

and the sacrificer fine women who are not naked (covered with clothes, jewels, &c.).

Both are closed with a Yajusmantra.[15] Thus the Adhvaryus do it with the said Yajus. When the Adhvaryu and Pratiprasthâtar on both sides (of the Havirdhânas) drive in the two stakes (*methi*), then he should conclude. For at that time the two Havirdhânas are closed.

These eight verses which he has repeated are complete in form. What is complete in form, that is, when the verse recited alludes to the ceremony which is being performed, that is successful in the sacrifice. Of these, he repeats ths first and last thrice, that makes twelve. For the year has twelve months. Prajâpati is the year. He who has such a knowledge thus prospers through these verses which reside in Prajâpati.

By repeating the first and last thrice, he ties the two ends (knots) of the sacrifice for giving it a hold, and tighten it to prevent it from falling down.

[68] 30

(The Bringing-of Agni and Soma[16] *to the Place of the Uttarâ Vedi.)*

When Agni and Soma are brought, the Adhyaryu calls upon (the Hotar) to repeat appropriate mantras.

He (first) repeats a verse addressed to Savitar *sâvîr hi deva prathamâya* (Âśv. Śr. S. 4, 10. Atharv. 7, 14, 3.) They ask: why does he repeat a verse addressed to Savitar, when Agni and Soma are brought? (The answer is:) Savitar rules over generation. Under the recital of this verse, they (the priests) carry both (Agni and Soma) as being produced by Savitar. Therefore he repeats a verse addressed to Savitar.

He repeats a verse addressed to Brahmaṇaspati: *praitu Brahmaṇaspatiḥ* (1, 40, 3). They ask: why does he repeat a verse addressed to Brahmaṇaspati when Agni and Soma are brought? (The answer is): Bṛihaspati (the same as Brahmaṇaspati) is Brahma. By repeating this verse, he makes Brahma the leader (*purogava*) of both (Agni and Soma), and the sacrificer, being provided with the Brahma, does not suffer any injury.

---

[15] This is, *viṣṇoḥ priṣṭham asi.* See Taitt. Saṁh. 6, 2, 9.

[16] In order to make the removal of Agni-Soma and the Havirdhânas clear it is to be remarked, that first Agni alone is carried to the Uttarâ Vedi. This ceremony is called *Agni-praṇayanam.* Then the two carts, called Havirdhânas, filled with ghee, Soma, and after oblations, are drawn by the priests to the place on the right side of the Uttarâ Vedi. This is the *Havirdhâna pravartaṇam.* Then the priests go a third time back to the Prâchîna-vaṁśa, and bring Agni (fire), and Soma again. Both, after having been removed from the Prâchîna-vaṁśa, are put down at the gate, facing their former place. The fire is to be put in the Agnîdhrîya hearth, in the place of the Uttarâ Vedi (on the left side), and the Soma in the place called Sadas, near the Agnîdhrîya hearth. This ceremony is called: *Agnîṣoma-praṇayanam.*

[69] By repeating the second half verse (of *praitu Brhmaṇaspatiḥ*) *pra devī etu sunritâ*, he provides the sacrifice with a good omen. Thence he repeats a verse addressed to Brahmaṇaspati.

He repeats a triplet in the Gâyatrî metre, which is addressed to Agni : *hotâ devo amartya* (3, 27, 7).

When the King Soma had been carried once (to the place of the Uttarâ Vedi), then the Asuras and demons sought to kill the king between the place called Sadas and the two Havirdhânas. Agni saved him by assuming an illusory form (*mâyâ*), as is said in the words of the mantra (just quoted) : *purastâd eti mâyayâ*, *i.e.*, he walks before him by assuming an illusory form. In this way Agni saved Soma. Therefore they hold before him (Soma) fire.

He repeats the triplet, *upa tvâ agne dive* (1, 1, 7, 9 11), and the single verse, *upa priyam* (9, 67, 29). For these two Agnis,[1] that one which has been taken first, and the other which was brought afterwards,[18] have the power of injuring the sacrificer, when they are fighting (with one another as to whom the oblation belongs). By repeating these three verses, and the single one (in addition to them), he thus reconciles them in a friendly way, and puts them (back) in their proper places, without any injury being done either to himself or the sacrificer.

When the oblation is given to the fire, he repeats : *agne juṣasva prati harya* (1, 144, 7). By repeating this verse, he gives (this) oblation to Agni as a "favour" (on account of the term "*juṣasva*," take it favourably ! contained in it).

[70] When the King Soma is carried (to the Sadas) the Hotar repeats the triplet of verses, commencing with : *somo jigâti gâtuvid* (3, 62, 13-15), which is in the Gâyatrî metre, and addressed to Soma. By repeating it, he thus makes prosper Soma by means of his own deity (the verses being addressed to Soma) and his own metre (Gâyatrî). The words (in the last verse of this triplet)—*Somaḥ sadastham âsadat*, "Soma sat on the seat," which express that Soma (at the time of the triplet in question being repeated) is just about taking his seat (in the Sadas), are to be repeated by the Hotar, after having gone beyond the place of the Agnîdhrîya hearth, when turning his back to it.

He repeats a verse addressed to Viṣṇu : *tam asya râjâ varuṇas* (1, 156, 4), *i.e.*, "the King Varuṇa and "the Aśvins follow the wisdom

[17] This first Agni is that one, which was brought to the Uttarâ Vedi, and put in the Nâbhi of it ; the other is that one, which was afterwards taken to the Agnîdhrîya hearth.

[18] This refers to the burnt-offering (*homa*) which is to be thrown into the *Agnîdhrîya* hearth.

"of the leader of the Maruts (Viṣṇu); Viṣṇu is possessed of the high-"est power, by means of which he, surrounded by his friends, uncovers "the stable of darkness (night) to make broad daylight." Viṣṇu is the door-keeper of the gods. Thence he opens the door for him (for Soma's admission), when this verse is being repeated.

He repeats: *antaścha prâgâ aditir* (8, 48, 2), when Soma is about to be put in the Sadas. When Soma has taken his seat, the Hotar repeats: *śyeno na yonim sadanam* (9, 71, 6), *i.e.*, "the god (Soma) "takes his golden seat just as the eagle is occupying for his residence "a nest wisely constructed; the hymns fly to him, when comfortably "seated on the grass spread; like a sacrificial horse he runs to the gods." By "golden seat" the black goat skin (on which Soma is put) is to be understood, which covers that which belongs to the gods (their food). Thence he repeats this mantra.

[71] He concludes with a verse addressed to Varuṇa: *astabhnât dyâm asuro* (8, 42, 1), *i.e.*, "the living god (Asura) established heaven, "he the all-possessing created the plain of the earth; as their "supreme ruler, he enforces upon all beings those (well-known) laws "of Varuṇa (laws of nature, birth and death &c.)." For Soma is in the power of Varuṇa, as long as he remains tied up (in a cloth), and whilst moving in a place shut up (by hanging kuśa grass over it). By repeating at that (time) this verse, the Hotar makes him (Soma) prosper through his own deity, and his own metre (Triṣṭubh).

If some persons should take their refuge with the sacrificer, or should wish for protection from him, the Hotar must conclude with: *evâ vandasva varuṇam* (8, 42, 2). He who, having such a knowledge, concludes with this verse, secures safety for as many persons as he wishes and contemplates. Thence he who knows it, should conclude with this verse.

All the seventeen verses which he has repeated on this occasion are complete in their form. What is complete in form, that is to say, when the mantra which is repeated alludes to the ceremony which is being performed, that is successful in the sacrifice. Of these (17 verses) he repeats thrice the first and last; that makes twenty-one. Prajâpati is twenty-one fold; for he consists of twelve months, five seasons, and these three worlds with that Âditya (sun) as the twenty-first. For he is the highest place (on the sky, occupied by Âditya), he is the field of the gods, he is fortune, he is sovereignty; he is the heaven of the bright one (sun), he is the residence of Prajâpati; he is independent rule. He (the Hotar) makes the sacrificer prosperous through these twenty-one verses.

[72]

SECOND BOOK

FIRST CHAPTER.

(The Animal Sacrifice.)

1.

(Erecting of the Sacrificial Post.)

The Gods went up to the celestial world by means of this sacrifice. They were afraid that Men and Ṛiṣis, after having seen their sacrifice (by means of which they ascended to heaven), might come after (they had gone), and inquire (whether they could not obtain some sacrificial knowledge). They debarred them[1] (from obtaining such a knowledge) by means of the *Yûpa, i.e.*, the sacrificial post. Thence the Yûpa is called so (from *yoyûpayan*, they debarred). The gods when going up to the celestial world, struck the Yûpa in (the earth), turning its points downwards. Thereupon Men and Ṛiṣis came to the spot where the gods had performed their sacrifice, thinking, that they might obtain some information (about the sacrifice). They found only the Yûpa struck in (the earth), with its point turned downwards. They learnt that the gods had by this means (*i.e.*, by having struck in the earth the Yûpa) precluded the sacrificial secret (from being known). They dug the Yûpa out, and turned its points upwards, where-[73]upon they got aware of the sacrifice, and beheld (consequently), the celestial world. That is the reason that the Yûpa is erected with its point turned upwards (it is done), in order to get aware of the sacrifice, and to behold the celestial world.

This Yûpa is a weapon. Its point must have eight edges. For a weapon (or iron club) has eight edges. Whenever he strikes with it an enemy or adversary, he kills him. (This weapon serves) to put down him (every one) who is to be put down by him (the sacrificer). The Yûpa is a weapon which stands erected (being ready) to slay an enemy. Thence an

[1] The term is : *yoyûpayan*, which word is only a derivation from *yûpa*, and proves, in fact, nothing for the etymology of the latter. The author had no doubt the root (*yu* "to avert, prevent") in view. It is possible that the word is ultimately to be traced to this root. The *Yûpa* itself is a high wooden post, decorated with ribands and erected before the Uttarâ Vedi. The sacrificial animal is tied to it.

enemy (of the sacrificer) who might be present (at the sacrifice) comes out ill after having seen the Yûpa of such or such one.

He who desires heaven, ought to make his Yûpa of Khâdira wood. For the gods conquered the celestial world by means of a Yûpa made of Khâdira wood. In the same way, the sacrificer conquers the celestial world by means of a Yûpa made of Khâdira wood.

He who desires food and wishes to grow fat, ought to make his Yûpa of Bilva wood. For the Bilva tree bears fruits every year; it is the symbol of fertility; for it increases (every year) in size from the roots up to the branches, therefore it is a symbol of fatness. He who having such a knowledge makes his Yûpa of Bilva wood, makes fat his children and cattle.

As regards the Yûpa made of Bilva wood (it is further to be remarked, that) they call "light" *bilva.* He who has such a knowledge, becomes a light among his own people, the most distinguished among his own people.

He who desires beauty and sacred knowledge ought to make his Yûpa of Palâśa wood. For the **[74]** Palâśa is among the trees beauty and sacred knowledge. He who having such a knowledge makes his Yûpa of Palâśa wood, becomes beautiful and acquires sacred knowledge.

As regards the Yûpa made of Palâśa wood (there is further to be remarked, that) the Palâśa is the womb of all trees. Thence they speak on account of the *palâśam* (foliage) of the Palâśa tree, of the *palâśam* (foliage) of this or that tree (*i.e.*, they call the foliage of every tree *palâśam*). He who has such a knowledge obtains (the gratification of) any desire he might have regarding all trees (*i.e.*, he obtains from all trees anything he might wish for).

2.

(*The Ceremony of Anointing the Sacrificial Post*).

The Adhvaryu says (to the Hotar): "We anoint the sacrificial post (*Yûpa*); repeat the mantra (required)." The Hotar then repeats the verse: "*Aṁjanti tvâm adhvare*" (3, 8, 1), *i.e.*, "The priests anoint thee, O tree! with celestial honey (butter); provide (us) with wealth if thou standest here erected, or if thou art lying on thy mother (earth)." The "celestial honey" is the melted butter (with which the priests anoint the *Yûpa*). (The second half verse from) "provide us," &c., means: "thou mayest stand or lie, [2] provide us with wealth."

[2] The Brâhmaṇam explains here only the two somewhat obscure verbal forms: *tiṣṭhâ* and *kṣayo* of the mantra, by *tîṣṭhâsi* (2nd person conjunctive, present tense), and *śayasâi* (2nd person conjunctive, middle voice, present tense), which are in the common Saṁskrit language equally obsolete: *tiṣṭhâ* stands instead of *tiṣṭhâs*, 2nd person conjunctive, present tense of the shorter form.

(The Hotar repeats the mantra.) *Uchchhrayasva*, &c. (3, 8, 3), *i.e.*, "be raised, O tree! on the surface of the soil; thou who hast well lain (on the ground), grant splendour to the carrying up of the **[75]** sacrifice (to heaven)." This (verse) is appropriate to (the occasion of) erecting the Yûpa (for it contains the words: "be raised!"). What is appropriate in the sacrifice, that is sure of success. (The words) "on the surface of the soil" mean the surface of that soil over which they raise the *Yûpa*. (By the words) "thou hast lain well, grant us," &c., the Hotar asks for a blessing (from the Yûpa).

(The Hotar repeats:) *samiddhasya śrayamâṇaḥ*" (3, 8, 2), *i.e.*, "placed before the (fire) which is kindled (here), thou grantest the Brahma power, which is indestructible and provides with abundance offspring. Stand erected, driving far off our enemies (*amati*), for our welfare." By the words: "placed before," &c., he means: placed before it (what is kindled, the fire). By the words: "thou grantest," &c., he asks for a blessing. The wicked enemy (*amati*) is hunger. By the words: "driving far off,' &c., he frees the sacrifice as well as the sacrificer from hunger. By the words: "stand erected," &c., he asks for a blessing.

(The Hotar repeats the mantra: *ûrdhva û ṣu na ûtaye* (1, 36, 13), *i.e.*, "Stand upright for our protection just as the sungod! Being raised, be a giver of food, when we invoke thee in different ways (metres), whilst the anointing priests are carrying on (the sacrifice)." (As to the expression), *deva na savitâ*, "just as the sungod," the (particle) *na* has with the gods the same meaning as *om* (yes) with these (men); [3] it means *iva*, "like as." By the words, **[76]** "being raised, be a giver of food," he calls him (the Yûpa) a dispenser of food; he is giving them (men) grain; he dispenses (*sanoti*) it. The words, "*aṁjayo vâghataḥ*" (the anointing priests are carrying) mean the metres; for by their means the sacrificers call the different gods: "Come to my sacrifice, to my sacrifice!" If many, as it were, bring a sacrifice (at the same time), then the gods come only to the sacrifice of him, at which (there is a Hotar), who having such a knowledge repeats this (mantra).

(The Hotar then repeats:) "*ûrdhvo*" *naḥ pâhi*[4] (1, 36, 14), *i.e.*,

[3] Sâyaṇa refers the demonstrative pronoun *eṣâm* to the Vedas. But there is no sufficient proof to show that the three Vedas are hinted at in this demonstrative. It stands in opposition to *devânâm*; thence it can only refer to men. The meaning of the explanatory remark, that "*na* has with the gods the same meaning as *om* (yes), with men," is, that *na* is here no negative particle, as is generally the case, but affirmative, excluding negation, just as *om*, which is used for solemn affirmation.

[4] This and the preceding verse properly refer to Agni, and not to the Yûpa, as the contents of both clearly show. They form part of a hymn addressed to Agni. They

"(Standing) upright protect us from distress; with thy beams burn down all carnivorous beings (ghosts). Make us (stand) upright, that we may walk and live! Mayst thou as messenger carry (our offerings) to the gods! The wicked carnivorous beings are the Rakṣas. He calls upon him (the Yûpa) to burn the wicked Rakṣas down. (In the second half verse) the word *charathâya*, "that he might walk," is equivalent to *charaṇâya*, "for walking."

(By the word "to live") he rescues the sacrificer, even if he should have been already seized, as it were (by death), and restores him to (the enjoyment of) the whole year. (By the words:) "mayst thou carry," &c., he asks for a blessing.

(The Hotar then repeats:) "*jâto jâyate sudinatve,*" &c. (3, 8, 5), *i. e.*, "After having been born, he (the Yûpa) is growing (to serve) in the prime of his life the [77] sacrifice of mortal man. The wise are busy in decorating (him, the Yûpa) with skill. He as an eloquent messenger of the gods, lifts his voice (that it might be heard by the gods)." He (the Yûpa) is called *jâta*, *i.e.*, born, because he is born by this (by the recital of the first quarter of this verse). (By the word) *vardhamâna*, *i.e.*, growing, they make him (the Yûpa) grow in this manner. (By the words:) *punanti* (*i.e.*, to clean, decorate), they clean him in this manner. (By the words:) "he as an eloquent messenger, &c.," he announces the Yûpa (the fact of his existence), to the gods.

The Hotar then concludes (the ceremony of anointing the sacrificial post) with the verse "*yuvâ suvâsâḥ parivîtaḥ*" (3, 8, 4.), *i.e.*, "the youth,[5] decorated with ribands, has arrived; he is finer (than all trees) which ever grew; the wise priests raise him up under recital of well-framed thoughts of their mind." The youth decorated with ribands, is the vital air (the soul), which is covered by the limbs of the body.[6] (By the words:) "he is finer," &c., he means that he (the Yûpa) is becoming finer (more excellent, beautiful) by this (mantra). By the wise priests (*Kavis*) those who have repeated the hymns are to be understood. Thus by this (mantra) they raise him up.

When the Hotar has repeated these seven verses, which are com-

---

appear to have been selected for being applied to the Yûpa, only on account of the word "*ûrdhva,*" "erected, upwards," being mentioned in them. The Yûpa, when standing upright, required mantras appropriate to its position, and these appear to have been the only available ones serving this purpose.

[5] There is a pun between *yuvâ*, young, a youth, and Yûpa. By this "youth" the Yûpa is to be understood.

[6] The limbs of the body are to correspond with the ribands to be put on the Yûpa.

plete in their form (corresponding to the ceremony for which they are used), the sacrifice is made successful; that is, the form is complete, when the verse recited alludes to the ceremony which is being performed. Of these seven (verses), he recites the first thrice, and the last thrice; **[78]** that makes eleven. The *Triṣṭubh* (metre) namely consists of eleven syllables (*i.e.*, each quarter of the verse). Triṣṭubh is Indra's thunderbolt.[7] He who has such a knowledge prospers through these verses which reside in Indra. By repeating the first and last verses thrice, he ties together both ends of the sacrifice to fasten and tighten them, in order to prevent (the sacrifice) from slipping down.

3.

(*Speculations on the Yûpa, and the Meaning of the Sacrificial Animal.*)

They (the theologians) argue the question: Is the Yûpa to remain standing (before the fire), or is it to be thrown (into the fire)? They answer:) For him who desires cattle, it may remain standing. (About this the following story is reported). Once upon a time cattle did not stand still to be taken by the gods for food. Having run away, they stood still (and turning towards the gods), said repeatedly: You shall not obtain us! No! no! Thereupon the gods saw that Yûpa-weapon which they erected. Thus they frightened the animals, which then returned to them. That is the reason, that up to this day, the (sacrificial) animals are turned towards the Yûpa, (*i.e.*, the head being bent towards the sacrificial post to which they are tied). Then they stood still to be taken by the gods for their food. The (sacrificial) animals of him who has such a knowledge, and whose Yûpa stands erected, stand still to be taken by him for his food. **[79]** He (the Adhvaryu) should afterwards throw the Yûpa of that sacrificer who desires heaven (into the fire). For the former (sacrificers) actually used to throw the Yûpa (into the fire), after it had been used for tying the sacrificial animal to it. For the sacrificer is the Yûpa, and the bunch [8] of Darbha grass (*prastara*) is the sacrificer (also), and Agni is the

---

[7] The Yûpa represents Indra's thunderbolt, see 2, 1. Thence the author is anxiously looking out for a relationship between the Yûpa and anything belonging to Indra. Here he finds it in the circumstance, that, if the repetitions are counted, the number of the mantras required for the ceremony of anointing, raising, and decorating the Yûpa, amounts to eleven, which is the principal number of Indra's sacred metre, Triṣṭubh.

[8] At the beginning of the sacrifice the Adhvaryu makes of the load of Darbha or sacred grass, which has been brought to the sacrificial compound, seven *muṣṭis* or bunches, each of which is tied together with a stalk of grass, just as the Baresma (Barsom) of the Parsis. The several names of these seven bunches are: (1) *yajamâna muṣṭi*, the bunch kept by the sacrificer himself in his hand as long as the sacrifice lasts. (2) Three bunches form the *Barhis*, or the covering of the Vedi on which the sacrificial vessels are put. These are unloosened and spread all over the Vedi. (3) *Prastara*. This

womb of the gods. By means of the invocation offerings (*âhuti*), the sacrificer joins the womb of the gods, and will go with a golden body to the celestial world.[9]

The sacrificers who lived after the ancient ones, observed that the *svaru*,[10] being a piece of the Yûpa (represents the whole of it). He (who now brings a sacrifice) should, therefore, throw it, at this time, afterwards (into the fire). In this way, any thing obtainable through the throwing of the Yûpa (into the fire), as well as that one obtainable through its remaining standing, is obtained.

[**80**] The man who is initiated (into the sacrificial mysteries) offers himself to all deities. Agni represents all deities, and Soma represents all deities. When he (the sacrificer) offers the animal to *Agni-Soma*,[11] he releases himself (by being represented by the animal) from being offered to all deities.[12]

They say : the animal to be offered to Agni-Soma, must be of two colours,[13] because it belongs to two deities. But this (precept) is not to be attended to. A fat animal is to be sacrificed ; because animals are of a fat complexion, and the sacrificer (if compared with them) certainly lean. When the animal is fat, the sacrificer thrives through its marrow.

They say : "do not eat from the animal offered to Agni-Soma." Who eats from this animal, eats from human flesh ; because the sacrificer re-

---

bunch, which must remain tied, is put over the Darbha of the Vedi. (4) *Paribhojani.* From this bunch the Adhvaryu takes a handful out for each priest, and the sacrificer and his wife, which they then use for their seat. [5) *Veda.* This bunch is made double in its first part ; the latter part is cut off and has to remain on the Vedi ; it is called *parivâsana.* The *Veda* itself is always wandering from one priest to another, and is given to the sacrificer and his wife. It is handed over to the latter only when one of the priests makes her recite a mantra. In our passage here, *prastara* cannot mean the bunch which is put on the Vedi, but we must understand by it the *Yajamanu muṣṭi.*

[9] If the Yûpa represents the sacrificer, then his ascent to heaven is effected by the throwing into the fire of the former.

[10] *Svaru* means "shavings." A small piece of the Yûpa is put into the *Juhu* (sacrificial ladle) and thrown into the fire by the words : "may thy smoke go to heaven."

[11] The name of the animal, or animals, sacrificed on the day previous to the Soma festival, as well as that of the day itself, is *Agniṣamîya.*

[12] The same idea is expressed in the Kauaṣîtaki Brâhmaṇam 10, 3. अग्नीषोमयोर्वा एष आस्यमापद्यते यो दीक्षते तद्यदुपवसथेऽग्नीषोमीयं पशुमालभत आत्मनिष्क्रयण एवास्यैष तेन आत्मानं निष्क्रीयानृणो भूत्वाथ भजते तस्मादु तस्य नाश्नीयात्, *i.e.*, He who is initiated (into the sacrificial mysteries) falls into the very mouth of Agni-Soma (to be their food). That is the reason, that the sacrificer kills on the day previous to the Soma festival an animal being devoted to Agni-Soma, thus redeeming himself (from the obligation of being himself sacrificed.) He then brings his (Soma) sacrifice after having thus redeemed himself, and become free from debts. Thence the sacrificer ought not to eat of the flesh of this (animal).

[13] White and black according to Sâyaṇa.

leases himself (from being sacrificed) by means of the animal." But this (precept) is not to be attended to.

The animal offered to Agni-Soma is an offering to Vṛitraghna (Indra). For Indra slew Vṛitra through Agni-Soma. Both then said to him: "Thou hast slain Vṛitra through us, let us choose a boon from thee." Choose yourselves, answered he. Thus they **[81]** chose this boon from him. Thus they receive (now as their food) the animal which is sacrificed the day previous to the Soma feast.

This is their everlasting portion chosen by them. Thence one ought to take pieces of it, and eat them.

4.

(*The Aprî verses.*[14])

The Hotar repeats the Aprî verses. These are brightness and sacred knowledge. Through brightness and sacred knowledge the Hotar thus makes thrive the sacrificer.

[82] (First) he recites a Yâjyâ verse for the wooden sticks (*samidhaḥ*) which are used as fuel.[15] These are the vital airs. The vital airs kindle

---

[14] The so called *Aprî* verses, *i.e.*, verses of invitation, occupy at the animal sacrifice the same rank which the *prayâjas* have at the Iṣṭis. By means of them certain divine beings (who do not get any share in the principal part of the sacrifice) are invited and satisfied chiefly with butter. The number of these *prayâjas* or *Aprî* verses varies according to the Iṣṭis, of which they are the introductory part. At the common Iṣṭis, such as *Darśa-pûrṇima*, there are five (see Âśv. Śr. S. 1, 5), at the *Châturmâsya-iṣṭi* we have nine (Âśv. 2, 16), and at the *Pasu-iṣṭi* (the animal sacrifice) there are eleven used (Âśv. 3, 2). The nnmber of the latter may, however, rise to twelve, and even thirteen (See Max. Müller's History of Ancient Saṁskrit Literature, p. 464). At all Prayâjas, at the common Iṣṭis as well as at the sacrificial sacrifice, there is a difference in the second deity. Certain Gotras must invoke *Tanûnapât*, others must choose instead of this deity *Narâśaṁsa*. This is distinctly expressed in the words **तनूनपादग्न आज्यस्य वेत्विति द्वितीयो (प्रयाजः) अन्यत्र वसिष्ठ शुनकात्रिवध्र्यश्वराजन्येभ्यो नराशंसो अग्न आज्यस्यवेत्वेति तेषां.** (Âśv. 1, 5), *i.e.*, the second Prayâja mantra (at the Darśa Pûrṇimâ Iṣṭi) is: "may Tanûnapât, O Agni, taste of this melted butter;" but a different mantra is used by the Vasiṣṭas, Sunakas, Atris, Vadhryasvas and individuals belonging to the royal caste. They use the mantra: May *Narâśaṁsu*, O Agni! taste of the melted butter!" On the distribution of the ten Aprî hymns of the Ṛigveda Saṁhitâ, according to the Gotras, see Max. Müller's History of Ancient Saṁskrit Literature, p. 466. It clearly follows from this distinction between the invocation of the two deities *Tanûnapât* and *Narâśaṁsa* (both representing a particular kind of Agni), that certain Gotras regarded Tanûnapât, others Narâśaṁsa as their tutelary deity, or rather as one of their deified ancestors. These Aprî verses seemed to have formed one of the earliest part of the Aryan sacrifices; for we find them in the form of *Afrîgân* also with the Parsis. See my 'Essays on the Sacred language, Writings and Religion of the Parsis. p. 241.

[15] The formula by which each Aprî verse is introduced, is **येऽ३यजामहे.** For each verse there is a separate *praiṣa*, *i.e.*, order, requisite. This is given by the *Maitrâvaruṇa* priest of the Hotar, which always begins with the words **होतायक्षत**, and the

this whole universe (give life to it). Thus he pleases the vital airs and puts them into the sacrificer.

He repeats a Yâjyâ verse for *Tanûnapât*. The air inhaled (*prâṇa*) is Tanûnapât, because it preserves (*apât*) the bodies (*tanvaḥ*).[16] Thus he pleases the air inhaled, and puts it into the sacrificer.

He repeats a Yâjyâ verse for *Narâśaṁsa*. *Nara* means offspring, *śaṁsa* speech. Thus he pleases offspring and speech, and puts them into the sacrificer.

He repeats the Yâjyâ for *Ilaḥ*. Ilaḥ means food. Thus he pleases food and puts food into the sacrificer.

He repeats a Yâjyâ for the *Barhis* (sacred grass). Barhis is cattle. Thus he pleases the cattle and puts it into the sacrificer.

He repeats the Yâjyâ for the gates (of the sacrificial place). The gates are the rain. Thus he pleases (fertility) and puts it into the sacrificer.

He repeats the Yâjyâ for Dawn and Night. Dawn and Night are day and night. Thus he pleases day and night and puts them into the sacrificer.

He repeats a Yâjyâ for the two Divine Hotars.[17] **[83]** The air inhaled and exhaled are the two Divine Hotars. Thus he pleases them and puts them into the sacrificer.

He repeats a Yâjyâ for three goddesses.[18] These three goddesses are the air inhaled, the air exhaled, and the air circulating in the body. Thus he pleases them and puts them into the sacrificer.

He repeats a Yâjyâ for *Tvaṣṭâr*. Tvaṣṭâr is speech. Speech shapes (*tâṣṭi*), as it were, the whole universe. Thus he pleases speech, and puts it into the sacrificer.

He repeats a Yâjyâ for *Vanaspati* (trees). Vanaspati is the life. Thus he pleases life and puts it into the sacrificer.

He repeats a Yâjyâ for the *Svâhâkṛitis*.[19] These are a firm footing Thus he puts the sacrificer on a firm footing.

---

name of the respective deity समिधं तनू नपातं, &c., in the accusative. See Vâjasaneya Saṁhitâ 21, 29-40.

[16] This etymology is apparently wrong. Sâyaṇa explains it in a similar way by *śarîrum na pâtayati*, he does not make fall the body.

[17] They are, according to Sâyaṇa's Commentary on the Rigveda Saṁhitâ, i. p. 162 (ed. Müller), the two Agnis, *i.e.*, the fire on earth, and that in the clouds. See also Mâdhava's Commentary on the Vâjasaneya Saṁhitâ, p. 678, ed. Weber.

[18] They are: *Ilâ* (food), *Sarasvatî* (speech), and *Mahî* or *Bhâratî* (earth). See Vâjasaneya Saṁhitâ 21, 37.

[19] In the last Prayâja, at every occasion, there occurs the formula *svâhâ* along with all the deities of the respective I.ṭi, of which the Prajâyas form part. There are as

He ought to repeat such Aprî verses, as are traceable to a Ṛiṣi (of the family of the sacrificer). By doing so the Hotar keeps the sacrificer within the relationship (of his ancestors).

5.

[34] *(The Carrying of Fire round the Sacrificial Animal.)*

When the fire is carried round[20] (the animal) the Adhvaryu says to the Hotar: repeat (thy mantras). The Hotar then repeats his triplet of verses, addressed to Agni, and composed in the Gâyatrî metre: *agnir hotâ ṇo adhvare* (4, 15, 1-3) *i.e.* (1) Agni, our priest, is carried round about like a horse, he who is among gods the god of sacrifices. (2) Like a charioteer Agni passes thrice by the sacrifice; to the gods he carries the offering. (3) The master of food, the seer Agni, went round the offerings; he bestows riches on the sacrificer.

When the fire is carried round (the animal) then he makes him (Agni) prosper by means of his own deity and his own[21] metre. "As a horse he is carried" means: they carry him as if he were a horse, round about. Like a charioteer Agni passes thrice by the sacrifice means: he goes round the sacrifice like a charioteer (swiftly). He is called *vajapati* (master of food) because he is the master of (different kinds of) food.

The Adhvaryu says: give Hotar! the additional order for despatching offerings to the god.[22]

(35) Then the Maitrâvaruṇa proceeds to give his orders by the words: may Agni be victorious, may he grant (us) food!

They ask: why does the Maitrâvaruṇa proceed to give his orders, if the Adhvaryu orders the Hotar to recite? (The answer is:) The

---

many *svâhâs* as there are deities mentioned. The pronunciation of this formula is called *svâhâkṛiti*. Besides the regular deities, there are mentioned the *devâ âjyapâ*, *i.e.*, the deities who drink melted butter. To make it clear, I write out the fifth Prayâja of the Dîkṣaṇîya Iṣṭi—ये३ यजामहे स्वाहाग्निं स्वाहा सोमं स्वाहाग्नाविष्णू स्वाहा देवा आज्यपा जुषाणा अग्न आज्यस्य व्यन्तु वौषट्: *i.e.* (may the Gods) for whom we sacrifice, Agni, Soma, Agni-Viṣṇu, and the gods who enjoy melted butter, become pleased and eat of (this) melted butter, "each of them being invited by (*Svâhâ*)".—*Sapta hautra*. The latter means nothing but "well spoken" (the εὐφημεῖν of the Greeks).

[20] This ceremony is called *paryagnikriyâ* and is performed by the *Agnîd* priest. He takes a firebrand from the Ahavanîya fire and carries it to the right side, thrice round the animal which is to be sacrificed.

[21] Agni himself is the deity of the hymn in question; it is in Agni's metre, *i.e.*, Gâyatrî.

[22] This second praiṣa, or order of one of the Hotars, who is here the Maitrâvaruṇa to the Hotar to repeat his mantras, is called *upapraiṣa*. At the Animal, as well as at the Soma sacrifices, the orders for repeating the Yâjyâ mantras are given by the Maitrâvaruṇa. As symbol of his power, he receives a stick which he holds in his hand. The Adhvaryu gives at these sacrifices only the order for repeating the Anuvâkyâs.

Maitrâvaruṇa is the mind of the sacrifice; the Hotar is the speech of the sacrifice; for speech speaks only if driven (sent) by the mind; because an other-minded[10] speaks the speech of the Asuras which is not agreeable to the Devas. If the Maitrâvaruna proceeds to give orders, he stirs up speech by means of the mind. Speech being stirred up by his mind, he secures the offering to the gods (by preventing the Asuras from taking possession of it).

6.

(*The Formula to be Recited at the Slaughter of the Animal.* See Âśv. Śr. S. 3, 3).[11]

The Hotar then says (to the slaughterers): *Ye divine slaughterers, commence* (your work), *as well as ye who are human!* that is to say, he orders all the slaughterers among gods as well as among men (to commence).

Bring hither the instruments for killing, ye who are ordering the sacrifice, in behalf of the two masters of the sacrifice.[12]

(86) The animal is the offering, the sacrificer the master of the offering. Thus he (the Hotar) makes prosper the sacrificer by means of his (the sacrificer's) own offering. Thence they truly say: for whatever deity the animal is killed, that one is the master of the offering. If the animal is to be offered to one deity only, the priest should say: *medha-pataye*[13] "to the master of the sacrifice (singular)"; if to two deities, then he should use the dual "to both the masters of the offering," and if to several deities, then he should use the plural "to the masters of the offering." This is the established custom.

Bring ye for him fire! For the animal when carried (to the slaughter) saw death before it. Not wishing to go to the gods, the gods said to it: Come, we will bring thee to heaven! The animal consented and said: One of you should walk before me.

---

[10] If "mind and speech" are unconnected.

[11] It is called the *Adhrigu-praiṣa-mantra, i.e.,* the mantra by which the *Adhrigu* is ordered to kill the animal. The word used for "killer, slaughterer," is "*Samitâ,*" lit, silence-maker. This peculiar term accurately expresses the mode in which the sacrificial animal is to be killed. They stop its mouth, and beat it severely ten or twelve times on the testicles till it is suffocated. During the act of killing, no voice is to be heard.

[12] Either the sacrificer and his wife, or the two deities, Agnîṣomâu, to whom the sacrificial animal is devoted. Sây. says: another Sâkhâ has *Medha-pataye.* In the Kauṣîtaki Brâhmaṇam 10, 4, there is also the dual.

[13] This change in the formula is called *ûha*. See Sâyaṇa's Introduction to Ṛigveda, vol. i., p. 10, 11, ed. Müller.

They consented. Agni then walked before it, and it followed after Agni. Thence they say, every animal belongs to Agni, for it followed after him. Thence they carry before the animal fire (*Agni*).

Spread the (sacred) *grass*! The animal lives on herbs. He (the Hotar) thus provides the animal with its entire soul (the herbs being supposed to form part of it).

The mother, father, brother, sister, friend, and *companion should give this* (animal) *up* (for being slaughtered)! When these words are pronounced, they seize the animal which is (regarded as) entirely given up by its relations (parents, &c.).

Turn its feet northwards! Make its eye go to the sun, dismiss its breath to the wind, its life to the air, its hearing to the directions, its body to the earth. **[87]** In this way he (the Hotar) places it (connects it) with these worlds.

Take of the skin entire (without cutting it). *Before opening the navel, tear out the omentum! Stop its breathing within* (by stopping its mouth)! Thus he (the Hotar) puts its breath in the animals.

Make of its breast a piece like an eagle, of its arms (two pieces, like) *two hatchets, of its forearms* (two pieces, like) *two spikes, of its shoulders* (two pieces, like) *two kaśyapas,* [14] *its loins should be unbroken* (entire); (make of) *its thighs* (two pieces, like) *two shields, of the two kneepans* (two pieces, like) *two oleander leaves; take out its twenty-six ribs according to their order; preserve every limb of it in its integrity.* Thus he benefits all its limbs.

Dig a ditch in the earth to hide its excrements. The excrements consist of vegetable food; for the earth is the place for the herbs. Thus the Hotar puts them (the excrements) finally in their proper place.

7

Present the evil spirits with the blood! For the gods having deprived (once) the evil spirits of their share in the Haviryajñas (such as the Full-and New-moon offerings) apportioned to them the husks and smallest grains,[15] and after having them turned out of the great sacrifice (such as the Soma and animal sacrifices), presented to them the blood. Thence the Hotar pronounces the words: *present the evil spirits with the blood!* By giving them this share he **88** deprives the evil spirits

---

[14] Probably another name for *kûrma, i.e.,* tortoise. See Śatapathabrâhm. 7, 5, 1, 2.

[15] The priest having taken these parts, addresses them as follows: "Thou art the share of the evil spirits!" By these words he throws them below the black goat-skin (always required at the sacrifices.) So do the Apastambas.—*Sây.*

of any other share in the sacrifice.[16] They say : one should not address the evil spirits at the sacrifice, any evil spirits, whichever they might be (Râkṣas, Asuras, &c.); for the sacrifice is to be without the evil spirits (not to be disturbed by them). But others say : one should address them; for he who deprives any one, entitled to a share, of this share, will be punished (by him whom he deprives); and if he himself does not suffer the penalty, then his son, and if his son be spared, then his grandson, will suffer it, and thus he resents at him (the son or grandson) what he wanted to resent at you.

However, if the Hotar addresses them, he should do so with a low voice. For both, the low voice and the evil spirits, are, as it were, hidden. If he addresses them with a loud voice, then such a one speaks in the voice of the evil spirits, and is capable of producing Râkṣas-sounds (a horrible, terrific voice). The voice in which the haughty man and the drunkard speak, is that of the evil spirits (Râkṣas). He who has such a knowledge will neither himself become haughty, nor will such a man be among his offspring.

Do not cut[17] *the entrails which resemble an owl* (when taking out the omentum), *nor should among your children, O slaughterers! or among their* **[89]** *offspring, any one be found who might cut them.* By speaking these words, he presents these entrails to the slaughterers among the gods as well as to those among men.

The Hotar shall then say thrice : *O Adhṛigu* (and ye others), *kill* (the animal), *do it well* ; *kill it, O Adhṛigâu.* After the animal has been killed, (he should say thrice :) *Far may it*[18] (the consequences of murder) be (from us). For *Adhṛigu* among the gods is he who silences[19] (the animal) and the *Apâpa* (away, away !) is he who puts it down. By speak-

---

[16] According to the Âpastamba Sûtras, the priest takes the thick ends of the sacrificial grass in his left hand, besmears them with blood, and by the recital of the words, *rakṣasam bhâgo sî, i.e.,* "thou art the share of the evil spirits," he shakes it up and down, and pours it out from the middle of the bunch. See also the *Hiraṇyakeśi Srâuta* Sûtras, 4, 12.

[17] *Râviṣṭha* is here to be traced to the root *ru=lu*, to cut, *r* being put instead of *l*, just as we have here *urûka* instead of *ulûka*, an owl. Sâyaṇa explains : *lavanam kuruta. Ravitâ*, a cutter, and *ravat* conjunct., are traced by Sây. to the root *ru*, to roar ; but there is no reason to take the word here in another sense than *râviṣṭha* in the preceding sentence.

[18] *Apâpa.* This formula is evidently nothing but the repetition of the particle *apa*, away ! It was very early misunderstood, as we may see from the very explanation given of it by the author of our Brâhmaṇam ; for he takes it as *apâpah, i.e.,* guiltless, and makes it the name of one of the divine slaughterers.

[19] He is the proper *Śamitâ* or silencer.

ing those words, he surrenders the animal to those who silence it (by stopping its mouth), and to those who butcher it.

The Hotar then mutters (he makes *japa*) : " O slaughterers ! may all good you might do abide by us ! and all mischief you might do go elsewhere." The Hotar [20] gives by (this) speech the order (for killing the animal), for Agni had given the order for killing (the animal) with the same words when he was the Hotar of the gods.

By those words (the *japa* mentioned) the Hotar removes (all evil consequences) from those who suffocate the animal and those who butcher it, in all that they might transgress the rule by cutting one **[90]** piece too soon, the other too late, or by cutting a too large, or a too small piece. The Hotar, enjoying this happiness, clears himself (from all guilt), and attains the full length of his life (and it serves the sacrificer) for obtaining his full life. He who has such a knowledge, attains the full length of his life.

8.

(The Animals fit for being Sacrificed. The Offering of the Purodâśa, formingpart of the Animal Sacrifice.)

The gods killed a man for their sacrifice. But that part in him, which was fit for being made an offering, went out and entered a horse. Thence the horse became an animal fit for being sacrificed. The gods then dismissed that man after that part which was only fit for being offered had gone from him, whereupon he became deformed. [21]

The gods killed the horse ; but the part fit for being sacrificed (the *medha*) went out of it, and entered an ox ; thence the ox became an animal fit for being sacrificed. The gods then dismissed (this horse) after the sacrificial part had gone from it, whereupon it turned to a white deer.

The gods killed the ox ; but the part fit for being sacrificed went out of the ox, and entered a sheep ; thence the sheep became fit for being sacrificed. The gods then dismissed the ox which turned to a gayal (bos goaevus).

The gods killed the sheep ; but the part fit for being sacrificed went out of the sheep, and entered **[91]** a goat ; thence the goat became fit for

---

[20] The Hotar must recite at the sacrifice the whole formula, from " Ye divine slaughterers," &c. The whole of it, consisting of many so called *Prâiṣas* or orders ought properly to be repeated, by the Adhvaryu, who generally calls upon the different priests to do their respective duties. This exception to the rule is here explained by a reference to what Agni, the model Hotar, had once done when officiating at a sacrifice brought by the gods.

[21] In the original : *kimpuruṣa*. According to the original etymological meaning, the word signifies "a deformed or low man." In later mythology, the *kimpuruṣas* or *kinnaras* were attached to Kuvera, the god of treasures. They were regarded as musicians. But this meaning is certainly not applicable here. The author very likely means a dwarf.

being sacrificed. The gods dismissed the sheep, which turned to a camel.

The sacrificial part (the *medha*) remained for the longest time (longer than in the other animals) in the goat; thence is the goat among all these animals pre-eminently fit (for being sacrificed).

The gods killed the goat; but the part fit for being sacrificed went out of it, and entered the earth. Thence the earth is fit for being offered. The gods then dismissed the goat, which turned to a *Śarabha*.[22]

All those animals from which the sacrificial part had gone, are unfit for being sacrificed, thence one should not eat (their flesh).[23]

After the sacrificial part had entered the earth, the gods surrounded it (so that no escape was possible). It then turned to rice. When they (therefore) divide the Purodâśa into parts, after they have killed the animal, then they do it, wishing "might our animal sacrifice be performed with the sacrificial part (which is contained in the rice of the Purodâśa)! might our sacrificial part be provided with the whole sacrificial essence!" The sacrificial animal of him who has such a knowledge becomes then provided with the sacrificial part, with the whole sacrificial essence.

[92] (*The Relation of the Rice Cake Offering to that of Flesh. The Vapâ and Purodâśa Offerings*).

The Purodâśa (offered at the animal sacrifice) is the animal which is killed. The chaff and straw of the rice of which it consists are the hairs of the animal, its husks[24] the skin, its smallest particles the blood, all the fine particles to which the (cleaned) rice is ground (for making, by kneading it with water, a ball) represent the flesh (of the animal), and whatever other substantial part[25] is in the rice, are the bones (of the animal). He who offers the Purodâśa, offers the sacrificial substance of all animals (for the latter is contained in the rice of the Purodâśa). Thence they say: the performance of the Purodâśa offering is to be attended to.

---

[22] A fabulous animal, supposed to have eight legs, and to kill lions.

[23] That is to say: all beings who owe their origin to a loss of the sacrificial part in a higher species of the same class, such as the dwarf, the gayal, the camel, &c., are unfit to be used as food. Here is a hint given as to why certain animals are allowed and others prohibited to be eaten. We see from this passage clearly, that animal food was very extensively used in the Vedic times.

[24] The husks, *tuṣa*, fall off when the rice is beaten for the first time; the thinnest particles, which fall off, when the grains are completely made bare and white by conti nued beating, are called *phalîkaraṇas*.

[25] *Kiñchitkam sâram. Kiñchitaka* is an adjective of the indefinite pronoun Kiñchit, having, as Sây. remarks, the sense of "all."

Now he recites the Yâjyâ for the Vapâ (which is about to be offered): *yuvam etâni divi, i.e.* Ye, O Agni and Soma, have placed, by your joint labours, those lights on the sky ! ye, Agni and Soma, have liberated the rivers which had been taken (by demons), from imprecation and defilement. (Ṛigveda 1, 93, 5.)

The man who is initiated into the sacrificial mystery (the Dîkṣita) is seized by all the gods (as their property). Thence they say: he should not eat of a thing dedicated (to the gods).[26] But others say: he should eat when the Vapâ is offered; for the Hotar [93] liberates the sacrificer from the gods by (the last words of the mantra just mentioned): "Ye, Agni and Soma, have liberated the (rivers) which had been taken." Consequently, he becomes a sacrificer (a yajamâna), and ceases to belong as a Dîkṣita exclusively to the gods.[27]

Now follows the Yâjyâ verse for the Purodâśa (mentioned): *ânyam divo mâtariśvâ* (1, 93, 6), *i.e.*, Mâtariśvâ brought from heaven another (Soma),[28] and the eagle struck out another (Agni, fire) of the rock, &c. (On account of the meaning of the last words "and the eagle," &c., the verse is used as Yâjyâ for the Purodâśa offering.) For it expresses the idea, that the sacrificial essence had gone out and had been taken away (from man, horse, &c.), as it were, just as (Agni) had come out (of the rock).

With the verse: Taste (O Agni) the offerings, burn them well, &c., (3, 54, 22), the Hotar makes the *Sviṣṭakrit* of the *Purodâśa.* By this mantra the Hotar makes the sacrificer enjoy such an offering (to be granted by the gods in return for the gift), and acquires for himself food and milky essences.

He now calls the *Iḷâ* (and eats from the Purodâśa). For *Iḷâ* means cattle; (by doing so) he therefore calls cattle, and provides the sacrificer with them.

---

[26] The text offers some difficulties; it literally means: he should not eat of the Dîkṣita, which latter word can here not be taken in its usual sense, "one initiated into the sacrificial rites," but in that of a thing consecrated to the gods. Sây. gets over the difficulty by inserting the word *grihe* after *dîkṣitasya*, and understands it of a meal to be taken in the house of a sacrificer when the Vapâ offering is performed.

[27] As a Yajamâna, he is allowed to eat again.

[28] This refers to the legend of Soma being abstracted from heaven by the Gâyatrî, in the shape of an eagle, or by Mâtariśvâ, the Prometheus of the Vedic tradition. See Kuhn, *Die Herabkunft des Feuers und Göttertranks.* Ait. Br. 3, 25-27.

10.

(*The Offering of Parts of the Body of the Animal. The Manotâ*).

The Adhvaryu now says (to the Hotar) : recite the verses appropriate to[29] the offering of the [**94**] parts of the sacrificial animal which are cut off for the *Manotâ.*[30] He then repeats the hymn : Thou, O Agni, art the first Manotâ (6, 1). (This hymn being exclusively devoted to Agni), and the sacrificial animal belonging to another deity (besides Agni, *viz.*, Soma), they ask : Why does he recite verses, (exclusively) addressed to Agni, when the sacrificial parts (of the animal) intended for the *Manotâ* are being cut off ? (The answer is :) There are three *Manotâs* among the gods, in which all their thoughts are plotted and woven, *viz.*, *Vâch* (speech), *Gâus* (the cow), and *Agni*, in every one of whom the thoughts of the gods are plotted and woven ; but Agni is the complete *Manotâ* (the centre for all [**95**] thoughts) ; for in him all Manotâs are gathered. For this reason the priest repeats verses as *anuvâkyâs* addressed to Agni at that occaṣion. By the verse : "O Agni-Soma, eat the food which is waiting (for you) &c. (1, 93, 7)," he makes the Yâjyâ to the offering, This verse ensures, on account of the words "food" (*haviṣo*) and "waiting for you" (*prasthitasya*), success. For the offering of him who has such a know-

---

[29] After the Vapâ (omentum) and the Purodâśa, which forms part of the animal sacrifice have been thrown into the fire, the Adhvaryus offer different parts of the body of the slaughtered animal. Most of them are put in the *Juhû*—ladle, some in the Upabhṛit. For the Adhvaryu generally holds, when giving an oblation, two ladles, Juhû and Upabhṛit, in his hand, placing the first over the latter. The names of the parts of the body which are to be sacrificed, are differently stated in the Kâtîya (6, 7, 6-11) and Hiraṇyankeśi Sutras (4, 14), but they appear to mean always the same parts. They are : the heart, tongue, the breast, the two sides (with the ribs which are not to be broken), the liver (called *yakṛit* in Kat., and *taniman* in the Hiraṇyankeśi and Bâudhâyana Sutras), the two reins (*vakkâu* in the K., *atasnû* in the H. and B. Sutras), the left shoulder blade (*savyam dos* in H. and B., *savyasakthîpûr-vanadakam* in K.), the right part of the loins, the middle part of the anus. These are put in the Juhû. The remainder, the right shoulder blade, the third part of the anus which is very small, and the left part of the loins are put in the Upabhṛit. Besides the penis (*varṣiṣṭha*), the straight gut (*vaniṣṭha*), and the tail are cut off for being sacrificed. If the parts to be given with the Juhû and Upabhṛit are fried and dripped over with melted butter, then is the Hotar ordered to repeat the Anuvâkyâ mantra by the words : *manotâyâi haviṣo avadîyamanasya anubrûhi*, *i.e.*, "repeat a mantra to the offering, which has been cut off for the Manotâ." This offering which is called the *angayâga*, is given to the Manotâ, the weaver of thoughts, who is said to be Agni.

[30] The word is explained by Sâyaṇa as a compound of *man* and *otâ*, which means, literally, the "weaving of thoughts," that is, the seat of intelligence. Here it is used as a feminine ; but in the hymn referred to, it is evidently a masculine : *prathamô manotâ*, "the first weaver of thoughts," which means about the same as "the first poet or priest," another denomination of Agni.

ledge ensures success and goes to the gods (only) by means of all parts of a particular ceremony being well performed.[31]

He gives an offering to Vanaspati[32] (the vegetable [96] kingdom). Vanaspati is the vital air; therefore, the offering of him who, knowing this, sacrifices to Vanaspati, goes endowed with life to the gods.

He gives an offering to the *Sviṣṭakṛit.*[33] The Sviṣṭakṛit is the footing on which he finally places the sacrificer.

---

[31] The verses should be always in accordance with the sacrificial act.

[32] The offering of melted butter to Vanaspati (in form of the Yûpa) takes place immediately after the so-called *vasâhoma*, or the offering of the water in which entrails (heart, &c.) of the slaughtered animal have been fried. In the Apastamba Sûtras, the performance is thus described as Sây. mentions. The Adhvaryu puts a plant on the *Juhû* (large ladle), takes once liquid âjyâ (melted butter), drips it twice about it (the plant), and says to the Hotar: address Vanaspati. He then first repeats an Anuvâkyâ: *devebhyo vanaspataye.* I give here the text of this mantra, which I found in its entirety only in the Sapta-hâutra prayoga.

देवेभ्यो वनस्पत हवींषि हिरण्यपर्ण प्रदिवस्ते अर्थम् । प्रदक्षिणिद्रशनया वियूय ऋतस्य वक्षि पथिभी रजिष्ठोम् ॥

i. e., Mayst thou, O tree (the Yûpa), with golden leaves of old, who art quite straight after having been freed from the bonds (with which thou wert tied), carry up, on the paths of right, turning towards the south, the offerings for thy own sake to the gods! (The "bonds" refer to the cord with which the animal was tied to the Yûpa; they are to be taken off. The golden leaves refer to the decoration of the Yûpa with ribands. "For thy own sake;" this offering belongs to himself.)

After the Hotar has repeated this Anuvâkyâ, the Maitrâvaruṇa then gives the *praiṣa* (orders) to repeat the Yâjyâ mantra by the words: होता यक्षद्वनस्पतिं, &c. (See the mantra in full in the Vâjasaneya-Saṁh. 21, 46, with some deviations.)

The Hotar thereupon repeats the Yâjyâ mantra, which runs as follows:

ये ३ यजामहे । वनस्पते रशनया नियूय पिष्टतमया वयुननानि विद्वान् ॥ वह देवत्रा दिधिषो हवींषि प्रचदातारममृतेषु वोचा । वौषट् ॥

O tree! after having been loosened from the nicely decorated cord, thou, who art experienced in wisdom and knowledge, carry up to the gods the offerings, and proclaim to the immortals the (name of the) giver!

[33] After the oblation to Vanaspati follows that to Agni Sviṣṭakṛit, including all the deities of the animal sacrifice, *viz.*, *Agni*, *Soma*, *Agni-Somâu*, *Indrâgnî*, *Aśvinâu' Vanaspati*, *Devâ âjyapâ* (deities which drink melted butter). The Anuvâkyâ of the Sviṣṭakṛit oblation is at the animal sacrifice the same as at other Iṣṭis, *viz*: पिप्रीहि देवानुशतो (Rigveda 10, 1, 2, Âśv. Śr. S. 1, 6). Then follows the *praiṣa* by the Maitrâvaruṇa, where the names of all the deities of the Iṣṭi (as given above) are mentioned. It runs as follows:

होता यक्षदग्निं स्विष्टकृतमयाळ् अग्निरग्नेराज्यस्य हविषः प्रिया धामान्ययाट् सोमस्याज्यस्य हविषः प्रिया धामान्ययाळग्नीषोमयोश्छागस्य हविषः प्रिया धामान्ययालिंद्राग्न्योश्छागस्य हविषः प्रिया धामान्यया अश्विनोश्छागस्य हविषः प्रिया धामान्ययाड्वनस्पतेः प्रिया पाथांस्ययाट् देवानामाज्यपानां प्रिया धामानि यक्षदग्नेर्होतुः प्रिया धामानि यक्षत्स्वं महिमानमायजतामेज्या इषः कृणोतु सो अध्वरा जातवेदा जुषतां हविर्होतर्यज Sapta Hâutra (compare Vâjasaneya S. 21, 47. On the form of the Sviṣṭakṛit, see Âśv. Śr. S. 1, 6), The Yâjyâ mantra is: अग्ने यदद्य (4, 15, 14). which is preceded by

He calles Iḷa.[34] The cattle are Iḷâ. By calling her, he calls cattle and provides the sacrificer with them.

---

[97] SECOND CHAPTER.

(The Remaining Rites of the Animal Sacrificè. The Prâtar-anuvâka).

11.

(Why fire is carried round the sacrificial animal.)

The Devas spread the sacrifice. When doing so, the Asuras attacked them, intending to put an obstacle in their way (to prevent the successful performance of the sacrifice). The attack was made against the sacrificial post from the eastern direction, after the animal had been consecrated by the Aprî verses (see 2, 4), and before the fire was carried round the animal. The Devas awoke, and surrounded, for their own protection, as well as for that of the sacrifice (the place) with a three-fold wall resembling fire. The Asuras seeing those walls shining and blazing, did not venture an attack, but ran away. Thus the Devas defeated the Asuras on the eastern side as well as on the western. For this reason the sacrificers perform the rite of carrying fire round (the animal, when consecrated), and have a mantra recited; for they thus surround (the animal) with a three-fold wall, shining like fire, for their own protection and that of the sacrifice.

After the animal is consecrated, and fire carried around it, they take it northwards. They carry before it a firebrand, meaning thereby that the animal is ultimately the sacrificer himself; they believe that he will go to heaven, having that light (the firebrand) [98] carried before him. And in this way he really goes to heaven.

The Adhvaryu throws sacred grass (*barhis*) on the spot where they are to kill the animal. When they carry it outside the Vedi, after having consecrated and carried fire round it, they make it sit on the sacred grass (barhis).

---

the *âgur* : ये ३ यजामहे, and followed by the Vaṣaṭkâra. One of the rules laid down for the Sviṣṭakṛit mantras and the respective *praiṣas*, as far as they are not taken from the Saṁhitâ of Rigveda, is, that all the deities of the Iṣṭi must be mentioned along with the expression : प्रिया धामानि, *i.e.*, beloved residence; the name of the deity always precedes it in the genitive.

[34] After the Sviṣṭakṛit is over, the remainder of the offerings, which are at the animal sacrifice, flesh is eaten by thé priests and the sacrificer. The Iḍâpâtra in which the dish is placed is held up and Ilâ, the personification of food, called to appear. This "calling," of Ilâ is always the same. The formula is given in the Âśval. Śr. Sûtras I, 7 : इळोपहूता सह दिवा०

1 Agnîdhra is performing this rite. See 2, 5.

They dig a ditch for its excrements. The excrements consist of herbs; the earth is the proper place for herbs; thus he puts them at the end in their proper place (by throwing them into a ditch, dug in the earth).

They say: when the animal is the offering, then many parts (of this offering) go off (are not used), such as hairs, skin, blood, half-digested food, hoofs, the two horns, some pieces of flesh which fall to the ground. (Such being the case) in what way then is the deficiency made up? The answer is: if they sacrifice Purodâśa, divided into its proper parts along with the animal, then the animal sacrifice is made complete. When the sacrificial essence had gone from the animals, both rice and barley sprang out of it. When they offer Purodâśa, divided into its proper parts along with the animal, then they should think, "our animal was sacrificed with the sacrificial essence in it; our animal has been sacrificed in its entirety." The animal of him who has this knowledge is sacrificed in its entirety.

12.

(The Offering of the Drops which fall from the Omentum).

After the Vapâ (omentum) has been torn out (of the belly), they bring it (to the fire for being fried). The Adhvaryu causes to drip out of a Sruva drops of hot melted butter. When the drops are falling **[99]** (to the ground), the Adhvaryu orders the Hotar to recite the mantra appropriate to the drops (falling down). For the drops belong to all deities. He might think, they are not mine. (I, the priest, have nothing to do with them); they may, therefore, uninvited go to the gods; (but he ought to repeat mantras for them).

He repeats the Anuvâkyâ (for the drops:) "Be favourable to our loud voice (to be heard at a distance) which is agreeable to the gods, when swallowing our offerings with thy mouth! (1, 75, 1.)" By this mantra he throws the drops into the mouth of Agni. He further repeats the hymn: "Bring this our sacrifice among the gods" (3, 21). By the words (of the second pada of the first verse:) "be favourable to our offerings, O Jâtavedas!" he begs for the acceptance of the offerings. In the words (in the third pada of the first verse:) "eat, O Agni, the drops of the marrow [2] (and the) melted butter," the drops of the marrow and the melted butter are mentioned. The words (of the fourth pada of the first verse:) "eat, O Hotar, having first taken thy seat!" mean: Agni (for he is the Hotar of the gods) eat, after having taken, &c.

(In the first half of the second verse:) "the drops of melted butter drip for thee, O purifier, from the marrow," the drops both of the melted

2 By *medas*, Sây. understands the Vapâ, which is ceatainly the right explanation

butter and the marrow are mentioned. (By the second half:) "grant us the best things which are desirable, for worshipping (thee) in the proper way," he pronounces a blessing.

(In the first half of the third verse:) "O! Agni! these drops are dripping melted butter for thee, the wise, who art to be worshipped with gifts," the drops (of marrow) are described as "dripping melted butter." **[100]** (By the second half:) "thou, the best Riṣi art kindled; be a carrier of the sacrifice!" he (the priest) orders the sacrifice to be successful.

(In the first half of the fourth verse:) "to thee, O Adhṛigu! drip the drops of marrow and melted butter, O Agni! thou strong one!" the drops both, of the marrow and melted butter, are mentioned. (By the second half:) "mayst thou, praised by poets, come (to us) with thy brightly shining flame! kindly accept our offerings, O wise!" the priest asks the acceptance of the offerings.

(After the recital of the fifth verses:) "we offer to thee the most juicy marrow (the Vapâ), taken out of the midst (of the belly); these drops (of melted butter) drip on this thin skin [3] (the Vapâ), carry them severally up to the gods!" the priest pronounces the formula *Vâuṣaṭ*! for the drops (and thus concludes the offering of the drops).

He then repeats the same formula (the Anuvaṣaṭkâra as is sacrificing the Soma), O Agni, enjoy the Soma! (using instead of "Soma" the word "drops.") These drops belong to all the gods. Thence the rain falls, divided in drops, down upon the earth.

13.

(*On the Svâhâkṛitiṣ and the Offering of the Vapâ*).

They ask: which are the Puronuvâkyâs, the Praiṣas and the Yâjyâs for the call: Svâhâ [4]? (The **[101]** answer is:) The Puronuvâkyâs

[3] From this passage it is clear that by *medas* in the whole of this hymn, the *Vapâ* or omentum is to be understood; for it is called here *tvach, i.e.*, skin, which (although it is very thin) it resembles.

[4] The author of the Brâhm. alludes here to a practice which appears to be contrary to the general rules established regarding the offering of oblations. To make it clear, I here extract the passage concerning it from the Manual, used by the seven Hotṛi priests (called *Sapta hautra*). On pp. 22, 23 of my manuscript is said, that the Hotar, after having repeated the hymn addressed to the drops dripping from the Vapâ, is requested by the Maitrâvaruṇa (who then gives the *praiṣa, i.e.*, order) to make the Svâhâs (*svâhâkṛitis, i.e.*, the pronunciation of the formula: svâhâ! of the *âjyâ*, the *medas* (Vapâ) of the drops dripping from the Vapâ, of the *Svâhâkṛitis* in general, and of the verses which are addressed to the oblations in the hymn mentioned (*imam no yajnam*, 3, 21, see above). This order the Maitrâvaruṇa concludes by the words: "Svâhâ! the gods pleased with the Âjyâ may first taste the Âjyâ! Hotar, repeat the Yâjyâ!" Thereupon the Maitrâvaruṇa repeats a Puronuvâkyâ for the offering of two portions of Âjya. Then the Maitrâvaruṇa orders the Hotar to recite two Yâjyâs, one for Agni, the other for Soma,

are just the same as those recited (for the drops), the Praiṣas and the Yâjyâs are also the same. They further ask: which are the deities for these Svâhâkṛitis? (To this) one should answer, the *Viśve devâh*; for there are (at the end) of the Yâjyâ the words, "may the gods eat the oblation over which Svâhâ! is spoken."

The gods conquered by means of the sacrifice, austerities, penances, and sacrificial oblations the heavenly world. After the Vapâ had been offered, the heavenly world became apparent to them. Regardless of all the other rites, they went up to heaven by means of the oblation of the Vapâ (alone). Thereupon Men and Riṣis went to the sacrificial place of the gods (to see) [**102**] whether they might not obtain something worth knowing. Having gone round about and searched all the place, they found nothing but a disembowelled animal lying there. Thence they learnt that verily the value of the animal (for sacrifices) consists only in its Vapâ, which part is just as much as the whole animal.

When they, at the third libation, fry the remaining portions (all save the Vapâ) of the animal and offer them, then they do so, wishing, "may our sacrifice be performed with many many oblations! may our sacrifice be performed with the entire animal!"

14.

The oblation of the Vapâ is just like an oblation of ambrosia; such oblations of ambrosia are (besides) the throwing of the fire [a] (produced by the friction of wooden sticks) into the sacrificial hearth, the oblation of Âjyâ and that of Soma. All these oblations are without an (apparent) body (they disappear at once when thrown into the fire). With such bodiless oblations the sacrificer conquers the heavenly world. The Vapâ is just like sperm; for just as the sperm (when effused) is lost (in the womb), the Vapâ is lost (disappears in the fire on account of its thinness). Further, the Vapâ is white like sperm, and, without a substantial body, just as

---

in order to induce these deities to accept the offering given after the recital of the Yâjyâ. After having repeated them, he is ordered to repeat the Yâjyâ for the medas (Vapâ), addressing *Agniṣomâu*.

Now the deviation from the general adopted rules of the sacrificial practice is, the formula Svâhâ is here several times used without having a proper Anuvâkyâ and Yâjyâ. To this practice some performers of sacrifices had raised some objections. But the author of our Brâhm. defends the practice, asserting that the Puronuvâkyâs required for the Svâhâkṛitis are included in those mentioned for the drops (p. 99), their *praiṣa* is contained in the general *praiṣa*, in the words: *hotar agnim yakṣat*, may the Hotar recite the Yâjyâ for Agni! &c., which formula the different Svâhâs follow, one of which is, *Svâhâ svâhâkṛitinâm* (see above); and their Yâjyâ comprised in the general Yâjyâ, which is according to the Âśvalây. Sutr. 3, 4, the last verse of the *Apriśûktâ*.

[a] See Ait. Br. 1, 15.

sperm. Blood and flesh making up the substance of the hody, the Hotar therefore should say (to the Adhvaryu): cut off all that has no blood.

The Vapâ oblation must consist of five parts, even if there are only four parts (all except the gold plate) at the sacrificer's disposal. The priest first puts melted **[103]** butter for the Vapâ in the ladle, then follows a thin gold plate, the Vapâ, the melted butter for the gold plate, and (lastly) the dripping of melted butter (on the whole).

They ask: if there is no gold to be had, what should he do then? (The answer is:) he should first put twice melted butter in the ladle, then the Vapâ, and drip twice hot melted butter on it. The melted butter is ambrosia, the gold is also ambrosia. Therefore everything wished for (by the sacrificer) when throwing the melted butter and the gold (into the ladle), is attainable. Together with the melted butter (to be taken twice), and the gold, the Vapâ oblation consists of five parts.[7]

Man is composed of five parts, *viz.* hairs, skin, flesh, bones, and marrow. The priest having (by the Vapâ oblation) made (the sacrificer) just such a man (composed of five parts), offers him in Agni, who is the womb of the gods. For Agni is the womb of the gods; after having grown together in Agni's womb with the (different other) oblations, he then goes up to heaven with a golden body.

15.

(*On the Repetition of the Prâtar-anuvâka, or Early Morning Prayer, on the Day of the Soma Libation.*)

The Adhvaryu orders the Hotar to repeat the mantras appropriate for the gods who appear in the early morning. These gods are Agni, Uṣâs (dawn), and the Aśvins (twilight); they come, if each of them is addressed in mantras of seven different **[104]** metres.[8] They come on the call of him who has such knowledge.

As Prajâpati, when he himself was (once) Hotar, was just about to repeat the Prâtar-anuvâka, in the presence of both the Devas and Asuras, he first thought, he will repeat the Prâtar-anuvâka for our benefit; the latter believed, he will do so for us. He then repeated it for the Devas. Thence the Devas became masters of the Asuras. He who has such a knowledge becomes master of his enemy, adversary, and

---

[6] The technical term for this proceeding is *upa-staraṇam.*

[7] The two others are the Vapâ itself and the hot melted butter dripped on it.

[8] To each of these three deities are mantras in the following seven metres addressed: *Gâyatrî, Anuṣṭup, Triṣṭup, Bṛhati, Uṣṇih, Jagatî* and *Paṅkti.*

gainsayer. It is called Prâtar-anuvâka (morning prayer); for Prajâpati prayed it early in the morning. It is to be repeated in the dead of night.[9] For people follow in their sayings him, who possesses the whole speech, and the full Brahma, and who has obtained the leadership.[10]

Therefore, the Prâtar-anuvâka is to be repeated in the dead of night: for it must be repeated before people commence talking. Should he, however, repeat the Prâtar-anuvâka after people have commenced talking, he would make the Prâtar-anuvâka (which should be the *first* speech uttered in the morning) follow the speech of another. (Such being contrary to its nature) it must be repeated in the dead of night. He should repeat it even before the voice of the cock is heard.[11] For all the birds, including the cock, are the [105] mouth (the very end) of the goddess *Nirriti* (destruction, death.) If he thus repeats the Prâtar-anuvâka before the voice of the cock is heard, (he should do so considering) that we cannot utter the sacred words required at a sacrifice, should others already (animals or men) have made their voices heard. Thence (to avoid this) the Prâtar-anuvâka should be repeated in the dead of night. Then verily the Adhvaryu should begin his ceremonies[12] (by calling on the Hotar to repeat the Prâtar-anuvâka), and the Hotar then should repeat it. When the Adhvaryu begins his work (by ordering the Hotar to repeat), he begins with Speech, and the Hotar repeats (the Prâtar-anuvâka) through Speech. Speech is Brahma. Thus every wish which might be attainable either by Speech or Brahma[13] is attained.

16.

Prajâpati being just about to repeat the Prâtar-anuvâka, when he was himself Hotar (at his own sacrifice), all the gods were in a state of anxious expectation, as to who of them would be first mentioned. Prajâpati looked about (and, seeing the state of anxiety in which the gods were, thought), if I commence by addressing (the mantra) to one deity only,

---

[9] This appears to be the meaning of: *mahatî râtryâḥ*. Sây. explains it rather artificially "as the great portion of the night following the day on which the animal sacrifice for *Agnîṣomîya* had been performed.

[10] The author alludes here to the relation of subjects to the king, and of pupils to their teacher.

[11] By *śakuni* only the cock is to be understood. The original form being *kakuni*, we are reminded of the very word "cock." Great importance is attached to this bird in the Zend-Avesta, where it is named *paro-dars*.

[12] The term used is, *upâkaroti*.

[13] Sây. understands here by *speech* the worldly common talk, by *Brahma* the sacred speech, the repetition of the mantras.

how will the other deities have a share (in such an invocation)? He then saw (with his mental eyes) the verse: *âpô revatîr*, *i.e.*, the wealthy waters (10, 30, 12). *Âpo*, *i.e.* waters, means all deities, and *revatîḥ* (rich) means also all deities. He thus commenced the Prâtar-anuvâka by this verse, at which all the gods felt joy: (for each of them thought), he first has mentioned *me*; they all then felt [**106**] joy when he was repeating the Prâtar-anuvâka. He who has such a knowledge (*i.e.*, who commences his Prâtar-anuvâka by the same verse), commences his Prâtar-anuvâka with a joint address to all the gods.

The Devas were afraid of the Asuras robbing them of their early morning sacrifice (the Prâtar-anuvâka), for they (the Asuras) were so very strong and powerful. But Indra said to them: "Do not be afraid! I shall strike them with the three-fold power of my morning thunderbolt." He then repeated the verse mentioned (10, 30, 12). This verse is in three respects a thunderbolt, *viz.*, it contains "the destroying waters"[14] (*apô naptryô*), it is in the Trisṭubh (Indra's metre, and it contains "speech"[15] (it is recited with a loud voice). With this thunderbolt he struck and destroyed them. Thence the Devas became masters of the Asuras. He who has such a knowledge, becomes master of his enemy, adversary, and gainsayer.

They say: he should be the Hotar who produces in this verse (when reciting it) the number containing all metres. This is the case, if it be repeated thrice. This is the production of the metres.

17.

He who wishes for long life, should repeat a hundred verses. For the (full) life of man is a hundred (years); he has (besides) a hundred powers, and a hundred senses.[16] (By repeating one hundred verses) [**107**], the priest secures to the sacrificer his full age, his (mental and bodily) powers, and his senses.

He who wishes for (performing successfully the subsequent great) sacrifices, should repeat 360 verses. For the year consists of 360 days; such a year (is meant here). The year is Prajâpati. Prajâpati is the sacrifice. The intelligent Hotar who recites 360 verses, turns (in this way) the sacrifice (regarded as a divine being, the mediator between gods and men) towards the sacrificer.

---

[14] In the Anukramaṇikâ, the deity of the song in which this verse occurs, is called *Apo naptryaḥ*.

[15] *Vâch* has the power of destroying, under certain circumstances, the sacrificer.

[16] According to Sây, the number of "a hundred" for the senses is to be obtained, if the senses are stated at ten, and if to each of them ten tubular vessels, in which they move, are ascribed.

He who wishes for children and cattle, should repeat 720 verses. For so many days and nights make a year (one of 360 days). Prajâpati is the year. For, after he is produced (*prâjayamâna*), the whole universe is produced (*prajâyate*).[17] He who has such a knowledge, obtains, if being born after Prajâpati (by means of the sacrifice), children and cattle.

If any one who is not recognized as a Brahman, or one who has a bad reputation on account of being charged with crimes, should bring a sacrifice, then 800 verses should be repeated. The Gâyatrî consists of eight syllables (three times eight). The gods being of the nature of the Gâyatrî, removed the evil consequences of sin and crime. He who has such a knowledge, removes the evil consequences of sin and crime from himself by means of the Gâyatrî.

He who wishes for heaven, should repeat a thousand verses. For the heavenly world is at a distance of about 1,000 days' travelling on horseback from here (this earth). (To repeat a thousand verses, is done) for reaching the heavenly world everywhere. (He who then wishes) for acquisition of things to be enjoyed, and of communion (with the gods), should recite an unlimited number (of verses). For Prajâpati is **[108]** boundless. To Prajâpati belongs the recitation which makes up the Prâtar-anuvâka. Therein are all desires contained. When he repeats an unlimited number (it is done) to obtain fulfilment of all desires. He who has such a knowledge, obtains fulfilment of all wishes.

Thence one should repeat an unlimited[18] number (of verses). He repeats verses of seven (kinds of) metres for Agni; for there are seven worlds of the gods. He who has such a knowledge becomes successful in all of them. He repeats verses of seven (kinds of metres) for Uṣas; for there are seven (kinds of) cattle[19] in villages. He who has such a knowledge, obtains these seven (kinds of) cattle in the villages.

He repeats seven (kinds of verses) for the Aśvins; for Speech spoke in seven (different tones). In as many tones (*i.e.*, seven) then spoke Speech (in all made men). (These seven tones are made) for comprising the whole speech (the worldly talk and singing), the whole Brahma. He repeats verses for three deities; for three worlds are three-fold. (This repetition therefore serves) for conquering (all) these worlds of the gods.

---

[17] He is the creator.

[18] As many as a Hotar can repeat from after midnight to sunrise.

[19] Such as goats, sheep, cows, horses, asses, camels, &c. As the seventh kind, Apastamba counts man.

18.

They ask : how should the Prâtar-anuvâka be repeated? It is to be repeated[20] according to the metres (verses of the same metre to be put together). The metres are the limbs of Prajâpati. He who brings the sacrifice is Prajâpati. For the benefit of the sacrificer, the several verses of the Prâtar-anuvâka are to be recited pada (foot) by pada.[21] For cattle **[109]** have four feet, (if he do so) he obtains cattle. He should repeat it by half verses. When he repeats it in this way, (then he does so for securing) a footing (to the sacrificer). Man has two legs, and animals have four. He thus places the two-legged sacrificer among the four-legged animals.[22] Thence he should repeat the Prâtar-anuvâka only by half verses.

They ask : the (metres of the) Prâtar-anuvâka being developed,[23] how do they become then undeveloped? The answer should be : if the Bṛihatî metre is not moved from its centre.

Some deities have a share in the invocation offerings, others in the Stomas (the chants of the Sâma singers), others in the metrical verses) (*chhandas*) repeated (by the Hotar). By means of the invocation offerings (*âhutis*), one makes pleased those deities who have a share in these offerings, and, by means of the chants and recitations, those also who have their shares in the Stomas and metres. He who has such a knowledge, makes pleased and well-disposed both parties of deities (those who have their share in the invocation offerings, and those who have theirs in the Stomas and metres).

[110] There are thirty-three gods who drink Soma and thirty-three who do not drink Soma.

The Soma-drinking gods are : eight Vasus, eleven Rudras, twelve

---

[20] That is to say : he should take together all the verses in the Gâyatrî, or in the Triṣṭubh or other metres, without mixing them.

[21] There are in most cases four.

[22] The four feet of animals are indicated by the division of each verse into four padas, and the two legs of the sacrificer by the stopping of the voice after the repetition of each half verse.

[23] Âśv. Sr. Sûtr. 4, 13. The regular order of metres which commences by Gâyatrî and goes on by Uṣṇih, Anuṣṭubh, &c., based on the increase by four syllables of each subsequent metre, is not kept in the Prâtar-anuvâka. Uṣṇih is here not second, but fifth ; Anuṣṭubh is second. The expression *vyûlha* means, one metre being produced by an increase of the number of syllables out of the preceding metre. This increase in the Prâtar-anuvâka goes as far as the fourth mentre, the Bṛihatî, which is the centre ; then the turn from the lower number to the higher commences again. The first turn is Gâyatrî, Anuṣṭubh, Triṣṭubh, and Bṛihatî ; the second Uṣṇih, Jagatî, and Paṅkti. There being after the Bṛihatî a return to lower numbers, the development is stopped : thence the Prâtar-anuvâka is *avyûlha* also.

Âdityas, Prajâpati and Vaṣaṭ-kâra. The not-Soma-drinking gods are: eleven Prayâjas,[24] eleven Anuyâjas,[25] and eleven Upayâjas.[26] They [111] have their share in the sacrificial animal. With Soma, he pleases the Soma-drinking deities; with the animal, those who do not drink Soma. Thus, he who has such a knowledge, makes both parties pleased and well-disposed.

---

[24] These are the eleven verses of the Aprî hymns, see 2, 4.

[25] At the animal sacrifice, there are eleven Anuyâjas required. This is briefly stated in Âśv. Śr. Sûtras 4, 6, where, however, in addition to those occurring at a previous sacrifice (Châturmâsya Iṣṭi), only two are mentioned; and on reference to the rules on the Châturmâsya Iṣṭi (2, 16), we find also, in addition to three which are supposed to be already known, only six mentioned. The three primitive ones are then to be found in the rules on the Darśa pûrnima-iṣṭis (1, 8). The formula is for all Anuyâjas the same. First comes the name of the respective deity in the nominative, then follow the words: *vasuvane vasudheyasya vetû* (or *vîtâm*, or *vyantû*). The first Anuyâja, which is addressed to the *barhis*, or sacrificial seat, runs for instance, as follows: देवं बर्हिर्वसुवने वसुधेयस्य वेतु *i. e.* "may the divine sacrificial seat, O giver of wealth (Agni)! taste of the wealth (food) which is to be put by." The latter expression refers to the remainder of the sacrificial food which had been eaten by the priests and the sacrificer just before the offering of the Anuyâjas. The gods are to have a share in the food already eaten. Food is regarded as the wealth to be put by; for it serves for the acquisition of vigour and strength. The term *vasu* is frequently used with reference to food at the time of eating the remainder of the sacrifice. See 2, 27. The order of the Anuyâjaḥ deities at the animal sacrifice is the following: (1) *devîr dvâraḥ* (the gates), (2) *uṣâsâ-naktâ* (dawn and night), (3) *devî joṣṭrî* (satiation), (4) *ûrj* and *âhuti* (vigour and oblation), (5) *daivyâ hotârâ* (the two divine Hotars, *i.e.*, the fire on earth and that in the sky), (6) *tisro devîr* (the three deities: *Ilâ, Sarasvatî*, and *Bhâratî*, see 2, 5), (7) *barhis*, (8) *narâśamsa* (see 2, 5), (9) *vanaspati*, (10) *barhir vâritînâm* (the stalks of kuśa grass, thrown in water jars, (11) *Agni Sviṣṭakṛit*.

[26] The *Upayâjas*, or supplementary offerings, accompany the Anuyâjas. At the same time that the Hotar is repeating the Anuyâja mantras, and the Adhvaryu is throwing at the end of each an oblation into the fire, the Pratiprasthâtar, who is the constant assistant of the Adhvaryu, offers eleven pieces of the guts of the slaughtered animal, and accompanies his offerings with eleven Yajusmantras (see them in the Vâjasaneya Saṁhitâ 6, 21, and Taittriîya Saṁh. 1, 3, 11). All conclude with: *svâhâ*. On comparing their text in the Vâjasaneya S., with that in the Taittirîya S., we find some differences in the order of these mantras. The deities are the same. They are according to the Taitt. S. the following ones: (1) Ocean, (2) Air, (3) Savitar, (4) Day and Night, (5) Mitrâvaruṇa, (6) Soma, (7) the Sacrifice, (8) the Metres, (9) Heaven and Earth, (10) the Divine Clouds (*nabhas*, invoked for giving rain according to Sâyaṇa's commentary on the Taitt. S. vol. i. p. 550, ed. Cowell), (11) Agni Vaiśvânara. The Hotar has nothing to do with the Upayâjas. All is performed by the Pratiprasthâtar. We find the whole ceremony minutely described in the Hiraṇyakeśi-Śrauta-Sûtras (4, 16, 17). The charcoals for kindling the fire for these offerings are taken from the fire which is on the place where the animal is slaughtered. These charcoals are (as I am orally informed) put on the so-called Dhiṣṇya, or small fire-place behind which the Hotar is sitting, and which is between the Agnîdhra and Mârjâli fires. On the same place the tail of the animal, the principal part of which belongs to the "wives of gods," is sacrificed.

He concludes with the verse: *abhûd uṣâ ruśatpâśur* (5, 75, 9), *i.e.*, aurora appeared with the roaring cattle.

They ask: if he repeats three liturgies (*kratus*)[27] addressed to Agni, Uṣâs, and the Aśvins, how can his concluding (the whole liturgy) with one verse only be accounted for? (The answer is:) all three deities are contained (in this verse). (The first pada:) "aurora appeared with the roaring cattle," is appropriate to Uṣâs. (The second pada:) "Agni is put in at the proper time," belongs to Agni. (The second half verse:) "O, ye mighty (brothers!), your immortal carriage is yoked, hear my sweet voice!" belongs to the Aśvins. When he thus concludes with (this) one verse, then all three liturgies have their place in it.

---

[112] THIRD CHAPTER.

(*The Apo Naptrîyam Ceremony. The Upâṁśu and Antaryâma Oblations. The Hotar has no share in the Bahiṣpavamâna Meal. The Libation for Mitrâ-Varuṇa to be mixed with milk. On the Purodâśas belonging to the Libations. Haviṣpaṅkti. Akṣara-paṅkti. Narâśaṁsa-paṅkti. Savana-paṅkti*).

19.

(*Story of the Śûdra Riṣi Kavaṣa*[1]).

The Riṣis, when once holding a sacrificial session on (the banks of) the Sarasvatî, expelled Kavaṣa, the **(113)** son of Ilûṣa, from (their) Soma

---

[27] This term denotes the parts of the Prâtar-anuvâka which introduces the Soma sacrifice.

[1] In the Kauṣîtakî Brâhmaṇam (12, 3), the story of Kavaṣa is reported in the following way:—

माध्यमाः सरस्वत्यां सत्रमासत तद्धापि कवषो मध्ये निषसाद । तं हेम उपोदुर्दास्या वै त्वं पुत्रोऽसि न वयं त्वया सह भक्षयिष्याम इति स ह क्रुद्धः प्रद्रवन्त्सरस्वतीमेतेन सूक्तेन तुष्टाव । तं हेयमन्वेयाय त उ हेमे निरागा इव मेनिरे तं हान्वावृत्योचुर्ऋषे नमस्ते अस्तु मा नो हिंसीस्त्वं वै नः श्रेष्ठोऽसि यं त्वेयमन्वेतीति । तं ह यज्ञपयांचक्रुस्तस्य ह क्रोधं विनिन्युः । स एष कवषस्यैष महिमा सूक्तस्य चानुवेदिता ॥

i.e., the Riṣis, called the "middle ones" (Gṛitsamada, Viśvâmitra, Vâmadeva, Atri, Bharadvâja, Vaśiṣṭha, see Âśv. Gṛihya Sûtras, 3, 4), held once a sacrificial session on the Sarasvatî. Amongst them there sat Kavaṣa. These (Riṣis) reproached him (that he had come among them) saying: "Thou art the son of a slave girl, we shall neither eat nor drink with thee." Having become angry, he ran to the Sarasvatî, and obtained her favour by means of this hymn (*pra devatrâ brahmaṇe*). She followed him. These Riṣis then thought that he was guiltless. Turning to him, they said, "Riṣi! adoration be to thee, do us no harm! thou art the most excellent among us, for she (Sarasvatî) follows thee." They made him the manager of the sacrifice, and thus appeased his wrath. This is the importance of Kavaṣa, and he it was who made that hymn known.

The occasion on which Kavaṣa had this hymn revealed to him, is thus related in the Kauṣîtakî Brâhm. (12, 1):

sacrifice (saying): How should the son of a slave-girl, a gamester, who is no Brahman, remain among us and become initiated (into all sacrificial rites)? They turned him out (of the place) into a desert, saying, that he should die by thirst, and not drink the water of the Sarasvatî. After having been driven (from this place), into a desert, he, being vexed by thirst, saw (the mantra called) Apo naptrîyam: *pra devatrâ brahmaṇe gâtur etu*, &c., *i.e.*, may there be a way leading to the gods for the Brahman (may he be received among them). By this means he obtained the favour of the waters. They went out (of their house) to (meet) him. Sarasvatî surrounded him on all sides. Therefore that place is called *Parisâraka* (from *enam-kavaṣam-parisasâra*). As Sarasvatî had surrounded him on all sides, the Riṣis said, the gods know him; let us call him back. All consented, and called him back. After having called him back, they made *Apo naptrîyam*, by repeating: *pra devatrâ brahmaṇe* (10, 30); by its means they obtained the favour of the waters and of the gods. He who, having this knowledge, makes the Apo naptrîyam,[2] obtains the favour of the waters and the gods, and conquers the highest world (the heavenly-world).

[**114**] He should repeat it without stopping. (If he do so) the god of rain (Parjanya) will bless his children with incessant rain. Should he stop at regular intervals, when repeating (the hymn, as usual), then the rain-god would keep away in the clouds the rain from his children. Thence it is to be repeated without stopping. If he repeats thrice the first verse of this (hymn) without stopping, in this manner the whole (of the hymn) becomes repeated without stopping.[3]

20.

(The Ceremony of Mixing the Vasatîvarî and Ekadhanâ Waters.)

After having repeated these (first) nine verses (of the hymn, 10, 30) in the same order as they follow (one another in the Saṁhitâ), he repeats the

---

तद्ध स्म पुरा यज्ञमुहो रक्षांसि तीर्थेष्वपो गोपायन्ति । तदेके ऽ पो ऽछ्ह जग्मुस्तत एव तान् सर्वान् जघ्नुस्तु एव तत् कवषः सूक्तमपश्यत्पंचदशर्चं प्र देवत्रा ब्रह्मणे गातुरेत्विति तदन्वब्रवीत्तेन यज्ञमुहो रक्षांसि तीर्थेभ्यो ऽ पाहन् ॥

Of old the Rakṣas, the disturbers of the sacrifice, guarded the waters on the bathing places. Some persons had come to the waters. Thereupon the Rakṣas killed them all. Kavaṣa then saw this hymn which comprises fifteen verses: *pra devatrâ.* He then repeated it, and by means of it turned the Rakṣas from the bathing places, and killed them.

[2] The priests take water from a river, putting it in an earthen vessel. This water serves for squeezing the Soma juice.

[3] He has to repeat only the first verse thrice without stopping, whilst all remaining verses of the hymn may be repeated in the usual manner. For, the repetition of the first holds good for the whole remaining part.

(11th verse), *hinotâ no adhvaraṁ*, &c., as the tenth, and (after it, he adds the 10th :) *âvarvṛitatîr*, when the waters[4] filled (in jars) by the *Ekadhanins* are **[115]** turned away (from the river or tank whence they have been taken to the sacrificial compound). When they are seen (by the Hotar), he repeats : *prati yad âpô adṛiśram* (10, 30, 13). When the waters approach (the Châtvâla), then he repeats the verse : *âdhenavaḥ payasâ* (5, 43). When the (Vasatîvarî and Ekadhanâ) waters are joined together (in the Chamasas of the Hotar and Maitrâvaruṇa), then the Hotar repeats : *sam anyâ yanti* (2, 35, 3).

(To illustrate the origin of this rite, the following story is related.)

Both kinds of waters, those called *Vasatîvarî*, which were brought the day previous (to the Soma feast), and those called *Ekadhanâs*, which were brought on the very morning (of the Soma feast), were once jealous of one another, as to which should first carry up the sacrifice. Bhṛigu, becoming aware of their jealousy, bade them to be quiet, with the verse : *sam anyâ yanti*, &c. He restored peace among them. The waters of him who, having such a knowledge, restores peace among them (in this manner) will carry his sacrifice.

[116] When (both kinds of waters) the *Vasatîvarîs* and the *Ekadhanâs* are poured together in the Chamasa of the Hotar, he repeats : *âpo na devîr upayanti* (1, 83, 2). Then the Hotar asks the Adhvaryu :

---

[4] I subjoin here a more detailed description of the *Apô naptrîyam* ceremony, or the joining of the water jugs. My statements are taken from a Soma prayoga (a manual of the Adhvaryu priests), the Hiraṇyakeśi Śrâuta Śûtras, and oral information. After the Hotar has finished the Prâtar-anuvâka, the Adhvaryu addresses to him the words : "Ask for (*iṣya*) the waters," to which the Hotar answers : "*Apô naptriya*" (calling upon them). The Adhvaryu continues his orders (before the Hotar can answer) : Chamasa-adhvaryu of the Maitrâvaruṇa, come hither ! ye Ekadhanins (bringer of the Ekadhanâ waters) come ! Neṣṭar bring the wife (of the sacrificer) ! Agnîd (Agnîdhra), turn the Chamasa (Soma cup) of the Hotar and the *vasatîvarî* waters towards one another in the *Châtvâla* (a hole, for making ablutions) ! The Chamasa-adhvaryu of the Maitrâvaruṇa then brings a Chamasa. The Ekadhanins, *i.e.*, those who carry the so-called Ekadhanâ waters, then come with three jugs for the *ekadhanâ*, that the Adhvaryu should first throw one stalk (ekadhana) into the jug, and thus consecrate it. Thence these waters are called *ekadhanâs*. The Neṣṭar brings the wife who holds a jug in her hand. After all have come, the Adhvaryu throws one stalk of kuśa grass into the waters, and after having repeated the mantra, *devir âpaḥ*, he puts four sruvafuls of ghee on the stalk, and sacrifices it. The Adhvaryu brings the Chamasa of the Hotar and that of the Maitrâvaruṇa, in which the Ekadhanâ waters are, into mutual contact, and puts the Vasatîvarî water jug near it. He pours water from it into the Chamasa of the Hotar, and leads it into that of the Maitrâvaruṇa, and again from that of the Maitrâvaruṇa into that of the Hotar. When the waters poured by the Adhvaryu from this jug come near the Hotar, the latter asks the Adhvaryu thrice, *adhvaryo aver apâ*—Hast thou brought the waters, Adhvaryu ? Instead of this formula, we find in the Kau îtakî Br. (12, 1,) अध्वर्य वैषीरपा । which means exactly the same.

Hast thou obtained the waters? For the waters are the sacrifice. (The question therefore means:) Hast thou obtained[5] the sacrifice? The Advharyu answers: These (waters) are completely obtained.[6] This means: see these waters.

(The Hotar now addresses to the Adhvaryu the following words:) "With these waters you will squeeze, O Adhvaryu, for Indra, the Soma, the honey-like, the rain-giving, the inevitably-successful-making[7] at the end, after having included so many ceremonies (from the first to the last); (you will squeeze) for him (Indra), who is joined by the Vasus, Rudras, Âdityas, Ribhus, who has power, who has food, who is joined by Bṛihaspati, and by all gods; (you will squeeze the Soma) of which Indra (formerly) drank, slew his enemies, and overcame his adversaries. Ôm!" (After having spoken these words) the Hotar rises from his seat (to show his respect). Respect is to be paid to the waters by rising, just as people rise to salute a distinguished
[**117**] person who is coming near. Thence the waters are to be saluted by rising from the seat, and turning towards them. For, in the same manner, people salute a distinguished man. Therefore the Hotar must go behind the waters for saluting them. For, the Hotar, even if another one brings the sacrifice, has (in this way) the power of earning fame. Therefore the repeater (of the mantra) should go behind them. When going behind them, he repeats: *ambayo yanty adhvabhiḥ* (1, 23, 16), *i.e.*, the waters which are the friends of the sacrificers come on (various) ways mixing their (own) liquid with honey. (In the word *madhu*, honey, there is an allusion to Soma.) If a man, who has not tasted (formerly) the Soma juice, should wish to earn fame (he ought to repeat this verse). If he wishes for beauty, or for the acquirement of sacred knowledge (Brahma splendour), he should repeat the verse, *amûr yâ upa sûrye* (1, 23, 17). If he wishes for cattle, he should repeat, *apo devîr upahvaye* (1, 23, 18).

---

[5] The word *aver*, in the formula used by the Hotar, is here explained by "*avidaḥ*," thou hast obtained.

[6] In the original, *Utem anannamur*. The formulas appear to be very ancient. *Anannamur* is an imperfect of the intensive of the root *nam*. In the Kaushîtakî Brâhmaṇam stands the same formula.

[7] *Tîvrântam*. The word, *tîvra*, "pungent," is here, no doubt, used in a figurative sense, as Sây. explains it. It means a thing that is ultimately to the point, that hits at its aim, just as the sting of an insect. Sây.'s explanation is, on the whole, certainly correct. That this is the true meaning, is corroborated by the following word, *bahura-madhyam*, *i.e.*, which has much (*i.e.*, many ceremonies) between the commencement and end. Both expressions seem to belong together, forming a sort of proverbial phrase, the import of which is that, notwithstanding the many ceremonies, the fruit of the Soma sacrifice is not lost, but ultimately sure.

Should he, when repeating all these verses, go behind (the waters), he would obtain fulfilment of (all) these wishes. He who knows this, obtains these wishes.

When the *Vasatívarí*, and *Ekadhanás* are being put (on the Vedi), then he repeats, *imâ agman revatîr jíva dhanyâ* (10, 30, 14); and with the verse, *âgmann âpaḥ* (10, 30, 15), he concludes when they are (actually) put (on the Vedi).

21.

(The Libations from the Upâṁśu and Antaryâma Grahas.
The Haling in and out of the Air by the Hotar).

The Prâtar-Anuvâka is the head of the sacrifice (Soma sacrifice). The Upâṁśu and Antaryâma [118] Grahas[8]) are the air inhaled (*prâṇa*) and the air exhaled (*apâna*[9]). Speech is the weapon. Therefore, the Hotar should not make his voice heard before the libations from the Upâṁśu and Antaryâma grahas are poured (into the fire). Should the Hotar make his voice heard before these two have

---

[8] *Upâṁśu* and *Antaryâma* are names of vessels from which the two first Soma libations are poured into the Ahavanîya fire, as soon as the juice is obtained by squeezing. Both libations which precede those from the other Soma vessels (Aindravâyava, &c.) poured into the fire of the Uttarâ Vedi, are not accompanied with mantras recited by the Hotar, as all other libations are, but they are performed by the Adhvaryu, whilst the Hotar is drawing in his breath; or haling out the air which was breathed in. When doing the first, the libation from the Upâṁśu graha is poured into the fire ; when doing the latter, that from the Antaryâma graha is given. The Adhvaryu repeats some sacrificial formulas (see the Taittirîya Saṁhitâ 1, 4, 2, 3), whilst the Hotar mutters only the two formulas (the technical name of such formulas repeated by the Hotar is *nigada*) which are mentioned here (2, 21), and also in the Âśv. Śr. Sûtras (5, 2).

In the books belonging to the Yajurveda, we meet the terms *upâṁśu graha* and *upâṁśu pâtra*, and likewise *antaryâma graha*, and *antaryâma pâtra*. These terms require some explanation. The *pâtra* is a vessel, resembling a large wooden jar with but a very slight cavity on the top, in which the Soma juice is filled. The *graha* is a small cup, like a saucer, made of earth, and put over the cavity of the Soma vessel, in order to cover the " precious " juice. The bottom of it is first put in water, and a gold leaf placed beneath it. There are as many grahas as there are pâtras ; they belong together just as cup and saucer, and are regarded as inseparable. The word *graha* is, however, taken often in the sense of the whole, meaning both *graha* and *pâtra*. On the different names of the grahas required at the three great libations, see the *Grahakâṇḍa* in the Śatap. Brâhm. 4, and the commentary on the Taittirîya Saṁhitâ (vol. i. p. 593-693 ed. Cowell). I am in possession of several grahas and pâtras.

[9] At the end of the Prâtar-anuvâka, the Hotar must, after having repeated with a low voice the mantra, *prâṇam yachha*, &c., draw in the breath as strongly as he can. Then he repeats with a low voice, *apânam yachha*, &c., and, after having finished, he exhales the air (through the nose) as strongly as he can. He repeats with a low voice, *vyânâya*, &c., and when touching the stone by which the Soma for the Upâṁśu graha is squeezed, he is allowed to speak aloud. (Oral information).

[119] been poured into the fire, then he would carry off the vital airs of the sacrificer by means of the speech, which is a weapon. For (if he do so) some one should say to the Hotar (afterwards), that he has made the vital airs of the sacrificer go off, (and he, the Hotar) would lose his life.[10] It happens always thus. Thence the Hotar should not make his voice heard, before the libations from the Upâṁśu and Antaryâma grahas are poured into the fire. He should, when the libation from the Upâṁśu graha is given, mutter the words: "Keep in the air inhaled! Svâhâ! (I emit) thee, O speech of good call for pleasing the sun (which is thy presiding deity)." He should then draw in the air, and say (with a low voice): "O breath, who goest in (my body), keep in (my body) the breath!" He should, when the libation from the Antaryâma graha is given, mutter the words: "Keep in the air exhaled! Svâhâ! (I emit) thee, O speech of good call for pleasing the sun." (After having spoken these words) he should hale out the air, and say, "O air, haled out, keep this very air (which is to be haled out, in my body)." By the words "(I emit) thee (O speech!) for the air, circulating (in my body)," he then touches[11] the stone used to squeeze the Soma juice for the Upâṁśu graha, and makes his voice heard. This stone to squeeze the Soma juice for the Upâṁśu graha is the soul. The Hotar, after having put (thus) the vital airs in his own self, emits his voice, and attains his full age (100 years). Likewise, does he who has such a knowledge.

22.

[120] (*The Hotar has no share in the Bahiṣ-pavamâna Meal. The Soma Libation for Mitrâ-Varuṇa to be mixed with Milk*).

(After the libations from the Upâṁśu and Antaryâma have been poured into the fire, the Soma squeezed, and poured into the different vessels—*grahas*—such as *Aindavayava*, &c., which are then kept in readiness for making the libations, five of the priests: Adhvaryu, Prastotar, Pratihartar, Udgâtar, and Brahmâ, one holding the hand of the other—*samanvârabdhâ*—walk in the direction of the *Châtvâla*, and ultimately take their seats for performing the ceremony of the *Stotra*, *i.e*, chanting a sacred verse—a *Sâman*. Now the question is, whether the Hotar is allowed to walk or not at the same time that the other priests just mentioned do so.)

At that (occasion, when the priests walk) they (the theologians) ask, whether he (the Hotar) ought to walk or not (together with the others).

---

[10] That is to say, some one might charge him afterwards with having murdered the sacrificer.

[11] Not struck against another, as is done when the Soma juice is being squeezed.

Some say, he ought to walk; for this meal[12] in honour of the *Bahiṣpavamâna-stotra*[13] (which is about to **[121]** be performed by the Sâma singers) is enjoyed equally by both gods and men; hence (both gods and men) participate in it. But those who say so are not to be attended to. Should he walk (along with the Sâma singers), then he would make the Rik (which is repeated by the Hotar) follow the Sâman. (If any one should see him do so) he at that occasion should tell him: "The Hotar here has been behind the Sâma singers, and ceded his fame to the Udgâtar; he has fallen from his place and will (in future) also fall from it." So it always happens to the Hotar (who walks after the Sâma singers).[14] Therefore he ought to remain where he is sitting, and repeat the following *Anumantraṇa*[15] verse: "which Soma draught here at the sacrifice, placed on the sacred grass, on the altar, belongs to the gods, of this we also enjoy a share." Thus the soul of the Hotar is not excluded from that Soma draught (which is drunk by the Sâma singers after the Bahiṣ-pavamâna Sâman is over). Then (after having repeated the mantra mentioned) he ought to repeat: "Thou art the mouth (of the sacrifice); might I become the **[122]** mouth (first among my people) also! For the Bahiṣ-pavamâna

---

[12] Thus I translate *bhakṣa*. It refers to the eating of Charu or boiled rice by the Sâma singers before they chant. The Hotars are excluded from it.

[13] This stotra consists of nine *ṛichas* commencing with: *upâsmâi gâyatâ naraḥ*, which all are found together in the *Sâmavedârchikam* ii. 1-9. All nine *ṛichas* are solemnly chanted by the three Sâma singers, *Prastotar*, *Udgâtar*, and *Pratihartar*. Each of these verses is for the purpose of chanting, divided into four parts: *Prastâva*, *i.e.*, prelude, the first being preceded by *huṁ*, to be sung by the Prastotar; *Udgîtha*, the principal part of the Sâman, preceded by *om*, to be chanted by the Udgâtar; the *Pratihâra*, *i.e.*, response introduced by *huṁ*, to be chanted by the Pratihartar, and the *Nidhana*, *i.e.*, finale, to be sung by all three. To give the student an idea of this division, I here subjoin the second of these *ṛichas* in the Sâma form, distinguishing its four parts :—

Prastâva : अभि ते मधुना पयें ॥

Udgîtha : ओमाथर्वाणो अशिश्रादेयुर्वंदेवायदा ॥

Pratihâra : हुं आवायो ॥

Nidhana : साम् ॥

The *Nidhanas*, *i.e.*, finals, are for the nine Pavamâna-stotra verses, the following ones: सात, साम् सुवाः, इडा, वाक्, and आ (for the four last verses).

[14] The Rik is regarded as a solid foundation on which the Sâman is put. See the passage in the *Chândogya-Upaniṣad* (1, 6, 1), here quoted by Sâyaṇa: "The Rik is the earth, the Sâman Agni; just as (the fire is put) on the earth, the Sâman is placed over the Rik (as its foundation); thence the Sâman is sung placed over the Rik." This means, before the singers can sing the Sâman, the Rik which serves for this purpose, is first to be repeated in the form in which it is in Rigveda. This is generally done. See, besides, Ait. Br. 3, 23.

[15] This is the repetition, with a low voice, of a verse or formula, by the Hotar, after a ceremony is over.

draught is the very mouth of the sacrifice (sacrificial personage)." He who has such a knowledge, becomes the mouth of his own people, the chief among his own people.

An Asura woman, *Dîrghajîhvî* (long-tongued), licked the morning libation of the gods. It (consequently) became inebriating everywhere. The gods wished to remedy this, and said to Mitra and Varuṇa: "Ye two ought to take off this (the inebriating quality from the Soma)." They said: "Yes, but let us choose a boon from you." The god said: Choose! They chose at the morning libation curd of milk whey (*payasyâ*) in milk. This is their everlasting share; that is, the boon chosen by them. What had been made by her (the Asura woman) inebriating, that was made good (again) by the curd; for both Mitra and Varuṇa removed, through this curd, the inebriating quality, as it were (from the Soma juice).[16]

23.

(*Purodâśa Offerings for the Libations.*)

The libations (*savanâni*) of the gods did not hold (they were about falling down). The gods saw the rice cakes (*Pûrodâśas*). They portioned them out for each libation, that they should hold together the libations. Thence their libations were held together. When, therefore (at the libations) rice cakes are portioned [123] out for holding together the libations, the libations offered by the sacrificers are then (really) held together. The gods made these rice cakes *before* (the Soma offering). Thence it is called *purodâśa* (from *puro*, before).

About this they say: for each libation one ought to portion out rice cakes, one of eight potsherds (a ball put on eight kapâlas) at the morning, one of eleven potsherds at midday, and one of twelve at the evening, libation. For the form of the libations is defined [17] by the metres. But this

[16] The translation of this sentence offers some difficulty. I follow here Sâyaṇa, who refers the one *asyâi* to *Dîrghajîhvî*, the other to *payasyâ*. We have here an allusion to mixing the Soma with sour milk (*dadhyâśih*), in order to make it less inebriating. The curds put in it, are Mitra's and Varuṇa's everlasting share. By the story which is here told, the author tries to account for the fact, that the libation for Mitra-Varuṇa is mixed with curds of milk whey. At present, the Soma is not generally mixed with sour milk. A large quantity of water is taken, in order to weaken its strength.

[17] That is to say, at the morning libation *Gâyatrî*, each pada of which consists of eight syllables, is the leading metre, whilst at the midday libation *Triṣṭubh* (with four padas, each of eleven syllables), and at the evening libation *Jagatî* (with four padas, each of twelve syllables), are the leading metres. Therefore, some sacrificial priests were of opinion that, in accordance with the number of syllables of the leading metre of each libation, the number of kapâlas (potsherds) should be eight at the morning, eleven at the midday, and twelve at the evening, libtaion.

(opinion) is not to be attended to For all the rice cakes, which are portioned out for each libation, are Indra's. Thence they ought to be put (at all three libations) on eleven potsherds only. [18]

About this they say: one ought to eat of such a portion of a rice cake which is not besmeared with melted butter, in order to protect the Soma draught. For Indra slew with melted butter as his thunderbolt Vṛitra. But this (opinion) is not to be attended to. [19] For the offering (besmeared with butter) is a liquid sprinkled (into the fire), and the Soma draught is such a liquid sprinkled (into the fire). (Both—Ghee and Soma—being thus of the same nature) the sacrificer [124] should eat of any part of the offering (whether besmeared with ghee or not).

These offerings, *viz.*, melted butter, fried grains of barley (*dhânâḥ*), *karambha*, [20] *parivâpa*, [21] *purodâśa*, and *payasyâ*, [22] come by themselves to the sacrificers from every direction. To him who has such a knowledge come these (offerings) by themselves.

24.

(*Haviṣ-paṅkti. Akṣara-paṅkti. Narâśaṁsa-paṅkti. Savana-paṅkti.*)

He who knows the offering consisting of five parts prospers by means of this offering. The offering consisting of five parts (*haviṣ-paṅkti*) comprises (the following five things): fried grains of barley, *karambha*, *parivâpa*, *purodâśa*, and *payasyâ*.

He who knows the Akṣara-paṅkti sacrifice (offering of five syllables), prospers by means of this very sacrifice. The Akṣara-paṅkti comprises (the following five syllables): *su, mat, pad, vag, de.* [23] He, who has such a knowledge, prospers by the sacrifice consisting of five syllables.

He who knows the *Narâśamsa-paṅkti* [24] sacrifice [125], prospers by

---

[18] The reason is that Indra's metre, Triṣṭubh, consists of eleven syllables.

[19] The Soma is not to be brought into contact with anything that is supposed to have been an instrument of murder, as in this case the melted butter was.

[20] This is a kind of pap, prepared of curds and barley juice (*saktu*) by kneading both together. Instead of curds, slightly melted butter (*sarpis*) might be taken. See Kâtyâyana Śrâuta Sûtra. 9, 1, 17.

[21] This is another kind of pap, prepared of fried grains and barley juice.

[22] See 2, 22. p. 122.

[23] These five syllables are to be muttered by the Hotar when making *japa* (the uttering of mantras with a low inaudible voice), after the *haviṣ-paṅkti* is over. They, no doubt, correspond to the five parts of the *haviṣ-paṅkti* offering.

[24] This means: the assemblage of five *Narâśaṁsas*. *Narâśaṁsa* is, as is well-known, a name of Agni, and of some other gods, identical with the *Nâiryô-śanha* of the Zend-Avesta (see Haug's "Essays on the Sacred Language, Writings, and Religion of the Parsees," p. 232). According to the explanation given by Sâyaṇa, who follows

means of it. For two Narâśaṁsa offerings belong to the morning, two to the midday, and one to the evening, libation. This is the Narâśaṁsa-paṅkti sacrifice. He who has such a knowledge prospers by it.

He who knows the *Savana-paṅkti* sacrifice, prospers by it. This *Savana-paṅkti* sacrifice consists of the animal which is sacrificed the day previous to the Soma feast (*paśur upavasathe*), the three libations (*savanâni*), and the animal to be sacrificed after the Soma feast is over (*paśur anûbandhyaḥ*). This is the Savana-paṅkti sacrifice. He who has such a knowledge prospers by means of the *Savana-paṅkti* sacrifice.

The Yâjyâ-mantra for the *haviṣ-paṅkti* is: [25] "May *Indra*, with his "two yellow horses, eat the fried grains (first part of the *haviṣ-paṅkti*), "with *Pûṣan*, the *karambha*; may the *parivâpa* (be enjoyed) by "*Sarasvatî* and *Bhâratî*, and the cake (*apûpa-purodâśa*) by Indra!" The two yellow horses (*harî*) of Indra are the *Rik* and *Sâman*. *Pûṣan* (the guardian of flocks, the divine herdsman) is cattle, and *karambhâ* is food.[26] As to the words: *sarasvatî-vân* and *bhâratîvan*, *Sarasvatî* is speech, [126] and *Bhârata* (bearer) means vital air. *Parivâpa* is food, and *apûpa* is sharpness of senses.

(By repeating this Yâjyâ-mantra) the Hotar makes the sacrificer join those deities, assume the same form, and occupy the same place with them. He (the Hotar) who has such a knowledge becomes (also) joined to the best beings and obtains the highest bliss.

The Yâjyâ-mantra for the Sviṣṭakṛit of the *Purodâśa* offering at each libation is "Agni, eat the offering."[27]

---

one of the masters (Âcharyas), the word *Narâśaṁsa*, *i.e.*, belonging to *Narâśaṁsa*, means the Soma cups (*chamasa*), after one has drunk out of them, sprinkled water over them, and put them down. For, in this condition, they belong to *Narâśaṁsa*. At the morning and midday libations, the Soma cups (*chamasa*) are filled twice each time, and at the evening libation only once. Thus the Soma cups become during the day of libations five times *Narâśaṁsas*. This is the *Narâśaṁsa-paṅkti* sacrifice.

[25] It is not in the Saṁhitâ. As it stands here, it appears to have been taken from another *Śâkhâ*. For, whilst we found above, five parts of the *haviṣ-paṅkti* mentioned, here in this mantra we have only four, the *payasyâ* being omitted.

[26] According to Sâyaṇa, the meaning of the latter sentence is: *Pûṣan* is called by this name from his feeding (*puṣ*) the cattle, and *karambha* is called food from being itself the nourishment.

[27] The Kauṣîtakî Brâhmaṇam (13, 3) furnishes us with a fuller report on the origin of the Sviṣṭakṛit formula required for the Purodâśa offerings which accompany the Soma libations. It is as follows:—

हविरग्ने वीहीत्यनुसवनं पुरोडाशः स्विष्टकृतो यजत्यवत्सारो प्राश्रवणो देवानां होतास । तमेतस्मिन् युम्ने मृत्युः प्रत्यालिल्येऽग्निर्वै मृत्युः स हविरग्ने वीहीति हविषाग्निं प्रीत्वाऽथातिमुमुचे तथो एवैवं विद्वान्होता हविरग्ने वीहीत्येव हविषाग्निं प्रीत्वाथातिमुच्यत एतैर्हवा अन्तराकाशैर्देवाः स्वर्गं लोकं अग्मु-

[**127**] By repeating this mantra, *Avatsâra* (an ancient Riṣi) obtained Agni's favour and conquered the highest world. The same happens to him who has such a knowledge, and who knowing it has this *haviṣ-paṅkti* offered (*i.e.*, the sacrificer), or repeats the Yâjyâ-mantra belonging to it (*i.e.*, the Hotar).

FOURTH CHAPTER.

(*The Dvidevatya Graha Libations, i.e., the Libations poured from the Aindravâyava, Maitrâvaruṇa, and Aśvina Grahas. Ṛituyâjas. The Silent Praise*).

25.

(*Story of a Race run by the Gods for obtaining the right to drink first from a Soma Libation. The Aindravâyava Graha. Explanation of a certain custom with the Bhâratas*).

The gods could not agree as to who of them should first taste the Soma juice. They (all) wished for it, (each saying) "Might I drink first, might I drink first." They came (at length) to an understanding. They said: "Well, let us run a race.[1] He of us who will be victor, shall first taste the Soma juice." So they did. Among all those who ran the race, *Vâyu* first arrived at the goal; next *Indra*; next *Mitra* and *Varuṇa*, then the *Aśvins*. Indra thinking he would be beforehand with Vâyu, (ran as fast as he could [**128**] and) fell down close to him. He

---

स्तानेतस्मिन् द्युम्ने मृत्यः प्रत्यालिल्येऽग्निर्वै मृत्युस्ते हविरग्ने वीहीति हविषाग्निं प्रीत्वाऽथातिमुमुचिरे। तथो एवैवं विद्वान्होता हविरग्ने वीहीत्येव हविषाग्निं प्रीत्वाथातिमुच्यते। तानि वा एतानि षडक्षराणि हविरग्ने वीहीति षळङ्गोऽयमात्मा षड्विधस्तदात्मनैवात्मानं निष्क्रीयानृणो भूत्वाथ यजते स एषोऽवत्सारस्य प्राश्रवणस्य मंत्रः।

i.e., The Hotar uses, as Yâjyâ of the Sviṣṭakṛit offering of the Purodâśa which accompanies the libations, the formula: "Agni, eat the offering."

(On the origin of this formula, the following is reported:) Avatsâra, the son of Praśravaṇa, was (once) the Hotar of the gods. In that abode of light, Death (one of the gods) attached himself to him; for Agni is Death. He pleased Agni with an offering, repeating: "Agni, eat of the offering," and was released.

(There is another story reported on the origin of this formula, which runs as follows:—)

The gods went by means of their innate light and splendour to the celestial world. In that abode of light, Death attached himself to them. Agni is Death. They pleased Agni with an offering, repeating "Agni, eat the offering," and were released.

This formula (*havir agne vîhi*) consists of six syllables; the soul consists of six parts,—is six-fold. Thus the sacrificer redeems (by means of this formula) through a soul (represented by this formula) his own soul, and clears off his debts. This is the mantra of Avatsâra, the son of Praśravaṇa.

[1] The expression in the original is: *âjim ayâma*. See 4, 7.

then said, "We both have (arrived at the goal) together; let both of us be winners of the race." Vâyu answered, "No! I (alone) am winner of the race." Indra said, "Let the third part (of the prize) be mine; let both of us be winners of the race!" Vâyu said, "No! I alone am winner of the race." Indra said, "Let the fourth part (of the prize) be mine; let us both be winners of the race!" To this Vâyu agreed, and invested him with the right to the fourth part (of the first Soma cup presented). Thence Indra is entitled only to the fourth part; but Vâyu to three parts. Thus Indra and Vâyu won the race together; next followed Mitra and Varuṇa together, and then the Aśvins.

According to the order in which they arrived at the goal, they obtained their shares in the Soma juice. The first portion belongs to Indra and Vâyu, then follows that of Mitra and Varuṇa, and (lastly) that of the Aśvins.

The *Aindravâyava* Soma jar (*graha*) is that one in which Indra enjoys the fourth part. Just this (fourth part as belonging to Indra) was seen (by means of revelation) by a Riṣi. He then repeated the mantra appropriate to it, *niyutvâñ Indraḥ sârathir*, *i.e.*, Vâyu[2] (and) Indra his carriage-driver! Thence, when now-a-days the Bharatas[3] spoil their enemies (conquered in the battle-field), those charioteers who **[129]** seize the booty, say, in imitation of that example set by Indra, who won his race only by becoming the charioteer (of Vâyu), "the fourth part (of the booty is ours) alone."[4]

26.

(*On the Meaning of the Libations from the Aindravâyava, Maitrâvaruṇa, and Aśvina Grahas. The two Anuvâkyâs for the Aindravâyava Graha.*)

The Soma jars (*graha*) which belong to two deities[5] are the vital airs. The *Aindravâyava* jar is speech and breath, the *Maitrâvaruṇa* jar is eye and mind; the *Aśvina* jar is ear and soul. Some (sacrificial priests) use two verses in the Anuṣṭubh metre as Puronuvâkyâs, and two in the Gâyatrî metre as Yâjyâs when offering (the Soma juice) from the

---

[2] *Niyutvân* is a frequent epithet of Vâyu. See the hymn 2, 41, meaning, one who has teams, oxen, cows, &c.

[3] Sâyaṇa does not take this word here as a proper name, in which sense we generally find it in the ancient Samskrit Literature, but as an appellative noun, meaning "warriors." He derives the word from *bhara* cattle, and *tan* to extend, stretch; to which etymology no modern philologist will give his assent. *Satvan* is here explained by Sâyaṇa as "charioteer;" but in his commentary on Rigveda 1. 62, 2, he takes it in the sense of "enemy" which is, we think, the right one.

[4] The author of the Brâhmaṇam explains here the reason of the custom why the charioteers are entitled to the fourth part of the booty made in a battle.

[5] These vessels are called: *Aindravâyava*, *Maitrâvaruṇa*, and *Aśvina*.

Aindravâyava jar. As the Aindravâyava jar represents speech and breath, thus the proper metres (Anuṣṭubh being speech, and Gâyatrî breath) will be applied. But this (practice) ought not to be observed. For, where the Puronuvâkyâ mantra exceeds in (syllables) the Yâjyâ mantra,[6] there is no success in the sacrifice; but where the Yâjyâ exceeds the Puronuvâkyâ (in syllables) there is success.

(Likewise success is not obtained) by using the same metres (for Anuvâkyâ and Yâjyâ mantras). In order to obtain any desire whatever, referring to speech and breath, the Hotar ought to do so (*i.e.*, [130] to repeat two verses in the Anuṣṭubh metre as Anuvâkyâs, and two in the Gâyatrî metre as Yâjyâ mantras). In this way (all he desires) will be fulfilled. The first Puronuvâkyâ belongs to Vâyu (1, 2, 1), the second to Indra and Vâyu (1, 2, 4). By that Yâjyâ[1] which belongs to Vâyu, the Hotar makes (produces) breath (in the sacrificer). For Vâyu (wind) is breath, and by means of that pada (foot) of the Indra-Vâyu-Yâjyâ mantra, which refers to Indra, he makes speech. For speech is Indra's. He (thus) obtains every desire (granted) which refers to breath and speech, without producing any inequality (by having the one set of mantras too long, the other too short) in the sacrifice.[2]

27.

(*The Rite of Drinking from the Aindravâyava, Maitrâvaruṇa, and Aśvina Grahas by the Hotar. The Formulas repeated at those occasions.*)

The Soma offerings belonging to two deities are the vital airs;[3] but they are offered in the same jar for both (deities); for the reason is, that (all) the vital airs are of one and the same nature. They are sacrificed from two[4] grahas (jars with small cups), for the vital airs are a pair (such as the

---

[6] This would be the case if the Anuṣṭubh metre should be used for the Puronuvâkyâ, and the Gâyatrî as Yâjyâ; for the Anuṣṭubh consists of thirty-two, and the Gâyatrî only of twenty-four syllables.

[1] The two first verses of 4, 46, are used as Yâjyâs.

[2] This latter remark refers to the opinion of those who maintained that the Puronuvâkyâ and Yâjyâ mantras ought to be of the same metres.

[3] By these, speech, eyes, and ears are meant.

[4] At the Soma offerings, there are always two *Grahas* required; one is held by the Adhvaryu, the other by his assistant Pratipasthâtar. The contents of both the grahas belong to the same pair of deities; both are therefore *dvidevatya*, belonging to two deities. The author of the Brâhmaṇa attempts here to explain the circumstance that, though the Soma offering contained in one graha belong to two deities (Vâyu and Indra, Mitra and Varuṇa, &c.), there are always two Grahas used, and their contents simultaneously sacrificed.

eyes). **[131]** When (after the Soma offering has been given to the two respective deities) the Adhvaryu hands over (the Soma cup to drink of the remainder of the juice) to the Hotār, he receives it with the same mantra by which the Adhvaryu presents it (to him). By the (words): " This is a good,[5] " this is a multitude of goods ; here is good, a multitude of goods ; in me is " the good (when the Soma is drunk), a multitude of goods ; rule of speech[6] ! " protect my speech ! " the Hotar drinks Soma from the Aindravâyava " graha. (Then he repeats) : ' Speech with breath is called hither (by me) ; " may speech with breath call also me ! The divine Riṣis, the protectors of " (our) bodies, [7] who are born from austerities (*tapoja*) are called hither (by " me) ! may the divine Riṣis, the protectors of our bodies, who are born " from austerities, call (also) mė !' By the divine Riṣis, who are the " protectors of (our) bodies, the vital airs are to be understood. Thus he " calls (invites) the Riṣis.

(By the words) : " This is a good which has knowledge ; here is a good " which has knowledge ; in me is a good which has knowledge ; ruler of the eye, protect my eye !" the Hotar drinks Soma from the Maitrâvaruṇa graha. (Then he repeats) : "The eye with the mind is called hither. May the " **[132]** eye with the mind call (also) me ! The divine Riṣis," &c. (just as above).

(By the words) : " This is a good, a good which is lasting ; here is a " good, a good which is lasting ; in me is a good, a good which is lasting ; " ruler of the sense of hearing ![8] protect my sense of hearing !" the Hotar drinks Soma from the Aśvina graha. (Then he repeats) : " The sense of " hearing with the soul is called hither : may the sense of hearing with the " soul call (also) me ! The divine Riṣis," &c. (just as above).

When drinking from the Aindravâyava graha, the Hotar facing the cup turns its mouth towards his face (and drinks) ; for the inhaled and exhaled airs are in his front. In the same manner, he drinks from the Maitrâvaruṇa jar ; for the two eyes are in his front. When drinking from

---

[5] This formula resembles very much one of the most sacred prayers of the Parsis, *viz.*, *ashem vohu vahistem asti* which is particularly repeated when the Zota priest (the Hotar of the Brahmans) is drinking the Homa (Soma) juice ; *vohû* is etymologically *vasu*, which is very frequently used in formulas repeated by the Hotar before he tastes the sacrificial food ; *vahistem* is the superlative of *vohû*, conveying the same sense as *purûvasu*.

[6] In this translation I followed the reading वाक्पा. One of my Manuscripts and Sâyaṇa read वाक्या, which appears to be only a lapsus calami for वाक्पा.

[7] The expression in the original is : *tanûpâvânas tanvaḥ*, the term "body" being thus put twice.

[8] Sâyaṇa explains संयत् by नियत.

the Aśvina jar, he turns its mouth * round about; for men and animals hear speech sounding from all sides.

28.

(On the Repetition of the Two Yâjyâ Mantras for Libation from the Dvidetyagrahas. No Anuvaṣaṭkâra allowed. On the Agur for those Yâjyâs).

The Soma jars belonging to two deities are the vital airs. The Hotar ought to repeat the (two) Yâjyâ mantras (for the offering poured out of such a jar) **[133]** without stopping (at the end of the first mantra), in order to keep together the vital airs and to prevent their being cut off. The Soma jars belonging to two deities are the vital airs. (Thence) the Hotar should not make the Anuvaṣaṭkâra (*i.e.*, not pronounce the formula: "Agni, eat the Soma!"[10] with the formula *Vauṣaṭ*! after the Yâjyâ has been repeated). If he do so, then he stops the (circulation of the) vital airs which are not stopped (in any other way). For this formula (the *anuvaṣaṭkâra*) is a stop. (If one should observe a Hotar repeat the Anuvaṣaṭkâra) one ought to tell him, that he had stopped the vital airs, which are not stopped (otherwise), and that he would (consequently) lose his life. This always happens. Thence he ought not to repeat that formula (the *anuvaṣaṭkâra*) when pouring oblations from the Soma jars belonging to two deities.

They ask, (what is the reason that) the Maitrâvaruṇa priest gives twice his assent that the Yâjyâ mantra should be repeated, and calls twice (upon the Hotar) to do so, whilst the Hotar declares his readiness to repeat the Yâjyâ mantra only once, and (concludes with) pronouncing twice, *Vauṣaṭ! Vauṣaṭ!* (instead of doing it once)? What is the (meaning) of the Hotar's declaration of his readiness to repeat the Yâjyâ mantra[11] (that he repeats it only **[134]** once at the beginning, and not before the second mantra)?

---

* The Aindravâyava graha has one, the Maitrâvaruṇa two, mouths. The drinking from the two latter ones is described as *purastât pratyañcham*, that is, to take the graha in one's hands, so that its mouth faces the mouth of the drinker, and, when drinking, to turn the lower part of the vessel aside.

The Aśvina graha has three mouths. The drinking from it is described as *parihâram*, that is, to turn its three mouths one after the other to one's mouth when drinking, so that the whole vessel becomes turned round. (*Oral information.*)

[10] The recital of this formula is called *anuvaṣaṭkâra.*

[11] The words "assent that the Yâjyâ mantra," &c., and "declaration of his readiness to repeat," &c., are only a translation of the term *âgur*, stating its full import. After the Hotar has repeated the two Puronuvâkyâ mantras, mentioned on p. 130, he is addressed by the Maitrâvaruṇa priest in two formulas, following immediately one another, which are called *Praiṣa-mantra, i.e*, mantras containing an order to repeat. Both commence by

(The answer is.) The Soma jars belonging to two deities are the vital airs. The Agur formula is the thunderbolt. If, therefore, the Hotar were to put between (the two Yâjyâ mantras) the Agur formula, he would deprive the sacrificer of his life (as if striking him) with (a weapon like) the thunderbolt. (If one should observe a Hotar doing so) one ought to tell him, that for having, by means of the Agur weapon, deprived the sacrificer of his life, he himself would also lose his life. Thus it always
[135] happens. (Therefore) the Hotar ought not to repeat the Agur formula in the midst of (the two Yâjyâ mantras).

And, further, the Maitrâvaruṇa priest is the mind of the sacrifice, and the Hotar its speech. Speech speaks only when instigated by the mind (to do so). If any one utters speech different from what he thinks, such a speech is liked only by the Asuras, but not by the Devas. The Agur formula of the Hotar is contained in the two Agur formulas (*hotâ yakṣat*) pronounced at this (occasion) by the Maitrâvaruṇa priest.

29.

(Rituyâjas.)

The mantras repeated for the offerings to the Ritus [12] (seasons) are

---

the formula: *Hotâ yakṣat*, *i.e.*, may the Hotar repeat the Yâjyâ mantra. The Hotar being obliged to repeat both Yâjyâ mantras *uno tenore* without stopping, he can declare his readiness to respond to the order given by the Maitrâvaruṇâ only before he commences to repeat the proper Yâjyâ mantras. His readiness he declares by the words ये ३ यजामहे. This is the *âgur* of the Hotar. That ये is to be pronounced with *pluti*, *i.e.*, with three moras, is remarked by Pâṇini 8, 2, 88 (ये यज्ञकर्मणि). Patañjali, in his Mahâbhâṣya, explains ये as an elliptical expression, implying the whole verse—ये देवासो दिव्येकादश स्थ (Rigveda, 1, 139, 11). On the *Agur* formula, see Âśval. Śrauta Sûtras 1, 5, where it is said that the *Agur* formula, ये यजामहे, is required at the so-called Prayâjas (at the first and fifth) and principally 5, 5. In this latter passage, the rule is given to which the author of the Brâhmaṇa refers, that the two Yâjyâs for the Aindravâyava graha require two Praiṣas, *i.e.* orders, one Agur, and two Vaṣaṭkâras; whilst the two other grahas, the Maitrâvaruṇa and the Aśvina, require each only one Yâjyâ, one Praiṣa, and one Vaṣaṭkâra. See also the *Sânkhâyana* Sûtras 7, 2. The formula ये यजामहे is always at the beginning of the Yâjyâ, as well as the words होता यक्षत् at that of the Praiṣa mantra. The proper order to repeat is conveyed at the end of the latter by the words होतर्यज, *i.e.*, Hotar, repeat the Yâjyâ mantra, whereupon the Hotar repeats the Yâjyâ. The repetition of this formula appears to go back to a very remote antiquity. For we find both the formula and its technical term in the Zend-Avesta. *Yajâmahe* is completely identical with the Zend *Yazamâidê*, which always precedes the names of Ahura-mazda, the archangels, and other divine beings, and the souls of the deceased, when homage is paid to them. The technical term for repeating this formula is: *â-ghare* (the same as *â-gur*). See the Fravardin Yasht 50, *kahê no idha nâmâ âghairyât*, *i.e.*, to whose name of us will he pay homage by repeating *Yazamâidê*, *i.e.*, we worship. That the word *âghairyât* has this meaning, is well-known to the Parsi Dasturs.

[12] There are twelve Grahas for the Ritus, from which the Soma juice is offered in three sections; first six, then four, and, lastly, two are taken. The mantras required

the vital airs. By performing **[136]** them, they (the priests) provide the sacrificer with vital airs. By repeating six mantras containing the singular *ritunâ* to the Ritus, they provide the sacrificer with the air inhaled (*prâṇa*); by repeating four mantras containing the plural *ritubhiḥ*, they provide him with the air exhaled (*apâna*); by repeating, at last, two mantras containing the singular *ritunâ*, they provide him with the circulating vital air (*vyâna*). For the vital airs are three-fold, *viz.*, air inhaled, air exhaled, and the air circulating in the body. (These Ritu offerings being made in three sections) in the first (series of mantras when six are given), the singular *ritunâ* is used; in the second, the plural *ritubhiḥ*; and in the third, the singular again *ritunâ* are applied. (This is done) to keep together the vital airs, to prevent them from being cut off.

are to be found among the so-called *praiṣa sûktas*. See Âśval. Śraut. S. 5, 8. Sânkhâyana 7, 8. About the particulars of the Ritu Yâjâs, see Taittirîya Saṁhitâ 1, 4, 14 and 6, 5, 3, with Sâyaṇa's commentary, ed. Cowell, i., p. 643-46. The Yâjyâ mantras and the Praiṣas for the Ritu offerings are essentially the same. All (12) Praiṣas are given by the Maitrâvaruṇa. The first is addressed to the Hotar, and runs as follows: होता यक्षदिन्द्रं होत्रात्सजूर्दिवः आ पृथिव्या ऋतुना सोमं पिबतु होतर्यज, *i.e.*, May the Hotar repeat the Yâjyâ mantra for Indra! May he drink Soma from the cup of the Hotar with the Ritu! The Yâjyâ contains the same words, with the only difference that, instead of *yakṣat*, the appropriate formula ये ३ यजामहे is used.

In the second Rituyâja, which is repeated by the Potar, the Marutas are invited to drink with the Ritu from the offering of the Potar. The third belongs to Tvaṣṭar and the wives of the gods. It is repeated by the Neṣṭar (ये ३ यजामहे ग्रावो नेष्ट्रात्त्वष्टा सुजनिमा सजूर्देवानां पत्नीभिर्ऋतुना सोमं पिबतु).

The fourth, which is repeated by the Agnîdhra, belongs to Agni. The fifth belongs to Indra-Brahmâ, and is repeated by the Brahmaṇâchhansi. The sixth is repeated for Mitra-Varuṇa (who are called प्रशास्तारौ) by the Maitrâvaruṇa. These six mantras contain the formula ऋतुना सोमं पिबतु.

The seventh, eighth, ninth and tenth Rituyâjas which are repeated by the Hotar, Potar, Neṣṭar and Achhâvâka respectively, belong to *deva draviṇodâh* (a name of Agni). These four mantras contain the term ऋतुभिः सोमं पिबतु. The eleventh and twelfth Rituyâjas are repeated by the Hotar with the term ऋतुना सेमं The eleventh belongs to the Aśvins as the two Adhvaryus; the twelfth to Agni Gṛihapati.

The first Soma libation for the Ritus is poured from the Hotrapâtra, the second from the Potra-pâtra, the third from that of the Neṣṭar, the fourth from that of the Agnîd, the fifth from the Brâhmaṇa-pâtra, the sixth from that of the Praśâstar (Maitrâvaruṇa).

The seventh, eighth and ninth from the Pâtras of the Hotar, Potar, and Neṣṭar respectively. The tenth libation is not poured from one of these Pâtras already mentioned, but in addition to the Pâtras of the Hotar, Potar, and Neṣṭar, a "fourth vessel" (*turîyam pâtram*) is mentioned, which is called *amartyam*, *i.e.*, immortal. The *devo draviṇodâḥ* (Agni) is called upon to prepare the Soma draught himself and repeat himself the Yâjyâ. The eleventh libation is poured from the Adhvaryava-pâtra, and the twelfth from the Gârhapatya. (*Sapta-Hautra*).

[137] The Ritu Yâjâs[13] are the vital airs. (Thence) the Hotar ought not to repeat the *Anuvaṣaṭkâra.* For the Ritus have no end ; one (always) follows the other. Were the Hotar to repeat this formula (the *anuvaṣaṭkâra*) when making the offerings to the Ritus, he would bring the endless seasons (their endless succession) to a stand still. For this formula is a stand still. Who (therefore) should repeat it, would bring the Ritus to a stand still, and difficulty would be created (for the sacrifice). This always happens. Thence he ought not to repeat that formula, when repeating the mantras for the offerings to the Ritus.

30.

(The Hotar Eats the Purolâśa and Drinks from the Grahas.)

The Soma jars belonging to two deities, are the vital airs, and cattle is food (*iḷâ*). (Thence) after having drunk from the Soma jars belonging to two deities, he calls *Iḷâ* (food).[14] *Iḷâ* is cattle. He thus calls cattle, and (consequently) provides the sacrificer with cattle.

They ask, Should the Hotar first eat the food (remainder of the Purodâśa offering previous to the Soma offering) which he has in his hand, or should he drink[15] first from his Soma cup (*chamasa*)? (The [138] answer is) he should first eat the food which he has in his hand, then he may drink Soma from his cup. In consequence of the circumstance that he first drinks from the Soma jars (*grahas*) belonging to two deities, the Soma draught is first (before he takes any other food) enjoyed by him. Therefore (after having tasted already the Soma juice by drinking from the Grahas belonging to two deities) he ought to eat the food (Purodâśa) which he has in his hand, and then drink from his own cup (*chamasa*). In this way, he takes (for himself) nourishment of both kinds (food and drink).

By taking both Soma draughts (from the *graha* and the *chamasa*) he obtains (for himself) nourishment (of all kinds).

(The Hotar pours some drops of Soma from the Graha into his Chamasa ; the meaning of this proceeding is given in the following :)

[13] The same speculations on the nature of the Rituyâjâs, *viz.*, that they are the vital airs, we find in the Kauṣîtakî Brâhm. 13, 9, and in the Gopatha Brâhm. 8, 7.

[14] The term used for "drinking" is *bhakṣayati*, which is also the common word for eating. That *bhakṣ* must have been used already in very ancient times for "drinking" the Soma juice, is shown in a passage in the Homa Yasht of the Zend-Avesta (see Yasna 10, 13.) *yase tê bâdha haoma zâirê gavâ iristahê bakṣaiti*, *i.e.*, who enjoys thee, O Homa, (Soma) when being dead (by bruising and squeezing) in the yellow milk. (The Homa juice of the Parsis is of yellow colour, and actually mixed with a little fresh milk).

[15] The formula for calling Ila is to be found in the Âsvalâyana Śrâuta Sûtra 1, 7 : *ilopâhûtâ*, &c.

The Soma jars belonging to two deities are the vital airs; the Chamasa of the Hotar is the soul. By pouring drops from the Soma jars belonging to two deities in the Chamasa of the Hotar, the Hotar puts (in his own body) the vital airs for obtaining his full age. He who has such a knowledge attains to his full age (100 years).

31.

(The Origin of the Tûṣṇîm Śaṁsa,[16] *i.e., Silent Praise, Explained.)*

The Asuras performed at the sacrifice all that the Devas performed. The Asuras became thus of equal **[139]** power (with the Devas), and did not yield to them (in any respect). Thereupon the Devas saw (by their mental eyes) the *tûṣṇîm śaṁsa, i.e.*, silent praise.[17] The Asuras (not knowing it) did not perform this (ceremony) of the Devas. This "silent praise" is the silent (latent) essence (of the mantras). Whatever weapon (*vajra*) the Devas raised against the Asuras, the latter got (always) aware of them.[18] The Devas then saw (by their mental eyes) the "silent praise" as their weapon; they raised it, but the Asuras did not get aware of it. The Devas aimed with it a blow at the Asuras and defeated the latter, who did not perceive (the weapon which was aimed at them). Thereupon the Devas became masters of the Asuras. He who has such a knowledge becomes master of his enemy, adversary, and hater.

The Devas thinking themselves to be victors spread the sacrifice (*i.e.*, made preparations for performing it). The Asuras came near it, intending to disturb it. When the Devas saw the most daring (of the Asuras) draw near from all quarters, they said: let us finish this sacrifice, lest the Asuras slay us. So they did. They finished it by repeating the "silent praise." (The words which constitute the "silent praise" now follow.) By the words, *bhûr agnir jyotir jyotir agniḥ*, they finished the Ajya and Pra-uga Śâstras (the two principal liturgies at the morning libation). By the words, *indro jyotir bhuvo jyotir indraḥ*, they finished the Niṣkevalya and Marutvatîya Śâstras **[140]** (the two principal liturgies at the midday libation). By the words, *sûrya jyotir jyotiḥ svaḥ*

[16] See about this particular part of the Soma service, Âśval. Śr. S. 5, 9, which passage is quoted by Sâyaṇa in his commentary on the Aitarêya Brâhmaṇam. The three formulas which constitute the Silent Praise (as mentioned here) form also, with the exception of the *vyâhṛitis* (the three great words *bhûr, bhuvaḥ, svaḥ*) a chant called the *Jyotirgâna*, which is sung by the Udgâtar when holding the cloth through which the Soma juice is strained (it is called *daśâpavitra*) in his hand. The metre of the three formulas (if all are taken together) is Gâyatrî. The Riṣi to whom it was revealed is said to be Puṣkala (Sâma prayoga).

[17] Mantras, sacred formulas and words, are always regarded as personages.

[18] The term in the original is: *pratyabudhyanta*. Sâyaṇa explains it by प्रतीकारं कुर्वन्ति, they retaliate, take revenge.

sûryaḥ, they finished the Vaiśvadeva and Agnimâruta Śâstras (the two liturgies of the evening libation).

Thus they finished the sacrifice by the "silent praise." Having thus finished the sacrifice by means "of the silent praise" they obtained the last mantra required for the safety of the sacrifice.[19] The sacrifice is finished when the Hotar repeats the "silent praise."

Should any one abuse the Hotar or curse him after having repeated the "silent praise," he should tell him (the man who abuses or curses him) that he (the abuser) would be hurt by doing so.

(In order to make abuses or curses retort upon their author, the Hotar repeats the following mantra :) "At morning we (the Hotars) finish to-day this sacrifice after having repeated the "silent praise." Just as one receives a guest (who comes to our houses) with ceremony, in the same way we receive (the sacrifice as our guest with due honours) by repeating this (silent praise)." He who having such a knowledge should abuse or curse the Hotar after he has repeated the " silent praise," suffers injury. Thence he who has such a knowledge should not abuse or curse, after the "silent praise" has been repeated.

32.

(On the Meaning of the Silent Praise.)

The "silent praise" are the eyes of the (three) libations. *Bhûr agnir*, &c., are the two eyes of the morning libation. *Indro jyotir*, &c., are the two eyes **[141]** of the midday libation. *Sûryo jyotir*, &c., are the two eyes of the evening libation. He who has such a knowledge, prospers by means of the three libations which are provided with eyes, and goes by means of such libations to the celestial world.

This " silent praise " is the eye of the sacrifice (the sacrificial man). There being only one of the " great words " (*bhûr, bhuvaḥ, svar*), (in the "silent praise" of every libation), it must be repeated twice, for, though the eye is (according to its substance) only one, it is double (in its appearance).

The " silent praise " is the root of the sacrifice. Should a Hotar wish to deprive any sacrificer of his standing place, then he must not at his sacrifice repeat the " silent praise ;" the sacrificer then perishes along with his sacrifice (the sacrificial personage) which thus has become rootless.

---

[19] The sacrifice is believed to be a chain ; none of its links is to be broken. If finished, it is rolled up. The last mantra represents the last link. Without the last link, a chain cannot be wound up.

About this they say: the Hotar ought to recite (it at any rate); for it is for the priest's own benefit when the Hotar repeats the "silent praise." In the priest rests the whole sacrifice, and the sacrificer in the sacrifice. Thence the "silent praise," ought to be repeated.

FIFTH CHAPTER.

The Different Parts of the Ajya Śâstra: Ahâva, Nivid, Sûkta.)

33.

The call, *śomsâvom*[1] (called *âhâva*) is the *Brahma*; **[142]** the address (*Nivid*)[2] is the *Kṣatram* (royal power), and the hymn (*sûkta*) are the subjects (*viś*). By repeating (first) the call *śomsâvom* (representing the Brahma), and then setting forth the titles (representing the royal power), the Hotar joins subsequently the Kṣatram to the Brahma. By repeating the Nivid before he recites the hymn, he joins subsequently the subjects to the Kṣatram, the Kṣatram being the Nivid, and the hymn the subjects.

Should the Hotar wish to deprive the sacrificer of his Kṣatram, he

---

[1] This formula, which is very frequently used, is only a corruption and contraction of शंसाव ओम् *i.e.*, let us both repeat the Śâstra. To this call by the Hotar the Adhvaryu responds with the words: शंस,मो दैव *i.e.*, we repeat, God! (*deva* meaning here only priest). This call of the Hotar is called *Ahâva*, and the response of the Adhvaryu *Pratigâra*. See Âśval. Sr. S. 5, 9, where the following rules regarding the repetition of the *Ahâva*, by which the Adhvaryu is informed that the Hotar is about to repeat his recitation, are given: एष आहाव: प्रात:सवने शस्त्रादिषु पर्यायप्रभृतीनांच सर्वत्रांत: शस्त्रं तेनचेापसंतान: this Ahâva (the call *śomsâvom* with a loud voice by the Hotar) takes place at the commencement of the Śâstras at the morning libation, and at the beginning of the several parts of the Śâstras (as in those of the Pra-uga Śâstra), and everywhere (at all Śâstras) within the Śâstra of which it forms an integral part. The first syllable शों is always *pluta*, *i.e.*, spoken with three moras, and also the *om* (*pranav*) at the end. In the Prayogas it is thus written: शों३ सावों३म. At the midday libation, the *âhâva* is preceded by the word अध्वर्यो Adhvaryu (Âśv. Sr. S. 5, 14), which is wanting at the morning libation. At the evening libation, there is another modification of the *âhâva*, *viz.*, अध्वर्यो शोशोंसवोम्, the syllable *śo* being repeated twice. This *âhâva* is regarded as a matter of great importance, and required at the beginning of all Śâstras, be they recited by the Hotar, or the Maitrâvaruṇa or Brâhmaṇâchhansi or the Achhâvâka. (See 3, 12.)

[2] The *Nivid* is an address either to a single deity or to a class of deities, inviting them to enjoy the Soma libation which had been prepared for them. It generally contains the enumeration of the titles and the qualities of the respective deities. Its proper place is only in the midday and evening libations. All the Nivids for these libations are given in full in the Sânkhâyana Sr. S. 8, 16-23. The twelve formulas addressed to Agni which are enumerated in 2, 34, are properly, speaking, no Nivid, but only a Puroruk, *i.e.* a mere preliminary address. They are actually called so in 2, 40. We find the word also in the Zend Avesta in the verbal form: *nivaêdayêmi i.e.*, I address my prayer to such and such beings (which are then mentioned).

has only to put in the midst of [143] the Nivid the hymn. By doing so, he deprives him of his Kṣatram.

Should the Hotar wish to deprive the sacrificer of his subjects (his income, &c.) he has only to put in the midst of the hymn the Nivid. By doing so, he deprives the sacrificer of his subjects.

But should he wish to perform the sacrifice in such a way as to keep the sacrificer in the proper possession of all he had (*Brahma*, *Kṣatra*, or *Viś*)[3], then he must first repeat the *âhâva* (*śomsâvom*,) then the *nivid*, and (lastly) the *sûkta* (hymn). This is the proper performance for all (the three castes).

Prajâpati was in the beginning only one (not distinguished from the world). He felt a desire of creating (beings) and (thus) multiplying himself. (Therefore) he underwent austerities, and remained silent. After a year had elapsed, he uttered twelve times (words) which constitute the Nivid of twelve sentences. After this Nivid had been pronounced, all creatures were produced.

(That the world had been created by means of the Nivid) this saw (also) a Riṣi (*Kutsa* by name) when repeating the following verse in which there is an allusion to it: *sa pûrvayâ nividâ* (1, 96, 2) *i.e.*, "he "(Agni) created through the first Nivid, through the praise of life in "songs, all the creatures of the Manus (regents of large periods of time); "through his lustre shining everywhere (he made) the heavens and "water; the gods (priests) kept Agni (back on earth), the giver of "treasures."

This is the reason that the Hotar gets offspring, when he puts the Nivid before the hymn (*sûkta*). He who has such a knowledge, is blessed with children and cattle.

34.

[144] (*The Several Words of the Nivid are Explained*).

The Hotar repeats: *Agnir deveddhaḥ*,[4] *i.e.*, Agni lighted by the gods. The Agni lighted by the gods is that Agni (in heaven); for the gods kindled him. By these words, he (the Hotar) has command over that Agni in that world (the fire in heaven).

The Hotar repeats: *Agnir manviddhaḥ*, *i.e.*, Agni lighted by men. The Agni lighted by men is this one (on earth); for men lighted him. Thus he has command over Agni who is in this world (on earth).

---

[3] That is to say, if he does not wish to deprive one of the royal caste of his nobility, or a Vaiśya of his caste.

[4] The address to Agni at the Darśapûrṇamâsa-iṣṭi, after the names of the chief patriarchs (*pravara*) of the sacrificer's family have been pronounced, is just like this one mentioned here, which is required at the Ajya Śâstra. Aśval. Śr. S. 1, 3.

The Hotar repeats: *Agniḥ suśamit, i.e.,* Agni who lights well. This is Vâyu. For Vâyu lights himself through himself and all that exists. Thus he has command over Vâyu in the airy region.

He repeats: *hotâ devaavṛitaḥ, i.e.,* the Hotar chosen by the gods. The Hotar chosen by the gods is that Agni (in heaven). For he is everywhere chosen by the gods. Thus he has command over him in that world (heaven).

He repeats: *hotâ manuvṛitaḥ, i.e.,* the Hotar chosen by men. The Hotar chosen by men is this Agni (on earth). For this Agni is everywhere chosen by men. Thus the Hotar has command over Agni in this world.

He repeats: *praṇîr yajñânâm, i.e.,* the carrier of sacrifices. Vâyu is the carrier of sacrifices. For, when he blows (*prâṇiti*), then the sacrifice exists, and consequently the *Agnihotram.* Thus he has command over Vâyu in the airy region.

He repeats: *rathir adhvarâṇâm, i.e.,* proprietor of the carriage
[**145**] laden with offerings. The proprietor of the carriage laden with offerings is that one (Agni in heaven, Âditya). For he moves to his place (to which he wishes to go), just as one who has a carriage. Thus the Hotar has command over him (Agni) in this world.

He repeats: *atûrto hotâ, i.e.,* the Hotar who is not to be overcome. This Agni (the Agni on earth) is the Hotar who is not to be overcome. None can come across his way. Thus the Hotar has command over Agni in this world (on earth).

He repeats: *tûrṇir havyâvaṭ, i.e.,* the runner who carries the offerings. Vâyu is the runner who carries the offerings. For Vâyu runs in an instant through the whole universe; he carries the offerings to the gods. Thus he has command over Vâyu in the airy region.

He repeats: *â devo devân vakṣat, i.e.,* may the god bring hither the gods. That god (Agni in heaven) is it who brings hither the gods. Thus he has command over that (Agni) in that world.

He repeats: *yakṣad agnir devo ḍevân, i.e.,* may Agni, the god, repeat the sacrificial mantras addressed to the gods. This Agni is it who repeats the sacrificial mantras addressed to the gods. Thus he has command over Agni in this world.

He repeats: *so adhvarâ karati, jâtavedâḥ, i.e.* may Jâtavedâs (Agni) prepare the sacred food. Vâyu is Jâtavedâs. Vâyu makes the whole universe. Thus he has command over Vâyu in the airy region.

35.

(On the Recitation of the Sûkta of the Ajya Śastra. The Peculiar Recitation of the First Verse Represents Copulation.)

(When the Hotar repeats) the (seven) Anuṣṭubh verses: *pra vo devâya agnaye* (3, 13), he separates [**146**] the first pada (from the second one). For a female divaricates her thighs (at the time of coitus.) He joins the two last padas (when repeating the hymn). For a male contracts his thighs (at the time of coitus). This (represents) copulation. Thus he performs the act of copulation (in a mystical way) at the very beginning of the recitation (of the Ajya Śastra), in order to produce (offspring and cattle for the sacrificer). He who has such a knowledge, is blessed with the production of offspring and cattle.

By separating, the two first padas when repeating (this hymn), he thus makes the hindpart of the weapon (represented by the Ajya Śastra) very thick, and by joining the two latter padas (of the hymn), he makes its forepart thin. (The same is the case with) an iron club or with an axe (that is to say, the forepart, the shaft is thin, and the (iron) part of them thick). Thus he strikes a blow with the weapon at his enemy and adversary. Whatever (enemy) of his is to be put down, this weapon will accomplish it.

36.

(Why the Hotṛi Priests Repair to the Dhiṣṇyas or Fire Places, stretching a Straight Line from the Agnîdhra Hearth. On the Name of the Ajya Śastra. The Śastra of the Achhâvâka belongs to Indra Agni).

The Devas and the Asuras were fighting in these worlds. The Devas had made the Sadas (sitting place) of the priests (on the right side of the Uttarâ Vedi) their residence. But the Asuras turned them out of it. They then repaired to the Agnîdhra[5] hearth (on the left of the Uttarâ Vedi). Thence they were [**147**] not conquered by the Asuras. Therefore, the priests take their seats near the Agnîdhra, and not in the Sadas. For, when sitting near the *Agnîdhra*, they are held (from *dhṛi* to hold). Thence that hearth is called Agnîdhra.

The Asuras extinguished the fires of the sitting place of the Devas. But the Devas took the fires (which they required) for their sitting places[6] from the Agnîdhra. By means of them they defeated

[5] The legend is here related, in order to account for the fact, that the priests when performing the Śastras, have their usual sitting place near the *Mârjâliya* fire and take their seats (*dhiṣṇya*) near the Agnîdhra fire.

[6] The places to which the Brâhmaṇam alludes are the so-called *Dhiṣṇyas*, extending in a straight line from the Mârjâli to the Agnîdhra fire. They are eight in number, all

the Asuras and Rakṣas, and drove them out. Thence the sacrificers, by taking out the different fires (required) from the Agnîdhra, defeat the Asuras and Rakṣasas and turn them out.

They conquered (*ajayanta*) by means of the (four) Ajya Śastras at the morning libation and entered (the place) which they had conquered. Thence the name *âjya* (from *ji* to conquer, and *â-yâ* to come near, enter).

Among the bodies of the minor Hotṛi priests (Maitrâvaruṇa, Brâhmaṇâchhansî, and Achhâvâka), that of the Achhâvâka was missing when they conquered and entered (the place); for in his body Agni and Indra had taken up their abode. Agni and Indra are of all the gods the strongest, mightiest, defeating best (the enemies), the most excellent, saving best (their friends). Thence the Śastra of the Achhâvâka[7] at the morning libation belongs to [148] Indra and Agni (whilst in those of the other Hotṛi priests, Agni alone is praised). For Indra and Agni took their abode in his (the Achhâvâka's) body. Thence the other Hotṛi priests walk first to their sitting places, and last comes the Achhâvâka. For he who is behind, is missing; he will join (the others) at a later time.

Thence the sacrificer should have a very strong Bahvṛicha[8] Brâhmaṇa to repeat the Achhâvâka Śastra, for only then (if he be strong) his (the priest's) body will not be missing.

37.

(*On the Meaning of the Ajya and Pra-uga Śastras. How they correspond with their respective Stotras. On the Yâjyâ of the Hotar.*)

The sacrifice is the carriage of the gods. The Ajya and Pra-uga Śastras are the two reins between (the carriage and the horses). By repeating the Ajya Śastra after the Pavamânaḥ Stotra (has been sung by the Sâma singers), and the Pra-uga after the Ajya Stotra,[9]

---

occupied by the so-called Hotṛi priests in the following order, commencing from the Mârjâli fire: Maitrâvaruṇa, Hotar, Brâhmaṇachhânsî, Potar, Neṣṭar, Achhâvâka, and Agnîd. Before each of these priests there is a small earthen ring, in which sand, dust, &c., are thrown and a little fire lighted on it for the protection of the Hotṛi priest who stands near it. See Mahîdhara's commentary on the Vâjasaneya Saṁhitâ, p. 151-52, ed. Weber, and the Katîyâ Sûtras 8, 6, 16-23. (p. 708-10, ed. Weber).

[7] The Śastra of the Achhâvâka consists of a hymn addressed to Indrâgnî, viz., *indrâgnî â gatam* (3, 12).

[8] This means a *Rigvedî*, *i.e.*, a repeater of the mantras, of which the Rigveda Saṁhitâ is made up.

[9] Each Śastram or recitation of one of the Hotṛi priests pre-supposes a Stotram, or performance of the Sâma singers. There are always as many Śastras as there are Stotras.

the Hotar holds asunder the reins of the carriage of the gods, in order to prevent it from being broken to pieces. In imitation thereof charioteers hold asunder the reins of human carriages. Neither the divine nor the human carriage of him who has such a knowledge will be broken.

They (the theologians) ask: How does the Ajya Śastra of the Hotar which belongs to Agni, correspond with the Pavamânya verses (for the fermentation of the Soma juice) which are chanted by the Sâma singers, (the rule being) that the Śastra **[149]** should be just like the Stotra?[10] (The answer is:) Agni is *pav mânaḥ*, *i.e.*, purifying, as even a Riṣi (already) said: *Agnir riṣiḥ pavamânaḥ* (9, 66, 20). The Ajya Śastra, which begins with verses addressed to Agni, thus corresponds with the Pavamânya verses of the Stotra (for Agni is also pavamânaḥ).

They ask: Why is the Stotram of the Sâma singers in the Gâyatrî, and the Ajya Śastra of the Hotar in the Anuṣṭubh metre, (the rule being) that the Stotram must be like the Śastram (*i.e.*, both must be of the same metre)? He ought to answer: one ought to look only to the total. There are seven verses (*i.e.*, the hymn of the Ajya Śastra) in the Anuṣṭubh metre; by repeating the first and last verses thrice, the number is brought to eleven; as the twelfth verse, the Yâjyâ, in the Virâṭ metre is to be counted, for the metres are not changed by an excess of one or two syllables.[11] These twelve (Anuṣṭubhs) are equal to sixteen Gâyatrîs. The Śastra being in the Anuṣṭubh metre, corresponds with the Gâyatrîs of the Stotram (the metres thus being equalized).

The Yâjyâ mantra (belonging to the Ajya Śastra of the Hotar) is, *agna indraścha dâśuṣo* (3, 25, 4.) (Instead of the regular order *indrâgnî*, there is *agna indraścha* in the Yâjyâ, *Agni* thus being first; but this must be so, for) these two (deities) did not conquer, as *Indrâgnî*, but they conquered, when being made, *Agnendrâu*. The reason that the Hotar repeats a Yâjyâ verse addressed to Agni-Indra is that he might be victorious. This verse is in the Virâṭ metre, which consists of thirty-three syllables. **[150]** There are thirty-three gods, *viz.*: eight Vasus, eleven Rudras, twelve Âdityas, one Prajâpati, and one Vaṣaṭkâra. Thus he makes the deities participate in the syllables at the very first recitation (the Ajya Śastra being the first among the twelve recitations of

[10] There appeared to be an exception to the rule in the fact that the Śastra and the Stotra have not the same deity, the first being addressed to Agni, and the latter to Indra, whilst, according to the rule, both Śastra and Stotra ought to refer to one and the same deity.

[11] The Anuṣṭubh has thirty-two syllables, but the Virâṭ thirty-three.

the Soma-day). According to the order of the (thirty-three) syllables, the gods severally (one after the other) drink (the Soma). Thus the deities are satisfied by the vessel holding the gods.[12]

They ask, Why is the Yâjyâ verse addressed to Agni-Indra, whilst the Ajya Śastra of the Hotar belongs to Agni alone, (the rule being) that the Yâjyâ verse is to correspond with the Śastra (to which it belongs)? (The answer is) The Agni-Indra-Yâjyâ is the same with the Indra-Agni one; and this Śastra belongs to Indra-Agni, as may be seen from the (Aindrâgna) Graha (mantra), and the "silent praise" (used at this occasion). For the Adhvaryu takes the Graha under the recital of the following mantra: *indrâgnî âgatam sutam*[13] (3, 12, 1. Vâjasaneya-Saṁhita 7, 31), *i.e.*, "Come ye, Indra and Agni! to the Soma juice, (which is like a) fine cloud. Drink of it, driven by your mind." The "silent praise" is, *bhûr agniṛ jyotir jyotir agnir, indro jyotir bhuvo jyotir indraḥ; sûryo jyotir jyotiḥ svaḥ sûryaḥ.* Thus the Yâjyâ verse is in accordance with the Śastram.

38.

(*The Japa which is Repeated before the Libations from the Dvidevatya Grahas are given. Its Several Sentences Explained.*)

The *Japa*[14] which the Hotar mutters, is the seed. **[151]** The effusion of seed is inaudible; so is the Japa. It is, as it were, the effusion of the seed.

---

[12] This mystical *devapâtra, i.e.*, vessel holding the gods, is here the Yâjyâ verse in the Virâṭ metre.

[13] This is the Yâjyâ mantra which is repeated by the Achhâvâka.

[14] This *Japa* or inaudible utterance of words is the very commencement of the Ajya Śastra. It is given in full, Aśval. Śr. S. 5, 9. First the Adhvaryu is called upon by the Hotar to turn away his face with the words: पराङ् अध्वर्यो, *i.e.*, Away, Adhvaryu! Then he commences the *Japa* with the words: *su-mat*, &c. (see 2, 24). We here give the whole of it:

सुमत्पद्वग्दे पिता मातरिश्वा छिद्रा पदा धादछिद्रोक्था कवयः शंसन्त्सोमो विश्वविन्नीथानि नेषद्बृहस्पतिरुक्था मदानि शंसिषद्वागायुर्विश्वायुर्विश्वमायुः क इदं शंसिष्यति स इदं शंसिष्यति.

i.e., "May the father Mâtariśvan (wind, breath) make the verse feet without a breach! May the Kavis repeat the recitations without a breach! May Soma, the all-possessing, guide our performances! May Bṛihaspati repeat the recitations (and) the joyful choruses! Vâch (speech) is life, she has the whole life. She is life. Who will repeat this (Śastra)? He (*i.e.*, I, the Hotar, representing Vâch) will repeat it." From the contents of this *Japa*, it is evident that the Hotar invokes the deities presiding over breath, speech, and literary skill, for a successful recitation of the whole Śastra, to accomplish which is regarded as an arduous task. In one of the sentences of this *Japa* the repeaters are called *kavis*, which appears to have been the more ancient name of the Hotṛi priests. It is mentioned as signifying a class of priests in the Zend-Avesta also.

He mutters the Japa before the call *śoṁsâvom*. For all that is repeated after the call, *śoṁsâvom,* forms part of the Śastra. The Hotar addresses this call (*śoṁsâvom*) to the Adhvaryu, when the latter with his face turned away is lying prostrate on the earth (using the two hands as his two forelegs like beasts). For four-footed beings (animals) emit their sperms (at the time of copulation) having turned their faces away from one another. He (the Adhvaryu) then stands upright on his two legs. For two-footed beings (men) emit their sperms when facing one another in a straight line.

(The several sentences of the Japa are now explained).

He mutters, *pitâ mâtariśvâ.* The breath is *pitâ* (father), and the breath is *mâtariśvâ* ; the breath is seed.

[152] By repeating these words, he (the Hotar) emits the seed (for a spiritual birth).

Achhidrâ padâ dhâ.[12] *Achhidrâ,* *i.e.,* without breach, is seed. Thence a being which is unbroken (a whole) rises out of the seed.

Achhidrâ ukthâ kavayaḥ śaṁsann. Those who have learnt by heart (the mantras) are called *kavis.* The sentence means: "They produced this unbroken (matter), *i.e.,* the seed."

Somo viśvavid—saṁśiṣat. Brihaspati is Bṛahma ; the Soma, who is praised by the singers, is the Kṣatram. The *nîthâni* and *ukthâ madâni* are the Śastras. By repeating this sentence, the Hotar recites his Śastras, instigated (*prasuta*) by the divine Brahma and by the divine Kṣatra. Both these (Bṛihaspati and Soma) preside over the whole creation, whatever exists. For all that the Hotar is doing without being incited by these two (deities), is not done. (Just as) they reproach one (in common life, when something is done without order, saying) he has done what was not done (not to be done). Of him who has such a knowledge all that is done will be done, and nothing that is done be undone.

Vâg-âyur. *Ayuḥ* (life) is breath ; seed is breath ; the womb is *vâch.* By repeating this sentence, he pours the seed into the womb.

Kaidam-śaṁsiṣyati. *Kaḥ* (who ?) is Prajâpati. The meaning of the sentence is, Prajâpati will generate.

39.

(*On the Meaning of the Six Members of the "Silent Praise," and the Twelve Members of the Puroruk. Why Jâtavedâs is mentioned in the Puroruk. The Meaning of the Ajya-sûkta.*)

Having called *śoṁsâvom,* he recites the "silent praise." This trans-

[12] Âśval., *dhât.*

forms the seed (represented by **[153]** the *Japa*). First the effusion of the seed takes place; then follows its transformation.

He repeats the "silent praise" without proper articulation of the voice [16] (in order to make its proper words unintelligible even to those who stand nearest). For, in the same way, the seeds are transformed (going across one another).

He repeats the "silent praise" in six padas[17] (*i.e.*, stopping six times). For man is six-fold, having six limbs. Thus he produces by transformation the soul as six-fold, consisting of six parts.

After having repeated the "silent praise," he repeats the *Puroruk* (Nivid 2, 34). Thus he brings forth (as a birth) the seed which had been transformed. The transformation (of the seed) occurs first; then follows birth.

He repeats the Puroruk with a loud voice. Thus he brings him (the mystical body of the sacrificer) forth with a loud voice (crying).

He repeats it in twelve padas. The year has twelve months; Prajâpati is the year; he is the producer of the whole universe. He who is the producer of the whole universe, produces also him (the sacrificer) and (provides him) with offspring and cattle for propagation. He who has such a knowledge, prospers in offspring and cattle.

He repeats a Puroruk addressed to *Jâtavedas*[18] (Agni), the word Jâtavedâs occurring in the last (twelfth part (of it).

[154] They ask, Why do they repeat at the morning libation a Puroruk addressed to Jâtavedâs, whereas this deity has its proper place at the evening libation? (The answer is) Jâtavedâs is life. For he knows (*veda*) all that are born. As many as he knows of are born (*jâtânâm*), so many (only) exist.[19] How could those exist of whom he does not know (that they are born?) Whosoever (what sacrificer) knows that he himself is made a new man (by means of the Ajya Śastra), he has a good knowledge.

40.

He repeats the (hymn), *pra vo devâya Agnaye* (3, 13).[20] (The word) *pra* means *prâṇa* (life). For all these beings move only after having been

---

[10] This is called: *tira iva*, *i.e.*, across as it were.

[17] Its six parts are as follows: (1) भूरग्निर्ज्योतिर् (2) ज्योतिरग्निर् (3) इन्द्रोज्योतिर्भुवो (4) ज्योतिरिन्द्रोस् (5) सूर्योज्योतिर् (6) ज्योतिः स्वःसूर्योम्. See Âśval. Śr. S. 5, 8. Properly speaking, the "silent praise" consists only of three padas. See Ait. Br. 2, 31.

[18] This refers to the last pada of the Puroruk or Nivid, where Agni is mentioned by the name of *Jâtavedâs*. See 2, 34.

[19] This is an explanation of the name "*Jâtavedâs*."

[20] This is the Ajya-sûkta, the chief part of the Ajya-śastra.

endowed with *prâṇa.* Thus the Hotar produces the *prâṇa* (for the sacrificer), and makes it ready (for use).

He repeats, *dîdivâṁsam apûrvyam* (3, 13, 5).[21] For the mind has become shining (*dîdâya*), and nothing exists anterior (*apûrvyam*) to the mind. Thus he produces the mind (of the sacrificer), and makes it (ready for use).

He repeats, *sa naḥ śarmâni vîtaye* (4). *Vâch* is *śarma* (refuge). For they say about one who is repeating with his speech (the words of another). "I have stopped his talkativeness (*śarmavat*)."[22] By **[155]** repeating this vsrse, the Hotar produces speech (in the sacrificer), and makes it ready (for use).

He repeats, *uta no brahman* (6). Brahma is the sense of hearing. For, by means of the ear, one hears the Brahma ;[23] Brahma is placed in the ear. By repeating this verse, he produces (in the sacrificer) the sense of hearing, and makes it ready (for use).

He repeats, *sa yantâ vipra* (3). The air exhaled is Yantâ, *i.e.*, restrainer. For the air inhaled (*prâṇa*) is held back by the air exhaled (*apâna*), and does (consequently) not turn away. By repeating this verse, he produces the *apâna* (in the sacrificer), and makes it ready (for use).

He repeats, *ritâvâ yasya rodasî* (2). *Rita, i.e.*, true is the eye. For if two men have a dispute with one another (about anything), they believe him who says, "I have seen it by the exertion of (my own) eyes." By repeating this verse, he produces the eye (in the sacrifice), and makes it ready (for use).

With the verse, *nû no râsva* (7), he concludes. The whole (man) "endowed with thousand-fold gifts, with offspring, and thriving well,"[24] is the *âtmâ* (soul). By repeating this verse, he thus produces the soul as the aggregate man, and makes it ready (for use).

He repeats a Yâjyâ mantra. The *Yâjyâ* is a gift, meritorious, and

---

[21] Though in the Sûkta the fifth verse, it is the second, if this hymn is used as the principal part of the Ajya Śastra.

[22] The words, शर्मवद्वास्माआयांसि are no doubt an idiomatical phrase of the ancient Sanskrit, the exact meaning of which it is now impossible to determine. Sâyaṇa expiains it in the following way: अस्मैगुरोत्तार्थस्य सम्यगनुवादिने शिष्याय शर्मवत् सुखयुक्तजीवनं संपन्नं । यस्मात् तस्मात् । हे शिष्य आयांसि समन्ततो नियतोऽस्मि The irregular form आस्म। instead of अस्मै he takes a Vedic anomaly. The phrase, he further adds, is applied in common life when one's speech is stopped. The author of the Brâhmaṇa adduces this phrase only in illustration of the supposed identity of *Vâch* with *Sarma.*

[23] Sây. takes it in the sense of *Veda*, which appears to be the right interpretation, if the word is restricted to the Mantras.

[24] These are words of the Mantra.

fortune. By repeating it, he makes him (the sacrificer) a pure (goddess) of fortune [25] and prepares her for assisting him.

He who has such a knowledge, merges in the deities, after having been identified with the metres, **[156]** the deites, the Brahma, and immortality. He who thus knows how to become identified with metres, &c., has (certainly) a good knowledge ; it is beyond the soul and beyond any deity (*i. e.*, this knowledge is of higher value than the soul, or any god).

41.

(*The Meaning of the Several Verses of the Ajya Sûkta.*)

He repeats the "silent praise" in six padas. There are six seasons. By doing so, he makes the seasons and enters them.

He repeats the Puroruk in twelve padas. There are twelve months. By doing so, he makes the months and enters them.

He repeats, *pra vo devâya* [26] (3, 13). *Pra* is the air. For all beings go after air. By repeating this verse, he makes the air and enters it.

He repeats, *dîdivâṁsam.* The sun is *dîdâya*, nothing is earlier[27] than the sun. By repeating this verse, he makes the sun and enters it.

He repeats, *sa naḥ śarmâṇi vîtaye.* *Śarmâṇi* (places of refuge) means Agni. He, gives nourishment. By repeating this verse, he makes Agni and enters Agni.

He repeats, *uta no brahman.* The moon is Brahma. By repeating this verse, he makes the moon and enters her.

He repeats, *sa yantâ.* Vâyu is *yantâ* (the restrainer) ; for by Vâyu (wind) the universe is kept up, who prevents the air from gathering in the atmosphere only. By repeating this verse, he makes Vâyu and enters him.

[157] He repeats, *ṛitâvâ yasya rodasî.* Heaven and earth are the two *rodas.* Thus he makes heaven and earth and enters them.

He concludes with the verse, *nû no râsva.* The year is a whole with thousand-fold gifts, produces, and well-being. Thus he makes the year as a whole and enters it.

He repeats a Yâjyâ mantra. The Yâjyâ is rain (and rain is) lightning. For lightning (produces) rain, and rain gives food. Thus he makes lightning and enters it. He who has such a knowledge, becomes identified with (all) these things [28] and with the deities.

---

[25] The word *lakṣmi* here evidently expresses the idea of "destiny" in general.

[26] The Ajya-sûkta (3, 13), which has been explained in the preceding chapter, is here explained again.

[27] This is an explanation of the term *apûrvyam* in the verse in question.

[28] Such as the seasons, months, Agni, &c., which are severally mentioned in this paragraph.

THIRD BOOK.

FIRST CHAPTER.

[**158**] *(The Pra-uga Śastra. Vaṣaṭkâra. The Nivids.)*

(The Pra-uga Śastra.) [1]

1.

(The deities of the Pra-uga Śastra.)

The Pra-uga Śastra is the recitation appropriate to the Soma offer-

---

[1] The Pra-uga Śastra is the most peculiar of all the recitations by the Hotar on the day of the Soma feast; for it comprises a larger number of deities, divided into regular sections, than any other one, and has neither a proper Nivid, nor Pragâthas, nor Dhâyyâs, nor Sûktas, as we constantly find at the Śastras of the midday and evening libations. It consists only of the verses in seven sections, mentioned in the Rigveda-Saṁhitâ (1, 2-3). Each section is preceded by a so-called Puroruk, along with the Ahâva. Before the Puroruk of the first section there are, besides, the Hiṁkâra and the three great words required. I here write these introductory words in the same order in which they are repeated by the Hotṛi-priests up to the present day: हिं भूर्भुवः स्वरों३ शों३ सावों३ वायुरग्रेगा यज्ञप्रीः साकं गन्मनसा यज्ञं । शिवो नियुद्भिः शिवाभों३ वायवायाहि॰ (see 1, 2, 1-3) *i.e.*, may Vâyu who walks first, be the enjoyer of the sacrificer, come with his mind to the sacrifice; (may he come) the happy with his happy crowd! Om! Come, O Vâyu, &c.

The Puroruk of the second triplet (1. 2, 4-6), which is addressed to Indravâyu, is:

शों३सावों३ हिरण्यवर्त्तनी नरा देवा पती अभिष्टये । वायु रथेंद्रश्च सुमखो३ मिंद्रवायू इमे सुता॰

i.e., the two divine men who come of golden paths, the two masters (who are) for protection, Indra and Vâyu, the happy ones, &c.

Puroruk of the third triplet, which is addressed to Mitra-Varuṇa (1, 2, 7-9):

शों३॰ काव्या राजाना क्रत्वा दक्षस्य दुरोणे। रिशादसा सधस्थयों३ मित्रंजहुवे॰ the two Kavyas (descendants of the Kavis), the two kings (who are distinguished) through skilful performance (of sacrifices) at home, and who destroy the enemies in the combat.

Puroruk of the fourth triplet, which is addressed to the Aśvin, (1, 3, 1-3):

शों३॰ दैव्या अध्वर्यु आगतं रथेन सूर्यत्वचा॰ । मध्वा यज्ञं समंजाथो३ माश्विना यज्वरी॰

Ye two divine Adhvaryus whose skin is sun-like, come up with (your) carriage; may ye anoint the sacrifice with honey!

Puroruk before the fifth triplet, which is addressed to Indra (1, 3, 4-6):

शों३॰ इंद्र उक्थेभिर्मंदिष्ठो वाजानां च वाजपतिः । हरिवां सुतानां सखो३मिन्द्रायाहि॰ Indra who is most stimulated (to action) through the recitations (of the Hotṛis), and is the lord of booty, he, with his two yellow horses, the friend of the Soma drops.

Puroruk before the sixth triplet, which is addressed to the Viśve Devâḥ (1, 3, 7-9):

शों३॰विश्वान्देवान्हवामहेऽस्मिन्यज्ञे सुपेशसः। त इमं यज्ञमागमन् देवासो दैव्या धिया। जुषाणा अध्वरे सदो ये यज्ञस्य तनूकृतः विश्व आ सोमपीतयो३ मोमासश्च॰ We call all the gods the well-adorned to this sacrifice; may these gods come to this sacrifice with divine thought, favourably accepting the seat (prepared for them) at the preparation (by cooking) of the self-making sacrifice (*i.e.*, of the sacrificial personage whose body is always restored by itself, when the sacrificial rites are performed); (may) all (come) to drink the Soma!

ings from the Grahas. Nine[2] such Grahas are taken at the morning. With nine [159] verses forming the Bahiṣ-pavamâna chant,[3] they are praised by singers. After the singers have finished [160] their chant, the Adhvaryu takes the tenth Graha (for the Aśvins); the sound "*hiṁ*" uttered by singers when chanting the other verses, counts as the tenth part. Thus, an equality[4] of the Grahas and verses of the chant is obtained.

The Hotar repeats a triplet addressed to Vâyu (1, 2, 1-3). By this the Vâyu graha is celebrated. He repeats a triplet addressed to Indra-Vâyu (1, 2, 4-6). By this the Indra-Vâyu graha is celebrated. He repeats a triplet addressed to Mitra, Varuṇa. By this the Mitra-Varuṇa graha is celebrated. He repeats a triplet addressed to the Aśvins (1, 3, 1-3). By this the Aśvin graha is celebrated. He repeats a triplet addressed to Indra (1, 3, 4-6). By this the Śukra and Manthi grahas are celebrated. He repeats a triplet addressed to the Viśve Devâḥ (1, 3, 7-9). By this the Agrayaṇa graha is celebrated. He repeats a triplet addressed to Sarasvatî (1, 3, 10-12), though there is no Sarasvatî graha (no such vessel as in the other cases). Sarasvatî is Speech. Whatever grahas are taken by means of Speech (under recital of a mantra), all these are celebrated by means of Śastras. He who has such a knowledge gets (thus) celebrated (all his Grahas).

2.

(On the Meaning of the Several Parts of the Pra-uga Śastra.)

By means of the Pra-uga Śastra one obtains food. In (each part of) the Pra-uga Śastra, there is always another deity praised, and (thus) always another being celebrated. He who has such a knowledge [161], keeps different kinds of food in his Grahas.[5] The Pra-uga Śastra is, as it were, most intimately connected with the sacrificer. Thence they say, the greatest attention is to be paid to it by the sacrificer. For by means of it the Hotar makes him (his new body) ready.

Puroruk before the seventh triplet, which is addressed to Sarasvatî (1, 3, 10-12):

ओं३ वाचमहं देवीं वाचास्मिन्यज्ञे सुपेशसा सरस्वतीं हवामहेंपावका ० I (invoke) the goddess of Speech with my excellent speech at this sacrifice; we invoke Sarasvatî, &c. (Saptahâutra).

[2] The nine Grahas here alluded to are the Upâṁśu, Antaryâma, Vâyava, Aindravâyava, Maitrâvaruṇa, Aśvina, Śukra, Manthis Agrayaṇa. The libations from these nine Grahas belong to the Bahiśpavamâna Stotra, and the Pra-uga Sastra.

[3] See page 120.

[4] The expression in the original is, *so sá sammá*, no doubt an idiomatical expression, implying "this and that is the same."

[5] The whole Pra-uga is intended for providing the sacrificer with food. A variety in food is produced by changing the deities in every part of the Śastra.

He repeats a triplet, addressed to Vâyu, because they say, life is Vâyu, seed is life. Seed is first produced (in the body) before a man is produced (out of it). By repeating a triplet addressed to Vâyu, the Hotar makes the *prâṇa* (air inhaled) of the sacrificer.

He repeats a triplet, addressed to Indra and Vâyu. Where there is *prâṇa* (air inhaled), there is *apâna* (air exhaled). By repeating a triplet, addressed to Indra and Vâyu, he thus makes the *prâṇa* and *apâna* of the sacrificer.

He repeats a triplet, addressed to Mitra-Varuṇa. That is done, because they say, the eye is first produced when a human being is being called into existence. By repeating a triplet, addressed to Mitra-Varuṇa, he thus makes eyes to the sacrificer.

He repeats a triplet, addressed to the Aśvins. Because parents say, in their conversations about a child when it is born, "it has the desire of listening (to us); it is very attentive." By repeating a triplet, addressed to the Aśvins, he makes to the sacrificer the sense of hearing.

He repeats a triplet, addressed to Indra. Because parents say, in their conversations about a child, when it is born, "it endeavours to raise its neck, then its head." By repeating a triplet, addressed to Indra, he makes to the sacrificer, strength.

He repeats a triplet, addressed to Viśve Devâḥ. Because a child when it is born, uses hands and feet **[162]** after (it has been able to use the eye, ear, and to raise its neck). The limbs (for they are many) belong to the Viśve Devâḥ, *i.e.,* All Gods. By repeating a triplet, addressed to the Viśve Devâḥ, he thus makes the limbs to the sacrificer.

He repeats a triplet, addressed to Sarasvatî. Because Speech enters the child, when it is born, last. Sarasvatî is speech. By repeating a triplet, addressed to Sarasvatî, he thus makes speech to the sacrificer.

The Hotar who has such a knowledge, as well as the sacrificer for whom the Hotṛi priests repeat the recitations (Śastras), are, though already born (from their mother), born again from all these deities, from all the recitations (Śastras), from all the metres, from all the triplets of the Pra-uga Śastra, from all the (three) libations.

3.

(*The Hotar has it in his power to deprive the Sacrificer of his life, &c., by not repeating the several parts of the Pra-uga Śastra in the proper way.*)

This Pra-uga Śastra represents the vital airs. The Hotar addresses this recitation to seven deities. For there are seven vital airs in the head. By doing so, the Hotar places the vital airs in the head (of the sacrificer).

There is the question asked, Whether the Hotar might be able to produce woe as well as happiness to the sacrificer? (The answer is) He who might be the Hotar of the sacrificer at that time (when the Pra-uga Śastra is to be repeated) can do with him what he pleases. If he think, "I will separate him from his vital airs," he need only repeat the triplet addressed to Vâyu confusedly, or forego a pada, by which means the (several parts of the) triplet become con-
[163] fused. In this manner, he separates him (the sacrificer) whom he wishes so to separate, from his vital airs.

Should he think, "I will separate him from his *prâṇa* and *apâna*," he need only repeat the triplet addressed to Indra-Vâyu confusedly, or forego a pada. In this way, the triplet becomes confused, and he thus separates the sacrificer, whom he wishes so to separate, from his *prâṇa* and *apâna*.

Should he think, "I will separate the sacrificer from his eye," he need only repeat the triplet addressed to Mitra-Varuṇa confusedly, or forego a pada. In this way the triplet becomes confused, and he thus separates the sacrificer, whom he wishes so to separate, from his eye.

Should he think, "I will separate him from the sense of hearing," he need only repeat the triplet addressed to the Aśvins confusedly, or forego a pada. In this way, the triplet becomes confused, and he separates the sacrificer, whom he wishes so to separate, from the sense of hearing.

Should he think, "I will separate him from his strength," he need only repeat the triplet addressed to Indra confusedly, or forego a pada. In this way, the triplet becomes confused, and he separates him, whom he wishes so to separate, from his strength.

Should he think, "I will separate him from his limbs," he need only repeat the triplet addressed to the Viśve Devâḥ confusedly, or forego a pada. In this way, the triplet becomes confused, and he separates the sacrificer, whom he wishes so to separate, from his limbs.

Should he think, "I will separate him from his speech," he need only repeat the triplet addressed to Sarasvatî confusedly, or forego a pada. In this way, the triplet becomes confused, and he separates the **[164]**
sacrificer, whom he wishes so to separate, from his speech.

Should he think, "I will keep him joined with all his limbs and his soul," he ought to repeat the triplet, as it was first told (to him by his master) in the right way. Thus he keeps him joined with all his limbs and his whole soul. He who has such a knowledge remains joined with all his limbs and the whole soul.

4

(*All the Deities of the Pra-uga Śastra are said to be forms of Agni.*)

They ask, How (can it be accounted for) that the verses addressed to Agni which the Sâma singers chant,[6] are celebrated by a recitation of the Hotar commencing with a verse addressed to Vâyu, (the rule being) that the Śastra exactly corresponds to the Stotra? (The answer is) Those deities are only the bodies of Agni. When Agni is blazing up, as it were, that is his Vâyu (wind) form. Thus he celebrates by means of this (Vâyu form) that (Agni form).

Divided into two halves, the fire burns. Indra and Vâyu are two. That is his Indra-Vâyu form. Thus he celebrates by means of this (Indra-Vâyu form) that (Agni form).

It moves up and down (when being lighted or extinguished); this is his Mitra-Varuṇa form. Thus he celebrates by means of this (Mitra-Varuṇa form) that (Agni form).

[165] The dangerous touch[7] of Agni is his Varuṇa form. His Mitra form is (shown in the fact) that men who make friends with him may sit near him, though his touch be dangerous. Thus he celebrates by means of these (Mitra and Varuṇa forms) that (Agni form).

His Aśvina form is that they produce him by friction through two arms and two wooden sticks, the Aśvins being two. Thus he celebrates by means of this (Aśvina form) that (Agni form).

That he burns with a loud crackling voice, imitating the sound *bababâ*, as it were, on account of which all beings flee trembling from him. This is his Indra form. Thus the Hotar celebrates by means of the (Indra form) that (Agni form).

That they divide him into many parts (when taking fire from the hearth), though he is only one. This is his Viśve Devâḥ form. Thus the Hotar celebrates by means of this (Viśve Devâḥ form) that (Agni form).

That he burns with a roaring noise, uttering speech, as it were. This is his Saravatî form. Thus the Hotar celebrates by means of this (Sarasvatî form) that (Agni form).

In this way, the triplet of the Sâma singers[8] becomes celebrated, notwithstanding these (different) deities in the several triplets, for him who thus has commenced (the Sastra) with a verse addressed to Vâyu.

---

[6] The recitation of the Pra-uga Śastra is preceded by the singing of the so-called *Ajya-stotra*: *agna âyâhi vîtaye* (Sâma-veda 2, 10-12). The deity of it is Agni, whilst the deities of the Pra-uga Śastra, to which it is said to stand in connection, are different.

[7] *Ghora-samsparśa.* See the Kauṣîtaki Brâhmaṇam 1, 1, where Agni says: अहं घोरसंस्पर्शतमो ऽस्मि.

[8] The Ajya Stotra, see note 1. It consists of three verses.

Having repeated the Śastra addressed to all the gods[9] (*Pra-uga*), he recites a Yâjyâ mantra addressed **[166]** to the Viśve Devâḥ (all gods): *viśvebhiḥ somyan madhvagna* (1, 14, 10). Thus he satisfies all deities, giving to each his due share.

5.

(*On the Vaṣaṭkâra and Anuvaṣaṭkâra.*)

The Vaṣaṭkâra[10] (the formula *vauṣaṭ!*) is the drinking vessel of the gods. By making the Vaṣaṭkâra, the Hotar satisfies the deities with (presenting) a drinking vessel.

He makes the Anuvaṣaṭkâra (the formula "Agni, eat!"). In this way, he satisfies the deities by repeatedly placing before them the Vaṣaṭkâra (representing the drinking vessel), just as men place before their horses or cows repeatedly grass, water, &c.[11]

They ask, Why do they sacrifice in the same Agni (the Agni of the Uttarâ Vedi) where they did it before, and make the Vaṣaṭkâra there, when sitting near the Dhiṣṇya[12] fires (after having left the place near the Uttarâ Vedi)? (The answer is) By making the Anuvaṣṭkâra, "Agni, taste the Soma!" he makes there the Vaṣaṭkâra and pleases the Dhiṣṇyas.

They ask, Which is the Sviṣṭakṛit portion of the Soma at those offerings,[13] of which the priest tastes without having finished them, and without making the Anuvaṣaṭkâra? (The answer is) By repeating the Anuvaṣaṭkâra (when repeating the Yâjyâs for the Śastras), "Agni, taste the Soma!" they (complete the ceremony and) drink from the Soma juice after the completion (of the **[167]** ceremony).[14] This very (Anuvaṣaṭkâra) is the Sviṣṭakṛit portion of the Soma. (Thence) he makes the Vaṣaṭkâra (and Anuvaṣaṭkâra).

---

[9] The Pra-uga Śastra is here called *vaiśvadevam, i.e.*, belonging to all the gods, on account of the large number of deities, comprising the Viśve Devâḥ contained in it.

[10] The paragraphs from 5, 8, are found also with very little change and a few omissions in the Gopatha Brâhmaṇam 3, 1—5. Both evidently come from one source only.

[11] This is the full meaning of पुनरभ्याकार as explained by Sâyaṇa.

[12] See above.

[13] These are the *dvidevatya grahas*, see 2.

[14] The priests are not allowed to eat from the sacrificial food, or drink of the Soma, before all the ceremonies pertaining to the offerings to the gods are completed. The Sviṣṭakṛit ceremony is regarded as the completion of the principal rites attending any oblation given to the gods. At this ceremony, the Anuvaṣaṭkâra does not take place. After it is completed, the priests are allowed to eat the remainder of the food or drink the remaining juice.

6.

(On the Meaning of the Vaṣaṭkâra and its Different Parts).

The Vaṣaṭkâra is a weapon. If one has an enemy (and wishes to destroy him), one has only to think of him when making the Vaṣaṭkâra, in order to strike him a blow with a weapon (in the form of the Vaṣaṭkâra).

The word *ṣaṭ* (six) is contained in the formula *vau-ṣaṭ*[15] (the so-called Vaṣaṭkâra). There are six seasons. Thus he makes the seasons and establishes them. He who is established in the seasons becomes afterwards (also) established in all other things. He who has such a knowledge, obtains a firm footing.

Hiraṇyadan, the son of Beda, said about this (the Vaṣaṭkâra) as follows: By this part *ṣaṭ* (six) of the formula (*vauṣaṭ*), the Hotar establishes these six (things). The sky rests on the air; the air on the earth; the earth on the waters; the waters [**168**] on the reality (*satya*); the reality on the Brahma; the Brahma on the concentrated heat of meditation (*tapas*). If these places are established, then all things are consequently established. He who has such a knowledge has a firm footing.

The part *vâu* of the formula *vauṣaṭ* means the six seasons. By repeating the Vaṣaṭkâra, the Hotar places the sacrificer in the seasons, gives him a footing in them. Just as he does unto the gods, the gods do unto him.

7.

(The Three Kinds of the Vaṣaṭkâra: Vajra, Damachhad, and Rikta. In what Tone the Vaṣaṭkâra is to be Repeated. The Hotar can, by not repeating it properly, injure the Sacrificer.)

There are three (kinds of the) Vaṣaṭkâra, *vajra* (weapon), *damachhad* (who covers beings), and *rikta* (empty, void).

It is a *vajra* (weapon), in consequence of its being pronounced with a loud and strong voice by the Hotar. With it he strikes, whenever he pleases, a blow to his enemy and adversary who is to be put down by him, in order to put him down. Thence is this weapon, in the form of the Vaṣaṭkâra, to be used by the sacrificer who has enemies.

It is *damachhad*, *i.e.*, protecting the beings, on account of its being pronounced as an integral part of the verse to which it belongs without

[15] The etymology which is here given of the word *vauṣaṭ* is of course quite fanciful. It is only a very much lengthened pronunciation of a conjunctive form *vokṣaṭ*, of the root *vah*, to carry, meaning, may he (Agni) carry it (the offering) up. Instead of the original *ôk*, *âu* was substituted.

omitting any part of it.[16] Children and cattle stand near (this part of **[169]** the Vaṣaṭkâra) and follow it. Thence ought he, who desires children and cattle, to make this Vaṣaṭkâra.

It is *rikta, i.e.*, void; the syllable *ṣaṭ* being pronounced with a low accent. He thus makes void (*rikta*) the soul, and the sacrificer. He who makes such a Vaṣaṭkâra becomes a great sinner, and also he for whom such a Vaṣaṭkâra is made. Thence he should not wish to make it.

As regards the question whether the Hotar might make the sacrificer happy or unhappy, the answer is, that he who might be the Hotar of any sacrificer can do so. At this (occasion, *i.e.*, at the sacrifice), the Hotar may just do with the sacrificer as he pleases.

Should he wish to deprive the sacrificer of the fruit of his sacrifice, he has only to repeat the (Yâjyâ) verse, and the Vaṣaṭkâra in the same tone[17] (*i.e.*, monotonously). If he do so, he deprives the sacrificer of the fruit of his sacrifice.

Should he wish to make the sacrificer liable to the consequences of a great guilt, he has only to repeat the (Yâjyâ) verse with a very loud voice, and the Vaṣaṭkâra with a very low one. (If he do so) he makes the sacrificer liable to the consequences of a great guilt.

Should he wish to make the sacrificer very happy, he has to repeat the (Yâjyâ) verse with a very low, and the Vaṣaṭkâra with a very loud, voice. (That is done) for obtaining fortune. By doing so, he puts the sacrificer in (the possession of) fortune.

The Vaṣaṭkâra is to form an integral part of the (Yâjyâ) verse (no stopping between the end of the **[170]** verse and *vauṣaṭ* being allowed), in order to have an uninterrupted whole. He who has such a knowledge becomes possessed of children and cattle.

8.

(*The Danger which might be imminent upon the Hotar and Sacrificer, in consequence of the Vaṣaṭkâra weapon, is to be averted by certain Formulas.*)

The Hotar ought to think of the deity to whom the oblation is given

---

16 The term in the original is *nirhâṇarcha, i.e.*, without losing any part of the *Rich*. This means, that no vowel is to be dropped at the end of the Yâjyâ verse when *Vauṣaṭ* is joined to it as an integral part. The remark is made on account of the way in which the syllable *om* (when *praṇava* is made) is joined to the last syllable of a verse. In that case, the last vowel disappears and *ô* is substituted in its stead. If, for instance, the last syllable of the *Rich* be *ya*, then in the Praṇava *yom* is pronounced. See the rules for making the Praṇava in the Sâmidhenî verses, Âśv. Śr. S. 1, 2.

17 The Yâjyâ is repeated monotonously, and, at the morning libation, in a low tone, whilst the Vaṣaṭkâra is pronounced with a loud voice.

when he is about to repeat the Vaṣaṭkâra. Thus he pleases the deity personally, and addresses the Yâjyâ mantra direct to it.

The Vaṣaṭkâra is a weapon.[18] The weapon is like a flash when one strikes with it without having conjured its evil effects.[19] Not every one knows how to conjure it, nor its (proper) place. Therefore the mantra, *vag ojaḥ* (Âśv. Śr. S. 1, 5) is at such occasions, when even many are killed (as is the case in a battle), the propitiation, and the assignation of the proper place (after the Vaṣaṭkâra). For this reason, the Hotar has, after every Vaṣaṭkâra, to repeat the Anumantraṇa[20] formula, *vâg ojaḥ*. If thus propitiated, the Vaṣaṭkâra does not hurt the sacrificer,[21]

[**171**] The sacrificer ought to repeat this Anumantraṇa formula : "O "Vaṣaṭkâra, do not sweep me away, I will not sweep thee away. I call "hither (thy) mind with great effort, thou art a shelter (having joined "thy) body with the air circulating (in my body). Go to (thy) place, let "me go to (my) place."

Some one (a theologian) has said : this (just mentioned *anumantraṇam*) is too long and has no effect. (Instead of it) the sacrificer ought to repeat after the Vaṣaṭkâra the words, *ojaḥ saha ojaḥ*. *Ojaḥ* (vigour) and *sahaḥ* (strength) are the two most beloved bodies (forms) of the Vaṣaṭkâra. By making him repeat this Anumantraṇa formula, he thus makes the sacrificer prosper through (the Vaṣaṭkâra's) own nature. He, who has such a knowledge, prospers through (the Vaṣaṭkâra's) own nature.

The Vaṣaṭkâra is speech, and *prâṇa* (air inhaled) and *apâna* (air exhaled). These (three) leave as often as a Vaṣaṭkâra is repeated. (But that ought to be prevented ; thence) he ought to include them (their names) in the Anumantraṇa formula. (This is done by repeating the following formula) *vâg ojaḥ saha ojo mayi prâṇâpânâu, i.e.*, May speech, vigour, strength (and) the prâṇa and apâna (be) in me ! Thus the Hotar puts speech, prâṇa and apâna in himself (he prevents them from going), and reaches his full age. He who has such a knowledge reaches his full age.

---

[18] This idea is clearly expressed in an Anumantraṇa formula : **वषट्कारेण वज्रेण योऽस्मान्द्वेष्टि यं च वयं द्विष्मस्तं हन्मि ;** *i.e.*, I slay, with the Vaṣaṭkâra as a weapon, him who hates us as well as him whom we hate (Âśv. Śr. S. 1, 3).

[19] For the mischief done by a weapon, he who strikes with it, is answerable. To guard himself against the evil consequences of such an act, propitiation (*śânti*) is required.

[20] This is the technical name of those formulas which are to be repeated by the Hotar and the sacrificer after the proper mantra has been recited. They *follow* the mantra. Thence the name, *anumantraṇa*. They must be always uttered with a low voice.

[21] Up to the present day, the Śrotriyas or sacrifical priests never dare to pronounce this formula save at the time of sacrificing. They say that, if they would do so at any other time, they would be cursed by the gods.

9.

(*Etymology of the words Praiṣa, Puroruk, Vedi, Nivid, Graha.*)

The sacrifice went away from the gods They wished it (to return) by means of the *Praiṣas.*[22] **[172]** That is the reason that the Praiṣas (orders to repeat a mantra given by the Adhvaryu or Mitra Varuṇa to the Hotar) are called so (from *pra*+*iṣ*, "to wish"). They made it shine forth (*prârochayanti*) by means of the *Puroruks*. Thence the Puroruk is called so (from *prârochayanti*). They found it on the Vedi. Thence this place is called Vedi (from *vid*, to find). After having found it, they caught it with the *Grahas*; thence they are called so (from *gṛih*, to catch, seize). Having found it, they announced it to the gods by means of the *Nivids*. Thence they are called *Nivids* (from *nivedayati*, he announces).

A person who wishes to recover something lost, wants either much (of it) or little. Among two, the elder (most experienced) wishes for the best (portion). He who knows that the Praiṣas are exceedingly strong (give most power), knows (at the same time) that they are the best portion. The Praiṣas being the desire to recover something lost, he (the Mitra-Varuṇa) repeats them with his head lowered (*prahvas*) (just as supplicants do).

10.

(*On the Proper Place of the Nivids in the Three Libations.*)

The Nivids are the embryos of the Śastras (*ukthas*). At the morning libation, they are put before the Śastras (*ukthas*), because the embryos are lying in the womb with their heads turned downward, and thus they are born (the head coming first out of the womb). At the midday libation, the Nivids are put in the midst (of the Śastras). This is done because the embryos have their hold in the middle of the womb. At the evening libation, the Nivids are repeated at the end (of the Śastras), because the embryos are coming down from thence (the womb) **[173]** when they are brought forth. He who has such a knowledge is blessed with children and cattle

The Nivids are the decorations of the Śastras. They are put, at the morning libation, before the Śastras, just as a weaver weaves decorations in the beginning of a cloth.

At the midday libation, they are put in the midst (of the Śastras), just as a weaver weaves decorations in the midst (of a cloth).

At the evening libation, they are put at the end (of the Śastras), just as the weaver weaves decorations in the end of a cloth (*avaprajjana*).

---

22 The Praiṣas here alluded to are those used at the animal sacrifice. They correspond to the Prayâja (Aprî) mantras. See the White Yajurveda 21, 29-40.

He who has such a knowledge is ornamented on all parts with the decoration of the sacrifice.

11.

(How the Nivids should be Repeated. How to Correct Mistakes Arising from Confusion.)

The Nivids are deities connected with the sun. When they are put at the morning libation at the beginning (of the Śastras), at the midday libation in the midst, and at the evening libation at the end, then they follow the regular course of the sun.

The gods had obtained (once) one portion of the sacrifice after the other (*pach-chhas*). Thence the Nivids are repeated pada by pada. When the gods had obtained the (whole of the) sacrifice, a horse came out of it. Thence they say, the sacrificer ought to give a horse to the reciter of the Nivids. By doing so (presenting a horse), they present really the most exquisite gift (to the reciter).

The reciter (of the Nivid) ought not to forego any of its padas. Should he do so, he would make a rupture in the sacrifice; if this (rupture) increases, the sacrificer then becomes guilty of the consequences [**174**] of a great sin. Thence the reciter ought not to forego any of the padas of the Nivid.

He ought not to invert the order of two padas of the Nivid. Should he do so, he would confound the sacrifice, and the sacrificer would become confounded. Thence he ought not to invert the order of two padas.

He ought not to take together two padas of the Nivid. Should he do so, he would confound the sacrifice, which would prove fatal to the sacrificer. Thence he ought not to take together two padas of the Nivid when repeating it.

He ought to take together only the two padas, *predam brahma* and *predam kṣatram.*[23] If he do so, it is (done) for joining together the Brahma and the Kṣatra. Thence the Brahma and Kṣatra become joined.

He ought, for the insertion of the Nivid, to select hymns consisting of more than a triplet, or stanza of four verses;[24] for the several padas of the Nivid ought to correspond, each to the several verses in the hymn.[25]

---

23 These two sentences form part of every Nivid, used at the midday or evening libation. They occur in the following connections: प्रेमां देवो देवहूतिमवतु देव्या धिया । प्रेदं ब्रह्म प्रेदं क्षत्रम् । प्रेदं सुन्वन्तं यजमानमवतु ।

24 This refers to the *sûkta* or hymn which stands in connection with the Nivid.

25 The expression *ṛicham sûktam prati* is evidently a Hendiadyoin; for the distributive meaning of *prati* can only refer to *ṛich*, but not to *sûkta*; because there are not as many sûktas as there are padas of the Nivid. The sentence, न तृचं न चतुरृचं अतिमन्येत

Thence he ought, for the insertion of the [175] Nivid, to select hymns consisting of more than of stanzas with three or four verses. Through the Nivid the celebration of the Sâman is made excessive.[26]

At the evening libation, he ought to put the Nivid when only one verse (of the Śastra) remains (to be recited). Should he recite the Nivid when two verses (of the Śastra) are still remaining, he would thus destroy the faculty of generation, and deprive the offspring of their embryos. Thence he ought to repeat the Nivid at the evening libation when only one verse (of the Śastra) remains (to be recited).

He ought not to let fall the Nivid beyond the hymn (to which it belongs).[27] Should he, however, do it, he ought not to revert to it again (not to use the hymn), the place (where the Nivid is to be put) being destroyed. He ought (in such a case) to select another hymn which is addressed to the same deity and in the same metre, to put the Nivid into it.

(In such a case) he ought, before (repeating the new) Nivid hymn, to recite the hymn : *mâ pragâma* [176] *patho vayam* (10, 57), *i.e.*, let us not go astray. For he loses his way who gets confounded at a sacrifice. (By repeating the second pada) *ma yajnâd indra saminaḥ* (10, 57, 1) *i.e.*, (let us not lose) O Indra, the Soma sacrifice, he prevents the sacrificer from falling out of the sacrifice. (By repeating the third pada) *mâ antaḥ sthur no arâtayaḥ*, *i.e.*, "May no wicked men stand among us !" he turns away all who have wicked designs, and defeats them.

In the second verse (of this hymn) *yo yajñasya prasâdhanas tantur*, *i.e.*, "Let us recover the same thread which serves for the performance

---

निविद्धानं, can easily be misunderstood. At the first glance it appears to mean "he ought not to think of selecting any other hymn for inserting the Nivid, save such ones as consist of three or four verses." Sây. followed this explanation which most naturally suggests itself to every reader. But, in consideration that all the Nivid hymns, actually in use, and mentioned in the Aitareya Br. exceed in number four verses (some contain eleven, others even fifteen verses), that explanation cannot be correct. The passage can only have the sense given to it in my translation.

[26] The Sastra thus obtains more verses than are properly required.

[27] The meaning is : he should not repeat the Nivid, after he might have repeated the whole of the hymn in which it ought to have been inserted. Should he, however, have committed such a mistake, then he must select another hymn, and put the Nivid in its proper place, *i.e.*, *before* the last verse of the hymn. The Hotar is more liable to commit such a mistake at the evening libation than at the two preceding ones. For, at the evening libation, there are seven Nivids (to Savitar, Dyâvâpṛithivî, Ribhus, Vaiśvânara, Viśvedevâḥ, Marutas, and Jâtavedâs) required, whilst we find at the morning libation only one (which is rather a Puroruk than a Nivid), and at the midday libation two (to the Marutas and Indra).

of sacrifice, and is spread among the gods[28] by means of which was ((hitherto) sacrificed (by us)," the expression *tantu* (thread) means offspring. By repeating it, the Hotar spreads (*saṁtanoti*) offspring for the sacrificer.

(The words of the third verse are) *mano nu â huvâmahe nârâśaṁsena somena, i.e.*, "Now we bring an offering[29] to the mind (*manas*) by pouring water in the Soma cups (devoting them thus to Narâśaṁsa)." By means of the mind, the sacrifice is spread; by means of the mind, it is performed. This is verily the atonement at that occasion (for the mistake pointed out above).

SECOND CHAPTER.

[177] (*The Marutvatîya and Niṣkevalya Śastras.*)

12

(*On the Âhâva and Pratigara.*)

They (the theologians) say: the subjects of the gods[1] are to be procured. (To achieve this end) one metre is to be put in another metre. (This is done when) the Hotar calls (the Adhvaryu) by *śoṁsâvom*, "Let us both repeat, yes!" which (formula) consists of three syllables. At the morning libation, the Adhvaryu responds (*prati-grihnâti*) (to this formula of three syllables) with one consisting of five: *śamsâmo daivôm.*[2] This makes eight on the whole. The Gâyatrî has eight syllables (*i. e.* each of its three padas). Thus these two (formulas) make the Gâyatrî at the commencement of the recitation at the morning libation. After the Hotar has finished his recitation, he uses this (formula of) four syllables: *uktham* [178] *vâchi,*[3] *i.e.*, the recitation has been read, to which the Adhvaryu

---

[28] Sây. has, in his commentary on the Rigveda Saṁhitâ, the following remark: देवैः स्तोत्रिभिः ऋत्विग्भिर्विस्तारितो वर्त्तते.

[29] Of आहुवामहे Sây. gives two different explanations in his commentaries on the Ait. Br. and in that on the Rigveda Saṁhitâ. In the first, he explains it by आह्वयामि I call hither (from *hvê* to call); in the other, he derives it from *hu*, to sacrifice. The latter explanation is preferable.

[1] See 1, 9.

[2] See about the *Pratigara, i.e.*, response by the Adhvaryu to the recitations of the Hotar, Âsv. Śr. S. 5, 9. The most common *pratigara* repeated by the Adhvaryu is *othâmo daiva*; but at the time of the *âhâva* (the call *śomsâvom*) it is: *śamsâmo daiva.* At the end of the *Pratigara*, the *praṇava*, (incorporation of the syllable *om*) required, is *daivôm.*

[3] The formula *uktham vâchi*, with some additional words, always concludes a Sastra. In the Kauṣîtaki Brâhmaṇam (14, 1), and in the Sânkhây. Śrauta Sûtras (8, 16, 17-20), this formula is called *achha viryam*. In the Âśval. Sûtras, no particular name is given to it. The Kauṣîtaki and Sânkhây. Śâkhas differ here a little from that of Âśvalâyana. According to the former, *uktham vâchi* is always preceded by a few sentences which are

(responds) in four syllables: *om ukthaśâ, i.e.*, thou hast repeated the recitation[4] (*uktham, śastram*). This makes eight syllables. The Gâyatrî consists of eight syllables. Thus the two (formulas) make at the morning libation [**179**] the Gâyatrî[5] at both ends (at the commencement and the end).

At the midday libation, the Hotar calls: *adhvaryo śoṁsâvom, i.e.*, "Adhvaryu, let us two repeat! Om!" with six syllables! to which the Adhvaryu responds with five syllables, the *śaṁsâmo daivom*. This makes eleven syllables. The Triṣṭubh has eleven syllables. Thus he makes the Triṣṭubh at the beginning of the Śastra at the midday libation. After having repeated it, he says, *uktham vâchi indrâya, i.e.*, the Śastra has been read for Indra, in seven syllables; to which the Adhvaryu responds in four syllables: *oṁ ukthaśâ*. This makes (also) eleven syllables. The Triṣṭubh has eleven syllables. Thus the two

---

not to be found in Âśval. Thus, we have, for instance there, at the end of the Marutvatîya Śastra, the following formulas: **रूपमनुरूपं प्रतिरूपं सुरूपमिहोपाये भद्रमाश्टण्वते चोकथमवार्चीद्राय** In the Âśval. Sûtras (5, 14), there is instead of it only: **उकथं वार्चीद्राय श्रुण्वते त्वा** At every Śastra repeated by the Hotar, there is a little difference in the appendages to this formula. The rules, as given here in this paragraph, refer only to the conclusion of the Śastras of the minor Hotṛi priests; they alone conclude in the way here stated, without any other appendage (see Âśval. 5, 10). The concluding formulas for the Hotar are, according to Âśval. Śr. S., as follows:

(*a*) For the Ajya Sastra: **उकथं वाचि घोषाय त्वा** (5, 9).

(*b*) For the Pra-uga Śastra: **उकथं वाचि श्लोकाय त्वा** (5, 10).

(*c*) For the Marutvatîya Śastra (see above).

(*d*) For the Niṣkevalya Śastra: **उकथं वाचीन्द्रायोपश्टण्वते त्वा** (5, 15).

(*e*) For the Vaiśvadeva Śastra: **उकथं वाचीन्द्राय देवेभ्य आश्रुत्यै त्वा** (5, 18).

(*f*) For the Agnimaruta Śastra: **उकथं वाचीन्द्राय देवेभ्य आश्रुताय त्वा** (5, 20).

All these appendages express the idea, that the god to whom the recitation is addressed should hear it, and take notice of it. So *ghoṣhâya tvâ* means that "it (the recitation) might be sounded to thee;" *upaśṛiṇvate tvâ*, "that it might be for thy hearing." The active participle in the present tense must here have something like the meaning of an abstract noun, corresponding with *ślokâya* and *âśrutyâi*. Literally, *upaśṛiṇvate* appears to mean that "the hearing (of this recitation might come) to thee."

After the repetition of these formulas which conclude all Śastras, the Yâjyâ verse belonging to the particular Śastra is recited.

[4] This alone can be the meaning of the obscure formula, *ukthaśâ*, which comes no doubt from the remotest antiquity. It is perhaps a corruption of *uktham śâs*, the neutral character *m* being left out. Sây. explains: **त्वं शास्त्रशंसी**, "thou art the repeater of the Śastra. But this meaning is not appropriate to the occasion at which the formula is used. This is done only when the recitation is over. The only proper meaning of the formula therefore is either "the recitation is repeated," or "thou hast repeated the recitation."

[5] The Gâyatrî is the characteristic metre of the morning libation; thence its form (eight syllables) is to appear in some shape at the commencement as well as at the end of the Śastra.

(formulas) make the Triṣṭubh at both ends of the Śastra at the midday libation.

At the evening libation, the Hotar calls: *adhvaryo śoṁ-śoṁsâvom*, in seven syllables, to which the Avdharyu responds in five syllables: *śaṁsâmo daivom*. This makes twelve syllables. The Jagatî has twelve syllables. Thus (with these two formulas taken together) he makes the Jagatî at the beginning of the Śastra at the evening libation. After having repeated the Śastra, he says, in eleven syllables: *uktham vâchi indrâya devebhyaḥ*, *i.e.*, "the Śastra has been repeated for Indra," for the Devas, to which the Adhvaryu responds in one syllable: *om!* This makes twelve syllables. The Jagatî has twelve syllables. Thus the two (formulas) make the Jagatî at both ends at the evening libation.

This (the mutual relation of the three chief metres to one another and to the sacrificer) saw a Riṣi, and expressed (his opinion) in the mantra: *yad gâyatre adhi* (1, 164, 23), *i.e.*, "those who know that **[180]** the Gâyatrî is put over a Gâyatrî, and that out of a Triṣṭubh a (another) Trishṭubh is formed, and a Jagat (Jagatî) is put in a Jagat, obtain immortality."[6]

In this way, he who has such a knowledge puts metre in metre, and procures "the subjects of the gods."

13.

(On the Distribution of the Metres among the Gods. Anuṣṭubh Prajâpati's Metre.)

Prajâpati allotted to the deities their (different) parts in the sacrifice and metres. He allotted to Agni and the Vasus at the morning libation the Gâyatrî, to Indra and the Rudras the Triṣṭubh at the midday libation, and to the Viśve Devâḥ and Âdityas the Jagatî at the evening libation.

His (Prajâpati's) own metre was Anuṣṭubh. He pushed it to the end (of the Śastra), to the verse repeated by the Achhâvâka (which is the last). Anuṣṭubh said to him: "Thou art the most wicked of all gods; for thou hast me, who am thy metre, pushed to the end (of the Śastra), to the verse repeated by the Achhâvâka." He acknowledged (that he had wronged her). (In order to give redress) he took his own Soma (sacrifice) and put at the beginning, at the very mouth of it,

[6] The meaning is, that no pada of a metre, neither that of the Gâyatrî nor Triṣṭubh, nor Jagatî can stand alone, but must be joined to another pada of the same metre. The *âhâva* and *pratigara* must, therefore, be at the beginning as well as at the end of the Śastra in the same metre; for each time they consist only of one pada, and that is not auspicious.

Anuṣṭubh. Thence Anuṣṭubh is joined (to the Śastras) as the first metre, as the very mouth-piece at all libations.

He who has such a knowledge becomes the first, the very mouth (of the others), and attains to supremacy. Prajâpati having thus made (the beginning **[181]** of all libations) at his own Soma sacrifice (with Anuṣṭubh), the sacrificer (who does the same) becomes master of the sacrifice, and the latter becomes (properly) performed. Wherever a sacrificer has a sacrifice performed, so that he remains master of it, it is performed for this (the whole) assemblage of men[7] (who might be with the sacrificer).

14.

(*How Agni, as Hotar of the Gods, Escaped the Meshes of Death.*)

When Agni was the Hotar of the Gods, Death sitting in the Bahiṣpavamâna Stotra[8] lurked for him. By commencing the Ajya Śastra[9] with the Anuṣṭubh metre, he overcame Death. Death repaired to the Ajya Śastra lurking for Agni. By beginning (to repeat) the Pra-uga Śastra, he overcame Death (again).

At the midday libation, Death sat in the Pavamâna Stotra[10] lurking for Agni. By commencing the Marutvatîya Śastra with Anuṣṭubh, he overcame Death. Death could not sit, at that libation, in the Bṛihatî verses (repeated by the Hotar at the commencement of the Niṣkevalya Śastra). For the Bṛihatîs are life. Thus Death could not take away the life. This is the reason that the Hotar begins (the Niṣkevalya Śastra) with the Stotriya triplet (corresponding to the Sâman which is sung) in the Bṛihatî metre. The Bṛihatîs are life. By commencing **[182]** his second Śastra (with Bṛihatîs), he has the preservation of (his) life in view.

At the evening libation, Death sat in the Pavamâna Stotra lurking for Agni. By commencing the Vaiśvadeva Śastra with Anuṣṭubh, Agni overcame Death. Death repaired to the *Yajnâ yajnîya Sâman.*[11] By

---

[7] The sacrificer is to make the sacrifice, *i.e.*, the sacrificial man, his own, *i.e*, he must subject it to his own will, just as Prajâpati did. Thus he makes it beneficial to others, just as Prajâpati benefited gods and men by it.

See page 120.

[9] See the hymn : *pra vo devâya agnaye*, 2, 35, which is in the Anuṣṭubh metre and which is meant here.

[10] *Uchchâ te jâtam andhaso.* Sâmaveda Saṁh. 2, 22-29.

[11] यज्ञा यज्ञा वो अग्नये । Sâmaveda Saṁh, 2, 53-54.

commencing the Agni-Mâruta Śastra, with a hymn addressed to Vaiśvânara, he overcame Death. For the hymn addressed to Vaiśvânara is a weapon; the Yajna yajnîya Sâman is the place. By repeating the Vaiśvânara hymn, he thus turns Death out of his place.

Having escaped all the meshes of Death, and his clubs, Agni came off in safety. The Hotar who has such a knowledge, comes off in safety, preserving his life to its full extent, and attains to his full age (of a hundred years).

15.

(*Marutvatîya Śastra. Indra Conceals Himself. How he was found.*)

Indra, after having killed Vṛitra, thought, 'I might perhaps not have subdued him' (apprehending his revival), and went to very distant regions. He (ultimately) arrived at the most distant place. This place is Anuṣṭubh, and Anuṣṭubh is Speech. He having entered Speech, lay down in her. All beings scattering themselves here and there went in search of him. The *Pitaras* (manes) found him one day earlier than the gods. This is the reason that ceremonies are performed in honour of the Pitaras previous to the day on which they sacrifice for the gods.[12] They (the gods) said, "Let us squeeze the **[183]** Soma juice; (then) Indra will come to us very quickly." So they did. They squeezed the Soma juice. By repeating the verse, *â tva ratham* (8, 57, 1), they made him (Indra) turn (towards the Soma juice). By the mantra, *idam vaso sutam* (8, 2, 1), he became visible to the gods on account of the term (*suta*), *i.e.*, squeezed (contained in it).[13] By the mantra, *indra nedîya ed ihi* (8, 53, 5),[14] they made him (Indra) come into the middle (of the sacrificial place).

He who has such a knowledge, gets his sacrifice performed in the presence of Indra, and becomes (consequently) successful by means of the sacrifice, having Indra (being honoured by his presence).

16.

(*Indra-Nihava Pragâtha.*)

As Indra had killed Vṛitra, all deities thinking that he had not conquered him, left him. The Maruts alone, who are his own relations,[15] did not leave him. The "*maruto svâpayaḥ*" (in the verse, *Indra*

---

[12] The Pitaras are worshipped on the Amâvasyâ day (New Moon), and the Darśapûrṇima iṣṭi takes place on the *pratipada* (first day after the New Moon).—Sây.

[13] These two first are called the *pratipad* and *anuchara* of the Marutvatîya Śastra, the beginning verse and the sequel.

[14] This mantra is called, *indra-nihava pragâtha*, *i.e.*, pragâtha for calling Indra near.

[15] Svâpi, which term occurs in the Indra-Nihava Pragâtha (8, 58, 5), is explained by Sây. सुषुप्तिकालेऽपि वर्त्तमानाः But this interpretation, which is founded on Vedantic ideas strange to the poets of the Vedic hymns, is certainly wrong; for, "being

nedîya) are the vital airs. The vital airs did not leave him [184] (Indra). Thence this Pragâtha, which contains the term *svâpi* (in the pada) *â svâpe svâpibhir*, is constantly repeated (at the midday libation of all Soma sacrifices). When, after this (Pragâtha), a mantra addressed to Indra is repeated, then all this (is termed) *Marutvatîya* (Śastra). If this unchangeable Pragâtha, containing the term *svâpi*, is repeated (then always the Marutvatîya Śastra is made).

17.

(*Brâhmaṇaspati Pragâtha. To what Stotras the Indra-Nihava and Brâhmaṇaspati Pragâtha belong. The Dhâyyâs.*)

He repeats the Pragâtha[16] addressed to Brâhmaṇaspati. Led by Bṛihaspati as Purohita (spirirual guide), the gods conquered the celestial world, and were (also) victorious everywhere in this world. Thus the sacrificer who is led by Bṛihaspati as his Purohita, conquers the celestial world, and is (also) victorious everywhere in this world.

These two Pragâthas,[17] not being accompanied by a chant, are recited with repetition[18] (of the last pada of each verse). They ask, "How is it that these two Pragâthas, which are not accompanied by a chant, are recited with repetition (of the last pada of each verse), the rule being that no Śastra verse can be recited with such a repetition, if it be not accompanied by a chant?" (The answer is) The Marutvatîya (Śastra) [185] is the recitation for the Pavamâna Stotra;[19] they perform this Stotra (in singing), with six verses in the Gâyatrî, with six in the Bṛihatî, and with three

in profound sleep," does not suit the sense of the passage at all. How could the Marutas assist Indra when they were in "profound sleep" (*suṣupti*)? In order to countenance his interpretation, Sây. refers to the meaning "*prâṇa*," life, attributed to the word by the author of the Ait. Br. itself in this passage. The word is, however, to be traceable only to *su-âpi* or *sva-âpi*. That *âpi* means "friend, associate," follows from several passages of the Saṁhitâ. See Boehtlingk and Roth's Saṁskrit Dictionary, i., p. 660.

[16] A Pragâtha comprises two *ṛichas*, according to Âśv. Śr. S. 5, 14: **तृचाः प्रतपदनुचरा द्वृचाः प्रगाथाः** *i. e.*, the Pratipad (opening of the Marutvatîya Śastra) and its Anuchara (sequel) consist of three *ṛichas*, the Pragâthas of two *ṛichas*.

[17] The Indra-Nihava and Brâhmaṇaspatyaḥ Pragâtha.

[18] The two Pragâtha verses are to be repeated, so as to form a triplet. This is achieved by repeating thrice the fourth pada of each verse, if it be in the Bṛihatî metre. In a similar way, the Sâma singers make of two verses three.

[19] The Pavamâna Stotra or the performance of the Sâma singers at the beginning of the midday libation, consists only of three verses in the Gâyatrî (*uchchâ te jâto*, Sâmaveda, 2, 22-24), of two in the Bṛihatî (*punânaḥ Soma*, S. V. 2, 25, 26) and three in the Triṣṭubh metre (*pra tu drava pari kośam*, S. V. 2, 27-29). The three Gâyatrîs are sung twice, thus six are obtained, and the two Bṛihatis are twice repeated in such a manner as to produce each time three verses (by repeating thrice the last pada of each verse), which makes also six. *Sâma prayoya.*

in the Triṣṭubh metres. Thus, the Pavamâna (Stoma) of the midday libation comprises three metres, and is fifteen-fold.[20] They ask, " How becomes this Pavamâna Stoma celebrated (by a Śastra) ?" The two last verses of the Pratipad triplet (8, 57, 1-3, *â tvâ ratham*) [**186**] are in the Gâyatrî metre (the first being Anuṣṭubh), and also the triplet which forms the sequel (of the Pratipad) is in the Gâyatrî metre. Thus the Gâyatrî verses (of the Pavamâna Stotra) become celebrated. By means of these two Pragâthas (the Indra-Nihava and Brâhmaṇaspati Pragâtha, which are in the Bṛihatî metre) the Bṛihatî verses (of the Pavamâna Stotra) become celebrated.

The Sâma singers perform this chant with these verses in the Bṛihatî metre, by means of the Raurava and Yaudhaja Sâmans (tunes[21]), repeating thrice (the last pada of each verse). This is the reason that the two Pragâthas, though they have no Stoma belonging to them, are recited with repeating thrice (the last pada of each verse). Thus the Stotra is in accordance with the Śastra.

Two *Dhâyyâs*[22] are in the Triṣṭubh metre, and also the hymn[23] in which the Nivid is inserted. By these verses (in the Triṣṭubh metre), are the Triṣṭubhs of the Stotra celebrated. In this way, the Pavamâna

---

[20] For the explanation of this and similar terms, Sâyaṇa refers always to the Brâhmaṇas of the Sâmaveda. Tha explanatory phrase of the *panchadas'aḥ stoma* of the Sâmaveda theologians is constantly the following : पंचभ्यो हिंकरोति सः तिसृभिः स एकया स एकया । पंचभ्यो हिंकरोति स एकया । स तिसृभिः स एकया पंचभ्यो हिंकरोति स एकया स एकया स तिसृभिः These enigmatical words are utterly unintelligible without oral information, which I was happy enough to obtain. They refer to the number of verses obtained by repetition of the triplet which forms the text of a Sâman. The Sâman consists of two verses only : it is first to be made to consist of three, by repetition of some feet of the two principal verses, before it can be used as a chant at the Soma sacrifices. After a triplet of verses has been thus obtained, it is to be chanted in three turns, each turn containing in three subdivisions a certain number of repetitions. This number of repetitions is indicated by three rows of wooden sticks of the Udumbara tree, called *kuśâ*, each row comprising five (if the Stoma is the *pañchadaśa*, the fifteen-fold), which the three Sâma singers must arrange according to a certain order before they can chant the Sâman. Each row is called a *paryâya*. The several sticks in each row are placed in the following order : 1st row—3 in a straight, 1 across, 1 in a straight, line ; 2nd row—1 in a straight, 3 across, 1 in a straight, line ; 3rd row—1 in a straight, 1 across, 3 in a straight, line. As often as the sticks of one row are laid, the Sâma singer utters the sound *him*. This apparatus is regarded as quite essential for the successful chanting of the Sâman. See more on this subject in the notes to 3, 42.

[21] These are the names of the two peculiar tunes in which the verses, *punânaḥ soma* and *duhâna ûdhar* (Sâmaveda S. 2, 25-26) are sung.

[22] See 3, 18 : the two first, *agnir netâ*, and *tvam Soma kratubhiḥ* are in the Triṣṭubh metre.

[23] The Nivid hymn is *janiṣṭha ugra* , see 3, 19 ; it is in the Triṣṭubh metre

Stoma, comprising three metres, being fifteen-fold, becomes celebrated for him who has such a knowledge.

18.

(On the Origin of the Dhâyyâs, their Nature and Meaning.)

He recites the Dhâyyâs. Prajâpati had (once) sucked up from these worlds everything he desired **[187]** by means of the Dhâyyâs (from *dhe*, to suck). Thus the sacrificer who has such a knowledge sucks up from these worlds everything he desires. The nature of the Dhâyyâs is, that the gods at a sacrifice, wherever they discovered a breach, covered it with a Dhâyyâ ; thence they are so called (from *dhâ*, to put). The sacrifice of him, who has such a knowledge, becomes performed without any breach in it.

As to the Dhâyyâs, we sew up with them (every rent in the) sacrifice, just as we sew up (a rent in) a cloth with a pin that it might become mended. A breach in the sacrifice of him who has such a knowledge becomes thus mended.

As to the Dhâyyâs, they are the recitations for the Upasads.[24] The verse, *Agnir netâ* (3, 20, 4), which is addressed to Agni, is the recitation for the first Upasad ; the verse, *tvam Soma kratubhiḥ*, which is addressed to Soma (1, 91, 2), is the recitation for the second Upasad ; the verse *pinvanty apo* (1, 64, 6), which is addressed to Viṣṇu, is the recitation for the third Upasad. Whatever place one may conquer by means of the Soma sacrifice, he who, having such a knowledge, recites the Dhâyyâs, conquers (it only) by the several Upasads.

About this last Dhâyyâ, some say, the Hotar ought (instead of *pinvanty apo*) to repeat *tân vo maho* (2, 34, 11), asserting, " we distinctly know that this verse is repeated (as the third Dhâyyâ) among the Bharatas." But this advice is not to be cared for. Should the Hotar repeat that verse (*tân vo maho*), he would prevent the rain from coming, for Parjanya has power over the rain (but there is no allusion to him in that verse). But if he repeat the verse *pinvanty apo*, where there is a pada referring to rain (the third *atyam na mihe*), and one referring to the Marutas **[188]** (the storms accompanying the rain, in the first pada), and the word *viniyanti*, " they carry off," which refers to Viṣṇu, whose characteristic feature is said to be *vichakrame, i.e.*, he strode (thrice through the universe), which meaning is (also) implied in the term *vinayanti*, and (where is further in it) the word, *vâjīe*, " being laden with booty," referring to Indra (then the rain would come). This vese has four padas, and (as we have seen) refers to rain, the Marutas, Viṣṇu,

---

[24] See Ait. Br. 1, 23-25.

and Indra, and, though (on account of these allusions just mentioned, and its being in the Jagatî metre) properly belonging to the evening libation, it is repeated at the midday libation. Therefore the cattle of the Bharatas which are at their stables at evening (for being milked) repair at noon to a shed erected for giving all the cows shelter (against heat). That verse (*pinvanty apo*) is in the Jagatî metre; cattle are of the Jagatî nature; the soul of the sacrificer is the midday. Thus the priest provides cattle for the sacrificer (when he recites this verse as a Dhâyyâ at the midday libation).

19.

(*The Marutvatîya Pragâtha. The Nivid hymn of the Marutvatîya Śastra. How the Hotar can injure the sacrificer by misplacing the Nivid.*)

He repeats the *Marutvatîya Pragâtha* (*pra va indrâya bṛîhate*, 8, 78, 3). The Marutas are cattle, cattle are the Pargâtha (that is to say, the Pragâtha is used) for obtaining cattle.

He repeats the hymn *janiṣṭhâ ugraḥ* (10, 73). This hymn serves for producing the sacrificer. For, by means of it, the Hotar brings forth the sacrificer from the sacrifice as the womb of the gods. By this (hymn) victory is obtained; with it the sacrificer remains victor, without it he is defeated.

[189] This hymn was (seen) by (the Riṣi) *Gaurivîti*. Gaurivîti, the son of Śakti, having come very near the celestial world, saw this hymn (*i.e.*, had it revealed); by means of it, he gained heaven. Thus the sacrificer gains by this (hymn) the celestial world.

Having repeated half the number of verses (of this hymn), he leaves out the other half, and inserts the Nivid [25] in the midst (of both

[22] This is not strictly in accordance with the rules laid down by Âśvalâyana, who in his Śrâuta Sutras, 5, 14: जनिष्ठा उग्रइत्येक भूयसी : शस्त्वा मरुत्वतीयां निविदं दध्यात्सर्वत्रैवमयुजासु माध्यान्दिने *i.e.*, the Nivid Sûkta is, *janiṣṭhâ ugrah.* After having repeated one verse more than half the number of verses (the whole has eleven verses) of which it consists, he ought to insert the Nivid. That ought always to be done at the midday libation, where the number of verses of the Nivid Sûkta is uneven. The Sûkta *janiṣṭha ugra* consists of eleven verses. The number being uneven, the Marutvatîya Nivid is put in the hymn *janiṣṭha ugra* after the sixth verse, which concludes with धन्य. The text of this Nivid (see the Sâṅkhâyâna Sûtras, 8, 16) is (according to Sapta Hâutra) as follows: शों३ सावो३ मिन्द्रो मरुत्वान्त्सोमस्य पिबतु । मरुत्स्तोत्रो मरुद्गणः । मरुत्सखा मरुद्वृधः । घ्नन्वृत्रा सृजदपः । मरुतामोजसा सह । य ईमेनं देवा अन्वमदन् । असूर्ये वृत्रतूर्ये । शंबरहत्ये गविष्टौ । अर्चंतं गुह्या पदा । परमस्यां परावति । आर्दीं ब्रह्माणि वर्धयन् । अनाधृष्टान्योजसा । कृण्वं देवेभ्यो दुवः । मरुद्भिः सखिभिः सह । इन्द्रो मरुत्वां इह श्रवदिह सोमस्य पिबतु । प्रेमां देवो देवहूतिमवतु देव्या धिया । प्रेदं ब्रह्म प्रेदं चत्रस् । प्रेदं सुन्वन्तं यजमानं अवतु । चित्रश्चित्राभिरूतिभिः । श्रवद् ब्रह्माण्यावसागमत् । *i.e.*, May Indra with the Marutas drink of the Soma. He has the praise of the Marutas; he has (with him) the assemblage of the Marutas. He is the friend of

parts). The Nivid is [190] the ascent to heaven; it is the ladder for climbing up to heaven. (Therefore) he ought to recite it (stopping at regular intervals) as if he were climbing up (a height) by means of a ladder. Thus he can take along with him (up to the celestial world) that sacrificer to whom he is friendly. Now, he who desires heaven, avails himself of this opportunity of going thither.

Should the Hotar intend to do any harm (to the sacrificer) thinking, "may I slay the Viś through the Kṣatra," he need only repeat the Nivid in three different places of the hymn (in the commencement, middle, and end) For the Nivid is the *Kṣatram* (commanding power), and the hymn the *Viś* (prototype of the Vaiśyas); thus he slays the Viś of any one whom he wishes through his Kṣatra.[26] Thus he slays the Viś through the Kṣatram.

Should he think, "may I slay the Kṣatram through the Viś," he need only thrice dissect the Nivid through the hymn (by repeating the hymn at the commencement, in the middle, and at the end of the Nivid). The Nivid is the Kṣatram, and the [191] hymn is Viś. He thus slays whosoever Kṣatra he wishes by means of the Viś.

Should he think, "I will cut off from the sacrificer the Viś (relation, subject, offspring) on both sides," he need only dissect (at the beginning and end) the Nivid by the call *śoṁsavom.* Thus he cuts the sacrificer off from his Viś on both sides (from father and mother, as well as from his children). Thus he should do who has sinister designs towards the

---

the Marutas, he is their help. He slew the enemies, he released the waters (kept back by the demons of the air) by means of the strength of the Marutas. The gods following him rejoiced at the (defeat of the) Asuras, the conquest of Vṛitra, at the killing of Śambara, at the battle (for conquering cows). Him (Indra) when he was repeating the secret verses, in the highest region, in a remote place, made the sacred rites and hymns (*brahmâṇi*) grow (increase in strength); these (sacred rites) are through their power inviolable. He makes presents to the gods, he who is with the Marutas his friends. May Indra with the Marutas here hear (our prayer), and drink of the Soma. May the god come to his oblation offered to the gods with (our) thoughts being directed to the gods. May he protect this Brahma (spiritual power), may he protect this Kṣatram (worldly power), may he protect the sacrificer who prepares this (the Soma juice), (may he come) with his manifold helps. May he (Indra) hear the sacred hymns (*brahmâṇi*), may he come with (his) aid!

[26] These sentences can be only understood when one bears in mind, that men of the higher caste are supposed to have a share in a certain prototype. Kṣatra represents the commanding power. A Brahman, deprived of his Kṣatra, loses all influence and becomes quite insignificant in worldly things; if deprived of his Viś, he loses his means of subsistence. A Kṣatriya loses his power, if deprived of his kṣatram, and his subjects, if deprived of his Viś.

sacrificer. But otherwise (in the manner first described) he should do to him who desires for heaven (if he be friendly to him).

He concludes with the verse, *vayaḥ suparṇâ upasedur* (10, 73, 11), *i.e.*, "the poets with good thoughts have approached Indra, begging like birds with beautiful wings; uncover him who is enshrouded in darkness; fill the eye (with light); release us who are bound (by darkness), as it were, with a rope (*nidhâ*)." When he repeats the words "uncover him," &c., then he should think that the darkness in which he is enshrouded, might go by means of his mind. Thus he rids himself of darkness. By repeating the words, "fill the eye," he should repeatedly rub both his eyes. He who has such a knowledge, keeps the use of his eyes up to his old age. In the words, "release us," &c., the word *nidhâ* means rope. The meaning is, release us who are tied with a rope, as it were.

20.

(*Why the Marutas are Honoured with a separate Śastra.*)

Indra, when he was about to kill Vṛitra, said to all the gods, "Stand near me, help me." So they did. They rushed upon Vṛitra to kill him. He perceived they were rushing upon him for the purpose of **[192]** killing him. He thought, "I will frighten them." He breathed at them, upon which all the gods were flung away and took to flight; only the Marutas did not leave him (Indra); they exhorted him by saying, "Strike, O Bhagavan! kill (Vṛitra)! show thy prowess!" This saw a Riṣi, and recorded it in the verse *vṛitrasya tvâ śvasathâd* (8, 85, 7), *i.e.*, "all the gods who were associated (with Indra) left him when flung away by the breathing of Vṛitra. If thou keepest friendship with the Marutas, thou wilt conquer in all these battles (with Vṛitra)."

He (Indra) perceived, "the Marutas are certainly my friends; these (men) love me! well, I shall give them a share in this (my own) celebration (Śastra)." He gave them a share in this celebration. Formerly both (Indra as well as the Marutas) had a place in the Niṣkevalya [27] Śastra. (But to reward their great services he granted them more, *viz.*, a separate Marutvatîya Śastra, &c.). The share of the Marutas (in the midday libation) is, that the Adhvaryu takes the Marutvatîya Graha, and the Hotar repeats the Marutvâtîya Pragâtha, the Marutvatîya hymn, and the Marutvatîya Nivid. After having repeated the Marutvatîya Śastra, he recites the Marutvatîya Yâjyâ. Thus he satisfies the deities by giving them their shares. (The Marutvatîya Yâjyâ is) *ye tvâhihatye maghavan* (3, 47, 4), *i.e.*, "drink Indra, the Soma juice, surrounded by thy host, the

[27] The second Śastra to be repeated by the Hotar at the midday libation.

Marutas who assisted thee, O Maghavan, in the battles with the huge serpent (Ahi)," &c. Wherever Indra remained victor in his various engagements, through their assistance, wherever he displayed his prowess, there (in the feast given in his honour) he announced them (the Marutas) as his associates, and made them share in the Soma juice along with him.

[193] 21.

(*Indra wishes for Prajâpati's rank. Why Prajâpati is called Kaḥ. Indra's share in the Sacrifice.*)

Indra, after having slain Vṛitra and remained victor in various battles, said to Prajâpati, "I will have thy rank, that of the supreme deity; I will be great!" Prajâpati said, "Who am I" (*ko aham*)? Indra answered, "Just, what thou hast told(*i.e.*, *kaḥ*, who ?)" Thence Prajâpati received the name *kaḥ*, who? Prajâpati is (the god) *kaḥ*, who? Indra is called *mahendra*, *i.e.*, the great Indra, because he had become great (greater than all the other gods).

He, after having become great, said to the gods, "Give me a distinguished reception!"[28] just as one here (in this world) who is (great) wishes for (honourable) distinction, and he who attains to an eminent position, is great. The gods said to him, "Tell it yourself what shall be yours (as a mark of distinction)." He answered, "This Mahendra Soma jar (Graha), among the libations that of the midday, among the Śastras the Niṣkevalya, among the metres the Triṣṭubh, and among the Sâmans the Pṛiṣṭha"[29] They thus gave him these marks of distinction. They give them also to him who has such a knowledge. [194] The gods said to him, "Thou hast chosen for thyself all; let some of these things (just mentioned) be our also." He said, "No, why should anything belong to you?" They answered, "Let it belong to us, Maghavan." He only looked at them (as if conniving).

---

[28] Of the words उद्वारं मे उद्धारत Sâyâṇa gives the following explanation: यः पुंसापूजाविशेषो ह्रियते संपाद्यते सोऽयं सत्कार उद्वारस्तं सत्कारभागं मे मदर्थं उद्धरत पृथक् कुरुतेति

[29] *Pṛiṣṭha* is a combination of two Sâma triplets for singing. Here the principal chant of the Niṣkevalya Śastra, which is the centre of the whole Soma feast, is to be understood. At the Agniṣṭoma, this chant is the Rathantaram. The four Stotras at the midday libation, which follow the Pavamâna Stotra, are called Pṛiṣṭha Stotras. For they are capable of entering into the combination, called Pṛiṣṭha, by putting in the midst of them another Sâman. At the Agniṣṭoma, the actual Pṛiṣṭha is, however, not required. The four Pṛiṣṭha Stotras of the midday libation are, the Rathantaram, Vâmadevyam Naudhasam, and Kaleyam.

22.

(Story of Prâsahâ, the wife of Indra. On the Origin of the Dhâyyâ verse of the Niṣkevalya Śastra. How a King can defeat a hostile army. All gods have a share in the Yâjyâ in the Virâṭ metre. On the Importance of the Virâṭ metre at this occasion.)

The gods said, "There is a béloved wife of Indra, of the Vâvâta [30] order, Prâsahâ by name. Let us inquire of her (what Indra's intention is)." So they did. They inquired of her (what Indra's intention was). She said to them, "I shall give you the answer to-morrow." For women ask their husbands; they do so during the night. On the morning the gods went to her (to inquire). She addressed the following (verses) to them: *yad vâvâna purutamam* [31] (10, 74, 6), *i.e.*, what Indra, the slayer of Vritra, the con-[**195**] queror in many battles of old has gained, filling (the world) with his name (fame), by what he showed himself as master in conquering (*prâsahaspati*), as a powerful (hero), that is what we beseech him to do (now); may he do it." Indra is the mighty husband of Prâsahâ.[32] (The last pada) "that is what we beseech him," &c., means, he will do what we have told him.[33]

Thus she (Prâsahâ) told them. The gods said, "Let her have a share here (in this Niṣkevalya Śastra) who has not yet obtained one in it (*na vâ vidat*).[34] So they did. They gave her (a share) in it; thence this verse, *yad vâvâna*, &c., forms part of the (Niṣkevalya) Śastra.[35]

The army (*senâ*) is Indra's beloved wife, Vâvâta, Prâsahâ by name. Prajâpati is by the name of *kaḥ* (who?) his father-in-law. If one wish

---

[30] The wives of a king are divided into three classes, the first is called *mahiṣî*, the second *vâvâta*, the third or last *parivṛikti*. Sây. *Vâvâta* is in the Rigveda Saṁhitâ, 8, 84, 14, a name of Indra's two horses. Sâyaṇa in his commentary on the passage, proposes two etymologies, from the root *van* to obtain, and *vâ* to go. The latter is the most probable.

[31] That part of the Saṁhitâ where it occurs, not being printed yet, I put this verse here in full :—

यद्वावान पुरुतमं पुराषाळावृत्रहेन्द्रो नामान्यप्राः ।
अचेति प्रासहस्पति स्तविष्मान्यदीमुश्मसि कर्त्तवे करत्तत् ॥

करत् is taken by Sâyaṇa in both his commentaries on the Aitareya Brâhmaṇam, and the Rigveda Saṁhitâ in the sense of a present tense करोति। But it is here conjunctive, which word alone gives a good sense. Besides, the present tense is never formed in this way.

[32] The author takes *prâsahaspati* in the sense of husband of a wife, Prâsahâ, abovementioned.

[33] I take here *akarat* in the sense of a future tense. *Let*, the Vedic conjunctive, has often this meaning. Sây. takes it in the sense of अकरोत्.

[34] This is nothing but an attempt at an etymology of the name *vâvâta*. That it is perfectly childish, every one may see at a glance.

[35] This verse, frequently used at various sacrifices, is the so-called *Dhâyyâ* of the Niṣkevalya Śastra at the midday libation.

that his army might be victorious, then he should go beyond the battle line (occupied by his own army), cut a stalk of grass at the top and end, and throw it against the other (hostile) army by the words, *prâsahe kas tvâ paśyati* ? *i.e.*, " O Prâsahâ, who sees thee ? " If one who has such a knowledge cuts a stalk of grass at the top and end, and throws (the parts cut) against the other (hostile) army, saying *prâsahe kas tvâ paśyati* ? it becomes split and dissolved, just as a daughter-in-law becomes abashed and faints, when seeing her father-in-law (for the first time).

[196] Indra said to them (the gods), " You also shall have (a share) in this (Śastra)." The gods, said, " Let it be the Yâjyâ verse,[36] in the Virâṭ metre of the Niṣkevalya Śastra." The Virâṭ has thirty-three syllables. There are thirty-three gods, *viz.*, eight Vasus, eleven Rudras, twelve Âdityas, (one) Prajâpati, and (one) Vaṣaṭkâra. He (thus) makes the deities participate in the syllables ; and according to the order of the syllables they drink, and become thus satisfied by (this) divine dish.

Should the Hotar wish to deprive the sacrificer of his house and estate, he ought to use for his Yâjyâ along with the Vaṣaṭkâra a verse which is not in the Virâṭ metre, but in the Gâyatrî or Triṣṭubh, or any other metre (save the Virâṭ); thus he deprives him of his house and estate.

Should he wish to procure a house and estate for the sacrificer, he ought to repeat his Yâjyâ in the Virât metre : *piba somam indra mandatu*, (7, 22, 1). By this verse, he procures for the sacrificer a house and estate.

23.

(*On the Close Relationship between Sâman and Rik. Why the Sâma Singers require three ṛichas. The five-fold division of both. Both are contained in the Virâṭ. The five parts of the Niṣkevalya Śastra.*)

First there existed the Rik and the Sâman (separate from one another) ; *sâ* was the Rik, and the name *amaḥ* was the Sâman. *Sâ*, which was Rik, said to the Sâman, " Let us copulate for begetting children." The Sâman answered, " No ; for my greatness exceeds (yours)." (Thereupon) the Rik became two ; both spoke (to the Sâman to the same effect); but **[197]** it did not comply with their request. The Rik became three (divided into three) ; all three spoke (to the Sâman to the same effect). Thus the Sâman joined the three Ṛichas. Thence the Sâma singers use for their chant three Richas,[37] (that is) they perform their work of chanting

---

[36] This is *piba somam indra* (7, 221).

[37] The Sâman, to which the Niṣkevalya Śastra of the Hotar refers, is the Rathantaram. It consists only of two *ṛichas* (verses), *viz.*, *abhi tvâ Śûra* and *na tvâvaṇ* (Sâmaveda Samh. 2, 30, 31), but by the repetition of certain parts of these two verses, three are produced. See about this process, called *punarâdâyam*, above.

with three Richas. (This is so also in worldly affairs.) For one man has many wives (represented by the Ṛichas), but one wife has not many husbands at the same time. From *sâ* and *amaḥ* having joined, *sâma* was produced. Thence it is called *sâman.*[38] He who has such a knowledge becomes *sâman, i.e.*, equal, equitous. He who exists and attains to the highest rank, is a *sâman*, whilst they use the word *asâmanya, i.e.*, inequitous, partial, as a term of reproach.

Both, the Rik as well as the Sâman, were prepared (for sacrificial use) by dividing either into five **[198]** separate parts: (1) *âhâva* (the call *śoṁṣâvom* at the commencement of the Śastras, and *hiṁkâra* (the sound *hum*, commencing every Sâman); (2) the *prastâva* (prelude, first part of the text of the Sâman) and the first *ṛich* out of the three, required for the Sâman of the Niṣkevalya Śastras); (3) the *udgîtha* (principal part of the Sâman), and the second *ṛich*; (4) the *pratihâra* (response of the Sâman), and the last *ṛich* (out of the three); (5) *nidhanam* (the finale of the Sâman) and the call *vauṣaṭ* (at the end of the Yâjyâ verses).[39] Thence they say, the sacrifice is

---

[38] The same etymology is given in the Chhândogya Upaniṣad, 3, 6, 1-6, p. 58 in the Calcutta edition of the Bibliotheca Indica): इयमेव सा ऽग्निरमस्तत्साम *i.e.*, the earth is *sa*, and fire *ama*, whence comes Sâma. The author of this Upaniṣad also supposes that the Sâma rests on the Rik, the latter being compared to the earth, the first to the fire burning on her. This etymology is wholly untenable from a philological point of view. The crude form is not *sâma*, but *sâman*; thence the derivation of the second part of the word from *ama* (a noun ending in *a*, not *an*) falls to the ground. The first part *sâ* is regarded as the feminine of the demonstrative pronoun, and said to mean *Rik*, for Rik is a feminine. But such monstrous formations of words are utterly strange to the Sanskrit language and sanctioned by no rules of the grammarians. In all probability we have to trace the word *sâman* to the root *so*, "to bind," whence the word *avasâna, i.e.*, pause, is derived. It thus means "what is bound, strung together," referring to the peculiar way of chanting the Sâmans. All sounds and syllables of one of the parts of a Sâman are so chanted, that they appear to be strung together, and to form only one long sound.

[39] Many Sâmans are divided into four or five parts. See the note to 2, 22. If five parts are mentioned, then either the *hiṁkâra*, which precedes the *prastâva*, is counted as a separate part, or the *pratihâra* part divided into two, *pratihâra* and *upadrava*, the latter generally only comprising a few syllables.

In order to better illustrate the division of Sâmans into five parts, I give here the Rathantaram, according to these divisions:

First ṛich—(1), *prastâva*:—हुम् ॥ आभि त्वा शूर नोनुमो वा ॥

(2) *udgîtha*: ओमादुग्धा इव धेनव ईशानमस्य जगतः सुवा ईशाम् ॥

(3) *pratihâra*: आईशानमा इंद्रा ।

(4) *upadrava*: सुस्थूषा ओवा हा उवा ।

(5) *nidhanam*: अस ।

Second ṛich—(1) *prastâva*: इशोवा ।

[199] five-fold (is a pentad). Animals are five-fold (consist of five parts, four feet and a mouth).

(Both, the Rik and the Sâman, either of which is divided into five parts, are contained in the Virâṭ, which consists of ten syllables).[40] Thence they say, the sacrifice is put in the Virâṭ, which consists of ten parts.

(The whole Niṣkevalya Śastra also consists of five parts, analogous to the five parts of the Sâman and the Rik at this Śastra.) The *stotriya* is the soul; the *anurûpa* is offspring, the *dhâyyâ* is the wife, animals are the *pragâtha*, the *sûktam* is the house.[41]

He who has such a knowledge, lives in his premises in this world, and in the other, with children and cattle.

24.

(The Stotriya, Anurûpa, Dhâyyâ, Sâma-Pragâtha and Nivid Sûkta of the Niṣkevalya Śastra.)

He repeats the Stotriya. He recites it with a half loud voice. By doing so, he makes his own soul (the Stotriya representing the soul).

---

(2) *udgîtha* :ओनामिंद्र सुस्थषो न त्वा वा ँ अन्योदिवियो न पार्थिवाः

(3) *pratihâra* : न जातो नाजा ।

(4) *upadrava* : नाहृष्याता ओवा हा उवा ।

(5) *nîdhanam* अस् ॥

Third ṛich : (1) *prastâva* नजोवा ।

(2) *udgîtha* : ओंतो न जनिष्यते अश्वायंतो मघवन्निंद्रवाजिनाः ॥

(3) *pratihâra* : गव्यंतस्त्वाहा ।

(4) *upadrava* : वामाहाओवा हा उवा ।

(5) *nidhanam*: अस् *Agniṣṭoma Sâm Prayaga.*

From this specimen the reader will easily learn in what way they make of two ṛichas three, and how they divide each into five parts. The prastâva is chanted by the Prastotar, the udgîtha by the Udgâtar (the chief of the Sâma singers), the pratihâra by the pratihartar, the upadrava by the Udgâtar, and the nidhanam by all three.

[40] This statement is not very accurate. In other passages it is said, that it consists of thirty-three syllables, see 3, 22. The metre is divided into three padas, each consisting of nine, ten, or eleven syllables.

[41] Here are the five parts of the Niṣkevalya Śastra severally enumerated. The *stotriya* are the two verses of which the Rathantara consists, but so repeated by the Hotar as to make three of them, just as the Sâma singers do. The substantive to be supplied to *stotriya* is *pragâtha, i.e.*, that pragâtha, which contains the same text as the *stotram* or performance of the Sâma singers. The *anurûpa pragâtha*, follows the form of the Stotriya; it consists of two verses which are made three. It must have the same commencing words as the Stotriya. The *anurûpa* is : *abhi tvâ pûrvapitaye* (8, 3, 7-8). The Dhâyyâ is already mentioned (3, 22). The Sâma pragâtha is : *pibâ sutasya* (8, 3, 12). The sûkta or hymn is mentioned in the following (24) paragraph.

He repeats the Anurûpa. The Anurûpa is offspring. It is to be repeated with a very loud voice. [200] By doing so, he makes his children more happy than he himself is (for the Stotriya representing his own self, was repeated by him with a half loud voice only.)

He repeats the Dhâyyâ. The Dhâyyâ is the wife. It is to be repeated with a very low voice. When he who has such a knowledge repeats the Dhâyyâ with a very low voice, then his wife does not quarrel with him in his house.

He repeats the (Sâma) Pragâtha. It is to be repeated with the proper modulation of the voice (*i.e.*, with the pronunciation of the four accents).[42] The accents are the animals, the Pragâtha are the animals. (This is done) for obtaining cattle.

He repeats the Sûkta[43] (hymn): *indrasya nu vîryâṇi* [201] (1, 32). This is the hymn liked by Indra, belonging to the Niṣkevalya Śastra, and (seen) by *Hiraṇyastûpa*. By means of this hymn, Hiraṇyastûpa, the son of Angiras, obtained the favour of Indra (and) gained the highest world. He who has such a knowledge, obtains the favour of Indra (and) gains the highest world. The hymn is the house as a firm footing. Thence it is to be repeated with the greatest slowness. (For a firm footing as a resting place is required for every one.) If, for instance, one happens to have cattle grazing in a distant quarter, he wishes to bring them (in the evening) under a shelter. The stables are the firm footing (the place where to put up) for cattle. That is the reason

[42] The mantras which form part of the Śastras are nearly throughout monotonously (*ekaśrutyâ*) repeated. Only in the recital of the Sâma pragâtha an exception takes place. It is to be repeated with all the four accents: *anudâtta, anudâttatara, udâtta,* and *svarita,* just as is always done when the Rigveda is repeated in the temple, or in private houses, without any religious ceremony being performed.

[43] In this hymn, the Nivid of the Niṣkevalya Śastra is to be inserted after its eighth verse. The Nivid is as follows:

इन्द्रो देवः सोम पिबतु । एकजानां वोरतमः । भूरिदानां तवस्तमः । हर्योः स्थाता । पृश्नेः प्रेता । वज्रस्य भर्त्ता । पुरां भेत्ता । पुरां दर्मा । अपां स्रष्टा । अपां नेता । सत्वनां नेता । निजघ्निर्दूरेश्रवाः । उपमातिकृद् सनावान् । इहोशं देवो बभूवान् । इन्द्रो देव इह श्रवदिह सोमस्य पिबतु । प्रेमां देवो देवहूतिमवतु देव्या धिया । प्रेद० (the conclusion being the same as in the Marutyutîya Nivid, see page 189) *i.e.*, May the god Indra drink of the Soma juice, he who is the strongest among those who are born only once; he who is the mightiest among those who are rich; he who is the master of the two yellow horses, he the lover of Priśni, he the bearer of the thunderbolt, who cleaves the castles, who destroys the castles, who makes flow the water, who carries the waters, who carries the spoil from his enemies, who kills, who is far-famed, who appears in different forms *upamâtikrit*, lit., making similes), who is busy, he who has been here a willing god (to listen to our prayers). May the god Indra hear, &c. *Sapta hâutra*. Instead of भूरिदानां, the Sânkhâyana Sûtras, 7, 17, read भूरिजानाः which is less correct, and appears to be a mistake.

that this hymn, which represents a firm footing, or shelter for cattle, which was represented by the Pragâtha, is to be repeated very slowly, so as to represent a firm footing.

THIRD CHAPTER.

(The Abstraction of Soma. Origin of the Three Libations. Evening Libation. The Vaiśvadeva and Agnimâruta Śastras.)

25.

(Story of the Metres which were despatched by the Gods to fetch the Soma from heaven. Jagatî and Triṣṭubh unsuccessful. Origin of Dîkṣâ, Tapas, and Dakṣiṇâ).

The king Soma lived (once) in the other world (in heaven). The Gods and Riṣis deliberated: how might the king Soma (be induced) to come to us? They said, "Ye metres must bring back to us this king Soma." They consented. They transformed themselves into birds. That they transformed themselves into birds (*suparṇa*), and flew up, is called [**202**] by the knowers of stories *sauparṇam* (*i.e.*, this very story is called so). The metres went to fetch the king Soma. They consisted (at that time) of four syllables only; for (at that time) there were only such metres as consisted of four syllables. The Jagatî, with her four syllables, flew first up. In flying up, she became tired, after having completed only half the way. She lost three syllables, and being reduced to one syllable, she took (from heaven) with her (only) the *Dîkṣâ* and *Tapas*,[1] and flew back (to the earth). He who has cattle is possessed of Dîkṣâ and possessed of Tapas. For cattle belong to Jagatî. Jagatî took them.

Then the Triṣṭubh flew up. After having completed more than half the way, she became fatigued, and throwing off one syllable, became reduced to three syllables, and taking (with her) the Dakṣiṇâ, flew back (to the earth). Thence the Dakṣiṇâ gifts (sacrificial rewards) are carried away (by the priests) at the midday libation (which is) the place of the Triṣṭubh; for Triṣṭubh alone had taken them[2] (the Dakṣiṇâ gifts.)

26.

(Gâyatrî successful; Wounded when Robbing the Soma. What became of her nail cut off, &c.)

The gods said to the Gâyatrî, "Fetch thou the king Soma." She consented, but said, "During the whole of my journey (up to the celestial

---

[1] These gifts are to be bestowed upon the sacrificer at the *Dîkṣaṇîyâ iṣṭi*. See 1, 1-5.

[2] The words त्रिष्टुब्ह्यभिता are to be parsed as follows: त्रिष्टुभ् । हि । ता

world), you must repeat the formula for wishing a safe passage for me." The gods consented. She flew up. The gods [**203**] repeated throughout her passage the formula for wishing a safe passage, *viz.*, *pra châ châ*, go, and come back, and come back. For the words, *pra châ châ*,[3] signify, that the whole journey will be made in safety. He who has a friend (who sets out on a journey) ought to repeat this formula; he then makes his passage in safety, and returns in safety.

The Gâyatrî, when flying up, frightened the guardians of Soma, and seized him with her feet and bill, and (along with him) she also seized the syllables which the two other metres (Jagatî and Triṣṭubh) had lost. Kṛiśânu, (one of) the guardians[4] of the Soma, discharged an arrow after her, which cut off the nail of her left leg. This became a porcupine.

(The porcupine, having thus sprung from the nail which was cut off), the Vaśâ (a kind of goat) sprang from the marrow (*vaśa*) which dripped from the nail (cut off). Thence this goat is a (suitable) offering. The shaft of the arrow with the point (discharged by Kṛiśânu) became a serpent which does not bite (*dundubha* by name). From the vehemence with which the arrow was discharged, the snake *svaja* was produced; from the feathers, the shaking branches which hang down (the airy roots of the Aśvattha); from the sinews (with which the feathers were fastened on the shaft) the worms called *gaṇḍûpada*, from the fulmination (of the steel) the serpent *andhâhi*. Into such objects was the arrow (of Kṛiśânu) transformed.

27.

[**204**] (*Origin of the Three Libations. They all are of equal strength.*)

What Gâyatrî had seized with her right foot, that became the morning libation; she made it her own place. Thence they think the morning libation to be the most auspicious (of all). He who has such a knowledge, becomes the first and most prominent (among his people) and attains to the leadership.

What she had seized with her left foot, became the midday libation. This (portion) slipped down, and after having slipped down, did not attain to the same (strength) as the first libation (held with the right foot). The gods got aware of it, and wished (that this portion should not be lost). They put (therefore) in it, of the metres, the Triṣṭubh, and of the deities.

---

[3] This formula is used for wishing to a friend who is setting out on a journey a safe passage and return in safety.

[4] Sâyaṇa here quotes an Adhvaryu mantra containing the names of the guardians of the Soma, among whom one is Kṛiśânu : स्वानभ्राजांघारे बंभारे हस्त सुहस्त कृशाने एते वः सोमक्रयणा-स्तान् रक्षध्वम् मा वो दभन, See Vâjasanêyi Saṁhitâ, 4, 27, with Mahîdhara's commentary on it (p. 117 in Weber's edition).

Indra. Therefore it (the midday libation) became endowed with the same strength as the first libation. He who has such a knowledge, prospers through both the libations which are of equal strength, and of the same quality.

What Gâyatrî had seized with her bill, became the evening libation. When flying down, she sucked in the juice of this (portion of Soma, held in her bill), and after its juice had gone, it did not equal (in strength) the two first libations. The gods got aware of that and wished (that the juice of this portion should be kept). They discovered it (the remedy) in cattle. That is the reason that the priests pour sour milk (in the Soma at the evening libation), and bring oblations of melted butter and of flesh (things coming from the cattle). In this way, the evening libation obtained equal strength with the two first libations.

He who has such a knowledge, prospers through all the libations which are of equal strength and of the same quality.

[205] 28.

(How Triṣṭubh and Gâyatrî obtained their proper number of syllables.)

The two other metres said to the Gâyatrî, "That which thou hast obtained of us, *viz.*, our syllables, should be restored to us." The Gâyatrî answered, "No." (They said) "As far as the right of possession is concerned, they (those syllables) are ours." They went to ask the gods. The gods said, "As far as the right of possession is concerned, they are yours." Thence it comes, that even here (in affairs of daily life), people say when they quarrel, "as far as the right of possession is concerned, this is ours."[5]

Hence the Gâyatrî became possessed of eight syllables (for she did not return the four which she had taken from the others), the Triṣṭubh had three, and the Jagatî only one syllable.

The Gâyatrî lifted the morning libation up (to the gods); but the Triṣṭubh was unable to lift up the midday libation. The Gâyatrî said to her, "I will go up (with the midday libation); let me have a share in it. The Triṣṭubh consented, and said, "Put upon me (who consists of three syllables), these eight syllables." The Gâyatrî consented, and put upon her (eight syllables). That is the reason that at the midday libation the two last verses of the triplet at the beginning of the Marutvatîya Śastra (the first verse being in the Anuṣṭubh metre), and its sequel

[5] This remark here is only made to illustrate a phrase which seems to have been very common in the Vedic Saṁskṛit : यथावित्तं नः

(the *anuchara* triplet) belong to the Gâyatrî. After having obtained thus eleven syllables, she lifted the midday libation up (to heaven).

The Jagatî which had only one syllable, was unable to lift the third libation (up). The Gâyatrî said **[206]** to her, " I will also go up (with thee); let me have a share in this (libation)." The Jagatî consented (and said), " Put upon me those eleven syllables (of the Gâyatrî and Trishṭubh joined). She consented and put (those eleven syllables) upon the Jagatî. That is the reason, that, at the evening libation, the two latter verses of the triplet with which the Vaiśvadeva Śastra commences (*pratipad*), and its sequel (*anuchara*) belong to the Gâyatrî. Jagatî, after having obtained twelve syllables, was able to lift the evening libation up (to heaven). Thence it comes that the Gâyatrî obtained eight, the Trishṭubh eleven, and the Jagatî twelve syllables.

He who has such a knowledge, prospers through all metres which are of equal strength and of the same quality. What was one, that became three-fold.[6] Thence they say, only he who has this knowledge, that what was one, became three-fold, should receive presents.

29.

(*Why the Âdityas and Savitar have a share in the evening libation. On Vâyu's and Dyâvâpṛithivî's share in it.*)

The gods said to the Âdityas, " Let us lift up this (the evening) libation through you." They consented. Thence the evening libation commences with the Âdityas.[7] At the commencement of it there is (the **[207]** libation from) the Âditya graha. Its Yâjyâ mantra is, *âdityâso aditîr madayantâm* (7, 51, 2), which contains the term *mad*, " to be drunk," which is complete in form (equal to the occasion). For the characteristic feature of the evening libation is, " to be drunk." He does not repeat the Anuvaṣaṭkâra,[8] nor does he taste the Soma (as is usual, after the libation has been poured into the fire); for the Anuvaṣaṭkâra is the completion, and the tasting (of the offering by the priests) is also the completion (of the ceremony). The Âdityas are the vital airs. (When the Hotar, therefore, does not repeat the Anuvaṣaṭkâra,

[6] This remark refers to the fact that the Gâyatrî, which consisted originally only of eight syllables, consists of three times eight, *i.e.*, twenty-four.

[7] The very commencement of the evening libation is the pouring of Soma juice from the so-called Âditya graha (a wooden jar). Then follows the chanting of the *Arbhavam*; then the offering of an animal, and that of Purodâśa to the manes, after which a libation is poured from the Sâvitri graha, and the Vaiśvadeva Śastra repeated. (Âśv. Śr. S. 5, 17.)

[8] See page 133.

nor taste the Âditya libation, (he thinks), I will certainly put no end [9] to the life (of the sacrificer).

The Âdityas said to Savitar, "let us lift up this (the évening) libation through thee." He consented. Thence the beginning (*pratipad* of the Vaiśvadeva Śastra at the evening libation) is made with a triplet of verses addressed to Savitar.[10] To the Vaiśvadeva Śastra belongs the Savitri graha. Before[11] the commencement (of this Śastra) he repeats the Yâjyâ for the libation (from the Savitri graha), *damûnâ devaḥ savitâ vareṇyam* (Âśv. Śr. S. 5, 18). This verse[12] contains **[208]** the term *mad* "to be drunk" which is complete in form. The term *mad* "to be druuk" is a characteristic of the evening libation. He does not repeat the Anuvaṣaṭkâra, nor does he taste (from the Soma juice in the Savitri graha). For the Anuvaṣaṭkâra is completion, the tasting (of the Soma by the priest) is completion. Savitar is the life. (He should do neither, thinking) I will certainly put no end to the life (of the sacrificer). Savitar drinks largely from both the morning and evening libations. For there is the term *piba*, "drink," at the commencement [13] of the Nivid addressed to Savitar at the

---

[9] The negation is here expressed by *net*, *i.e.*, *na it*, the same word, which is almost exclusively used in the Zend-Avesta, in the form *noit.*, for expressing the simple negative.

[10] The Pratipad, or beginning triplet of verses of the Vaiśvadeva Śastra is: *tat savitur vṛiṇîmahe* (5, 82, 1-3).

[11] The Yâjyâ is to be repeated before the Vaiśvadeva Śastra is repeated.

[12] It is also, with some deviations, found in the Atharvaveda Saṁhitâ (7, 14, 4). According to the Âśv. Sûtras, it runs as follows :

दमूना देवः सविता वरेण्यो दधद्रत्ना दक्षपितृभ्यो आयुनि । पिवात्सोमं ममदन्नेनमिष्टयः परिज्मा चिद्रमते अस्य धर्मणि ॥ The deviations of the text in the Atharvaveda consist in the following : instead of रत्ना : रत्नं ; for दक्षपि० : दक्षपो० ; for ममदन्नेनमिष्टयः it has ममदद्देनमिष्टेः ; instead of रमते, it has क्रमते. It is evident that the readings of the Atharvaveda are corrupt ; for it will be impossible to make out the sense of the mantra from its text presented in the Atharvaveda : but it may be done from that one given in the Âśvalâyana Sûtras. I translate it as follows : "The divine house-father Savitar, who is chosen (as tutelary deity by men), has provided people (*âyu*) with precious gifts to make offerings to Dakṣa (one of the Âdityas) and the manes. May he drink the Soma! May the (Soma) offerings inebriate him, when on his wanderings, he pleases to delight in his (the Soma's) quality !"

[13] In the words, *savitâ devaḥ somasya pibatu.* The hymn, in which the Nivid for Savitar is inserted, is, *abhûd devaḥ savita* (4, 54). The whole Nivid is as follows :

सविता देवः सोमस्य पिबतु । हिरण्यपाणिः सुजिह्वः । सुबाहुः स्वंगुरिः । त्रिरहन्सत्यसवनः । यः प्रासुवद्वसुधितो । उभे जोत्री सवोमनि । श्रेष्ठं सावित्रमासुवं । दोग्ध्रीं धेनुं । वोळ्हारमनड्वाहं । आशुं सप्तिं । पुरंधिं योषां । जिष्णुं रथेष्ठां । सभेयं युवानं । परामीवां साविषत्पराघशंसं । सविता देव इह अवदिह सोमस्य मत्सत् । प्रेमां देवो० (The conclusion is just as in the other Nivids). Sapta Hâutra. In the Sânkhay. Śr. Sûtras (8, 18), there are, before परामी० the words :

[209] evening libation), and at the end[14] the term *mad*, "to be drunk." Thus he makes Savitar share in both the morning and evening libations.

At the morning and evening libations, verses addressed to Vâyu are repeated, many at the morning, one only[15] at the evening, libation. That is done because the vital airs (represented by Vâyu, the wind) in the upper parts (represented by the morning libation) of the human body are more numerous than those in the lower parts (represented by the evening libation).

He repeats a hymn addressed to Heaven and Earth.[16] For Heaven and Earth are stand-points. [210] Earth is the stand-point here, and Heaven is the stand-point there (in the other world). By thus repeating a hymn addressed to Heaven and Earth, the Hotar establishes the sacrificer in both places (in earth and heaven).

30.

(*Story of the Ṛibhus. On their Share in the Evening Libation.*)

He repeats the Ṛibhu hymn (*takṣan ratham*, 1, 111).[17] The (beings

---

सविता देव : I translate it as follows: May the god Savitar drink of the Soma juice he with his golden hands and his good tongue, with his fine arms and fine fingers, he who produces thrice a day the real objects (*i.e.*, the external world is visible in the morning, at noon, and in the evening), he who produced the two treasures of wealth, the two loving sisters (night and dawn), the best things that are created, the milking cow, the ox-drawing cart, the swift septad (of horses for drawing the carriage of the sun-god), the female (called) *purandhi*, *i.e*, meditation, the victorious warrior, the youth in the assemblage (of men), &c.

[14] In the words, *savitâ devaḥ iha śravad iha somasya matsat.*

[15] This remark refers to the last words which are appended to the Nivid hymn for Savitar, *viz.*, *niyudbhir vâyaviha.* The whole appendage, which is to be found in the Âsv. Śr. S. 5, 18, and in Sapta Hâutra is: एकया च दशभिश्च स्वभूते । द्वाभ्यामिष्टये विंशत्याचोंं३ तिस्टभिश्च वहसे त्रिंशताच । नियुद्भिर्वायविह ता मुंचोंं३, *i.e.*, Vâyu, come hither with (thy) steeds, unloosen them, (come) with eleven for thy own sake, with twenty-two for (making) the sacrifice om! with thirty-three for carrying (the sacrifice).

[16] This is *pradyâvâ yajnâiḥ* (1, 159). The Nivid to be inserted before the lost verse of the Dyâvâpṛithivî hymn is:

द्यावापृथिवी सोमस्य मत्सतां । पिता च माता च पुत्रश्च प्रजननं च । धेनुश्च ऋषभश्च । धन्या च धिषणा च । सुरेताश्च सुदुघा च । शंभूच मयोभूश्च । ऊर्जस्वती च । पयस्वतीच रेतोधाश्च रेतोभिश्च । द्यावा पृथिवी इह श्रुतामिह सोमस्य मत्सतां । प्रेमां देवी देवहूतिमवतां देव्या धिया । प्रेदं ब्रह्म प्रेदं क्षत्रं । प्रेदं सुन्वन्तं यजमानमवतां । चित्रे चित्राभिरूतिभिः । श्रुतां ब्रह्माण्यावसागतां ॥ May Heaven and Earth enjoy the Soma which are the father and mother, the son and generation, the cow and the bull, the grain and the wood, the well-provided with seed, and the well-provided with milk, the happy and the beneficial, the juicy and milky, the giver of seed, and (holder) of seed. May both Heaven and Earth here hear (me)! May they here enjoy the Soma, &c.

[17] The Nivid inserted before the last verse of the Ribhu hymn is:

ऋभवो देवाः सोमस्य मत्सन । विष्ट्वी स्वपसः । कर्मणा सुहस्ताः । धन्या धनिष्ठाः । शम्या

called) Ṛibhus among the gods, had, by means of austerities, obtained the right to a share in the Soma beverage. They (the gods) wished to make room for them in the recitations at the morning libation; but Agni with the Vasus (to whom this libation belongs), turned them out of the morning libation. They (the gods) then wished to make room for them in the recitations at the midday libation; but Indra with the Rudras (to whom this libation belongs), turned them out of this libation. They then wished to make room for them in the **[211]** recitations at the evening libation; but the Viśve Devâḥ (to whom it belongs), tried to turn them out of it, saying, "They shall not drink here; they shall not." Prajâpati then said to Savitar, "These are thy pupils; thou alone (among the Viśve Devâh), therefore, shalt drink with them." He consented, and said (to Prajâpati), "Drink thou also, standing on both sides of the Ribhus." Prajâpati drank standing on both sides of them. (That is the reason that) these two Dhâyyâs (required for the Vaiśvadeva Śastra) which do not contain the name of any particular deity, and belong to Prajâpati, are repeated, one before the other, after the Ṛibhu hymn. (They are) *surûpakṛtnuṁ ûtaye* (1, 4, 1) and *ayam venaś chodayat* (10, 123, 1).[18] Prajâpati thus drinks on both their sides. Thus it comes that a chief (*śreṣṭhî*) favours with a draught from his goblet whom he likes.

The gods, however, abhorred them (the Ṛibhus), on account of their human[19] smell. (Therefore) they placed two (other) Dhâyyâs between the Ṛibhus and themselves. (These are) *yebhyo mâtâ madhumat* (10, 63 3), and *evâ pitre viśva devâya* (4, 50, 6).[20]

शमिष्ठाः। शच्या शचिष्ठाः। ये धेनुं विश्वजुवं विश्वरूपामतक्षन्। अतक्षं धेनुमभवद्विश्वरूपी। अयुंजत हरी अयुदवानुप। अबुध्रनत्सं कनीनां अदंतः। संवत्सरे स्वपसो यज्ञियं भागमायन्। ऋभवो देवा इह श्रवन्निह सोमस्य मत्सन्। प्रेमां देवा देवहूतिमवंतु॰ May the divine Ṛibhus enjoy the Soma, who are busy and clever, who are skilful with their hands, who are very rich, who are full of bliss, full of strength, who cut the cow which moves everywhere, and has all forms (*i.e.*, the earth), who cut the cow (that) she became of all forms, who yoked the two yellow horses (of Indra) who went to the gods, who when eating got aware of the girls, who entered by their skill upon their share in the sacrifice in the year (at the sacrificial session lasting for one year); may the divine Ṛibhus hear (us) here and enjoy the Soma, &c.

[18] This whole story is invented for explaining the position assigned to certain verses and hymns in the Vaiśvadeva Śastra. After the hymn addressed to Savitar, *abhûd devaḥ savitâ* (4, 54), there follows the verse *surûpakṛitnum*, which is called a Dhâyyâ; then comes the hymn addressed to the Ṛibhus, *takṣan ratham*, and then the verse *ayam venaś*, which is also a Dhâyyá. See Âśv. Śr. S. 5, 8.

[19] They are said to have been men, and raised themselves to an equal rank with the gods by means of sacrifice and austerities.

[20] These two verses immediately follow: *ayam venaś chodayat*. Âśv. Śr. S. 5, 18.

[212] 31.

(The Nivid hymn for the Viśve Devâḥ. On the Dhâyyâs of the Vaiśvadeva Śastra. To what deities it belongs. On the concluding verse of this Śastra).

He repeats the Vaiśvadeva hymn.[21] The Vaiśvadeva Śastra shows the relationship of subjects (to their king) Just as people represent the interior part **[213]** (of a kingdom), so do also the hymns (represent the interior, the kernel, of the Śastra). The Dhâyyâs, then, are like what is in the desert (beasts, &c.) That is the reason why the Hotar must repeat before and after every Dhâyyâ the call *śomsâvom* (for every Dhâyyâ is

---

[21] This is *â no bhad âh kratavo* (1, 89). The Nivid inserted before the last verse of this Viśvedevâḥ hymn is:

विश्वे देवाः सोमस्य मत्सन् । विश्वे वैश्वानराः । विश्वे हि विश्वमहसः । महिमहान्त : । तक्वान्नानेमतिथीवान : । आस्क्राः पचतवाहस : । वातात्मानो अग्निदूताः । ये द्यांच पृथिवींच तस्थु : । अपश्च स्वश्च । ब्रह्म च क्षत्रं च । बर्हिश्च वेदिं च । यज्ञंचोरुचांतरिक्षं । येस्थ त्रय एकदशा : । त्रयश्च त्रिंशच्च । त्रयश्च त्रीच शता । त्रयश्च त्रीच सहस्रा । तावन्तो भिषाचः । तावन्तो रातिषाचः । तावतोः पत्नी : । तावतोर्ग्नाः । तावन्त उदरणे । तावन्तो निवेशने । अतो वा देवा भूयांसः स्थ । मा वो देवा अपिशसामापरिशसावृक्षि । विश्वे देवा इह अवस्विह सोमस्य मत्सन् । प्रेमां देवा०

(Sapta Hâutra). The text as given in the Sânkhâya. Śr. S. 8, 21, differs in several passages. Instead of तक्वान्न ० it has पक्वान्ना ० which is, no doubt, more correct. The words तावन्त उदरणे तावन्तो निवेशने are transposed; they follow after तावतीर्ग्नाः, after which तावभिष० and ताव० रा० are put. Instead of अपिशस०, there is अविशासामाविशसा पुरा वक्षि The translation of some terms in this Nivid, which is doubtless very old, is extremely difficult. Now and then the reading does not appear to be correct. It is, however, highly interesting, as perhaps one of the most ancient accounts we have of the number of Hindu deities. They are here stated at 3 times 11; then at 33, then at 303, then at 3003. It appears from this statement, that only the number 3 remained unchanged, whilst the number 30 was multiplied by 10 or 100. Similarly, the number of gods is stated at 3339 in a hymn ascribed to the Ṛiṣi Viśvâmitra Ṛigveda, 3, 9, 9. This statement appears to rely on the Vaiśvadeva Nivid. For, if we add 33+303+3003 together, we obtain exactly the number 3339. This coincidence can hardly be fortuitous, and we have strong reasons to believe that Viśvâmitra perfectly knew this Viśve Devâh Nivid. That it contains one of the most authoritative passages for fixing the number of Hindu deities follows from quotations in other Vedic books. So we read in the Bṛihad Araṇyaka Upanishad (page 642-49, edited by Roer, Calcutta, 1849) a discussion by Yâjñavalkya on the number of gods, where he appeals to the Nivid of the Vaiśvadeva hymn as the most authoritative passage for settling this question. Perhaps the oldest authority we have for fixing the number of the Hindu deities, on the first instance, at thirty-three, is Ṛigveda, 8, 28, 1. The hymn to which this verse belongs is said to have descended from Manu, the progenitor of the human race. Its style shows traces of high antiquity, and there can be hardly any doubt, that it is one of the earliest Vedic hymns we have. The division of these thirty-three deities into three sets, each of eleven, equally distributed among the three worlds, heaven, air, and earth, (see 1, 139, 11) appears to be the result of later speculations. According to the Nivid in question, the gods are not distributed among the three worlds, but they are in heaven and earth, water, and sky, in the Brahma and Kṣatra, in the Barhis, and on the Vedi, in the sacrifice, and in the air.

considered as a separate recitation distinct from the body of the Śastra). (Some one might object) how can verses, like the Dhâyyâs, which are life, be compared to a desert ? Regarding this, he (the Aitareya Ṛiṣi) has told that the deserts (*araṇyâni*) are properly speaking no deserts, on account of the deer and birds to be found there.

The Vaiśvadeva Śastra is to be likened to man. Its hymns are like his internal parts; its Dhâyyâs are like the links (of his body). That is the reason that the Hotar calls *śomsâvom* before and after every Dhâyyâ (to represent motion and flexibility). For the links of the human body are loose; these are, however, fastened and held together by the Brahma. The Dhâyyâ[22] and Yâjyâ verses are the root of the **[214]** sacrifice. When they use Dhâyyâs and Yâjyâs different from those which are prescribed, then they uproot the sacrifice. Therefore, they (the Dhâyyâs and Yâjyâs) should be only of the same nature (they should not use other ones than those mentioned).

The Vaiśvadeva Śastra belongs to five classes of beings. It belongs to all five classes of beings, *viz.*: Gods and Men, Gandharvas (and) Apsaras,[23] Serpents and Manes. To all these five classes of beings belongs the Vaiśvadeva Śastra. All beings of these five classes know him (the Hotar who repeats the Vaiśvadeva Śastra). To that Hotar who has such a knowledge come those individuals of these five classes of beings who understand the art of recitation (to assist him). The Hotar who repeats the Vaiśvadeva Śastra belongs to all deities. When he is about to repeat his Śastra, he ought to think of all directions (have them before his mind), by which means he provides all these directions with liquid (*rasa*) But he ought not to think of that direction in which his enemy lives. By doing so, he consequently deprives him of his strength.

He concludes (the Vaiśvadeva Śastra) with the verse *aditir dyâur aditir antarikṣam* (1, 89, 10), *i.e.*, Aditi is heaven, Aditi is the air, Aditi is mother, father and son; Aditi is all gods; Aditi is the five classes of creatures; Aditi is what is born; Aditi is what is to be born." She (Aditi) is mother, she is father, she is son. In her are the Vaiśvadevas, in her the five classes of creatures. She is what is born, she is what is to be born.

(When reciting this concluding verse which is to be repeated thrice), he recites it twice (for the second and third times) so as to stop at each (of the four) padas. (He does so) for obtaining cattle, which are

[22] Here the regular Dhâyyâs (see 3, 18), are to be understood, not those extraordinary additions which we have in the Vaiśvadeva Śastra.

[23] Gandharvas and Apsaras are counted as one class only.

[215] four-footed. Once (the first time) he repeats the concluding verse, stopping at the end of each half of the verse only. (That is done) for establishing a firm footing. Man has two feet, but animals have four. (By repeating the concluding verse twice in the said manner) the Hotar places the two-legged sacrificer among the four-legged animals.

He ought always to conclude (the Vaiśvadeva Śastra) with a verse addressed to the five classes of beings (as is the case in *aditir dyâur*); and, when concluding, touch the earth. Thus he finally establishes the sacrifice in the same place in which he acquires the means of his performance.

After having repeated the Vaiśvadeva Śastra, he recites the Yâjyâ verse addressed to the Viśve Devâs: *viśve devâḥ śriṇuta imam havam me* (6, 52, 13). Thus he pleases the deities according to their shares (in the libation).

32.

(The Offerings of Ghee to Agni and Viṣṇu, and the Offering of a Charu to Soma.)

The first Yâjyâ verse for the offering of hot butter is addressed to Agni, that for the offering of Charu is addressed to Soma, and another for the offering of hot butter is addressed to Viṣṇu.[24]

[216] The Yâjyâ verse for the offering of Charu to Soma is *tvam soma pitṛibhih* (8, 48, 13); it contains the word "*pitaras*," *i.e.*, manes (This Charu is an oblation to the dead Soma). The priests kill the Soma, when they extract its juice. This (oblation of Charu) is therefore the cow which they use to kill (when the body of a sacrificer is laid on the funeral pile.[25]) For this Charu oblation has, for the Soma,

[24] After the Soma juice has been offered to the Visvedevâs, an offering of hot butter (ghee) is given to Agni; then follows the oblation of Charu or boiled rice to Soma, and then another oblation of hot butter to Viṣṇu. The chief oblation is that of Charu to Soma, which is put in the midst of the two offerings of hot butter. The Yâjyâ verses addressed at this occasion to Agni and Viṣṇu are not to be found in the Samhitâ of the Ṛigveda; but they are given by Âśval. in the śrauta Sûtras, (5, 19). The following is addressed to Agni: घृताहवनो घृतपृष्ठो अग्निर्घृतैश्रितो घृतम्वस्य धाम । घृतप्रुषस्त्वां हरितो वहन्तु, घृतं पिबन् यजसि देव देवान्, *i.e.*, Agni is it who receives oblations of hot butter, who has (as it were) a back laden with hot butter, by whom hot butter abides, whose very house is hot butter. May thy butter drops, sputtering horses, carry thee! Thou, O God! offerest up the sacrifice to the gods, by drinking the hot butter.

The Yâjyâ verse addressed to Viṣṇu is: उरु विष्णो विक्रमस्वोरुक्षयाय नस्कृधि । घृतं घृतयोने पिब प्र प्रयज्ञपतिं तिर, *i.e.*, take, O Viṣṇu! thy wide strides; make us room for living in ease. Drink the hot butter, O thou, who art the womb of hot butter; prolong (the life of) the master of the sacrifice (the sacrificer).

[25] The term is *anustaraṇî (gauḥ)*, *i.e.*, a cow put down *after*, *i.e.*, accompanying the dead to the other world. See Âśv. Gṛihya Sûtra, 4, 3.

the same significance as the cow sacrificed at the funeral pile for the manes. This is the reason that the Hotar repeats (at this occasion) a Yâjyâ verse, containing the term "*pitaras*," *i.e.*, manes. Those who have extracted the Soma juice, have killed the Soma. (By making this oblation) they produce him anew.

They make him fat[26] in the form of a siege (by putting him between Agni and Viṣṇu); for (the order **[217]** of) the deities Agni, Soma, and Viṣṇu, has the form of a siege.

After having received (from the Adhvaryu) the Charu for Soma for being eaten by him, the Hotar should first look at himself and then (offer it) to the Sâma singers. Some Hotṛi-priests offer first this Charu (after the oblation to the gods is over) to the Sâma singers. But he ought not to do that; for he (the Hotar) who pronounces the (powerful) call *vauṣaṭ*, eats all the remains of the food (offered to the gods). So it has been said by him (the Aitareya Ṛiṣi). Therefore the Hotar who pronounces the (powerful) formula *vauṣaṭ* should, when acting upon that injunction (to offer first the Charu remains to the Sâma singers), certainly first look upon himself. Afterwards the Hotar offers it to the Sâma singers.[27]

33.

(Prajâpati's Illegal Intercourse with his Daughter, and the Consequences of it. The Origin of Bhûtavân.)

Prajâpati thought of cohabiting with his own daughter, whom some call "Heaven," others "Dawn," (Uṣâs). He transformed himself into a buck or a kind of deer (*ṛiśya*), whilst his daughter assumed the shape of

---

[26] The term is *âpyayanti*. This is generally done by sprinkling water over him before the juice is squeezed, for the purpose of making the Soma (mystically) grow. When he is already squeezed and even sacrificed, water itself cannot be sprinkled over him. But this is mystically done, by addressing the verses just mentioned to the deities Agni, Soma, and Viṣṇu, so as to put Soma in the midst of them, just as a town invested on all sides. When they perform the ceremony of *âpyâyanam*, the Soma plant is on all sides to be sprinkled with water. This is done here symbolically by offering first ghee, and giving ghee again after the Charu for Soma is sacrificed. So he is surrounded everywhere by ghee, and the two gods, Agni and Viṣṇu.

The remark about the *âpyâyanam* is made in the Brâhmaṇam for the sole purpose of accounting for the fact, that the first Yâjyâ is addressed to Agni, the second to Soma, and the third to Viṣṇu; that this was a sacrificial rule, see Âśv. Śr. S. 5, 19.

[27] The mantras which the Hotar has to repeat at this occasion, are given in full by Aśvalâyana Śr. S. 5, 19. After having repeated them, he besmears his eyes with melted butter, and gives the Charu, over which butter is dripped, to the Sâma singers, who are called here and in Âśvalâyana *Chandogas*

a female deer (*rohit*).[28] He approached her. **[218]** The gods saw it (crying), " Prajâpati commits an act never done (before)." (In order to avert the evil consequences of this incestuous act) the gods inquired for some one who might destroy the evil consequences (of it). Among themselves they did not find any one who might do that (atone for Prajâpati's crime). They then put the most fearful bodies (for the gods have many bodies) of theirs in one. This aggregate of the most fearful bodies of the gods became a god, *Bhûtavân*,[29] by name. For he who knows this name only, is born.[30] The gods said to him, "Prajâpati has committed an act which he ought not to have committed. Pierce this[31] (the incarnation of his evil deed)." So he did. He then said, "I will choose a boon from you."—They said, "Choose." He then chose as his boon sovereignty over cattle.[32] That is the reason that his name is *paśumân*), *i.e.*, having cattle. He who knows on this earth only this name (*paśumân*), becomes rich in cattle.

He (Bhûtavân) attacked him (the incarnation of Prajâpati's evil deed) and pierced him (with an arrow). After having pierced him, he sprang up (and became a constellation). They call him *mṛiga*, *i.e.*, deer (stars in the Orion), and him who killed that being[33] (which **[219]** sprang from Prajâpati's misdeeds), *mṛiga vyâdha*, *i.e.*, hunter of the deer (name of star). The female deer *Rohit* (into which Prajâpati's daughter had been transformed) became (the constellation) Rohiṇî.

---

[28] Sâyaṇa gives another explanation. He takes *rohitam*, not as the name of a female deer, but as an adjective, meaning *red*. But then we had to expect *rohitâm*. The crude form is *rohit*, not *rohita*. He explains the supposed *rohita* as *ṛitumatî*.

[29] Sây. takes him as Rudra, which is, no doubt, correct.

[30] This is only an explanation of the term *bhûtavân*.

[31] This refers to the *pâpman*, *i.e.*, the incarnate evil deeds, a kind of devil. The evil deed of Prajâpati had assumed a certain form, and this phantom, which is nothing but a personification of remorse, was to be destroyed.

[32] This appears to confirm Sâyaṇa's opinion that Rudra or Śiva is here alluded to. For he is called *paśupati*, master of cattle.

[33] Sây. refers the demonstrative pronouns *tam imam*, by which alone the incarnation of Prjâpati's evil deed is here indicated, to Prajâpati himself, who had assumed the shape of a buck. But the idea that Prajâpati was killed (even in the shape of a buck) is utterly inconsistent with the Vedic notions about him : for in the older parts of the Vedas he appears as the Supreme Being, to whom all are subject. The noun to be supplied was *pâpman*. But the author of the Brâhmaṇam abhorred the idea of a *pâpman* or incarnation of sin of Prajâpati, the Lord of the Universe, the Creator. Thence he was only hinted at by this demonstrative pronoun. The mentioning of the word *pâpman* in connection with Prajâpati, was, no doubt, regarded by the author, as very inauspicious. Even the incestuous act committed by Prajâpati, he does not call *pâpa*, sin, or *doṣa*, fault, but only *akritam*, " what ought not to be done," which is the very mildest term by which a crime can be mentioned.

The arrow (by which the phantom of Prajâpati's sin was pierced) which had three parts (shaft, steel, and point) became such an arrow (in the sky). The sperm which had been poured forth from Prajâpati, flew down on the earth and became a lake. The gods said, "May this sperm of Prajâpati not be spoilt (*mâduṣat*)." This became the *maduṣam*. This name *mâduṣa* is the same as *mânuṣa*, *i.e.*, man. For the word *mânuṣa*, *i.e.*, man, means "one who should not be spoiled" (*mâduṣan*). This (*mâduṣa*) is a (commonly) unknown word. For the gods like to express themselves in such terms unknwn (to men).

34.

(*How Different Creatures Originated from Prajâpati's Sperm. On the Verse addressed to Rudra. Propitiation of Rudra.*)

The gods surrounded this sperm with Agni (in order to make it flow); the Marutas agitated it; but Agni did not make it (the pool formed of Prajâpati's sperm) move. They (then) surrounded it with *Agni Vaiśvânara*; the Marutas agitated it; Agni Vaiśvânara (then) made it move. That spark which first blazed up from Prajâpati's sperm became that *Âditya* (the **[220]** sun); the second which blazed up became *Bhṛigu*. Varuṇa adopted him as his son. Thence Bhṛigu is called *Varuṇi*, *i.e.*, descendant of Varuṇa. The third which blazed up (*âdidevatâ*)[24] became the Âdityas (a class of gods). Those parts (of Prajâpati's seed after it was heated) which were coals (*aṅgâra*) becane the *Aṅgiras*. Those coals whose fire was not extinguished, and which blazed up again, became *Bṛihaspati*. Those parts which remained as coal dust (*parikṣâṇâni*) became black animals, and the earth burnt red (by the fire), became red animals. The ashes which remained became a being full of links, which went in all directions (and sent forth) a stag, buffalo, antelope, camel, ass, and wild beasts.

This god (the Bhûtavân), addressed them (these animals), "This is mine; mine is what was left on the place." They made him resign his share by the verse which is addressed to Rudra: *â te pitâ marutâm* (2, 33, 1), *i.e.*, "may it please thee, father of the Marutas, not to cut us off from beholding the sun (*i.e.*, from living); may'st thou, powerful hero (Rudra)! spare our cattle and children, that we, O master of the Rudras!" might be propagated by our progeny."

The Hotar ought to repeat (in the third pada of the verse) *tvam no vîro* and not *abhi no vîro* (as is the reading of another Śâkhâ). For, if he do not repeat the words *abhi naḥ*, *i.e.*, towards us, then this god

[24] This strange intensive form of the root *div*, to shine, is here chosen only for explaining the origin of the name, "*âdityâs*."

(Rudra) does not entertain any designs against (*abhi*) our children and cattle (*i.e.*) he does not kill them. In the fourth half-verse he ought to use the word *rudriya*, instead of *rudra*, for diminishing the terror (and danger) arising from (the pronunciation of) the real name Rudra.[35]

[**221**] (But should this verse appear to be too dangerous) the Hotar may omit it and repeat (instead of it) only *śaṁ naḥ karati* (1, 43, 6), *i.e.*, "may he be propitiated (and) let our horses, rams and ewes, our males and females, and cows go on well." (By repeating this verse) he commences with the word *śam*, *i.e.*, propitiated, which serves for general propitiation. *Narah* (in the verse mentioned) means *males*, and *nâryaḥ* females.

(That the latter verse and not the first one should be repeated, may be shown from another reason.) The deity is not mentioned with its name, though it is addressed to Rudra, and contains the propitiatory term *śam*. (This verse helps) to obtain the full term of life (100 years). He who has such a knowledge, obtains the full term of his life. This verse (*śaṁ naḥ karati*) is in the Gâyatrî metre. Gâyatrî is Brahma. By repeating that verse, the Hotar worships him (Rudra) by means of Brahma (and averts consequently all evil consequences which arise from using a verse referring to Rudra).

35.

(The Vaiśvânara and Mâruta Nivid Hymns, and the Stotriya and Anurûpa of the Agnimâruta Śastra.)

The Hotar commences the Agni-mâruta Śastra with a hymn addressed to Agni-Vaiśvânara.[36] [**222**] Vaiśvânara is the seed which

---

[35] In the Rigveda Saṁhitâ which is extant at present, the mantra has in the third pada the word *abhi no*, and not *tvam no*, and in the fourth pada *rudra*, and not *rudriya*. The readings of the verse as they are in our copies of the Saṃhita, seem to have been current already at the time of the author of the Aitareya Brâhmaṇam. But he objects to using the verse so, as it was handed down, for sacrificial purposes, on account of the danger which might arise from the use of such terms as *abhi*, *i.e.* (turned) towards, and *rudra*, the proper name of the fearful god of destruction. He proposes two things, either to change these dangerous terms, or to leave out the verse altogether, and use another one instead of it.

[36] This is *vaiśvânarâya pṛithu* (3, 3). The Nivid for the Vaiśvânara hymn is :—

अग्निर्वैश्वानरः सेामस्य मत्सत् । विश्वेषां देवानां समित् । अजस्रं दैव्यं ज्योतिः । येा विड्भ्येा मानुषीभ्यो अदीदेत् । द्युषु पूर्वासु दिद्युतानः । अजर उषसामनीके । आ येा द्यां भात्यापृथिवीं । ओर्वंतरिक्षं । ज्योतिषा यज्ञाय शर्म यंसत् । अग्निर्वैश्वानर इह अवदिह सेामस्य मत्सत् । प्रेमां देवो देवहूतिमवतु॰

"May Agni Vaiśvânara enjoy the Soma, he who is the fuel for all gods (for he as the vital spirit keeps them up), he who is the imperishable divine light, who lighted to the quarters of men, who (was) shining in former skies (days), who is never decaying in the

was poured forth. Thence the Hotar commences the Agni-mâruta Sastra with a hymn addressed to Vaiśvânara. The first verse is to be repeated without stopping. He who repeats the Agni-mâruta Śastra, extinguishes the fearful flames of the fires. By (suppressing) his breath (when repeating the first verse) he crosses the fires. Lest he might (possibly) forego some sound (of the mantra) when repeating it, it is desirable that he should appoint some one to correct such a mistake (which might arise). By thus making him (the other man) the bridge, he crosses (the fires, even if he should commit some mistake in repeating). Because of no mistake in repeating being allowed in this, there ought to be some one appointed to correct the mistakes, when the Hotar repeats it.

The Marutas are the sperm which was poured forth. By shaking it they made it flow. Thence he repeats a hymn addressed to the Marutas.[37]

[223] In the midst (of the Śastra, after having repeated the two hymns mentioned) he repeats the Stotriya[38] and Anurûpa Pragâthas, *yajnâ yajnâ vo agnaye* (1, 168, 1-2), and *devo vo dravinodâ* (7, 16, 11-12). The reason that he repeats the "womb" (the Stotriya) in the midst (of the Śastra), is because women have their wombs in the middle (of their bodies). By repeating it, after having already recited two hymns (the Vaiśvanara and Agni-mâruta), he puts the organ of generation between the two legs in their upper part for producing offspring. He who has such a knowledge will be blessed with offspring and cattle.

---

course of the auroras (during all days to come), who illumines the sky, the earth, and the wide airy region. May he, through his light, give (us) shelter! May Agni Vaiśvânara here hear (us), &c."

[37] This is the Sûkta : *pratvakṣasaḥ pratavasaḥ* (1, 87). The Nivid of the hymn for the Marutas at the evening libation, is :

मरुतो देवाः सोमस्य मत्सन् । सुष्टुभः स्वर्काः । अर्कस्तुभो बृहद्वयसः । सूरा अनाधृष्टरथीः । त्वेषासः पृश्निमातरः । शुभ्राहि-रण्यखादय : तव सो भंददिष्टयः : । नभस्यावर्ष निर्णिज : । मरुतो देवा इह श्रवन्निह सोमस्य मत्सन् । प्रेमां देवा देवहूतिमवंतु ०

"May the divine Marutas enjoy the Soma, who chant well and have fine songs, who chant their songs, who have large stores (of wealth), who have good gifts, and whose chariots are irresistible, who are glittering, the sons of Priśni, whose armour shines with the brilliancy of gold, who are powerful, who receive the offerings (to carry them up), who make the clouds drop the rain. May the divine Marutas hear (my invocation). May they enjoy the Soma, &c."

[38] The Stotriya is here mentioned by the term of *yoni*, womb. It is called so on account of its containing the very words of the Sâman in whose praise the whole Śastra is recited, and forming thus the centre of the whole recitation. The name of the Sâman in question is *yajnâ yajniya* (Sâmaveda Saṁhitâ, 2, 53, 54.)

36.

(*The Jâtavedâs Nivid Hymn*).

He repeats the hymn addressed to Jâtavedâs.[39] All beings, after having been created by Prajâpati **[224]**, walked, having their faces turned aside, and did not turn (their backs). He (Prajâpati) then encircled them with fire, whereupon they turned to Agni. After they had turned to Agni, Prajâpati said, " The creatures which are born (*jâta*), I obtained (*avidam*) through this one (Agni)." From these words came forth the Jâtavedâs hymn. That is the reason that Agni is called Jâtavedâs.[40]

The creatures being encircled by fire, were hemmed in walking. They stood in flames and blazing. Prajâpati sprinkled them with water. That is the reason that the Hotar, after having recited the Jâtavedâs hymn, repeats a hymn addressed to the waters: *âpô hiṣṭha mayobhuvaḥ* (10, 9). Thence it is to be recited by him as if he were extinguishing fire (*i.e.*, slowly).

Prajâpati, after having sprinkled the creatures with water, thought that they (the creatures) were his own. He provided them with an invisible lustre, through *Ahir budhnya.* This Ahir budhnya (lit., the serpent of the depth) is the Agni Gârhapatya (the household fire). By repeating therefore a verse addressed to Ahir bundhnya, [41] the Hotar

---

[39] This is: *pra tavyasîm*, 1, 143. The Nivid for Jâtavedâs is:

अग्निर्जातवेदाः सोमस्य मत्सत् । स्वनीकश्चित्रभानु :। अप्रोषिवान्गृहपतिः । तिरस्तमांसि दर्शतः । घृताहवन ईड्यः । बहुलवर्मास्तृत यज्वा प्रतीत्या शत्रूञ्जेतापराजितः । अग्ने जातवेदोऽभिद्युम्नमभिसह आयच्छस्व । तुशोअप्तुशः । समेद्धारं स्तोतारमंहसस्पाहि । अग्निर्जातवेदा इह श्रवदिह सोमस्य मत्सत् । प्रेमां देवो देव हूतिमवतु ॰

"May Agni Jâtavedâs enjoy the Soma! he who has a beautiful appearance, whose splendour is apparent to all, he, the house-father, who does not flicker (when burning, *i.e.*, whose fire is great and strong), he who is visible amidst the darkness, he who receives the offerings of melted butter, who is to be praised, who performs the sacrifices without being disturbed by many hindrances, who is unconquerable and conquers his enemies in the battle. O Agni Jâtavedâs! extend (thy) splendour and strength round us, with force and pluck (*tuśaḥ* and *aptuśaḥ* are adverbs); protect him who lights (thee), and praises (thee) from distress! May Agni Jâtavedâs here hear (us): may he enjoy the Soma.

[40] The etymology of the word as here given is fanciful. The proper meaning of the word is, "having possession of all that is born," *i.e.*, pervading it. With the idea of the fire being an all-pervading power, the Ṛiṣis are quite familiar. By *Jâtavedâs* the "animal fire" is particularly to be understood.

[41] This is *uta no ahir budhnyaḥ śrinotu* (6, 50, 14), which forms part of the Agnimâruta Śastra. See Âśv. Śr. S. 5, 20.

puts the invisible lustre in the **[225]** offspring (of the sacrificer). Thence they say, "One who brings oblations is more shining than one who does not bring them." [42]

37.

(*The Offerings to the Wives of the Gods and to Yama and the Kâvyas, a Class of Manes.*)

After having addressed (in the Ahir budhnya verse) Agni, the house-father, he recites the verses addressed to the wives of the gods. [43] For the wife (of the sacrificer) sits behind the Gârhapatya fire.

They say : he should first address *Râkâ* [44] with a verse, for the honour of drinking first from the Soma belongs (among the divine women) to the sister (of the gods). But this precept should not be cared for. He should first address the wives of the gods. By doing so, Agni, the house-father, provides the wives with seed. By means of the Gârhapatya, Agni, the Hotar thus actually provides the wives with seed for production. He who has such a knowledge will be blessed with offspring (and) cattle. (That the wives have precedence of a sister is apparent in worldly things.) For a sister who has come from the same womb is provided with food, &c., after the wife, who has come from another womb, has been cared for.

He repeats the Râkâ verse. [45] She sews that seam (in the womb) which is on the penis, so as to form a man. He who has such a knowledge obtains male children.

[226] He repeats the *Pâvîravî* verse.[46] Speech is *Sarasvatî pâvîravî.* By repeating this verse, he provides the sacrificer with speech.

They ask, Should he first repeat the verse addressed to Yama, or that one which is devoted to the Manes? [47] He should first repeat the verse addressed to Yama : *imam yama prastara* (10, 14, 4). For a king (Yama being a ruler) has the honour of drinking first.

Immediately after it, he repeats the verse for the *Kâvyas* : *mâtalî kavyâir yamo* (10, 14, 3). The Kâvyas are beings inferior to the gods, and superior to the manes. Thence he repeats the verses for the manes, *udiratâm avara utparâsaḥ* (10, 15, 1-3), after that one addressed to the Kâvyas. By the words (of the first verse), "May the Soma-loving

[42] This, no doubt, refers to the so-called Agni-hotṛis, to whom daily oblations to the fire, in the morning and evening, are enjoined.

[43] These are two in number, *devânâm patnîr uśatîr avantu* (5, 46, 7, 8).

[44] See the note to 7, 11.

[45] This is *râkâm aham*, 2, 32, 4.

[46] *Pâvîrâvî Kanyâ*, 6, 49, 7.

[47] This is *udîratâm avara utparâsaḥ* (10, 15, 1).

manes who are of low as well as those who are of a middling and superior character, rise," he pleases them all, the lowest as well the middling and highest ones, without foregoing any one. In the second verse, the term *barhiṣado*, "sitting on the sacred grass," implies, that they have a beloved house. By repeating it, he makes them[48] prosper through their beloved house. He who has such a knowledge prospers through his beloved house. The verse (out of three) which contains the term "adoration," "this adoration be to the manes," he repeats at the end (though it be second in order). That is the reason, that at the end (of funeral ceremonies), the manes are adored (by the words) "adoration to you, O manes!"

They ask, Should he, when repeating the verses to the manes, use at each verse the call *śoṁsâvom*, or [**227**] should he repeat them without that call? He should repeat it. What ceremony is not finished in the *Pitri yajña* (offering to the manes), that is to be completed. The Hotar who repeats the call *śoṁsâvom* at each verse, completes the incomplete sacrifice. Thence the call *śoṁsâvom* ought to be repeated.

38.

On Indra's Share in the Evening Libation. On the Verses Addressed to Viṣṇu and Varuṇa, to Viṣṇu alone, and to Prajâpati. The Concluding Verse and the Yâjyâ of the Agnimâruta Śastra.)

The Hotar repeats the *anu-pânîya* verses addressed to Indra and his drinking of the Soma juice after (the other deities have been satisfied), *svâduṣ kilâyam madhuman* (6, 47, 1-4). By their means, Indra drank from the Soma after the third libation (*anupibat*). Thence the verses are called *anu-pânîyat*, "referring to drinking after." The deities are drunk, as it were, at this (third libation) when the Hotar repeats those verses. Thence has the Adhvaryu, when they are repeated, to respond to the Hotar (when calling *śoṁsâvom*) with a word derived from the root *mad*, "to be drunk."[49]

He repeats a verse referring to Viṣṇu and Varuṇa, *yayor ojasâ.*[50]

---

[48] The MSS have एनंस्, instead of एनांस् (acc. pl.), as Sây. reads in his Commentary.

[49] This refers to the two phrases, *madâmo deva*, "we are drunk, O God!" and *modâmo daivom*, "we rejoice, O divine! Om!" which are the responses of the Adhvaryu to the Hotar's call *śoṃsâvom* in the midst of the four Anu-pânîya verses abovementioned. See Âśv. Śr. S. 5, 20. The usual response of the Adhvaryu to the Hotar's *âhâva*, *śoṁsâvom*, is *śoṁsâmo daivom*, see Âśv. Śr. S. 5, 9.

[50] It is not found in the Saṁhitâ of the Rigveda, but in the Âśv. Śr. S. 5. 20, and in the Atharvaveda, S. 7, 25, 1. Both texts differ a little. Âśvalâyana reads:

ययोरोजसा स्कभिता रजांसि वीर्येभिर्वीरतमा शविष्ठया पत्येते अप्रतीता सहोभिर्विष्णू अगन्वरुणा पूर्वहूतौ, *i. e.*, "The two, through whose power the atmosphere was framed, the

Viṣṇu protects the defects in the **[228]** sacrifices (from producing any evil consequences) and Varuṇa protects the fruits arising from its successful performance. (This verse is repeated) to propitiate both of them.

He repeats a verse addressed to Viṣṇu: *viṣṇor nu kam vîryâṇî* (1, 154, 1). Viṣṇu is in the sacrifice the same as deliberation in (worldly things). Just (as an agriculturist) is going to make good the mistakes in ploughing, (and a king) in making good a bad judgment by devising a good one, so the Hotar is going to make well recited what was badly recited, and well chanted what was badly chanted, by repeating this verse addressed to Viṣṇu.

He repeats a verse addressed to Prajâpati, *tantum tanvan rajaso* (10, 53, 6). *Tantu, i.e.*, thread, means offspring. By repeating this verse, the Hotar spreads (*santanoti*) for him (the sacrificer) offspring. By the words of this verse, *jyotiṣmataḥ patho rakṣa dhiyâ kṛitaṁ, i.e.*, "protect the paths which are provided with lights, and made by absorption in meditation" wherein the term "the paths provided with lights" means the roads of the gods (to heaven), the Hotar paves these roads (for the sacrificer to go on them on his way to heaven).

By the words *anulbanam vayata, i.e.*, "weave ye the work of the chanters and repeaters[51] so as to rid **[229]** it from all defects, become a Manu, produce a divine race," the Hotar propagates him through human offspring. (That is done) for production. He who has such a knowledge will be blessed with offspring and cattle.

---

two who are the strongest in power and most vigorous, who rule unconquerable through their strength; may these two, Viṣṇu and Varuṇa, come on being called first." There is a grammatical difficulty in this translation: *agan*, which can be only explained as a third person plural of the aorist in the conjunctive, is here joined to nouns in the dual. The Atharvaveda shows the same form. Here is an evident incorrectness, which perhaps was the reason for its being excluded from the Saṁhitâ.

[51] The word translated by "chanters and repeaters" is *jogu*. Sây. explains it in his commentary on this passage of the Ait. Br. in the following manner:

कर्मसु गच्छंति प्रवर्त्तंत इति अनुष्ठानशीला जोगुशब्देनोच्यन्ते.

In his commentary on the Ṛigveda Saṁhitâ (10, 53, 6, page 8 of my manuscript copy of the commentary on the 8th Aṣṭaka), he explains it simply by स्तोतृणाम् । But I think the first definition is too comprehensive, the latter too restricted, For, strictly speaking, the term *stotar* is only applicable to the chanters of the Sâmans. But the recital of the Ṛik mantras by the Hotars, and the formulas of the Yajurveda by the Adhvaryu and his assistants is about as important for the success of the sacrifice. All that is in excess (*ulbanam*), above what is required, is a hindrance to the sacrifice. Thence all mistakes, by whatever priest they might have been committed, are to be propitiated. The word *jogu*, being a derivative of the root *gu*, "to sound," cannot mean "a sacrificial performer" in general, as Sây. supposes in his commentary on the Ait. Br., but such performers only as require principally the aid of their voice.

He concludes with the verse *evâ na indro maghavâ virapśî* (4, 17, 20). This earth is *Indra maghavâ virapśî, i.e.*, Indra, the strong, of manifold crafts. She is (also) *satyâ*, the true, *charṣaṇîdhṛit, i.e.*, holding men *anarvâ*, safe. She is (also) the *râjâ*. In the words, *śravo mahinâm yaj jaritre, mahinâm* means the earth, *śravo* the sacrifice, and *jaritâ* the sacrificer. By repeating them, he asks for a blessing for the sacrificer. When he thus concludes, he ought to touch the earth on which he employs the sacrificial agency. On this earth he finally establishes the sacrifice.

After having repeated the Agni-Mâruta Śastra, he recites the Yâjyâ: *agne marudbhiḥ* (5, 60, 8). Thus he satisfies (all) the deities, giving to each his due.

---

[230] FOURTH CHAPTER.

(*On the Origin, Meaning, and Universal Nature of the Agniṣṭoma as the model for other Sacrifices. On the Chatuṣṭoma and Jyotiṣṭoma.*)

39.

(*On the Origin of the name "Agniṣṭoma," and its Meaning.*)

The Devas went to war with the Asuras, in order to defeat them. Agni was not willing to follow them. The Devas then said to him, "Go thou also, for thou art one of us." He said, "I shall not go, unless a ceremony of praise is performed for me. Do ye that now." So they did. They all rose up (from their places), turned towards Agni, and performed the ceremony of praising him. After having been praised, he followed them. He having assumed the shape of three rows, attacked in three battle lines the Asuras, in order to defeat them. The three rows were made only of the metres (*Gâyatrî, Triṣṭubh, Jagatî*). The three battle lines are only the three libations. He defeated them beyond expectation. Thence the Devas put down the Asuras. The enemy, the incarnate sin (*pâpman*), the adversary of him who has such a knowledge, perishes by himself.

The Agniṣṭoma is just as the Gâyatrî. The latter has twenty-four syllables (if all its three padas are counted) and the Agniṣṭoma has twenty-four Stotras and Śastras.[1]

---

[1] That is to say, twelve Stotras or performances of the Sâma singers, and twelve Śastras or recitations of the Hotṛi-priests. To each Stotra a Śastra corresponds. The twelve Śastras are as follows:—(*A*) At the morning libation—1) the Ajya and 2) Pra-uga to be repeated by the Hotar, 3) the Śastra of the Maitrâvaruṇa, 4) of the Brâhmaṇâchhansi, and 5) of the Achhâvâka. (*B*) At the midday libation—6) the Marutvatîya and 7) Niṣkevalya Sastras to be recited by the Hotar, 8) the Sastras of the Maitrâvaruṇa, 9) of the Brâhmaṇâchhansi, and 10) that of the Achhâvâka. (*C*) At the evening libation—11) the Vaiśvadeva, and 12) Agnimâruta Sastras to be repeated by the Hotar alone

[231] It is just as they say : a horse if well managed (*suhitâ*) puts the rider into ease (*sudhâ*). This does also the Gâyatrî. She does not stop on the earth, but takes the sacrificer up to heaven. This does also the Agniṣṭoma ; it does not stop on earth, but takes the sacrificer up to heaven. The Agniṣṭoma is the year. The year has twenty-four half-months, and the Agniṣṭoma twenty-four Stotras and Śastras. Just as waters flow into the sea, so go all sacrificial performances into the Agniṣṭoma (*i. e.*, are contained in it).

40.

(*All Sacrificial Rites are Contained in the Agniṣṭoma.*)

When the Dîkṣhaṇîya Iṣṭi is once performed in all its parts (lit., is spread), then all other Iṣṭis, whatever they may be, are comprised in the Agniṣṭoma.[2]

When he calls Iḷâ,[3] then all Pâkayajñas,[4] whatever they may be, are comprised in the Agniṣṭoma.

[232] One brings the Agnihotram [5] in the morning and evening. They (the sacrificers when being initiated) perform in the morning and

[2] The meaning is, the Dîkṣaṇîya Iṣṭi is the model Iṣṭi or *prakṛiti*, of all the other Iṣṭis required at the Agniṣṭoma, such as the Prâyaṇîya, &c., and is, besides, exactly of the same nature as other independent Iṣṭis, such as the Darśpûrṇima Iṣṭi.

[3] This is always done at every occasion of the Agniṣṭoma sacrifice, as often as the priests and the sacrificer eat of the sacrificial food, after having first given an oblation to the gods, by the words : *ilopahûtâ saha divâ bṛiha âdityena*, &c. (Âśv. Śr. S. 1, 7).

[4] This is the general name of the oblations offered in the so-called *smârta agni* or domestic fire of every Brahman, which are always distinguished from the sacrifices performed with the Vaitânika fires (Gârhapatya, Dakṣina, and Ahavanîya). They are said to be seven in number. According to oral information founded on Nârâyaṇa Bhaṭṭa's practical manual for the performance of all domestic rites, they are for the Ṛigveda as follows : 1) *Śrâvaṇâkarma* (an oblation principally given to Agni in the full moon of the month of Śrâvaṇa), 2) *Sarpabali* (an oblation of rice to the serpents), 3) *Âśvayuji* (an oblation to Rudra, the master of cattle), 4) *Agrayaṇa* (an oblation to Indrâgni and the Viśvedevas), 5) *Pratyavarohaṇam* (an oblation to *Svaita Vaidârava*, a particular deity connected with the sun), 6) *Piṇḍapitṛiyajña* (an oblation to the manes), 7) *Anvaṣṭaka* (another oblation to the manes). See Âśval. Gṛihya Sûtras, 2, 1-4. The meaning of the word *pâka* in the word *pâkayajña* is doubtful. In all likelihood, *pâka* here means "cooked, dressed food," which is always required at these oblations. Some Hindu Scholars whom Max Müller follows (History of Ancient Saṁskṛit Literature, p. 203), explain it as "good." It is true the word is already used in the sense of "ripe, mature, excellent" in the Saṁhitâ of the Ṛigveda (see 7, 104, 8-9). In the sense of "ripening" we find it 1, 31, 14. But it is very doubtful to me whether by *pâka*, a man particularly fit for performing sacrifices can be understood. The difference between the Śrâuta and Smârta oblations is, that at the former no food, cooked in any other than the sacred fires, can be offered to the gods, whilst at the latter an oblation is first cooked on the common hearth, and then offered in the sacred *Smârta agni*.

[5] The sacrificer who is being initiated (who is made a Dîkṣita) has to observe fast for several days (three at the Agniṣṭoma) before he is allowed to take any substantial

evening the religious vow (of drinking milk only), and do that with the formula *svâhâ*. With the same formula one offers the Agnihotram. Thus the Agnihotram is comprised in the Agniṣṭoma.

At the Prâyaṇîya Iṣṭi [6] the Hotar repeats fifteen **[233]** verses for the wooden sticks thrown into the fire (*sâmidhenis*). The same number is required at the New and Full Moon offerings. Thus the New and Full Moon offerings are comprised in the Prâyaṇîya Iṣṭi.

They buy the king Soma (the ceremony of *Somakraya*[7] is meant). The king Soma belongs to the herbs. They cure (a sick person) by means of medicaments taken from the vegetable kingdom. All vegetable medicaments following the king Soma when being bought, they are thus comprised in the Agniṣṭoma.

At the Atithya Iṣṭi [8] they produce fire by friction, and at the Châturmâsya Iṣṭis (they do the same). The Châturmâsya Iṣṭis thus following the Atithya Iṣṭi, are comprised in the Agniṣṭoma.

At the Pravargya ceremony they use fresh milk, the same is the case at the *Dâkṣâyaṇa* yajña. [9] Thus **[234]** the Dâkṣâyaṇa sacrifice is comprised in the Agniṣṭoma.

---

food. He drinks in the morning and evening only milk, which is taken from the cow after sunrise and after sunset. He is allowed but a very small quantity, as much as remains from the milk of one nipple only after the calf has sucked. This fast is called a *vrata*, and as long as he is observing it he is *vrataprada*, *i.e.*, fulfilling a vow. See Hiraṇyakeśi Sûtras, 7, 4. When doing this he repeats the mantra, *ye devâ manojâta* (Taitt. S. 1, 2, 3, 1), which concludes with *tebhyo namas tebhyo svâhâ*, *i.e.*, worship be to them, Svâhâ be to them. The Agnihotram being offered in the morning and evening always with the formula *svâhâ*, the author of the Brâhmaṇam believes that by these incidents the Agnihotram might be said to be contained in the Agniṣṭoma.

[6] There are fifteen Sâmidhenî verses required at the Prâyaṇîya Iṣṭi, whilst at the Dîkṣaṇîyâ seventeen are requisite. Fifteen is the general number at most Iṣṭis. This number is therefore to be regarded as the *prakṛiti*, *i. e.*, standard, model, whilst any other number is a *vikṛiti*, *i.e.*, modification.

[7] On the buying of the Soma, see 1, 12-13.

[8] On the producing of fire by friction at the Atithya Iṣṭi, see 1. 16-17. The same is done at the Châturmâsya Iṣṭis., See Kâtîya-Śr. S. 5, 2, 1.

[9] The *Dâkṣâyaṇa yajña* belongs to that peculiar class of Iṣṭis which are called *iṣṭyayanâni*, *i.e.*, oblations to be brought regularly during a certain period. They are, as to their nature, only modifications of the Darśapûrṇamâsa Iṣṭi. It can be performed either on every Full and New Moon during the life-time of the sacrificer, or during a period of fifteen years, or the whole course of oblations can be completed in one year. The rule is, that the number of oblations given must amount to at least 720. This number is obtained either by performing it every day twice during a whole year, or by making at every Full Moon day two oblations, and two others on every New Moon day during a space of fifteen years. The deities are, Agni-Soma at the New Moon, and Indra-Agni and Mitra-Varuṇa at the Full Moon oblations. The offerings consist of Puroḍâśa, sour milk (*dadhi*), and fresh milk (*payas*). On every day on which this sacrifice is performed, it must be performed twice. See Kâtîya. Śr. S. 4, 4, 1-30 and Aśv. Śr. S. 2, 14.

The animal sacrifice takes place the day previous to the Soma feast. All animal sacrifices[10] which follow it are thus comprised in the Agniṣṭoma.

Iḷâdadha [11] by name is a sacrificial rite. They perform it with thick milk (*dadhi*), and they also take thick milk at the time of making the *Dadhigharma*[12] rite (in the Agniṣṭoma). Thus the Iḷâdadha is, on account of its following the Dadhigharma rite, comprised in the Agniṣṭoma.

41.

(*The Other Parts of Jyotiṣṭoma, such as Ukthya, Atirâtra, Comprised in the Agniṣṭoma.*)

Now the first part (of the Agniṣṭoma) has been explained. After that has been performed, the fifteen Stotras and Śastras of the *Ukthya* ceremony **[235]** fllow. If they (the fifteen Stotras and fifteen Śastras) are taken together, they represent the year as divided into months (each consisting of thirty days). Agni Vaiśvânara is the year ; Agniṣṭoma is Agni. The Ukthya by following (also) the order of the year is thus comprised in the Agniṣṭoma.

After the Ukthya has entered the Agniṣṭoma, the Vâjapeya [13] follows it ; for it exceeds (the number of the Stotras of) the Ukthya (by two only).

The twelve turns of the Soma cups [14] at night (at the Atirâtra Soma

---

[10] On the animal sacrifice, see 2, 1-14. The animal sacrifices are called here, *paśubandha*. Some such as the *Nirûḍha Paśubandha* can precede the Agniṣṭoma.

[11] *Ilâdadha* is another modification of the Darśapûrṇamâsa Iṣṭis. Its principal part is sour milk. See Áśv. 2, 14.

[12] On the Dadhi-gharma, the draught of sour milk, see Âśv. 5, 13, and Hiraṇyakeśi Śr. Sûtr. 9, 2. It is prepared and drunk by the priests after an oblation of it has been thrown into the fire, at the midday libation of the Soma feast just before the recital of the Marutvatîya Śastra. The ceremony is chiefly performed by the Pratiprasthâthar, who, after having taken sour milk with a spoon of Udumbara wood, makes it hot under the recital of the mantra, *vâkcha tvâ manaścha śriṇitâm*, &c., in which Speech and Mind, the two vital airs (*prâṇa* and *apâna*), eye and ear, Wisdom and Strength, Power and Quickness in action, are invoked to cook it. After having repeated this mantra and made hot the offering, he says to the Hotar, " The offering is cooked, repeat the Yâjyâ for the Dadhi-gharma." The latter repeats, " The offering is cooked ; I think it cooked in the udder (of the cow) and cooked in the fire. Vauṣaṭ ! Agni, eat the Dadhi-gharma, Vauṣaṭ !" Then the Hotar repeats another mantra, *mayi tyad indriyam bṛihas* (Asv. Sr. 5, 13), whereupon the priests eat it.

[13] This is a particular Soma sacrifice, generally taken as part of Jyotiṣṭoma, which is said to be *sapta-saṁsthâ*, *i.e.*, consisting of seven parts.

[14] This refers to the arrangement for the great Soma banquets held at night when celebrating the Atirâtra. In the evening, after a Soma libation has been given to the fire from the Ṣolaśî Graha, the Soma cups are passed in a certain order. There are four such orders called *gaṇas*. At the first, the cup of the Hotar takes the lead, at the seco nd that

feast) are on the whole joined to the fifteen verses by means of which the Stotras are performed. Two [15] of those turns belonging always together, the number of the Stotra verses to which they (the turns) belong, is brought to thirty (by multiplying the number fifteen with these two). (But the number thirty is to be obtained in another way also for the Atirâtra). The Ṣolaśi Sâman is twenty-one-fold, and the Sandhi (a Sâman at the end of Atirâtra) is *trivṛit, i.e.*, nine-fold, which amounts in all to thirty. There are thirty nights in every month all the year round. Agni Vaiśvânara is the year, and Agni is the Agniṣṭoma. The Atirâtra is, by thus following (the order of) the year, comprised **[236]** in the Agniṣṭoma, and the Aptoryâma sacrifice follows the track of the Atirâtra when entering the Agniṣṭoma. For it becomes also an Atirâtra. Thus all sacrificial rites which precede the Agniṣṭoma, as well as those which come after it, are comprised in it.

All the Stotra verses of the Agniṣṭoma amount, if counted, to one hundred and ninety. For ninety are the ten *trivṛitas* (three times three=nine). (The number hundred is obtained thus) ninety are ten (*trivṛitas*), but of the number ten one Stotriyâ verse is in excess ; the rest is the Trivṛit (nine), which is taken twenty-one-fold [16] (this makes 189) and represents by this number that one (the sun) which is put over (the others), and burns. This is the *Viṣuvan* [17] (equator), which has ten Trivṛit Stomas before it and ten after it, and, being placed in the midst of both, turns above them, and burns (like the sun). The one Stotriyâ verse which is in excess, is put in that (Viṣuvan which is the twenty-first) and placed over it (like a cover). This is the sacrificer. This (the twenty-one-fold Trivṛit Stoma) is the divine Kṣatram (sovereign power), which has the power of defying any attack.

He who has such a knowledge obtains the divine Kṣtram, which has the power for defying any attack, and becomes assimilated to it, assumes its shape, and takes the same place with it.

42.

(Why Four Stomas are Required at the Agniṣṭoma.)

The Devas after having (once upon a time) been defeated by the Asuras, started for the celestial world.

---

of the Maitrâvaruṇa, at the third that of the Brâhmaṇâchhansi, and at the fourth that of the Achhâ vâka. This is thrice repeated, which makes twelve turns in all.—*Sây.*

[15] Always two turns are presided over by one priest, the first two by the Adhvaryu, the following two by the Pratiprasthâtar.

[16] The 190 Stotriya verses of the Agniṣṭoma comprise the number 21 nine times taken, one being only in excess.

[17] See about it in the Ait. Br. 4, 18-22.

[237] Agni touching the sky (from his place on earth), entered the upper region (with his flames), and closed the gate of the celestial world; for Agni is its master. The Vasus first approached him and said: "Mayest thou allow us to pass over (thy flames) to enter (heaven); give us an opportunity (*âkâśa.*)" Agni said, "Being not praised (by you), I shall not allow you to pass (through the gate). Praise me now." So they did. They praised him with nine verses (the Trivṛit Stoma).[18] After they had

[13] The Trivṛit Stoma consists of the nine verses of the *Bahiṣpavamâna* Stotra (see Sâmaveda Saṁh. 2, 1-9), which are sung in three turns, each accompanied by the Hiṁkâra. In this Stoma, the same verses arenot sung repeatedly, as is the case with all other Stomas. There are three kinds (*viṣṭuti*) of this Stoma mentioned in the *Tâṇdya Brâhmaṇam* 2, 1-2, called the *udyatî trivṛito viṣṭuti, parivarttinî,* and *kulâyinî.* The difference of these three kinds lies in the order which is assigned to each of the three verses which form one turn (*paryâya*), and in the application of the Hiṁkâra (the sound *hum* pronounced very loudly) which always belongs to one turn. The arrangement of all the verses which form part of the Stoma (the whole musical piece), in three turns, each with a particular order for its several verses, and their repetition, is called in the technical language of the Sâma singers a *viṣṭuti.* Each Stoma has several variations. The first variation of the Trivṛit Stoma is the *udyatî, i.e.,* the rising. This kind is very simple. The Hiṁkâra is pronounced in the first *paryâya* at the first verse (*tisṛibhyohiṁkaroti sa prathamayâ*), in the second at the middle verse of the triplet (*tisṛibhyo hiṁkaroti sa madhyamayâ*), and in the third, at the last verse (*tisṛibhyo himkaroti sa uttamayâ*). The *parivarttinî viṣṭuti* consist in singing the several verses of the triplet in all three turns in the inverted order, that is to say, the first is always made the last, and the last the first (*tisṛibhyo hiṁkaroti sa parâchibhih*). The *kuṭâyinî viṣṭuti* is more complicated than the two others. In the first turn, the order of the verses is inverted (*tisṛibhyo hiṁkaroti sa parâchibhiḥ*), in the second turn the middle verse is made the first, the last becomes the middle verse and the first becomes the last (*tisṛibhyo hiṁkaroti yâ madhyamâ sa prathamâ, yâ uttamâ sâ madhyamâ, yâ prathamâ sâ uttamâ*); in the third turn, the last becomes the first, the first the second, and the second the last. The Sâma singers mark the several turns, and the order of each verse in it as well as the number of repetitions by small sticks cut from the wood of the Udumbara tree, the trunk of which must always be placed behind the seat of the Udgâtar. They are called *kuśâs.* Each of the three divisions of each set in which they are put is called *viṣṭâva.* Their making is minutely described in the *Lâṭyâyâna Sûtras,* 2, 6.

प्रस्तोता कुशाः कारयेद्यज्ञियस्य वृक्षस्य। खदिरस्य दीर्घसत्रेष्वेके। प्रदेशमात्रीः कुशपृष्ठास्त्वक्तः समा मज्जतोऽङ्गुष्ठपर्वपृथुमात्रीः प्रज्ञाताग्राः कारयित्वा गंधैः प्रलिप्य सर्पिषा सत्रेष्वेके वैष्टुतेन वसनेन परिवेष्ट्य क्षौमशाणकार्पासेन केनचिदुपर्यौदुंबर्यां वासयेत्।

i.e., the Prastotar ought to get made the kuśâs (small piece of wood) from a wood which is used at sacrifices. Some are of opinion that at sacrificial sessions (*sattras*) which last long, they ought to be made of Khadira wood only. After having got them made of the length of a span (the space between the thumb and forefinger stretched), so that the part which is covered with bark resembles the back of the kuśa grass, the fibre part of the stick being quite even, as big as the link of the thumb, the ends being prominent (easily to be recognized), he should besmear them with odoriferous substances, but at the Sattras, as some say, with liquid butter, put the cloth used for the Viṣṭutis, which is made of linen, or flax, or cotton, round them and place them, above the Udumbara branch (always required when singing).

done, so he allowed [238] them to pass (the gate), that they might enter the (celestial) world.

The Rudras approached him and said to him, "Mayest thou allow us to pass on ; give us an opportunity (by moderating thy flames)." He answered, "If I be not praised, I shall not allow you to pass. Praise me now." They consented. They praised him with fifteen verses.[19] After they had done so, he allowed [239] them to pass, that they might enter the (celestial) world.

The Âdityas approached and said to him, "Mayest thou allow us to pass on ; give us an opportunity." He answered, "If I be not praised, I shall not allow you to pass. Praise me now!" They consented. They praised him with seventeen verses. After they had done so, he allowed them to pass, that they might enter the (celestial) world.

The Viśve Devâs approached and said to him, "Mayest thou allow us to pass on ; give us an opportunity." He answered: If I be not praised, I shall not allow you to pass. Praise me now!" They consented. They praised him with twenty-one verses. After they had done so, he allowed them to pass, that they might enter the (celestial) world.

The gods having praised Agni each with another Stoma (combination of verses), he allowed them to pass.

The sacrificer who praisesgni with all (four) Stomas, as well as he (the priest) who knows it (the Agniṣṭoma) will pass on beyond him (Agni, who watches with his flames the entrance to heaven).[20]

To him who has such a knowledge, he (Agni) allows to pass and enter the celestial world.

43.

(On the Names " Agniṣṭoma, Chatuṣṭoma, Jyotiṣṭoma." The Agniṣṭoma is Endless).

The Agniṣṭoma is Agni. It is called so, because they (the gods)

---

[19] This is the so-called *Pânchadaśa Stoma.* The arrangement is the same as with the Trivṛit Stoma. The same triplet of verses is here reuired for each of the three turns. Each turn is to consist of five verses. In the first turn, the first verse is chanted thrice, the second once, the third once (*pâṇchabhyo hiṁkaroti sa tisṛibhiḥ sa ekayâ sa ekayâ*); in the second turn the first verse is chanted once, the second thrice, the third once ; in the third turn the first and second verses are chanted each once, but the third thrice. This Stoma is required for those Sâmans of the morning libation which follow the *Bahiṣpâvamánas.* The *saptadaśa* and *ekaviṁśa stomas* follow the same order as the panchadaśa. The several verses of the triplet are in three turns chanted so many times as to obtain respectively the number 17 and 21. The former is appropriate to the midday libation, the latter to the evening libation.

[20] In this sentence, we have two peculiar forms : *atí*, instead of *ati*, beyond, and *arjâtâi*, 3rd pers. conjunct. middle voice, in the sense of a future.

praised him with this Stoma. They called it so to hide the proper meaning of the word ; **[240]** for the gods like to hide the proper meaning of words.

On account of four classes of gods having praised Agni with four Stomas, the whole was called *Chatuḥstoma* (containing four Stomas). They called it so to hide the proper meaning of the word ; for the gods like to hide the proper meaning of words.

If (the Agniṣṭoma) is called *Jyotiṣṭoma*, for they praised Agni when he had risen up (to the sky) in the shape of a light (*jyotis.*) They called it so to hide the proper meaning of the word ; for the gods like to hide the proper meaning of words.

This (Agniṣṭoma) is a sacrificial performance which has no beginning and no end. The Agniṣṭoma is like the endless wheel of a carriage. The beginning (*prâyaṇîya*) and the conclusion (*udayanîya*) of it are alike (just as the two wheels of a carriage.)

About this there is a sacrificial stanza sung, "What is its (of the Agniṣṭoma) beginning, that is its end, and what is its end, that is its beginning ; just as the Sâkala serpent, it moves in a circle, that none can distinguish its first part from its last part." For its opening (the *prâyaṇîya*) was (also) its conclusion.[21]

But to this some raise objections, saying, "they make the beginning (of the Stotras of the Soma day) with the Trivṛit Stoma, and conclude with the twenty-one-fold Stoma (at the evening libation) ; how are they (the beginning and conclusion) then alike ?" To this one should answer, "They are alike as far as the twenty-one-fold Stoma is also a Trivṛit Stoma, for both contain triplets of verses, and have their nature. [22]

44.

[241] (*How the Śastras should be Repeated at each of the Three Libations. The Sun never rises nor sets. How the Phenomena of unrise and Sunset are to be Explained.*)

The Agniṣṭoma is that one who burns (the sun). The sun shines

---

[21] This refers to the Charu oblation to be given to Aditi at the Prâyaṇîya as well as at the Udayanîya Iṣṭi. See 1, 7.

[22] For performing the Trivṛit Stoma at the commencement of the morning libation, the nine Bahiṣ-pavamna verses are required which consist of three triplets (*tṛichas*). For performing the twenty-one-fold Stoma at the evening libation, the *Yajñayajnîya* Sâman is used, which consists only of two verses, but by repeating some parts of them twice, the number of three verses is obtained. The same triplet being canted in thr ee turns (*paryâya,*) the twenty-one-fold Stoma appears to be like the *Trivṛit.*

during the day, and the Agniṣṭoma [23] should be completed along with the day. It being a *sâhna, i.e.*, going with the day, they should not perform it hurriedly (in order to finish it before the day is over), neither at the morning, nor midday, nor evening libations. (Should they do so) the sacrificer would suddenly die.

When they do not perform hurriedly (nly) the rites of the morning and midday libations, but hurry over the rites of the evening libation, then this, *viz.*, the villages lying in the eastern direction, become largely populated, whilst all that is in the western direction becomes a long tract of deserts, and the sacrificer dies suddenly. Thence they ought to perform without any hurry the rites of the morning and midday, as well as those of the evening libation. (If they do so) the sacrificer will not suddenly die.

In repeating the Śastras, the Hotar ought to be guided by the (daily) course (of the sun). In the **[242]** morning time, at sunrise, it burns but slowly. Thence the Hotar should repeat the Śastras at the morning libation with a feeble voice.

When the sun is rising higher up (on the horizon), it burns with greater force. Thence the Hotar should repeat the Śastras at the midday libation with a strong voice.

When the sun faces men most (after having passed the meridian), it burns with the greatest force. Thence the Hotar should repeat the Śastras at the third (evening) libation with an extremely strong voice. He should (only) then (commence to) repeat it so (with the greatest force of his voice), when he should be complete master of his full voice. For the Śastra is Speech. Should he continue to repeat (the Śastras of the third libation) with the same strength of voice with which he commenced the repetition, up to the end, then his recitation will be admirably well accomplished.

The sun does never set nor rise. When people think the sun is setting (it is not so). For, after having arrived at the end of the day, it makes itself produce two opposite effects, making night to what is below and day to what is on the other side.

When they believe it rises in the morning (this supposed rising is

---

23 Agniṣṭoma is here taken in the strictest sense, as meaning only a Soma festival, lasting for one day, and comleted by means of the f our Stomas mentioned. Therefore, Agniṣṭoma is often called th model (*prakṛiti*) of the *Aikâhika* Soma sacrifices, or such ones which last for one day only. But in a more comprehensive sense all the rites which precede it, such as the Dîkṣaṇîya and other Iṣṭis, and the animal sacrifice, are regarded as part of the Agniṣṭoma. For, without these rites, nobody is allowed to perform any Soma sacrifice.

thus to be accounted for). Having reached the end of the night, it makes itself produce two opposite effects, making day to what is below and night to what is on the other side.[24] In fact, the sun never sets. Nor does it set for him who has such a knowledge. Such a one becomes united with the sun, assumes its form, and enters its place.

---

[243] FIFTH CHPTER.

(On the Gradual Recovery of the Sacrifice. What Men are Unfit to Officiate as Sacrificial Priests. The Offerings to the Devîs and Devikâs. The Ukthya Sacrifice.)

45.

(How the Gods recoveredt he Sacrifice whih had gone from them. How they Performed Different Rites. Under what Conditions the Sacrifice is Effectual.)

The sacrifice once left the gods and went to nourishing substances. The gods said, " The sacrifice has gone from us to nourishing substances, let us seek both the sacrifice and the nourishment by means of a Brâhmaṇa and the metres." So they did. They initiated a Brâhmaṇa by means of the metres. They performed all the rites of the Dikṣaṇîya Iṣṭi up to the end, including even the *Patnî-saṁyâjas.*[1] On account of the gods having at that occasion performed all the rites at the Dikṣaṇiyâ Iṣṭi up to the end, including even the Patnî-saṁyâjas,[2] men followed afterwards the same practice. The gods (in their search for the sacrifice) came very near it by means of the Prâyaṇîya Iṣṭi. They performed the ceremonies with great haste and finished the Iṣṭi already with the Śaṁyuvâka.[3] This is the reason that the Prâyaṇîya Iṣṭi ends with Śaṁyuvâka ; for men followed (afterwards) this practice.

244 The gods performed the rites of the Atithya Iṣṭi, and came by means of it very near the sacrifice. They concluded hastily the ceremonies with the *Iḷâ* [4] (the eating of the sacrificial food). This is the

---

24 This passage is of considerable interest, containing the denial of the existence of sunrise and sunset. The author ascribes a daily course to the sun, but supposes it to remain always in its high position in the sky, making sunrise and sunset by means of its own contrarieties.

1 See page 24.

2 The Patnî-saṁyâjas generally conclude all Iṣṭis an sacrifices.

3 This is a formula containing the words *śam yoḥ* which is repeated before the Patnî-saṁyâjas. Âśv. Śr. S. 1, 10. The mantra which is frequently used at other occasions also, runs as follows :

तच्छंयोरावृणीमहे गातुं यज्ञाय गातुं यज्ञपतये दैवीः स्वस्तिरस्तु नः स्वस्तिर्मानुषेभ्यः । ऊर्ध्वं जिगातु भेषजं शन्नो अस्तु द्विपदे शं चतुष्पदे ॥

4 See page 41. This rite precedes the Śaṁyuvâka.

reason that the Atitbya Iṣṭi is finished with the Iḷâ ; for men followed (afterwards) this practice.

The gods performed the rites of the Upasads [5] and came by means of them very near the sacrifice. They performed hastily the ceremonies, repeating only three Sâmidhenî verses, and the Yâjyâs for three deities. This is the reason that at the Upasad Iṣṭi only three Sâmidhenîs are repeated, and Yâjyâ verses to three deities ; for men followed (afterwards) this practice.

The gods performed the rites of the *upavasatha* [6] (the eve of the Soma festival). On the *upavasatha* day they reached the sacrifice. After having reached the sacrifice (*Yajña*), they performed all its rites severally, even including the Patnî-saṁyâjas. This is the reason that they perform at the day previous to the Soma festival all rites to the end, even including the Patnî-saṁyâjas.

This is the reason that the Hotar should repeat the mantras at all ceremonies preceding the Upavasatha day (at which the animal sacrifice is o ff ere) with a very slow voice. For the gods came at it (the sacrifice) by performing the several rites in such a manner as if they were searching (after something, *i.e.*, slowly)

This is the reason that the Hotar may repeat on the Upavasatha day (after having reached the sacrifice) **[245]** the mantras, in whatever tone he might like to recite them. For, at that occasion the sacrifice is already reached (and the "searching" tone of repeating not required).

The gods, after having reached the sacrifice, said to him, "Stand still to be our food." He answered, "No. How should I stand still for you (to be your food)?" He then only looked at them. They said to him, "Because of thy having become united with a Brâhmaṇa and the metres, thou shalt stand still." He consented.

That is the reason that the sacrifice (only) when joined to a Brâhmaṇa and metres carries the oblations to the gods. [7]

---

[5] See 41, 23-26. At the Upasad Iṣṭi only three Sâmidhenî verses are required, whilst their number in other Iṣṭis amounts to fifteen, and now and then to seventeen. See page 56.

[6] This is the day for the animal sacrifice, called Agnîṣomîya. See 2, 1-14.

[7] The drift of this paragraph is to show, that, for the successful performance of the sacrifice, Brâhmaṇas, as well as the verses composed in the different metres and preserved by Brâhmaṇas only, are indispensible. The Kṣattriyas and other castes were to be deluded into the belief that they could not perform any sacrifice with the slightest chance of success, if they did not appoint râhmaṇas and employ the verses of the Ṛigveda, which were chiefly preserved by the Brâhmaṇas only.

46.

(On Three Mistakes which might be made in the Appointment of Priests. How they are to be Remedied.)

Three things occur at the sacrifice: offals, devoured food, and vomited food. Offals (*jagdha*) occur when one appoints to the office of a sacrificial priest one who offers his services, thinking "he (the sacrificer) give me something, or he should choose me for the performance of his sacrifice." [8] This (to appoint such a man to the office of a priest) is as should perverse as (to eat) the offals of a meal (which are generally not touched by others). For the acts of such a one do not benefit the sacrificer.

[246] Devoured (*gîrṇam*) is that, when a sacrificer appoints some one to the office of a priest out of fear, thinking, "he might kill me (at some future occasion), or disturb my sacrifice (if I do not choose him for the office of a priest)." This is as perverse as if food is devoured (not eaten in the proper way). For the acts of such a one do not benefit the sacrificer (as little as the devouring of food with greediness benefits the body).

Vomited (*vânta*) is that, when a sacrificer appoints to the office of a priest a man who is ill-spoken of. Just as men take disgust at anything that is vomited, so the gods take also disgust at such a man. This (to appoint such a man) is as disgusting as something vomited. For the acts of such a man do not benefit the sacrificer.

The sacrificer ought not to cherish the thought of appointing any one belonging to these three classes (just described). Should he, however, involuntarily (by mistake) appoint one of these three, then the penance (for this fault) is the chanting of the Vâmadevya Sâman. For this Vâmadevyam is the whole universe, the world of the sacrificer (the earth), the world of the immortals, and the celestial world. This Sâman (which is in the Gâyatrî metre) falls short of three syllables. [9] When going to perform this chant, he hould divide the word *puruṣa*, denoting his own self, into three syllables, and insert one of them at the end of each pada (of the verse *abhi ṣu ṇa*). Thus he puts himself in these worlds, *viz.*, **[247]** the world of the sarificer, that o the immortals, and

---

[8] The sacrificer must always himself choose his priests by addressing them in due form. No one should offer his services; but he must be asked by the man who wishes to perform a sacrifice.

[9] The Vâmadevyam consists of the three verses, *kayâ naśchitra*, *kas tvâ satyo*, and *abhi ṣu ṇaḥ* (See Sâmaveda Saṁh. 2, 32-34). All three are in the Gâyatrî metre. But the last *abhî ṣu* has, instead of twenty-four, only twenty-one syllables, wanting in every pada one syllable. To make it to consist of twenty-four also, the repeater has at this occasion to add to the first pada *pu*, to the second *ru*, to the third *ṣa*.

the celestial world. (By chanting this Sâman) the sacrificer overcomes all obstacles arising from mistakes in the performance of the sacrifice (and obtains nevertheless what he was sacrificing for).

He (the Ṛiṣi of the Aitareyins), moreover, has told that the sacrificer should mutter (as *japa*) the Vâmadevyam in the way described (above), even if the performing priests were all of unexceptionable character.

47.

The Offerings to Dhâtar and the Devikâs : Anumati, Râkâ, Sinîvâlî, Kuhû.)

The metres (*chhandânsi*), having carried the offerings to the gods, became (once) tired, and stood still on the latter part of the sacrifice's tail, just as a horse or a mule after having carried a load (to a distant place) stands still.

(In order to refresh the fatigued deities of the metres) the priest ought, after the Purodâśa belonging to the animal slaughtered for Mitra-Varuṇa [10] has been offered, portion out the rice for the *devikâ havîṁṣi* (offerings for the inferior deities).

For *Dhâtar*, he should make a rice ball (the Purodâśa) to be put on twelve potsherds. Dhâtar is the Vaṣaṭkâra.

To *Anumati* (he should offer) a portion of boiled rice *charu* ; for Anumati is Gâyatrî.

To *Râkâ* (he should offer) a portion of boiled rice ; for she is Triṣṭubh.

The same (he should offer) to *Sinîvâlî* and *Kuhû* ; for *Sinîvâlî* is Jagatî, and *Kuhû* Anuṣṭubh. These are all the metres. For all other metres (used at the sacrifice) follow the Gâyatrî, Triṣṭubh, Jagatî, and [**248**] Anuṣṭubh, as their models. If, therefore, one sacrifices for these metres only, it has the same effect as if he had sacrificed for all of them.

The (common) saying, " the horse if well managed (*suhita*) puts him (the rider) into ease," is applicable to the metres ; for they put (if well treated) the sacrificer into ease (*sudhâ*, comfort or happiness of any kind). He who has such a knowledge, obtains such a world (of bliss) as he did not expect.

Regarding these (*devikâ*) oblations, some are of opinion that before each oblation to all (the several) goddesses, the priest ought to make an oblation of melted butter to Dhâtar ; for thus he would make all the goddesses (to whom oblations are given along with the Dhâtar) cohabit with the Dhâtar.

---

[10] This is done at the end of the Agniṣṭoma sacrifice.

About this they say : it is laziness [11] (at a sacrifice) to repeat the same two verses (the Puronuvâkyâ and Yâjyâ for the Dhâtar) on the same day (several times).[12] (It is sufficient to repeat those two verses once only.) For even many wives cohabit with one and the same husband only. When the Hotar, therefore, repeats, before addressing the (four) goddesses, the Yâjyâ verse for the Dhâtar, he thus **[249]** cohabits with all goddesses. So much about the oblations to the minor goddesses (*devikâ*).

48.

(*The Offerings for Sûrya and the Devîs, Dyâus, Uṣâs, Gâus, Pṛithivî, who are Represented by the Metres. When Oblations should be given to both the Devikâs and Devîs. Story of Vṛiddhadyumna.*)

Now about the offerings to the goddesses (*devî*). [13]

The Adhvaryu ought to portion out for *Sûrya* (the sun) rice for a ball to be put on one potsherd (*ekakapâla*). Sûrya is Dhâtar (creator), and this is the Vaṣaṭkâra.

To *Dyâus* (Heaven) he ought to offer boiled rice. For Dyâus is Anumati, and she is Gâyatrî.

To *Uṣâs* (Dawn) he ought to offer boiled rice. For Uṣâs is Râkâ, and she is Triṣṭubh.

To *Gâus* (Cow) he ought to offer boiled rice. For Gâus is Sinîvâlî, and she is Jagatî.

To *Pṛithivî* (Earth) he ought to offer boiled rice. For Prithivî is Kuhu, and she is Anuṣtubh.

All other metres which are used at the sacrifice, follow the Gâyatrî, Triṣṭtubh, Jagatî and Anuṣṭubh as their models (which are most frequently used).

---

[11] The word *jâmi* is explained by *âlasyam*.

[12] Both the Anuvâkyâ and Yâjyâ for the Dhâtar are not in the Saṁhitâ, but in the Âval. Śr. S. 6, 14. The Anuvâkyâ is :

धाता ददातु दाशुषे प्राचीं जीवातुमक्षितां ।

वयं देवस्य धीमहि सुमतिं वाजिनीवतः ॥ (Atharvaveda S, 7, 17, 2).

The Yâjyâ is :

धाता प्रजानामुत्तराय ईशे धातेदं विश्वं भुवनं जजान ।

धाता कृष्टोरनिमिषाभिचष्टे धात्र इद्धव्यं घृतवज्जुहोता ॥

The oblations to the Dhâtar who is the same as Tvaṣṭar, and the four goddesses mentioned, form part of the *Udayanîya* or concluding Iṣṭi. The ceremony is called *Maitrâvaruṇî âmikṣâ*, (*i.e.*, the âmikṣâ dish for Mitra-Varuṇa). Mitra-Varuṇa are first invoked, then follow Dhâtar and the goddesses.

[13] Instead of the *devikâ* offerings those for the *devîs* might be chosen. The effect is the same. The place of the Dhâtar is occupied by Sûrya, who himself is regarded as a Dhâtar, *i.e.*, Creator.

The sacrifice of him who, having such a knowledge, gives oblations to these metres, [14] includes (then) oblations to all metres.

The (common) saying, " the horse, if well managed, puts him (the rider) into ease," is applicable to the metres ; for they put the sacrificer (if well treated) [**250**] into ease (*sudhâ*). He who has such a knowledge, obtains such a world (of bliss) as he did not expect.

Regarding these (oblations to the Devîs), some are of opinion that, before each oblation to all (the several) goddesses, one ought to offer melted butter to Sûrya ; for thus one would make all goddesses cohabit with Sûrya.

About this they say, it is laziness at a sacrifice to repeat (several times) the same two verses (the Puronuvâkyâ and Yâjyâ for Sûrya) on the same day. (It is sufficient to repeat those verses once only). For even many wives cohabit with one (and the same) husband only. When the Hotar, therefore, repeats before addressing the (four) goddesses, the Yâjyâ verse for Sûrya, he thus cohabits with all goddesses.

These (Sûrya with Dyâus, &c.) deities are the same as those others (Dhâtar with Anumati, &c.) One obtains, therefore, through one of these (classes of deities), the gratification of any desire which is in the gift of both.

The priest ought to portion out a rice-cake ball for both these classes (of deities) for him who desires the faculty of producing offspring (to make him obtain) the blessings contained in both. But he ought not to do so for him who sacrifices for acquiring great wealth only. If he were to portion out a rice-cake ball for both these classes (of deities) for him who sacrifices for acquiring wealth only, he has it in his power to make the gods displeased (jealous) with the wealth of the sacrificer (and deprive him of it) ; for such one might think (after having obtained the great wealth he is sacrificing for), ' I have enough (and do not require anything else from the gods).'

Suchivṛikṣa Gaupâlâyana had once portioned out the rice ball for both classes (of deities) at the sacrifice [**251**] of *Vṛiddhadyumna Pratârina*. As he (afterwards) saw a prince swim (in water), he said, " This is owing to the circumstance that I made the goddesses of the higher and lower ranks (*devîs* and *devikâs*) quite pleased at the sacrifice of that king ; therefore the royal prince swims (in the water). (Moreover, he saw not only

---

14 The instrumental *etâiḥ chhandobhiḥ* must here be taken in the sense of a dative. For the whole refers to oblations given to the metres, not to those offered through them to the gods.

him) but sixty-four (other) heroes always steel-clad, who were his sons and grandsons. [15]

49.

(*Origin of the Ukthya. The Sâkamaśram Sâmans. The Pramaṁhiṣṭhiya Sâman.*) [16]

The Devas took shelter in the Agniṣṭoma, and the Asuras in the Ukthyas. Both being (thus) of **[252]** equal strength, the gods could not turn them out. One of the Ṛiṣis, Bharadvâja, saw them (and said), "These Asuras have entered the Ukthas (Śastras); but none (else) sees them." He called out Agni with the mantra: *ehy û ṣu bravâṇi* (6, 16,

---

15 The king had performed the sacrifice for obtaining offspring, and became blessed with them.

16 The *Ukthya* is a slight modification of the Agniṣṭoma sacrifice. The noun to be supplied to it is *kratu*. It is a Soma sacrifice also, and one of the seven Saṁsthas or component parts of the Jyotiṣṭoma. Its name indicates its nature. For *Ukthya* means "what refers to the Uktha," which is an older name for Śastra, *i.e.*, a recitation of one of the Hotṛi priests at the time of the Soma libations. Whilst the Agniṣṭoma has twelve recitations, the Ukthya has fifteen. The first twelve recitations of the Ukthya are the same as those of the Agniṣṭoma; to these, three are added, which are wanting in the Agniṣṭoma. For, at the evening libation of the latter sacrifice, there are only two Śastras, the Vaiśvadeva and Agni-Mâruta, both to be repeated by the Hotar. The three Śastras of the so-called *Hotrakas*, *i.e.*, minor Hotṛi-priests, who are (according to Âs'val. Śr. S. 5, 10), the *Praśâstar* (another name of the *Maitrâvaruṇa*), the *Brâhmaṇâchhansi*, and *Achhâvâka*, are left out. But just these three Śastras which are briefly described by Âśvalâyana (Śr. S. 6, 1) form a necessary part of the Ukthya. Thus this sacrifice is only a kind of supplement to the Agniṣṭoma.

There is some more difference in the Sâmans than in the Ṛik verses required at the Ukthya. Of the three triplets which constitute the Bahiṣpavamâna Stotra (see page 120) at the morning libation of the Agniṣṭoma, only the two last are employed: for the first another one is chosen, *pavasva vâcho agriyaḥ* (Sâm. Saṁh. 2, 125—27). The four remaining Stotras of the morning libation, the so-called *Ajya-stotrâṇi*, are different. They are all together in the Sâmaveda Saṁh. (2, 140-152). At the midday libation, there is the *Bṛihat-Sâma* (*tvâm iddhi havâmahe*, Sâm. S. 2, 159-160) used instead of the Rathantaram; the *Śyaitam* (*abhi pra vaḥ surâdha-sam*, Sâm. S. 2, 161-62 (instead of the Vâmadevyam). At the evening libation, there are three Stotras required, in addition to those of the Agniṣṭoma. (See note 18 to this chapter).

In the Hiraṇyakeśi Sûtras (9, 18), the following description of the Ukthya is given :—

उकथ्येन पशुकामो यजेत । तस्याग्निष्टोमे कल्पो व्याख्यातः । पंचदश छदिसदः क्रतुकरणं हुत्वा एतेन मंत्रेण मध्यमे परिधावभ्यंतरखेपं निर्माष्ट्यैन्द्राग्नमुकथ्ये द्वितीयं सवनीयमालभते । तृतीयसवने धाराग्रहकाल आग्रयणं गृहीत्वोकथ्यं गृह्णात्येग्निष्टोमचमसानुन्नयं श्चिभ्यश्चमसगणेभ्यो राजानमतिरेचयति सर्वं राजानमुन्नय मातिरो रिचो दशाभिः कलशौ मृष्ट्वा न्युब्जेति च लुप्यत एतदग्निष्टोमचमसानां संप्रैषस्य यो य उत्तमः संस्थानचमसगणास्तमुन्नयन्नेतत्संप्रेष्यत्यग्निष्टोमचमसैः प्रचर्यं त्रिभिरुक्थ्यविग्रहैः प्रचरतो यथा पुरस्तादिंद्राय वरुणाभ्यां त्वेति प्रथमे ग्रहणसादनौ संनमन्तीन्द्राबृहस्पतिभ्यां त्वेति द्वितीय इन्द्राविष्णुभ्यां त्वेति तृतीये.

16). The *itarâ girah, i.e.*, other voices (mentioned in this verse) are those of the Asuras. Agni rose thereupon [17] and said : " What is it, then, that the lean, long, pale has to tell me ? " For Bharadvâja was lean, of high stature, and pale. He answered, " These Asuras have entered the Ukthas (Śastras) ; but nobody is aware of them."

Agni then turned into a horse, ran against them and overtook them. This act of Agni became the *Sâkamaśvam* [18] Sâman. Thence it is called so from *aśva*, a horse).

[253] About this they say, the priest ought to lead the Ukthas by means of the Sâkamaśvam. For if the Ukthas (Śastras) have another head save the Sâkamaśvam, they are not led at all.

They say, the priest should lead (the Ukthas) with the *Pramaṁhiṣṭhiya* Sâman (Sâm. Saṁh. 2, 228, 229=2, 2, 2, 17, 1, 2); for, by means of this Sâman, the Devas had turned the Asuras from the Ukthas.

(Which of both these opinions is preferable, cannot be settled.) He is at liberty[19] to lead (the Ukthas) by means of the *Pramaṁhiṣṭhîya* or the *Sâkamaśva*.[20]

50.

(The Śastras of the Three Minor Hotri-priests at the Evening Libation of the Ukthya Sacrifice.)

The Asuras entered the Uktha (Śastra) of the Maitrâvaruṇa. Indra said, " Who will join me, that we both might turn these Asuras out from here (the Śastra of the Maitrâvaruṇa) ? " " I," said Varuṇa. Thence the Maitrâvaruṇa repeats a hymn for Indra-Varuṇa [21] at the evening libation. Indra and Varuṇa then turned them out from it (the Śastra of the Maitrâvaruṇa).

[254] The Asuras having been turned out from this place, entered the Śastra of the Brâhmaṇâchhaṁsi. Indra said, " Who will join me, that we both might turn the Asuras out from this place?" Bṛihaspati answered, " I (will join you)." Thence the Brâhmaṇâchhaṁsî repeats at

---

17 Sây. reads *upottiṣṭhann*, but my MSS. have all *upottiṣṭhanu*, *u* being an encilitic.

18 This Sâman consists of the three verses, *ehy û ṣu bravâṇi yatra kvacha te* and *na hi te pûrtam* (Sâmaveda Saṁh. 2, 55-57). This Sâman is regarded as the leader of the whole Ukthya ceremony, that is to say, as the principal Sâman. Thence the two other Sâmans, which follow it at this ceremony, the *Sâubharam* (*vâyam u tvâm*, Sâṁh, 2, 58-59), 5 and the *Nârmadhasam* (*adhâ hîndra girvaṇa* 2, 60-62), are called in the Sâma prayogas the second and third *Sâkamaśvam*.

19 At the Ukthya ceremonies which were performed in the Dekkhan, more than ten years ago, only the Sâkamaśvam Sâman was used.

20 This meaning is conveyed by the particle *aha*, which has here about the same sense as *athavâ*, as Sây. justly remarks.

21 This is *Indrâ-Varuṇâ yuvam* (7, 82).

the evening libation an Aindra-Bârhaspatya hymn[22]. Indra and Bṛihaspati turned the Asuras out from it.

The Asuras, after having been turned out from it, entered the Śastra of the Achhâvâka. Indra said, "Who will join me, that we both might turn out the Asuras from here?" Viṣṇu answered, "I (will join you.)" Thence the Achhâvâka repeats at the evening libation an Aindrâ-Vaiṣṇava hymn.[23] Indra and Viṣṇu turned the Asuras out from this place.

The deities who are (successively) praised along with Indra, form (each) a pair with (him). A pair is a couple, consisting of a male and female. From this pair such a couple is produced for production. He who has such a knowledge, is blessed with children and cattle.

The Ṛituyâjas of both the Potar and Neṣṭar amount to four.[24] The (Yâjyâs to be recited by them along with the other Hotars) are six verses. This is a Virâṭ which contains the number ten. Thus they complete the sacrifice with a Virâṭ, which contains the number ten (three times ten).

---

[22] This is *ud apruto na vayo* (10, 68).

[23] This is *saṁ vâm karmanâ* (6, 69).

[24] The Potar has to repeat the second and eighth, the Neṣṭar the third and ninth Ṛituyâja, see page 135-36. At each of the three Śastras of the Ukthya, each of these two priests has also to recite a Yâjyâ. This makes six. If they are added to the four Rituyâjas, then the number *ten* is obtained, which represents the Virâṭ.

[255] FOURTH BOOK.

FIRST CHAPTER.

(On the Ṣoḷaśî and Atirâtra Sacrifices.)

1.

(On the Nature of the Ṣoḷaśi, and the Origin of its Name. On the Anuṣṭubh Nature of the Ṣoḷaśî Śastra.)

The gods prepared for Indra, by means (of the Soma ceremony) of the first day[1], the thunderbolt; by means (of the Soma ceremony) of the second day, they cooled it (after having forged it, to increase its sharpness); by means (of the Soma ceremony) of the third day, they presented it (to him); by means (of the Soma ceremony) of the fourth day, he struck with it (his enemies).

Thence the Hotar repeats on the fourth day the *Ṣoḷaśî*[2] *Sastra.* The Soḷaśî is the thunderbolt. [256] By reciting the Ṣoḷaśî on the fourth day, he strikes a blow at the enemy (and) adversary (of the sacrificer), in order to put down any one who is to be put down by him (the sacrificer).

The Ṣoḷaśî is the thunderbolt; the Śastras (Ukthas) are cattle. He repeats it as a cover over the Śastras (of the evening libation). By doing so he surrounds cattle with a weapon (in the form of) the Ṣoḷaśî (and tames them). Therefore cattle return to men if threatened round about with the weapon (in the form) of the Ṣoḷaśî.

---

[1] The first, second day, &c. refer to the so-called *Sal-aha* or six days' sacrifice, about which see the 3rd chapter of this Pañchikâ.

[2] The Ṣolaśî sacrifice is almost identical with the Ukthya. The Sâmans and Śastras at all three libations are the same. The only distinctive features are the use of the Ṣolaśî graha, the chanting of the Gaurivîtam or Nânadam Sâman, and the recital of the Ṣolaśî Śastra, after the Ukthâni (the Sâmans of the evening libation) have been chanted, and their respective Śastras recited. The Ṣolaśî Śastra is of a peculiar composition. It is here minutely described, and also in the Âśv. Śr. S. 6, 2. The number *sixteen* prevails in the arrangement of this Śastra, which is itself the sixteenth on the day on which it is repeated. Thence the name. " The substantive to be supplied is, *kratu*. The whole term means, the sacrificial performance which contains the number sixteen." The Anuṣṭubh metre consisting of twice sixteen syllables, the whole Śastra has the Anuṣṭubh character. It commences with six verses in the Anuṣṭubh metre, called by Âśv. though improperly, Stotriya and Anurûpa (for the Stotriya verse of the Śastra is always chanted by the Sâma singers, but this is not the case with the verse in question). These are: *asâvi soma indra te* (1, 84, 1-6).

Thence a horse, or a man, or a cow, or an elephant, after having been (once) tamed, return by themselves (to their owner), if they are only commanded (by the owner) with the voice (to return).

He who sees the weapon (in the form of) the Ṣoḷaśî (Śastra), is subdued by means of this weapon only. For voice is a weapon, and the Ṣoḷaśî is voice (being recited by means of the voice).

About this they ask, Whence comes the name "Ṣoḷaśî" (sixteen)? (The answer is) There are sixteen Stotras, and sixteen Śastras. The Hotar stops after (having repeated the first) sixteen syllables (of the Anuṣṭubh verse required for the Soḷaśî Śastra), and pronounces the word *om* after (having repeated the latter) sixteen syllables (of the Anuṣṭubh). He puts in it (the hymn required at the Ṣoḷasî Śastra) a Nivid of sixteen padas (small sentences). This is the reason that it is called Ṣoḷaśî. But two syllables are in excess (for in the second-half there are eighteen, instead of sixteen) in the Anuṣṭubh, **[257]** which forms a component part of the Ṣoḷaśî Śastra. For Speech (represented by the Anuṣṭubh) has (as a female deity) two breasts; these are truth and untruth. Truth protects him who has such a knowledge, and untruth does no harm to such one.

2.

(On the Way of Repeating the Ṣoḷaśî Sastra. On the Application of the Gaurivîti or Nânada Sâman.)

He who desires beauty and the acquirement of sacred knowledge ought to use the *Gaurivîtam* [3] as (the proper) Sâman at the Ṣoḷaśî (ceremony). For the Gaurivîtam is beauty and acquirement of sacred knowledge. He who having such a knowledge uses the Gaurivîtam as (the proper Sâman at the Ṣoḷaśî ceremony) becomes beautiful and acquires sacred knowledge.

They say, the *Nânadam* [4] ought to be used as (the proper) Sâman at the Ṣoḷaśî (ceremony). Indra lifted his thunderbolt to strike Vṛitra; he struck him with it, and, hitting him with it, killed him. He, after having been struck down, made a fearful noise (*vyanadat*). Thence the Nânada Sâman took its origin, and therefore it is called so (from *nad* to scream). This Sâman is free from enemies; for it kills enemies. He who having such a knowledge uses the Nânada Sâman at the Ṣoḷaśî (ceremony) gets rid of his enemies, (and) kills them.

If they use the Nânadam (Sâman), the several padas of verses in two metres at the Ṣoḷaśi Śastra are not to be taken out of their natural

[3] This is *Indra juṣasva pra vahâ* (Sâm. Saṁh. 2, 302-304). These verses are not to be found in the Ṛigveda Saṁhitâ, but in Âsv. Śr. S. 6, 2.

[4] This is *praty asmâi pipishate* (Sâm. Saṁh. 2, 6, 3, 2, 1, 4).

connection to **[258]** join one pada of the one metre to one of the other [5] (*avihṛita*). For the Sâma singers do the same, using verses which are not joined in the *vihṛita* way for singing the Nânada Sâman.

If they use the Gaurivîtam, several padas of verses in two metres used at the Ṣoḷaśî are to be taken out of their natural connection, to join one pada of the one metre to one of the other (*vihṛita*). For the Sâma singers do the same with the verses which they use for singing. [6]

3.

The Way in which the Padas of Two Different Metres are Mixed in the Ṣoḷaśî Sastra is Shown.)

Then (when they use the Gaurivîti Sâman) the Hotar changes the natural position of the several padas of two different metres, and mixes them (*vyatiṣajati*). He mixes thus Gâyatrîs and Paṅktîs, *â tvâ vahantu* (1, 16, 1-3), and *upa ṣu śriṇuhi* (1, 82, 1-3-4). [7] Man has the nature of the Gâyatrî, **[259]** and cattle that of the Paṅktî. (By thus mixing together Gâyatrî and Paṅktî verses) the Hotar mixes man among cattle, and gives him a firm footing among them (in order to become possessed of them).

As regards the Gâyatrî and Paṅktî, they both form two Anuṣṭubhs (for they contain as many padas, viz., eight, as both Gâyatrî and Paṅktî taken together). By this means, the sacrificer becomes neither separated from the nature of Speech which exists in form of the Anuṣṭubh, nor from the nature of a weapon (Speech being regarded as such a one).

He mixes verses in the Uṣṇih and Bṛihatî metres, *yad indra pṛitanâjye* (8, 12, 25-27) and *ayam te astu haryata* (3, 44, 1-3). Man has the nature of Uṣṇih, and cattle that of Bṛihatî. (By thus mixing together Uṣṇih and Bṛihatî verses) he mixes man among cattle, and gives him a firm footing among them.

---

[5] All the words from "the several padas" to "other" are only a translation of the term *avihṛita*, in order to make it better understood.

[6] The reason of this is, that the recitations of the Hotṛi-priest must correspond with the performances of the Sâma singers.

[7] Sây. shows the way in which the metres are mixed in the two verses:
(Gâyatrî) *imâ dhânâ ghṛitasnuvo harî ihopa vakṣataḥ indram sukhatame rathe* (1, 16, 2).
(Paṅkti) *susaṁdṛiśam tvâ vayam maghavan vandiṣimahi.*
pra nûnaṁ pûrṇavandhuraḥ stuto yâhi viśân anu yojânvindra to harî.

The Gâyatrî has three, the Paṅktî five feet (padas), each consisting of eight syllables. The two padas which the Paṅktî has in excess over the Gâyatrî, follow at the end without any corresponding Gâyatrî pada. After the second pada of the Paṅktî, there is the *praṇava* made (*i.e.*, the syllable *om* is pronounced), and, likewise, after the fifth. The two verses, just mentioned, are now mixed as follows: *imâ dhânâ ghṛitasnuvaḥ susaṁdriśam tvâ vayam harî ihopa vakṣato maghavan vandiṣimahom indram sukhatame rathe pra nûnaṁ pûrṇavandhuraḥ stuto yâhi viśan anu yojânvindra to harom.*

As regards the Uṣnih and Bṛihatî, they both form two Anuṣṭubhs. By this means the sacrificer becomes neither separated, &c.

He mixes a Dvipâd (verse of two padas only) and a Triṣṭubh, *â dhûrṣv asmâi* (7, 34, 4), and *brahman vîra* (7, 29, 2). Man is *dvipâdin* *i.e.*, has two feet, and strength is Triṣṭubh. (By thus mixing a Dvipâd and Triṣṭubh), he mixes man with Strength (provides him with it) and makes him a footing in it. That is the reason that man, as having prepared for him a footing in Strength, is the strongest of all animals. The Dvipâdv erse consisting of twenty syllables, and the Triṣṭubh (of forty-four), make two Anuṣṭubhs (sixty-four syllables). By this means, the sacrificer becomes neither separated, &c.

He mixes Dvipâdas and Jagatîs, viz., *eṣa brahmârya hitvyam* (Âśv. Śr. S. 6, 2) [8] and *pra te mahe* **[260]** 10, 96, 1-3). (Man is Dvipâd, and animals have the nature of the Jagatî. (By thus mixing Dvipâd and Jagatî verses) he mixes man among cattle, and makes him a footing among them. That is the reason that man, having obtained a footing among cattle, eats (them) [9] and rules over them, for they are at his disposal.

As regards the Dvipâd verse consisting of sixteen syllables and the Jagatî (consisting of forty-eight), they both (taken together) contain two Anuṣṭubhs. By this means, the sacrificer, &c.

He repeats verses in metres exceeding the number of padas of the principal metres, [10] viz., *trikadrukeṣu mahiṣo* (2, 22, 1-3), and *proṣvasmai puro ratham* (10, 133, 1-3). The juice which was flowing from the metres, took its course to the *atichhandas*. Thence such metres are called *atichhandas*, (*i. e.*, beyond the metre, what has gone beyond, is in excess).

This Ṣolaśî Śastra being formed out of all metres, he repeats verses in the Atichhandas metre.

Thus the Hotar makes (the spiritual body of) the sacrificer consist of all metres.

---

[8] These verses are not to be found in the Ṛigveda Saṁhitâ. I, therefore, write them out from my copies of the Âśval. Sûtras : –

एष ब्रह्मा य ऋत्विय । इन्द्रो नाम श्रुतो गृणे ॥
विस्रुतयो यथा पथ । इन्द्र त्वद्यन्ति रातयः ॥
त्वामिच्छवसस्पते । यन्ति निरोग संयत ॥

[9] That *atti* "he eats," put here without any object, refers to "*paśavaḥ*," animals, follows with certainty from the context. Sây. supplies *kṣîra*, milk, &c., for he abhorred the idea that animal food should be thus explicitly allowed in a sacred text.

[10] Thus I have translated the term *atichhandâsaḥ*, *i.e.*, having excess in the metre. The verses mentioned contain seven padas or feet, which exceeds the number of feet of all other metres.

He who has such a knowledge prospers by means of the Ṣoḷaśî consisting of all metres.

4.

[261] (*The Upasargas taken from the Mahânâmnîs. The Proper Anuṣṭubhs. Consequences of Repeating the Ṣoḷaśî Sastra in the Vihṛita and Avihṛita way. The Yâjyâ of the Ṣoḷaśî Sastra.*)

He makes the additions [11] (*upasarga*), taking (certain parts) from the *Mahânâmnî* verses.

The first Mahânâmnî (verse) is this world (the earth), the second the air, and the third that world (heaven). In this way, the Śoḷaśî is made to consist of all worlds.

By adding parts from the Mahânâmnîs (to the Ṣoḷaśî), the Hotar makes the sacrificer participate in all worlds. He who has such a knowledge, prospers by means of the Ṣoḷaśî being made to consist of all the worlds.

He repeats (now) Anuṣṭubhs of the proper form,[12] viz., *pra pra vas trîṣṭubham* (8, 58, 1), *archata prârchata* (8, 58, 8-10), and *yo vyatîñr aphâṇayat* (8, 58, 13-15).

[262] That the Hotar repeats Anuṣṭubhs of the proper form (after having obtained them only in an artificial way) is just as if a man, after having gone here and there astray, is led back to the (right) path.

He who thinks that he is possessed (of fortune) and is, as it were, sitting in fortune's lap (*gataśrîr*), should make his Hotar repeat the Ṣoḷaśî in the *avihṛita* way, lest he fall into distress for the injury done to the metres (by repeating them in the *vihṛita* way).

But if one wishes to do away with the consequences of guilt (to get out of distress and poverty), one should make the Hotar repeat the Ṣoḷaśî in the *vihṛita* way.

---

[11] These additions are called *upasargas.* They are five in number, and mentioned by Âśv. 6, 2. They are all taken from different verses of the so-called Mahânâmnîs, commencing with विदा मघवन्विद गातुं which make up the fourth Araṇyaka of the Aitareya Brâhm. These five *upasargas* make together one Anuṣṭubh. They are: (1) प्रचेतन (2) प्रचेतय (3) आयाहि पिब मत्स्व. (4) क्रतुश्छन्द ऋतं वृहत् (5) सुम्नआधेहि नो वसो. Their application is different according to the *avihṛita* or *vihṛita* way of repeating the Ṣolaśî Sastra. If the Sastra is to be repeated in the former way, they are simply repeated in the form of one verse, after the recital of the Atichhandas verses. But if it be repeated in the *vihṛita* way, the several *upasargas* are distributed among the five latter of the six Atichhandasa verses, in order to bring the number of syllables of each such verse to sixty-four, to obtain the two Anuṣṭubhs for each

[12] As yet the Anuṣṭubhs were only artificially obtained by the combination of the padas of different other metres.

For (in such cases) man is, as it were, intermixed with the consequences of guilt (with the *papman*). By thus repeating the Ṣoḷaśî in the *vihṛita* way, the Hotar takes from the sacrificer all sin and guilt. He who has such a knowledge becomes free from (the consequences of) guilt.

With the verse *ud yad bradhnasya viṣṭapam* (8, 58, 7) he concludes. For the celestial world is the "*bradhnasya viṣṭapam.*" Thus he makes the sacrificer go to the celestial world.

As Yâjyâ verse he repeats *apâḥ purveṣâm harivaḥ* (10, 96, 13).[13] By repeating this verse as Yâjyâ (of the Ṣoḷaśî Śastra) he makes the Ṣoḷaśî to consist of all libations (*savanâni*). The term *apâḥ*, thou hast drunk (used in this verse) signifies the Morning Libation. Thus he makes the Ṣoḷaśî to consist of [**263**] the Morning Libation. The words *atho idam savanam kevalam te, i.e.*, this libation here is entirely thy own, signifies the Midday Libation. Thus he makes the Ṣoḷaśî to consist of the Midday Libation. The words, *mamaddhi somam, i.e.*, enjoy the Soma, signify the Evening Libation, which has its characteristic the term *mad*, to enjoy, to be drunk. Thus he makes the Ṣoḷaśî to consist of the Evening Libation. The word *vṛiṣan, i.e.*, bull (contained in the last pada), is the characteristic of the Ṣoḷaśî.

By repeating as Yâjyâ (for the Ṣoḷaśî), the verse just mentioned, the Ṣoḷaśî is made to consist of all Libations. Thus he makes it to consist of all Libations. He who has such a knowledge prospers through the Ṣoḷaśî, which consists of all Libations.

(When repeating the Yâjyâ) he prefixes to each (of the four) pada,[14] consisting of eleven syllables, an *upasarga* of five syllables (taken) from the Mahânâmnîs. Thus he makes the Ṣoḷaśî to consist of all metres. He who has such a knowledge prospers by means of the Ṣoḷaśî, which is made to consist of all metres.

---

[13] The whole of the verse is as follows :—

अपाः पूर्वेषां हरिवः सुतानामथो इदं सवनं केवलं ते ।
ममद्धि सोमं मधुमन्तमिन्द्र सत्रा वृषन् जठर आवृषस्व ॥

i.e., "Thou hast drunk, O master of the two yellow horses (Indra)! of the Soma drops formerly prepared for thee. This libation here is entirely thy own (thou hast not to snare it with any other god). Enjoy, O Indra! the honey-like Soma. O bull! increase thy strength by (receiving) all this (quantity of Soma) in (thy) belly.

[14] These four upasargas are :

a) एवाह्येव *b*) एवहीन्द्रं *c*) एवाहि शक्रो *d*) वशो हि शक्र.

They are thus prefixed :

एवा ह्येवापाः पूर्वेषां॰ एवहोन्द्राथो इदं॰ &c

These Upasargas are prefixed to the Yâjyâ, in order to obtain two Anuṣṭubhs (sixty-four syllables).

5.

(Atirâtra. Its origin. The three Paryâyas.)

The Devas[15] took shelter with Day, the Asuras with Night. They were thus of equal strength, and [**264**] none yielded to the other. Indra said, " Who, besides me, will enter Night to turn the Asuras out of it ?" But he did not find any one among the Devas ready to accept (his offer), (for) they were afraid of Night, on account of its darkness being (like that of) Death. This is the reason that even now one is afraid of going at night even to a spot which is quite close. For Night is, as it were, Darkness, and is Death, as it were. The metres (alone) followed him. This is the reason that Indra and the metres are the leading deities of the Night (of the nightly festival of Atirâtra). No Nivid is repeated, nor a Puroruk, nor a Dhâyyâ ; nor is there any other deity save Indra and the metres who are the leading (deities). They turned them out by going round (*paryâyam*) with the *Paryâyas* (the different turns of passing the Soma cups). This is the reason that they are called *paryâya* (from *i* to go, and *pari* around).

By means of the first Paryâya they turned them out of the first part of the night; by means of the middle Paryâya out of midnight, and by means of the third Paryâya out of the latter part of the night. The metres said to Indra, "Even we (alone) are following (thee, to turn the Asuras) out of the Dark one (*śarvarâ*, night)." He (the sage Aitareya) therefore called them (the metres) *apiśarvarâṇi*, for they had Indra, who was afraid of the darkness of night (as) of death, safely carried beyond it. That is the reason that they are called *apiśarvaâṇi*.

6.

(The Sastras of Atirâtra at the Three Paryâyas. Sandhi Stotra.)

The Hotar commences (the recitations at Atirâtra) with an Anuṣṭubh verse containing the term *andhas, i.e.*, darkness, viz., *pântâm â vo andhasaḥ* (8, 81, 1.) [**265**] For night belongs to Anuṣṭubh ; it has the nature of night.

As appropriate Yâjyâ verse (at the end of each turn of the three Paryâyas) [16] Triṣṭubhs containing the terms—*andhas*, darkness, *pâ* to, drink,

---

[15] The same story with some trifling deviations in the wording only is recorded in the Gopatha Brâhmaṇam of the Atharvaveda, 10, 1.

[16] There are four turns of the Soma cups passing the round in each Paryâya, or part of the night. At the end of each, a Yâjyâ is repeated, and the juice then sacrifieed. There is at each turn (there are on the whole twelve) a Śastra repeated, to which a Yâjyâ belongs. The latter contains always the terms indicated. See, for instance, the four Yâjyâs used at the first Paryâya (Âśv. Śr. S. 6,4) *adhvaryavo bharata indriya*, 2, 14, 1. (repeated by the Hotar). In the second pada, there are the words, *madyam andhaḥ*, " the inebriating

and *mad*, to be drunk, are used. What is appropriate at the sacrifice, that is successful.

The Sâma singers repeat when chanting at the first Paryâya twice the first padas only of the verses (which they chant). By doing so they take from them (the Asuras) all their horses and cows.

At the middle Paryâya, they repeat twice the middle padas. By doing so, they take from them (the Asuras) their carts and carriages.

At the last Paryâya, they repeat twice when chanting the last padas (of the verses which they chant). By doing so, they take from them (the Asuras) all things they wear on their own body, such as dresses, gold and jewels.

He who has such a knowledge deprives his enemy of his property, (and) turns him out of all these worlds (depriving him of every firm footing).

[266] They ask, How are the Pavamâna Stotras [17] provided for the night, whereas such Stotras refer only to the day, but not to the night? In what way are they both made to consist of the same parts (to have the same number of Stotras and Śastras)?

The answer is, (They are provided for) by the following verses, which form part of the Stotras as well of the Śastras (at the Atirâtra): *indrâya madvane sutam* (8, 81, 19. Sâmaveda Samh. 2, 72), *idam vsao sutam andhaḥ* (8, 2, 1, Sâm. S. 2, 84), *idam hyanvojasâ sutam* (3, 51, 10. Sâm, S. 2, 87). In this way, the night becomes also provided with *Pavamânas* (for the verses mentioned contain the term *suta*, *i.e.*, squeezed, referring to the squeezing of the Soma juice, which term is proper to the Pavamâna Stotra); in this way, both (day and night) are provided with Pavamânas, and made to consist of the same (number of) parts.

They ask, As there are fifteen Stotras for the day only, but not for

---

darkness" (symbolical name of the Soma juice). The Yâjyâ of the Maitrâvaruṇa is, *asya made puruvarpâṁsi* 6, 44, 14). It contains the term *made*, "to get drunk," and *pâ*, "to drink," in the last pada. The Yâjyâ of the Brâhmaṇâchhaṁsî is *âpsu dhûtasya harivaḥ piba* (10, 104, 2). This verse contains both the terms *pâ*, "to drink" (in *piba* of the first pada), and *mad*, "to be drunk" (in the last pada). The Yâjyâ of the Achhâvâka is, *indra piba tubhyam* (6, 40, 1). It contains both the terms, *pâ*, and *mad*. The Yâjyâ of the Hotar in the second Paryâya is, *apâyyasyândhaso madâya* (2, 19, 1); it contains all three terms, "darkness, to drink, and to be drunk."

17 This question refers to the Stotras to be chanted for the purification of the Soma juice, which are, at the morning libation, the Bahis-pavamâna, at midday, the Pavamâna, and in the evening, the Arbhava-pavamâna. At night, there being no squeezing of the Soma juice, there are, properly speaking, no Pavamâna Stotras required. But to make the performance of day and night alike, the Pavamâna Stotras for day and night are to be indicated in one way or other in the Stotras chanted at night. This is here shown.

the night, how are there fifteen Stotras for both (for day as well as for night)? In what way are they made to consist of the same (number of) parts?

The answer is, The *Apiśarvaras*[18] form twelve Stotras. (Besides) they chant, according to the Rathantara tune, the Sandhi[19] Stotra which contains **[267]** (three sets of) verses addressed to three deities. In this way, night comprises (also) fifteen Stotras. Thus both (day and night) comprise each fifteen Stotras. Thus both are made to consist of the same (number of) parts.

The number of verses for making the Stotras is limited, but the number of recitations which follow the Stotras) is unlimited. The past is, as it were, limited, defined; the future is, as it were, unlimited (not defined). In order to secure the future (wealth, &c.,) the Hotar repeats more verses (than the Sâma singers chant). What goes beyond the Stotra is offspring, what goes beyond one's self (represented by the Stotra), is cattle. By repeating, when making his recitation, more verses (than the Sâma singers chant) the Hotar acquires all that he (the sacrificer) has beyond his own self on this earth (*i.e.*, all his cattle, children, fortune, &c.)

---

18 See 4, 5. They are the metres used for Śastras and Stotras during the night of Atirâtra.

19 This Stotra which is chanted after the latter part of the night is over, when the dawn is commencing (thence it is called *saṁdhi*, *i.e.*, the joining of night and day), consists of six verses in the Bṛihatî metre, with the exception of the two last which are kakubha (a variety of the Bṛihatî). They are put together in the Sâmav. Saṁh. 2, 99-104. The two first of them, *ena vo âgnim* (2, 99-100) are addressed to Agni, the third and fourth, *pratyu adarśy âyatyû* (101-102) to Uṣâs, and the fifth and sixth, *imâ u vâṁ divistaya* (103-104) to the Aśvins. The Stoma required for singing it, is the *trivṛit parivarttinî* (see page 237). Two verses are made three by means of the repetition of the latter padas. This Sâman is chanted just like the verses of the Rathantaram, which are in the same metre. It follows throughout the musical arrangement of the Rathantaram. The musical accents, the crescendos, and decrescendos, the stobhas, *i. e.*, musical flourishes, and the finales (*nidhana*) are the same. Both are for the purpose of chanting equally divided into five parts, *viz.*, Prastâva, Udgîtha, Pratihâra, Upadrava, and Nidhana (see page 198). For instance, the Prastâva or prelude commences in both in the low tone, and rises only at the last syllable (at *mo* in the *nonumo* of the Rathantaram, and at the *so* in the *namaso* of the first Sandhi Stotra); at the end of the Prastâva of both there is the Stobha, *i.e.*, flourish *va.* At the end of the Upadrava both have the Stobhas *vâ hâ uvâ.* The finale is in both throughout, as, in the rising tone.—(*Sâma prayoga* and *Oral information.*)

[268] SECOND CHAPTER.

(The Aśvina Sastra. The Beginning Day of the Gavâm Ayanam. The Use of the Rathantara and Bṛihat Sâmans and their kindreds. The Mahâvrata Day of the Sattra.) [1]

---

[1] The Aśvin Śastra is one of the longest recitations by the Hotar. It is only a modification of the Prâtaranuvâka. Its principal parts are the same as those of the Prâtaranuvâka, the *Agneya kratu*, *Uṣasya kratu* and *Aśvina kratu* (see page 111), *i.e.*, three series of hymns and verses in seven kinds of metre, addressed to Agni, Uṣâs, and the Aśvins, which deities rule at the end of the night, and at the very commencement of the day. In addition to these three *kratus* of the Prâtaranuvâka, in the Aśvina Śastra, there are verses addressed to other deities, chiefly the sun, repeated. Before commencing to repeat it, the Hotar (*not* the Adhvaryu) must sacrifice thrice a little melted butter, and eat the rest of it. These three oblations are given to Agni, Uṣâs, and the two Aśvins. Each is accompanied with a Yajus-like mantra. That one addressed to Agni is: अग्निरज्वी गायत्रेण छन्दसा तमश्यां तमन्वारभे तस्मै मामवतु तस्मै स्वाहा । " Agni is driving with the Gâyatrî metre (this metre being his carriage), might I reach him ; I hold him ; may this (melted butter) help me to him ; Svâhâ to him." The mantras repeated for the Ajya offerings to Uṣâs and the Aśvins differ very little.

उषा अज्विनी त्रैष्टुभेन छन्दसा तामाश्यां तामन्वारभे तस्यै मामवतु तस्यै स्वाहा । अश्विनावज्विनौ जागतेन छन्दसा तावश्यां तावन्वारभे ताभ्यां मामवतु ताभ्यां स्वाहा. (Âśv. Śr. S. 6, 5.) After having eaten the rest of the melted butter, he touches water only, but does not rinse his mouth in the usual way (by *āchamana*). He then sits down behind his Dhiṣṇya (fire-place) in a peculiar posture, representing an eagle who is just about flying up. He draws up his two legs, puts both his knees close to each other, and touches the earth with his toes. I saw a priest, who had once repeated the Aśvin Śastra (there are scarcely more than half a dozen Brâhmaṇs living all over India who actually have repeated it), make the posture with great facility, but I found it difficult to imitate it well.

The whole Aśvina Śastra comprises a thousand Bṛihatî verses. The actual number of verses is, however, larger. All verses in whatever metre they are, are reduced to Bṛihatîs by counting their aggregate number of syllables and dividing them by 36 (of so many syllables consists the Bṛihatî). The full account is cast up in the Kauṣîtaki Brâhmaṇam, 18, 3.

The first verse of the Śastra is mentioned in the text. It is to be repeated thrice and to be joined, without stopping, to the first verse of the Gâyatrî part of the *Agneya kratu* (घृतयाग्नेयं गायत्रमुपसंतनुयात् Âśv. Śr. S. 6, 5). After the opening verse which stands by itself altogether, just as the opening verse in the prâtaranuvâka, the three *kratus* or liturgies of the Prâtaranuvâka (*âgneya*, *uṣasya*, and *aśvani*) are repeated. These form the body of the Aśvin Śastra. Each *kratu* is preceded by the Stotriya Pragâtha, *i.e.*, that couple of verses of the Sandhi Stotra (see page 266) which refers to that deity, to which the respective *kratu* is devoted. So the *âgneya kratu*, *i.e.*, the series of hymns and verses, addressed to Agni, in seven different kinds of metre, is preceded by the first couple of verses of the Sandhi Stotra, which are, *enâ vo agnim namasâ* (Sâm. Saṁh. 2, 99-100); the *uṣasya kratu* is preceded by *praty u adarśy âyati* (Sâm. Saṁh. 2, 101, 102), the deity being Uṣâs, and the *âśvina-kratu* by *ima u vam diviṣṭaya* (Sâm. Saṁh. 2, 103-104) being addressed to the two Aśvins. Each couple of these verses is to be made a

[269] 7.

(The Marriage of Prajâpati's Daughter, Sûrya. The Aśvina Śastra was the Bridal Gift. In What Way the Hotar has to Repeat it. Its Beginning Verse.)

Prajâpati gave his daughter, Sûrya Sâvitrî, [2] in **[270]** marriage to the king Soma. All the gods came as paranymphs. Prajâpati formed, according to the model of a *vahatu, i.e.*, things (such as turmeric, powder, &c., to be carried before the paranymphs), this thousand (of verses), which is called the Aśvina (Śastra). What falls short of *(arvâk)* one thousand verses, is no more the Aśvin's. This is the reason that the Hotar ought to repeat only a thousand verses, or he might repeat more. He ought to eat ghee before he commences repeating. Just as in this world a cart or a carriage goes well if smeared (with oil), thus his repeating proceeds well if he be smeared (with ghee, by eating it.) Having taken the posture of an eagle when starting up, the Hotar should recite (when commencing) the call *śomsâvom (i.e.*, he should commence repeating the Aśvina Śastra).

The gods could not agree as to whom this (thousand verses) should belong, each saying, "Let it be mine." Not being able to agree (to whom it should belong), they said, "Let us run a race for it. He of us who will be the winner shall have it." They made the sun which is above Agni, the house-father (above the Gârhapatya fire [3]), the goal. That is the reason that the Aśvina Śastra commences with a verse addressed to Agni, viz., *agnir hotâ gṛihapatiḥ* (6, 15, 13).

---

triplet, by repeating the last pada several times, just as the Sâma singers do.

(बार्हताश्चयस्तृचा : । स्तोत्रिया : प्रगाथा वा तान्पुरस्ताद्दनुदैवतं स्वस्य छन्दसो यथा स्तुतं शंसेत (Âśv. 6, 5).

The Hotar must repeat less than a thousand verses before sunrise : सहस्त्रावममोदेतो : After sunrise, he repeats the verses addressed to Sûrya, which all are mentioned in the Aitareya Brâhmaṇam, as well as all other remaining verses of the Aśvina Śastra. The whole order of the several parts of this Śastra is more clearay stated in the Kusîtaki Brâhm., (18, 2), than in the Aitareya. The verses addressed to Indra follow after the Sûrya verses (4, 10). At the end of the Śastra, there are two Puronuvâkyâs and two Yâjyâs, for there are two Aśvins.

The Aśvina Śastra is, as one may see from its constituent parts, a Prâtaranuvâka, or early morning prayer, including the worship of the rising sun, and a Śastra accompanying a Soma libation. It follows the Sandhi Stotra at the end of the Atirâtra, and is regarded as the Śastra belonging to this Stotra. To the fact of its containing far more verses than the Sandhi Stotra, the term *atiśaṁsati, i.e.*, "he repeats *more* verses" (used in 4, 6) refers.

[2] This is the model marriage. It is described in the well-known marriage hymn *satyenottabhitâ* (10, 85).

[3] That is to say, they started when running the race from the Gârhapatya fire, and ran up as far as the sun, which was the goal (*kâṣṭhâ*).

According to the opinion of some (theologians), the Hotar should (instead of this verse) commence (the recitation of the Aśvina Śastra) with *agnim manye pitaram* (10, 7, 3); for they say, he reaches the goal by means of the first verse through the words (contained in its fourth pada): *divi śukram yajatam sûryasya, i.e.*, the splendour of the sun in heaven which deserves worship. But this opinion is not to **[271]** be attended to. (If one should observe a Hotar commencing the Aśvina Śastra with the verse *agnim manaye*) one should say to him, "If (a Śastra) has been commenced with repeatedly mentioning *agni*[4] fire, the Hotar will (ultimately fall into the fire (be burnt by it)." Thus it always happens. Thence the Hotar ought to commence with the verse: *agnir hotâ grihapatiḥ*. This verse contains in the terms *gṛihapati*, house-father, and *janima*, generations, the propitiation (of the word *agni*, fire, with which it commences, and is therefore not dangerous) for attaining to the full age.

He who has such a knowledge attains to his full age (of one hundred years).

8.

(*The Race Run by the Gods for Obtaining the Aśvina Śastra as a Prize.*)

Among (all) these deities who were running the race, Agni was with his mouth (the flames) in advance (of all others) after they had started. The Aśvins (closely) followed him, and said to him, "Let us both be winners of this race." Agni consented, under the condition that he should also have a share in it (the Aśvina Śastra). They consented, and made room also for him in this (Aśvina Śastra). This is the reason that there is in the Aśvina Śastra a series of verses addressed to Agni.

The Aśvins (closely) followed Uṣâs. They said to her, "Go aside, that we both may be winners of the race." She consented, under the condition that they should give her also a share in it (the Aśvina Śastra). They consented, and made room also for **[272]** her in it. This is the reason that in the Aśvina Śastra a series of verses is addressed to Uṣâs.

The Aśvins (closely) followed Indra. They said to him, "Maghavan, we both wish to be winners of this race." They did not dare to say to him, "Go aside." He consented, under the condition that he should also obtain a share in it (the Aśvina Śastra). They consented, and made room also for him. This is the reason that in the Aśvina Śastra there is a series of verses addressed to Indra.

Thus the Aśvins were winners of the race, and obtained (the prize). This is the reason that it (the prize) is called Aśvinam (*i. e.*, the Aśvina

[4] The verse in question contains four times the word *agni*. This is regarded as inauspicious. The deity should not be always mentioned with its very name, but with its epithets.

Śastra). He who has such a knowledge obtains what he may wish for.

They ask, Why is this (Śastra) called Aśvinam, notwithstanding there being in it verses addressed to Agni, Uṣâs, and Indra? (The answer is) the Aśvins were the winners of this race, they obtained it (the prize). This is the reason that it is called the Aśvina Śastra. He who has such a knowledge obtains what he may wish for.

9.

(What Animals were Yoked to the Carriages of the Gods when they were Running the Race for the Aśvina Śastra. The Verses Addressed to Sûrya in this Śastra.)

Agni ran the race, with a carriage drawn by mules. When driving them he burnt their wombs; thence they do not conceive.

Uṣâs ran the race with cows of a reddish colour, thence it comes that after the arrival of Uṣâs (Dawn), there is a reddish colour shining as it were (spread over the eastern direction) which is the characteristic of Uṣâs.

[273] Indra ran the race with a carriage drawn by horses. Thence a very noisy spectacle (represented by the noise made by horses which draw a carriage) is the characteristic of the royal caste, which is Indra's.

The Aśvins were the winners of the race with a carriage drawn by donkeys; they obtained (the prize). Thence (on account of the excessive efforts to arrive at the goal) the donkey lost its (original) velocity, became devoid of milk, and the slowest among all animals used for drawing carriages. The Aśvins, however, did not deprive the sperm of the ass of its (primitive) vigour. This is the reason that the male ass (*vâjî*) has two kinds of sperm (to produce mules from a mare, and asses from a female ass).

Regarding this (the different parts which make up the Aśvina Śastra), they say, "The Hotar ought to repeat, just as he does for Agni, Uṣâs, and the Aśvins also, verses in all seven metres for Sûrya. There are seven worlds of the gods. (By doing so) he prospers in all (seven) worlds."

This opinion ought not to be attended to. He ought to repeat (for Sûrya) verses in three metres only. For there are three worlds which are three-fold. (If the Hotar repeats for Sûrya verses in three metres only, this is done) for obtaining possession of these worlds.

Regarding this (the order in which the verses addressed to Sûrya are to be repeated), they say, "The Hotar ought to commence (his recitation of the Sûrya verses) with *ud u tyam jâtavedasam* (1, 50, in the Gâyatrî metre)." But this opinion is not to be attended to. (To commence with this verse) is just as to miss the goal when running. He ought to commence with *suryo no divas pâtu* (10, 158, 1, in the Gâyatrî metre). (If he do so) he is just as one who reaches the goal when running. He repeats: *ud u tyam* as the second hymn.

[274] The Triṣṭubh hymn is, *chitram devânâm ud âgâd* (1, 115). For that one (the sun) rises as the *chitram devânâm, i.e.*, as the manifestation of the gods. Thence he repeats it.

The hymn is, *namo mitrasya varuṇasya* (10, 37). In this (hymn) there is a pada (the fourth of the first verse, *sûryâya śaṁsata*) which contains a blessing (*âśîḥ*). By means of it, the Hotar imparts a blessing to himself, as well as to the sacrificer.

10.

(*The Verses which Follow those Addressed to Sûrya in the Aśvina Śastra Must Bear some Relation to Sûrya and the Bṛihatî Metre. The Pragâthas to Indra. The Text of the Rathantara Sâman. The Pragâtha to Mitrâvaruṇa. The Two Verses to Heaven and Earth. The Dvipadâ for Nirṛiti.*)

Regarding this (the recitations for Sûrya), they say, Sûrya is not to be passed over in the recitation; nor is the Bṛihatî metre (of the Aśvina Śastra) to be passed over. Should the Hotar pass over Sûrya, he would fall beyond (the sphere of) Brahma splendour (and consequently lose it). Should he pass over the Bṛihatî, he would fall beyond the (sphere of the) vital airs (and consequently die).

He repeats the Pragâtha, addressed to Indra, viz., *indra kratum na* (7, 32, 26), *i.e.*, "Carry, O Indra! our (sacrificial) performance through, just as a father does to his sons (by assisting them). Teach us, O thou who art invoked by many, that we may, in this turn (of the night) reach alive the (sphere of) light."[5] The word "light" (*jyotis*) in this verse, is **[275]** that one (the sun). In this way, he does not pass over the sun.

By repeating a Bârhata Pragâtha he does not pass over the Bṛihatî. By repeating the principal text of the Rathantara Sâman (which is in the Bṛihatî metre, viz., *abhi tvâ śûra*, 7, 32, 22-23), according to whose tune

[5] This verse evidently refers to the Atirâtra feast, for which occasion it was in all likelihood composed by Vasiṣṭha. Sây., in his commentary on this passage in the Ait. Br. takes the same view of it. It forms part of the Aśvina Śastra which is repeated at the end of the night. *Kratu* means the Atirâtra feast; for Atirâtra is actually called a *kratu*; *yâman* is the last watch of the night. That Atirâtra was well-known to the great Riṣis, we may learn from the well-known "praise of the frogs" (7, 103), which is by no means one of the latest hymns, as some scholars have supposed.

the Sâma singers chant the Sandhi Stotra for the Aśvina Śastra, he does not overpraise the Bṛihatî. This is done in order to have provided (for the Sandhi Stotra) its principal text (lit., its *womb*). In the words of the Rathantara Sâman, *îśâṇam asya jagataḥ svardṛiśam, i.e.*, the ruler of this world who sees the sky, there is an allusion made to Sûrya by "*svardṛiśam*," *i.e.*, who sees the sky. By repeating it, he does not pass the sun. Nor does he by its (the Rathantaram) being a Bârhata Pragâtha pass over the Bṛihatî.

He repeats a Maitrâvaruṇa Pragâtha, viz., *bahavaḥ śûrachakṣase* (7, 66, 10). For Mitra is the day, and Varuṇa the night. He who performs the Atirâtra, commences (his sacrifice) with both day and night. By repeating a Maitrâvaruna Pragâtha, the Hotar places the sacrificer in day and night. By the words *sûrachakṣase* he does not overpraise Sûrya. The verse being a Bṛihatî Pragâtha, he does not pass over the Bṛihatî.

He repeats two verses addressed to Heaven and Earth, viz., *mahî dyâuḥ prithivî* (1, 22, 13), and *te hi dyâvâ prithivî viśvaś ambhuva* (1, 160, 1). Heaven and Earth are two places for a firm footing; Earth being the firm footing here, and Heaven there (in the other world). By thus repeating two verses [276] addressed to Heaven and Earth, he puts the sacrificer in two places on a firm footing. By the words, *devo devî dharmaṇâ sûryaḥ śuchiḥ* (in the last pada of 1, 160, 1), *i.e.*, "the divine brilliant Sûrya passes regularly between the two goddesses (*i.e.*, Heaven and Earth)," he does not pass over Sûrya. One of these verses being in the Gâyatrî, the other in the Jagatî, metre, which make two Bṛihatîs,[6] he does not pass over the Bṛihatî.

He repeats the Dvipadâ verse: *viśvasya devî mṛichayasya* (not to be found in the Saṁhitâ, but in the Brâhmaṇam), *i.e.*, may she who is the ruler of all that is born and moves (*mṛichaya*) not be angry (with us), nor visit us (with destruction). They (the theologians) have called the Aśvina Śastra a funeral pile of wood (*chitaidhâ*). For, when the Hotar is about to conclude (this Śastra), *Nirṛiti* (the goddess of destruction) is lurking with her cords, thinking to cast them round (the Hotar). (To prevent this) Bṛihaspati saw this Dvipadâ verse. By its words, "may she not be angry (with us), nor visit us (with destruction)," he wrested from Nirṛiti's hands her cords and put them down. Thus the Hotar wrests also from the hands of Nirṛiti her cords, and puts them down when repeating this Dvipadâ verse, by which means he comes off in safety. (He does so) for

[6] The Bṛihatî contains thirty-six syllables, the Gâyatrî twenty-four, and the Jagatî forty-eight. Two Bṛihatîs make seventy-two, and one Gâyatrî and Jagatî make together seventy-two syllables.

attaining to his full age. He who has such a knowledge attains to his full age. By the words, *mṛichayasya janmanaḥ, i.e.*, "what is born and moves," he does not pass over the sun in his recitation, for that one (the sun) moves (*marchayati*) as it were.

As regards the Dvipadâ verse, it is the metre corresponding to man (on account of his two padas, *i.e.*, [277] feet). Thus it comprises all metres (for the two-legged man is using them all). In this way, the Hotar does not (by repeating the Dvipadâ) pass over the Bṛihatî.

11.

(The Concluding Verses of the Aśvin Śastra. The Two Yâjyâs of it. In What Metre They Ought To Be.)

The Hotar concludes with a verse addressed to Brahmaṇaspati. For Brahma is Bṛihaspati. By repeating such a verse he puts the sacrificer in the Brahma. He who wishes for children and cattle should conclude with, *evâ pitre viśvâderâya* (4, 50, 6). For, on account of its containing the words, " O Bṛihaspati, might we be blessed with children and strong men, might we become owners of riches," that man becomes blessed with children, cattle and riches, and strong men, at whose sacrifice there is a Hotar, knowing that he must conclude with this verse (in order to obtain this object wished for).

He who wishes for beauty and acquirement of sacred knowledge ought to conclude with, *bṛihaspate atiyad* (2, 23, 15). Here the word *ati, i. e.*, beyond, means that he acquires more of sacred knowledge than other men do. The term, *dyumat* (in the second pada), means "acquirement of sacred knowledge," and *vibhâti* means, that the sacred knowledge shines everywhere, as it were. The term *dîdayat* (in the third pada) means, that the sacred knowledge has been shining forth (in the Brahmans). The term, *chitra* (in the fourth pada), means that the sacred knowledge is, as it were, apparent (*chitram*).

He, at whose sacrifice there is a Hotar knowing that he must conclude with this verse, becomes endowed with sacred knowledge and famous for sanctity. Thence a Hotar who has such a knowledge ought to conclude with this Brahmaṇaspati verse. [278] By repeating it, he does not pass over the sun. The Trishṭubh,[7] when repeated thrice, comprises all metres. In this way, he does not pass over the Bṛihatî (by repeating this Trisṭubh).

He ought to pronounce the formula, *Vauṣaṭ*, along with a verse

[7] The verse *bṛihaspate ati* is in the Trisṭubh metre. On account of its being the last verse of the Śhastra, it is to be repeated thrice.

in the Gâyatrî, and one in the Triṣṭubh metre. Gâyatrî is the Brahma, and Triṣṭubh is strength. By doing so, he joins strength to the Brahma.

He, at whose sacrifice there is a Hotar knowing that he (in order to obtain the objects mentioned) must pronounce the formula, *Vauṣaṭ*,[8] with a verse in the Gâyatrî, and one in the Triṣṭubh metre, becomes endowed with sacred knowledge and strength, and famous for sanctity. (The Triṣṭubh verse is) *aśvinâ vâyunâ yuvam* (3, 58, 7); (the Gâyatrî is) *ubhâ pibatam* (1, 46, 15).

(There is another way of pronouncing the formula *Vauṣaṭ*.)

He ought to pronounce the formula *Vauṣaṭ* along with a verse in the Gâyatrî, and one in the Virâṭ metre. For Gâyatrî is Brahma, and Virâṭ is food. By doing so, he joins food to the Brahma.

He, at whose sacrifice there is a Hotar knowing that he must pronounce the formula *Vauṣaṭ* along with a verse in the Gâyatrî, and one in the Virâṭ metre, becomes endowed with sacred knowledge, and famous for sanctity and eats Brahma food (*i.e.*, pure food). Therefore, one who has such a knowledge ought to pronounce the formula *Vauṣaṭ* along with a verse in the Gâyatrî, and one in the Triṣṭubh metre. They are, *pra vâṁ andhâṁsi* (7, 68, 2, Virâṭ) and *ubhâ pibatam* (1, 46, 15, Gâyatrî).

[279] 12.

(*The Chaturviṁśa*[9] *Day of the Sacrificial Session, called Gavâm Ayanam.*)

On this day[10] (which follows the Atirâtra ceremony) they celebrate

---

[8] That is to say, he should then make the Yâjyâs ; for only at that occasion the formula *vauṣaṭ* is pronounced.

[9] This is the name of a day, and a Stoma, required at the Sattra or sacrificial session, called the *gavâm ayanam* (see more about it, 4, 17). It lasts for a whole year of 360 days, and consists of the following parts : 1) The Atirâtra at the beginning. 2) The Chaturviṁśa or beginning day ; it is called in the Aitareya Br. *ârambhaṇîya*, in the Tâṇḍya Br. (4, 2,) *prâyaṇîya*. 3) The periods of six days' performance (*Ṣalaha*) continued during five months, so that always the four first *Ṣalaha*s are *Abhiplava*s, and the fifth a *Pṛiṣṭhya* (see on these terms 4, 15-17). 4) In the sixth month, there are three Abhiplava Ṣalahas, and one Pṛiṣṭhya Ṣalaha. 5) The Abhijit day. 6) The three Svarasâman, days. 7) The Viṣuvan or central day which stands quite apart. 8) The three Svarasâman days again. 9) The Viśvajit day. 10) A Pṛiṣṭhya Ṣalaha, and three Abhiplavas during four months continuously. 12) In the last month (the twelfth of the Sattra) there are three Abhiplavas, one Goṣṭoma, one Âyuṣṭoma, and one Daśarâtra (the ten days of the Dvâdaśâha). 13) The Mahâvrata day, which properly concludes the performance ; it corresponds to the Chaturviṁśa at the beginning. 14) The concluding Atirâtra. See Aś v. Sr. S. 11, 7.

[10] *Ahaḥ*, has, according to Sây., the technical meaning of the Soma ceremony, which is performed on every particular day of a sacrificial session.

the Chaturviṁśa (Stoma). It is the beginning day (of the year during which the sacrificial session is to last). For by this day they begin the year, and also the Stomas and metres, and (the worship of) the deities. If they do not commence (the Sattra) on this day, the metres have no (proper) beginning and the (worship of the) deities is not commenced. Thence this day is called *ârambhaṇîya*, *i. e.*, the beginning day. On account of the Chaturviṁśa (twenty-four-fold) Stoma being used on it, it is (also) called Chaturviṁśa. There are twenty-four half months. (By beginning the Sattra with the Chaturviṁśa Stoma, *i.e.*, the chant, consisting **[280]** of twenty-four verses) they commence the year as divided into half-months.

The Ukthya (performance of the Jyotiṣṭoma) takes place (on that day). For the *ukthas* (recitations) are cattle. (This is done) for obtaining cattle.

This (Ukthya sacrifice) has fifteen Stotras and fifteen Śastras.[11] (These make, if taken together, one month of thirty days.) By (performing) this (sacrifice) they commence the year as divided into months. This (Ukthya sacrifice) has 360 Stotriya verses[12] as many as the year has days. By (performing) this (sacrifice) they commence the year as divided into days.

They say, "the performance of this (first) day ought to be an Agniṣṭoma. Agniṣṭoma is the year. For no other sacrifice, save the Agniṣṭoma, has kept (has been able to keep) this day (the performance of this day), nor developed its several parts (*i.e.*, has given the power of performing all its several rites).

Should they perform (on the beginning day) the Agniṣṭoma, then the three Pavamâna Stotras[13] of the morning, midday, and evening libations are to be put in the Aṣṭachatvâriṁśa Stoma (*i.e.*, each of the Stotriya triplets is made to consist of forty-eight verses by means of repetition), and the other (nine) Stotras in the Chaturviṁśa Stoma. This makes (on the whole) 360 Stotriyas, as many as there are days (in the year). (By performing the Agniṣṭoma in this way) they commence the year as divided into days.

[281] The Ukthya sacrifice should, however, be performed (on the beginning day of the Sattra, not the Agniṣṭoma). (For) the sacrifice is wealth in cattle, the Sattra is (also) wealth in cattle (and cattle is represent-

---

[11] See page 234.

[12] Each of the fifteen Stotra triplets is made to consist of twenty-four verses by repetition, according to the theory of the *Chaturviṁśa Stoma*. 24 times 15 makes 360.

[13] These are, the Bahiṣ-pavamâna, the Pavamâna, and Arbhavapavamâna.

ted by the Ukthya). If all Stotras are put in the Chaturviṁśa Stoma (as is the case when the Ukthya is performed), then this day becomes actually throughout a Chaturviṁśa (twenty-four-fold). Thence the Ukthya sacrifice ought to be performed (on the beginning day of the Sattra).

13.

(On the Importance of the Two Sâmans, Rathantaram and Bṛihat. They are Not to be Used at the Same Time. The Succession of the Sacrificial Days in the Second-Half of the Year is Inverted.)

The two (principal) Sâmans at the Sattra are the Bṛihat and Rathantaram. These are the two boats of the sacrifice, landing it on the other shore (in the celestial world). By means of them, the sacrificers cross the year (just as one crosses a river). Bṛihat and Rathantara are the two feet (of the sacrifice); the performance of the day is the head. By means of the two feet, men gain their fortune (consisting of gold, jewels, &c.) which is to be put (as ornament) on their heads.

Bṛihat and Rathantaram are two wings; the performance of the day is the head. By means of these two wings, they direct their heads to fortune, and dive into it.

Both these Sâmans are not to be let off together. Those performers of the sacrificial session who would do so, would be floating from one shore to the other (without being able to land anywhere), just as a boat, whose cords are cut off, is floating from shore to shore. Should they let off the Rathantaram, then, by means of the Bṛihat, both are kept. Should he let off [282] the Bṛihat, then, by means of the Rathantaram both are kept.[14] (The same is the case with the other Sâma Pṛiṣṭhas.) Vairûpam[15] is

[14] This refers to the so-called *Sâma pṛiṣṭhas, i.e.*, combination of two different Sâmans, in such a way, that one forms the womb (*yoni*), the other the embryo (*garbha*). This relationship of both Sâmans is represented by repeating that set of verses which form the womb in the first and third turns (*paryâyas*) of the Stomas (see 237-38), and that one which is the embryo, in the second turn. In this way, the embryo is symbolically placed in the womb which surrounds it on both sides. The two Sâmans which generally form the womb, are the Bṛihat and Rathantaram. Both are not to be used at the same time; but only one of them. Both being the two ships which land the sacrificer on the other shore (bring him safely through the year in this world), they cannot be sent off at the same time: for the sacrificer would thus deprive himself of his conveyance. One of them is tied to this, the other to the other shore. If he has landed on the other shore, he requires another boat to go back. For, before the end of the year, he cannot establish himself on the other shore, nor, as long as he is alive, on the shore of the celestial world. By going from one shore to the other, and returning to that whence he started, he obtains a fair knowledge of the way, and provides himself with all that is required for being received and admitted on the other shore after the year is over, or the life has terminated.

[15] The Vairûpa Sâma is, *yadyâva indra te śatam* (Sâm. Saṁh. 2, 212-13).

the same as Bṛihat, Vairâja[16] is the same as Bṛihat, Śâkvaram[17] is the same as Rathantaram, and Raivatam[18] is the same as Bṛihat.

Those who, having such a knowledge, begin the Sattra (sacrificial session) on this day, hold their (sacrificial) year in performing austerities, enjoying the Soma draught, and preparing the Soma juice, after having reached the year as divided into half-months, months, and days.

[283] When they (those who hold the Sattra) begin the performance of the other part[19] (of the sacrifice), they lay down their heavy burden, for the heavy burden (if they are not released) breaks them down. Therefore, he who, after having reached this (the central day of the yearly sacrificial session) by means of performing the ceremonies one after the other, begins (the second part of the sacrificial session) by inverting the order of the ceremonies, arrives safely at the end of the year.

14.

(On a Modification of the Niṣkevalya Śastra on the Chaturviṁśa and Mahâvrata Days of the Sattra.

This Chaturviṁśa day is (the same as) the Mahâvrata[20] (the Niṣkevalya Śastra being the same as in the Mahâvrata sacrifice). By means of the Bṛihad-deva hymn,[21] the Hotar pours forth the seed. Thus he makes the seed (which is poured forth) by means of the Mahâvrata day produce offspring. For seed if effused every year is productive (every year). This is the reason that (in both parts of the Sattra) the [284] Bṛihad-deva hymn forms equally part of the Niṣkevalya Śastra.

He who having such a knowledge performs, after having reached the central day by performing the ceremonies one after the other, the

[16] The Vairâja Sâma is, *pibâ somam indra mandatu* (Sâm. Saṁh. 2, 277-79).

[17] The Śâkvara Sâma is, *pro ṣvasmâi puroratham* (Sâm. Saṁh. 2, 9, 1, 14, 1-3).

[18] The Raivata Sâma is, *revatir naḥ sadhamâda* (Sam. Sâṁh. 2, 434-36).

[19] This sense is implied in the words, *ata ûrdhvam*, "beyond this," *i. e.*, beyond the ceremonies commencing on the *ârambhanîya* day of the Sattra. The first six months of the sacrificial session lasting all the year, are the first, the second six months the other turn; in the midst of both is the *Viṣuvan* day (see 4, 18.), *i. e.*, the equator. After that day the same ceremonies begin anew, but in an inverted order; that is to say, what was performed immediately before the Viṣuvan day, that is performed the day after it, &c.

[20] This sacrifice is described in the Araṇyaka of the Ṛigveda. It refers to generation and includes, therefere, some very obscene rites. Its principal Śastra is the *Mahaduktham*, *i. e.*, the great Śastra, also called the Bṛihatî Śastra. The Mahâvrata forms part of a Sattra. It is celebrated on the day previous to the concluding Atirâtra, and has the same position and importance as the Chaturviṁśa day after the beginning Atirâtra. The Bṛihad-deva hymn is required at the Niṣkevalya Śastra of both. But, instead of the Chaturviṁśa Stoma, the Pañchaviṁśa (twenty-five-fold) Stoma is used at the Mahâvrata sacrifice. (See Aitar. Araṇyaka 1, 2.)

[21] This Is, *tad id âsa bhuvaneṣu*, 10, 120.

ceremonies of the second part in an inverted order, using the Bṛihad-deva hymn also, reaches safely the end of the year.

He who knows this shore and that shore of (the stream of) the year, arrives safely on the other shore. The Atirâtra at the beginning (of the Sattra) is this shore (of the year), and the Atirâtra at the end (of the Sattra) is the other shore.

He who has such a knowledge, arrives safely at the end of the year. He who knows how to appropriate the year (according to half-months, months, and days), and how to disentangle himself from it (after having passed through it) arrives safely at the end of the year. The Atirâtra at the beginning is the appropriation, and that at the end is the disentanglement.

He who has such a knowledge, safely reaches the end of the year. He who knows the *prâṇa* (air inhaled) of the year and its *apâna* (air exhaled) safely reaches the end of the year. The Atirâtra at the beginning is its *prâṇa*, and the Atirâtra at the end its *udâna* (*apâna*). He who has such a knowledge, safely reaches the end of the year.

THIRD CHAPTER.

(The Ṣaḷaha and Viṣuvan Day of the Sattras with the Performance of the Days Preceding and Following the Viṣuvan.)

15.

(The Tryaha and Ṣaḷaha, i. e., periods of three and six days at the Sattra. The Abhiplava.)

They (those who hold the sacrificial session) perform **[280]** (now) the *Jyotiṣ-Go* and *Ayuṣ-Stomas*. This world is the *Jyotis* (light), the airy region the *Go* (Stoma), that world *âyus* (life). The same Stomas (as in the first three days out of the six) are observed in the latter three days. (In the first) three days (the order of the stomas is), Jyotiṣ-Go and Ayuṣ Stomas. (In the latter) three days (the order is) Go-Ayuṣ-Jotiṣ-Stomas. (According to the position of the Jyotiṣ Stoma in both parts) the Jyotiṣ is this world and that world; they are the two Jyotiṣ (lights) on both sides facing (one another) in the world.

They perform the *Ṣaḷaha* (six days' Soma sacrifice), so that in both its parts (each consisting of three days) there is the Jyotiṣ Stoma (in the first at the beginning, in the latter at the end). By doing so, they gain a firm footing in both worlds, in this one and that one, and walk in both.

Abhiplava Ṣaḷaha[1] is the revolving wheel of the gods. Two Agniṣ-

---

[1] The Sattra is divided into periods of six days, of which period every month has five. Such a period is called a *Ṣalaha*, *i.e.*, six days' sacrificial work. The five times repetition within a month is *abhiplava*.

ṭomas form the circumference (of this wheel); the four Ukthyas in the midst are then the nave. By means of this revolving (wheel of the gods) one can go to any place one may choose. Thus he who has such a knowledge, safely reaches the end of the year. He who has a (proper) knowledge of the first *Ṣaḷaha* safely reaches the end of the year, and so does he who has a (proper) knowledge of the second, third, fourth, and fifth Ṣaḷahas, *i.e.*, all the five Ṣaḷahas of the month.

16.

(On the Meaning of the Celebration of Five Ṣaḷahas during the Course of a Month.

They celebrate the first Ṣaḷaha. There are six seasons. This makes six days. Thus they secure **[286]** the year (for themselves) as divided into seasons, and gain a firm footing in the several seasons of the year.

They celebrate the second Ṣalaha. This makes (in addition to the previous six days) twelve days. There are twelve months. Thus they secure the year as divided into months, and gain a firm footing in the several months of the year.

They celebrate the third Ṣaḷaha. This makes (in addition to the previous twelve days) eighteen days. This makes twice nine. There are nine vital airs, and nine celestial worlds. Thus they obtain the nine vital airs, and reach the nine celestial worlds, and gaining a firm footing in the vital airs, and the celestial worlds, they walk there.

They celebrate the fourth Ṣaḷaha. This makes twenty-four days. There are twenty-four half-months. Thus they secure the year as divided into half-months, and, gaining a firm footing in its several half-months, they walk in them.

They celebrate the fifth Ṣaḷaha. This makes thirty days. The Virâṭ metre has thirty syllables. The Virâṭ is food. Thus they procure *virâṭ* (food) in every month.

Those who wished for food, were (once) holding a sacrificial session. By obtaining in every month the Virâṭ (the number thirty), they become possessed of food for both worlds, this one and that one.

17.

(Story of the Sacrificial Session held by the Cows. Different kinds of the great Sattras, such as the Gavâm Ayanam, Âdityânâm Ayanam, and Aṅgirasâm Ayanam).

They hold the *Gavâm Ayanam*, *i.e.*, the sacrificial session, called "cow's walk." The cows are the **[287]** Âdityas (gods of the months). By holding the session called the "cow's walk," they also hold the walk of the Âdityas.

The cows being desirous of obtaining hoofs and horns, held (once) a sacrificial session. In the tenth month (of their sacrifice) they obtained hoofs and horns. They said, " We have obtained fulfilment of that wish for which we underwent the initiation into the sacrificial rites. Let us rise (the sacrifice being finished)." When they arose they had horns. They, however, thought, " let us finish the year," and recommenced the session. On account of their distrust, their horns went off, and they consequently became hornless (*tûpara*). They (continuing their sacrificial session) produced vigour (*ûrj*). Thence after (having been sacrificing for twelve months and) having secured all the seasons, they rose (again) at the end. For they had produced the vigour (to reproduce horns, hoofs, &c., when decaying). Thus the cows made themselves beloved by all (the whole world), and are beautified (decorated) by all.[2]

He who has such a knowledge, makes himself beloved by every one, and is decorated by every one.

The Âdityas and Aṅgiras were jealous of one another as to who should (first) enter the celestial world, each party saying, " we shall first enter." The Âdityas entered first the celestial world, then the Aṅgiras, after (they had been waiting for) sixty years.

(The performance of the sacrificial session called Âdityânâm ayanam agrees in several respects with the Gavâm ayanam). There is an Atirâtra at the beginning, and on the Chaturvimśa day the Ukthya is [**288**] performed ; all the (five) Abhiplava Ṣaḷahas[3] are comprised in it ; the order of the days is different, (that is to, say, the performance of the first, second days, &c., of the Abhiplava are different from those of the Gavâm ayanam). This is the Âdityânâm ayanam.

The Atirâtra at the beginning, the Ukthya on the Chaturviṁśa day, all (five) Abhiplava performed with the Pṛiṣṭhas, the performance of the ceremonies of the several days (of the Abhiplava) being different (from the Gavâm ayanam, &c.): this is the Aṅgirasâm ayanam.

The Abhiplava Ṣaḷaha is like the royal road, the smooth way to heaven. The Pṛiṣṭhya Ṣaḷaha is the great pathway which is to be

---

[2] It is an Indian custom preserved up to this day to decorate cows, chiefly on the birth-day of Kṛiṣṇa (Gokul aṣṭamî).

[3] In the Gavâm ayanam there are only four Abhiplava Ṣalahas ; but in the Âdityânâm ayanam there are all five Abhiplava Ṣalahas required within a month. The last (fifth) Ṣalaha of the Gavâm ayanam is a *Pṛiṣṭhya*, that is, one containing the Pṛiṣṭhas. The difference between an *Abhiplava Ṣalaha*, and a *Pṛiṣṭhya Ṣalaha*, is, that during the latter, the Sâma Pṛiṣṭhas is required, that is to say, that on every day at the midday libation the Stomas are made with a combination of two different Sâmans in the way described above (page 282), whilst this is wanting in the Abhiplava.

trodden everywhere to heaven. When they avail themselves of both roads, they will not suffer any injury, and obtain the fulfilment of all desires which are attainable by both, the Abhiplava Ṣaḷaha and the Pṛiṣṭhya Ṣaḷaha.[4]

18.

(*The Ekaviṁsa or Viṣuvan Day.*)

They perform the ceremonies of the Ekaviṁśa day, which is the equator, dividing the year (into two equal parts). By means of the performance of this day, the gods had raised the sun up to the heavens. This Ekaviṁśa day on which the Divâkîrtya mantra **[289]** (was produced), is preceded by ten days, [5] and followed by ten such days, and is in the midst (of both periods). On both sides, it is thus put in a Virâṭ (the number ten). Being thus put in a Virâṭ (in the number ten) on both sides, this (Ekaviṁśa, *i.e.*, the sun) becomes not disturbed in his course through these worlds.

The gods being afraid of the sun falling from the sky, supported him by placing beneath three celestial worlds to serve as a prop. The (three) Stomas [6] (used at the three Svarasâman days which precede the Viṣuvan day) are the three celestial worlds. They were afraid, lest he (the sun) should fall beyond them. They then placed over him three worlds (also), in order to give him a prop from above. The (three) Stomas (used at the three Svarasâman days which follow the Viṣuvan day) are the three worlds. Thus there are before (the Viṣuvan day) three seventeen-fold Stomas (one on each of the preceding Svarasâman days), and after it (also), three seventeen-fold Stomas. In the midst of them there is the Ekaviṁśa day (representing the sun) held on both sides by the Svarasâman days. On account of his being held by the three Svarasâmans (representing the three worlds below and the three above the sun) the sun is not disturbed in his course through these worlds.

The gods being afraid of the sun falling down from the sky, supported him by placing beneath the highest worlds. The Stomas are the highest worlds.

The gods being afraid of his falling beyond them being turned

---

[4] In the Gavâm ayanam, both the Abhiplava Ṣalaha and the Pṛiṣṭhya Ṣalaha are required. Thence the sacrificers who perform the Gavâm ayanam, avail themselves of both the roads leading to heaven.

[5] The ten days which precede the Ekaviṁśa are, the three *Svarasâmânaḥ*, *Abhijit*, and a *Ṣalaha* (a period of six days). The same days follow, but so, that Svarasâmânaḥ, which were the last three days before the Ekaviṁśa, are the first three days after that day, &c.

[6] On Stomas, see the note to 3, 42.

upside down, supported him by **[290]** placing above him the highest worlds (also). The Stomas are the highest worlds.

Now there are (as already mentioned) three seventeen-fold Stomas before, and three after (the Viṣuvan day). If two of them are taken together, three thirty-four-fold Stomas are obtained. Among the Stomas the thirty-four-fold is the last.[7]

The sun being placed among these (highest worlds) as their ruler, burns with (his rays). Owing to this position, he is superior to everything in creation that has been and will be, and shines beyond all that is in creation. (In the same way, this Viṣuvan day) is superior (to all days which precede or follow).

It is on account of his being prominent as an ornament, that the man who has such a knowledge, becomes superior (to all other men).

19.

(The Svarasâmans. Abhijit. Viśvajit. Viṣuvan.)[8]

They perform the ceremonies of the Svarasâman days. These (three) worlds are the Svarasâman days. On account of the sacrificers pleasing these worlds by means of the Svarasâmans, they are called Svarasâman (from *asprinvan*,[9] they made pleased).

By means of the performance of the Svarasâman days, they make him (the sun) participate in these worlds.

[291] The gods were afraid lest these seventeen-fold Stomas (employed at the Svarasâman days) might, on account of their being all the same, and not protected by being covered (with other Stomas), break down. Wishing that they should not slip down, they surrounded them, below with all the Stomas, and above with all the Pṛiṣṭhas. That is the reason that on the *Abhijit* day which precedes (the Svarasâman days) all Stomas are employed, and on the Viśvajit day which follows (the Svarasâman days after the Viṣuvan day is over) all Pṛiṣṭhas are used. These (Stomas and Pṛiṣṭhas) surround the seventeen-fold Stomas (of the Svarasâman days), in order to keep them (in their proper place) and to prevent them from breaking down.

---

[7] This is not quite correct. There is a forty-eight-fold Stoma, besides.

[8] See the Âśval. Śr. S. 8, 5-7.

[9] This etymology is certainly fanciful ; *Svara* cannot be traced to the root *sprin*, a modification of *prî*, to love. The name literally means, "The Sâmans of the tones." This appears to refer to some peculiarities in their intonations. These Sâmans being required only for the great Sattras, which have been out of use for at least a thousand years, it is difficult now to ascertain the exact nature of the recital of these Sâmans.

(*The Performance of the Viṣuvan Day.*)[10]

The gods were (again) afraid of the sun falling from the sky. They pulled him up and tied him with five ropes.[11] The ropes are the Divâkîrtya Sâmans,[12] among which there is the Mahâdivâkîrtya Pṛiṣṭha;[13] the others are, the Vikarṇa, the Brahma, the Bhâsa,[14] and the Agniṣṭoma[15] Sâma; **[292]** the Bṛihat and Rathantara Śâmans are required for the two Pavamâna Stotras (the Pavamâna at the midday, and the Arbhava-pavamâna at the evening, libations).

Thus they pulled up the sun, tying him with five cords,[16] in order to keep him and to prevent him from falling.

(On this day, the Viṣuvan) he ought to repeat the Prâtaranuvâka after the sun has risen; for only thus all prayers and recitations belonging to this particular day become repeated during the day-time (the day thus becomes *divâkîrtyam*).

As the sacrificial animal belonging to the Soma libation (of that day) and being dedicated to the sun, they ought to kill such an one as might be found to be quite white (without any speck of another colour). For this day is (a festival) for the sun.

He ought to repeat twenty-one Sâmidhenî verses (instead of fifteen or seventeen, as is the case at other occasions); for this day is actually the twenty-first (being provided with the twenty-one-fold Stoma).

---

[10] See the Âśval. Śr. S. 8, 6.

[11] The term is *raśmi*, ray, which Sây. explains by *parigraha*.

[12] Sây. explains the words by: दिवैव पटनियानि पंच नामानि *i.e.*, the five Sâmans which are to be repeated only at day. This explanation may appear at first somewhat strange, but it is quite correct. For the employment of the different tunes is regulated by the different parts of the day. Up to this time, certain tunes (*râga*, the word *sâman* being only the older denomination for the same thing) are allowed to be chanted only at day, such as the *Sâranga*, *Gaurasâranga*, &c., others are confined to the early morning, others to the night.

[13] This is the triplet *vibhraḍ bṛihat pibatu* (Sâm. Saṁh. 2, 802-804).

[14] The Vikarṇam Sâma is, *pṛikṣasya vṛiṣṇo* (6, 8, 1). The same verse is used, according to Sây., for the Brahma, as well as for the Bhâsa, Sâmans.

[15] The Agniṣṭoma Sâma is not especially mentioned by Sây. He simply says in the same manner in which the Pandits up to this day explain such things: येन साम्नाग्निष्टोमसंस्था समाप्यते तदग्निष्टोमसाम Now the Sâman with which the Agniṣṭoma becomes completed, *i.e.*, the last of the twelve Stotras is the so-called Yajñâ Yajñîya Sâman; *yajñâ yajñâ vo agnaye* (Sâm. Saṁ. 2, 53-54). This one is expressly called (in the Sâma prayogas) the *Agniṣṭoma-sâma*, being the characteristic Sâman of the Agniṣṭoma.

[16] The five tunes or Sâmans representing the five cords are, the Mahâdivâkîrtyam, the Vikarṇa, Brahma, and Bhâsa tunes, being regarded only as one on account of their containing the same verse; the Agniṣṭoma Sâma, and the Bṛihat, and Rathantaram.

After having repeated fifty-one or fifty-two verses [17] of the Śastra (of this day), he puts the Nivid (addressed **[293]** to Indra) in the midst (of the hymn *indrasya nu vîryâni*, 1, 32). After this (the repetition of the Nivid) he recites as many verses (as he had recited before putting the Nivid, *i. e.*, fifty-one or fifty-two). (In this way the total number of verses is brought to above a hundred.) The full life of man is a hundred years; he has (also) a hundred powers and a hundred senses. (By thus repeating above a hundred verses) the Hotar thus puts the sacrificer in (the possession of his full) life, strength, and senses.

20.

(The Haṁsavati Verse or the Târkṣya Triplet to be Repeated in the Dûrohaṇa way. Explanation of both the Haṁsavatî and Târkṣya.)

He repeats the Dûrohaṇam as if he were ascending (a height). For the heaven-world is difficult to ascend (*dûrohaṇam*). He who has such a knowledge ascends to the celestial world.

As regards the word *dûrohaṇam*, that one who there burns (the sun) has a difficult passage up (to his place) as well as any one who goes there (*i. e.*, the sacrificer who aspires after heaven).

By repeating the Dûrohaṇam, he thus ascends to him (the sun).

He ascends with a verse addressed to the *haṁsa* (with a *haṁsavatî*.)[18] (The several terms of the **[294]** *haṁ savatî* are now explained). This (Âditya, the sun) is "the swan sitting in light." He is the "Vasu (shining being) sitting in the air." He is the "Hotar sitting on the Vedi."

---

[17] The number fifty-one or fifty-two depends on the circumstance that of the Nivid hymn, *indrasya nu vîryâṇi*, either eight or nine verses might be recited before the insertion of the Nivid. The rule is that at the midday libation the Nivid should be inserted after the first half of the hymn has been exceeded by about one verse. The song in question has fifteen verses. The insertion can, therefore, not take place before the eighth, and not after the ninth.

[18] This verse forms the Dûrohaṇa mantra. Its repetition is described by Âśval. Śr. S. 8, 2, in the followin way :

आहूय दूरोहणं रोहेद्धंसः शूचिषदिति पच्छोऽर्धर्चशस्त्रिपद्याचतुर्थमनवानमुक्त्वा प्रणुत्यावस्येत्पुनस्त्रिपद्यार्धर्चशः पच्छ एव सप्तममेतद्दूरोहणं; *i. e.*, after having called śomsâvom, he should repeat the verse *haṁsaḥ śuchîṣad* (4, 40, 5) in the Dúrohaṇa way first by padas, then by half verses, then taking three padas together, and, finally, the whole verse without stopping, and conclude (this first repetition) with the syllable *om*. Then he ought to repeat it again, commencing with three padas taken together, then by half verses (and ultimately) by padas, which makes the seventh repetition (of the same verse). This is the Dûrohaṇam. See Ait. Br. 4, 21. The Maitrâvaruṇa has it to repeat always on the sixth day of the Abhiplava Ṣalaĥas. On the Viṣuvan day it is repeated by the Hotar. The *haṁsavatî* forms part of a hymn addressed to *Dadhikrâvan*, which is a name of the sun; *haṁsa*, *i. e.*, swan, is another metaphorical expression for "sun."

He is the "guest sitting in the house." He is "sitting among men." He "sits in the most excellent place" (*varasad*), for that place, in which sitting, he burns, is the most excellent of seats. He is "sitting in truth" (*ṛitasad*). He is "sitting in the sky" (*vyomasad*), for the sky is among the places that one where sitting he burns. He is "born from the waters" (*abjâ*), for in the morning he comes out of the waters, and in the evening he enters the waters. He is "born from cows" (*gojâ*). He is "born from truth." He is "born from the mountain" (he appears on a mountain, as it were, when rising). He is "truth" (*ṛitam*).

He (the sun) is all these (forms). Among the metres (sacred verses) this (*haṁsavatî* verse) is, as it were, his most expressive and clearest form. Thence the Hotar should, wherever he makes the Dûrohaṇam, make it with the Haṁsavatî verse.

He who desires heaven, should, however, make it with the Târkṣya verse (10, 178, 1). For Târkṣya showed the way to the Gâyatrî when she, in the form of an eagle, abstracted the Soma (from heaven). When he thus uses the Târkṣya (for [**295**] making the Dûrohaṇam), he does just the same as if he were to appoint one who knows the fields as his guide (when travelling anywhere). The Târkṣya [19] is that one who blows (*i. e.*, the wind), thus carrying one up to the celestial world.

The Târkṣya hymn is as follows :)—(1) "Let us call hither to (our) "safety the Târkṣya, that horse instigated by the gods, (the horse) which "is enduring, makes pass the carriages (without any impediment), which "keeps unbroken the spokes of the carriage wheel, which is fierce in battle "and swift."

He (the Târkṣya) is the horse (*vâjî*) instigated by the gods. He is enduring, makes pass the carriage (without any impediment); for he crosses the way through these worlds in an instant. He keeps the spokes of the carriage wheel unbroken, conquers in battle (*pṛitanâja* being explained by *pṛitanâjit*). By the words, "to (our) safety," the Hotar asks for safety. By the words, "let us call hither the Târkṣya," he thus calls him.

(2) "Offering repeatedly gifts (to the Târkṣya) as if they were for "Indra, let us for (our) safety embark in the ship (represented by the "Dûrohaṇam) as it were. (May) the earth (be) wide (to allow us free "passage). May we not be hurt when going (our way) through you two "(heaven and earth) who are great and deep (like an ocean)."

---

[19] It is often identified with the *Garuḍa*, *i. e.*, the celestial eagle. According to Naigh. 1, 14, it means "horse." Whether it is a personification of the sun, as is assumed in the Saṁskṛit Dictionary of Boehtlingk and Roth, iii, page 310, is very doubtful to me

By the words, "for safety," he asks for safety. By the words, "let us embark in the ship," he thus mounts him (the Târkṣya), in order to reach the heavenly world, to enjoy it and to join (the celestial **[296]** inhabitants). By the words, "(may) the earth (be) wide, may we not be hurt," &c., the Hotar prays for a (safe) passage and (a safe) return.[20]

(3) "He (the Târkṣya) passes in an instant by dint of his strength "through the regions of all five tribes (*i. e.*, the whole earth), just as the sun "extends the waters (in an instant) by its light. The speed of him (the "Târkṣya) who grants a thousand, who grants a hundred, gifts, is as irre-"sistible as that of a fresh arrow."

By the word, *sûrya*, he praises the sun openly. By the words, "the speed of him," &c., he asks for a blessing for himself and the sacrificers.

21.

(*On the Way of Repeating the Dûrohaṇam.*)

After having called *soṁsâvom*, he makes the Dûrohaṇam (representing the ascent to heaven). The celestial world is the Dûrohaṇam (for it is to ascend). Speech is the call *soṁsâvom* ; (Brahma is Speech). By thus calling *soṁsâvom*, he ascends through the Brahma, which is this call, to the celestial world. The first time he makes his ascent by stopping after every pada (of the Dûrohaṇa mantra). Thus he reaches this world (the earth). Then he stops after every half verse. Thus he reaches the airy region. Then he stops after having taken together three padas. Thus he reaches that world. Then he repeats the whole verse without stopping. Thus he gains a footing in him (the sun) who there burns.

(After having thus ascended) he descends by stopping after three padas, just as one (in this world) holds the branch of the tree (in his hand when **[297]** descending from it). By doing so, he gains a firm footing in that world. By then stopping after each half verse, he gains a firm footing in the airy region, (and by stopping) after each pada (he gains a firm footing) in this world (again). After having thus reached the celestial world, the sacrificers obtain thus a footing (again) in this world.[21]

For those who aspire only after (a footing) in one (world), that is,

---

[20] **श्राच पराच मेष्यन्** are explained by Sây. as **आगमिष्यन्** and **पुनरपि परावृत्य गमिष्यन्**.

[21] One has to bear in mind that the sacrificer does not wish to reside permanently in heaven before the expiration of his full life-term, *viz.*, one hundred years. But by means of certain sacrifices he can secure for himself, even when still alive, lodgings in heaven, to be taken up by him after death. He must already, when alive, mystically ascend to heaven, to gain a footing there, and to be registered as a future inhabitant of the celestial world. After having accomplished his end, he descends again to the earth. His ascent and descent are dramatically represented by the peculiar way in which the Dûrohaṇa mantra is repeated.

after heaven, the Hotar ought to repeat (the Dûrohaṇam) without making the descent (in the way described, by stopping first after three padas, &c.) They (thus) conquer only the celestial world, but they cannot stay long, as it were, in this world.

Hymns in the Triṣṭubh and Jagatî metre are mixed to represent a pair. For cattle are a pair; metres are cattle. (This is done) for obtaining cattle.

22.

(To What the Viṣuvan Day is like. Whether or not the Śastras of the Viṣuvan Day are to be Repeated on other Days during the Sattra also. On the Merit of Performing the Viṣuvan Day. On this Day an Ox is to be Immolated for Viśvakarma.)

The Viṣuvan day is like a man. Its first half is like the right half (of a man) and its latter half like the left half. This is the reason that it (the performance **[298]** of the six months' ceremonies following the Viṣuvan day) is called the "latter" (half).

The Viṣuvan day is (just as) the head of a man whose both sides are equal.[22] Man is, as it were, composed of fragments (*bidala*). That is the reason that even here a suture is found in the midst of the head.

They say, He ought to repeat (the recitation for) this day only on the Viṣuvan day.[23] Among the Śastras this one is Viṣuvan. This Śastra (called) Viṣuvan is the equator (*viṣuvan*). (By doing so) the sacrificers become *viṣuvat* (*i.e.*, standing like the head above both sides of the body) and attain to leadership.

But this opinion is not to be attended to. He ought to repeat it (also) during the year (the Sattra is lasting). For this Śastra is seed. By doing so, the sacrificers keep their seed (are not deprived of it) during the year.

For the seeds produced before the lapse of a year which have required (for their growth) five or six months, go off (have no productive power). The sacrificers will not enjoy them (the fruits which were expected to come from them). But they enjoy (the fruits of) those seeds which are produced after ten months or a year.

---

[22] The term in the original is *pràbâhuk*, which appears to mean, literally, measured by the length of arms (which both are equal). Sây. explains it in the following way:

प्रवाहुक् सतो वामदक्षिणभागौ समौ कृत्वाऽवस्थितस्य शिरो यथोन्नतं सन्मध्येऽवतिष्ठते.

[23] That is to say, the performance of the Viṣuvan day must be distinguished from that of all other days of the Sattra. The Mahâdivâkîrtyam Sâman, the Dûrohaṇam, &c, ought to be peculiar to it. *Ahas* here clearly means "the performance of the ceremonies," or more especially the "Śastras required for the Soma day."

[24] This is implied in the term (उपावभेरन्) *upa*, meaning, "in addition."

[299] Therefore, the Hotar ought to repeat the (Śastra for the) Viṣuvan day during the year (also). For this day's Śastra is the year. Those who observe this day's performance (during the year) obtain the (enjoyment of the) year.

The sacrificer destroys, by means of the Viṣuvan day's performance, during the year, all consequences of guilt (*pâpman*).

By means of (the performance of the Sattra ceremonies in) the months (during which the Sattra is lasting), he removes the consequences of guilt from his limbs (the months being the limbs of the year). By means of the Viṣuvan day's performance during the year he removes the consequences of guilt from the head (the Viṣuvan being the head). He who has such a knowledge removes, by means of the Viṣuvan day's performance, the consequences of guilt.

They ought (on the Mahâvrata day) to kill for the libations an ox for Viśvakarman (Tvaṣṭar), in addition (to the regular animal, a goat, required for that occasion); it should be of two colours, on both sides.

Indra, after having slain Vṛitra, became Viśvakarman. Prajâpati, after having produced the creatures, became (also) Viśvakarman. The year is Viśvakarman.[25] Thus (by sacrificing such a bullock) they reach Indra, their own Self, Prajâpati, the year, Viśvakarman (*i.e.*, they remain united with them, they will not die), and thus they obtain a footing in Indra, in their own Self (their prototype), in Prajâpati, in the year, in Viśvakarman. He who has such a knowledge, obtains a firm footing.

---

[300] FOURTH CHAPTER.

(*The Dvâdaśâha Sacrifice. Its Origin, and General Rules for its Performance. The Initiatory Rites.*)

23.

(*Origin of the Dvâdaśâha. Its Gâyatrî Form.*)

Prajâpati felt a desire to create and to multiply himself. He underwent (in order to accomplish this end) austerities. After having done so, he perceived the Dvâdaśâha sacrifice (ceremonies to be) in his limbs and vital airs. He took it out of his limbs and vital airs, and made it twelvefold. He seized it and sacrificed with it. Thence he (Prajâpati) was produced (*i.e.*, that form of his which enters creatures, his material body). Thus he was reproduced through himself in offspring and cattle. He who

---

[25] *Viśvakarman* means "who does all work." Generally, the architect of the gods is meant by the term.

has such a knowledge, is reproduced through himself in offspring and cattle.

Having the desire to obtain, through the Gâyatrî, throughout the Dvâdaśâha everywhere, the enjoyment of all things, (he meditated) how (this might be achieved.)

(It was done in the following way.) The Gâyatrî was at the beginning of the Dvâdaśâha in (the form of) splendour, in the midst of it, in (that of the) metre, at its end in (that of) syllables. Having penetrated with the Gâyatrî the Dvâdaśâha everywhere, he obtained the enjoyment of everything.

He who knows the Gâyatrî as having wings, eyes, light, and lustre, goes by means of her, being possessed of these things, to the celestial world.

The Dvâdaśâha (sacrifice) is the Gâyatrî with wings, eyes, light, and lustre. The two wings (of the Dvâdaśâha) are the two Atirâtras which are at the beginning and end of it (lit., *round about*). The two Agniṣṭomas (within the two Atirâtras) are the two **[301]** eyes. The eight Ukthya days (between the Atirâtra and Agniṣṭoma at the beginning, and the Agniṣṭoma and Atirâtra at the end) are the soul.

He who has such a knowledge, goes to heaven by means of the wings, the eyes, the light, and lustre of the Gâyatrî.

24.

(On the Different Parts, and the Duration of the Dvâdaśâha Sacrifice. On the Bṛihatî Nature of this Sacrifice. The Nature of the Bṛihatî.)

The Dvâdaśâha consists of three Tryahas (a sacrificial performance lasting for three days) together with the "tenth day" and the two Atirâtras. After having undergone the Dîkṣâ ceremony (the initiation) during twelve days, one becomes fit for performing (this) sacrifice. During twelve nights he undergoes the Upasads[1] (fasting). By means of them, he shakes off (all guilt) from his body.

He who has such a knowledge, becomes purified and clean, and enters the deities, after having during (these) twelve days been born anew and shaken off (all guilt) from his body.

The Dvâdaśâha consists (on the whole) of thirty-six days. The Bṛihatî has thirty-six syllables. The Dvâdaśâha is the sphere for the Bṛihatî (in which she is moving). By means of the Bṛihatî, the gods

[1] He keeps the fasting connected with the Upasad ceremony. At this occasion he must live on milk alone. The Upasads are, at the Dvâdaśâha, performed during four days, on each day thrice, that makes twelve. See about them 1, 25.

obtained (all) these worlds; for by ten syllables they reached this world (the earth), by (other) ten they reached the air, by (other) ten the sky, by four they reached the four directions, and by two they gained a firm footing in this world.

[302] He who has such a knowledge, secures a firm footing (for himself).

About this they (the theologians) ask, How is it, that this (particular metre of thirty-six syllables) is called Bṛihatî, *i.e.*, the great one, there being other metres which are stronger, and exceed the (Bṛihatî) in number of syllables? (The answer is) It is called so on account of the gods having reached by means of it (all) these worlds, by ten syllables, this world (the earth), &c. He who has such a knowledge, obtains anything he might desire.

25.

(*Prajâpati Instituted the Dvâdaśâha. The Nature of this Sacrifice. By Whom it should be Performed.*)

The Dvâdaśâha is Prajâpati's sacrifice. At the beginning, Prajâpati sacrificed with it. He said to the Seasons and Months, "Make me sacrifice with the Dvâdaśâha (*i.e.*, initiate me for this sacrifice)."

After having performed on him the Dîkṣâ ceremony, and prevented him from leaving (when walking in the sacrificial compound) they said to him, "Now give us (first something), then we shall make the sacrifice." He granted them food, and juice (milk, &c.). Just this juice is put in the Seasons and Months.

When he granted them that, then they made him sacrifice. This is the reason that only the man who can afford to give something is fit for performing this sacrifice.

When receiving his gifts, they (the Seasons and Months) made him (Prajâpati) sacrifice. Thence must he who receives gifts, sacrifice for another. Thus both parties succeed those who, having such a knowledge, bring sacrifices for others, as well as those who have them performed for themselves.

[303] The Seasons and Months felt themselves burdened, as it were (with guilt), for having accepted at the Dvâdaśâha (which they performed for Prajâpati) a reward. They said to Prajâpati, "Make us (also) sacrifice with the Dvâdaśâha." He consented and said to them, "Become ye initiated (take the Dîkṣâ)!" The deities residing in the first (the so-called bright) half of the months first underwent the Dîkṣâ ceremony, and thus removed the consequences of guilt. Thence they are in the daylight as it were; for those who have their guilt (really) removed, are in the daylight, as it were (may appear everywhere).

The deities residing in the second half (of the months) afterwards underwent the Dîkṣâ. But they (could) not wholly remove the evil consequences of guilt. Thence they are darkness, as it were; for those who have their guilt not removed are darkness, as it were (comparable to it).

Thence he who has this knowledge ought to have performed his Dîkṣâ first and in the first half (of the month). He who has such a knowledge, thus removes (all) guilt from himself.

It was Prajâpati who, as the year, resided in the year, the seasons, and months. The seasons and months thus resided (also) in Prajâpati as the year. Thus they mutually reside in one another. He who has the Dvâdaśâha performed for himself resides in the priest (who performs it for him). Thence they (the priests) say, "No sinner is fit for having the Dvâdaśâha sacrifice performed, nor should such an one reside in me."

The Dvâdaśâha is the sacrifice for the first-born. He who first had the Dvâdaśâha performed (became) the first-born among the gods. It is the sacrifice for a leader (a *śreṣṭha*). He who first performed it (became) the leader among the gods. The first-born, [304] the leader (of his family or tribe) ought to perform it (alone); then happiness lasts (all the year) in this (the place where it is performed).

(They say) "No sinner ought to have the Dvâdaśâha sacrifice performed; no such one should reside in me (the priest)."

The gods (once upon a time) did not acknowledge that Indra had the right of primogeniture and leadership. He said to Bṛihaspati, "Bring for me the Dvâdaśâha sacrifice." He complied with his wish. Thereupon the gods acknowledged Indra's right of primogeniture and leadership.

He who has such a knowledge, is acknowledged as the first-born and leader. All his relations agree as (to his right) to the leadership.

The first three (Soma) days (of the Dvâdaśâha) are ascending (*i.e.*, the metres required are from the morning to the evening libation increasing in number); the middle three (Soma) days are crossed, (*i. e.*, there is no regular order of increase nor decrease in the number of syllables of the metres); the last three (Soma) days are descending (*i.e.*, the number of syllables of the metres from the morning to the evening libations is decreasing).[2]

---

[2] Here are the nine principal days of the Dvâdaśâha sacrifice mentioned. They constitute the *Navarâtra*, *i.e.*, sacrifice lasting for nine nights (and days). It consists of

On account of the (metres of the) first three days (*tryaha*) being ascending, the fire blazes up, for the upward region belongs to the fire. On account of the (metres of the) middle three days being crossed, the wind blows across; the wind moves across (the other [305] regions), and the waters flow (also) across; for the region which is across (the others) belongs to the wind. On account of (the metres of) the three last days being descending, that one (the sun) burns downwards (sending his rays down), the rain falls down, (and) the constellations (in heaven) send (their light) down. For the region which goes down belongs to the sun.

The three worlds belong together, so do these three Tryahas. These (three) worlds jointly shine to the fortune of him who has such a knowledge.

26.

(*When the Dîkṣâ for the Dvâdaśâha is to be Performed. The Animal for Prajâpati. Jamadagni Sâmidhenî verses required. The Puroḍâsa for Vâyu. On Some Peculiar Rite when the Dvâdaśâha is Performed as a Sattra.*)

The Dîkṣâ went away from the gods. They made it enter the two months of spring, and joined it to it; but they did not get it out (of these months for using it). They then made it subsequently enter the two hot months, the two rainy months, the two months of autumn, and the two winter months, and joined it to them. They did not get it out of the two winter months. They then joined it to the two months of the dewy season (Śiśira); they (finally) got it out of these (two months for using it).

He who has such a knowledge, reaches any one he wishes to reach, but his enemy will not reach *him*.

Thence the sacrificer who wishes that the Dîkṣâ for a sacrificial session[3] should come (by itself) to him, should have the Dîkṣâ rites performed on himself [306] during the two months of the dewy season. Thus he takes his Dîkṣâ when the Dîkṣâ herself is present, and receives her in person.

(The reason that he should take his Dîkṣâ during the two months

---

three *Tryahas*, *i.e.*, three days' performance of the Soma sacrifice. The order of metres on the first three days is, at the morning libation, Gâyatrî (twenty-four syllables); at the midday libation, Triṣṭubh (forty-four syllables); at the evening libation, Jagatî (forty-eight syllables). On the middle three days the order of metres is, Jagatî, Gâyatrî, and Triṣṭubh, and on the last three days, Triṣṭubh, Jagatî, and Gâyatrî.

3 The Dvâdaśâha is regarded as a *Sattra* or session. The initiation for the performance of a Sattra is a Sattra dîkṣâ.

of the dewy season is) because both tame and wild animals are, in these two months (for want of green fodder), very thin and show only bones, and present in this state the most vivid image of the Dîkṣâ (the aim of which ceremony is to make the sacrificer lean by fasting).

Before he takes his Dîkṣâ, he sacrifices an animal for Prajâpati. For (the immolation of) this (animal) he ought to repeat seventeen Sâmidhenî[4] verses. For Prajâpati is seventeen-fold. (This is done) for reaching Prajâpati. Aprî verses which come from Jamadagni are (required) for (the immolation of) this animal. About this they say, Since at (all) other animal sacrifices only such Aprî verses are chosen as are traceable to the Ṛiṣi ancestors (of the sacrificer), why are at this (Prajâpati sacrifice) only Jamadagni verses to be used by all? (The reason is) The Jamadagni verses have a universal character, and make successful in everything. This (Prajâpati) animal is of a universal character, and makes successful in everything. The reason that they use (at that occasion) Jamadagni verses, is to secure all forms, and to be successful in everything.

The Puroḍâśa belonging to this animal is Vâyu's. About this they ask, Why does the Puroḍâśa, which forms part of the animal sacrifice, belong to Vâyu, whilst the animal itself belongs to another deity (Prajâpati)? (To this objection) one ought to reply, Prajâpati is the sacrifice; (that Puroḍâśa is given to Vâyu) in order to have the sacrifice performed without any mistake. Though this **[307]** Puroḍâśa belongs to Vâyu, it is not withheld from Prajâpati. For Vâyu is Prajâpati. This has been said by a Ṛiṣi in the words, *pavamânaḥ prajâpatiḥ* (9, 5, 9), *i.e.*, Prajâpati who blows.

If the Dvâdaśâha be (performed as) a Sattra, then the sacrificers[5] should put all their several fires together, and sacrifice in them. All should take the Dîkṣâ, and all should prepare the Soma juice.

He concludes (this sacrifice) in spring. For spring is sap. By doing so, he ends (his sacrifice) with (the obtaining of) food (resulting from the sap of spring).

27.

(The Rivalry of the Metres. The Separation of Heaven and Earth. They Contract a Marriage. The Sâma Forms in which they are Wedded to one another. On the Black Spot in the Moon. On Poṣa and Ûṣa.)

Each of the metres (Gâyatrî, Triṣṭubh, and Jagatî) tried to occupy

---

[4] See 1, 1.

[5] At a Sattra or sacrificial session all the sixteen priests in their turn become sacrificers. They perform the ceremonies for one another.

the place of another metre. Gâyatrî aspired after the place of Triṣṭubh and Jagatî, Triṣṭubh after that of Gâyatrî and Jagatî, and Jagatî after that of Gâyatrî and Triṣṭubh.

Thereupon Prajâpatî saw this Dvâdaśâha with metres being removed from their proper places (*vyûḷhachhandasa*). He took it and sacrificed with it. In this way, he made the metres obtain (fulfilment of) all their desires. He who has such a knowledge, obtains (fulfilment of) all desires.

The Hotar removes the metres from their proper places, in order that the sacrifice should not lose its essence.

This circumstance that the Hotar changes the proper place of the metres has its analogy in the fact **[308]** that (great) people when travelling (to a distant place) yoke to their carriages, at every stage, fresh horses or oxen which are not fatigued. Just in the same way, the sacrificers travel to the celestial world by employing at every stage fresh metres (representing the horses or oxen) which are not fatigued. (This results) from changing the places of the metres.

These two worlds (heaven and earth) were (once) joined. (Subsequently) they separated. (After their separation) there fell neither rain, nor was there sunshine. The five classes of beings (gods, men, &c.) then did not keep peace with one another. (Thereupon) the gods brought about a reconciliation of both these worlds. Both contracted with one another a marriage, according to the rites observed by the gods.

In the form of the Rathantara Sâman, this earth is wedded to heaven; and in the form of the Bṛihat Sâman, heaven is wedded to the earth. (And again) in the form of the Naudhasa Sâman, the earth is wedded to heaven; and in the form of the Śyâita Sâman, heaven is wedded to the earth.

In the form of smoke, this earth is wedded to heaven; in the form of rain, heaven is wedded to the earth.

The earth put a place fit for offering sacrifices to the gods into heaven. Heaven (then) put cattle on the earth.

The place fit for offering sacrifices to the gods which the earth put in heaven is that black spot in the moon.

This is the reason that they perform their sacrifice in those half months in which the moon is waxing and full (for only then that black spot is visible); for they only wish to obtain that (black spot).

Heaven (put) on the earth herbs for pasturage. About them Tura, the son of Kavaṣa, said: O Janamejaya, what is (to be understood by the words) **[309]** *poṣa* (fodder) and *ûṣa* (herbs of pasturage)? This is the reason that those who care for what proceeds from the cow (such as milk, &c.)

put the question (when sending a cow to a pasturage), are there ûṣâs, *i.e.*, herbs of pasturage? For *ûṣa* is fodder.

That world turned towards this world, surrounding it. Thence heaven and earth were produced. Neither came heaven from the air, nor the earth from the air.

28.

(On the Sâma Pṛiṣṭhas.) [6]

At the beginning, there were Bṛihat and Rathantaram; through them there were Speech and Mind. Rathantaram is Speech, Bṛihat is Mind. Bṛihat being first created, thought Rathantaram to be inferior; the Rathantaram put an embryo in its body and brought forth Vairûpam. These two, Rathantaram and Vairûpam joined, thought Bṛihat to be inferior to them; Bṛihat put an embryo in its own body, whence the Vairâjam was produced. These two, Bṛihat and Vairâjam joined, thought Rathantaram and Vairûpam to be inferior to them. Rathantaram then put an embryo in its body, whence the Śâkvaram was produced. These three, Rathantaram, Vairûpam, and Śâkvaram thought Bṛihat and Vairâjam to be inferior to them. Bṛihat then put an embryo in its body, whence the Raivatam was produced. These three Sâmans on each side (Rathantaram, Vairûpam, Śâkvaram, and Bṛihat, Vairâjam, Raivatam) became the six Pṛiṣṭhas. [7]

At this (time, when the Sâma Pṛiṣṭhas originated) the three metres (Gâyatrî, Triṣṭubh, and Jagatî) **[310]** were unable to get hold of these six Pṛiṣṭhas. Gâyatrî put an embryo in herself and produced Anuṣṭubh. Triṣṭubh put an embryo in hereself and produced Paṅkti. Jagatî put an embryo in herself and produced the Atichhandas (metres). The three metres having thus become six, were thus able to hold the six Pṛiṣṭhas.

The sacrifice of him becomes (well) performed and (also) becomes well performed for the whole assemblage (of sacrificer), who at this occasion takes his Dîkṣâ when knowing this production of the metres and Pṛiṣṭhas.

FIFTH CHAPTER.

(The Two First Days of the Dvâdaśâha Sacrifice)

29.

(The Śastras of the Morning and Midday Libations on the First Day.)

Agni is the leading deity of the first day. The Stoma (required) is

---

[6] See page 214.

[7] The purport of this paragraph is to show why on certain days of the Dvâdaśâha the Rathantara Sâman, and on others the Bṛihat Sâman, is required for forming a Pṛiṣṭha with another Sâman. See on these different Sâmans 4, 13.

Trivṛit (the nine-fold), the Sâman Rathantaram, the metre Gâyatrî. He who knows what deity, what Stoma, what Sâman, what metre (are required on the first day), becomes successful by it. The words *â* and *pra* are the characteristics of the first day. (Further) characteristics of this day are: *yukta* joined, *ratha* carriage, *âśu* swift, *pâ* to drink, the mentioning of the deities in the first padas (of the verses repeated) by their very names, the allusion to this world (earth), Sâmans akin to Rathantaram, metres akin to Gâyatrî, the future of *kṛi* to make.

The Ajya hymn of the first day is, *upa prayanto adhvaram* (1, 74); for it contains the term *pra*, which is a characteristic of the first day.

[311] The Pra-uga Śastram is, *vâyavâyâhi darśateme* (1, 2-3); for it contains the term *â*, a characteristic of the first day.

The Pratipad (beginning) of the Marutvatîya Śastra is, *â tvâ ratham yathotaye* (8, 57, 1-3); its Anuchara (sequel), *idaṁ vaso sutam andhaḥ* (8, 2, 1-3); they contain the terms *ratha* and *piba* (drink), which are characteristics of the first day.

The Indra-Nihava Pragâtha is, *indra nedîya ed ihi* (Vâlakh. 5, 5-6); here the deity is mentioned in the first pada, which is a characteristic of the first day.

The Brâhmaṇaspatya Pragâtha is, *praitu Brahmaṇaspatiḥ* (1, 40, 3-4); it contains the term *pra*, which is a characteristic of the first day.

The Dhâyyâs are, *agnir netâ, tvam Soma kratubhiḥ, pinvanty apaḥ* (Ait. Br. 3, 18); here are the deities mentioned in the first padas, which is a characteristic of the first day.

The Marutvatîya Pragâtha is, *prava indrâya bṛihate* (8, 78, 3-4); it contains the term *pra*, which is a characteristic of the first day.

The (Nivid) hymn is, *â yâtv indro vase* (4, 21); it contains the term *â*, which is a characteristic of the first day.

(*Niṣkevalya Śastra*)

The Rathantara Pṛiṣṭham is, *abhi tvâ śûra nonumo* (7, 32, 22-23) and *abhi tvâ pûrvapîtaye* (8, 3, 7-8); (this is done) at a Rathantara day, of which characteristic the first day is.

The Dhâyyâ is, *yad vâvâna* (Ait. Br. 3, 22); it contains the term *â*, which is a characteristic of the first day.

The Sâma Pragâtha is, *piba sutasya* (8, 3, 1-2); it contains the term *piba*, "drink," which is a characteristic of the first day.

The Târkṣyam is, *tyam û ṣu râjinam* (Ait. Br. 4, 20). The Hotar repeats it before the (Nivid) hymn **[312]** (of the Niṣkevalya Śastra). The Târkṣyam is safe journey. (It is repeated) for securing safety.

He who has such a knowledge makes his journey in safety and reaches the end of the year in safety.

30.

(The Rest of the Niṣkevalya Śastra, and the Śastras of the Evening Libation)

The (Nivid) hymn (of the Niṣkevalya Śastra) is, *â na indro dûrâd* (4, 20); it contains the term *â*, which is a characteristic of the first day.

Both Nivid hymns, that of the Marutvatîya as well as that of the Niṣkevalya Śastras are (so called) *Saṁpâtas.*[1] Vâmadeva, after having seen (once) these (three) worlds, got possession of them (*samopatat*) by means of the *Saṁpâtas.* On account of his getting possession of (*saṁpati*) by means of the Saṁpâtas, they are called by this name (saṁpâtas).

The reason that the Hotar, on the first day, repeats two Saṁpâta hymns, is, to reach the celestial world, to get possession of it, and join (its inhabitants).

The Pratipad (beginning verse) of the Vaiśvadeva Śastra on the first day, which is a Rathantara day[2] **[313]** is, *tat savitur vṛiṇimahe*, (5, 82, 1-3); its Anuchara (sequel) is, *adya no deva savitar* (5, 82, 4-6). It is used at a Rathantara day, which is characteristic of the first day.

The (Nivid) hymn for Savitar is, *yuñjate mana uta* (5, 81); it contains the term *yuj* to join, which is a characteristic of the first day.

The (Nivid) hymn for Heaven and Earth is, *pra dyâvâ yajñâiḥ* (1, 159); it contains the *pra*, which is a characteristic of the first day.

The (Nivid) hymn for the Ribhus is, *iheha vo manasâ* (3, 60). If it would contain *pra*, and *â*, the (proper) characteristics of the first day, then all would be *pra, i. e.*, going forth, and consequently the sacrificers would depart (*prâiśyan*) from this world. This is the reason that the Hotar repeats on the first day (as Nivid hymn for Heaven and Earth) *iheha mano* though it does not contain the term characteristic of the first day).

---

[1] See Ait. Brâhm. 6, 18.

[2] The so-called Rathantara days of the Dvâdaśâha are the first, third and fifth. Sây. here remarks that the Pratipad of the Vaiśvadeva Śastras is joined to the Rathantara Sâman. This is, however, an erroneous statement, as I can prove from the Sâma prayoga of the Dvâdaśâha (the last sacrifice of this kind has been, in this part of India, performed about fifty years ago) which is in my possession. The triplet addressed to Savitar is always (at all Soma sacrifices) the opening of the Vaiśvadeva Śastra on the evening libation; but on the first day of the Dvâdaśâha, there is besides the Arbhava Pavamâna Stotra, only the Yajña yajñîya Sâma used, the same which is required at the evening libation of the Agniṣṭoma. Sây. wrote that explanation only to explain the term *râthantara*. This means only that this is done on the " Rathantara day." The Rathantara is on this day required at the midday libation.

Iha, *i.e.*, here, is this world. By doing so, the Hotar makes the sacrificers enjoy this world.

The (Nivid) hymn for the Viśvedevâh is, *devân huve brihach chhavasah svastaye* (10, 66). The deities are mentioned in the first pada, which is a characteristic of the first day.

The reason that the Hotar repeats this hymn (as Nivid Sûkta) for the Viśvedevâh on the first day, is to make the journey (of the sacrificers) safe, because those who hold a session lasting for a year, or who perform the Dvâdaśâha, are going to set out on a long journey. Thus the Hotar makes (for them) the journey safe.

He who has such a knowledge reaches in safety the end of the year, as well as those who have a Hotar knowing this and acting accordingly.

The Partipad of the Agnimâruta Śastra is, *vaiś vânarâya prithupâjase* (3, 3). The deity (Vaiśvânara) **[314]** is mentioned in the first pada, which is a characteristic of the first day.

The (Nivid) hymn for the Marutas is, *pra tvakṣasaḥ pra tavasah* (1, 87). It contains the term *pra*, which is a characteristic of the first day.

He repeats the Jâtavedâs verse, *jâtavedase sunavâma* (1, 99, 1) before (the Jâtavedâs) hymn. The Jâtavedâs verse is safe journey. (It is repeated) for securing a safe journey. Thus he secures a safe journey (for the sacrificer). He who has such a knowledge reaches in safety the end of the year.

The (Nivid) hymn for Jâtavedâs is, *pra tavyasîm navyasîm* (1, 143). It contains the term *pra*, which is a characteristic of the first day.

The Agnimâruta Śastra (of the first day of the Dvâdaśâha) is the same as in the Agniṣṭoma[3]. The creatures live on what is performed equally in the sacrifice (*i.e.*, in several different kinds of sacrifices). Thence the Agnimâruta Śastra (of the first day of the Dvâdaśâha) is identical (with that of the Agniṣṭoma).

31

(The Characteristics of the Second Day of the Dvâdaśâha. The Śastras of the Morning and Midday Libations. Story of Sâryâta, the son of Manu)

Indra is the leading deity of the second day; the Stoma (required) is the fifteen-fold (*pañchadaśa*), the Sâman is Bṛihat, the metre is Triṣṭubh. He who knows what deity, what Stoma, what Sâman, what metre (are required for the second day) succeeds by it. On the second day, neither *â* nor *pra* (the characteristics of the first day) are used, but *sthâ* (derivations from this root) "to stand," is the characteristic. Other

---

[3] See 3, 35-38.

characteristics of the second day are, *ûrdhva* **[315]** upwards, *prati* towards, *antar* in, between, *vṛiṣan* male, *vṛidhan* growing, the deities mentioned (by their names) in the second pada, the allusion to the airy region, what has the nature of the Bṛihat Sâman, what has the nature of the Triṣṭubh the present tense[4].

The Ajya (hymn) of the second day is, *agnim dûtam vṛiṇîmahe* (1, 12); this contains the present tense (in *vṛiṇîmahe*), which is a characteristic of the second day.

The pra-uga Śastra is, *vâyo ye te sahasriṇo* (2, 41); it contains the term *vṛidhan* growing, increasing, in the words *sutaḥ soma ṛitâ ṛidha* (2, 41, 4), which is a characteristic of the second day.

The Pratipad (beginning) of the Marutvatîya Śastra is, *viśvânarasya vaspatîm* (8, 57, 4-6), and its Anuchara (sequel), *indra it Somapâ* (8, 2, 4-6). They contain the terms *vṛidhan* (8, 57, 5) and *antar* (8, 2, 5), which are characteristics of the second day.

The constant (Indra-Nihava) Pragâtha is, *indra nedîya edîhi.*

The Brahmaṇaspati Pragâtha is, *uttiṣṭha brahmaṇaspate ;* it contains the term *ûrdhva* up, upwards, (in the word *uttiṣṭha, i.e.*, rise), which is a characteristic of the second day.

The constant Dhâyyâs are, *agnir netâ tvam soma kratubhiḥ, pinvanty apaḥ.*

The Marutvatîya Pargâtha is, *bṛihad indrâya gâyata* (8, 87, 1-2) ; it contains the term *vṛidhan* increasing, in the word *ritarridhâ*.

The (Nivid) hymn (of the Marutvatîya Śastra) is, *indra somam soma pate* (3, 32); it contains the **[316]** term *vṛiṣan* in the word *â vṛiṣasva* "gather strength" (show yourself as a male 3, 32, 2), which is a characteristic of the second day.

The Bṛihat Pṛiṣṭham (*i. e.*, Stotriyam, and Anurûpam) is *tvâm iddhi havâmohe* (6, 46, 1-2) and *tvam hyehi cherave* (8, 50, 7-8) ; (this is done) on the Bârhata day,[5] of which kind the second day is (the use of the Bṛihat *pṛiṣṭha*), being a characteristic of the second day.

The constant Dhâyyâ (of the Niṣkevalya Śastra) is, *yad vâvâna.*

The Sâma Pragâtha is, *ubhayam śṛiṇavachcha* (8, 50, 1-2) ; (the term *ubhayam, i. e.* both) means, what is today and what was yesterday. It belongs to the Bṛihat Sâman, which is a charateristic of the second day.

The constant Târkṣya is, *tyam û ṣu vâjinam.*

---

[4] The word for "present tense" in the original is *kurvat*, which is the participle of the present tense of the root *kri* to make. That it cannot have any other meaning, undoubtedly follows from the application of this term to the hymn *agnim dutam vriṇ mahe*, in the whole of which there is nowhere any present tense or present participle of the root *kri*, but present tenses of other verbs.

[5] The Bârh ata days are the second, fourth, and sixth.

32

(The Remainder of the Niṣkevalya Śastra and the Śastras of the Evening Libation on the Second Day)

The (Nivid) hymn (of the Niṣkevalya Śastra) is, *ya ta ûtir avamâ* (6, 25); it contains the term *vṛiṣan*, in the word *vṛiṣṇyâni* (6, 25, 3), which term is a characteristic of the second day.

The Pratipad of the Vaiśvadeva Śastra is, *viśvo devasya netus* (5, 50, 1), and *tat savitur vareṇyam* (3, 62, 10-11), the Anuchara (sequel) is, *â viśvadevam satpatim* (5, 82, 7-9). It belongs to the Bṛihat day, and is thus a characteristic of the second ḍay (which is a Bṛihat day).

The (Nivid) hymn for Savitar is, *ud u Ṣya devaḥ savitâ* (6, 71); it contains the trem " up upwards " (in *ut*), which is a characteristic of the second day.

[317] The Nivid hymn for Dyâvâpṛithivî is, *te hi dyâvâpṛithivî* (1, 160); it contains the term *antar*, which is a characteristic of the second day.

The (Nivid) hymn for the Ribhus is, *takṣan ratham* (1, 111), it contains the term *vṛiṣan*, in the word *vṛiṣanvasû*, which is a characteristic of the second day.

The (Nivid) hymn for the Viśvedevâh is, *yajñasya yo rathyam* (10, 92); it contains the term *vṛiṣâ* in the words *vṛiṣa ketur*, which is a characteristic of the second day. This hymn is by Śâryâta. As the Aṅgiras were engaged in a sacrificial session for going to heaven, they became always confounded (in their recitations) as often as they were going to perform the ceremonies of the second day (of the Ṣaḷaha). Śâryâta, the son of Manu, made them repeat the hymn, *yajñasya rathyam* on the second day, whereupon they got aware of the sacrifice (the sacrificial personage), and (by means of it) of the celestial world. The reason that the Hotar repeats this hymn on the second day is (to help the sacrificer), to get aware of the sacrifice, and consequently to see the celestial world (of which he wishes to became an inhabitant).

The Pratipad (beginning) of the Agnimâruta Śastra is, *pṛikṣasya vṛiṣṇo* (6, 8); it contains the term *vṛiṣan*, which is a characteristic of the second day.

The (Nivid) hymn for the Marutas in the Agnimâruta Śastra is, *vṛisṇe śardhâya* (1, 64); it contains the term *vṛiṣan*, which is a characteristic of the second day.

The constant Jâtavedâs verse is, *Jâtavedase sunavâma*.

The (Nivid) hymn for Jâtavedâs is *yajñena vardhatu* (2, 2); it contains the term *vridh*, which is a charcteristic of the second day.

[318] FIFTH BOOK.

FIRST CHAPTER.

(The Characteristics and Śastras of the Third and Fourth Days of the Dvâdaśâha)

1

(The Characteristics of the Third-Day. The Śastras of the Morning and Midday Libations)

The leading deities of the third day are the Viśvedevâḥ; its (leading) Stoma is the so-called Saptadaśa (seventeen-fold), its Sâman the Vairûpam, its metre, the Jagatî. He who knows what deity, what Stoma, what Sâman, what metre (are required on the third day), becomes successful by it.

What hymn has a refrain, that is a characteristic of the third day. Other characteristics are: *aśva* horse, *anta* end, repetition, (*punarâvṛitti*) consonance (in the ending vowels), cohabitation, the term "covered, closed," (*paryasta*), the term *three*, what has the form of *anta* (end), the mentioning of the deity in the last pada, an allusion to that world, the Vairûpam Sâman, the Jagatî metre, the past tense.

The Ajya Śastra is, *yukṣvâ hi devahûtamân* (8, 64). The gods went to heaven by means of the third day. The Asuras (and) Râkṣas prevented them (from entering it). They said (to the Asuras), "Become deformed, become deformed" (*virûpa*); when the Asuras were becoming deformed, the Devas entered (heaven). This produced the Sâman called Vairûpam, thence it is called so (from *virûpa* deformed). He who has become deformed in consequence of his own guilt, destroys it (his deformity) by means of this knowledge.

[319] The Asuras persecuted the Devas again, and came into contact with them. The Devas turned horses (*aśva*) and kicked them with their feet. Thence the horses are called *aśva* (from *aś* to reach). He who knows this obtains (*aśnute*) all he desires. Thence the horse is the swiftest of animals, because of its kicking with the hind legs. He who has such a knowledge destroys the consequences of guilt. This is the reason that the Ajya hymn on the third day contains the term *aśva* horse, which is a characteristic of the third day.

The Pra-uga Śastra consists of the following triplets : *vâyavâyâhi vîtayê* (5, 51, 5-7) *vâyô yâhi śivâd* (8, 26, 23-25), *indraś cha vâyav eşâm sutânâm* (5, 51, 6-8), *â mitre varuṇê vayam* (5, 72, 1-3), *aśvinâveha gachhatâm* (5, 75, 7-9), *âyâhy adribhiḥ* (5, 40, 1-3), *sajûr devebhir viśvebhir* (7, 34, 15-17), *uta naḥ priyâ* (6, 61 10-12). They are in the Uṣṇih metre, have a refrain (*samânodarkam*), which is a characteristic of the third day.

Tam tam id râdhase (8, 57, 7-9), *traya indrasya Soma* (8, 2, 7-9) are the beginning and the sequel of the Marutvatîya Śastra, which contain the terms, *nṛtâ*, *i.e.*, consonance (8, 57, 7) and *traya*, *i.e.*, three, which are characteristics of the third day. *Indra nedîya* (Vâl. 5, 5-6) is the constant (Indra-Nihava) *pragâthaḥ*.[1] *Pranûnam Brahmaṇaspatir* (1, 40, 5-6) is the Brâhmaṇaspatya Pragâtha which has a consonance (of vowels), is a characteristic of the third day. *Agnir netâ* (3, 20, 4), *tvaṁ Soma kratubhiḥ* (1, 91, 2), and *pinvanty apô* (1, 64, 6) are the immovable Dhâyyâs. *Nakiḥ Sudâsô ratham* (7, 32, 10) **[320]** is the Marutvatîya Pragâtha, which contains the term *prayasta*, *i.e.*, covered, closed. *Tryaryamâ manuşo devatâtâ* (5, 29) is the (Nivid) hymn (for the Marutvatîya Shastra) ; it contains the term "three." *Yad dyâva indra* (8, 59, 5-6), *yad indra yâvatas* (7, 32, 18-19) form the Vairûpam Pṛiṣṭham on the third day, which is a Rathantara day, which is a characteristic of the third day.

Yad vâvâna (10, 74, 6) is the constant Dhâyyâ. By repeating (after this Dhâyyâ) : *abhi tvâ śûra nonumaḥ* (7, 32, 22-23) the Hotar turns back the womb (of this day), because this (third) day is, as to its position, a Rathantara day which Sâman is, therefore, the womb of it. *Indra tridhâtu śaraṇam* (6, 46, 9-10) is the Sâma Pragâtha ; it contains the term "three" (in *tridhâta*). *Tyam û şu vâjinam* (10, 178) is the constant Târkṣya.

2

(The Nivid Hymn of the Niṣkévalya Śastra, and the Śastras of the Evening Libation of the Third Day)

Yo jâtô eva prathamô manasvân (2, 12) is the (Nivid) hymn, every verse of which ends in the same words (*sa janâsa Indraḥ*), which is a characteristic of the third day. It contains the words *sa jana* and *Indra*. If this be recited, then Indra becomes possessd of his Indra (peculiar) power. The Sâma singers, therefore, say, the Rigvedis (the Hotars) praise Indra's peculiar nature (power, *indrasya indriyam*). This hymn is by the Riṣi Gṛitsamada. By means of it, this Riṣi obtained Indra's favour

[1] Sayaṇa explains *panarninritam* as follows : पुनर्निवृत्तं स्वरविशेषेणाक्षराणां, पुनः पुनरावर्त्तनेन वा नर्त्तनसादृश्यं, This clearly expresses what we call consonance ; the recurrence of the same vowel at the end is compared to the movements of a dancer (*ninrittam*).

and conquered the highest world. He who has this knowledge obtains Indra's favour and conquers the highest world.

Tat Savitur vriṇîmahe vayam (5, 82, 1-3) and *adyâ nô deva savitaḥ* (5, 82, 3-5), are the beginning and the **[321]** sequel of the Vaiśvadeva Śastra on the third day, which is a Rathantara day.

Tad devasya Savitur vâryam mahad vriṇîmahe (4, 53, 1) is the (Nivid) hymn for Savitar. Because the end (which is aimed at) is a great one (*mahad*); and the third day is also an end. *Ghritena dyâvâ prithivî* (6, 70) is the (Nivid) hymn for Dyâvâprithivî. It contains the words *ghritaśriyâ, ghrita prichâ, ghritavridhâ,* in which there is a repetition (because the word *ghrita* is three times repeated) and the consonance of the terminating vowels (because there is three times *â* at the end), which are characteristics of the third day.

Anaśvô jâtô anabhîśur (4, 36) is the (Nivid) hymn for the Ribhus. It contains, in the words *rathas trichakraḥ*, the term "three" (*tri*), which is a characteristic of the third day.

Parâvatô ye didhiṣanta (10, 63) is the (Nivid) hymn for the Viśvedevâḥ. Because the word *anta* (the end) is to be found in the word *paravatô* (*atô* in the strong form *antô*), and the third day is an end (an object). This is the Gayasûkta, by which Gaya, the son of Plata, obtained the favour of the Viśvedevâḥ and conquered the highest world. He who has this knowledge obtains the favour of the Viśvedevâḥ and conquers the highest world.

Vaisvanarâya dhiṣaṇâm (3, 2) is the beginning of the Agnimâruta Śastra. The *anta* (end) is in *diṣaṇâ* (but the *t* is wanting). The third day is also an "end" (to a *Tryaha* or period of three days).

Dhârâvarâ marutô (2, 34) is the (Nivid) hymn for the Marutas. Here by *anta* is the plural (most of the nominatives of this verse are in the plural) to be understood, because the plural is the end (the last among the terminations, following the singular and dual). The third day is also the end (of the Tryaha).

[322] *Jâtavedase sunavâma* (1, 99, 1) is the constant verse for Jâtavedâs. *Tvam agne prathamo aṅgirâ* (1, 31) is the (Nivid) hymn for Jâtavedâs, where each verse begins by the same words (*tvam agne*), which is a characteristic of the third day. By repeating *tvam tvam* (in every verse), the Hotar alludes to the following three days (from the fourth to the sixth) for connecting (both series of three days). Those who, with such a knowledge, repeat (at the end of the last Śastra of the third day a hymn every verse of which contains the term *tvam*) have both series of three days performed without interruption and breach.

3.

(On the Nyûñkha)

(Sây. These periods of three days form part of the *Navarâtra*—nine nights included in the Dvâdaśâha. **[323]** The first Tryahaḥ or period of three days is now explained, and the very same is the first part of the pṛisṭhyam, comprising six days. Now the middle part of the Navarâtra (the second three days) are to be explained.

The Stomas and Chhandas are at an end (*i.e.*, all the Stoma combinations, and the metres are exhausted) on the third day; that one only remains. This "that one" is the syllable *vách*, which consists of three sounds; vâch is one syllable, [a]and (this) syllable consists of three sounds, which represent the latter thre days (out of the six), of which Vâch (Speech) is one, and Gâus (Cow) is one, and Dyaus (Heaven) is one. Therefore, Vâch alone is the leading deity of the fourth day.

On just the fourth day, they make *Nyûñkha* of this syllable by pronouncing it with a tremulous voice, increasing and decreasing (dividing) the tone. It serves for rising the fourth day (to make it particularly important). Because the Nyûñkha is (produces) food, for the singers seeking a livelihood wander about, in order to make food grow (by their singing for rain).

By making Nyûñkha on the fourth day, they produce food; (because it is done) for producing food. Thence the fourth day is *jâtavat, i.e.*, productive. Some say, one must make Nyûñkha with a word comprising four sounds; for the animals are fourfooted, in order to obtain cattle. Others say, one must make Nyûñkha with three sounds. These three *sounds* are the three worlds. In order to conquer these worlds, they say,

---

[a] The rules for making the Nyûñkha are laid dwon in Aśval. Śr. S (7, 11), They are प्रातरनुवाक प्रतिपद्यद्वर्चा द्योयूँखो द्वितीयस्वरमोंकारं त्रिमात्रमुदात्तं त्रिस्तस्य तस्य चोपरिष्टादपरिमितान्पं-चवाद्वौँकारानुदात्तानुत्तमस्य, तु त्रीन् पूर्वमक्षरन्निहन्यते न्यूख्यमाने, *i.e.*, "on the fourth day is the second sound (syllable) of each of the two first half verses in the beginning of the Prâtaranuvâke to be pronounced with Nyûñkha. (This Nyûñkha is made in the following manner). The *ô* (in *âpô revatir* and *râyô*) is pronounced thrice with three moras, in the high tone (*udâtta*); this (*ô* thus pronounced in the high tone with three moras is each time followed by an indefinite number of half *os* (*i.e.*, the vowel *o* pronounced very abruptly with half a mora only) or by five only, the last *ô* (with three moras) being, however, followed by three half *os* only; the first sound is pronounced with some impetus, when a syllable is spoken with Nyûñkha.

This description which is quite exact, as I can assure the reader from my having heard the Nyûñka pronounced by a Śrotriya, is illustrated in Aśv by several instances. It occurs twice in the first verse of the Prâtaranuvâka (after the words *yajña râyas*, the last syllable of both being changed into *ô*), and once in the Ajva Sukta (*âgnim na* 10 21), after the *â* of the word *yajñâya*, and in the Niṣkevalya Śastra. The Nyûñkha is always followed by a pratigara, pronounced by the Adhvaryu, containing also the Nyûñkha.

one must make Nyûñkha with one sound only. Sângalâyana, the son of Mudgala, a Brahman, said "The word 'Vâch' comprises one syllable only; therefore he who makes Nyûñkha by one sound only, does it in the right way." They say, one must make Nyûñkha with two sounds for [324] obtaining a stand-point, for man has two legs, and the animals have four; thus he places the two-footed man among the four-footed animals. Therefore, the Hotar ought to make Nyûñkha with two sounds. At the beginning, he makes Nyûñkha in the morning prayer (Prâtaranuvâka); because creatures first eat food with the mouth. In this way, the Hotar places the sacrificer with his mouth (ready for eating) towards food.

In the Ajya Śastra, the Nyûñkha is made in the middle; for, in the middle, he makes the creatures fond of food, and he places thus the sacrificer in the midst of food. In the midday libation, the Hotar makes Nyûñkha at the beginning, because animals eat food with their mouth. Thus he places the sacrificer with his mouth towards food. Thus he makes Nyûñkha at both the libations (morning and midday) for obtaining food.

4.

(The Characteristics of the Fourth Day. The Śastras of the Morning and Midday Libations)

The leading deity of the fourth day is the Vâch. The Stoma is the twenty-one-fold, the Sâman is Vairâja, the metre is Anuṣṭubh. He who knows what deity, what Stoma, what Sâman, what metre (are required) on the fourth day, succeeds through it (the fourth day). The terms *â pra* are the characteristics of the fourth day. The fourth day has all the characteristics of the first, *viz.*, *yukta ratha âśu pâ* (to drink); the mentioning of the deity in first pada, an allusion to this world. Other characteristics of the fourth day are the *jâta, hava, śukra* what has the form of speech (the Nyûñkha), what is by Vimada *viriphita,* what has different metres (*vichhandas*), what is wanting in syllables, and [325] what has an excess of them; what refers to Virâj and to Anuṣṭubh; the tense in future (*kariṣyat*).

Agnim na svavṛiktibhiḥ (10, 21) is the Ajya hymn of the fourth day.

It is by the Risi Vimada, whose name is contained in an alliteration in it (in *vi vo made*), and has alliterations, consonances, and assonances (*viriphitam*).[3] Such a hymn is a characteristic of the fourth day. It con-

[3] The word *viriphitam* has, it appears, been misunderstood by Sâyaṇa, who explains it by "*nyûñkhita,*" *i. e.*, in which the Nyûñkha is made. It is true, the Nyûñkha is made by the Hotar, when repeating the two Vimada hymns (*âgnim na svavṛiktibhir* 10, 21, and *kuha śruta indraḥ* 10, 22) on the morning and midday of the fourth day (See Aśv.

sists of eight verses, and is in the Paṅkti metre; because the sacrifice is a Paṅkti (series of ceremonies); and cattle are of the Paṅkti nature (*i. e.*, they consist of five parts); (it is done) for obtaining cattle.

These eight verses make ten Jagatîs, because **[326]** this morning libation of the middle three days (from the fourth to the sixth) belongs to the Jagat (*i. e.*, *Jagatî*). This (the connection of the Jagatî with the morning libation) is a characteristic of the fourth day.

These eight verses comprise ten Anuṣṭubhs; for this is the Anuṣṭubh day, in the application of which metre one of the characteristics of the fourth day consists.

These eight verses contain twenty Gâyatrîs; for this day is, again, a day of commencement (like the first, where Gâyatri is the metre). In this consists a characteristic of the fourth day.

Although this hymn is neither accompanied by the chants of the Sâma singers, nor by the recitations of the Hotṛi priests, the sacrifice does not lose its essence by it, but the sacrificial personage is even actually present (in it); thence it serves as the Ajya Sastra of the fourth day. They thus develop (stretch) out (of the form of) the sacrifice (contained in this hymn), the sacrifice (*i. e.*, this hymn is the external shape, in the boundary of which the sacrifice—conceived as a being—extends and thrives), and obtain (through the medium of this hymn) the Vâch again. (This is done) for establihshing a connection (between the several periods of three days. Those who have such a knowledge move continually within the closely connected and uninterrupted periods of three days (required for having success in the sacrifice).

Śr. S. 7, 11). But the term *nyûṅkha* being perfectly known to the author of our Brâhmaṇam, and its application even being accurately described by him (in 5, 3), it is surprising only why he should call this peculiar way of lengthening the syllable *ô* (*m*) in the midst of a verse, here *viriphita*. Besides, the Nyûṅkha does not take place in the Vimada hymn only, but in the beginning verses, the Prâtaranuvâka of which verse is by the Śûdra Riṣi Kavaṣa Ailûṣa. *Viriphita* must refer to some peculiarities which lie in the two hymns alluded to. On reference to them, every one will observe that in the first of them, each verse concludes with the word *vivakṣase*, and contains the words *vi vo made*, which are an allusion to the name of the Riṣi Vimada, who is therefore also called *viriphita*; in the second, there occurs in the two first verses in the same place (in the commencement of the second pada) the term *adya*, and at the end of several padas in the following verses, the word *vajrivaḥ*. These repetitions of the same words, generally commencing with *va*, *vi*, *vo* is, no doubt, the proper meaning of the term "*viriphitam*," as understood by the author of our Brâhmaṇam.

4. This is brought about by repeating thrice the first and last verses. The paṅkti consists of 41 syllables. In this way of computation, one obtains 480 syllables, just as many as 10 Jagatîs comprise (Sây.) If they are divided by 32 (the number of syllables for the Anuṣṭubh metre), then we obtain 15 Anuṣṭubhs, and if divided by 24, 20 Gâyatrîs.

The Pra-uga Śastra, which is in the Anuṣṭubh metre, is composed of the following verses: *Vâyô śukro* (4, 47, 1), *vihi hotrâ avitâ* (4, 48, 1) *vâyô śatam harînâm* (4, 48, 5), *índraś cha vâyav eṣâm* (4, 48 2-1), *â chikitâna sukratû* (5, 66, 1-3), *â no viśvâbhir ûtibhiḥ* (7, 24, 4-6), *tyam u vo aprahanam* (6, 44, 4-6), *apa tyam vṛijinam ripum* (6, 51, 13-15) *ambitame nadîtame* (2, 41, 1-3). In them, there occur the words, **[327]** *â pra*, and *śukra*, which are characteristics of the fourth day.

Tam tvâ yajñebhir îmahe (8, 57. 10) is the beginning (*pratipad*) of the Marutvatîya Śastra. The word *îmahe* " we ask for " in this verse, means that this day's work is to be made long (in consequence of the multitude of rites) as it were (just as one has to wait long before a request is acceded to). This is a characteristic of the fourth day (for it indicates the multitude of its rites).

The verses, *Idam vaso sutam andhaḥ* (8, 2, 1-2), *Indra nedîya* (Vâl 5. 5-6), *prâitu Brahmaṇaspatir* (1,4, 34), *Agnir netâ* (3, 20, 4), *tvaṁ Soma kratubhiḥ* (1, 91, 2), *pinvanty apô* (1, 64, 6), *pra va indrâya bṛihate* (8, 78, 3), which form part of the Marutvatîya Śastra of the first day, are also required for the fourth day, and are a characteristic of it. *Śrudhi havam mâ riṣanya* (2, 11, 1) is the hymn which contains the word *hava* (call), being a characteristic of the fourth day. In the hymn *Marutvâṁ Indra vriṣabhô* (3, 47), there is, in its last quarter (47, 5), in the word *huvema*, the root *hu* perceptible, which is a characteristic of the fourth day. This hymn is in the Triṣṭubh metre.

By means of the padas of this hymn which stand firm, the Hotar keeps the libation lest it fall from its proper place (it should be kept in its proper place, like a piece in machinery). *Imam nu mâyinam huva* (8, 65, 13) is the setting (*paryâsa*), containing the word *huva*, which is a characteristic of the fourth day. The verses (of this hymn) are in the Gâyatrî metre, for the Gâyatrî verses are the leaders of the midday libation in these latter three days. That metre is the leading one in which the Nivid is placed; therefore one puts in (these) Gâyatrî verses the Nivid.

Piba Somam Indra mandatu (7, 22, 1-2) and *śrudhi havam vipipânasyâdrer* (7, 22, 4-5) is the Vairâja Pṛiṣṭham of the Bṛihat days, to which the fourth day belongs. **[328]** This (reference to the Bṛihat) is a characteristic of the fourth day.

Yad vâvâna (10, 74, 6) is the immovable Dhâyyâ.

Tvâm iddhi havâmahe (6, 46, 1) forms the womb (central verse) to which the Hotar brings (all) back, after the Dhâyyâ has been recited; for this is a Bṛihat Sâma day, according to its position (thence the Pragâtha, constituting the text of the Bṛihat Sâman, is its womb).

Tvam Indra pratûrtiṣu (8, 88, 5) is the Sâma Pragâtha; (the third pada) *aśastihâ janitâ* contains the term "*jâta*," which is a characteristic of the fourth day. *Tyam û ṣu vâjinam* (10, 178) is the immovable Târkṣya.

5.

(The Remainder of the Niṣkevalya Śastra, and the Śastras of the Evening Libation)

Kuha śruta indraḥ (10, 22) is the Vimada hymn, with alliterations, assonances, and consonances, by the Riṣi whose (name) is contained in an alliteration (*vi vo made* in 10, 21 being taken as equal to *vimada*). This is one of the characteristics of the fourth day. The hymn *yudhmasya te vṛiṣabhasya* (3, 46) contains (in the fourth verse) the word *januṣâ* (from the root *jan* "to be born"), which is a characteristic of the fourth day. It is in the Triṣṭubh metre. By means of the padas of this hymn which stand firm, the Hotar keeps the libation, lest it fall from its proper place.

Tyam uvaḥ satrâsâham (8, 81) is the setting. Its words, *viśvâsu gîrṣv âyatam*, indicate that this day's work is to be made long, as it were, which is one of the characteristics of the fourth day. They are in the Gâyatrî metre; the Gâyatrîs are the leaders of the midday libation in these three (latter) days.

[329] The Nivid is to be put in that metre which leads (the day); therefore they put the Nivid in the Gâyatrîs. *Viśvô devasya netus* (5, 50, 1), *tat savitur varenyam* (3, 62, 10-18), *â viśvadevam saptatim* (5, 82, 7-9), are the beginning and sequel of the Vaiśvadeva Śastra on the fourth day, which is a Bṛihat day, being one of the characteristics of the fourth day. *A devô yâtu* (7, 45) is the (Nivid) hymn for Savitar; it contains the term *â*, which is a characteristic of the fourth day.

Pra dyâvâ yajñâiḥ prithivî (7, 53) is the (Nivid) hymn for Dyâvâ-priṭhivî; it contains the term *pra*, which is a characteristic of the fourth day. *Pra ṛibhubhyô dûtam iva vâcham iṣya* (4, 33) is the (Nivid) hymn for the Ribhus; it contains the words *pra* and *vâcham iṣya*, which are characteristics of the fourth day. *Pra śukrâitu devîmanîṣâ* (7, 34) is the (Nivid) hymn for the Viśvedevâḥ; it contains the terms *pra* and *śukra*, which are characteristics of the fourth day. It has different metres, such as consist of two padas, and such as consist of four padas. This is a characteristic of the fourth day.

Vaiśvânarasya sumatâu syâma (1, 98) is the beginning of the Agni-mâruta Śastra; it contains the term *jâta*, which is a characteristic of the fourth day. *Ka îm vyaktâ* (7, 56) is the (Nivid) hymn for the Marutas.

(In the third pada of its first verse) there are the words, *nakir hy eṣâm janânṣi veda*, which contain the root *jan* to be born (in *janânṣi*), which is a characteristic of the fourth day. The verses of this hymn are in unequal metres; some have two padas, some four. This constitutes a characteristic of the fourth day.

Jâtavedase sunavâma somam (1, 99, 1) is the immovable Jâtavedâs verse. *Agnim narô didhitibir* (7, 1) is the (Nivid) hymn for Jâtavedâs; it contains the term *janayanta*, which is a characteristic of the fourth **[330]** day. Its meters are unequal; there are in it Virâjas and Triṣṭubhs. This constitutes a characteristic of the fourth day.

SECOND CHAPTER.

(The Characteristics and Śastras of the Fifth and Sixth Days of the Dvâdaśâha)

6

The Characteristics of the Fifth day. The Śastras of the Morning and Midday Libations)

The leading deity of the fifth day is *Gâus* (the cow). Its Stoma is the Triṇava (twenty-seven-fold), the Sâman is the Śâkvaram, the metre is Pañkti. He who knows what deity, what Stoma, what Sâman, what metre (are required on this day), succeeds by it. What is not *â* and not *pra*, what is fixed (standing), that is a characteristic of the fifth day. Besides, the characteristics of the second day re-occur in the fifth, such as *ûrdhva, prati, antar, vriṣan, vridhan*: the mentioning of the deity in the middle pada, an allusion to the airy region. (In addition to these, there are the following peculiar characteristics), *dugdha*, (*duh* to milk) *udha* (udder), *dhenu* (cow) *priśni* (cloud, cow) *mad* (drunk), the animal form, an increase (*adhyâsaḥ*),[1] for the animals differ in size, as it were, one being smaller or bigger than the other.[2] This (fifth) day is *jâgatam, i.e.*, it refers to the movable (*jagat*) things (or the Jagatî metre), for **[331]** the animals are movable; it is *bârhatam*, for the animals have reference to the Bṛihatî metre; it is *pâñktam*, for the animals refer to the Pañkti metre; it is *vâmam, i.e.*, left, because the animals are of this quality.[3] It is *haviṣmat, i.e.*, having offerings; because the animals

---

[1] The *Paśu* is considered to have five feet, the mouth being reckoned as the fifth. *Sây.*

[2] The original *vikṣudrâ iva hi pâśavô* cannot be literally translated. I therefore must content myself with a paraphrase, based chiefly on Sâyaṇa; *kṣudra* means small, low; and *vi* expresses " different, manifold."

[3] Sây. interprets the word *vâma* here differently. He takes it to mean "lovely, beautiful." This, he says, refers to the song (what song, he does not specify) which is pleasing to hear on account of its sweet tones and sounds; or to the beautiful view which animals, such

are an offering (serve as an offering); it is *vapuṣmat*, *i.e.*, having a body ; for the animals have a body ; it is *śákvaram pâṅktam*, and has the present tense, just as the second day.

Imam û ṣuvo atithim (6, 15) is the Ajya Śastra. It is in the Jagatî metre with additional other metres (such as Śakvarî, Atiś akvarî, &c.) ; this is the animal characteristic of the fifth day.

The Pra-uga Śastra of the fifth day, which is in the Bṛihatî metre, consists of the following verses : *A no yajñam divispṛiśam* (8, 90, 9-10), *à no vâyo* (8, 46, 25), *rathena prithapâjasâ* (4, 46, 5-7) *bahavaḥ sûrachakṣasâ* (7, 66, 10-12), *imâ u vâm diviṣṭaya* (7, 74, 1-3), *pibâ sutasya rasinô* (8, 3, 1-3), *devam devam vo vase devam* (8, 27, 13-15) *bṛihad u gâyiṣe vacha* (7, 96, 1-3).

In the verse *yat pâñchajanyayâviśá* (8, 52, 7), which is the beginning of the Marutvatîya Śastra, there is the word *pâñchajanyayâ* (consisting of five families) which (five) is a characteristic of the fifth day (it being *pâṅkta*, *i. e.*, five-fold.)

Indra it somapa ekaḥ (8, 2, 4), *Indra nedîya edihi* (Vâl. 5, 5), *uttiṣṭha Brahmaṇaspate* (1, 40, 1), *Agnir netâ* (3, 20, 1), *tvam soma kratubhiḥ* (1, 91, 2), **[332]** *pinvanty apô* (1, 64, 6), *bṛihad Indrâya gâyata* (8, 78, 1) is the extension (of the Marutvatîya Śastra) of the fifth day, which is identical with that of the second day.

Avîtâsi sunvatô (8, 36) is a· hymn which contains the word *mad* "to be drunk." There are (in the first verse) five padas, which is in the Paṅkti metre, all these are characteristics of the fifth day. *Itthâ hi soma in mada* (1, 80) is another hymn in the Paṅkti metre, consisting of five padas which contains the word *mad* also.

The hymn *Indra piba tubhyam suto madâya* (6, 40), composed in the Triṣṭubh metre, contains the word *mad* also. By means of this pada which remained firm, the Hotar keeps the libation in its proper place, preventing it from slipping down. The triplet *marutvâm indra mîdhva* (8, 65, 7-9) is the setting containing neither the word *â* nor *pra* which is a characteristic of the fifth day. These verses are in the Gâyatrî metre, which lead the midday libation of the three days' sacrifice. The Nivid is placed in that metre which is the leading one. Therefore the Hotar places the Nivid in (these) Gâyatrîs.

---

as cows, horses, &c., represent to the eye of the spectator. But these explanations have no sense at all, and appear to be mere guesses. I think it better to take the word in the meaning "left" according to which the animals are the "left part" in creation, opposed to men and gods who represent the right.

7.

(*On the Śâkvara Sâman and the Mahânâmnîs. The Niṣkevalya Śastra.*)

On the fifth day, which is a Rathantara day, the Sâma singers chant the Mahânâmnî verses[4] according to the Śâkvara tune; this is a characteristic of the fifth day. Indra (having had once a desire of becoming great), made himself great by means of these verses; therefore they are called Mahânâmnî. These worlds (also) are Mahânâmnîs, for they are great.

[333] Prajâpati had, when he created the universe, the power (of making all) this and everything. The power possessed by Prajâpati to make all this and everything when creating these worlds, became the Śakvarî verses. Thence they are called Śakvarîs (from *śaknoti*, he has the power). He (Prajâpatî) made them (these Mahânâmnîs) to extend beyond the frontiers. All that he created as extending beyond the frontiers, turned cords (*sima*). Thence comes the word *sîman*, from *sima* a cord.

The verses *Svâdor itthâ viṣûvato* (1, 84, 10), *upa no haribhiḥ sutam* (8, 82, 31), *indram viśvâ avîvṛidhann* (1, 111, 1), are the Anurûpa (of the Niṣkevalya Śastra); they contain the words *vṛiṣan, pṛiśni, mad, vṛidhan*, which are characteristics of the fifth day. *Yad vâvâna* (10, 74, 6) is the immovable Dhâyyâ. By repeating *Abhi tvâ śûra nonumo* after the Dhâyyâ, the Hotar returns to the womb of the Rathantaram (as the receptacle of all ceremonies), this (fifth) day being a Rathantara day by its position. *Mô ṣu tvâ vâghataś chana* (7, 32, 1-2) is the Sâma Prâgatha with an additional foot, having the animal form (five parts), which is a characteristic of the fifth day. *Tyam û ṣu vâjinam* is the immovable Târkṣya.

8.

(*The Remainder of the Niṣkevalya Śastra. The Śastras of the Evening Libation.*)

The hymn, *predam brahma* (8, 37) is in the Paṅkti metre, comprising five padas. The hymn, *Indro madâya vâvṛidha* (1, 81) is in the Paṅkti metre, consisting of five padas, and containing the term "*mad.*" By means of the hymn *Satrâ madâsas tava* (6, 36, 1) which contains the term "*mad*" also, and is in the Triṣṭubh metre, the Hotar keeps through its padas which remain firm, the libation in its proper place, [334] thus preventing it from falling down. The triplet, *tam Indram vâjayâmasi* (8, 82, 7-9) is the setting (*paryâsa*). (Its third pada) *sa vṛiṣâ vṛiṣabho bhuvat*, contains the animal from (there is the word *vṛiṣan, i. e.,*

[4] These are *vidâ maghavan*. See 4, 4.

male, in it). It is in the Gâyartî metre, for the Gâyatrîs are the leading metres at the midday libation in this Tryaha (the three days from the fourth to the sixth). The Nivid is placed in that metre which is the leading. Therefore the Hotar places the Nivid in (these) Gâyatrîs.

The verses, *tat savitur vṛinîmahe* (5, 82, 1-3) *adyâ no deva savitar* (5, 82, 13-15), are the beginning and sequel of the Vaiśvadeva Śastra on the Rathantara day, of which the fifth is one. *Ud u ṣya devaḥ savitâ damûnâ* (6, 71, 4-6) is the (Nivid) hymn for Savitar. In it there is the word *vâmam* (in the last pada), *i.e.*, left, which is a characteristic of the animal form. In the Dyâvâpṛithivî hymn, *mahî dyâvâprithivî* (4, 56) the words *ruvad dhokṣâ* (in the last pada) contain the animal form (because the word *dhokṣâ*, from the root *duh*, to milk, is in it).

Ribhur vibhvâ vâja (4, 34) is the Ribhu hymn. Because the auimals are *vâjaḥ*, *i. e.*, property, booty, which (*vâjaḥ*) is an animal form. *Stuṣe janaṁ suvrataṁ navyasîbhir* (6, 49, 1) is a hymn (in the Triṣṭubh metre) with an additional pada (in the last verse, which is in the Śakvarî, instead of in the Triṣṭubh metre). This is the animal form (animals being supposed to have five feet instead of four, the mouth being counted as the fifth) which is a characteristic of the fifth day. *Haviṣ pântam ajaram* (10, 88, 1) is the beginning of the Agnimâruta Śastra. It contains the word *haviṣ*, *i. e.*, offering, which is a characteristic of the fifth day. *Vapur na tachchikituṣê* (6, 66) is the (Nivid) hymn for the Marutas, which contains the word *vapus*, *i. e.*, from. *Jâtavedase sunavâma* is the invariable Dhâyyâ. *Agnir hotâ* **[335]** *gṛihapatiḥ* (6, 15, 13) is the (Nivid) hymn for Jâtavedâs, with an additional pada (at the end); this is the animal form, which is a characteristic of the fifth day.

9.

(On the Rituyâjas of the Sixth Day.)

The sixth day is *deva kṣetra*, *i. e*, the field of the gods. Those who enter on the sixth day, enter the field of the gods who do not live together, but each in his own house. They say, No Ritu (season) lives in the house of another Ritu. Therefore the priests perform the Rituyâjas (offerings to the Ritus), each for himself, without appointing another one to do it for them.[5] Thus the priests prepare all the Ritus

[5] This refers to the circumstance that at the common Soma sacrifices, such as the Agniṣṭoma, the Rituyâja mantra for the Adhvaryu and the sacrificer are repeated by the Hotar, and not by the Adhvaryu and the sacrificer themselves. But at a Sattra, to which class of sacrifices the Dvâdaśâha belongs, this is not allowed; each must act for himself, each member of the body of priests who are performing a Sattra, being alternately priest and sacrificer. The Rituyâja mantras for the Adhvaryu and sacrificer are the eleventh and twelfth in order. See the note on page 135-36.

without foregoing such or such one (and make them fit for their own use), that the whole assemblage enjoys happiness, each in his own place. They say, No order for making the Ritu offering is required, nor is the formula "*vâuṣaṭ*" to be repeated. Because the order given (by the Maitrâvaruṇa), for the Ritu offerings are the Vâch, who is wearied on the sixth day. When they would give the order (for repeating the Yâjyâs) for the Ritu offerings, and call "*vâuṣaṭ*," then they would have Vâch wearied, tired, sinking under her load[6] (the number of mantras recited on the previous days) and faltering in her **[336]** voice.[7] But if the priests do not repeat the order for the Ritu offerings, nor repeat *vâusat* after the Yâjyâs, then they fall from the line of the sacrifice which should not be broken and (consequently they fall) from the sacrifice, from the prâṇa (breath), Prajâpati and cattle, and will (henceforth) walk crooked. Therefore the order (praiṣa) to repeat the mantras, as well as the Yâjyâ verse (at the end of which the Vaṣaṭkâra occurs) should be preceded by a Rik verse.[8] Thus they will not have the Vâch wearied, tried, sinking beneath her load, faltering in her voice, nor will they fall from the line of sacrifice which should not be broken, nor from the sacrifice, nor from the prâṇa, nor from Prajâpati, nor from the cattle, nor walk crooked.

10.

(On the Nature and Meaning of the Paruchhepa Verses.)

They place at the two first libations a Paruchhepa verse (one seen by the Riṣi Paruchhepa) before each of the Yâjyâs, which are repeated by the seven Hotars in their order (the so-called *prasthitas*).[9] The name of their metre is *Rohita*. By means of it Indra ascended the seven heavens. Thus he who has this knowledge ascends the seven heavens. They say, Verses which consist of five padas (steps) are a characteristic of the fifth day, and such ones as consist of six padas are fit for the sixth day, why then are metres of seven padas (as the Rohita is) **[337]** recited on the sixth day? (The reason is) By six steps the sixth day is reached; but by cutting off, as it were, the seventh day (by taking it single) they settle with the seventh step down (in heaven after having reached it by six). Thus they regain the Vâch for the connection (of the whole). Those who are possessed of such a knowledge have the three days connected and unbroken.

---

[6] *Rikṇavahi*; *rikna=bhagna*, broken, stands, as Sây. observes, instead of *vṛikna*.

[7] *Vaharâviṇî*.

[8] The verse to be prefixed to the Praiṣa and Yâjyâ is *tubhyam hinvânâ* (2, 36, 1).

[9] Previous to the recital of every Yâjyâ, one of the Paruchhepa verses is to be repeated. These are, *vṛiṣann indra vṛiṣa pânâsa indavaḥ* (1, 139, 6-11) and *pibâ somam indra suvânam*(1, 130, 2-10).

11.

(On the Origin of the Paruchhepa Verses.)

The Devâs and Asuras waged war in these worlds. The Devas turned the Asuras by means of the sixth day's ceremonies out of these worlds. The Asuras seized all things which they could grasp, took them and threw them into the sea. The Devas following them behind[10] seized by means of this metre (of the Paruchhepa verses which have seven padas) all they (the Asuras) had grasped. Just this pada, *viz.*, the additional pada (the seventh in the Paruchhepa verses) became a hook for the purpose of gathering the treasures (thrown into the sea by the Asuras). Therefore he who has this knowledge, deprives his enemy of his fortune and turns him out of all these worlds.

12.

(The Characteristics of the Sixth Day. The Śastras of the Morning and Midday Libations.)

Heaven (*Dyâus*) is the leading deity of the sixth day. The Stoma is the thirty-three-fold, the Sâman is Raivatam, Atichhandâs the metre. What has the same end (refrain) is a characteristic of the sixth day. **[338]** The sixth day has the same characteristics as the third, *viz.* the words, *aśva*, *anta*, end, repetition, consonance, cohabitation, *paryasta* (set), three, what has the form of *anta*; the mentioning of the deity in the last pada, an allusion to that world (heaven). The peculiar characteristics of the sixth day are, the *Paruchhepa* hymns comprising seven padas, the *Naraśaṁsam*, the *Nâbhânediṣṭham*, the *Raivatam* the *Atichhandâḥ*, and the past tense.

Ayam jâyata manuṣo dharîmaṇi (1, 128) is the Ajya Śastra, which is a Paruchhepa hymn, an Atichhandâḥ (a metre exceeding the normal measure) comprising seven padas, which is a characteristic of the sixth day.

The Pra-uga Śastra consists of the following verses, which all are Paruchhepa, and Atichhandâḥ, comprising seven padas: *stîrṇam barhir up no yâhi vîtaye* (1, 135, 1-3), *â vâm ratho niyutvân* (1, 135, 4-6); *suṣumâ yatam adribhir* (1, 137, 1-3); *yuvâm stomebhir devayanto* (1, 139, 4-6); *avar maha* (1, 133, 6-7); *astu śrâuṣaḷ* (1, 139, 1); *o ṣu no agne śriṇuhi tvâm îḷitô* (1, 139, 7); *ye devâso divy ekâdaśa* (1, 139, 11); *iyam adadâd rabhasam* (6, 61, 1-3).

Sa pûrvyô mahânâm (8, 52, 1-3) is the beginning of the Marutvatîya Śastra, because *mahan* is a word in *anta* (acc. *mahántam*), and *anta*, *i. e.*,

---

[10] *Anuhâya=priṣṭhato gatvâ S.*

end, is a characteristic of the sixth day, being the *end* (the last of the second series of three days). The verses, *Traya indrasya Soma* (8, 2, 7-9) *Indra nedîya edihi* (Vâl. 5, 5-6); *pra nûnam Brahmaṇaspatir* (1, 40, 5-6); *Agnír netâ* (3, 20, 4); *tvam Soma kratubhiḥ* (1, 91, 2), *pinvanty apô* (1, 64, 6); and *nakiḥ sudâsô ratham* are the extension (*âtânaḥ* of the Marutvatîya Śastra) and identical with those of the third day.

Yam tvaṃ ratham indra medhasâtaye (1, 129) is a Paruchhepa hymn in the Atichhandâḥ metre, consisting **[339]** of seven padas. *Sa yo vriṣâ-vriṣṇyebhiḥ* (1, 100) is the hymn whose verses have the same refrain[11] (*samânodarka*). *Indra Marutvâ iha pâhi* (3, 51, 7) is the hymn,[12] which contains an *anta*, (a participle of present tense form in *ant*, or its equivalent) in the words (verse 9), *tebhiḥ sâkam pibatu vṛitrakhâdaḥ*; because *vṛitrakhâdô* (*âdô* being taken as equivalent to *anta*) is the *anta*, and the sixth day is the end (*anta*). By means of this hymn, which is in the Triṣṭubh metre, the Hotar keeps through its padas which remain firm, the libation in its proper place, preventing it from falling. *Ayaṁ ha yena* (10, 65, 4-6) is the triplet which serves as a setting, for in its words, *svar marutvatâ jitam*, there is an *anta*, *jita* is an *anta*.[13] These verses are in the Gâyâtrî metre; the Gâyatrîs are the leading metres at the midday libation during these three days. The Nivid is put in the leading metre; thence the Hotar puts the Nivid in the Gâyâtrî metre.

The verses, *revatîr na sadhamâde* (1, 30, 13-15), and *revân id* (8, 2, 13-15), form the Raivata Pṛiṣṭha (the Raivaita Sâma), which is used on a Bṛihat day, to which the sixth day belongs. The verse *yad vâvâna* is the invariable Dhâyyâ. By "*tvâṁ iddhi havâmahê*" (6, 46, 1-2) which follows the Dhâyyâ, the Hotar returns all to the womb of the Bṛihat Sâma; for this is a Bṛihat day according to its position. *Indram id devatâtaya* (8, 3,5-6) is the Sâma Pragâtha which has the characteristic of *ninṛita* (has a consonance).[14] *Tyam û ṣu vâjinam* is the invariable Târkṣya.

13

[340] (*The Remainder of the Niṣkevalya Śastra and the Śastras of the Evening Libation.*)

Endra yâhy upa naḥ (1, 130) is the Paruchhepa hymn, in the Atichhandâḥ metre, comprising seven padas. *Pra gha nvasya* (2, 15) is the hymn whose several verses have the same refrain.[15] In the hymn *abhúr eko*

---

[11] This is *Marutvân no bhavatv indra ûti.*

[12] In the present state of the Samhitâ it is incorporated with another one.

[13] This appears to be an error, the form *ant* is to be sought in *marutvatâ.*

[14] Because in every pada there is the word *Indra*, the repetition of which resembles the sounding of a bell metal instrument.— *Sây.*

[15] This is *mada indra chakâra.*

rayipate (6, 31), the words occur (verse 5) *ratham âtiṣṭha tuvinṛimna bhîmam* ; in it the word *sthâ* " to stand, " marks an end (standing being the end of going) which is a characteristic of the sixth day. By means of this hymn, which is in the Triṣṭubh metre, the Hotar keeps, through its padas which remain firm, the libation in its proper place, preventing it from falling. *Upa no haribhiḥ stutam* (8, 82, 31-33) is the setting which has the same refrain. It is in the Gâyatrî metre, which is the leading one of the midday libation of the three (latter) days. Therefore the Nivid is to be placed in it. *Abhi taym devam Savitâram* (Vaj. Saṁh. 4, 25) is the beginning of the Vaiśvadeva Śastra, in the Atichhanda metre. *Tat Savitur vareṇyam* (3, 62, 10-11) and *doṣô agât* from the sequel, because *gata, i.e.*, gone, signifies an end, which is a characteristic of the sixth day.

Ud u ṣya devaḥ savitâ savâya (2, 38) is the (Nivid) hymn for Savitar ; the words therein, *śaśvattamam tadapa vahnir asthât,* contain an *anta,* for *sthita, i.e.*, standing is an *anta.*

Katarâ pûrvâ (1, 185, 1) is the (Nivid) hymn for Dyâvâpṛithivî, whose verses have the same refrain.[16]

Kim u śreṣṭhaḥ kiṁ yaviṣṭhô (1, 161) and *upa no vâjâ adhvaram ṛibhukṣa* (4, 37) form the Arbhavam **[341]** Narâśaṁsam hymns, in which the term " three " occurs, being a characteristic of the third day.

The two hymns *Idam itthâ râudram* (10, 61), and *ye yajñena dakṣiṇayâ samaktâ* (10, 62) form the Vaiśvadeva (Nâbhânediṣṭha) hymns.

14.

(The Story of Nâbhânediṣṭha, the son of Manu.)

He recites the Nâbhânediṣṭham. Nâbhânediṣṭha was a son of Manu, who was given to the sacred study (after his investiture in the house of his Guru) ; [17] his brothers deprived him of his share in the paternal property. He went (to them) and said, " What portion is left to me ? " They answered, " Go to the adjudicator [18] and arbitrator. " By " adjudicator and arbitrator " they meant their father. He went to his father and said, " They have divided the property including my share among themselves." The father answered, " My dear son, do not mind that. There are the Angirasaḥ just engaged in holding their sacrificial session (Sattra) for going to heaven. As often as they commence the ceremonies of the sixth day, they are puzzled (frustrated in their design). Let them recite on the sixth day those two hymns (abovementioned, Rigveda 10, 61-62), then they will give thee the sum of a thousand which is contributed by all the

[16] This is *dyâvâ rakṣatam pṛithivi no abhvât.*
[17] This is the meaning of the term *brahmacharyam vasantam.*
[18] *Niṣṭâva.*

sacrificers who participate in the sacrificial session, [19] when they go to heaven." He said, "Well, let it be so." He then went to them, saying, "Receive me, the son of Manu, among you, O ye wise!" They said, "What dost thou wish, that thou speakest thus?" He answered, [342] "I will show you how to perform the sixth day, then give me the reward for the sacrificial session of a thousand (cows or other valuables), when you go up to heaven." They said, "Well, let it be so." He made them recite on the sixth day those two hymns; then they became aware of the Yajña (the sacrifice regarded as a person, leading to heaven), and of the heaven-world. Therefore the Hotar recites those two hymns on the sixth day, in order that the sacrificer might become aware of the sacrifice, and to have subsequently pointed out the heaven-world. When they were going up, they said, "This thousand, O Brâhmaṇa, belongs to thee." When he was putting all together (the thousand pieces), a man clothed in a blackish (dirty) dress [20] alighted and approaching him, said, "This is mine; I have left it here." He answered, "The Angirasaḥ have given it to me." The man said "Then it belongs to either of us, thy father may decide." He went to his father. He asked him, "Have they not, my dear son, given you (the reward)?" He said, "They have given me; but a man clothed in a blackish dress alighted, and approaching me said, 'This is mine, I have left it here.' So saying, he took it." The father said, "It is his, my dear son! but he will give it to thee." He went back to him, and said, "Sir, this belongs only to you; so says my father." He said, "I give it to thee, because you have spoken the truth, (*i.e.*, acknowledged that it is my property)." Therefore a man who is learned must speak only the truth. This is the mantra of "the thousand gifts," the Nâbhânediṣṭha hymn. Upon that man who has this knowledge, a thousand gifts shower, and he gets a glimpse of heaven by means of the sixth day.

15.

[343] *On the auxiliary Śastras at the Evening Libation, Nâbhânediṣṭha, Vâlakhilyâ, the Sukîrti Hymn, Vṛiṣâkapi, and Evayâmarut. The Agnimâruta Śastra of the Sixth Day.* (*See 6, 27-30.*)

The Hotar ought to repeat those Śastras which are called the accompaniments (of the others on the sixth day), *viz.*, the Nâbhânediṣṭham, Vâlakhilyâ, Vṛiṣâkapi and Evayâmaruta only as auxiliaries (to the Vaiśvadeva-Śastra). If the Hotar foregoes only one of them,

---

[19] This is the translation of *sattra-pariveṣaṇam*.

[20] Sây. says that according to another Śâkhâ, this man is Rudra, the master of cattle.

(these additional Śastras), the sacrificer will lose something. If he foregoes the Nâbhânediṣṭham, then the sacrificer will lose his semen; if he foregoes the Vâlakhilyâs, then the sacrificer will lose his breath; if he foregoes the Vṛiṣâkapi, the sacrificer will lose his soul; and if he foregoes the Evayâmarutam, then he will turn the sacrificer out of his divine and human position. By means of the Nâbhânediṣṭham, he (the priest) poured the semen into the sacrificer; by means of the Vâlakhilyâ verses, he transformed them (to make an embryo). By means of the hymn [21] by Sukîrti, the son of Kakṣîvat, he made the womb set forth the child, because therein (in the first verse is said), "Let us rejoice in thy shelter, Indra! (just as people find pleasure in a large commodious room)." Thence the child (*garbha*), though being larger, does not damage the womb which is (much) smaller. If the womb is prepared by (this) sacred hymn (Brahma, the Sukîrti hymn), then the Hotar imparts to the sarcificer the faculty of walking by means of the Evayâmaruta hymn (5, 87). If he has done all required for making the sacrificer walk, then he walks (he has obtained the faculty of walking).

Ahaścha kṛiṣṇam ahar arjunam (6, 9, 1-33) is the beginning of the Agnimâruta Śastra, because *ahas* **[344]** is a repetition, and a consonance, which is a characteristic of the sixth day. *Madhvo vo nâma mârutam yajatrâ* (7, 57) is the Maruta hymn. Here is the plural (because the Marutas are many) to be urged; because the plural is an *anta*, and this is a characteristic of the sixth day.

Jâtavedase sunavâma (1, 99, 1), is the invariable Jâtavedâs verse. *Sa pratnathâ sahasâ* (1, 96, 1) is the (Nivid) hymn for Jâtavedâs, whose verses have the same refrain, which is a characteristic of the sixth day.

The priest, apprehending the *anta*, *i. e.*, ends of the sacrifice, might fall down, keeps them up by repeating twice the word *dhârayan*,[22] *i. e.*, they may hold, just as one ties and unties successively the ends of a cord, [23] or just as one (a tanner) is driving in the end of a (wetted) skin a peg, in order to keep it (expanded). It is done to keep the sacrifice uninterrupted Those who have such a knowledge have the three days continuous and unbroken (undisturbed).

---

[21] *Apa prâcha Indra* (*10, 131*).

[22] It is in the last pada of all verses of this hymn.

[23] In order to make of them a large ring.

THIRD CHAPTER.

(The Characteristics and Śastras of the Seventh and Eighth Days.)

16.

(The Characteristics of the Seventh Day. The Śastras of the Morning and Midday Libation.)

The terms *â* and *pra* are the characteristics of the seventh day. The seventh day is just like the first, *yukta*, *ratha*, *âśu*, *piba*, the deity mentioned in the first pada, the allusion to this world (earth,) *jâta*, *anirukta*, *kariṣyat* (future), these are the characteristics of the seventh day.

[345] *Samudrâd ûrmim* (10, 123, 2) is the Ajya hymn. Here is something hidden (*aniruktam*, *i. e.*, not explicitly stated) which is a characteristic of the seventh day. In the sea (Samudra) is Vâch; because neither the sea becomes (ever) extinct, nor Vâch. Thence this (hymn) is the Ajya (Śastra) of the seventh day. From the Yajña (sacrifice) only, the Hotar thus extends the sacrifice,[1] and thus they recover Vâch again (to continue the sacrifice). The Stomas are at an end, the meters are at an end on the sixth day. Just as (at the Darśapûrnamâsa Iṣṭi) they cause to drip upon the pieces of sacrificial food drops of melted butter (*âjya*), in order to make them hot again[2] for recovering its essence already gone; in the same way, they recover the Stomas and meters for regaining (the essence of) the sacrifice again by this Ajya Śastra of the seventh day. It is in the Triṣṭubh metre; because this is the metre at the morning libation during the (last) three days.

The Pra-uga Śastra consists of the following mantras: *â vâyo bhûṣa* (7, 92, 1), *prayâbhir yâsi* (7, 92, 3) *â no niyudbhiḥ śatinîr* (7, 92, 5), *pra sotâ jiro adhvareṣv asthât* (7, 92, 2), *ye vâyava indra mâda nâsa* (7, 92, 4), *yâ vâm śatam* (7, 91, 6),[3] *pra yad vam Mitrâvaruṇâ* (6, 67, 9-11), *â gomatâ nâsatyâ* (7, 72, 1-3), *â no deva śavasâ* (7, 30, 1-3) *pra vo yajñeṣu* (7, 43, 1-3), *pra kṣodasâ dhâyasâ* (7, 95, 1-3). In these verses there are the characteristics of the **[346]** seventh day, *â* and *pra*, contained. They are in the Triṣṭubh metre, because this is the metre at the morning libation during the (last) three days.

---

[1] With the sixth day, the sacrifice is finished. Vâch is done up; but the priest commences now developing the Yajña again. This can be done only by starting from the Yajña itself (without any other help), and recovering the Vâch in the form of this allusion.

[2] All this is implied in the expression *pratyabhighârayan*.

[3] These six verses form two triplets; they all are so called *ekapâtinîs*, and constitute the two triplets for Vâyu and Indra respectively, which are always required at the Pra-uga Śastra.

Â tvâ ratham yathotaya, (8, 57, 1-2) *idam vaso sutam andaḥ* (8, 2, 1-2), *Indra nedîya ed ihi* (Vâl. 5, 5-6), *praitu Brahmanaspatir* (1, 40, 3-4), *Agnír netâ* (3, 20, 4), *tvam soma kratubhiḥ* (1, 91, 2), *pinvanty apaḥ* (1, 64, 6), *pra va indrâya bṛihate* (8, 78, 3), are the extension (of the Marutvatîya Śastra) of the seventh day, identical with that of the first.

In the hymn, *Kayâ śubhâ savayaśaḥ* (1, 165) (9th verse), in the words *na jâyamâno naśate, na jâta* the term *jâta* occurs, which is one of the characteristics of the seventh day. This is the *Kayâśubhîya* hymn which effects unanimity (among people) and prolongs life. By means of it Indra, Agastya, and the Maruts became (unanimous). By reciting the *Kayâśubhîyam* hymn, the Hotar produces unanimity. But it bears upon the prolongation of life also. Who desires that, may have repeated the *Kayâśubhîyam*. It is in the Triṣṭubh metre. By means of its pada which remains firm, the Hotar keeps the libation in its proper place, preventing it from falling down.

The hymn, *tyam su meṣam mahayâ* (1, 52) contains (in the second pada of the first verse) the words *atyaṁ na vâjam havanasyadaṁratham*, the term *ratha*, *i.e.*, carriage, being a characteristic of the seventh day. It is in the Jagatî metre, for the Jagatîs are the leading metres at the midday libation of these three last days. The Nivid is placed in that metre which is the leading; thence one places (here) the Nivid in the Jagatîs.

The hymns representing cohabitation are now repeated; they are in the Triṣṭubh and Jagatî metres. Because cattle is represented by cohabitation and **[347]** the Chandomâs[4] are cattle and calculated for obtaining cattle. *Tvâm iddhi havâmahe*, and *tvam hy ehi* **[348]** *cherave* (8, 50, 1-2) form the Bṛihat Pṛiṣṭha on the seventh day. The same Pṛiṣṭhas take place as on the sixth day. The Vairûpam (Sâma) belongs

[4]The Chandomâḥ are three peculair Stomas, which are required on the three last days of Navarâtra, or the seventh, eighth, and ninth days of the Dvâdaśâha and the name of these three days themselves. They are minutely described in the Tâṇḍya Brâhmaṇam 3, 8-13. These Stomas are, the twenty-four-fold (*chaturviṁśa*), the forty-four-fold (*chatuśchatvâriṁśa*), and the forty-eight-fold (*aṣṭâchatvâriṁśa*). The verses required for chanting the Chandomâḥ on the three last days of Navarâtra are (according to the *Udgâtri prayoga* of the *Dvâdaśâha*) all put together in the second part of the Sâmavedârchikam, commencing with the second Ardha of the fourth Prapâṭhaka (*pra kâvyam uśaneva*), and ending with the fifth Prapâṭhaka (with the verse *Yuṅkṣvâ hi keśinâ hari*). The order is, on the seventh day, all Sâma verses are put in the twenty-four-fold Stoma, on the eighth all are chanted according to the forty-four-fold Stoma in three varieties, on the ninth all are put in the forty-eight-fold Stoma, of which there are two varieties enumerated. There is here no change of the Stomas according to the libations, as it is in the Agniṣṭoma and the cognate sacrifices. That Stoma, in which the first Stotram

to the Rathantaram ; the Vairâjam to the Bṛihat ; the Sâkvaram to the Rathantaram, and the Raivatam to the Bṛihat. Therefore (because the Raivatam representing the Bṛihat was chanted on the sixth day) the Bṛihat Pṛiṣṭha takes place (on the seventh day) ; for they fasten through that Bṛihat (of the sixth day), the Bṛihat (of the seventh day) to prevent the cutting off of the Stomas ; for, if the Rathantaram (which is opposed to the Bṛihat) is used, then the union (of the sixth and seventh days) is destroyed. Therefore only the Bṛihat is to be used (on the seventh day.)

Yad vâvâna is the immovable Dhâyyâ. By the subsequent recital of the Rathantaram *abhi tvâ śûra nonumaḥ*, the Hotar brings all back to the womb ; for this is a Rathantara day according to its position. *Pibâ sutasya rasinaḥ* (8, 3, 1-2) is the Sâma Pragâtha, which has *piba*, one of the characteristics of the seventh day. *Tyam û ṣu vâjinam* is the invariable Târkṣya.

17

(The Remainder of the Niṣkevalya Śastra. The Śastras of the Evening Libation.)

Indrasya nu vîryâṇi (1, 32) is a hymn which has the characteristic word *pra* of the seventh day. It is **[349]** in the Triṣṭubh metre. By

(the Bahiṣ-pavamâna) is chanted, remains in force for the whole day. The Bahiṣ-pavamânas of all three days, generally contain as many verses as the Stoma has members. So, for instance, the Bahiṣ-pavamâna of the seventh day consists of 24 verses (Sâmaveda ii. 465-88), for the twenty-four-fold Stoma is reigning during this day ; the Bahiṣ-pavamâna of the eighth day consists of forty-four verses (Sâmaveda ii. 524-67), for the Stoma reigning during this day is the forty-four-fold, &c. The four Sâmans which follow the Bahiṣ-pavamâna Stotras at the midday libation, are called *âjyâni*, the four which follow the Pavamâna Stotras at the midday libation, go by the name of *Pṛiṣṭhâni*, and the four which follow the Arbhava-pavamâna Stotra at the evening libation are called *ukthâni*. Now the *âjyâni*, *pṛiṣṭhâni* and *ukthâni* generally consist either of three or even only two verses. If they consist of only two verses, they are to be made three, just as is the case with the Rathantara, Nâudhasa, and Kâleya Pṛiṣṭha at the Agniṣṭoma. The three verses then are, in three turns, so often to be repeated, as to yield twenty-four, forty-four, or forty-eight. Each turn of the twenty-four-fold Stoma contains, for instance, eight verses, in three divisions, in the following order :—

I. 8—*a*, 3 ; *b*, 4 ; *c*, 1 : II. 8—*a*, 1 ; *b*, 3 ; *c*, 4 : III. 8—*a*, 4 ; *b*, 1 ; *c*, 3.

In the forty-four-fold Stoma, the repetitions are arranged in the following way :—

I. 15—*a*, 3 ; *b*, 11 ; *c*, 1 : II. 14—*a*, 1 ; *b*, 3 ; *c*, 10 : III. 15—*a*, 11 ; *b*, 1 ; *c*, 3.

The forty-eight-fold Stoma is as follows :—

I. 16—*a*, 3 ; *b*, 12 ; *c*, 1 : II. 16—*a*, 1 ; *b*, 3 ; *c*, 12 : III. 16 —*a*, 12 ; *b*, 1 ; *c*, 3.

The forty-eight-fold Stoma is the last of the Stomas ; thence it is called *anta*. The Chandomâḥ are said to have the animal form. According to the Tâṇḍya Brâhm. (3, 8), the animals have eight hoofs, thence are eight verses required in each turn when the twenty-four-fold Stoma is made ; or, they are said (3, 12) to consist of sixteen pieces ; thence are sixteen verses in each turn required when the forty-eight-fold Stoma is made.

means of the pâdas which remain firm, the Hotar keeps the libation in its proper place, preventing it from falling down.

Abhi tyam meṣam puruhûtam (1, 51, 1) is a hymn in which *pra* is replaced by *abhi*, forming a characteristic of the seventh day. It is in the Jagatî metre, because the Jagatîs are the leading metres at the midday libation. Therefore the Nivid is to be placed in it.

These hymns representing cohabitation are now repeated, which are in the Triṣṭubh and Jagatî metres; because cohabitation represents cattle, and the Chandomâs represent cattle; (this is done) in order to obtain cattle.

Tat savitar vinîmahe (5, 82, 1-3), *adya no deva Savitar* (5, 82, 3-5) are the beginning and sequel of the Vaiśvadeva Śastra in the Rathantara days, on the seventh day. *Abhi tvâ deva Savitar* (1, 24, 3) is the (Nivid) hymn for Savitar, which contains instead of *pra* the word *abhi*, which is identical with *pra*, a characteristic of the seventh day.

Pretâm yujñasya (2, 41, 19) is the (Nivid) hymn for Dyâvâpṛithivî, which contains the word *pra*. *Ayam devâya janmana* (1, 20 is the (Nivid) hymn for the Ribhus, which contains the word *jan*, to be born.

He repeats now the verses, consisting of two pâdas, commencing *âyâhi ranasâ saha*, (10, 172, 1); for man has two feet, and animals have four; animals are represented by the Chandomâs. (This is done) for obtaining cattle. If he repeats these verses which consist of two feet, then he places the sacrificer, who has two legs, among the four-footed cattle.[6]

Abhir agne duvo (1, 14) is the (Nivid) hymn for the Viśvedevâh, which has the characteristic *â* of the seventh day. It is in the Gâyatrî metre; for **[350]** the third libation is headed by the Gâyatri during these three days.

Viśvânaro ajîjanat is the beginning of the Agnimâruta Śastra, which contains the word *jan*, to be born. *Pra yad vas triṣṭubham* (8, 7) is the (Nivid) hymn for the Marutas, which has the word *pra*. *Jâtavedase sunavâma* (1, 99, 1) is the invariable Jâtavedâs verse. *Dûtam vo viśvavedasam* (4, 8) is the (Nivid) hymn for Jâtavedâs, where the name (Jâtavedâs) is not explicitly mentioned (only hinted-at). All these are in the Gâyatrî metre; for the third libation on these three days is headed by the Gâyatrî.

---

[6] He makes him obtain them.

18.

(The Characteristics of the Eighth day. The Śastras of the Morning and Midday Libations.)

Neither the words *â* nor *pra*, but what is "standing" is the characteristic of the eighth day; because the eighth is identical with the second. The characteristics are, *ûrdhva*; *prati*, *antar*, *vṛiṣan*, *vṛidhan*, the mentioning of the deity in the middle pâda, an allusion to the airy region, twice the name Agni (in the same pâda), the words *mahad*, *vihûta punar*, the present tense.

Agnim vo devam agnibhiḥ (7, 3) is the Ajya of the eighth day; bacause it contains twice the word *agni*. It is in the Triṣṭubh metre; for the Triṣṭubh is the leading metre at the morning libation during these three days. The Pra-uga Śastra is composed of the following verses: *Kuvid aṅga namasâ* (7, 91, 1,) *pîvo annân* (7, 91, 3,) *uchhan uṣasaḥ* (7, 90, 4), *uśantâ dûtâ* (7, 91, 2,) *yâvat taras* (7, 91, 4-5,) *prati vâṁ sûra udite* (7, 65, 1-3,) *dhenuḥ pratnasya* (3, 58, 1-3), *Brahmâna indropa* (7, 28, 1-3,) *ûrdhvo agniḥ sumatim* (7, 39, 1-3) *uta syâ naḥ sarasvatî* (7, 95, 4-6). In these verses are the characteristics **[351]** *prati*, *antar*, *vihûta*, *urdhvai* contained; they are in the Triṣṭubh metre, which is the leading metre at the morning libation on these three days.

The extension (of the Marutvatîya Śastra) consists of the following verses: *Viśvânarasya vaspatim* (8, 57, 4), *Indra it Somapâ ekah* (8, 2, 4), *Indra nedîya ed ihi* (Vâl. 5, 5-6), *uttiṣtha Brahmanspate* (1, 40, 1-2), *agnir netâ tvam Soma kratubhiḥ*, *pinvanty apo*, *brihad indrâya gâyata*. This Śastra is identical with that of the second day.

Now follow the *Mahadvat* hymns, *i. e.*, such ones as contain the word *mahat*, great. (These are) *saṁsâ mahâm* (3, 49), *mahaśchit tvâm* (1, 169), *pibâ somam abhi yam* (6, 17), in the words *ûrvam gavyam mahi*, *mahâṁ indro nṛivat* (6, 19). This hymn is in the Triṣṭubh metre; by means of its pâdas which remain firm, the Hotar keeps the libation in its proper place, preventing it from falling down.

Tam asya dyâvâ prithivî (10, 113) is a *mahadvat* hymn also; for, in the second pâda of the first verse, the word *mahîmâno* occurs. It is in the Jagatî metre. The Jagatîs are the leading metres at the midday libation during the three last days (above-mentioned). Thence the Nivid is placed in it. These hymns represent cohabitation; they are in the Triṣṭubh and Jagatî metres, for cattle is represented by cohabitation, and, for obtaining cattle, the *mahadvat* hymns are repeated. The air is *mahad*; in order to obtain the airy region, *five* hymns (there are five, four in Triṣtubh, and one in Jagatî) are required. For the Paṅkti metre comprises five pâdas, the sacrifice belongs to this metre, cattle belong to it; cattle is represented by the Chandomâs.

Abhi tvâ śûra nonumaḥ, and *abhi tvâ pûrvapîtaye* form the Rathantaram Pṛiṣṭham of the eighth day. *Yad vâvâna* is the invariable Dhâyyâ. By *tvâm iddhi havâmahe* all is brought back to the womb; **[352]** for this day is a Bâṛhata day according to its position. *Ubhayaṁ sriṇâvachcha* (8, 50, 1-2) is the Sâma Pragâtha; the meaning of *ubhayam i. e.*, both, in it is, what is to-day and what was yesterday. This is a characteristic of the eighth day, which is a Bṛihat day. *Tyam û ṣu vâjinam* is the invariable Târkṣya.

19.

(*The Mahadvat Hymns of the Niṣkevalya Śastra. The Śastras of the Evening Libation.*)

The five Mahadvat hymns are, *apûrvyâ purutamâni* (6, 32), *tâm su te kîrtim* (10, 54), *tvaṁ mahân Indra yo ha* (1, 63), *tvaṁ mahân indra tubhyam* (4, 17). These (four) hymns are in the Triṣṭubh metre; by means of its pâdas which remain firm, the Hotar keeps the libation in its proper place, preventing it from falling down. The fifth is in the Jagatî metre, *viz.*, *divaśchid asya varimâ* (1, 55), which contains in the words, *indram na mahnâ*, the term *mahat*, great. For obtaining cattle these Mahadvat hymns are repeated. The air is *mahat*, and for obtaining the airy region two times five hymns must be repeated. Because a Paṅkti (a collection of five hymns) has five feet, the Yajña consists of five parts, cattle consist of five parts. Twice five makes ten;[6] this decade is Virâṭ, Virâṭ is food, cattle are food, the Chandomâs are cattle.

Viśvo devasya netus (5, 50, 1), *tat savitur vareṇyaṁ â vis vedçvam saptatim* (5, 82, 7-8), are the beginning and sequel of the Vaiśvadeva Śastra. *Hiranyapâṇim ûtaye* (1, 22, 5-7), which contains the word *ûrdhva*, is the (Nivid) hymn for Savitar. *Mahi dyâuḥ pṛithivî chana* (1, 22, 13-15) is the (Nivid) hymn for Dyâvâpṛithivî, which contains the word *mahat*. *Yuvânâ* **[353]** *pitarâ punar* (1, 20, 4-8) is the (Nivid) hymn for the Ribhus, which has the characteristic word "*punah*."

Imâ nu kam bhuvanâ (10, 157) is the hymn which contains only verses of two feet.[7] For man has two feet, whilst the animals have four, and by

---

[6] *Sây*—The five Mahadvat hymns of the Marutvatîya, and the five of the Niṣkevalya Śastras are to be understood.

[7] It contains five verses, which are called Dvipadâ Triṣṭubh. (Sây, in his Commentary on the Saṁhitâ.)

means of this hymn he places the two-footed sacrificer among the four-footed cattle. *Devânâm id avo mahad* (8, 72, 1) is the (Nivid) hymn for the Viśvedevâs, which contains the term *mahat*. These verses are in the Gâyatrî metre (except the Dvipâds), because the Gâyatrî is the leading metre at the evening libation during these three (last) days.

By *ṛitâvânam vaiśvânaram* (Aśv. Śr. S. 8, 10), commences the Agnimâruta Śastra ; because in the word *agnir vaiśvânaro mâhón*, there is the word *mahat* contained. *Krîlaṁ vaḥ śardho mârutam* (1, 37) is the (Nivid) hymn for the Marutas ; because it contains (in the fifth verse) the word *vavṛidhe*, which is a characteristic of the eighth day.

Jâtavedase sunavâma is the invariable Jâtavedâs verse. *Agne mrila mahân asi* (4, 9) is the (Nivid) hymn for Jâtavedâs ; it contains the characteristic term *mahad*. All these verses are in the Gâyatrî metre, which is the (leading) metre at the evening libation during these three (last) days.

FOURTH CHAPTER.

(The Ninth and Tenth Days of the Dvâdaśâha. Conclusion of this Sacrifice.)

20.

(The Characteristics of the Ninth Day. The Śastras of the Morning and Midday Libations.)

What has the same refrain, is a characteristic of the ninth day. This day has the same characteristics as **[354]** the third, *viz.*, *aśva*, *anta*, *punarâvrittam*, *punarninṛittam*, *rata*, *paryasta*, the number three, *antarûpa*, the mentioning of the deity in the last pada, an allusion to that world, *śuchi* splendour, *satya* truth, *kṣeti* to reside, *gata* gone, *oka* house, the past tense.

Aganma mahâ namaśâ (7,12, 1) is the Ajya hymn of the ninth day, because it contains the word "gone" (in *aganma*, we went), it is in the Triṣṭubh metre.

The Pra-uga Śastra consists of the following verses : *pra vîryâ* (7, 90, 1), *te te satyena manasâ* (7, 90, 5), *divi kṣayanta* (7, 64, 1), *â viśva vârâ* (7, 70, 1-3), *ayam soma indra tubhyam sunva* (7, 29, 1-3), *pra Brâhmaṇo* (7, 42, 1-3), *Sarasvatîm devayanto* (10, 17, 7-9), *â no divo bṛihataḥ* (5, 43, 11-13), *Sarasvaty abhi no* (6, 61, 14-16). These verses have the characteristics, *śuchi* *i.e.*, splendour ; *satya*, *i.e.*, truth ; *kṣeti*, *i.e.*, residence ; *gate*, *i.e.*, gone ; *oka*, *i.e.*, house. They are in the Triṣṭubh metre, which is the (leading) metre at the morning libation, during the three (last) days.

The extension (of the Marutvatîya Śastra) is the same as on the third day. The five hymns representing cohabitation which contain the characteristics of this day, and represent cattle, are, *Indra svâhâ pibatu* (3, 50); *svâhâ* here is an *anta*; *gâyat sâma nabhanyam* (1, 173), which contains an *anta* in the word *svar*; *tiṣṭhâ hari ṛatha* (335), which contains an *anta* in *sthâ*, to stand; *ima u tvâ purutam asya* (6, 21), which contains an *anta* in *rathestha*. These four are in the Triṣṭubh metre. The fifth is in the Jagatî metre, *pra mandine pitumat* (1, 101), whose verses have the same refrain. The Jagatîs being the leading metre on the three (last) days, the Nivid is to be put in them. These hymns in the Triṣṭubh and Jagatî metres are repeated as (representing) cohabitation. For cattle is cohabitation; the Chandomâs are **[355]** cattle. (This is done) for obtaining cattle. Five (such) hymns are repeated. For the Paṅkti consists of five pâdas; the sacrifice has the nature of the Paṅkti, and so have cattle (also); the Chandomâḥ are cattle; (this is done) for obtaining cattle.

Tvâm iddhi havâmahe and *tvâm hyehi cherave*, form the Bṛihat Pṛiṣṭha. *Yad vâvâna* is the invariable Dâyyâ. By *abhi tvâ śûra nonumo* all is brought to the womb, because the ninth day is a Rathantara day according to its position. *Indra tridhâtu śaraṇam* (6, 46, 9-10) is the Sâma Pragâtha containing the characteristic "three." (The Târkṣya just as on the other days.)

21.

(The Remainder of the Niṣkevalya Śastra. The Śastras of the Evening Libation.)

There are five other pair-hymns enumerated, the four first are in the Triṣṭubh, the fifth in the Jagatî metre. These are, *saṁ cha tve jagmur* (6, 34), which contains the word "gone;" *kadâ bhuvan* (6, 35) which contains the word "*kṣi*" to reside, (in *kṣayaṇi*), which is an *antarûpa*, "he resides as it were, gone to an end (having gained his object)," *â satyo yâtu* (4, 16) which contains *satya* truth, *tat ta indṛiyam paramam* (1, 103), which contains an *anta* in the word "*paramaṁ*," *i. e.*, highest. *Ahaṁ bhuvaṁ* (10, 48, 1), which contains an *anta* in *jayâmi*, I conquer[1].

The commencement and sequel of the Vaiśvadeva Śastra is, *tat Savitur vriṇîmahe*, and *adyâ no deva Savitar*. (The Nivid) hymn for Savitar is *doṣo âgât* (?). The (Nivid) hymn for Dyâvâprithivî is, *pravâm mahi dyavî abhî* (4, 56, 5-7).

[356] *Indra iṣe dadâtu naḥ* (8, 82, 34), *te no ratnâni* (1, 20, 7-8) form the (Nivid) hymn for the Ribhus, the words *trir â saptâni* (1, 20, 7) contain

1 For the sentences here omitted in the translation (they are only repetitions) see 5, 19. 5

the characteristic "three." *Babhrur eko viṣuṇaḥ* (8, 29) is the Dvipadâ. By repeating a Dvipâd, the Hotar puts the two-legged sacrificer among the four-legged animals. *Ye trimsati trayas para* (8, 28) is the (Nivid) hymn for the *viśvedevâh*, because it contains the term "three." *Vaiśvânaro na ûtaye* (Aśv Sr. S. 8, 11) is the Pratipad of the Agnimâruta Śastra ; it contains the term *parâvataḥ*, which is an *anta.*

Maruto yasya hi kṣaya (1, 86) is the (Nivid) hymn for the Marutas. It contains the term *kṣi*, to reside, which is an *antarûpam* ; for one resides, as it were, after having gone to a (certain) object.

The (Nivid) hymn for Jâtavedâs is, *prâgnaye vâcham iraya* (10, 187) (each verse of which ends with) *sa naḥ pârṣad ati dviṣaḥ*, *i. e.*, may he (Agni) overcome our enemies, and bring (safely our ceremonies) to a conclusion. He repeats this refrain twice. For in this Navarâtra sacrifice (which is lasting for nine days), there are so many ceremonies, that the committal of a mistake is unavoidable. In order to make good (any such mistake, the pâda mentioned must be repeated twice). By doing so, the Hotar makes them (the priests and sacrificers) free from all guilt. These verses are in the Gâyatrî metre ; for the Gâyatrî is the (leading) metre at the evening libation during the three (last) days.

22.

(To What the Different Parts of the Dvâdaśâha are to be likened. The Tenth Day.)

The six Pṛiṣṭha days (the six first in the Dvâdaśâha) represent the mouth ; the Chandomâḥ days, from the seventh to the ninth, are then what is **[357]** in the mouth, as tongue, palate, and teeth ; but that by which one produces articulate sounds of speech, or by which one distinguishes the sweet and not sweet, this is the tenth day. Or the six Pṛiṣṭha days are comparable to the nostrils, and what is between them, to the Chandomâḥ days ; but that by which one discerns the different smells, this is the tenth day. Or the six Pṛiṣṭha days are comprable to the eye ; the Chandomâḥ are then the black in the eye, and the tenth day then is the pupil of the eye, by which one sees. Or the six Pṛiṣṭha days are comparable to the ear ; while the Chandomâḥ represent what is in the ear ; but by what one hears, that is the tenth day.

The tenth day is happiness ; those who enter on the tenth day, enter on happiness, therefore silence must be kept during the tenth day ; for "we shall not bespeak the (goddess of) fortune,"[2] because a happy thing is not to be spoken to.

Now the priests walk, clean themselves, and proceed to the place of the sacrificer's wife (*patnîśâlâ*).[3] That one of the priests, who should know this invocation offering (*âhuti*), shall say :

"Hold one another ;" then he shall offer the oblation by repeating the mantra, "here be thou happy, here be ye happy, here may be a hold, here may be a hold for all that is yours ;[4] may Agni carry it (the sacrifice) up ! Svâhâ ![5] may he take it up ! "

When he says, "be happy here," then he makes happy (joyful) all those (sacrificers) who are in this **[358]** world. When he says, "enjoy yourselves," then he makes joyful their offspring in these worlds. When he says, "here may be a hold, a hold for all that is yours," then he provides the sacrificers with children, and speech (the power of speech). By the words "may Agni carry it up" (*vâṭ*), the Rathantaram Sâman is to be understood, and by "Svâhâ ! may he carry it up !" the Bṛihat Sâman is meant. For the Rathantaram and Bṛihat Sâman are the cohabitation of the gods ; by means of this cohabitation of the gods one obtains generation ; by means of this cohabitation of the gods generation is produced. (This is done) for production. He who has this knowledge, obtains children and cattle.

Now they all go and make ablution and proceed to the place of the Agnîdhra. That one who knows the invocation offering (*âhuti*) shall say "hold now one another," then he should bring the offering and recite, "he who produced besides us this ground (our) mother, he, the preserver who feeds (us), may preserve in us wealth, vigour, health, and strength, Svâhâ !" Who knowing this, recites this formula, gains for himself, as well as for the sacrificers, wealth, vigour, health, and strength.

23.

(*The Chanting and Repeating of the Serpent Mantra. The Chaturhotṛi Mantra. Its effect. Who Ought to Repeat it.*)

All the other priests (except the Udgâtṛis) go from thence (the Agnîdhrîya fire) and proceed to the *Sadas* (a place in the south-east of the Utta-

---

[2] This is a very common superstition spread in Europe ; not to speak, for instance, on finding some treasure in the earth. Sây. explains *avavad* by "to blame ;" but this is not required, and is not good sense.

[3] To make Homa.

[4] All that you have, all your possessions may be upheld and remain in the same prosperous state.

[5] The formula Svâhâ is personified, and taken as a deity.

râvedi) all walking each in his own way, in this or that direction. But the Udgâtṛis walk together. They chant the verses (seen) by the Queen of the Serpents (*Sarpa-râjñî*) ; because the earth (*iyam*) is the Queen of the Serpents, for she is the queen of all that **[359]** moves (*sarpat*). She was in the beginning without hair, as it were (without trees, bushes, &c.) She then saw this mantra, which commences, *áyam gâuḥ priśnir akramît* (10, 189). In consequence of it, she obtained a motley appearance, she became variegated (being able to produce) any form she might like (such as) herbs, trees, and all (other) forms. Therefore the man who has such a knowledge obtains the faculty of assuming any form he might choose.

The three Udgâtris, Prastotar Udgâtar, and Pratihartar, repeat their respective parts in their mind (*i. e.* they do not utter words), but the Hotar repeats (aloud) with his voice ; for *Vâch* (speech) and *Manas* (mind) are the cohabitation of the gods. By means of this cohabitation of the gods, he who has such a knowledge, obtains children and cattle.

The Hotar now sets forth the Chaturhotṛi mantras;[6] he repeats them as the Śastra accompanying the Stotram (the chanting of the verses just mentioned) by the Udgâtṛis. The sacrificial name of the deities in the Chaturhotris was concealed. Therefore the Hotar now sets forth these names, and makes public the appropriate sacrificial name of the deities, and brings what has become public, to the public. He who has this knowledge, becomes public (*i.e.*, celebrated).

A Brahman who, after having completed his Vedic studies, should not attain to any fame, should go to a forest, string together the stalks of Dharba grass, with their ends standing upwards, and sitting on the right side of another Brahman, repeat with a loud voice, the Chaturhotṛi mantras. (Should he do so, he would attain to fame).

24.

(**[360]** *When and How the Priests Break their Silence on the Tenth Day*)

All touch now the branch of an Udumbara tree (which is at the sacrificial compound behind the seat of the Udgâtar) with their hands, thinking "I touch food and juice ; " for the Udumbara tree represents juice[7] and food. At the time that the gods distributed (for the earth)

[6] This is generally done before the singing of a mantra by the Udgâtar ; but the Udgâtar not being allowed at this occasion to utter words, his office is taken by the Ḥotar.

[7] The sap of the Udumbara tree is to be understood. It grew out of the food scattered by the gods on the earth.—*Sây.* compare 7, 32.

food and juice, the Udumbara trees grew up; therefore it brings forth every year three times ripe fruits. If they take the Udumbara branches in their hands, they then take food and juice. They suppress speech, for the sacrifice is speech; in suppressing the sacrifice (by abstaining from it) they suppress the day; for the day is the heaven-world, and (consequently) they subdue the heaven-world. No speech is allowed during the day; if they would speak during the day, they would hand over the day to the enemy; if they would speak during the night, they would hand over the night to the enemy. Only at the time when the sun has half set, they should speak; for then they leave but this much space (as is between the conjunction of day and night) to the enemy. Or they should speak (only) after the sun has completely set. By doing so, they make their enemy and adversary share in the darkness. Walking round the Ahavanîya fire, they then speak; for the Ahavanîya fire is the sacrifice, and the heaven-world; for by means of the sacrifice, which is the gate of the heaven-world, they go to the heaven-world. By the words, "if we have failed, by omission, or improper application, or by excess, of **[361]** what is required, all that may go (be taken away) to (our) father, who is Prajâpati," they recommence speaking. For all creatures are born after Prajâpati (he being their creator). Prajâpati, therefore, is the shelter from (the evil consequences of) what is deficient, or in excess (in his creatures); and thence these two faults do no harm to the sacrificers. Therefore all that is deficient or in excess with them who have this knowledge, enters Prajâpati. Thence they should commence speaking by (repeating) this (mantra).

25.

(*The Chaturhotṛi Mantras. The Bodies of Prajâpati. The Brahmodyam. The Sacrificers take their Seats in Heaven.*)

When the Hotar is about to repeat the Chaturhotṛi mantra, he cries, "Adhvaryu!" This is the proper form of *âhâva* (at this occasion, and not *śoṁsâvôm*). The Adhvaryu then responds, "*Om*, Hotar! *tathâ* Hotar!" The Hotar (thereupon) repeats (the Chaturhotṛi mantras), stopping at each of the ten padas!

(1) Their sacrificial spoon was intelligence!

(2) Their offering was endowed with intellect!

(3) Their altar was speech!

(4) Their Barhis (seat) was thought!

(5) Their Agni was understanding!

(6) Their Agnîdhra was reasoning!

(7) Their offering (*havis*) was breath!
(8) Their Adhvaryu was the Sâman!
(9) Their Hotar was Vâchaspati!
(10) Their Maitrâvaruṇa (*upa-vaktâ*) was the mind!
(11) They (sacrificers) took (with their mind) the Graha!
(12) O ruler Vâchaspati, O giver, O name!
(13) Let us put down thy name!
(14) May'st thou put down our (names); with (our) [362] names go to heaven (announce our arrival in heaven)!
(15) What success the gods who have Prajâpati for their master, gained, the same we shall gain!"[8]

The Hotar now reads the *Prajâpati tanu* (bodies) mantras, and the *Brahmodyam.*

(1 & 2) *Eater of food, and mistress of food.* The eater of food is Agni; the mistress of food is Âditya.

(3 & 4) *The happy and fortunate.* By "happy" Soma, and by "fortunate" cattle are meant.

(5 & 6) *The houseless and the dauntless.* "Houseless" is Vâyu, who never lives in a house, and "fearless" is Death, for all fear him.

(7 & 8) *The not reached, and not to be reached.* "The not reached" is Earth, and "the not to be reached" is Heaven.

(9 & 10) *The unconquerable, and the not to be stopped.* "The unconquerable" is Agni, and "the not to be stopped" is Âditya (sun).

(11 & 12) *Who has no first (material) cause (apûrvâ), nor is liable to destruction.* "Who has no first (material) cause" is the mind (*manas*) and "what is not liable to destruction" is the year.

These twelve bodies of Prajâpati make up the whole Prajâpati. On the tenth day, one reaches the whole Prajâpati.

They now repeat the Brahmodyam.[9] "Agni is **[363]** the house-father;
" thus say some, for he is the master (house-father) of the world (earth).
" Vâyu is the house-father, thus say others; for he is the ruler of the airy
" region. That one (Âditya, the sun) is the house-father; for he burns

8. Heaven-world. The gods ascended to heaven by sacrifice. The same is the object of the sacrificers. This is the *Graha mantra*, recited by the Hotar. Now follow the Prajâpati tanu mantras, and the Brahmodyam. There are twelve Prajâpati tanu mantras; they are repeated by pairs, every time two.

9. That is, what Brahmans ought to repeat. It begins with the words, *Agnir grihapatiḥ*, and ends with *arâtsma.* This Brahmodyam is no proper mantra, but a kind of Brâhmaṇam, or theological exposition. However, the whole is repeated by the Hotar as a mantra. See the whole of it also in the Aśv. Sr. S. 8, 13.

"(with his rays). The Ritus are the houses. He who knows what "god is their (the Ritu's) house-father, becomes their house-father, and "succeeds. Such sacrificers are successful (they become masters them-"selves). House-father (master) becomes he who knows the god who "destroys the evil consequences of sin (Âditya, the sun). This house-"father destroys the evil consequences of sin and becomes (sole) "master. These sacrificers destroy the evil consequences of their sin "(and say), O Adhvaryu ! we have succeeded, we have succeeded."

FIFTH CHAPTER.

(The Agnihotram. On the Duties of the Brahmâ Priest).

26.

(The Agnihotram.[1] *When the Sacrificer has to Order his Priest to Bring Fire to the Ahavanîya. The Sixteen Parts of the Agnihotram.)*

The Agnihotrî says to his Adhvaryu, "Take from" (here the Gârhapatya fire) the Ahavanîya fire." Thus he says at evening ; for what good he was doing during the day, all that is taken away (together with **[364]** the fire and brought) eastwards and put in safety. If he says at morning time, "Take from (here) the Ahavanîya," then he takes with him all the good he was doing during the night (brings it) eastwards and puts it in safety. The Ahavanîya fire is the sacrifice (sacrificial fire) ; the Ahavanîya is the heaven-world. He who has this knowledge, places the heaven-world (the real heaven) in the heaven-world, which (is represented by) the sacrifice alone. Who knows the Agnihotram which belongs to all gods, which consists of sixteen parts, and is placed among cattle, is successful by means of it.

What in it (the offering of which the Agnihotram consists) is of the cow (such as milk) belongs to Rudra. What is joined to the calf, belongs to Vâyu. What is being milked, belongs to the Aśvins. What has been milked, belongs to Soma. What is put on the fire to boil, belongs to Varuṇa. What bubbles up (in boiling) belongs to Pûṣan. What is dripping down, belongs to the Maruts. What has bubbles, belongs to Viśvedevas. The cream (of the milk) gathered, belongs to Mitra. What

[1] The Agnihotram is a burnt offering of fresh milk, brought every day, twice during the whole term of life. Before a Brahman can take upon himself to bring the Agnihotram, he has to establish the three sacred fires, Garhapatya, Dakṣiṇa and Ahavanîya. This ceremony is called *Agnyâdhâna*. The performers of these daily oblations are called "Agnihotrîs". They alone are entitled to bring the Iṣṭis and Soma sacrifices. There are, up to this day, Agnihotrîs in the Dekkhan, who may be regarded as the true followers of the ancient Vedic religion.

falls out (of the pot), belongs to Heaven and Earth. What turns up (in boiling), belongs to Savitar. What is seized (and placed in the vessel) belongs to Viṣṇu. What is placed (on the Vedi) belongs to Bṛihaspati. The first offering is Agni's, the latter portion is Prajâpati's, the offering itself (chief portion) belongs to Indra. This is the Agnihotram, belonging to all gods, which comprises sixteen parts.

27.

(How the priest has to make good certain casualties which may happen when the Agnihotram is offered.)

If the cow of an Agnihotrî [2] which is joined to her calf, sits down during the time of being milked, what is the penance for it? He shall repeat over it this **[365]** mantra. "Why dost thou sit down out of fear? From this grant us safety! Protect all our cattle! Praise to Rudra the giver!" (By repeating the following mantra) he should raise her up. "The divine Aditi (cow) rose, and put long life in the sacrifice, she who provides Indra, Mitra and Varuṇa with their (respective) shares (in the sacrifice)." Or he may hold on her udder and mouth a vessel filled with water and give her (the cow) then to a Brahman. This is another Prâyaśchitta (penance).

If the cow of an Agnihotrî, which is joined to her calf, cries during the time of being milked, how is this to be atoned for? If she cries out of hunger, to indicate to the sacrificer what she is in need of, then he shall give her more food in order to appease her. For food is appeasing. The mantra *sûyavasâd bhagavatî* (1, 164, 40) is to be repeated. This is the Prâyaśchitta.

If the cow of an Agnihotrî which is joined to her calf moves during the time of being milked, what is the Prâyaśchitta? Should she in moving spill (some milk) then he shall stroke her, and whisper (the following words), "What of the milk might have fallen to the ground to-day, what "might have gone to the herbs, what to the waters,—may this milk be in 'my houses, (my) cow, (my) calves, and in me." He shall then bring a burnt offering with what has remained, if it be sufficient for making the burnt offering (Homa).

Should all in the vessel have been spilt (by the moving of the cow) then he shall call another cow, milk her and bring the burnt offering with that milk, and sacrifice it. It is to be offered alone in faith.[3]

---

[2] The cow herself is called Agnihotrî.

[3] The meaning of the sentence : आत्वेव श्रद्धायै होतव्यं is : this (substitute) is to be offered (completely) even including the *śraddhâ*. This is the formula : अहं श्रद्धा जुहोमि (*i.e.*) "I offer (this) in faith (as a believing one)."

[366] This is the Prâyaśchitta. He who with such a knowledge offers the Agnihotram, has (only) offerings in readiness (which are fit) and has (consequently) all (accepted by the gods).

28.

(*On the Meaning of the Agnihotram, if Performed in Perfect Faith. It represents Dakṣiṇâ. The Aśvina Śastra, Mahâvrata, and Agnichayana are hinted at in it.*)

That Âditya (the sun) is his (the Agnihotrî's) sacrificial post, the earth is his altar, the herbs are his Barhis (seat of grass), the trees are his fuel, the waters his sprinkling vessels, the directions the wooden sticks laid round about (the hearth). If anything belonging to the Agnihotrî should be destoryed, or if he should die, or if he should be deprived of it, then he should receive all this in the other world, placed, as it were, on the Barhis (sacrificial litter). And the man who, having this knowledge, performs the Agnihotram, will actually obtain (all this).

He brings as Dakṣiṇâ (donation) both gods and men mutually, and everything (the whole world). By his evening offering he presents men to the gods, and the whole world. For men, if being fast asleep without shelter, as it were, are offered as gifts to the gods. By the morning offering he presents the gods as gifts to men, and the whole world. The gods, after having understood the intention (of men that the gods should serve them) make efforts (to do it), saying " I will do it, I will go." What world a man, who has presented all this property to the gods, might gain, the same world gains he who, with this knowledge, performs the Agnihotram.

By offering the evening oblation to Agni, the Agnihotrî commences the Aśvina Śastra (which **[367]** commences with a verse addressed to Agni). By using the term *vâch*, *i. e.*, speech (when taking out the Agnihotram) he makes a (*pratigara*), *i. e.*, response (just as is done at the repetition of a Śastra).

By (thus) repeating every day " Vâch," the Aśvina Śastra [4] is recited by Agni at night, for him who, having this knowledge, brings the Agnihotram.

---

[4] The Aśvina Śastra is required at the commencement of the Gavâm ayanam, when making Atirâtra. See 4, 17-11. The author of our Brâhmaṇa here tries to find out some resemblance between the performance of the evening Agnihotram and the Aśvina Śastra. He finds it in the circumstance, that this offering belongs to Agni, and the Aśvina Śastra commences with a verse addressed to Agni (4, 7). Having thus obtained the commencement of the Śastra, he must find out also the *pratigara* or response which belongs to every Śastra. This he discovers in the formula : *vâchâ tvâ hotre*, which the Agnihotrî repeats as often as the offering is taken out for being sacrificed.

By offering the morning oblation to Âditya, he commences the Mahâvrata [5] ceremony. By using (a term equivalent to) *prâṇa*, *i. e.*, life (when eating the remainder of the Agnihotram) he makes a *pratigara* (also). By (thus) repeating every day the word "food" (life), the Mahâvrata (Śastram) is recited by Âditya at day for him who, with this knowledge, performs the Agnihotram.

The Agnihotrî has to perform during the year 720 evening offerings and also 720 morning offerings, just as many bricks (1440) marked by sacrificial formulas as are required at the Gavâm ayanam. He who with such a knowledge brings the Agnihotram, has the sacrifice performed with a Sattra **[368]** lasting all the year (and) with Agni Chitya [6] (the hearth constructed at the Chayana ceremony).

29.

(Whether the Morning Oblation of the Agnihotrî is to be Offered Before or After Sunrise.

Vriṣaśuṣma, the son of *Vatavata*, the son of *Jâtukarna*, said, "We shall tell this to the gods, that they perform now the Agnihotram, which was brought on both days (on the evening of the preceding, and the morning of the following, day) only every other day." And a girl, who was possessed by a Gandharva, spoke thus, "We shall tell it to the Pitaras (ancestors), that the Agnihotram which was performed on both days, is now performed every other day."

The Agnihotram performed every other day is performed at evening after sunset, and at morning before sunrise. The Agnihotram performed on both days is performed at evening after sunset, and at morning after sunrise. Therefore, the Agnihotram is to be offered after sunrise. For he who offers the Agnihotram before sunset, reaches in the twenty-fourth year the Gâyatrî world, but if he brings it after sunrise, in the

[5] This concludes the Gavâm ayanam. See the note to 4, 12. The resemblance between the Mahâvrata and the morning Agniṣṭoma is found by our author in the following points: The morning Agnihotram belongs to Âditya, and the Niṣkevalya Śastra of the Mahâvrata commences with a mantra addressed to the same deity. The Pratigara he finds in the mantra, *annam payo reto smâsu*, which the Agnihotri repeats as often as he eats the remainder of his offering.

[6] At each Atirâtra of the Gavâm ayanam, the so-called *Chayana* ceremony takes place. This consists in the construction of the Uttarâ Vedi (the northern altar) in the shape of an eagle. About 1440 bricks are required for this structure, each being consecrated with a separate Yajus mantra. This altar represents the universe. A tortoise is buried alive in it, and a living frog carried round it and afterwards turned out. The fire kindled on this new altar is the *Agni Chitya*. To him are the oblations of flesh and Soma to be given. The whole ceremony is performed by the Adhvaryu alone.

twelfth. When he brings the Agnihotram before sunrise during two years, then he has actually sacrificed during one year only. But if he sacrifices after sunrise, then he completes the yearly amount of offerings in one year. Therefore **[369]** the Agnihotram is to be brought after sunrise. He who sacrifices after sunset at evening, and after sunrise in the morning, brings the offering in the lustre of the day-night (Ahorâtra). For the night receives light from Agni, and the day from the sun (Âditya). By means of this light the day is illuminated. Therefore he who sacrifices after sunrise, performs the sacrifice only in the light of Ahorâtra (that is, he receives the light only once, instead of twice, the offering brought before sunrise belonging to the night, and being illuminated by Agni, not by Âditya).

30.

(Several Stanzas Quoted Regarding the Necessity to bring the Agnihotram After Sunrise).

Day and night are the two wheels of the year. By means of both, he passes the year. He who sacrifices before sunrise, goes by one wheel, as it were, only. But he who sacrifices after sunrise, is going through the year with both wheels, as it were, and reaches his destination soon. There is a sacrificial Gâthâ (stanza) which runs as follows:

" All that was, and will be, is connected with the two Sâmans, *Bṛihat* "and *Rathantaram*, and subsists through them. The wise man, after having " established the sacred hearths (the Agnihotrî), shall bring a different " sacrifice at day, and a different one at night (*i. e.*, devoted to different " deities)."

The night belongs to the Rathantaram, the day to the Bṛihat. Agni is the Rathantaram, Âditya the Bṛihat. Both these deities cause him to go to the heaven-world, to the place of splendour (*bradhna*), who with this knowledge sacrifices (the Agnihotram) after sunrise. Thence it is to be sacrificed after sunrise. Regarding this, there is a sacrificial Gâthâ chanted, which runs as follows:

" Just as a man who drives with one pack-horse **[370]** only without " purchasing another one, act all those men who bring the Agnihotram " before sunrise."

For all beings whatever follow this deity (Âditya) when he stretches (the arms at sunrise and sunset). He who has this knowledge, is followed by this deity, after whom all follows, and he follows her. For this Âditya is the "one guest" who lives among those who bring the sacrifice after sunrise. Concerning this there is a Gâthâ (stanza, which runs as follows):

"He who has stolen lotus fibres, and does not receive (even) one guest "on the evening, will charge with this guilt the not guilty, and take off the "guilt from the guilty."[7]

This Âditya is the "one guest" (*ekâtithiḥ*) he is it "who lives among the sacrificers." The man who **[371]** thinking, it is enough of the Agnihotram, does not sacrifice, to this deity (Âditya), shuts him out from being his guest. Therefore this deity, if shut out, shuts such an Agnihotrî out from both this world and that one.

Therefore he who thinks, it is enough of the Agnihotram, may nevertheless bring sacrifices. Thence they say, a guest who comes at evening is not to be sent away. It happened that once a learned man, *Jânaśruteya*, a resident of a town (a Nagarî), said to an *Aikâdaśâkṣa*, a descendant of *Manutantu*, "we recognise from the children, whether one brings the Agnihotram with or without the proper knowledge." Aikâdaśâkṣa had as many children as are required to fill a kingdom. Just as many children will he obtain who brings the Agnihotram after sunrise.

31.

(*The Agnihotram is to be Offered After Sunrise*).

In rising, the sun joins his rays to the Ahavanîya fire. Who, therefore, sacrifices before sunrise, is like a female giving her breast to an unborn

---

[7] Sayaṇa makes the following remarks on this rather obscure stanza:

पुरा कदाचित्सप्तर्षीणां संवादप्रसंगे कश्चित्पुरुषो बिसस्तैन्यलक्षणमपवादं प्राप्य तत्परिहारार्थमृषीणामग्रे शपथं चकार । तदीयशपथोक्तिरूपेयं गाथा बिसानि पद्ममूलानि तेषामपहर्ता प्रत्यवायपरंपरां प्राप्नोतु ॥ पापरहिते पुरुषे बिसविषयमपवादं कृतवतो यः प्रत्यवायः पापिनः पुरुषस्य संबंधी पापं स्वीकुर्वतो यः प्रत्यवायः सायंकाले गृहे समागच्छत एवातिथेर्वैदेशिकस्यापरोधने यः प्रत्यवायः सेयं प्रत्यवायपरंपरा बिसस्तैन्ये सति मम भूयादित्येवं शपथः । अक्षरार्थस्तु अप्रसिद्धो मादृशः पुरुषस्तेनश्चोरो भूत्वा बिसान्यपजहार चेत् स पुमान् अनेनसं पापरहितं पुरुषं श्रोत्रियं एनसा ओभिशस्तात् पापेनाभिशंसनमपवादं कुर्यात् । तथैव स बिसापहारसायंकाले गृहे समागतं एकातिथिमपरुणद्धि भोजनमदत्वा निःसारयेत् ॥

The stealing of *bisâni*, *i.e.*, lotus fibres, from a tank appears to have been a great offence in ancient times. Not to receive one guest (at least) on the evening was considered as equally wicked. The man who has committed such crimes will, in order to clear himself from all guilt, charge an innocent man with it. The forms *abhiśastât* and *apaharât* have evidently the sense of a future tense, as is the case in other instances also. The stanza in question appears to be very old, and was hardly intelligible even to the author of our Brâhmaṇam. He means by *ekâtithiḥ* "the one guest," the sun, which, according to the context, cannot have been the original sense.

child, or a cow giving her udder to an unborn calf. But he who sacrifices after sunrise is like a female giving her breast to a child which is born, or like a cow giving her udder to a calf which is born. The Agnihotram being thus offered to him (Sûrya), he (Sûrya) gives to the Agnihotrî in return, food in both worlds, in this one and that one. He who brings the Agnihotram before sunrise, is like such an one who throws food before a man or an elephant, who do not stretch forth their hands (not caring for it). But he who sacrifices after sunrise, is like such an one who throws food before a man or an elephant who stretch forth their hands. He who has this knowledge, and sacrifices after sunrise, lifts up with this hand (Âditya's hand) his sacrifice, and puts it down **[372]** in the heaven-world. Therefore the sacrifice is to be brought after sunrise.

When rising, the sun brings all beings into motion (*praṇayati*). Therefore he is called *prâṇa* (breath). The offerings of him who, knowing this, sacrifices after sunrise, are well stored up in this *prâṇa* (Âditya). Therefore it is to be sacrificed after sunrise.

That man is speaking the truth, who in the evening after sunset, and in the morning after sunrise, brings his offering. He commences the evening sacrifice by the words, "*Bhûr, Bhuvaḥ, Svar, Om! Agni is Light, Light is Agni*;" and the morning sacrifice by "*Bhûr, Bhuvaḥ, Svar, Om! Sun is Light, Light is Sun.*" The truth-speaking man offers thus in truth, when he brings his sacrifice after sunrise. Therefore it must be sacrificed after sunrise. This is well expressed in a sacrificial stanza which is chanted.

"Those who sacrifice before sunrise tell every morning an
" untruth ; for, if celebrating the Agnihotram at night which ought to be
" celebrated at day, they say, Sun is Light, but then they have no light
" (for the sun has not risen)."

32.

(*On the Creation of the World. The Origin of the Vedas and the Sacred Words. The Penances for Mistakes committed at a Sacrifice.*)

Prajâpati had the desire of creating beings and multiplying himself. He underwent (consequently) austerities. Having finished them, he created these worlds, *viz.*, earth, air and heaven. He heated them (with the lustre of his mind, pursuing a course of austerities); three lights were produced: Agni from the earth, Vâyu from the air, and Âditya from heaven. He heated them again, in consequence of which the three Vedas were produced. The Rigveda came from Agni, the Yayurveda from

Vâyu, and the Sâmaveda from Âditya. He heated these Vedas, [373] in consequence of which three luminaries arose, *viz.*, Bhûr came from the Rigveda, Bhuvaḥ from the Yajurveda, and Svar from the Sâmaveda. He heated these luminaries again, and three sounds came out of them *â*, *u* and *m*. By putting them together, he made the syllable *om*. Therefore he (the priest) repeats "Om ! Om !," for Om is the heaven-world, and Om is that one who burns (Âditya).

Prajâpati spread the sacrifice[8] (extending it), took it, and sacrificed with it. By means of the Rich (Rigveda), he performed the duties of the Hotar; by means of the Yajus, those of the Adhvaryu; and by means of the Sâman, those of the Udgâtar. Out of the splendour (seed) which is inherent in this three-fold knowledge (the three Vedas), he made the Brahma essence.

Prajâpati offered then the sacrifice to the gods. The gods spread it, took it, and sacrificed with it, and did just as Prajâpati had done (regarding the office of the Hotar, &c). The gods said to Prajâpati, "If a mistake has been committed in the Rik, or in the Yajus, or in the Sâman in our sacrifice, or in consequence of ignorance, or of a general misfortune, what is the atonement for it ? " Prajâpati answered, " When you commit a mistake in the Rik, you shall sacrifice in the Gârhapatya, saying *Bhûḥ*. When you commit one in the Yajus, then you shall sacrifice in the Agnîdhriya fire[9] or (in the absence of it, as is the case) in the Havis offerings, [10] in the cooking fire (Dakṣiṇa Agni) saying, *Bhuvaḥ*. When a mistake is committed in the Sâman, then it is to be sacrificed in the Ahavanîya fire by saying, *Svar*. When a mistake has been committed out of ignorance, or in consequence of a general [374] mishap, then you shall sacrifice in the Ahavanîya fire, reciting all three words, *Bhûh, Bhuvaḥ, Svar*. These three " great words " (*vyâhṛiti*) are like nooses to tie together the Vedas. It is just like joining one thing to another, one link to another link, like the stringing of anything made of leather, or of any other thing, and connecting that which was disconnected, that one puts together by means of these great words all that was isolated in the sacrifice. These Vyâhṛitis are the general Prâyaśchitta (penance); thence the penances (for mistakes) at a sacrifice are to be made with them.

---

[8] It is regarded as a person.

[9] This is used only in the Soma sacrifices.

[10] Such as the Darśapûrṇamâsa iṣṭi, Châturmâsya iṣṭi, &c.

33.

(On the Office of the Brahmâ Priest. He ought to remain Silent during all the Principal Ceremonies.)

The great sages (*mahâvadaḥ*) ask, "When the duties of a Hotar are performed by the Rik, those of the Adhvaryus by the Yajus, and those of the Udgâtar by the Sâman, and the three-fold science is thus properly carried into effect by the several (priests employed), by what means then are the duties of the Brahmâ priest performed?" To this one should answer, "This is done just by means of this three-fold science."

He who blows (Vâyu) is the sacrifice. He has two roads, *viz.*, speech and mind. By their means (speech and mind), the sacrifice is performed. In the sacrifice there are both, speech and mind, required. By means of speech the three priests of the three-fold science perform one part (assigned to Vâch); but the Brahmâ priest performs his duty by the mind only. Some Brahmâ priests, after having muttered the Stomabhâgas [11] when all arrangements have been made for [375] the repetition of the Prâtaranuvâka (the morning prayer) sit down, and speak (without performing any of the ceremonies).

Respecting this (the silence on the part of the Brahmâ priests), a Brahman, who saw a Brahmâ priest at the Prâtaranuvâka talk, said (once) "they (the priests and the sacrificer) have made one-half of this sacrifice to disappear." Just as a man who walks with one foot only, or a carriage which has one wheel only, falls to the ground, in the same manner the sacrifice falls to the ground (*bhreṣan nyeti*), and if the sacrifice has fallen, the sacrificer falls after it too (if the Brahmâ priests talk during the time they ought to be silent). Therefore the Brahmâ priest should, after the order for repeating the Prâtaranuvâka has been given, refrain from speaking till the oblations from the Upâṁśu and Antaryâma (Grahas) are over. After the order for chanting the Pavamâna Stotra has been given (he ought also to refrain from speaking) till the last verse (of the Stotra) is done. And [376] again, he should during, the chanting of the (other) Stotras, and the repeating of the Śastras, refrain from speaking, till the Vaṣaṭkâra (at the end of the Yâjyâ verse of the Śastra) is pronounced. Likewise, as a man walking on both his legs,

---

[11] The Stomabhâgas are certain Yajus-like mantras which are to be found in the Brâhmaṇas of the Sâmaveda only (not in the Yajus or Rigveda). Each of these mantras consists of four parts: (*a*) To what the Stoma is like, such as a cord, a joint, &c.; (*b*) To what it is devoted or joined; (*c*) An order to the Stoma to favour the object to

and a carriage going on both its wheels, does not suffer any injury; in the same way such a sacrifice (if performed in this manner), does not suffer any injury, nor the sacrificer either, if the sacrifice be not injured.

34.

(On the Work done by the Brahmâ. He Permits the Chanters to Chant)

They say, When the sacrificer has the reward (*dakṣiṇâ*) given to the Adhvaryu, he thinks, "this priest has seized with his hands my Grahas (Soma cups), he has walked for me, he has sacrificed for me." And when he has the reward given to the Udgâtar, he thinks, "he has sung for me;" and when he has the reward given to the Hotar, he thinks, "this priest has spoken for me the Anuvâkyâs, and the Yâjyâs, and repeated the Śastras." But on account of what work done is the Brahmâ priest to receive his reward? Shall he receive[12] the reward, thinks the sacrificer, without having done any work whatever? Yes, he receives it for his medical attendance upon the sacrifice, for the Brahmâ is the physician of the sacrifice (which is regarded as a man). Because of the Brahmâ priest performing his priestly function with the Brahma, which is the quintessence of the metres. He does one-half of the work, for he was at the head of the other priests, and the others (Adhvaryu, Hotar, Udgâtar) do the other half. (The Brahmâ priests tell if any mistake has been commit-
[377] ted in the sacrifice, and perform the Prâyaśchittas, as described above.)[13]

---

which it is joined; (*d*) An order to the chanters to chant the Stoma by the permission of Savitar in honour of Bṛihaspati. The last (fourth) part is in all the Stomabhâga mantras the same. I give here some of these mantras, which are all to be found in the Tândya Brâhmaṇam (1, 8-9). They commence:

1 (*a*) रश्मिरसि (*b*) क्षयाय त्वा (*c*) क्षयं जिन्व (*d*) सवितृप्रसूता बृहस्पतये स्तुत
2 (*a*) प्रेतिरसि (*b*) धर्मणे त्वा (*c*) धर्मं जिन्व (*d*) सव॰
3 (*a*) अन्वितिरसि (*b*) दिवे त्वा (*c*) दिवं जिन्व (*d*) सव॰
4 (*a*) सन्धिरसि (*b*) अन्तरिक्षाय त्वा (*c*) अन्तरिक्षं जिन्व (*d*) सव॰
5 (*a*) विष्टम्बोऽसि (*b*) वृष्ट्यै त्वा (*c*) वृष्टिं जिन्व &c.

The proper meaning of the repetition of these and similar mantras by the Brahmâ priests is, to bring the chant (Stoma), which is about to be performed, into contact with the external world, with day, night, air, rain, the gods, and secure the favour of all these powers and beings.

[12] In the original, *haratâ*, which is to be taken in the sense of a future.

[13] I have not translated the passage regarding the Prâyaśchitta to be performed by the Brahmâ priest if any mistake has been committed; for it is only a repetition from 5, 32.

The Prastotar[13] says, after the order for chanting the Stotram has been given, " O Brahmâ, we shall now chant, our commander ! " The Brahmâ then shall say at the morning libation, " Bhûr ! filled with the thought of Indra, ye may sing !" and at the evening libation, [378] he says, " Svar ! filled with the thought of Indra, ye may sing."

At the time of the Ukthya or Atirâtra sacrifice, all the three great words, *Bhûr Bhuvaḥ Svar* are required. If the Brahmâ says, " Filled with the thought of Indra, ye may sing," this means, that the sacrifice is Indra's, for Indra is the deity of the sacrifice. By the words, " filled with the thought of Indra," the Brahmâ priest connects the Udgîtha (the principal part of the chant) with Indra. This saying of the Brahmâ means, " Do not leave Indra ; filled with him, ye may sing." Thus he tells them.

---

[14] The announcement of the Prastotar, that the chanters are ready to perform their chant, as well as the orders to do so given by the Brahmâ and Maitrâvaruṇa, are contained in full in the Aśval. Śr. S. (5, 2), and in the Sânk. Śr. S. (6, 8). I here give the text from the Aśv. S. :—

ब्रह्मन् स्तोष्यामः प्रशास्तरिति स्तोत्रायातिसर्जितावतिसृजतो भूरिन्द्रवन्तः सवितृप्रसूता इति जपित्वा स्तुध्वमिति ब्रह्मा प्रातःसवने भुव इति माध्यन्दिने स्वरिति तृतीयसवने भूर्भुवः स्वरिन्द्रवन्तः सवितृप्रसूता इत्यूर्ध्वमाग्निमारुतात् । स्तुतदेवेन सवित्रा प्रसूता ऋतं च सत्यं च वदत । आयुष्मत्य ऋचो मा गात तनू पात्साम्न ओ३मिति जपित्वा मैत्रावरुणः स्तुध्वमित्युच्चैः ॥

(When the Prastotar calls) " Brahmâ, we shall chant, O commander !" then the two priests (the Brahmâ and Maitrâvaruṇa) whose duty it is to allow (the chanters to sing) give their permission. The Brahmâ, after having first muttered the words " *bhûr*, be ye filled with Indra, created by Savitar (or permitted by Savitar)," at the morning libation, says, "chant ;" at the midday libation he uses, instead of *bhûr*, *bhuvaḥ* ; and at the evening libation, *svar* (the remainder of the Japa being the same). Before all the Stotras which follow the Agnimâruta Śastra (which concludes the Śastras of the Agniṣṭoma), that is to say, at the Ukthya, Śolaśî, Atirâtra sacrifices, &c., the Brahmâ mutters all the three great words (*bhûr*, *bhuvaḥ*, *svaḥ* along with the remainder of the formula) at the same time. The Maitrâvaruṇa, after having muttered, " Speak what is right and true, ye who are created by Savitar, the god to whose honour praises are chanted, do not lose the sacred verses (chanted by you) which are life, may he protect both bodies of the Sâman (the verses and the tune) Om !" says aloud " chant !"

[378] SIXTH BOOK.

FIRST CHAPTER.

(On the Offices of the Grâvastut and Subrahmaṇyâ.)

1

(On the Origin of the Office of the Grâvastut.[1] *The Serpent Riṣi Arbuda.)*

The gods held (once upon a time) a sacrificial session in Sarvacharu. They did not succeed in [380] destroying the consequences of guilt. Arbuda, the son of Kadru, the Serpent Risi, the framer of mantras, said to them, "You have overlooked one ceremony which is to be performed by the Hotar. I will perform it for you, then you will destroy the consequences of guilt." They said, "Well, let it be done." At every midday libation, he then came forth (from his hole), approached them, and repeated spells over the Soma, squeezing stones. Thence they repeat spells at every midday libation over the Soma squeezing stones, in imitation of him (the Serpent Riṣi). The way on which this Serpent Riṣi used to go when coming from (his hole) is now known by the name *Arbudodâ Sarpaṇî* (at the sacrificial compound).

[1] See also him about Aśv, Śr. S. 5, 12. His services are only required at the midday libation. He performs his function of repeating mantras over the Soma, squeezing stones before the so-called Dadhi Gharma ceremony. He enters through the eastern gate, and passes on to the two Havirdhânas (the two carts, on which the sacrificial offerings are put, and the two covered places, in which these two carts are). Having arrived north-east of the exterior front of the axe (*akṣaśiras*) of the southern Havirdhâna, he throws off a stalk of grass held in his hand, which ceremony is called *nirasanam* (it is performed often by other priests also). He then faces the Soma shoots, assuming a peculiar posture. The Adhvaryu gives him a band (*uṣṇîṣa*), which he ties round his face. As soon as the Adhvaryu and his assistants take the Soma sprouts from below, the *adhiṣavaṇa* board (see the note to 7, 32), he ought to repeat the mantras over the Grâvâṇas, which are now being employed for extracting the Soma juice. He commences with verses containing the term *su*, to squeeze, or derivatives of it. The first is: *abhi tvâ deva savitar* (1, 24, 3). After some more single verses follow, the three principal Grâvâṇa hymns, *viz.*, *praite vadantu* (10, 94), *â va ṛiṁjase* (10, 76), and *pra vo grâvâṇaḥ* (10, 175). The first and the last are said to have been seen by *Arbuda*, the Serpent Riṣi, the second by *Jarat karṇa*, one of the Serpent tribe also. These hymns very likely formed part of the so-called *Sarpaveda* or Serpent Veda (see the Gopatha Brâhmaṇam 1, 10, according to whose statement this Veda came from the east), and were originally foreign to the Rigveda. They may be, nevertheless, very ancient. The two latter hymns are to be repeated before the last verse of the first, and are thus treated like a Nivid at the evaning libation. Either in the midst, or before, or, after these two hymns, the Grâvastut must repeat the

The King (Soma) made the gods drunk. They then said, "A poisonous serpent (*aśîviṣa*) looks at our King! Well, let us tie a band round his eyes." They then tied a band round his eyes. Therefore they recite the spells over the Soma squeezing stones, when having tied (round the eyes) a band in imitation (of what the gods did). The King (Soma) made them drunk. They said, "He (the Serpent Riṣi) repeats his own mantra over the Soma squeezing stones. Well, let us mix with his mantra other verses." They then mixed with his mantra other verses, in consequence of which he (Soma) did not make them drunk.[2] By mixing his mantra with other verses for effecting propitiation, they succeeded in destroying the consequences of guilt.

[381] In imitation of this feat achieved by the gods, the Serpents destroyed all consequences of their own guilt. Having in this state (being quite free from guilt and sin) left off the old skin torn, they obtain a new one. Who knows this, destroys the consequences of his own guilt.

2

(*How Many Verses are to be Repeated over the Grâvaṇas. How they ought to be Repeated. They are Required only at the Midday Libation. No Order for Repeating them Necessary.*)

They say, With how many mantras should he (the Grâvastut) pray over the Soma squeezing stones? The answer is, with a hundred; for the life of a man is a hundred years, he has a hundred powers, and a hundred bodily organs; by doing so, he makes man participate in age, strength, and bodily organs. (Others) say, He ought to repeat thirty-three verses, for he (the Serpent Rishi) destroyed the sins of thirty-three gods, for there are thirty-three gods. (Others) say, He ought to recite an unlimited number of such mantras. For Prajâpati is unlimited; and this recital of the mantras referring to the Soma squeezing stones belongs to Prajâpati, and in it all desires are comprised. Who does so, obtains all he desires. Thence he ought to repeat an unlimited number of such mantras.

Now they ask, In what way should he repeat these mantras (over the Soma squeezing stones)? Syllable by syllable, or should he take four syllables together, or pâda by pâda, or half verse by half verse, or

---

so-called Pâvamânî verses (Rigveda 9.) He has to continue his recitation as long as the squeezing of the juice lasts, or he may go on till it is filled in the Grahas (*â vâ graha grahaṇât*); he then must conclude with the last verse of the first Grâvâṇa hymn. Besides this ritual for the Grâvastut, another one is given by Aśvalâyana, which he traces to *Gâṇagâri*.

[2] These mantras were the antidote.

verse by verse? With whole verses (repeated without stopping) one does not perform any ceremony, nor with stopping at every pâda. If the verses are repeated with stopping at every syllable, or every four syllables, then the metres become mutilated, for **[382]** many syllables (sounds) would thus be lost. Thence he ought to (repeat) these mantras one half verse by another. For man has two legs, and cattle are four-footed. By doing so, he places the two-legged sacrificer among the four-legged cattle. Thence he ought to repeat these mantras by half verses.

Since the Grâvastut repeats only at every midday libation mantras over the Soma squeezing stones, how do mantras become repeated over them at the two other (morning and evening) libations? By repeating verses in the Gâyatrî metre, he provides for the morning libation; for the Gâyatrî metre is appropriate to the morning libation; and by repeating verses in the Jagatî metre, he provides for the evening libation; for the Jagatî metre is appropriate to the evening libation. In this way he who, with this knowledge, repeats the mantras over the Soma squeezing stones only at the midday libation, supplies these praises for the morning and eveving libations.

They say, What is the reason, that, whilst the Adhvaryu calls upon the other priests to do their respective duties, the Grâvastut repeats this mantra without being called upon (without receiving a *prâiṣa*)? The ceremony of repeating mantras over the Soma squeezing stones is of the same nature as the mind which is not called upon. Therefore the Grâvastut repeats his mantra without being called upon.

3

(The Subrahmaṇyâ Fomula. On its Nature. By whom it is to be Repeated. The Oblation from the Pâtnîvata Graha. The Yâjyâ of the Agnîdhrâ.)

The Subrahmaṇyâ [2] is Vâch. Her son is the **[383]** king Soma. At the time of buying Soma, they call the Subrahmaṇyâ (thither), just as one calls a cow.

---

[2] The Subrahmaṇyâ formula is contained in the Kâtyâyana Śrauta Sûtras (1, 3), the Agniṣṭoma Sâma Prayoga, the Śatapatha Brâhm. (3, 3, 4, 17-20), and the Taittirîya Araṇyaka (1, 12, 3-4). The peculiar pronunciation of this formula is noted by Pâṇini (1,2, 37-38). The most complete information on its use being only to be found in the Sâmaveda Sûtras, I here give the passages from Kâtyâyana referring to it, along with the formula itself:—

आतिथ्यायां संस्थितायां दक्षिणस्य द्वारबाहोः पुरस्तात्तिष्ठन्नन्तर्वेदिदेशेऽन्वारब्धे यजमाने पत्न्यां च सुब्रह्मण्योमिति त्रिरुक्त्वा निगदं ब्रूयात् । इन्द्रागच्छ हरिव आगच्छ मेधातिथेर्मेष वृषणश्वस्य मेने गौरावस्कन्दिन्नहल्यायै जार कौशिक ब्राह्मण गौतम ब्रुवाणैतावदहे स्तुत्यामिति यावदहे स्यात् ।

[384] Through this son, the Subrahmaṇyâ priest milks[3] (obtains) all desires for the sacrificer. For Vâch grants all desires of him who has this knowledge. They ask, What is the nature of this Subrahmaṇyâ ?

After the Atithya Iṣṭi has been finished, he (the Subrahmaṇyâ) should stand in the front part of the enclosure made for the wife of the sacrificer inside the Vedi, and when touching the sacrificer and his wife, after having called thrice " *subrahmaṇyom*," recite the following formula, " Come, Indra ! come owner of the yellow horses ! " ram of Me-" dhâtithi ! Menâ of Vriṣaṇaśva ! thou buffalo (*gaura*) who ascendest the female " (*avaskandin*), lover of Ahalyâ ! son of Kuśika ! Brâhmaṇa ! son of Gotama ! (come) " thou who art called " (to appear) at the Soma feast in so and so many days how many there might intervene (between the day on which the Subrahmaṇyâ calls him, and that of the Soma festival at which his presence is requested). The Subrahmaṇyâ is required on the second, third, fourth and fifth day of the Agniṣṭoma, and almost on every day of the other Soma sacrifices. On the second day, the terms, *tryahe sutyâm*, " three days hence," *i.e.*, on the fifth) ; on the third day, *dvyahe sutyâm*, *i.e.*, two days hence ; on the fourth, *śvas*, *i. e.*, to-morrow ; and on the fifth (the day of the Soma feast) *adya*, *i. e.* to-day, are used to mark the time when the Soma banquet, to which Indra is by this formula solemnly invited, is to come off. As far as ब्रुवाण which is followed by the mentioning of the time appointed त्र्यहे, द्व्यहे, &c., there is no difference anywhere observable. But the few sentences which follow, and which conclude the formula, differ according to different schools. Some were (according to Kâtyâyana) of opinion, that only आगच्छ " come hither " is to follow; others recommended आगच्छ मघवन्, " come hither, O Maghavan." Others, such as Gautama, were of opinion, that either is to be omitted, and the concluding formula, देवा ब्रह्माण आगच्छतागच्छतागच्छत " come, ye divine Brahmâ priests, come, come." has to follow immediately upon सुत्यां,

The name of the tune (Sâman), according to which it is chanted (or rather recited) is *Brahmaśrî*, the metre is called *Sampât*, the Risi is Âditya, and Indra is the deity.

At the so-called Agnishṭut sacrifices, which open the Chaturdaśarâtra Sattras (sacrificial sessions lasting for a fortnight), (Aśv. Śr. S, 11, 2), the Subrahmaṇyâ calls Agni instead of Indra (Kâtyây. 1, 4), according to Gautama, by the following formula :

अग्न आगच्छ रोहिताभ्यां बृहद्भानो धूमकेतो जातवेदो विचर्षण आंगिरस ब्राह्मणांगिरस ब्रुवाण ।

i. e., " Come, O Agni, with (thy) two red ones (horses), thou brightly shining, thou blazing in smoke, Jâtavedâs, thou wise ! Aṅgiras ! Brâhmaṇa, (come) called, " &c. In the concluding formula देवा ब्रह्म०, अग्नय fires, is used instead of देवा According to Dhânañjay the Subrahmaṇyâ formula for Agni runs as follows : अग्नआगच्छ रोहितव आगच्छ भरद्वाजस्याज सहसः सूनो वारावस्कन्दिन्नुषसो जारांगिरस, (the remainder as above), *i. e.*, " Come, Agni ! master of the red horses, goat of Bhardvâja, son of power, thou who ascendest (the female) ; lover of Uṣas, " &c. The latter formula is just like that one addressed to Indra. Agni, as well as Indra, are in both these formulas, which must be very ancient, invoked as family deities, the first pre-eminently worshipped by the Aṅgirasa, the latter by the Kuśikas. Both gods are here called " Brâhmans." In later books, Indra appears as a Kṣattriya, and as a model of a king.

On the so-called Agniṣṭomîya day, of all sacrifices (in the Agniṣṭoma, it is the fourth and precedes the Soma day), on which day the animal for Agni and Soma is slain and sacrificed, an extension of the Subrahmaṇyâ formula takes place. The Subrahmaṇyâ priest has on this day to announce to the gods, that such and such one (the name of the sacrificer must be mentioned), the son of such and such one, the grandson of such and such one, offers, as a Dikṣita, (as initiated into the sacrificial rites) a sacrifice (दीक्षितो यजते) The term, 'Dikṣita,' forms then henceforth part of the name of the sacrificer, and his descendants down to the seventh degree. In this part of India, there are many Brâhmans distinguished by this honorary epithet, which always indicates that, either the bearer of it or his immediate ancestors have performed a Soma sacrifice, and have been proclaimed (*dikṣita* by the Subrahmaṇyâ in all due form.

[3] *Duhe* must be a 3rd person singulur, as Sây. explains it.

[385] One should answer, She is Vâch. For Vâch is Brahma, and Subrahma (good Brahma).

They ask, Why does one call him (the Subrahmaṇyâ priest) who is a male, a female? (They answer) Subrahmaṇyâ represents Vâch (which is in the feminine gender).

They further ask, When all the other priests are to perform their respective duties within the Vedi, and the Subrahmaṇyâ outside the Vedi, how is it that the duty of the Subrahmaṇyâ (in this particular case) becomes performed inside the Vedi)? One should answer, The Vedi has an outlet where things (which are no more required) are thrown; if the Subrahmaṇyâ priest calls (the Subrahmaṇyâ) when standing in this outlet, then, in this way (his duty is performed within the bounds of the Vedi). They ask, Why does he, standing in the outlet, repeat the Subrahmaṇyâ? On this, they tell the following story.)

The Riṣis held once a sacrificial session. They said to the most aged man among them, "Call the Subrahmaṇyâ. Thou shalt call the gods standing among us (on account of thy age), as it were, nearest to them." In consequence of this, the gods make him (the Subrahmaṇyâ) very aged. In this way, he pleases the whole Vedi.

They ask, Why do they present to him (the Subrahmaṇyâ) a bull as a reward for his services? (The answer is) The bull is a male (*vṛiṣa*), the Subrahmaṇyâ is a female, both making thus a couple. This is done for producing offspring from this pair.

The Agnîdhra repeats the Yâjyâ mantra for the Pâtnîvata Graha (a Soma vessel), with a low voice. For the Pâtnîvata is the semen virile, and the effusion of the semen virile passing on without noise, as it were, he does not make the Anuvaṣaṭkâra. For [386] the Anuvaṣaṭkâra is a stop. Thinking, I will not stop the effusion of the semen, he does not make the Anuvaṣaṭkâra, for the semen which is not disturbed in its effusion, bears fruit. Sitting near the Neṣṭar, he then eats, for the Neṣṭar is in the room of women. Agni (Agnîdhra) pours semen in women, to produce children. He who has this knowledge, provides through Agni his females with semen, and is blessed with children and cattle.

The Subrahmaṇyâ ends after the distribution of the Dakṣiṇâ,[5] for she is Vâch. The Dakṣiṇâ is food; thus they place finally the sacrifice in food, which is Speech.

---

[4] He represents Agni.

[5] The Dakshiṇâ is distributed at the midday libation.

SECOND CHAPTER.

(On the Śastras of the Minor Hotṛi-priests at the Sattras.)

4.

(On the Śastras of Minor Hotṛi-priests at the Morning and Evening Libations.)

The Devas spread the sacrifice. When doing so, the Asuras approached them, thinking, let us obstruct their sacrifice. They attacked them from the right side, thinking this to be the weak point. The Devas awoke, and posted two of their number, Mitra and Varuṇa, on the right side. Through the assistance of these two, the Devas drove the Asuras and Rakṣasas away from the morning libation. And thus the sacrificers drive them away (if they have the Maitrâvaruṇa Śastra repeated); thence the Maitrâvaruṇa priest repeats the Maitrâvaruṇa Śastra **[387]** at the morning libation. The Asuras, defeated on the right side, attacked the centre of the sacrifice. The Devas awoke, posted then Indra, and defeated through his assistance the enemies. Therefore the Brâhmaṇâchchhaṁsi repeats at the morning libation the Indra Shastra.

The Asuras, thus defeated, attacked the sacrifice on the northern side. The Devas posted on this side Indrâgnî, and defeated thus the Asuras. Therefore the Achhâvâka repeats the Aindrâgna Śastra at the morning libation. For, by means of Indrâgni, the Devas drove the Asuras and Rakṣasas away from the northern side.

The Asuras, defeated on the northern side, marched, arrayed in battle lines towards the eastern part. The Devas awoke and posted Agni eastwards at the morning libation. Through Agni, the Devas drove the Asuras and Rakṣasas away from the eastern front. In the same way, the sacrificers drive away from the eastern front the Asuras and Rakṣasas. Thence the morning libation is Agni's. He who has such a knowledge, destroys the evil consequences of his sin.

The Asuras, when defeated eastwards, went westwards. The Devas awoke and posted the Viśve Devâḥ themselves (westwards) at the third libation, who thus drove the Asuras and Rakṣasas away from the western direction at the third libation. Likewise, the sacrificers drive through the Viśve Devâḥ themselves at the third libation the Asuras and Rakṣas away. Thence the evining libation belongs to the Viśve Devâḥ. He who has such a knowledge, destroys the consequences of his sin.

In this manner, the Devas drove the Asuras out of the whole sacrifice. Thence the Devas became masters of the Asuras. He who has this knowledge becomes therefore through himself (alone) master of his adversary and enemy, and destroys the consequences [388] of his sin. The Devas drove away the Asuras and destroyed the consequences of sin by means of the sacrifice arranged in such a way, and conquered the heaven-world. He who has this knowledge, and he who, knowing this, prepares (these) libation required in the said manner, drives away his enemy and hater, destroys the consequences of his guilt, and gains the heaven-world.

5.

(*The Stotriya of the Following Day is made the Anurûpa of the Preceding Day in the Śastras of the Minor Hotṛi-priests at Soma Sarcrifices lasting for Several Days.*)

They use at the morning libation the Stotriya (triplet) (of the following day) as Anurûpas[1] (of the preceding day). They make in this way the following day the Anurûpa (corresponding to the preceding day). Thus they commence the performance of the preceding day with a view to that of the following. But this is not done at the midday libation; for the Pṛiṣṭhas[2] (used then) are happiness (they are independent); they have at this (the midday libation) not that position (which the verses have at the morning libation) that they could use the Stotriya (of the following day) as Anurûpa (of the preceding day). Likewise they do not use at the third libation, the Stotriya (of the following day) as Anurûpa (of the preceding day).

6.

[389] (*The Opening Verses of the Śastras of the Minor Hotṛi-priests at the Ahargaṇa Soma Sacrifice, i.e., such ones as last for a Series of Days.*)

Now follow the opening verses (of these Śastras after the Stotriyas have been repeated). *Rijunîtî no Varuṇa* (1, 90, 1) is that of the Maitrâvaruṇa Śastra; for in its second pâda is said, "Mitra, the wise, may lead!" for the Maitrâvaruṇa is the leader of the Hotṛi-priests. Therefore is this the leading verse.

By *Indram vo visvatas pari* (1, 7, 10) commences the Brâhmaṇâchchhaṁsi; for by the words "we call him (Indra) to the people" they call

---

[1] See on the meaning of the terms *stotriya* and *anurûpa*, note 41 on page 199. The first contains always those verses which the Sâma singers chant, the latter follows its form, and is a kind of supplement.

[2] The Sâmans of the midday libation are called Pṛiṣṭhas; and the Stotriyas and Anurûpas which accompany them, go by the same name.

Indra every day. When the Brâhmaṇâchchhaṁsi, with this knowledge, recites this verse every day, then no other sacrificer, notwithstanding he (Indra) might be called by different parties (at the same time), can get Indra away.

Yat soma â sute nara (7, 94, 10) is the verse of the Achchhâvâka. By its words "they called hither Indrâgnî," every called Indrâgnî every day. When the Achchhâvâka is doing this every day, no other one can wrest (from them) Indrâgnî. These verses (*rijunîtî* &c.) are the boats which lead to the shores of the heavenly world. By their means the sacrificers cross (the sea) and reach the heavenly world.

7.

(*The concluding verses of the same Śastras at the Ahargaṇa Soma sacrifices.*)

Now follow the concluding verses of these Śastras: *Te syâma deva varuṇa* (7, 66, 9) is that of the Maitrâvaruṇa Śastra. For by its words, "we contemplate food (*iṣam*) and light (*svar*)," they get [390] hold of both worlds; for "food" is this world, and "light" is that world.

By the triplet *vyantarikṣam atirad* (8, 14, 7-9), which has the characteristic *vi*, *i.e.* asunder, the Brâhmanâchchhaṁsî opens the gates of the heavenly world. The words, "Indra, inebriated by Soma, cleft the hole and made appear the lights" (8, 14, 7), refer to the passionate desire of those who are initiated into the sacrificial art (for heaven); thence it is called the *Balavatî* verse.[3] The words, "He drove out the cows, and revealed them which were hidden, to the Aṅgiras, and flung away Bala", contain the expression of a gift to them (the Aṅgiras). By the words, "*indrena rochanâ divi* (verse 9) the heaven-world is alluded to." By the words, "The fixed lights (stars) of heaven have been fastened by Indra, the fixed ones he does not fling away," the sacrificers approach every day heaven and walk there.

Aham sarasvatîvator (8, 38, 10), is the verse of he Achchhâvâka. For Ṣarasvatî is the voice; (the dual is used) for this day belongs to the "two who have the voice." (As to who they are is expressed by the words) "I choose the tone of Indrâgnî." For the voice is the beloved residence of Indrâgnî. Through this residence one makes both successful. Who has this knowledge, will be successful in his own residence (his own way).

---

[3] There is the word *vala* hole, in it, which may be regarded as a proper name of an Asura also.

8.

(*On the Ahina and Aikâhika concluding verses of the Śastras of the minor Hotṛi-priests.*)

The concluding verses of the Hotṛi-priests (Maitrâvaruṇa, Brâhmaṇâchchhaṁsi, and Achchhâvâka) are, at **[391]** the morning and midday libations of two kinds, *viz. âhîna* (which are proper for Soma sacrifices, which last for several days successively) and *aikâhika* (which are proper for Soma sacrifices which last for one day only). The Maitrâvaruṇa uses the aikâhikas preventing (thus) the sacrificer from falling out of this world. The Achchhâvâka uses the âhînas for making (the sacrificer obtain heaven). The Brâhmaṇâchchhṁsi uses both ; for thus he holds both worlds (with his hands) and walks in them. In this way he (the Brâhmaṇâchchhaṁsi) walks holding both, the Maitrâvaruṇa and the Achchhâvâka, the Ahîna and Ekâha, and (farther) the sacrifical session lasting all the year round (such as the Gavâm ayanam) and the Agniṣṭoma (the model of all Aikihikas).

The Hotṛi-priests require at the third libation Ekâhas only for concluding. For the Ekâha is the footing, and thus they place the sacrifice at the end on a footing.*

At the morning libation he must read the Yâjyâ verses without stopping (*anavânam*). The Hotar shall not recite one or two additional verses (*atiśamsanam*) for the Sṭoma. It is just the same case as if one who asks for food and drink must be speedily supplied. Thinking, I will quickly supply the gods their food, he speedily gets a footing in this world. He should make the Śastram at the two latter libations with an unlimited number of verses ; for the heaven-world is unlimitted. (This is done) for obtaining the heaven-world. The Hotar may, if he like, recite those verses which the minor Hotṛi-priests used to repeat on a previous day. Or the Hotṛi-priests (may, if they like, repeat those verses) which the Hotar (used to repeat on the previous day) (For Hotar as well as the Hotṛi-priests form parts of one **[392]** body only). For the Hotar is the breath, and the Hotṛi-priests are the limbs. This breath goes equally through the limbs. Thence the Hotar should, if he like, receite those verses which the minor Hotṛi-priests used to recite on the previous day. Or the Hotṛi-priest (may, if they like, repeat those verses) which the Hotar (used to repeat on the previous day). The last verses of the hymns with which the Hotar concludes, are the same with the concluding verses of the minor Hotṛî-priests at the evening

*For the Ekâha sacrifices are the models of the others.

libation. For the hotar is the soul, and the Hotṛi-priests are the limbs; the ends of the limbs are equal, therefore the (three) Hotri-priests use, at the evening libation, the same concluding verses.

THIRD CHAPTER.

(The hymns for lifting the Chamasa (Soma cups). The Prasthita Yâjyâs of the seven Hotars concluding this ceremony. The two different kinds of Hotars. Explanation of some apparent anomalies in the performances of the minor Hotṛis. The Jagatî hymns for Indra. The concluding verses of the minor Hotṛi-priests. On a peculiarity in the Śastras of the Achchhâvâha.)

9

(The number of verses which the Hotar has to repeat at the time of the Soma cups being lifted at the three libations.)

When at the morning libation the Soma cups are lifted and filled he (the Maitrâvaruṇa) recites the hymn *â tva vahantu harayaḥ* (1, 116.) the several verses of which contain the words *vriṣan* (male), *pîta* (drunk), *suta* (squeezed), *mad* (drunk), are complete in their form and are addressed to Indra, for **[393]** the sacrifice is Indra's. He repeats Gâyatrîs; for Gâyatrî is the metre of the morning liabation. At the morning libation he recites nine verses only; one less (than ten). For the semen is poured in to a place made narrow (*nyûna*). At the midday libation he repeats ten verses [1]; for the semen which was poured in a narrow place grows very large, after having reached the centre of the woman's body. At the evening libation he repeats nine[2] verses, one less (than ten); for from a narrow place (represented by the third libation) men are born. If he recites these hymns complete, than he makes the sacrificer bring forth the embryo of his (spiritual body) begotten in the sacrifice, which is the womb of the gods.

Some recite every time only seven verses at the morning, midday and evening libations, asserting that there must be as many Puronuvâkyâs as there are Yâjyâs. Seven (Hotṛi priests) having their faces turned (towards the fire) receite the Yâjyâs, and pronounce Vauṣat! Now they assert that those (seven verses) are the Puronuvâkyâs of these (seven

[1] They are the hymn, *asâvi devam goṛichîkam* (7, 21).

[2] They are the hymn, *ihopayâta śavaso* (4, 35).

Yâjyâs) ; but the Hotar ought not to do so (to recite only seven verses.) For in this way they spoil the semen of the sacrificer, and conseqnently the sacrificer himself.

The Maitrâvaruṇa carries in this way the sacrificer, for the sacrificer is the hymn, by means of nine verses from this world to the airy region ; but by means of ten he carries him further on to that (heaven) world ; for the airy region is the oldest ; from that world he takes him by means of nine verses up to the celestial world. Those who recite [395] only seven verses, do not wish to raise the sacrificer to heaven. Therefore the hymns are to be recited complete only[3].

10.

(On the Prasthita Yâjyâs[4] of the Hotars at the morning libation.)

Some one (a theologian) has asked, When the sacrifice is Indra's, why do only two, the Hotar and Brâhmaṇâchhaṁsi, at the morning libation, for the Soma drops which are in readiness, repeat Yâjyâs where Indra's very name is mentioned, the Yâjyâ of the Hotar being *idam te somyam madhu* (8, 54, 8), that of the Brâhmaṇâchchhaṁsî, *indra tva vṛiṣabham vayam* (3, 40, 1) ?

When the other (priests) repeat verses addressed to different deities, how do they concern Indra ? For the Yâjyâ of the Maitrâvaruṇa is *mitram vayam havâmahe* (1, 23, 4), " we invoke Mitra ;" but in its words *varuṇam somapîtaye i.e.* " we call Varuṇa to the Soma beverage;" there is an allusion to Indra ; for whatever word refers to "drinking", hints at Indra, and pleases him.

The Yâjyâ of the Potar is, *Maruto yasa hi kṣaye* (1, 86, 1) ; its words *sa sugopâtamo janaḥ i.e.* " he is the best protector," allude to Indra ; for Indra is the *gopâ*, which is a characteristic of Indra. Thus he pleases Indra.

The Yâjyâ of the Neṣṭar is, *agne patnîr ihâ vahâ* (1, 22, 9) ; in its words, *tvaṣṭâram somapîtaye,* [395] there is an allusion to Indra ;

---

[3] The hymns mentioned for the morning and evening libations contain each nine, that mentioned for the midday libation ten verses.

[4] These Yâjyâs are at each libation seven in number, and repated successively by the so called 'seven Hotars' (Hotar, Maitrâvaruṇa, Brâhmaṇâchchhaṁsi, Potar, Neṣṭar Agnidhra, and Achchhâvâka) when the Chamasa Adhvaryu or cup-bearers, are holding up the cups filled with Soma. As often as one of them has repeated his Yâjyâ, libations from seven cups are thrown at the same time in the fire. The rest is to be drunk by them.

for Indra is Tvaṣṭar, which is a characteristic of Indra. Thus he pleases him.

The Yâjyâ of the Agnîdhra is, *Ukṣânnâya* (8, 43, 11); in its words *Soma priṣṭhâya vedhase*, there is an allusion to Indra; for Indra is Vedhâs (striker, beater) which is a characteristic of Indra. Thus he pleases him.

The verse of the Achchhâvâka, which is directly addressed to Indra, is complete, *viz*: *prâtaryâvabhir* (8, 38, 7), (for in the last part of it there is the term *Indrâgnî*). Thus all these verses refer to Indra. Though there are different deities mentioned (in them) (such as Mitra, Varuṇa, &c.) the sacrificer does not satisfy other deities (alone). The verses being in the Gâyatrî metre, and this being sacred to Agni, sacrificer gains, by means of these verses, the favour of three deities, *i. e.* Indra, the *nânâdevatâs* or different deities, and Agni.

11.

(*The hymn to be repeated over the Soma cups being lifted, and the Prasthita Yâjyâs at the midday libation.*)

At the midday libation, when the Soma cups are being lifted, the Hotar repeats, *Asâvi devam goṛichîkam* (7, 21. 1.). This hymn contains the words, *vṛiṣan, pita, suta, mad*; its verses are complete in form and addressed to Indra. For the sacrifice belongs to Indra. The verses are in the Triṣṭubh metre; for this metre is appropriate to the midday libation. They say, if the term *mad* "to be drunk" is only appropriate to the third libation, why do they recite such verses (containing this term) at the midday libation as Anuvâkyâs and Yâjyâs? The gods get drunk, as it were, at the midday libation, and are then consequently at the third libation in a state of **[396]** complete drunkenness. Thence he repeats verses containing the term *mad* as Anuvâkyâs and Yâjyâs at the midday libation.

At the midday libation all the priests repeat Yâjyâs addressed to Indra by his very name (for the Soma drops) which are in readiness. Some (the Hotar, Maitrâvaruṇa, and Brâhmaṇâchchhaṁsi) make the Yâjyâs with verses containing (besides the name of Indra) the words, *abhi trid.* So the Hotar repeats, *pibâ somam abhi yam ugra tarda* (6, 17, 1); the Maitrâvaruṇa, *sa îm pâhi ya ṛîjishi* (6, 17, 2); and the Brâhmaṇâchhaṁsi, *evâ pâhi pratnathâ* (6, 17, 3).

The Yâjyâ of the Potar is, *arvâṅg ehí somakâmam* (1, 104, 9). The Yâjyâ of the Neṣṭar is, *tavâ yam somas tvam* (3, 35, 6). The Yâjyâ of the Achchhâvâka is, *indrâya somaḥ pra divo vidânâ* (3, 36, 2). The Yâjyâ of the Agnîdhra is, *âpûrnô asya kalaśaḥ svâhâ* (3, 32, 15).

* These three verses contain forms of the verb *tṛid* (Lat. trudere) "to injure, to kill," with the preposition *abhi*.

Among these verses there are those containing the words *abhi tṛid.* For Indra once did conquer at the morning libation; but by means of these verses he broke down the barriers and made himself master (*abhi triṇat*) of the midday libation. Thence these verses.

12.

(The hymn and the Prasthita Yâjyâs at the evening libation.)

At the third libation the Hotar repeats at the time when the Soma cups are being lifted, the hymn *ihopayâta śavasô napâtaḥ* (4, 35, 1). Its verses which are complete in form, are addressed to Indra, and belong to the Ribhus, contain the words *vṛiṣan, pîta,* **[397]** *suta mad.* They ask, Why is the Pavamâna Stotra at the evening libation called Arbhava, though they do not sing Ribhu verses? (The answer is) Prajâpati, the father, when transforming the Ribhus who were mortals, into immortals, gave them a share in the evening libation. Thence they do not sing Ribhu verses, but they call the Pavamâna Stotra Arbhava.

One (great Riṣi) asked about the application of metres, *viz.* for what reason does he use the Triṣṭubh metre at the third libation, whilst the appropriate metre for this libation is Jagatî, as well as the Gâyatrî that for the morning, and the Triṣṭubh for the midday libation? One ought to say (in reply), At the third libation the Soma juice is done; but if they use a sparkling (*śukriyam*) metre as the Triṣṭubh, the juice of which is not done, then they provide the (third) libation with juice (liquor). Then he makes Indra participate in this libation also. One says, Why, since the third libation belongs to Indra and the Ribhus, and the Hotar alone makes the Yâjyâs for the Soma which are in readiness (*prasthita*) with an Indra-Ribhu verse, at the third libation, do the other Hotṛi-priests use verses addressed to various other deities for their Yâjyâs? In the Yâjyâ of the Hotar, *ribhubhir vajadbhiḥ samukṣitam* (not in the Rigveda) the Ribhus are mentioned, but in the Yâjyâs of the other priests they are only hinted at.

The Maitrâvaruṇa repeats, *indrâvaruṇa sutapâvimam sutam* (6, 68, 10); in the words, *yuvo ratho adhvaram devavîtaye,* there is a plurality (in the words *devavîtaye=devânâm vîtaye, i.e.* for the enjoyment of the gods) which is a characteristic of the Ribhus.

The Brâhmanâchchhaṁsi repeats the verse, *indraścha somam pibatam* (4, 50, 10); in its words, *viśantu iṇdavaḥ, i. e.* "may the drops come," a **[398]** plurality is expressed, which is a characteristic of the Ribhus.

The Yâjyâ of the Potar is, *â vo vahantu saptayo* (1, 85, 6); in its words, *raghu atvânaḥ prajigâta bâhubhir* there is a plurality (these three words are in the plural) expressed, which is the characteristic of the Ribhus.

The Yâjyâ of the Neṣṭar is, *ameva naḥ suhavâ* (2, 36, 3), in it the word *gantana* "go ye!" expresses a plurality.

The Yâjyâ of the Achchhâvâka is, *indrâviṣṇu pibatam madhvo* (6, 69, 7); its words, *â vâm amdhâmsi madirâṇi* expresses a plurality.

The Yâjyâ of the Agnîdhra is, *imam stomam arhate* (1, 94, 1); in its words *ratham iva saṁmahemâ* (this is first person plural) there is a plurality expressed.

In this way all these verses become Aindra—Arbhavah. By repeating verses being (apparently) addressed to various deities, he pleases other deities (also), save Indra and the Ribhus. They are the conquerors of the *jagat i. e.* world; therefore the Jagatî metre is required for the evening libation, to make it successful.

13.

(On the relationship of those Hotars who have to repeat a Śastra to those who have none. How the Śastras of the minor Hotṛi-priests are supplied at the evening libation.)

Some one asks, Some of the duties of the Hotṛi-priests being performed without Śastra,[6] some with Śastra, how are then all these ceremonies (as it **[399]** should be) provided with their respective Śastras, and consequently equal and complete? (The answer is) They call the performance (*i.e.* the repetition of Yâjyâs) of those (Hotṛis) who like the Potar, Neṣṭar, and Agnîdhra, have no Śastra (to repeat) *Hotrâ* (also), on account of their reciting their (respective) verses along with (the other Hotṛi-priests, such as the Hotar, Maitrâvaruṇa &c. who repeat proper Śastras). In this way they are equal. But in the fact that some Hotṛi-priests perform their duties with Śastras, others without Śastras, lies their inequality. Thus (both kinds of Hotṛi performances) become provided with Śastras, equalised and successful (for the Yâjyâs of all seven Hotṛi-priests are repeated one after the other).

---

6 Besides the Hotar only the Maitrâvaruṇa, Brâhmaṇâchhaṁsi, and Achhâvâka repeat Shastras; the others, such as the Potar, &c. do not do it. But the former repeat them at the Agnishṭoma, only at the morning and midday libations.

Now the Hotṛi-priests (Maitrâvaruṇa, Brâhmaṇâchchhaṁsi, Achchhâvâka) repeat Śastras at the morning and midday libations only, in what way is this duty performed at the third libation? One ought to answer, in this way, that they (these three priests just mentioned) repeat at the midday libation two hymns each. Some one may ask, In what way do the Hotṛi-priests (who properly speaking repeat one Śastra only) repeat two Śastras, as many as the (chief) Hotar[7] does? One ought to answer, Their Yâjyâs are addressed to two deities.

14.

[400] (*How the Śastras of the Agnîdhra, Potar and Neṣṭar are supplied. On the two Praiṣas to the Potar and Neṣṭar. On the additional verse of the Achchhâvâka. How the Praiṣa formula, hotâ yakṣat, is applicable to the Potar, Neṣṭar, and Agnidhra. The Praiṣa for the chanters. The Praiṣa for the Achchhâvâka. On the inequality of the the deities of the Śastras and Stotriyas of the evening libation.*)

Some one asks further. If there are the performances of three Hotṛi-priests only provided with a Śastra, how are these Śastras supplied for the performances of the others (the three remaining Hotṛi-priests)? (The answer is) The Ajyam is the Śastra for the Yâjyâ repeated by the Agnîdhra; the Marutvatîya that one for the Potar's Yâjyâ; the Vaiśvadevam that one for the Neṣṭar's. These Yâjyâs have the characteristic sign of the respective Śastra.[7]

Some one asks further, If the other Hotṛi-priests are requested only once (to repeat their Śastras), why are the Potar and Neṣṭar requested twice?

(Regarding this the following story is reported). At the time when the Gâyatri having assumed the shape of an eagle, abstracted the Soma (from heaven), Indra (out of anger) cut off from these (three) Hotṛi-priests (Agnidhra, Potar and Neṣṭar) their Śastras, and transferred them to the Hotar, saying, "Do not call me, you are quite ignorant of it." The gods said, "Let us give more strength to the performances of these two Hotṛi-priests (Potar and Neṣṭar) through Speech (by requesting them once

[7] The Agnîdhra addresses the Yâjyâ to Agni, to whom the Ajya Śastra belongs; the Potar to the Marutas, to whom the Marutvatîya Śastra belongs, and the Neṣṭar to the Viśvedevas, to whom the Vâiśvadeva Śastra belongs.

[7] The Hotar repeats at the morning libation the Ajya and Pra-uga Śastra, at the midday libation the Marutvatiya and Niṣkevalya Śastra, and at the third libation the Vaiśvadeva and Agnimâruta Śastra.

The Agnidhra addresses the Yâjyâ to Agni, to whom the Ajya Śastra belongs; the Potar to the Marutas, to whom the Marutvatiya Śastra belongs, and the Neṣṭar to the Viśvedevas, to whom the Vaiśvadeva Śastra belongs.

[401] more than the others). Thence come the two requests (for Neṣṭar and Potar). The performance of the Agnîdhra was strengthened by one additional verse to his Yâjyâ; therefore his Yâjyâs are supernumerary by one verse.

Some one asks, When the Maitrâvaruṇa calls upon the Hotar by the words, "may the Hotar repeat the Yâjyâ! may the Hotar repeat the Yâjyâ!" why does he call upon those who are no Hotras, but only the repeaters of Hotṛi verses, by the same words, "may the Hotar repeat the Yâjyâ?" (The answer is) The Hotar is life, and all the (other) sacrificial priests are life also. The meaning (of the formula "may the Hotar repeat his Yâjyâ," is) "may the life repeat the Yâjyâ, may the life repeat the Yâjyâ!"

If some one asks further, Are there requests for the Udgâtṛi priests (to chant)? One should answer, Yes, there are. For if all (the priests) are ordered to do their respective duties, then the Maitrâvaruṇa, after having muttered with a low voice (a mantra), says, "praise ye!"[8] These are the summons for the Udgâtṛi priests.

Some one asks, Has the Achchhâvâka any preference (to the other priests)?[9] The answer is, Yes, he has; for the Adhvaryu says to him, "Achchhâvâka, speak what you have to speak (and no more)!"

Some one asks, Why are at the evening libation the Stotriya and Anurûpa verses addressed to Agni, whilst the Maitrâvaruṇa at that time repeats an Indra-Varuṇa Śastra? (The answer is) The Devas turned the Asuras out of the Śastras by means of Agni as their mouth. Therefore the Stotriya and Anurûpa are addressed to Agni.

[402] Some one asks, Why are both the Stotrîya and Anurûpa of the singers devoted to Indra at the evening libation, whilst the Śastram repeated by the Brâhmaṇâchchhaṁśi is addressed to Indra and Bṛihaspati, and that of the Achchhâvâka to Indra and Viṣṇu? (The answer is) Indra turned the Asuras out from the Śastras (of which they had got hold) and defeated them. He said to the Devas, "Which (from among you) follows me?," They said, "I, I,[10] (we will follow)," and thus the Devas fellowed. But on account of Indra having first defeated (the Asuras) the Stotriya and Anurûpa of the singers (they precede the Shastram) are addressed to Indra. And on account of the other deities having said, "I, I, (will follow)" and (actually) followed, both the Brâhmaṇâchhaṁsi and Achchhâvâka repeated hymns addressed to several deities.

---

[8] See note to 5, 34.

[9] That is, is there anything exceptional to be seen in the performance of his duties? This refers to the peculiar praiṣa given to him, which is mentioned in the context. See also Aśv. Śr. S. 5, 7.

[10] Viṣṇu and Bṛihaspati.

15.

(On the Jagatî hymns addressed to Indra at the evening libation. On the hymn of the Achchhâvâka. The concluding verses of the Maitrâvaruṇa Brâhmaṇâchchhaṁsi, and Achchhâvâka. The last four syllables of the last Śastra of the Soma day to be repeated twice.)

Some one asks further, For what reason do they repeat at the commencement of the evening libation hymns addressed to Indra, and composed in the Jagatî metre, whereas the evening libation belongs to the Viśvedevas? (The answer is) Having got hold of Indra (*ârabhya* having commenced with him) by means of these (hymns), they proceed to act, being sure of success). The Jagatî metre is used because the evening libation belongs to the Jagatî, implying a desire for this world (*Jagat*); and any metre **[403]** which is used after (this commencement) becomes related to the Jagatî (*jagat*) if, at the beginning of the evening libation, hymns in the Jagatî metre are repeated which are addressed to Indra.

At the end (of the Śastra) the Achchhâvâka repeats a hymn in the Triṣṭubh metre, *saṁvâṁ karmaṇâ* (6, 69, 1.) The word *karma* (ceremony) alludes only to the praise of drinking (the Soma).[11] In the words *sam iṣâ* the word *iṣâ* means food; it (serves) for obtaining food (by means of this mantra.) (By the words of the last pâda) " both (Indra and Viṣṇu) carry us through on safe paths," he pronounces every day[12] something relating to welfare.

Some one asks, Why do they conclude the evening libation by Triṣṭubhs, if properly the Jagatî metre should be used at it? Triṣṭubh is strength; (by repeating at the end Triṣṭubhs) the priests (who are at the Sattras the sacrificers themselve) get finally possessed of strength.

The concluding verses of the Maitrâvaruṇa is, *iyam Indram Varuṇam* (7, 84, 5.) That of the Brâhmaṇâchhaṁsi is, *Brihaspatir na paripâtu* (10, 42, 11.) That of the Achchhâvâka is, *ubhâ jigyathur* (6, 69, 8.) For "both (Indra and Viṣṇu) had been victorious *jigyathuḥ*, *i. e.*, they had not sustained any defeat, neither of them was defeated."[13]

---

[11] The word alluded to is, *panâyya*, which is traced to a root *paṇ=pan* to praise; but it hardly can mean "praising" in general. It refers, as Sâyaṇa justly remarks, to the " drinking of the Soma juice." In the fifth verse of the hymn in question, we have the word *panayâyya*, which is the same as *panâyya*, where the words *indrâviṣṇû tat panayâyyam vâm* evidently mean, " this is your praise for having drunk the Soma."

[12] The hymn is to be repeated every day on the Soma sacrifices which last for several days.

[13] This is a paraphrase by the author of the Brâhmaṇam of the first half of the verse 6, 69, 8 (*ubhâ jigyathur.*) It differs little from the original, and retains most of the terms

[404] In the words *indraś cha Viṣṇo yad apaspridhethâm*[14] (there is hinted) that Indra and Viṣṇu fought with the Asuras. After they had defeated them, they said to them, "Let us divide!" The Asuras accepted the offer. Indra then said, "All through which Viṣṇu makes his three steps is ours, the other part is yours." Then Indra stepped through these (three worlds), then over the Vedas, and (lastly) over Vâch.

They ask, What is meant by the "*sahasram*,"[15] a thousand? One should say in reply, these worlds, the Vedas, and Vâch. The Achchhâvâka repeats twice the (last) word *airayethâm*, *i.e.*, "you both (Indra and Viṣṇu) strode," at the Ukthya sacrifice; for the part (repeated) by the Achhâvâka, is the last in it; whereas at the Agniṣṭoma and Atirâtra the Hotar (repeats twice the four last syllables of his Śastra); for (the part recited by him) is in these [405] sacrifices, the last. At the Ṣolaśî there it is questionable whether or not (the last four syllables) are to be repeated twice. They say, He ought to repeat them twice, for why should he repeat them twice on the other days, and not on this one? Therefore he should repeat them twice (also at the Ṣolaśî.)

16.

(*Why the Achchhâvâha at the end of his Śilpa-Śastra does not recite verses addressed to Narâśaṁsa.*)

Some one further asks, Why does the Achhâvâka at the end, in his Śilpas, recite verses not addressed to Narâśaṁsa at the third libation, although this libation belongs to Narâśaṁsa? The Narâśaṁṣa part represents the change (of the semen into the human form); for the semen becomes by and by somewhat changed; that which then has undergone the

of the verse without giving any substitute for them. This shows, that many verses and turns of speech in the mantras were perfectly intelligible to the author of the Brâhmaṇas. The only difference of the paraphrase from the original is the substitution of *tayoḥ* for *enoḥ*, which is an uncommon dual form (gen.) of a demonstrative form; one ought to expect *enayoḥ*.

[14] This is the second half of the last verse of 6, 69, 8, which concludes the hymn repeated by the Achchhâvâka. The author of the Brâhmaṇam explains it also by reporting a story to which he thinks the contents of this latter half allude. However he does not quite overlook the meaning of several terms; *apaspṛidhetâm* he explains by *yuyudhâte*, "they two have fought," and *vyairayethâm* by *vichakrame*, "he stepped through." The meaning of these words is certainly correct; but the grammatical structure is misunderstood by our author; *airayethâm* is taken by him as a singular, though it is a dual, for it refers to both Indra and Viṣṇu, and not to Viṣṇu alone.

[15] In the last pada of the last verse *ubhá jigyathur*. There the words *tredhâ sahasram vi tad airayethâm* mean "ye both strode thrice through this thousand." The "thousand" refers to the booty they made in the battle, or perhaps to the "thousand cows" given as reward at great sacrifices.

change becomes the *prajâtam* (the proper form.)[16] Or the Narâśaṁsam is a soft and loose metre, as it were; and the Achchhâvâka is the last reciter; therefore (it cannot be used), for (the priests think) We must put the end in a firm place for obtaining stability. Therefore the Achhâ vâka does not repeat at the end, in his Śilpas, verses referring to Narâśaṁsa.[17]

---

[406] FOURTH CHAPTER.

(*The Saṁpâta hymns. The Vâlakhilyas. The Dûrohaṇaṁ.*)

17.

(See 6, 5.)

When they make at Soma sacrifices, which require several days for their performance (*ahînas*) in order to make them continuous, at the morning libation, the singing verse (Stotriya) of the following day, the Anurûpa of the preceding day, it is just the same as with the performance of a Soma sacrifiice which lasts for one day only (*ekâha.*) For just as the (three) libations of the one day's Soma sacrifice are connected with each other, in the same way are the days of a Soma sacrifice which lasts for several days connected with one another. The reason that they make at the morning libation, the singing verse (Stotriya) of the following day, the Anurûpa of the preceding day, is to make the days during which the sacrifice lasts one continuous series. Thus they make the days of the Ahîna sacrifices one continuous whole.

The Gods and Riṣis considered. Let us make the sacrifice continuous by equalising (its several days.) They then saw this equality (of the several parts) of the sacrifice, *viz.* the same Pragâthas, the same Pratipads (beginning triplets), the same hymns. For Indra walks in the sacrifice on the first as well as on the following day, just as one who has occupied a house. (The Soma days are thus equalised) in order to have (always) Indra (present.)

---

[16] Sây. says, "For seven nights after the coition the semen has the form of a bubble a fortnight after it is changed into a ball, which, if the change has been completed, assumes the proper (human or animal) form." The Narâśaṁsaṁ is the state of transition for the semen from the bubble into the ball form. Therefore in order not to disturb and stop the course of this change, no verses, referring to the imperfect state, can be repeated.

[17] See on them 6, 32.

18.

On the Saṁpâta hymn. The counter-Saṁpâta hymns. On a peculiarity in the use of the hymn of the Achchhâvâka.

Viśvâmitra saw for the first time (the so-called) **[407]** Saṁpâta hymns; but Vâmadeva made those seen by Viśvâmitra known to the public (*aśrijata*). These are the following: *evâ tvâm indra* (4, 19); *yanna indro* (4, 22); *kathâ mahâm avṛidhat* (4, 23). He went at once after them (*samapatat*) and taught them his disciples.[1] Thence they are called *Saṁpâtas*.

Viśvâmitra then looked after them, saying, "The Saṁpâta hymns which I saw, have been made public[2] by Vâmadeva; I will counteract these Saṁpâtas by the publication of other hymns which are like them. Thus he made known as counterparts the following hymns: *sadyô ha jâto vṛiṣabhaḥ* (3, 48); *indraḥ pûrbhid âtirad* (3, 34); *imâmû ṣu prabhṛitim* (3, 36); *ichhanti tvâ somyâsaḥ sakhâyaḥ* (3, 30); *śâsad vahnir duhitur* (3, 31); *abhi taṣṭeva didhayô manîṣâm* (3, 38); (Other Saṁpâta hymns are), the hymn of Bharadvâja, *ya eka id dhavyas* (6, 22); those of Vasiṣṭha, *yas tigmaśriṁgo vṛiṣabho na bhîma* (7, 19), *ud u brahmâṇairata* (7, 23); and that of Nodhâs *asmâ id u pratavase* (1, 61).

These Hotṛi-priests (Maitrâvaruṇa, Brahmaṇâchhaṁsi, and Achchhâvâka) after having recited at the morning libation of the six days' sacrifice the Stotriya verses, repeat at the midday libation the hymns or the several days' sacrifices (*ahîna*). These hymns are *â satyo yâtu maghavan* (4, 16); for the Maitrâvaruṇa (by whom it is to be repeated) is endowed with *satya*, *i. e.* truth. The Brâhmaṇâchhaṁsî repeats, *asma id u pratavase* (1, 61); for in this hymn there occur the words *indrâya brahmâṇâ râtatama* (in the fourth pada of the first verse), and *Indra brahmâṇi Gotamâso akrann* (verse 16), *i. e.* the Gotamas have made the prayers, Indra! in which the word "*brahma*" is mentioned. The Achchhâvâka **[408]** repeats *śâsad vahnir* (3, 31), in which the words *janayanta vahnim* (verse 2) occur; for he is the *Vahni* (guide).

Some one asks, Why does the Achchhâvâka repeat in both kinds of days[3] (of the Gavâm ayanam sacrifice) this Vahni hymn in those days which stand by themselves (*parâñchi*) as well as those which form

[1] This is the meaning of the expression *samapatat*.

[2] The term is *sṛij* to emit.

[3] This refers to two classes of days of which a great Sattra consists, *i. e.* single days, which only once occur in the course of the session, and regular periods of the same length which follow one another. See page 279.

regular periods (of six days) one following the other (*abhyâvarti*)? The answer is, the Bahvṛicha (Rigveda) priest (*i.e.* one of the Hotṛis) is endowed with power, and the Vahni hymn leads (*vahati*); for the *Vahni* (guide horse) draws the beams to which he is yoked. Therefore the Achchhâvâka repeats the Vahni hymns in both classes of days.

These Ahîna[4] hymns are required during the five days (in the Gavâm ayanam), *viz.* on the Chaturviṁśa, Abhijit, Viṣuvat, Viśvajit and Mahâvrata days; for these (five) days (though the performance of each lasts for one day only) are *ahînas*, for nothing is left out (*na-hîyate*)[5] in them; they (further) "stand aloof" and do not re-occur in the other turn (as is the case with the Śaḷahas). Thence the Hotṛi-priests repeat on these (five) days the Ahîna Sûktas. When they repeat them, then thay think, "may we obtain the heaven-worlds undiminished, in their full forms and integrity." When they repeat them, they call hither Indra by them, just as one calls a bullock to a cow. They repeat them for making uninterrupted the series of sacrificial days. Thus they make them uninterrupted.

[409] 19.

(*On what days, in what order, and by whom the Saṁpâta hymns are to be repeated. The Avapana hymns.*)

Thereupon the Maitriâvaruṇa repeats on every day (of the Śaḷaha, but not on those five days mentioned) one of the three Saṁpâtas, inverting their order[6] (in the second three days' performance of the Śa-ḷaha). On the first day he repeats *evâ tvâm indra*; on the second, *yanna indro jujuṣe*; and on the third, *kathâ mahâm avṛidhat.*

The Brâhmaṇâchchhaṁsi repeats three Saṁpâta hymns, every day one, inverting their order (in the second three days performance), *viz. pûrbhid âtirad* on the first day; *eka id dhavyas* on the second; and *yas tigmaś-riṁgo*, on the third day.

In the same manner the Achchhâvâka repeat three Saṁpâtas, every day one, *viz. imâm û ṣu prabhritim* on the fisrt day, *ichhanti tvâ somyâsaḥ* on the second day, and *śâsad vahni* on the third day.

These three (for there are every day three to be repeated) and nine (nine is the number of all taken together) hymns, to be recited day after day, make twelve in all. For the year consists of twelve months, Prajâpati is

---

[4] The Saṁpâtas which are mentioned here are meant.

[5] They are here called *ahînas* from a purely etymological reason. Strictly speaking, they are *aikâhikas*.

[6] This is the real meaning of the term *viparyâsam*. In the second Tryaha of the Salaha, the hymn which was the first in the first Tryaha is made the last, and the last the first.

the year, the sacrifice is Prajápati. They obtained thus this sacrifice, which is Prajâpati, who is the year, and they place thus every day's performance in the sacrifice, in Prajapati, and in the year.

Between these hymns they ought to insert the Virâj verses by Vimada, to be recited without Nyûṅkha on the fourth, the Pañkti verses on the fifth, and the Paruchhepa verses on the sixth day. Then on the **[410]** days when the Mahâstomas are required (the Chhandomâ days) the Maitrâvaruṇa inserts *ko adya naryo devakâma* (4, 25, 1), the Brahmaṇâchchhaṁsi, *vanena vāyo nyadhâyi* (10, 29, 1), and the Achchhâvâka, *âyâhy arvâṁg upa* (3, 43, 1). These are the Avapana hymns (intercalary hymns), by means of which the Gods and Riṣis conquered the heaven-world, and by means of which the sacrificers conquer heaven (also).

20.

(On the hymns repeated by the Maitrâvaruṇa, &c. which precede the Saṁpâtas).

Before the (Ahîna) hymns are repeated, the Maitrâvaruṇa repeats every day, *sadyo ha jâto vriṣabhaḥ* (3, 48). This hymn leads to heaven; for by means of this hymn the Gods conquered the heavenly world, and the Riṣis did the same; by means of it the sacrificers also conquer the heavenly world. This is a Viśvâmitra hymn, for Viśvâmitra (all-friend) was the friend of all; therefore all will be friendly towards him who has this knowledge, if the Maitrâvaruṇa knowing this repeats (this hymn) every day before the Ahîna Sûktas. This hymn (*sadyo ha*) contains the word "bull," and is therefore a*paśumat* (having cattle), serving for obtaining cattle. It consists of five verses; five-hood comprises five feet, and five-hood is food for obtaining (which this hymn is useful). The Brâhmaṇâchhaṁsi repeats every day the Brahmâ hymn, whice is complete, *ud u brahmâṇy airata* (7, 23).

This hymn leads to heaven; by means of it the Gods conquered the heavenly world, and the Riṣis did the same; by means of it the sacrificers conquered the heavenly world. It is a Vasiṣtha hymn; by means of it Vasiṣtha obtained Indra's favour, and conquered the highest world. He who has such a **[411]** knowledge, obtains Indra's favour, and conquers the highest world. It consists of six verses; for there are six seasons; in order to gain the seasons (*ritus*), he repeats it after the Sampâtas. For the sacrifiers have thus a firm footing in this world, in order to reach the heavenly world (after death).

The Achchhâvâka repeats every day, *abhi taṣṭeva dîdhayâ* (3, 38). This hymn contains the characteristic *abhi* (towards) in order to establish a connection (with the other world). Its words "*abhi priyâṇi marmṛiśat parâṇi*," mean that the other days (those in the other world) are lovely, and that they are seizing them (securing them). Beyond (*para*) this world is the heaven-world, to which he thus alludes.

When repeating the words, *kavimrichchhâmi saṁdriśe sumedhâ*, *i. e.* "I wish to see the wise prophets," he means by *kavis* the departed Riṣis. This hymn (*abhi taṣṭeva*) is a Viśvâmitra hymn, for Viśvâmitra was friend to all; every one will be friendly to him who has this knowledge.

He repeats this hymn which belongs to Prajâpati, though his name is not expressly mentioned (*aniruktam* only hinted at) in it. For Prajâpati cannot be expressed in words. (This is done) in order to obtain (communion with) him. In this hymn the name "Indra" is once mentioned[7]; but this is only for the purpose of preserving the Indra form of the sacrifice (to Indra chiefly belongs the sacrifice). It consist of ten verses. For the Virâj consists of ten syllables, and the Virâj is food; it serves for obtaining food. As regards the number ten (of these) verses, it is to be remarked that there are ten vital airs. The sacrificers thus obtain the vital airs, and connect them with one another.

[412] The Achchhâvâka repeats this hymn after the Saṁpâtas in order to secure the heavenly world (for the sacrificers), whilst the sacrificers move in this world.

21.

(The Kadvat hymns.[8] The Triṣṭubhs).

The beginning Pragâthas of every day are the *kadavntas* (containing the interrogative pronoun *kas* who?) *viz. kas tam Indra* (7, 32, 14-15), *kannvayo* (8, 3, 13-14), *kad û nv asya* (8, 55, 9-10). By *kas i.e.*, who? Prajâpati is meant; these Kadvantaḥ Pragâthas are suitable for obtaining

---

[7] In the last verse (3, 38, 10); but several times alluded to by the name "*vriṣabha*," *i. e.* bull.

[8] The Śastras of the minor Hotṛi-priests being at the Dvâdaśâha and Sattras rather complicated, I here give some hints as to the order of their several parts. At the midday libation, after the Hotar has finished his two Śastras, the Maitrâvaruṇa, Brâhmaṇâchhaṁsi, and Achchhâvâka repeat one after the other the several parts of their Śastras in the following order: (1) Stotriya and Anûrupa. (2) One of the three Triṣṭubh verses as introductory to the Ahîna hymns and the Kadvantaḥ Pragâthas. (3) The Ahîna hymns, of which each has to repeat two, *viz.* the Maitrâvaruṇa *sadyo ha jâta*, the Brâhmaṇâchhaṁsi *aśmâ id u pra tavase*, and the Achchhâvâka *śâsad vahnir*; and further, the

Prajâpati. *Kam* (old neuter form of *kas*) signifies food; the *kadvantas* therefore serve for obtaining food. For the sacrificers are every day joined to the Ahîna hymns, which become (by containing the term *kam i. e.* happy) propitiated. They make by means of the *kadvad* Pragâthas propitiation (for the sacrificers). When thus propitiated, these (Ahîna hymns) become (a source of) happiness for them (the sacrificers) and thus carry them up to the celestial world.

[413] They ought to repeat the Triṣṭubhs as the beginning of the (Ahîna) hymns. Some repeat them before these Pragâthas, calling them (these Trṣhṭubhs) Dhâyyâs. But in this way one should not proceed. For the Hotar is the ruler, and the performances of the minor Hotṛi-priests are the subjects. In this way (by repeating Dhâyyâs which ought to be repeated by the Hotar alone) they would make the subject revolt against his ruler, which would be a breach of the oath of allegiance.[9]

(The repetition of these Triṣṭubhs by the minor Hotṛi-priests is, however, necessary). He ought to know, " these Triṣṭubhs are the helm (*pratipad*) of my hymns," just as (one requires a helm) if crossing the sea. For those who perform a session lasting for a year or the Dvâdaśâha, are floating like those who cross the sea. Just as those who wish to land on the shore enter a ship having plenty of provisions,[10] in the same manner the sacrificers should enter (*i.e.*, begin with) these Triṣṭubhs. For if this metre, which is the strongest, has made the sacrificer go to heaven, he does not return (to the earth). But he does not repeat (at the beginning) of the several Triṣṭubhs the call *somśavoms*; for the metre must run in one and the same strain (without any interruption, through the call *somśavom*, in order to be successful).

The Hotar further ought to think, I will not make the Dhâyyâs, if they recite those (Triṣṭubhs), and further, let us use as a conveyance the hymns with their well known introductory verses (the Triṣṭubhs). If they then repeat these verses (Triṣṭubhs), they **[214]** call hither by them Indra, just as a bullock is called to the cow. If they repeat them,

---

Maitrâvaruna *a satya yâtu*, the Brâhmaṇâchhamsi, *u du brahmaṇi*, and the Achchhâvâka *abhi taṣteva* (see the reference in 6, 18.) (4) The three Kadvantah Pragâtha, of which each has to repeat one. (5) The Sampâta hymns, see 6, 19. The principal parts of the Śastras of the minor Hotṛi-priests are only the two latter, the hymns and verses which precede being regarded only as intercalary (*âvapana*); thence the Kadvantaḥ Pragâthas are here called *ârambhaṇîya*, *i. e.* beginning Pragâthas. See on the whole Aśval. Śr. S. 7, 4.

[9] This is the translation of *pâpa vasyasam*.

[10] Thus Sây. explains, *Sairavati*, tracing it to *ira=annam*. But I doubt the correctness of this explanation; very likely the front of the ship which might have had the form of a plough (*sira*) is to be understood.

it is for making the sacrificial days continuous. Thus they make the sacrificial days continuous.

22.

(*The Triṣṭubhs of the minor Hotṛis.*)

The Maitrâvaruṇa repeats every day before the hymns (the Triṣṭubh) *apa prâcha Indra* (10, 131, 1), in which the idea of safety is expressed; in the words, " Drive away from round about us all enemies · drive them away, O conqueror! May they be in the south or north, prostrate (all) O hero! that we may enjoy thy far-extended shelter!" For he (the Maitrâvaruṇa) wishes to be in safety (thence he has to repeat this verse).

The Brâhmanâchchhaṁsi repeats every day *Brahmâṇa te brahmayujâ* (3, 35, 4). By the word *yunajmi*, " I join," the idea of " joining " is intimated; for the sacrificial days are joined, which is the characteristic of (all) sacrifices which last for a series of days (the Ahînas).

The Achchhâvâka repeats every day, *urum no lokam anuneshi* (6. 47, 8). For the term *anu* " after," implies the idea of going (after), as it were, which is a characteristic of the Ahîna sacrifices (for one day follows the other); whereas *neṣi* is a characteristic of a six monthly period of a sacrificial session.

These verses are recited every day, as well as the concluding[11] verses, which are every day the same.

Indra is the occupant of their (of the sacrificer's) house, he is at their sacrifice. Just as the bull goes [415] to the cow, and the cow to her well-known stable, so does Indra go to the sacrifice. He ought not to conclude the Ahîna with the verse *śunam havema* (3, 30, 22); for the king loses his kingdom if he calls him who becomes his enemy (rival).

23.

How to join and disconnect the Ahînas.

There is a joining as well as a disconnecting of the Ahîna sacrifice. By the mantra *vy antarikṣam atirad* (8, 14, 7-9) the Brâhmaṇâchchhaṁsî joins the Ahînas (at the morning libation); by *eved Indra* (7. 23, 6) he dissolves them (at the midday libation).

11 These are according to Say., *nu ṣṭuta indra* (4, 16, 21) repeated by the Maitrâvaruṇa; *eved indram* (7, 23, 6) repeated by the Brâhmaṇâchchhaṁsi; and *nûnam sâ te* (2, 11 22) repeated by the Achchhâvâka.

By the mantra *â ham sarasvatîvator* (8, 38, 10) the Achchhâvâka joins them, and by *nûnam sâ te* (2, 11, 22) (he dissolves them).

By *te syâma deva Varuṇa* (7, 66, 9) the Maitrâvaruṇa (joins them), and by *nu ṣṭuta* (4, 16, 21) he dissolves them.[12]

He who knows how to join (at the morning libation) and to disconnect (at the midday libation) is enabled to spread the thread of the sacrificial days (Ahînas). Their (general) junction consists in their being joined on the Chaturviṁśa day; and their (general) disconnection in disconnecting them before the concluding Atirâtra (on the Mahâvrata) day When the Hotri-priests would conclude on the Chaturviṁśa day with verses appropriate to the *Ekâhas*, then they would bring the sacrifice to a close, without performing the ceremonies referring to the Ahînas. When they would conclude with the concluding verses of the Ahîna days, then the sacrificers [**416**] would be cut off, just as (a bullock) who is tired must be cut off, (from the rope, for he does not move). They ought to conclude with both the Ekâha and Ahîna verses, just as a man setting out on a long journey takes from station to station fresh animals. Thence their sacrifice becomes connected, and they themselves (the sacrificers) find relaxation.

He ought not to overpraise the stoma (*i. e.* not to repeat more verses than the singers chant) at the two (first) libations by (more than) one or two verses. When the Stoma is overpraised with many verses, (*i. e.* more than two) then they become for the Hotar like extensive forests (through which he has to pass without a resting place). At the third libation (he ought to overpraise the stoma) with an unlimited number of verses. For the heavenly world has no limits. (This serves) for obtaining the celestial world. The Ahîna sarifice of him who with such a knowledge extends it, remains, if once commenced, undisturbed.

(*The nature of the Vâlakhilya Śastra.* 13 *How to repeat it.*)

---

[12] The verbs *vimuñchati* as well as *yuṅkte* are here used in an elliptical sense (उपलक्षनार्थे To the former, *yuṅkte*, and to the latter, *vimuñchati* is to be supplied, each thus implying its contrariety.

[13] The way of repeating the so called Vâlakhilya Sastra, the text of which consists of the Vâlakhilya verses, now arranged in eight hymns, is very artificial, and considered as the most difficult task to be achieved by a Hotṛi-priest. It is repeated in a manner similar to the repetition of the Ṣolaśî Śastra (see page 258). The most general term for the peculiar way of repeating both the Vâlakhilya and Ṣolaśî Śastras is *vihâra*, that is, the dissecting of a verse by joining to each of its pâdas, a pâda taken from another verse, and reciting then both parts in such a way as if they were forming only one verse. The way in which the Vâlakhilyas are repeated is a modification of the *vihâra*. It is called *vyatimarśa*. This consists in a mutual transposition of the several pâdas or half verses, or whole verses of the first and second Vâlakhilya hymns, which are repeated in sets, always two being taken together. The first two are to be repeated pâda by

24.

The gods after having perceived the cows to be in the cavern,[14] wished to obtain them by means of a sacrifice. They obtained them by means of the sixth day.[15] They bored at the morning libation the cavern with the bore mantra (*nabhâka*). After having succeeded in making an opening, they loosened (the stones), and then, at the third libation, broke up the cavern by means of the Vâlakhilya verses, with the Ekapadâ as *vâchaḥ kûṭa*, which served as a weapon and drove the cows out. In this way the sacrificers bore the cavern at the morning libation by means of the Nabhâka, and make, by boring, its structure loose. Hence the Hotṛi-priests repeat at the morning libation the Nabhâka triplet. The Maitrâvaruṇa repeats, *yaḥ kakubho nidhâraya* (8, 41, 4-6); the Brâhhmaṇâchchhaṁsi), *pûrvîṣṭa indra* (8, 40, 9-11); the Achchhâvâka, *tâ hi madhyam bharâṇâm* (8, 40, 3-5).

---

pâda; the third and fourth by half verses; the fifth and sixth by whole verses (Aśv, Śr. S. 8. 2). The general rule for this transposition is expressed by Aśval पूर्वस्थ प्रथमा-मुत्तरस्य द्वितीयवोत्तरस्थ प्रथमां पूर्वस्थ द्वितीया *i. e.* he must join the first verse (or half verse or pâda, as the case may be) of the first hymn with the second verse of the following hymn, and then the first of the following hymn with the second of the first. Two such verses form then one Pragâtha.

In order to better illustrate the way of transposition, I here subjoin an instance The first verse of the first Vâlakhilya hymn is as follows:

Abhi pra vah surâdhasam indram archa yathâ vide-
Yo jaritṛibhyo maghavâ purûvasuḥ sahasreṇeva śikṣati

The second verse of the second hymn is:

Śatanîka hetaya asya duṣṭarâ indrasya samiṣo mahîḥ.
Girir na bhujmâ maghavastu pinvate yadiṁ sutâ amandiṣuḥ.

If the several pâdas of these two verses are to be mutually transposed, it is then done in the following way:

(1) *Abhi pra vaḥ surâdhasam indrasya samiṣo mahîḥ.*
Śatanika hetayo asya duṣṭarâ indram urchâ yathâ vidom.
(2) *Yo jaritribhyo maghavâ purûvasar yadiṁ suta amandiṣuḥ.*
Girir na bhujmâ maghavatsu pinvate sahasreṇa śikṣatom.

At the end of the five first Pragâtha verses an Ekapadâ or verse containing one pâda only is added. Four of them belong to the performance of the tenth day. These are according to Aśval. (8, 2): (1) *indra viśvasya gopatiḥ*; (2) *indra viśvasya bhûpatiḥ*; (3) *indra viśvasya chetati*; (4) *îndra viśvasya râjati*. The fifth is from the Mahâvrata day, *sânvendro viśvam virajati*. These five Ekapadâs are not joined to the Pragâtha without a stop after the latter. (प्रगाथांतेषु चानुपसंतान ऋगावानमेकपदः शंसेत Aśv. 8, 2.)

The Pragâtha with the Ekapadâ belonging to it is the *vâchaḥ kûṭaḥ*, *i.e.* the point of speech, according to Sâyaṇa. But this appears not to be quite correct. According to an unmistakable indication in Ait. Br. 6, 24 (*upâpto vâchaḥ kûṭa ekapadâyâm*) it can mean only the Ekapadâ which is added to the Pragâtha.

[14] This story is frequently alluded to in the Saṁhitâ of the Rigveda.

[15] See page 335.

At the third libation they break up the cavern with the Vâlakhilya verses, and the one footed *Vâchaḥ kûṭa* which served as a weapon, and obtain the cows. There are six Vâlakhilya hymns. He repeats them in three terms; for the first time he repeats them foot by foot, dissecting the verse by insertion; for the second time half verse by half verse; and for the third time verse by verse. When he repeats them foot by foot, dissecting the verse by insertion, then he ought to put in every Pragâtha verse (of which each hymn is composed) one additional foot (*ekapadâ*), which is the *Vâchaḥ kûṭaḥ, i.e.* the point of the Vâch. There are five such Ekapadâs, four of them being taken from the tenth day and one from the Mahâvrata sacrifice.

He ought (if the two verses joined should fall short of a proper Pragâtha by eight syllables) to supply the eight syllables from the Mahânâmnîs[16] as often as they might be wanting; for the other pâdas (of the Mahânâmnîs which he does not require for filling up the deficiency in the Pragâtha) he ought not to care.

When reciting the Vâlakhilyas half verse by half verse, he ought to repeat those Ekapadâs; and the **[419]** pâdas from the Mahânâmnis which consist of eight syllables. When repeating the Vâlakhilyas verse by verse, he ought (also) to repeat those Ekapadâs, and the pâdas of eight syllables which are taken from the Mahânâmnis. When he repeats, for the first time, the six Vâlakhilya hymns, then he mixes (*viharati*) breath and speech by it. When he repeats them for the second time, then he mixes the eye and mind by it. When he repeats them for the third time, then he mixes the ear and the soul by it. Thus every desire regarding the mixing (of the verses) becomes fulfilled, and all desires regarding the Vâlakhilyas, which serve as a weapon, the Vâchaḥ kûṭa in the form of an Ekapadâ and the formation of life will be fulfilled (also).

He repeats the (Vâlakhilya) Pragâthas for the fourth time without mixing the verses of two hymns. For the Pragâthas are cattle. (It serves) for obtaining cattle. He ought not to insert (this time) an Ekapadâ in it Were he to do so, then he would cut off cattle from the sacrificer by slaying them. (If one should observe a Hotri-priest doing so) one ought to tell him at this occasion, thou hast cut off cattle from the sacrificer by slaying them with the point of speech (*vâchaḥ kûṭa*) thou hast deprived him of cattle (altogether). And thus it always happens. Thence one ought never to insert the Ekapadâs at this occasion.

---

[16] See page 281.

The two last Vâlakhilya hymns (the seventh and eighth[17]) he adds as a setting (cover). Both are mixed. In such a way, *Sarpi*, the son of *Vatsa*, repeated them for a sacrificer, *Subala* by name. He said, "I have now grasped for the sacrificer the largest number of cattle, the best ones (as a reward for my skill) will come to me." He then gave **[420]** him (Sarpi) as much Dakṣiṇâ[18] as to the great priests (Hotar, Adhvaryu, Udgâtar, Brahmâ). This Śastra procures cattle and heaven. Thence one repeats it

25.

(*What kind of hymn ought to be chosen for the Dûrohaṇam.*)

He recites a hymn in the Dûrohaṇa way, about which a Brâhmaṇam has been already told (4, 20). If the sacrificer aspires to cattle, then an Indra hymn is required for this purpose. For cattle belong to Indra ; it should be in the Jagatî metre, for cattle have the nature of Jagatî, they are (movable) ; it should be a great hymn (a *mahâsukta*) ;[19] for then he places, by it, the sacrificer among the largest number of cattle. He may choose for making Dûrohaṇam the Baru hymn (seen by the Riṣi Baru), which is a large hymn and in the Jagati metre.[20]

For one who aspires after a firm footing, an Indra-Varuṇa hymn is required ; for this performance of the Maitravaruṇa (his *hotrâ*) belongs to this deity ; (and) the Indra-Varuṇa[21] (Yâjyâ) is the conclusion of it. It is the Dakṣiṇâ of the great priests.

[421] This (Dûrohaṇa repetition) puts (the reciter) finally in his own place (keeps him in his position). As regards the Indra-Varuṇa hymn, it is at this occasion (when performing the Dûrohaṇam) a Nivid (*i.e.* like it). By means of the Nivid all desires become gratified. When he should use an Indra-Varuṇa hymn for the Dûrohaṇam, then he ought to choose a hymn by Suparṇa. Thus a desire regarding Indra-Varuṇa and one regarding Suparṇa [22] become gratified (at the same time).

---

[17] The order of both is only inverted, the eighth Sukta is first to be repeated, and then follows the seventh.

[18] The term is only *ninâya*, to which *dakṣiṇâ* "on the right side" is to be supplied. Cows horses, &c., which are given as a sacrificial reward, are actually carried to the right side of the recipient. The word *dakṣiṇâ* itself is only an abbreviation of *dakṣiṇâ nîta*, "what has been carried to the right side." Very soon the word was used as a feminine substantive. The noun to be supplied is *diś*, direction. The repeater of the Vâlakhilya Śastra is the Maitrâvaruṇa, who as one of the minor Hotṛi-priests, obtains generally only half the Dakṣiṇâ of the great priests.

[19] Hymns which exceed the number of ten verses are called by this name. Those which fall short of this number, are the *kshudra sûktas* (small hymns). *Sây.*

[20] It commences *pra te mahe* (10, 96).

[21] This is, *indrâvaruṇâ madhumattamasya* (6, 68, 11).

[22] The hymn is, *imâni vâṁ bhâyâdheyâni* (Vâlak. 11). It is addresed to Indra Varṇua

26.

(Whether or not the Maitrâvaruṇa should repeat the Ahîna and Ekâha hymns along with the Dûrohaṇam.)

They (the interpreters of Brahmâ) ask, Shall he recite together (with these Durohaṇas the Ahîna hymns which are required on the sixth day) or shall he not do so? To this question they answer, he shall recite them; for why should he recite them on all other days, and not do so on this day? But (others) say he ought not to recite them together with these hymns;[23] for the sixth day represents the heavenly world; the heaven-world is not accessible to every one (*asamâyî*); for only a certain one (by performing properly the sacrifices) meets there (the previous occupants). Therefore, when the other hymns are repeated together with the Dûrohaṇas, then he (the priest) would make all equal (make all those who sacrifice and those who do not sacrifice go to heaven). Not to repeat these other hymns along with the Dûrohaṇas is a characteristic of the heaven-world (the celestial world being accessible to but few). Therefore, one ought not to repeat them.

[422] That is the reason that he does not repeat them. (Should he do so, he would destroy the sacrificer); for the singing verse (Stotriya) is his soul, and the Vâlakhilyas are his breath. When he repeats (the Ahîna hymns) along (with the Dûrohaṇa) then he takes away the life of the sacrificer through those two deities (Indra-Varuṇa, to whom the Dûrohaṇa belongs.) (If one should observe a Hotṛi-priest doing so), one ought to tell the priest that he has deprived the sacrificer of his vital airs through those two deities (who get angry at it), and that he will lose his life. And thus it always happens. Thence he ought not to repeat (them).

If the Maitrâvaruṇa should think, "I have repeated the Vâlakhilyas (which was a very arduous task), well, I will now repeat before the Dûrohaṇa the Ekâha hymns,"[24] he should not entertain such a thought (for it is useless). But, however, should he pride himself too much of his skill, that he would be able to repeat after the Dûrohaṇa (the repetition of which is very difficult) is over, many hundred mantras, he may do so for gratifying that desire alone which is (to be gratified by repeating many mantras). He then obtains what he was wishing to obtain by repeating many mantras. He would, however, do better not to recite them. For the Vâlakhilyas

---

[23] Śastram of the Maitrâvaruṇa is to be understood.

[24] These are, *charṣaṇîdhritam* (3, 51), and *â vâm râjânâu* (7, 84).

belong to Indra; in them there are pâdas of twelve feet[25] and every wish to be gratified by an Indra hymn in the Jagatî metre, is contained therein (therefore no other Indra hymn is required).

[423] (Another reason that he had better not recite them) is the Indra-Varuṇa hymn (of the Dûrohaṇa), and the Indra-Varuṇa (Yâjyâ) which concludes (for these represent a firm footing, of which the sacrificer might be deprived, when repeating hymns which serve for connecting the several days).

They say, The Śastra must always correspond with the Stotra. Now the Vâlakhilyas being repeated by mixing verses of two hymns (vihṛita) are then the Stotras to be treated in the same way or not? The answer is, There is such a mixing in (the Stotra), a pâda of twelve syllables being joined to one of eight.[26]

They say, The Yâjyâ must correspond with the Śastra. If in (the Śastra) there are three deities, *viz.* Agni, Indra, and Varuṇa mentioned, how does he make the Yâjyâ with a verse addressed to Indra-Varuṇa alone, and omit Agni? (The answer is) Agni and Varuna are one and the same being. So said a Rishi in the mantra, "Thou Agni! art born as Varuṇa" (5, 3, 1). If he therefore makes his Yâjyâ with an Indra-Varuṇa mantra, then Agni is not left out.

FIFTH CHAPTER.

(The so-called Śilpas, viz. the Nâbhânediṣṭha, Narâśaṁsa, Vâlakhilya, Sukîrti, Vṛiṣâkapi, and Evayâmarut hymns. The Kuntâpa Śastra.)

27.

(The Nâbhânediṣṭha and Narâśaṁsa hymns repeated by the Hotar)

They repeat the Śilpas (hymns for producing **[424]** wonderful pieces of art). There are such wonder-works of the gods, and the arts in this world are to be understood as an imitation thereof. The gilded cloth spread over an elephant, the carriage to which a mule is yoked, are such a wonder-work. This work is understood in this world by him, who has such a knowledge. The Śilpas make ready the soul, and imbue it with the knowledge of the sacred hymns. By means of them the Hotṛi-priest prepares the soul for the sacrificer.

---

[25] Some of the Vâlakhilyas are in the Pragâtha metre, which consists of two strophes, called Bṛihatî and Satobṛihatî. In the first the third pâda comprises twelve syllables, and in the second the first and third contain as many. Twelve syllables four times taken constitute the Jagatî metre. Thence the author supposes the Jagatî metre to be contained in the Vâlakhilyas.

[26] The Stotra alluded to is, *agne tvaṁ no antamaḥ* (5, 24, 1) which is a Dvipadâ, the first pâda comprising eight, the second twelve feet.

He repeats the Nâbhânediṣṭha hymn (one of the Śilpas). For Nâbhânediṣṭha is the sperm. In such a way he (the priest) effuses the sperm. He praises him (Nâbhânediṣṭha) without mentioning his name. For the semen is like something unspeakable secretly poured forth into the womb. The sperm becomes blended. For when Prajâpati had carnal intercourse with his daughter, his sperm was poured forth upon the earth (and was mixed up with it).[1] This was done for making the sperm produce fruit.

He then repeats the Narâśaṁsa,[2] for *naraḥ* means "offspring," and *śaṁsaḥ* "speech." In this way he (the priest) places speech into children (when they are born.) Thence chidren are born endowed with the faculty of speech.

Some repeat the Narâśaṁsa before (the Nâbhânediṣṭha,) saying, Speech has its place in the front (of the body); others repeat it after (the Nâbhânediṣṭha), saying, Speech has its place behind (in the hinder part of the head). He shall recite it in the middle; for speech has its place in the middle (of [**425**] the body). But speech being always, as it were, nearer to the latter part (of the Nâbhânediṣṭha hymn), the Narâśaṁsa must be repeated before the Nâbhânediṣṭha is finished)[3]

The Hotar having effused the sacrificer in the shape of sperm (symbolically), gives him up to the Maitrâvaruṇa, saying, "form his breaths."

28.

(*The Vâlakhilyas repeated by the Maitrâvâruṇa.*)

He (the Maitrâvaruṇa) now repeats the Vâlakhilyas. For the Vâlakhilyas are the breaths. In this way he forms the breaths of the sacrificer. He repeats them by mixing two verses together. For these breaths are mutually mixed together,[4] with the Prâṇa the Apâna, and with the Apâna the Vyâna. The two first hymns are repeated pâda by pâda; the second set (third and fourth) half verse by half verse, and the third set (fifth and sixth) verse by verse. By repeating the first set, he makes the breath and speech. By repeating the second set, he makes the eye and mind. By repeating the third set, he makes the ear and soul. Some take,

---

1 This is mentioned in the fifth verse of the Nâbhânediṣṭha hymn (10, 61). Prajâpati's intercourse with his daughter is alluded to in this hymn.

2 This is called the second Nâbhânediṣṭha hymn (10, 62), beginning *ye yajñena*. There the birth of the Aṅgiras is spoken of.

3 The Nâbhânediṣṭha hymn, *idam itthâ roûdram* (10, 61) consists of twenty-seven verses; after the twenty-fifth verse is finished, the following Narâśaṁsa hymn is repeated. Repeater of both the Nâbhânediṣṭha and Narâśaṁsa hymns is the Hotar.

4 The six first Valakhilya hymns are repeated in three sets, each comprising two hymns, see page 419.

when repeating these Vâlakhilya Pragâthas, always two Bṛihatîs, and two Satobṛihatîs together. Though the wish obtainable by mixing the verses is obtained by this way of recital, yet no Pragâthas[5] are thus formed.

[426] He must repeat them by inserting an additional pâda;[6] then thus are the Pragâthas formed. The Vâlakhilya verses are the Pragâthas. Therefore he must repeat them by inserting a pâda (in order to obtain the Pragâtha metre). The Bṛihatî of the Pragâtha is the soul, the Satobṛihatî the life. If he has repeated the Bṛihatî, then the soul, (is made); and if he has repeated the Satobrihatî, the vital airs (are made). By thus repeating the Bṛihatî and the Satobṛihatî, he surrounds the soul with the vital airs. Therefore he must repeat the Vâlakhilyas in such a way as to obtain the Pragâtha metre. The Bṛihatî is the soul, and the Satobṛihatî cattle. If he has repeated the Bṛihatî, then the soul (is made); and if he has repeated the Satobṛihatî, then cattle (is made). By repeating both he surrounds the soul with cattle. The two last hymns are repeated in an inverted order (first the eighth and then the seventh.)

The Maitrâvaruṇa after having made in this way the vital airs of the sacrificer, hands him over to the Brâhmaṇâchchhaṁsî, saying, "create him now (in the human form)."

29

(The Sukîrti and Vṛiṣâkapi hymns repeated by the Brâhmaṇâchhaṁsî.)

The Brâhmaṇâchchhaṁsi repeats the *Sukîrti* hymn;[7] for the Sukîrti is the womb of the gods. He thus causes the sacrificer to be born out of the sacrifice, which is the womb of the gods.

He repeats the *Vṛiṣâkapi* hymn.[8] For Vṛiṣâkapi is the soul. In this way he makes the soul of [427] the sacrificer. He repeats it with Nyûṅkha.[9] The Nyûṅkha is food. In this way he provides him when born with food, just as (a mother) gives the breast to her child. That hymn is in the Paṅkti *i.e.* five-hood) metre; for man consists of five parts, *viz.* hair, skin, flesh, bones and marrow. He prepares the sacrificer just in the same way, as man (in general) is prepared.

The Brâhmaṇâchchhaṁsî, after having created the sacrificer, hands him over to the Achchhâvaka, saying, " make a footing for him. "

[5] The form required for the Pragâtha metre is the combination of the Bṛihatî with the Satobṛihatî. If two Bṛihatîs are taken together, no Pragâtha is formed, nor if two Satobṛihatîs are joined.

[6] See above page 419. This is called Atimarśa.

[7] This is the hymn, *apa prâcha* (10, 131). It is repeated by the Brâhmaṇachchhaṁsi.

[8] This is the hymn *vihi sotor* (10, 86.)

[9] This Nyûṅkha differs somewhat from the usual way of making it. The sound is uttered sixteen times, three times with three moras, and thirteen times with half moras See Aśval. Sr. S. 8, 3.

30.

(*The Evayâmarut repeated by the Achchhâvâka. Story of Bulila*)

The Achchhâvâka now repeats the Evayâmarut hymn.[10] This hymn is the footing; by repeating it the Achchhâvâka makes a footing to the sacrificer. He repeats it with Nyûṅkha. The Nyûṅkha is food. Thus he provides the sacrificer with food. In this hymn there is the Jagatî and Atijagatî metre, which metres comprise the whole universe what falls in the sphere of movable things as well as what falls beyond it. It is addressed to the Marutas. The Marutas are the waters; and water is food which is to be filled (in the sacrificer like water in a pot). In this way he provides the sacrificer with food.

The Nâbhânediṣṭha, Vâlakhilyas, Vṛiṣâkapi, and Evayâmaruta are called "auxiliary hymns." The priest ought to recite them (all) along with (the other hymns); (if he does not like that) he ought not to repeat any (of them along with the other hymns).

[428] But if he should repeat them on different (days or occasions) it is just as if one would separate a man from his sperm. Thence he ought either to repeat them along with (the other hymns) or omit them entirely.

That (famous) *Bulila*, the son of *Aśvâtara*, the son of *Aśva*, being once Hotar at the Viśvajit sacrifice, speculated about this matter, that is to say, these Śilpas (these auxiliary hymns). He thought, "There having been added two Śastras (that of the Maitrâvaruṇa and that of the Brâhmaṇâchchhaṁsî) to the midday libation in the Viśvajit of the sacrificial sessions for a year, I thus (in further addition) will repeat the Evayâmaruta." Thus he recited it. Whilst he was repeating it *Gauśla* came near him, and said, "Hotar! Why does thy Śastra proceed without wheels? How has it come (that thou art acting in such a way)?" The Evayâmaruta is repeated by the Achchhâvâka standing north from the Hotar. He further said, "The midday libation belongs to Indra. Why dost thou wish to turn out Indra from it?" He answered, "I do not wish to turn out Indra from the midday libation." He said, (Yes, you do), for this particular metre being the Jagatî and Atijagatî is not fit for the midday libation,[11] and the hymn is besides addressed to the Marutas (not to Indra, as it should be); therefore one should not repeat it now. Bulila then said, "Stop, Achhâvâka, I wish to carry out Gauśla's order.". Gauśla then said, "He shall repeat an Indra hymn, in which

---

[10] *Pravo mahe matayaḥ* (5, 87).

[11] The proper metre for the midday libation is the Triṣṭubh, whilst the Jagatî is used at the evening libation.

the mark of Viṣṇu is impressed.[12] Thence thou, Hotar, shalt leave [429] out from thy Śastra this Evayâmaruta, which was recited after the Rudra Dhâyyâ, and before the Maruta Śastra." He did so, and so they proceed now.

31

(Queries on some particulars of the application of these auxiliary hymns. Their meaning).

They ask, Why do they not repeat the Nâbhânediṣṭha in the Viśvajit, Atirâtra, and on the sixth day of the Ṣaḷaha, when they make the sacrifice complete and reproduce the sacrificer (in a mystical way), although the Maitrâvaruṇa repeats the Vâlakhilyas which represent the breaths, but not the sperm (as the Nâbhânediṣṭha does), whilst the sperm must precede the breaths (in the act of generation)? In the same way why does the Brâhmaṇâchchhaṁsi repeat the Vṛiṣâkapi when the Nâbhânediṣṭha is not repeated? For the Vṛiṣâkapi is the soul, whilst the sperm represented by the Nâbhânediṣṭha hymn precedes the making of the soul. How then can the sacrificer be reproduced in this way? How can that be effected, if his life is not formed (by the act of generation)? For the priests produce the sacrificer (make him anew) by means of the sacrificial process. Therefore the whole being of the sacrificer cannot be made at once at the beginning, but just as an embryo which, lying in the womb, developes itself (grows gradually). If h has all limbs (only then he is entire). The priests should make them all on the same day. If thus the sacrifice is made ready, then the reproduction of the sacrificer is effected.

The Hotar repeats the Evayâmarut at the third libation. For this is the sacrificer's footing on which the Hotar places him at the end.

32

(On the origin and nature of the so-called Kuntapa[13] hymns, Atharvaveda 20, 127-136. The Narasaṁsî, Raibhî and Pârikṣiti, Diśâm klripti and Janakalpa verses; the Indra-gâthâs.)

[430] The juice of the metres which were all done by the sixth day (at the Ṣaḷaha) was running (over the brim). Prajâpati got afraid lest the

[12] Instead of the Evayâmarut, the Achchhâvâka is to repeat, *dyaur naya* (6, 20,) which is an Indra hymn. Viṣṇu is mentioned in the fourth pâda of the second verse by the words. *v ṣṇunâ sachânaḥ*.

[13] The so-called Kuntâpa hymns are to be repeated by the Brâhmaṇâchchhmsi after he has finished the Vṛiṣâkapi. Their repetition has several peculiarities regarding the response, which all are noted by Aśval. Śr. S. (8, 3). The response for the first 14 verses beginning with *iduṁ anâ upa sruta* is at the end of each verse only, it is simply *othâmo daivom*. The verses which immediately follow up to *etâ asvâ âplavanta* have two

juice of the metres might go away and run over the worlds. Therefore he kept it down by means of metres placed on another part (above them). With the *Narâśaṁsî* he kept down (the juice) of the Gâyatrî, with the *Raibhî* that of the Triṣṭubh, with the *Pârikṣiti* that of the Jagatîs, with the *Kâravyâ* that of the Anuṣ **[431]** ṭubhs. Thus he provided again the metres with good juice. The sacrifice of him who has this knowledge becomes performed with metres keeping their juice, and he spreads it with metres keeping their juice, (*i.e.*, the essence of the sacrifice is not lost).

The priest now repeats *Narâśaṁsi* verses.[14] For *naraḥ* (men) means children and *śaṁsaḥ* speech. He thus places speech in children. Therefore children of him who has this knowledge are born with the faculty of speaking. The Gods and Riṣis having gained the heavenly world by repeating the Narâśaṁsa verses, the sacrificers who repeat them go to the heavenly world also. The priest stops when repeating these verses, after each of the two or three first pâdas, and after the two or three last taken together,[15] just as he does when repeating the Vṛiṣâkapi. For what is of the same nature as the Vṛiṣâkapi (as the Narâśaṁsîs are

responses each, after every half verse. The seventy pâdas commencing with *etâ aśvâ* have each a response. The six verses commencing with *vitatâu kiraṇâu* have each a peculiar response after the first half verse. So the response to *vitatâu* is *dundubhim âhananâbhyâm jaritar othâmo daiva*; that to the second is *kośabile jaritar*, &c. They are all given in the Atharvaveda Saṁhitâ (20, 133) along with the text of which they form, however, no part. For the response (*pratigara*) is repeated by the Adhvaryu. Similar responses occur in all verses which follow as far as the *devanitham, âdityâha jaritar*; they all are given in the Atharvaveda, such as *pipilakâvataḥ, śvâ, parṇaśadaḥ*, &c., which all are followed by *jaritar othâmo daivom*. In the Devanîtha (Athar. 20, 135, 6-10) the response is in the first pâda of each verse; it is *om ha jaritar othâmo daiva*. These Kuntâpa songs do not bear a strictly religious character; they are praise songs, principally referring to Dakṣiṇâ and belong to that class of ancient poetry which bears the name *nârâśaṁsi*. This may be clearly seen from the commencement of the whole collection, *idam janâ upaśruta nârâśaṁsaḥ, taviṣyate, i. e.*, hearken ye people to this; Narâśaṁsaḥ will be praised with chants. The recitation of these pieces is accompanied with musical instruments, such as *dundubhi, karkari*, &c. The repeater must have been originally the chanter; for in the response he is always addressed by "*jaritar*," *i. e.*, singer.

[14] *Idam jana upa śruta nârâśaṁsa* A. V. 20, 127, 1-3.

[15] This is a translation of the term *pragrâha*. Several of the verses are in the Paṅkti metre; then the three last pâdas are taken together. As far as this goes, they are just recited as the Vṛiṣâkapi hymn. Only the Nyûṅhka is not made, but instead of it the Ninarda, which is a substitute for it. This peculiar pronunciation of the vowel takes place in the second syllable of the third, and the fourth of the fourth pada. The Pratigara is *madethama daivom othâmo daivom.*

supposed to be) follows the same rule. In repeating them, he shall not make Nyûṅkha,[16] but pronounce them with a kind of **[432]** Ninarda,[17] for this is the Nyûṅkha of the Narâśaṁsîs verses.

The priest repeats the *Raibhî* verses.[18] For the Gods and Riṣis went by making a great noise (*rebhantaḥ*) to the celestial world; in the same way, therefore, the sacrificers go to the celestial world. (The recital is just the same as that of the Narâśaṁsîs, and subject to the same rules.)

He repeats the *Pârikṣiti* verses.[19] For Agni is the dweller round about (*parikṣit*); he lives round the people, and the people live round (*parikṣi*) him. He who has such a knowledge, obtains union with Agni, and shares the same character and abode with him. As to these Pârikṣiti verses (they may have another meaning too . For the year is *Parikṣit* (dwelling round about); for it dwells round about men, and men dwell round about the year. Therefore he who has this knowledge, obtains union with the year (*saṁvatsara*) and shares its character and abode. (The Pârikṣiti verses are repeated in the same way as the Narâśaṁsîḥ.)

He repeats the *Kâravyâ* verses.[20] For any work of the gods crowned with success was performed by means of the Kâravyâs; and the same is then the case with the sacrificers. (The recital is the same as that of the Narâśaṁsîḥ.)

The priest now repeats the "directions forming verses" (*diśâm klṛiptis*). For in this way he **[433]** forms the directions. He repeats five such verses; for there are five directions, *viz.*, the four points (east, west, south and north)

---

[16] In repeating the Vṛiṣâkapi hymn, both the Nyûṅkha and Ninarda are used. The Nyûṅkha takes place at the second syllable of the third pada, which is the proper place for the Ninarda also. (On the Nyûṅkha see page 322). The Ninarda is described by Aśval. Śr. S. 7, 11, as follows: *okâraś chaturninarda udâttân prathamottamâv anudâttâvitasâ uttaro snudâttataraḥ plutaḥ prathamo makârânta uttamaḥ*, *i. e.*, the vowel *o* has four times the Ninarda sound; the first and last times it has the *udâtta* accent, the two others the *anudâtta*; the latter of which has even the anudâttatara (lowest *anudâtta*); the first (and last) is pronounced with three moras. There is another way of making the Ninarda by pronouncing the *o* successively first with the udâtta, then with the anudâtta, then with the svarita, and lastly with the udâtta accent again.

[17] *Nivîva* is to be parsed *ni vi iva*, the *ni* and *vi* belonging to the verb *nardet*. The whole means, literally, he ought to make a peculiar species of the Ninarda, as it were.

[18] *Vachyasva rebha*, A. V. 20, 127, 4.

[19] *Râjño viśvajanîyasya*, A. V. 20, 127, 7-10. In every verse the word *pârikṣit*, *i. e.*, dwelling round about (said of Agni) occurs.

[20] *Indraḥ kârum abûbudhat*, A. V. 20, 127, 11-14. Because of the word *kâru*, *i. e.*, singer, praiser, occurring in the first verse, they are called *kâravyâs*.

[21] These are *yaḥ sabheyo vidathya*, A. V. 20, 128, 1-5.

and one direction above crossing (them all). He ought not to repeat (these verses) with Nyûṅkha, nor make the Ninarda in the same way as above. Thinking, I will not mutilate (*nyûṅkhayâni*) [22] these directions, he repeats these verses, half verse by half verse.

For making a footing, he then repeats the *Janakalpa* verses.[23] For children are *janakalpa* (production of men). Having made the directions in the above manner, he places people in them. He shall not repeat these verses with Nyûṅkha, nor with the Ninarda, but just in the same way and for the same reasons as the *diśâm klripti*.

He repeats the *Indra-gâthâs.*[24] For by means of the Indra songs, the Devas sang the Asuras down and defeated them. In the same way, the sacrificers put down their enemies by these songs. They are repeated, half verse by half verse, to obtain a footing for the sacrificer.

33.

(*Aitaśa-pralâpa. The Pravahlika Ajijñâsenya Pratirâdha, and Ativâda Verses.*)

The priest (Brâhmaṇâchhaṃsi) repeats the *Aitaśapralâpa.* Aitaśa was a Muni. He saw the mantras, called "the life of Agni" (*agner âyuḥ*), which should remove all defects from the sacrifice, as some say. He said to his sons, "O my dear sons, I saw 'the life of Agni;' I will talk about it; but pray do not scorn at me for anything I might speak. He then commenced to repeat, *etâ aśvâ âplavante, pratîpam* **[434]** *prâti sutvanam* (A. V. 20, 129, 1 *et seq.*).[25] Then one of his family, *Abhyagni* by name, went to him at an improper time (before Aitaśa had finished his talk) and stopped his mouth by putting his hand on it, saying, "Our father has become mad." Then his father said to him, "Go away, become infected with leprosy, thou who hast murdered my speech. I would be able to prolong the life of a cow to a hundred, and that of a man to a thousand years (if thou wouldst not have stopped my mouth), but thou, my son, who hast overpowered me (in such an improper way), I curse: thy progeny shall come into the condition of the lowest among the most wicked." Therefore they say, that among the Aitaśâyanas the Abhyagnis are most burdened with sins, in the whole Aurva-Gotra (to which they belong). Some priests lengthen this Aitaśa-pralâpa (repeating eighteen

---

[22] From *ukh, unkh,* to move, go.

[23] *Yo nâktâkṣo anabhyakto,* A. V. 20, 128, 6-11.

[24] *Yad indrâdo dasurâjñe,* A. V. 20, 128, 12-16.

[25] According to Sâyana, the Aitaśa-pralâpa consists of 70 pâdas.

more pâdas). (If they choose to do so) one should not prevent them ; but say, "repeat as long as you like. For the Aitaśa-pralâpa is life." Therefore, he who has this knowledge, prolongs in this way the life of the sacrificer.

As to the Aitaśa-pralâpa, there is another meaning in it. For it is the essence (juice) of the metres ; by repeating it, the reciter puts speech in the metres. He who has this knowledge, will keep the essence in the metres, when the sacrifice is performed, and will spread the sacrifice with the essence in the metres.

But there is still another meaning in the Aitaśa-pralâpa ; it is fit for removing defects in the sacrifice, and for restoring its entirety. For the Aitaśa-pralâpa is imperishableness. (Therefore when it is recited, the sacrificer wishes) "May my sacrifice be lasting and all its defects be removed." He repeats **[435]** this Aitaśa-pralâpa, stopping after every pâda, just as the Nivid is repeated ; at the last pâda he, pronounces "*om*," just as it is done in the Nivid.

He repeats the *Prâvahlika* verses.[26] For the gods made the Asuras benumbed (*pravahlya*) by means of the Pravahlikâs, and, consequently, defeated them. In the same way, the sacrificers benumb and defeat their enemies by repeating these verses. They are repeated, half verse by half verse for obtaining a footing.

He repeats the *Ajijñâsenya* verses.[27] For, by means of these verses, the Devas recognised (*Âjñâya*) the Asuras and defeated them. In the same way, the sacrificers recognise and defeat their enemies. They are repeated half verse by half verse.

He now repeats the *Pratirâdha*.[28] For, by means of it, the Devas frustrated (*prati-râdh*) the efforts of the Asuras, and consequently defeated them. The same effect is produced by the sacrificers who have repeated it.

He repeats the *Ativâda*.[29] For, by means of it, the Devas abused (*ativad*) the Asuras so much as to defeat them. The same effect is produced by the sacrificers who repeat it. They are repeated, half verse by half verse, for obtaining a footing.

---

[26] *Vitatâu kiraṇâu dvâu*, A. V. 20, 133, 1-6.

[27] *Iha itthâ prâg apâg udak*, A. V. 20, 134, 1-4

[28] *Bhugiti abhigataḥ*, A. V. 20, 135, 1-3.

[29] *Vime devâ akran*, A. V. 20, 135, 4.

34

(*Story of the Sacrifices of the Âdityas and Añgirasas for reaching Heaven.*)

He repeats the *Devanîitham.*[30] (About this, the following story is reported.) The Âditiyas and Añgirasas **[436]** were contending with one another as to who should gain first the heavenly world. The Añgirasas had seen (in their mind) that, by dint of the Soma sacrifice they were about to bring on the next day, they would be raised to heaven first. They therefore despatched one from among themselves, Agni by name, instructing him thus: "Go to the Âdityas and announce to them that we shall, by dint of our to-morrow's Soma sacrifice, go to heaven." As soon as the Âdityas got sight of Agni, they at once saw (in their minds) the Soma sacrifice by which they would reach heaven. Having come near them, Agni said, "We inform you of our bringing to-morrow that Soma sacrifice, by means of which we shall reach heaven." They answered, "And we announce to you that we are just now contemplating to bring that Soma sacrifice, by means of which we shall reach heaven; but thou (Agni) must serve as our Hotar, then we shall go to heaven. He said, "Yes," (and went back to the Añgiras). After having told (the Añgiras the message of the Âdityas) and received their reply, he went back to the Âdityas). They asked him, "Hast thou told our message?" He said, "Yes, I have told it (to the Añgiras); and they answered, and asked, 'Did'st thou not promise us thy assistance (as a Hotar),' and I said, 'Yes, I have promised.' (But I could not decline the offer of the Âdityas). For he who engages in performing the duty of a sacrificial priest, obtains fame; and any one Who prevents the sacrifice from being performed, excludes himself from his fame. Therefore I did not prevent (by declining the offer)." If one wishes to decline serving as a sacrificial priest, then this resfusal is only justified on account of oneself being engaged in a sacrifice, or because of being legally prohibited to perform the sacrificial duties.

35

[437] (*On the Dakṣiṇâ given by the Âdityas to the Añgirasas. The Devanîtha Hymn.*)

The Añgirasas, therefore, assisted the Âdityas in their sacrifice. For this service, the Âdityas gave them the earth filled with presents (*dakṣiṇâ*) as reward. But when they had accepted her, she burnt them. Therefore they flung her away. She then became a lioness, and, opening her

---

[30] *Aditya ha jaritar añgirobhyo*, **A. V., 20, 135, 6** *et seq.* **17 verses, according to Sây.**

mouth, attacked people. From this burning state of the earth came those ruptures (which are now visible on her), whereas she had been previously quite even.[31] Thence one shall not retake a sacrificial reward which one has once refused to accept. (For he must think) the Dakṣiṇâ being penetrated by a flame, shall not penetrate me with it. But should he take it back, then he may give it to his adversary and enemy, who will be defeated, for it burns him.

That (Âditya, the sun) then assuming the shape of a white horse with bridle and harness, presented himself to the other Âdityas, who said, "Let us carry this gift to you (the Aṅgirasas)." Therefore this Devanîtha, *i.e.*, what is carried by the gods, is to be recited.

(*Now follows the Devanîtha, with Explanatory Remarks.*)

"The Âdityas, O singer! brought the Aṅgirasas their reward. The Aṅgirasas, O singer, did not go near," *i.e.*, they did not go near to that first gift (the earth).

"But, O singer! (afterwards) they went near it," *i.e.*, they went near the other gift (the white horse).

[438] "They did not accept it, O singer," *i.e.*, they did not accept this earth. "But they accepted it," *i.e.*, they accepted that white horse.

"He (Âditya, the sun), being carried away,[32] the days disappeared;" for he (the sun) makes the days visible.

"He being carried away, the wise men were without a leader (*purogava*)." For the reward (Dakṣiṇâ) is the leader in the sacrifices. Just as a carriage without having a bullock as a leader yoked to it, becomes damaged, a sacrifice at which no reward (Dakṣiṇâ) is given, becomes damaged also. Therefore, the sacrificial reward must be given (to the performers of a sacrifice), and even if it should be but very little (on account of the poverty of the sacrificer).

"And, further, this horse is white, with quickly running feet, the swiftest (of all). He quickly discharges the duties incumbent on him. The Âdityas, Rudras and Vasavas praise (him). Accept, therefore, this gift, O Aṅgiras!" They now intended accepting this gift.

---

[31] Here we have an attempt to explain the unevenness of the earth. It is interesting to see the theories of modern geology foreshadowed in this certainly ancient myth.

[32] Instead of *neta sann*, which reading is to be found here, as well as in the Atharvaveda, *netaḥ sann* must be read; *neath*, then, is an irregular form of the past part. of *nî*, to carry, standing for *nita*.

"This gift is large and splendid. This present which the gods have given, shall be your illuminator. It shall be with you every day. Thence consent to accept it!" (After having heard these words) the Aṅgiras accepted the reward.

In reciting this Devanîtha, the priest stops at every pâda, just as is done when the Nivid is repeated, and pronounces "*om*" at the last pâda, just as is the case with the Nivid.

36.

[439] (*Bhûte-chhad, Ahanasya, Dadhikrâvan, Pâvamânya, and the Indra Brihaspati Verses.*)

He now repeats the *Bhûte-chhad* [33] (dazzling power) verses. By means of these verses, the Devas aproached the Asuras by fighting and cunning. For, by means of them, they dazzled the power of the Asuras, and consequently overcame them. In the same way, the sacrificer who repeats these verses, overcomes his enemy. They are repeated half verse by half verse, to obtain a footing.

He now repeats the *Ahanasya* [34] verses. For the sperm is poured forth from the Ahanasya (penis); and from the sperm creatures are born. In this way, the priest makes offspring (to the sacrificer). These verses are ten in number; for the Virâj has ten syllables, and the Virâj is food; from food the sperm (is produced) and can (consequently) be poured forth, and from sperm creatures are produced. He repeats them with Nyûṅkha; for this is food.

He now repeats the *Dadhikrâvan* verse, *dadhikrâvano akârsiham* (Atharv. V. 20, 137, 3). For the Dadhikra is the purifier of the gods. For he (the priest) spoke such (words[35]) as are to be regarded as the speech containing the most excellent semen.[36] By means of this purifier of the gods, he purifies speech (*vâch*). The verse is in the Anuṣṭubh metre; for Vâch is Anuṣṭubh, and thus she becomes purified by her own metre.

He now repeats the *Pâvamânya* verses, *sutâso madhumatamâ* (9, 101,4); for the Pâvamânyas (purification verses) are the purification of the gods. For he spoke such (words) as are to be regarded as the speech containing the most excellent semen. By means of this purifier of the gods, he purifies speech. They are Anuṣṭubhs; for the Vâch is Anuṣṭubh, and thus she becomes purified by her own metre.

---

[33] *Tvam indra Śarma riṇa*, A. V. 20, 135, 11-13.

[34] Lit., penis; for *âhanas, âhana*, means penis, derived just as *jaghanyâ*, *i.e.*, from the root *han*, to strike. Sây. explains it by "*maithunam*," *i.e.*, cohabitation.

[35] *Yad asya aṁhubhedyâḥ*, A. V. 20, 136, 1-10,

[36] The repetition of the Ahanasya verses is to be understood.

[440] He now repeats the *Indra-Bṛihaspati* triplet of verses commencing, *avâ drapso aṁśumatîm* (8, 85, 13-15). At the end of it (verse 15) there is said, "Indra, assisted by Bṛihaspati, conquered the tribes of the despisers of the Devas when they encountered (the Devas on the battle-field)." For the Asura nation, when they had marched out to fight against the Devas, was everywhere subjugated by Indra with the assistance of Bṛihaspati, and driven away. Therefore the sacrificers subdue and drive away by means of Indra and Bṛihaspati the nation of the Asuras (*asurya varṇa*).[37]

They ask, Should the Hotṛi-priest, on the sixth day, repeat (the hymns) along (with the additional Śastras ?). See 6, 26.

He concludes with a Bṛihaspati verse; thence he ought not to repeat (the hymns) along (with the additional Śastras).

---

[37] That these are the Zoroastrians, is beyond any doubt. See my Essays on the Sacred Language, Writings, &c., of the Parsis, page 226-30.

[441] SEVENTH BOOK.

FIRST CHAPTER.

(The Distribution of the Different Parts of the Sacrificial Animal among the Priests.)

1

Now follows the division of the different parts of the sacrificial animal (among the priests). We shall describe it[1]. The two jawbones with the tongue are to be given to the Prastotar; the breast in the form of an eagle to the Udgâtar; the throat with the palate to the Pratihartar; the lower part of the right loins the Hotar; the left to the Brahmâ; the right thigh to the Maitrâvaruṇa; the left to the Brahmaṇâchhaṁsî; the right side with the shoulder to the Adhvaryu; the left side to those who accompany the chants;[2] the left shoulder to the Pratipasthâtar; the lower part of the right arm to the Neṣṭar; the lower part of the left arm to the Potar; the upper part of the right thigh to the Achhâvâka; the left to the Agnîdhra; the upper part of the right arm to Atreya[3]; the left to the Sadasya; the back bone [442] and the urinal bladder to the Gṛihapati (sacrificer); the right feet to the Gṛihapati who gives a feasting; the left feet to the wife of that Gṛihapati who gives a feasting; the upper lip is common to both (the Gṛihapati and his wife), which is to be divided by the Gṛihapati. They offer the tail of the animal to wives, but they should give it to a Brâhmaṇa; the fleshy processes (*maṇikâh*) on the neck and three gristles (*kâkasâḥ*) to the Grâvastut; three

[1] The same piece is found in Aśv. Śr. S. 12, 9.

[2] The Upagâtris accompany the chant of the Sâma singers with certain syllables which correspond to the Pratigâra of the Adhvaryu This accompaniment is called *upagânam.* It differs according to the different Sâmans. At the Bahiṣ-pavamâna Stotra at the morning libation, the *upagânam* of the Upagâtris is *ho.* Besides, the sacrificer has to make an *upagânam* also. This is *om* at the Bahiṣ-pavamâna Stotra.

[3] The Atreya who is here mentioned as a receiver of a share in the sacrificial animal, is no officiating priest. But the circumstance that he receives gold for his Dakṣiṇâ, and that it is given to him before the other priests (save the Agnîdhra), as we learn from the Kâtîya Śrâuta Sutras 10, 2, 21 shows, that he had a certain right to a principal share in all sacrificial donations. *Atreya,* meaning only a descendant of the Atrigotra, the right appears to have been hereditary in the family of the ancient Riṣi Atri.

other gristles and one-half of the fleshy part on the back (*vaikurtta* [4]) to the Unnetar; the other half of the fleshy part on the neck and the left lobe (*kloma* [5]) to the slaughterer, who should present it to a Brâhmaṇa, if he himself would not happen to be a Brâhmaṇa. The head is to be given to the Subrahmṇyâ), the skin belongs to him (the Subrahmaṇyâ), who spoke, *śvaḥ sutyâm* (to-morrow at the Soma sacrifice); [6] that part of the sacrificial animal at a Soma sacrifice which belongs to Iḷâ (sacrificial food) is common to all the priests; only for the Hotar it is optional.

All these portions of the sacrifical animal amount to thirty-six single pieces, each of which represents the pâda (foot) of a verse by which the sacrifice is carried up. The Bṛihatî metre consists of thirty-six syllables; and the heavenly worlds are of the Bṛihatî nature. In this way (by dividing the animal into thirty-six parts), they gain life (in this world) and the heavens, and having become established in both (this and that world), they walk there.

[443] To those who divide the sacrificial animal in the way mentioned, it becomes the guide to heaven. But those who make the division otherwise, are like scoundrels and miscreants who kill an animal merely (for gratifying their lust after flesh).

This division of the sacrificial animal was invented by the Riṣi *Devabhâga*, a son of Śruta.[7] When he was departing from this life, he did not entrust (the secret to any one). But a supernatural being communicated it to *Girija*, the son of *Babhru*. Since his time, men study it.

SECOND CHAPTER.

The Penances for Mishaps to the Performer of the Agnihotram).

2.

(*What Penances are required when an Agnihotri Dies*)

They ask, If a man who has already established a sacred fire (an Agnihotri) should die on the day previous to a sacrifice (*upavasatha*), what is to become of his sacrifice (to which all preparations had been made)?

[4] A large piece of flesh.—*Sây.*

[5] The piece of flesh which is on the side of the heart.—*Sây.*

[6] See the note to 6, 3.

[7] Thus Sây., but the translation, a Śrotriya, *i.e.*, sacrificial priest (acquainted with the Śruti)would suit better.

One should not have it brought; thus say some; for he (the owner) himself has no share in the sacrifice.

They ask, If an Agnihotri should die after having placed the intended fire offering, be it the *Sânnâyya* [1] or (other) offerings (on the fire), how is [444] this to be atoned for? One shall put all these things one after the other round the fire (like sticks, *paridhas*) and burn them all together. This is the penance.

They ask, If an Agnihotri should die after having placed the sacrificial offerings (ready made) on the Vedi,[2] what is the atonement? One ought to sacrifice them all in the Ahavanîya fire, with the formula *Svâhâ*, to all those deities for whom they were intended (by the deceased Agnihotri).

They ask, If an Agnihotri should die when abroad, what is to become of his burnt offering (*agnihotram*)? (There are two ways.) Either one shall then sacrifice the milk of a cow to which another (as its own) calf had been brought (to rear it up), for the milk of such a cow is as different as the oblation brought in the name of an Agnihotri deceased. Or, they may offer the milk of any other cow. But they mention another way besides. (The relatives of the deceased Agnihotri) should keep burning the (three) constantly blazing fires (Ahavanîya, &c.) without giving them any offering till the ashes of the deceased shall have been collected. Should they not be forthcoming, then they should take three hundred and sixty footstalks of Palâśa leaves and form of them a human figure, and perform in it all the funeral ceremonies required (*âvṛt*). After having brought the members of this artificial corpse into contact with the three sacred fires, they shall remove (extinguish) them. They shall make this human [445] figure in the following way: one hundred and fifty footstalks are to represent the trunk of the corpse, one hundred and forty both the thighs, and fifty both the loins, and the rest are instead of the head, and are therefore to be placed accordingly. This is the penance.

---

[1] *Sânnâyya* is the technical term for a certain offering of the Agnihotris. It is prepared in the following way: The Adhvaryu takes the milk from three cows, called *Gaṅgâ*, *Yamunâ* and *Sarasvatî*, on the morning and evening, and gives it to the Agnîdhra. Half the mik is first drawn from the udder of each of the three cows under the recital of mantras; then the same is done silently (*tûṣṇim*). The milk is taken from these cows on the evening of the New Moon day, and on the morning of the following day, the so-called Pratipad (the first day of the month). The milk drawn on the evening is made hot, and lime-juice poured over it, to make it sour, whereupon it is hung up. The fresh milk of the following morning is then mixed with it, and both are sacrificed along with the Purodâśa. Only he who has already performed the Agniṣṭoma, is allowed to sacrifice the Sânnâyya at the Darśapurṇima iṣṭi. (*Oral information.*)

[2] The place for all the offerings.

3.

(This Paragraph is identical with 5, 27.)

4.

(On the Penances in the case of the Sânnâyya being Spoiled.)

They ask, If the Sânnâyya which was milked on the evening becomes spoiled or is lost (during the night), what is the penance for it? (The answer is) The Agnihotṛi shall divide the milk of the morning into two parts, and after having curdled one part of it, he may offer it. This is the penance.

They ask, If the Sânnâyya which was milked on the morning becomes spoiled or is lost, what is the penance? (The answer is) He must prepare a Puroḍâśa, for Indra and Mahendra, divide it instead of the milk, into the parts required, and then sacrifice it. This is the penance.

They ask, If all the milk (of the morning and evening) of the Sânnâyya becomes spoiled or is lost, what is the penance for it? The penance is made in the same way by offering the Indra or Mahendra Puroḍâśa (as in the preceding case).

They ask, If all the offerings (Puroḍâśa, curds, milk) become spoiled or are lost, what is the penance for it? He ought to prepare all these offerings with melted butter, and, having apportioned to the several gods their respective parts, should sacrifice this Ajyahavis (offerings with melted butter) as an Iṣṭi. [446] Then he ought to prepare another Iṣṭi all smooth and even. This sacrifice performed (in the regular way) is the penance for the first which had been spoiled.

5.

(The Penance required when Anything of the Agnihotram is Spilt, or the Spoon is Broken, or the Gârhapatya Fire Extinguished.)

They ask, If anything improper for being offered should fall into the fire offering when placed (over the fire to make it ready), what is the penance for it? The Agnihoti then ought to pour all this into a Sruch (sacrificial spoon), go eastwards and place the usual fuel (*samidh*) into the Ahavanîya fire. After having taken some hot ashes from the northern part of the Ahavanîya fire, he shall sacrifice it by repeating either in his mind (the usual Agnihotra mantra), or the Prajâpati verse.[3] In this

---

[3] *Prajâpate na tvad etâni* (10, 121, 10).

way (by means of the hot ashes), the offering becomes sacrificed and is not sacrificed.[4] (It is of no consequence) whether only one or two turns of the oblation (become spoiled); the penance for it is always performed in the way described. Should the Agnihotri be able to remove thus (the unclean things fallen into the offering) by pouring out all that is spoiled, and pour in what is unspoiled, then he ought to sacrifice it just as its turn[5] is. This is the penance.

They ask, If the fire offering when placed over the fire (for being made ready) is spilt or runs over (by boiling), what is then the penance for it? He [447] shall touch what fell down with water for appeasing (arresting the evil consequences); for water serves for this purpose. Then moving with his right hand over what fell out, he mutters the mantra, "May a "third go to heaven to the gods as a sacrifice; might I obtain thence "wealth! May a third go to the air, to the Pitaras, as a sacrifice; might I "obtain thence wealth! May a third go to to the earth, to men; might I "obtain thence wealth!" Then he mutters the Viṣṇu-Varuṇa verse, *yayor ojasâ skabhitâ rajâṁsi* (A. V. 7, 25, 1).[6] For Viṣṇu watches over what is performed badly in the sacrifice, and Varuṇa over what is performed well. To appease both of them, this penance (is appropriate).

They ask, When the fire offering, after having been made ready, at the time when the Adhvaryu takes it eastward to the Ahvanîya fire (to sacrifice it), runs over or is spilt altogether, what is the penance for it? (The Adhvaryu is not allowed to turn back his face). If he would turn his face backward, then he would turn the sacrificer from heaven. Therefore (some other men) must gather up for him when he is seated (having turned the face eastward) the remainder of the offering, which he then sacrifices just in its turn. This is the penance for it.

They ask, If the sacrificial spoon (*sruch*) should be broken, what is the penance for it? He ought to take another Sruch and sacrifice with it. Then he shall throw the broken Sruch into the Ahavanîya fire, the stick being in the front, and its cavity behind. This is the penance for it.

They ask, If the fire in the Ahavanîya only is burning, but that in the Gârhapatya is extinguished, what is the penance for it? When he

[4] It is only burnt by the ashes, but not sacrificed in the proper way.

[5] *Unniti.* Sây. understands by it the placing of the offering into the Agnihotrâ-havaṇî, which is a kind of large spoon.

[6] See 3, 38.

[7] Four times a portion is to be poured into the Agnihotrâ-havanî.

takes off the [448] eastern portion of the Ahavanîya (for the Gârhapatya), then he might lose his place; if he takes off the western portion, then he would spread the sacrifice in the way the Asuras do; if he kindles (a new fire) by friction, then he might produce an enemy to the sacrificer; if he extinguishes it, then the vital breath would leave the sacrificer. Thence he must take the whole (Ahavanîya fire) and, mixing it with its ashes, place it in the Gârhapatya, and then take off the eastern part as Ahavanîya. This is the penance for it.

6.

(The Penances for a Firebrand taken from a Sacred Fire, for Mingling the Sacred Fires with one another, or with Profane Fires.)

They ask, If they take fire from that belonging to an Agnihotri,[8] what is the penance for it? Should another Agni be at hand, then he should put him in the place of the former which has been taken. Were this not the case, then he ought to portion out to *Agni Agnivat* a Puroḍâśa, consisting of eight pieces (kapâlas). The Anuvâkyâ and Yâjyâ required for this purpose are, *agninâ agniḥ samidhyate* (fire is kindled by fire, 1, 12, 6); *tvâm hy âgne âgninâ* (8, 43, 14). Or, he may omit the Anuvâkyâ and Yâjyâ verses and (simply) throw (melted butter) into the Ahavanîya, under the recital of the words, *to Agni Agnivat Svâhâ!* This is the penance for it.

They ask, When some one's Ahavanîya and Gârhapatya fires should become mutually mingled together, what is the penance for it? One must portion out to *Agni vîti* a Puroḍâśa, consisting of eight pieces, under the recital of the following [449] Anuvâkyâ and Yâjyâ verses: *agna âyâhi vîtaye*) 6, 16, 10); *yo agnim devavîtaye* (1, 12, 9). Or, he may (simply) sacrifice (melted butter), under the recital of, *to Agni vîti Svâhâ!* in the Ahavanîya fire. This is the penance for it.

They ask, When all the (three) fires of an Agnihotri should become mutually mingled together, what is the penance for it? One must portion out to *Agni Virichi* (Agni, the separater) a Puroḍâśa, consisting of eight pieces, and repeat the following Anuvâkyâ and Yâjyâ verses: *svar ṇa vastor uṣasâm arochi* (7, 10, 2); *tvâm agne mânuṣîr îḷate viśaḥ* (5, 8, 3). Or, he may (simply) offer (melted butter), under the recital of, *to Agni Virichi Svâhâ!* in the Ahavanîya fire. This is the penance for it.

---

[8] Sây. understands the fire which is taken from the Ahavanîya and placed in the Gârhapatya.

They ask, When some one's fires are mingled together with other fires, what is the penance for it? One must portion out to *Agni kṣmâvat* a Puroḍâśa, consisting of eight pieces, under the recital of the following Anuvâkyâ and Yâjyâ: *akrandad agnis tanayan* (10, 45, 4); *adhâ yathâ naḥ pitaraḥ parâsaḥ* (4, 2, 16). Or, he may (simply) sacrifice (melted butter), under the recital of, *Agni kṣmâvat Svâhâ!* in the Ahavanîya fire. This is the penance for it.

7.

(The Penance for a Sacred Fire becoming Mixed with those of a Conflagration in a Village, or in a Wood, or with Lightning, or with those Burning a Corpse.)

They ask, When the fires of an Agnihotri should burn together with the fire of a general conflagration in the village, what is the penance for it? He ought to portion out a Puroḍâśa consisting of eight pieces to *Agni Saṁvarga* (Agni, the mingler), under the recital of the following Anuvâkyâ and Yâjyâ: *kuit su no gaviṣṭaye* (8, 64, 11), *mâ no asmin mahâdhane* (8, 64, **[450]** 12). Or, he may (simply) sacrifice (melted butter) under the recital of, *to Agni Saṁvarga Svâhâ!* in the Ahavanîya fire. This is the penance for it.

They ask, When the fires of an Agnihotri (have been struck) by lightning, and become mingled with it, what is the penance for it? He must offer to *Agni apsumat* (water Agni) a Puroḍâśa consisting of eight pieces, under the recital of the following Anuvâkyâ and Yâjyâ: *Apsv agne* (8, 43, 9); *mayô dadhe* (3, 1, 3). Or, he may (simply) sacrifice (melted butter), under the recital of, *to Agni apsumat Svâhâ!* in the Ahvanîya fire. This is the penance for it.

They ask, When the fires of an Agnihotri should become mingled with the fire which burns a corpse, what is the penance for it? He must offer to *Agni śuchi* a Puroḍâśa, consisting of eight pieces, under the recital of the following Anuvâkyâ and Yâjyâ: *Agniḥ śuchi vratatamaḥ* (8, 44, 21); *ud agne śuchayas tava* (8, 44, 17). Or, he may (simply) sacrifice (melted butter), under the recital of, *to Agni śuchi Svâhâ!* in the Ahavanîya fire. This is the penance for it.

They ask, When the fires of an Agnihotri should burn together with those of a forest conflagration, what is the penance for it? He shall catch the fires with the Araṇis (the two wooden sticks used for producing fire), or (if this be impossible) he should save a firebrand from either the

Ahavanîya or Gârhapatya. Where this is impossible, then he must ofer to *Agni Saṁvarga* (Agni, the mixer) a Puroḍâśa, consisting of eight pieces, under the recital of the abovementioned Anuvâkyâ and Yâjyâ (which belong to the Agni Saṁvarga). Or, he may (simply) sacrifice (melted butter), under the recital of, *to Agni Saṁvarga Svâhâ* in the Ahavanîya fire. This is the penance for it.

8.

[451] (*The Penances when the Agnihotri Sheds Tears, or Breaks his Vow, or Neglects the Performance of the Darśapûrṇima Iṣṭi, or when he allows his Fires to go out.*)

They ask, When an Agnihotri on the day previous to the sacrifice should shed tears, by which the Puroḍâśa might be sullied, what is the penance for it? He must offer to *Agni Vratabhṛit* (Agni, the bearer of vows) a Puroḍâśa, consisting of eight pieces, under the recital of the following Anuvâkyâ and Yâjyâ: *tvam agne vratabhṛit śuchir* (Aśv. Śr. S. 3, 11) *vratâni bibhrad vratapâ* (Aśv. Śr. S. 3, 11).[9] Or, he may sacrifice (melted butter), under the recital of, *to Agni vratabhṛit Svâhâ!* in the Ahavanîya fire. This is the penance for it.

They ask, When an Agnihotri should do something contrary to his vow (religion) on the day previous to the sacrifice, what is the penance for it? He must offer a Puroḍâśa, consisting of eight pieces to *Agni vratapati* (Agni, the lord of vows), under the recital of the following Anuvâkyâ and Yâjyâ: *tvam agne vratapâ asi* (8, 11, 1); *yad vo vayam pramināma* (10, 2, 4). Or, he may sacrifice (melted butter), under the recital of, *to Agni vratapati Svâhâ!* in the Ahavanîya fiire. This is the penance for it.

They ask, When an Agnihotri should neglect the celebration of the New Moon or Full Moon sacrifices, **[452]** what is the penance for it? He must offer to *Agni pathikṛit* (paver of ways) a Puroḍâśa, consisting of eight pieces, under the recital of the following Anuvkâyâ and Yâjyâ:

---

[9] The Anuvâkyâ is according to Aśval:

त्वमग्ने व्रतभृच्छुचिरग्ने देवानिहावह ।
उप यज्ञं हविश्च नः ॥

The Yâjyâ is:

व्रतानि बिभ्रद्व्रतपा अदब्धो यजानो देवानजरः सुवीरः ।
दधद्रत्नानि सुमृलीको अग्ने गोपाय नो जीवसे जातवेदः ॥

vettha hi vedho adhvana (6 , 16, 3) ; *â devânâm api* (10, 2, 3). Or, he may sacrifice (melted butter), under the recital of, *to Agni Pathikrit Svâhâ!* in the Ahavanîya fire. This is the penance for it.

They ask, When all (three) fires of an Agnihotri should go out, what is the penance for it? He must offer to *Agni tapasvat, janadvat* and *pâkavat,* a Puroḍâśa, consisting of eight pieces, under the recital of the following Anuvâkyâ and Yâjyâ: *âyâhi tapasâ janeṣu* (Aśv. Śr. S. 3, 11) ; *â no yâhi tapasâ* (Aśv. Śr. S. 3, 11).[10] Or, he may sacrifice (melted butter) in the Ahavanyîa fire, under the recital of, *to Agni tapasvat, janadvat pâkavat, Svâhâ!* This is the penance for it.

9.

(*Penances for an Agnihotri when he Eats New Corn without bringing the Sacrifice prescribed, and for Various Mishaps and Neglect when sacrifising.*)

They ask, When an Agnihotri eats new corn without having offered the Agrayaṇa [11] iṣṭi, what is the penance for it? He must offer to *Agni Vaiśvânara* a Puroḍâśa, consisting of twelve pieces, under the **[453]** recital of the following Anuvâkayâ and Yâjyâ: *Vaiśvânaro ajîjanat* (?) ; *priṣṭo divi priṣṭo* (1, 98, 2). Or, he may offer to *Agni Vaiśvânara* (melted butter) in the Ahavanîya fire, under the recital of, *to Agni viaśvânâra Svâhâ!* This is the penance for it.

They ask, When one of the potsherds (*kapâlas*) containing the Puroḍâśa should be destroyed, what is the penance for it? He must offer a Puroḍâśa, consisting of two pieces, to the Aśvins, under the recital of the following Anuvâkyâ and Yâjyâ: *aśvinâ vartir* (1, 92, 16) ; *â gomâtâ nasatya* (7, 72, 1). Or, he may sacrifice (melted butter) in the Ahvanîya fire under the recital of, *to the Aśvins Svâhâ!* This is the penance for it.

---

[10] The Anuvâkyâ is:

आयाहि तपसा जनेष्वग्ने पावको अर्चिषा ।

उपेमां सुष्टुतिं मम ॥

The Yâjyâ is:

आ नो याहि तपसा जनेष्वग्ने पावक दीद्यत् ।

हव्या देवेषु नो दधत् ॥

[11] This Iṣṭi is prescribed to be performed before the Agnihotri is allowed to eat new corn.

They ask, When the stalks of kuśa grass (*pavitra*) (on which the offering is placed) should be destroyed, what is the penance for it? He must offer to *Agni pavitravat* a Puroḍâśa, consisting of eight pieces, under the recital of the following Anuvâkyâ and Yâjyâ: *pavitram te vitatam* (9, 83, 1); *tapoṣ pavitram* (9, 83, 2). Or, he may offer (melted butter) in the Ahavanîya fire under the recital of, *to Agni pavitravat Svâhâ!* This is the penance for it.

They ask, When the gold of an Agnihotri should be destoryed, what is the penance for it? He must offer to *Agni hiraṇyvat* Puroḍâśâ, consisting of eight pieces, under the recital of the following Anuvâkyâ and Yâjyâ: *hiraṇyakeśo rajaso visâra* (1, 79, 1); *â te suparṇâ aminantam* (1, 79, 2). Or, he may offer (melted butter) in the Ahavanîya fire, under the recital of, *to Agni hiraṇyavat Svâhâ!* This is the penance for it.

They ask, When an Agnihotṛi offers the fire oblation without having performed in the morning the usual ablution, what is the penance for it? He must offer to *Agni Varuṇa* a Puroḍâśa, consisting of eight pieces, under the recital of the following **[454]** Anuvâkyâ and Yâjyâ: *tvam no agne varuṇaṣa* (4, 1, 4); *sa tvaṁ no agne avamo* (4, 1, 5). Or, he may offer (melted butter) in the Ahavanîya fire, under the recital of, *to Agni Varuṇa Svâhâ!* This is the penance for it.

They ask, When an Agnihotri eats food prepared by a woman who is confined (*sûtaka*), what is the penance for it? He must offer to *Agni tantumat* a Puroḍâśa, consisting of eight pieces, under the recital of the following Anuvâkyâ and Yâjyâ: *tantum tanvaṇ rajaso* (10, 53, 6); *akṣânaho nahy tanota* (10, 53, 7). Or, he may sacrifice (melted butter) in the Ahavanîya fire, under the recital of, *to Agni tantumat Svâhâ!* This is the penance for it.

They ask, When an Agnihotri hears, when living, any one, an enemy, say, that he (the Agnihotri) is dead, what is the penance for it? He must offer to *Agni surabhimat* a Puroḍâśa, consisting of eight pieces, under the recital of the following Anuvâkyâ and Yâjyâ: *Agnir hotâ nyasîdad* (5, 1, 6); *sâdhvîm akar deva vîtim* (10, 53, 3.) Or, he may sacrifice (melted butter) in the Ahavanîya fire, under the recital of, *to Agnir surabhimat Svâhâ!* This is the penance for it.

They ask, When the wife or the cow of an Agnihotri give birth to twins, what is the penance for it? He must offer to *Agni marutvat* a Purodâśa, consisting of thirteen pieces, under the recital of the following Anuvâkyâ and Yâjyâ : *maruto yasya hi kṣye* (1, 86, 1) ; *arâ ived* (5, 58, 5). Or, he may sacrifice (melted butter) in the Ahavanîya fire, under the recital of, *to Agni marutvat Svâhâ!* This is the penance for it.

They ask, Should an Agnihotri, who has lost his wife, bring the fire oblation, or should he not? He should do so. If he does not do so, then he is called [**455**] an Anaddhâ[12] man. Who is an Anaddhâ? He who offers oblations to neither the gods, nor to the ancestors, nor to men. Therefore, the Agnihotri who has lost his wife, should nevertheless bring the burnt offering (*agnihotram*). There is a stanza concerning sacrificial customs, where is said, "He who has lost his wife may bring the Sâutrâmaṇi[13] sacrifice ; for he is not allowed to drink Soma! But he must discharge the duties towards his parents."[14] But, whereas the sacred tradition (*śṛuti*) enjoins sacrifice,[15] let him bring the Soma sacrifice.

10.

[**456**] *How the Agnihotram of Him Who has no Wife becomes Performed).*[16]

They ask, In what way does an Agnihotri who has no wife, bring his oblations with Speech (*i. e.*, by repeating the mantras required with his voice)? In what way does he offer his (daily) burnt offering, when his wife dies, after he has already entered on the state of an Agnihotri, his wife

[12] By this term, a man is to be understood who, from reasons which are not culpable, does not discharge his duties towards the gods, ancestors and men. All the MSS. read *manuṣyâ*, instead of *manuṣyân*.

[13] The *Sâutrâmaṇi* (*iṣṭi*) is a substitute for the Soma sacrifice. Some spirituous liquor is taken instead of Soma, and milk. Both liquids are filled in the Soma vessels. It is performed in various ways. It is mentioned, and its performance briefly described in the Aśval. Śr. S. 3, 9, and in the Kâtîya Sûtras (in the 19th Adhyâya). From three to four animals are immolated, one to the Aśvins, one to Sarasvatî, one to Indra, and one to Bṛihaspati. The Paśupuroḍâśa are for Indra, Savitar and Varuṇa. The Puronuvâkyâ for the offering of the spirituous liquor is, *yuvaṁ surâmam aśvinâ* (10, 11, 4). The Praiṣa for repeating the Yâjyâ mantra is as follows :—

होता यक्षदश्विना सरस्वतीमिन्द्रं सुत्रामाणं सोमानां सुराम्णां
जुषन्तां व्यन्तु पिबन्तु मदन्तु सोमान्सुराम्णो होतर्यज

(The offering to be presented to the Aśvins, Sarasvatî, and Indra Sutrâman, are here called *somâḥ surâmaṇaḥ, i. e.*, Soma drops which are spirituous liquor). The Yâjyâ is *putram iva pitarâu* (10, 131, 5). The sacrifice is brought up to the present day in the Dekkhan

[14] In another Śâkhâ, there is said, that a Brâhman has incurred three debts, the Brahmachâryam or celibacy as a debt to the Riṣis, the sacrifice as a debt to the gods, and the necessity of begetting children as a debt to the Pitaras.—*Sây.*

[15] "Worship the gods by sacrificing, read the Vedas, and beget children!" This is the sacred tradition (Śruti) here alluded to.—*Sây.*

[16] This paragraph offers considerable difficulties to the translator. Its style is not plain and perspicuous, and it appears that it is an interpolation as well as the following (11th) paragraph. But, whether it is an interpolation of later times is very doubtful. The piece may (to judge from its uncouth language) even be older than the bulk of the Aitarêya

having (by her death) destroyed the qualification for the performance of (the daily) burnt offering? [17]

They say, That one has children, grand-children, and relations in this world, and in that world. In this world, there is heaven (*i. e.*, heaven is to be gained in this world by sacrificing). (The Agnihotri who [457] has no wife, says to his children, &c:) "I have ascended to heaven by means of what was no heaven (*i. e.*, by the sacrifice performed in this world)." He who does not wish for a (second) wife (for having his sacificial ceremonies continuously performed), keeps thus (by speaking to his children, &c., in the way indicated) his connection with the other world up. Thence they (his children) establish (new fires) for him who has lost his wife.

How does he who has no wife, bring his oblations (with his mind)? (The answer is) Faith is his wife, and Truth the sacrificer. The marriage of Faith and Truth is a most happy one. For by Faith and Truth joined, they conquer the celestial world.

11.

(*On the Different Names of the Full and New Moon.*)

They say, If an Agnihotri, who has not pledged himself by the usual vow, makes preparations for the performance of the Full and New Moon sacrifices, then the gods do not eat his food. If he, therefore, when making his preparations, thinks, might the gods eat my food,[18] (then they

---

Brâhmaṇam. Sây., who inverts their order, says, that they are found in some countries, whereas they are wanting in others. In his Commentary on the 10th paragraph, Sây. does several times violence to grammar. He asserts, for instance, that आहुः after पुत्रान्° is to be taken in the sense of the third person singular of the potential, standing for ब्रूयात्. The same sense of a potential he gives to the perfect tense, *âruroha*. Both these explanations are inadmissible. The purport of this paragraph is to show, in what way an Agnihotri may continue his sacrificial career, though it be interrupted by the death of his wife. For the rule is, that the sacrificer must always have his wife with him (their hands are tied together on such an occasion) when he is sacrificing.

[17] This is the translation of the term, *naṣṭâvâgnihotram*, which I take as a kind of compound. Sây. explains it, *naṣṭam eva bhavati pûrvasiddhair agnibhiḥ patnidahapakṣe punaragnihotrahetûnâm agninâm abhâvat*. *Naṣṭâ* is to be takon in the sense of an active past participle, "having destroyed," *vâ* appears to have the sense of *ava*, as Sây. explains. That *vâ* can form part of a compound as the word, *abhivânyavatsâ* proves (7, 2).

[18] All this refers to an Agnihotri, who has lost his wife and is continuing his sacrifice.

eat it). He ought to make all the preparations on the first part of the New Moon day; this is the opinion of the *Paiṅgyas*: he shall make them on the latter part; this is the opinion of the *Kâuṣîtakis*. The first part of the Full Moon day is called *Anumati*,[19] the latter *Râkâ*; the first [**458**] part of the New Moon day is called *Sinîvâlî*, and its latter part *Kuhû*. The space which the moon requires for setting and rising again is called *Tithi* (lunar day). Without paying any attention (to the opinion of the Paiṅgyas) to make the preparations on the first part of the Full Moon day, he brings his sacrifice when he meets (sees) the Moon (rising) on the New Moon day;[20] on this (day) they buy the Soma. Therefore he must always make his preparations on the second part of either the Full or New Moon days (*i. e.*, on the days on which the moon enters into either phase). All days which follow, belong to Soma (the Soma sacrifice may be completed.) He brings the Soma sacrifice as far as the Soma is a deity; for the divine Soma is the moon. Therefore, he must make the preparations on the second part of that lunar day.

12.

(On Some Other Penances for Mishaps occurring to an Agnihotri. Where the Agnihotri must Walk between his Fires. Whether the Dakṣiṇa Agni is to be Fed with the other Fires also. How an Agnihotri should Behave when absent from his Fires.)

They ask, If the sun rise or set before an Agnihotri takes fire out of (the Gârhapatya to bring it to the Ahavanîya), or should it, when placed (in the Ahavanîya), be extinguished before he brings the burnt offering (Homa), what is the penance for it? He shall take it out after sunset, after having placed a piece of gold before it; for light is a splendid [**459**] body (*śukram*), and gold is the splendid light, and that body

---

[19] The lunar day on which either the Full Moon or New Moon takes place, is divided into two parts, and is consequently broken. For the fourteenth *tithi* (or lunar day) is at an end, though it might not have been lasting for the usual time of thirty Muhûrtas, as soon as the disk of the moon appears to the eye, either completely full, or (at the New Moon) distinctly visible. The broken lunar day (the fourteenth) is then called *Anumati* at the Full Moon time, and *Sinîvâlî* at the New Moon time; the remaining part of the day (till the moon sets) is then either *Râkâ* or *Kuhû*. This part of the day forms, then, part either of the proper Full Moon or New Moon day (the fifteenth).

[20] That is, on the fifteenth.

(the sun) is just this light. Seeing it shining, he takes out the fire. At morning time (after sunrise), he may take out the fire when he has put silver below it; for this (silver) is of the same nature with the night (representing the splendour of the moon and the stars). He shall take out (of the Gârhapatya) the Ahavanîya before the shadows are cast together (before it has grown completely dark). For the shadow of darkness is death. By means of this light (the silver), he overcomes death, which is the shadow of darkness. This is the penance.

They ask, When a cart, or a carriage, or horses go over the Gârhapatya and Ahavanîya fires of an Agnihotri, what is the penance for it? He shall not mind it at all, thus they say, believing that these things (their types) are placed in his soul. But should he mind it, then he shall form a line of water drops from the Gârhapatya, to the Ahavanîya under the recital of *tantum tanvam rajaso* (10, 53 6). This is the penace.

They ask, Shall the Agnihotri, when feeding the (other) fires with wood, make the Dakṣiṇa Agni (*anvâhârya pachanad*) also to blaze up brightly, or shall he not do so? Who feeds the fires, puts into his soul the vital breaths; of these fires, the Dakṣiṇa Agni provides (the feeder) best with food. He gives him therefore an offering, saying, "*to Agni, the enjoyer of food, the master of food, Swâhâ!*" He who thus knows, becomes an enjoyer of food, and a master of food, and obtains children and food.

The Agnihotri must walk between the Gârhapatya and Ahavanîya when he is about to sacrifice; for the Agnis (fires) when perceiving him walk thus, know, "he is about to bring us a sacrifice." By this both these fires destroy all wickedness of him who is thus walking (between them). Whose wickedness **[460]** is thus destroyed, goes up to the heavenly world. Thus it is declared in another Brâhmaṇam which they quote.

They ask, How can an Agnihotri, who intends going abroad, be near his sacred fires (established at his home)? Can he do it when absent, or is he to return to them every day? He shall approach them silently (in his mind, without repeating the mantras). For, by keeping silence, they aspire after fortune. But some say (he should go to them) every day. For the Agnis of an Agnihotri lose all confidence in him by his absence, fearing lest they be removed or scattered. Therefore he must approach them, and, should he not be able to return, he must repeat the words, "May you be safe! may I be safe!" In this way, the Agnihotri is safe.

THIRD CHAPTER.

(The Story of Sunaḥśepa)

13

(King Hariśchandra wishes for a Son. Stanzas praising the Possession of a Son).

Hariśchandra, the son of Vedhas, of the Ikṣvâku race, was a king who had no son. Though he had a hundred wives, they did not give birth to a son. In his house there lived the Riṣis, Parvata and Nârada. Once the king addressed to Nârada (the following stanza):

"Since all beings, those endowed with reason (men) as well as those who are without it (beasts) wish for a son, what is the fruit to be obtained by having a son? This tell me, O Nârada?"

Nârada thus addressed in one stanza, replied in (the following) ten:

1. The father pays a debt in his son, and gains immortality, when he beholds the face of a son living who was born to him.

2. The pleasure which a father has in his son, exceeds the enjoyment of all other beings, be they on the earth, or in the fire, or in the water.

3. Fathers always overcome great difficulties through a son. (In him) the Self is born out of Self. The son is like a well-provisioned boat, which carries him over.

4. "What is the use of living unwashed,[1] wearing the goatskin,[2] and beard[3]? What is the use of performing austerities?[4] You should wish for a son, O Brahmans!" Thus people talk of them[5] (who forego the married life on account of religious devotion).

5. Food preserves life, clothes protect from cold, gold (golden ornaments) gives beauty, marriages produce wealth in cattle;[6] the wife is the friend, the daughter object of compassion, but the son shines as his light in the highest heaven.

---

[1] Here the *Gṛihastha* is meant.

[2] The *Brahmachâri* is alluded.

[3] The *Vanaprustha,* or hermit is to be understood.

[4] The *Parivrâjaka,* or religious mendicant is meant.

[5] *Avadavadaḥ, i. e.,* pronouncing a blame. Sây. takes the word in a different sense, "not deserving blame on account of being free from guilt." This explanation is artificial.

[6] At certain kinds of marriages, the so-called *Arṣa* (the Riṣi marriage), a pair of cows was given as a dowry. See Aśval. Grihy. Sûtr. 1, 6.

6. The husband enters the wife (in the shape of seed), and, when the seed is changed to an embryo, he makes her mother, from whom, after having become regenerated, in her, he is born in the tenth month.

7. His wife is only then a real wife (*jâyâ*, from *jan*, to be born) when he is born in her again. The [**462**] seed which is placed in her, she developes to a being and sets it forth.

8. The Gods and the Riṣis endowed her with great beauty. The gods then told to men, this being is destined to produce you again.

9. He who has no child, has no place (no firm footing). This even know the beasts. Thence the son cohabits (among beasts even) with his mother and sister.

10. This is the broad, well-trodden path on which those who have sons walk free from sorrows. Beasts and birds know it; thence they cohabit (even) with their own mothers.

Thus he told.

14.

(*A Son is Born to Hariśchandra. Varuṇa repeatedly requests the King to sacrifice his Son to him; but the Sacrifice is under different pretences always Put Off by the King.*)

Nârada then told him, "Go and beg of Varuṇa, the king, that he might favour you with the birth of a son (promising him at the same time) to sacrifice to him this son when born." He went to Varuṇa, the king, praying, "Let a son be born to me; I will sacrifice him to thee." Then a son, Rohita by name, was born to him. Varuṇa said to him, "A son is born to thee, sacrifice him to me." Hariśchandra said, "An animal is fit for being sacrificed, when it is more than ten days old. Let him reach this age, then I will sacrifice him to thee." After Rohita had passed the age of ten days, Varuṇa said to him, "He is now past ten days, sacrifice him to me." Hariśchandra answered, "An animal is fit for being sacrificed when its teeth come. Let his teeth come, then I will sacrifice [**463**] him to thee." After his teeth had come[1], Varuṇa said to Hariśchandra, "His teeth have now come, sacrifice him to me." He answered, "An animal is fit for being sacrificed when its teeth fall out. Let his teeth fall out, then I will sacrifice him to thee." His teeth fell out. He then said, "His teeth are falling out, sacrifice him to me." He said, "An animal is fit for being sacrificed when its teeth have come again. Let his teeth come again, then I will sacrifice him to thee." His teeth

[1] The words, *ajnatavâi* and *apatsatavâi*, are a kind of infinitive.

came again. Varuṇa said, "His teeth have now come again, sacrifice him to me." He answered, "A man of the warrior caste is fit for being sacrificed only after having received his full armour. Let him receive his full armour, then I will sacrifice him to thee." He then was invested with the armour. Varuṇa then said, "He has now received the armour, sacrifice him to me." After having thus spoken, he called his son, and told him, "Well, my dear, to him who gave thee unto me, I will sacrifice thee now." But the son said, 'No, no," took his bow and absconded to the wilderness, where he was roaming about for a year.

15.

(*Continuation of this story. Rohita, Hariśchandra's Son, Purchases, after Six Years of fruitless Wanderings in the Forest, a Brahman boy, Śunaḥśepa by name, from his parents, to be sacrificed in his stead by Hariśchandra to Varuṇa. Stanzas.*)

Varuṇa now seized Hariśchandra, and his belly swelled (*i. e.*, he was attacked by dropsy). When Rohita heard of it, he left the forest, and went to a village, where Indra in human disguise met him, and said to him, "There is no happiness for him who does not travel, Rohita! thus we have heard. Living **[464]** in the society of men, the best man (often) becomes a sinner (by seduction, which is best avoided by wandering in places void of human dwellings); for Indra surely is the friend of the traveller. Therefore, wander!"

Rohita thinking, a Brâhman told me to wander, wandered for a second year in the forest. When he was entering a village, after having left the forest, Indra met him in human disguise, and said to him, "The feet of the wanderer are like the flower, his soul is growing and reaping the fruit; and all his sins are destroyed by his fatigues in wandering. Therefore, wander!"

Rohita thinking, a Brâhman told me to wander, wandered then a third year in the forest. When he was entering a village, after having left the forest, Indra met him in human disguise, and said to him, "The fortune of him who is sitting, sits; it rises when he rises; it sleeps when he sleeps; it moves when he moves. Therefore, wander!"

Rohita thinking, a Brâhman told me to wander, wandered then a fourth year in the forest. When he was entering a village, after having left the forest, Indra said to him, "The Kali is lying on the ground, the Dvâpara is hovering there; the Tretâ is getting up, but the Kṛita happens to walk (hither and thither).[8] Therefore, wander, wander!"

Rohita thinking, a Brâhman told me to wander, wandered for a fifth year in the forest. When he was **[465]** entering a village, after having left the forest, Indra said to him, "The wanderer finds honey and the sweet Udumbara fruit; behold the beauty of the sun, who is not wearied by his wanderings. Therefore, wander, wander!"

Rohita then wandered for a sixth year in the forest. He met (this time) the Riṣi *Ajîgarta*, the son of *Suyavasa*, who was starving, in the forest. He had three sons, *Śunaḥpuchha*, *Śunaḥśepa*, and *Śunolangûla*. He told him, "Riṣi! I give thee a hundred cows; for I will ransom myself (from being sacrificed) with one of these (thy sons)." Ajîgarta then excepted the oldest, saying, "Do not take him," and the mother excepted the youngest, saying, "Do not take him." Thus they agreed upon the middle one, *Śunaḥśepa*. He then gave for him a hundred cows, left the forest, entered the village, and brought him before his father, saying, "O my dear (father)! by this boy I will ransom myself (from being sacrificed)." He then approached Varuṇa, the king (and said), "I will sacrifice him to thee!" He said, "Well, let it be done: for a Brâhmaṇ is worth more than a Kṣattriya!" Varuṇa then explained to the king the rites of the Râjasûya sacrifice, at which, on the day appointed for the inauguration (*abhiṣechanîya*), he replaced the (sacrificial animal) by a man.

16.

(The Sacrifice with the intended Human Victim comes off. Four Great Riṣis were officiating as Priests. Śunaḥśepa prays to the Gods to be Released from the Fearful Death. The Rik verses which he used mentioned, and the different Deities to whom he applied).

At this sacrifice, *Viśvâmitra* was his Hotar, *Jamadagni* his Adhvaryu, *Vasishṭha* his Brahmâ, and *Ayasya* his Udgâtar. After the preliminary cere- **[466]** monies had been performed, they could not find a person willing to bind him to the sacrificial post. Ajîgarta, the son of Suyavasa, then

[8] Sây. does not give any explanation of this important passage, where the names of the Yugas are mentioned for the first time. These four names are, as is well known from other sources (see the Sanscrit Dictionary by Boehtlingk and Roth, s. v. *kali, dvâpara*, &c.,) names of dice, used at gambling. The meaning of this Gâtha is, There is every success to be hoped; for the unluckiest die, the Kali, is lying, two others are slowly moving and half fallen, but the luckiest, the Kṛita, is in full motion. The position of dice given here is indicatory of a fair chance of winning the game.

said, "Give me another hundred (cows), and I will bind him." They gave him another hundred, whereupon he bound him. After he had been bound, the Aprî verses recited, and the fire carried round him,[9] they could not find a slaughterer. Ajîgarta then said, "Give me another hundred, and I will kill him." They gave him another hundred. He then whetted his knife and went to kill his son. *Śunaḥśepa* then got aware that they were going to butcher him just as if he were no man (but a beast.) "Well" said he, "I will seek shelter with the gods." He applied to Prajâpati, who is the first of the gods, with the verse, *kasya nûnam hatamasya* (1, 24, 1). Prajâpati answered him, "Agni is the nearest of the gods, go to him." He then applied to Agni, with the verse, *agner vayam prathamasya amritânâm* (1, 24, 2). Agni answered him, "Savitar rules over the creatures, go to him." He then applied to Savitar with the three verses (1, 24, 3-5) beginning with, *abhi tvâ deva Savitar*. Savitar answered him, "Thou art bound for Varuṇa, the King, go to him." He applied to Varuṇa with the following thirty-one verses (124, 6-25, 21). Varuṇa then answered him, "Agni is the mouth of the gods, and the most compassionate of them. Praise him now! then we shall release you." He then praised Agni with twenty-two verses (1, 26, 1 = 27, 12). Agni then answered, "Prasise the Viśve Devas, then we shall release you." He then praised the Viśve Devas with the verse (1,27,13), *namo mahadbhyo namo arbhakebhyo*. The Viśve Devas answered, "Indra is the strongest, the most powerful, the most enduring, the most true of the
[467] gods, who knows best how to bring to an end anything. Praise him, then we shall release you." He then praised Indra with the hymn (1, 29), *yach chid dhi satya somapâ*, and with fifteen verses of the following one (1, 30, 1-15). Indra, who had become pleased with his praise, presented him with a golden carriage. This present he accepted with the verse, *śaśvad indra* (1, 30, 16). Indra then told him, "Praise the Aśvins, then we shall release you." He then praised the Aśvins, with the three verses which follow the abovementioned (1, 30, 17-19. The Aśvins then answered, "Praise Uṣâs (Dawn), then we shall release you." He then praised Uṣâs with the three verses which follow the Aśvin verses (1, 30, 20-22). As he repeated one verse after the other, the fetters (of Varuṇa) were falling off, and the belly of Hariśchandra became smaller. And, after he had done repeating the last verse, (all) the fetters were taken off, and Hariśchandra restored to health again.

---

[9] See Ait. Br. 2, 3-5.

17

(*Śunaḥśepa is Released. He Invents the Añjaḥ Sava Preparation of the Soma. Viśvâmitra Adopts him as his Son. Stanzas.*)

The priests now said to Śunaḥśepa, "Thou art now only ours (thou art now a priest like us); take part in the performance of the particular ceremonies of this day (the *abiṣechanîya*)." He then saw (invented) the method of direct preparation of the Soma juice (*añjaḥ sava* without intermediate fermentation) after it is squeezed, and carried it out under the recital of the four verses, *yach chid dhi tvam gṛihe gṛihe* (1,285-8). Then, by the verse, *uchchhiṣṭam chamvor* (1, 28, 9), he brought it into the Droṇakaḷasa.[10] Then [**468**], after having been touched by Hariśchandra, he sacrificed the Soma, under the recital of the four first verses (of the hymn, *yatra grâvâ pṛithubudhna* (1, 28, 1-4), which were accompanied by the formula *Swâhâ*. Then he brought the implements required for making the concluding ceremonies (*avabhṛitha*) of this sacrifice to the spot, and performed them under the recital of the two verses, *tvaṁ no agne Varuṇasya* (4, 1, 4-5). Then, after this ceremony was over, Śunaḥśepa summoned Hariśchandra to the Ahavanîya fire,[11] and recited the verse, *Śunaḥ chichchhepam niditam* (5, 2, 7).

Śunaḥśepa then approached the side of Viśvâmitra (and sat by him). Ajîgarta, the son of Suyavasa, then said, "O Ṛiṣi! return me my son." He answered, "No, for the gods have presented (*devâ arâsata*) him to me." Since that time, he was *Devarâta*, Viśvâmitra's son. From him come the *Kapileyas* and *Babhravas*. Ajîgarta further said, "Come, then, we (thy mother and I myself) will call thee," and added, "Thou art known as the seer from Ajîgarta's family, as a descendant of the Aṅgirasaḥ. Therefore, O Ṛiṣi, do not leave your ancestral home; return to me." Śunaḥśepa answered, "What is not found even in the hands of a Śûdra, one has seen in thy hand, the knife (to kill thy son); three hundred cows thou hast preferred to me, O Aṅgiras!" Ajîgarta then answered, "O my dear son! I repent of the bad deed I have committed; I blot out this stain! one hundred of the cows shall be thine!"

Śunaḥśepa answered, "Who once might commit such a sin, may commit the same another time; thou art still not free from the brutality of a Śûdra, for thou hast committed a crime for

---

[10] The large vessel for keeping the Soma in readiness for sacrificial purposes, after it has been squeezed.

[11] They returned from the place of the Uttarâ Vedi to the Vedi, where the Iṣṭis are performed.

which no reconcilia- [469] tion exists." "Yes, irreconcileable (is this act)," interrupted Viśvâmitra.

Viśvâmitra then said, "Fearful was Suyavasa's son (to look at) when he was standing ready to murder, holding the knife in his hand; do not become his son again; but enter my family as my son." Śunaḥśepa then said, "O prince, let us know, tell (us) how I, as an Añgirasaḥ, can enter thy family as thy (adopted) son?" Viśvâmitra answered, "Thou shalt be the first-born of my sons, and thy children the best. Thou shalt now enter on the possession of my divine heritage. I solemnly instal thee to it." Śunaḥśepa then said, "When thy sons should agree to thy wish that I should enter thy family, O thou best of the Bharatas! then tell them for the sake of my own happiness to receive me friendly." Viśvâmitra then addressed his sons as follows: "Hear ye now, *Madhuchhandaḥ, Riṣabha, Renu, Aṣṭaka,* and all ye brothers, do not think [12] yourselves (entitled) to the right of primogeniture, which is (Śunaḥśepa's)."

18

(*On Viśvamitra's Descendants. How the Reciters of the Śunaḥśepa story are to be Rewarded by the King. Stanzas. On the Pratigara for the Ṛichas and Stanzas at this Occasion.*)

This Riṣi Viśvâmitra had a hundred sons, fifty of them were older than Madhuchhandâs, and fifty were younger than he. The older ones were not pleased with (the installation of Śunaḥśepa to the primogeniture). Viśvâmitra then pronounced against [470] them the curse, "You shall have the lowest castes for your descendants." Therefore are many of the most degraded classes of men, the rabble for the most part, such as the *Andhras, Puṇḍras, Śabaras, Palindas,* and *Mûtibas,* descendants of Viśvâmitra. But Madhuchhandâs, with the fifty younger sons, said, "What our father approves of, by that we abide; we all accord to thee (Śunaḥśepa) the first rank, and we will come after thee!" Viśvâmitra, deligated (at this answer) then praised these sons with the following verses:

"Ye my sons will have abundance of cattle and children, for you have made me rich in children by consenting to my wish."

---

[12] I have parsed the word *sthana* as *stha na.* If *sthana* is taken as a 2nd person plural, as Max Müller (following Sâyaṇa) does in his translation of the story of Śunaḥsepa (History of Ancient Sanscrit Literature, page 418), the passage is to be translated as follows: "and all you brothers that you are, think him to be entitled to the primogeniture."

"Ye sons of Gâthi, blessed with children, you all will be successful when headed by Devarâta; he will (always) lead you on the path of truth."

"This Devarâta, is your master (man); follow him, ye Kuśikas! He will exercise the paternal rights over you as his heritage from me, and take possession of the sacred knowledge that we have."

"All the true sons of Viśvâmitra, the grandsons of Gâthi, who forthwith stood with Devarâta, were blessed with wealth for their own welfare and renown."

"Devarâta is called the Riṣi who entered on two heritages, the royal dignity of Jahnû's house, and the divine knowledge of Gâthi's stem."[13]

This is the story of Śunaḥśepa contained in the stanzas which are beyond the number of the hundred Rik verses [14] (recited along with them) The Hotar **[471]** when sitting on a gold embroidered carpet, recites them to the king, after he has been sprinkled with the sacred water. The Adhvaryu who reapeats the responses sits likewise on a gold embroidered carpet. For gold is glory. This procures glory for the king (for whom these Gâthâs are repeated). *Om* is the Adhvaryu's response to a Rich (repeated by the Hotar), and *evam tathâ* (thus in this way it is) that to a Gâthâ (recited by the Hotar). For *Om* is divine (therefore applied to *ṛichas*, which are a divine revelation), and *tathâ* human. By means of the divine (*om*) and human (*tathâ*) responses, the Adhvaryu makes the king free from sin and fault. Therefore any king who might be a conqueror (and consequently by shedding blood a sinner), although he might not bring a sacrifice, should have told the story of Śunaḥśepa. (If he do so) then not the slightest trace of sin (and its consequences) will remain in him. He must give a thousand cows to the teller of this story, and a hundred to him who makes the responses (required); and to each of them the (gold embroidered) carpet on which he was sitting; to the Hotar, besides, a silver decked carriage drawn by mules. Those who wish for children, should also have told this story; then they certainly will be blessed with children.

[13] Jahnû is the ancestor of Ajîgarta, and Gâthi the father of Viśvâmitra.

[14] Sây. says that ninety-seven out of them had been seen by Śunaḥśpea and three by another Riṣi. The term *parariк-śata gâtham âkhyânam* means, the "story which contains besides one hundred Ṛik verses Gâthâs (stanzas) also." The number of the latter is thirty-one.

FOURTH CHAPTER.

(The Preliminary Rites of the Râjasûya Sacrifie.)

19.

(The Relationship between the Brahma aud Kṣattra.)

After Prajâpati had created the sacrifice, the *Brahma* (divine knowledge) and the *Kṣattṛa* (sovereignty) were produced. After both two kinds of **[472]** creatures sprang up, such ones as eat the sacrificial food, and such ones as do not eat it. All eaters of the sacrificial food followed the Brahma, the non-eaters followed the Kṣattra. Therefore, the Brahmans only are eaters of the sacrificial food ; whilst the Kṣattriyas, Vaiśyas, and Śûdras do not eat it.

The sacrifice went away from both of them. The Brahma and Kṣattra followed it. The Brahma followed with all its implements, and the Kṣattra followed (also) with its implements. The implements of the Brahma are those required for performing a sacrifice. The implements of the Kṣattra are a horse, carriage, an armour, and a bow with arrow. The Kṣattra not reaching the sacrifice, returned ; for, frightened by the weapons of the Kṣattra, the sacrifice ran aside. The Brahma then followed the sacrifice, and reached it. Hemming thus the sacrifice in its further course, the Brahma stood still ; the sacrifice reached and hemmed in its course, stood still also, and recognising in the hand of the Brahma its own implements, returned to the Brahma. The sacrifice having thus remained only in the Brahma, it is therefore only placed among the Brahmans (*i.e.*, they alone are allowed to perform it.)

The Kṣattra then ran after this Brahma, and said to it, "Allow me to take possession of this sacrifice (which is placed in thee)." The Brahma said, " Well, let it be so ; lay down thy own weapons, assume by means of the implements of the Brahma (the sacrificial implement) which constitute the Brahma, the form of the Brahma, and return to it ! " The Kṣattra obeyed, laid down its own weapons, assumed, by means of the implements of the Brahma which constitute the Brahma, its form, and returned to it. Therefore even a Kṣat **[473]** triya, when he lays down his weapons and assumes the from of the Brahma by means of the sacrificial implements, returns to the sacrifice (he is allowed a share in it.)

20

(*On the Place of Worshiping the Gods asked for by the King at the Râjasûya.*)

Then the king is to be requested to worship the gods. They ask, If a Brahman, Kṣattriya, or Vaiśya, who is to be initiated into the sacrificial rites, requests the king to grant a place for the worship of the gods, whom must the king himself request to do so? He must request the divine Kṣattra. Thus they say. This divine Kṣattra is Âditya [the sun]; for he is the ruler of all these beings. On the day on which the king is to be consecrated, in the forenoon, he must post himself towards the rising sun, and say, "This is among the lights the best light! [Rigveda 10, 1, 70, 3.] O god Savitar, grant me a place for the worship of gods."[1] By these words he asks for a place of worship. When Âditya, requested in this way, goes northwards, saying, "Yes, it may be so, I grant it," then nobody will do any harm to such a king, who is permitted [by Savitar to do so].

The fortune of a king who is consecrated in such a way by having secured the place of divine worship previously by the recital of the verse (mentioned above) and by addressing that request (to Savitar), will increase from day to day; and sovereign power over his subjects will remain with him.

21.

[474] (*The Iṣṭâpûrta Aparijyâni Offerings.*)

Then the burnt offering, called the *Iṣṭapûrta aparijyâni*[2] is to be performed by the king who brings the sacrifice. The king should perform this ceremony before he receives the sacrificial inauguration (*dikṣâ*). (When performing it) he throws four spoonfulls of melted butter in the Ahavaniya fire, saying, "to the preservation of the *Iṣṭapûrta*! May Indra the mighty

[1] The verse is evidently a Yajus, (and so it is termed by Sâyaṇa) but I do not find it in the Yajurveda.

[2] Lit., the recompensation (*aparijyâni*) of what has been sacrificed (*iṣṭa*) and filled (*iṣṭâpûrta*). *Iṣṭa* means only "what is sacrificed," and *âpûrta* "filled up to." For, all sacrifices go up to heaven, and are stored up there to be taken possession of by the sacrificer on his arrival in heaven (See Rigveda, 10, 14, 1 *saṁgachhasva—iṣṭâpûrtena*, join thy sacrifices which were stored up). The opinions of the ancient Acharyas or Brahmanical Doctors, about the proper meaning of this word, were already divided, as Sâyaṇa says. Some understood by it the duties of the castes and religious Brahmanical orders, as far as the digging of wells and making of ponds are concerned (which was a kind of religious obligation). Others meant by *iṣṭa* what refers to Smârta (domestic) offering, and *pûrta* they interpreted as referring to the solemn sacrifices (*śrâuta*.)

give us again (recompensate us for what we have sacrificed). May the Brahma give us again full compensation for what has been sacrificed."

Then, after having recited the Samiṣṭa Yajus mantras[3] which are required when binding the sacrificial animal to the pillar, he repeats the words, "May Agni Jâtavedâs, recompensate us! May the Kṣattra give us full compensation for what we have sacrificed, Svâhâ." These two Âhutis are the Iṣṭâpûrta aparijyâni for a princely person when bringing a sacrifice. Therefore both are to be offered.

22.

(The Ajîtapunarvaṇya [4] Offerings.)

[475] *Sujâta*, the son of *Arâlha*, said that it is optional for the king to perform (besides the ceremony mentioned in 21) the two invocation offerings, called *Ajîtapunarvaṇya*. He may bring them if he like to do so. He who, following the advice of Sujâta, brings these two invocation offerings, shall say, "I turn towards the Brahma, may it protect me from the Kṣattra, Svâhâ to the Brahma!" "This, this is certainly the case;" thus say the sacrificial priests (when this mantra is spoken by the king). The meaning of this formula is, He who turns towards the sacrifice, turns towards the Brahma; for the sacrifice is the Brahma; he, who undergoes the inauguration ceremony, is born again from the sacrifice. He who has turned towards the Brahma, the Kṣattra does not forsake. He says, "May the Brahma protect me from the Kṣattra," that is, the Brahma should protect him from the Kṣattra (which is persecuting him). By the words, *Swâhâ to the Brahma!* he pleases the Brahma; and, if pleased, it protects him from the Kṣattra. Then, after the recital of the Samiṣṭa Yajus mantras, required for binding the sacrificial animal to the pillar, he repeats, "I turn towards the Kṣattra, may it protect me from the Brahma, Svâhâ to the Kṣattra." "This, this is certainly the case;" thus they say. He who turns towards the royal power (to assume it again) turns towards the Kṣattra. For the Kṣattra is the royal power. When he has reached the Kṣattra, the Brahma does not leave him. If he

[3] The Adhvaryu takes Darbha grass and melted butter (in a spoon) in his hands, and sacrifices for them. This is called *Samiṣṭa*. The Yajus or sacrificial formula required at the time is *devâ gâtuvido*. *Svâhâ* must be repeated twice. (*Oral information.*)

[4] In some MSS. and in Sâyaṇa's commentary, this name is written: *ajîtapunarvarṇya*. It means "the recovering of what is not to be lost." This refers to the Kṣattra which the Kṣattriya first lost by his turning towards the Brahma, but regained by his subsequently embracing the Kṣattra again, which he cannot throw off if he otherwise wish to retain his sovereignty.

[476] repeats the words, "May the Kṣattra protect me from the Brahma," that is, the Kṣattra should protect him from the Brahma, "*Svâhâ to the Kṣattra!*" he pleases this Kṣattra. Pleased in this way, the Kṣattra protects him from the Brahma. Both these offerings (*ajîta-punarvaṇyam*) are also calculated to preserve the sacrificing king from the loss of the Iṣṭâpûrta. Thence these two are (also) to be sacrificed.

23.

(*The King is, Before Sacrificing, Made a Brahman, but he must Lose his Royal Qualifications.*)

As regards the deity, the royal prince (Kṣattriya) belongs to Indra; regarding the metre he belongs to the Triṣṭubh; regarding the Stoma, he belongs to that one which is fifteen-fold. As to his sovereignty, he is Soma (king of the gods); as to his relationship, he belongs to the royal order. And, if inaugurated into the sacrificial rites, he enters even the Brahmanship at the time when he covers himself with the black goatskin, and enters on the observances enjoined to an inaugurated one, and Brahmans surround him.

When he is initiated in such a manner, then Indra takes away from him sharpness of senses, Triṣṭubh strength, the fifteen-fold Stoma the life, Soma takes away the royal power, the Pitaras (manes) glory and fame. (For they say) "he has estranged himself from us; for he is the Brahma; he has turned to the Brahma." The royal prince then, after having brought an invocation offering before the inauguration, shall stand near the Ahavanîya fire, and say, "I do not leave Indra as my deity, nor the Triṣṭubh as (my) metre, nor the fifteen-fold Stoma, nor the king Soma, nor the kinship of the Pitaras. May therefore Indra not take from me the skill, nor the Triṣṭubh the strength, nor the fifteen-fold Stoma the life, nor Soma the royal power, nor the Pitaras glory and [477] renown. I approach here Agni as (my) deity with sharpness of senses, strength, life (vigour), renown and kinship. I go to the Gâyatri metre, to the three-fold Stoma, to Soma the king, to the Brahma, I become a Brâhmaṇa." When he, standing before the Ahavanîya fire, brings this invocation offering, then, although he be Kṣattriya (by birth, no Brahman), Indra does not take from him sharpness of senses, nor Triṣṭubh strength, &c.

24.

(How the King becomes a Kṣattriya again after the Sacrifice is over.)

The royal prince belongs, as regards the deity, to Agni; his metre is the Gâyatrî, his Stoma the Trivṛit (nine-fold), his kinsman the Brâhmana. But when performing the concluding ceremony of the sacrifice, the royal prince (who was during the sacrifice a Brâhmaṇa) assumes (by means of another offering) his royal dignity (which was lost) again. Then Agni takes away from him the (Brahmanical) lustre, Gâyatrî the strength, the Trivṛit Stoma the life, the Brâhmaṇas the Brahma, and glory and renown; for they say, this man has forsaken us by assuming the Kṣatra again, to which he has returned.

Then, after having performed the Samiṣṭa offerings[5] which are required for the ceremony of binding the sacrificial animal to the pillar he presents himself to the Ahavanîya fire (again), saying, "I do not leave, Agni as (my) deity, nor the Gâyatrî as my metre, nor the Trivṛit Stoma, nor the kindred of the Brahma. May Agni not take from me the lustre, nor the Gâyatrî the strength, nor the Trivṛit Stoma the life, nor the Brâhmaṇas glory and renown. With lustre, strength, life, the Brahma, glory, and renown, I turn to Indra as my deity, to the Triṣṭubh **[478]** metre, to the fifteen-fold Stoma, to Soma the king, I enter the Kṣattra, I become a Kṣattriya! O ye Pitaras of divine lustre! O ye Pitaras of divine lustre! I sacrifice in my own natural character (as a Kṣattriya, not as a Brâhmaṇa); what has been sacrificed by me, is my own, what has been completed as to wells, tanks, &c., is my own, what austerities have been undergone are my own, what burnt offerings have been brought are my own. That this is mine, this Agni will see, this Vâyu will hear, that Âditya will reveal it. I am only what I am (*i. e.*, a Kṣattriya, no Brâhmaṇa)." When he speaks thus and gives an invocation offering to the Ahavanîya fire, Agni does not take away from him the lustre, nor the Gâyatrî strength, nor the Trivṛit Stoma the life, nor the Brâhmaṇas the Brahma, glory and renown, though he concludes the sacred rites as a Kṣattriya.

25.

(The Pravaras of a Kṣattriya's House-priest are Invoked at the Time of his Sacrifice.)

Thence (if the sacrificer be a Kṣattriya) they (the Brahma speakers) ask as to how the inauguration *(dîkṣâ)*, which is, in the case of a Brah-

---

[5] See page 474.

man being initiated, announced by the formula, "the Brâhmaṇa is initiated,"[6] should be promulgated in the case of the sacrificer being a Kṣattriya? The answer is, The formula, "the Brâhmaṇa is initiated," is to be kept when a Kṣattriya is being initiated; the ancestral fire of the Kṣattriya's house-priest is to be mentioned.[7] This, this is certainly so.

[479] Having laid aside his own implements (weapons), and taking up those of the Brahma, and having thus become Brahma, by means of the Brahma form, he returned to the sacrifice. Therefore they should proclaim him as a Dîkṣita, with the name of his house-priest's ancestral fires, and invoke them also in the Pravara[8] prayer.

---

[6] This is, according to Sây., thrice low and thrice aloud to be repeated. By repeating the formula low, the inauguration is made known to the gods alone, but by repeating it aloud, it is announced to gods and men alike.

[7] For the Kṣattriya cannot claim descent from the Riṣis, as the Brahmans alone can do.

[8] By *pravara*, which literally means "choice, particular address," (see 6, 14), we have to understand the invocation of the sacrificial fires lighted by the principal Riṣi ancestors of the sacrificer. This invocation may comprise only one, or two, or three, or five ancestral fires, the name of which is *ârṣeya*; the pravara becomes accordingly *ekârṣeya, dvyârṣeya, tryârṣeya, and pañchârṣeya, i.e.*, having one or two, &c. Riṣis. This invocation takes place at the very commencement of the sacrifice, after the fire has been kindled under the recital of the Sâmidhenî verses, and at the time of the Subrahmaṇyâ proclamation (see 6, 3), after the sacrificer has become, in consequence of the initiatory rites, such as Dîkṣâ, Pravargya, &c., a Dîkṣita. Aśval. gives in his Śrâúta Sutras (1, 3), the following rules regarding this rite: यजमानस्यार्षेयान्प्रवृणीते यावन्तः स्युः परं परं प्रथमं । पौरोहित्यान्राजविशां राजर्षीन्वा राज्ञां सर्वेषां मानवेति संशये, *i.e.*, the Hotar particularly mentions the fires of the Riṣi ancestors of the sacrificer, as many as he may have (one, or two, or three, or five). He mentions one after the other, but the first (in the general enumeration) is to be made the last (at the time of sacrificing). If the sacrificers happen to be Kṣattriyas or Vaiśyas, he mentions the fires of the Riṣi ancestors of their Purohitas (house-priests), or the princely Riṣis (*râjarṣis*, who might have been their ancestors). If there should be any doubt, the word *mânava*, *i.e.*, descended from or made by Manu, may be used in the case of all kings.

This explanation of the terms *pravara* and *ârṣeya* have been already given by Max Müller (History of Ancient Sanscrit Literature, page 386) according to the authority of Aśvalâyana and *Baudhâyana*. It has been doubted, of late, by Dr. Hall (in his paper on three Sanscrit Inscriptions in the Journal of the Asiatic Society of Bengal of 1862, page 115), but without any sufficient reason. He says "*pravaras*" appear to be names of the families of certain persons from whom the founders of Gotras were descended, and of the families of the founders themselves." But if this were the case, it would be surprising, that the founders of certain Gotras should claim to descend not only from one but from several Riṣi ancestors. All the Gotras have eight great ancestors only, *viz.*, Viśvâmitra, Jamadagni, Bharadvâja, Gautama, Atri, Vasiṣṭha, Kaśyapa, and Agastya. These occupy with the Brahmans about the same position as the twelve sons of Jacob with

26

[**480**]—(*The Kṣattriya is Not Allowed to Eat Sacrificial Food. The Brahma Priest Eats his Portion for Him.*)

As regards the portion of sacrificial food which is to be eaten by the sacrificer, they ask, whether the Kṣattriya should eat, or whether he should not eat it? They say, if he eat, then he commits a great sin, as having eaten sacrificial food, although he is an *ahutâd* (one not permitted to eat). If he do not eat, then he cuts himself off from the sacrifice (with which he was connected). For the portions to be eaten by the sacrificer, is the sacrifice. This is to be made over to the Brahma priest. For the Brahma priest of the Kṣattriya is in the place of (his) Purohita. The Purohita is the one-half of the Kṣattriya; only [**481**] through the intervention of another (the Brahma priest) the portion appears to be eaten by him, though he does not eat it with his own mouth. For the sacrifice is there where the Brahma (priest) is. The entire sacrifice is placed in the Brahma, and the sacrificer is in the sacrifice. They throw the sacrifice (in the shape of the portion which is to be eaten by the sacrificer) into the sacrifice (which has the form of the Brahma), just as they throw water into water, fire into fire, without making it overflow, nor causing any injury to the sacrificer. Therefore, is this portion to be eaten by the sacrificer (if he be a Kṣattriya) to be given up to the Brahmâ.

---

the Jews. Only he whose descent from one of these great Riṣis was beyond doubt, could become the founder of a Gotra. In this genealogy there is no proper place for the *pravaras* according to Dr. Hall's opinion; for a family calls itself generally only by the name of its founder. From a genealogical point of view, therefore, only the names of the patriarch (one of the great Riṣis) and those of the founders of the Gotras were important. The institution of the Pravaras is purely religious, and sacrificial. The *pravaras* or *ârṣeyas*, which are used as synonymous terms, are those sacrificial fires which several Gotras had in common; it was left to their own choice, to which they wished to repair. This had a practical meaning, as long as fire-worship was the prevailing religion of the Aryas, which was the case before the commencement of the properly so-called Vedic period. In the course of time it became a mere form, the original meaning of which was very early lost. That the *ârṣeyas* refer to the sacrificial fire, may be clearly seen from the context, in which they occur. Their names are mentioned in the vocative, as soon as the fire is kindled. After they have been invoked, the Hotar begins at once the invocation of Agni, the fire, by various names, such as *deveddho, manviddho*, &c., kindled by gods, kindled by Manu, &c. (Aśv. Śr. S. 1, 3). That this rite of invoking the *ârṣeyas* must be very ancient, proves the occurrence of a similar, or even the same, rite with the Parsis. They invoke up to this day, in their confession of faith, those ancestors and beings who were of the same *varena, i.e.*, choice, religion, as they are. The term for "I will profess (a religion)" is *fravarânê*, which is exactly of the same origin as *pravara* (See Yaśna 12 in my Essays, page 164).

Some sacrificial priests, however, sacrifice this portion to the fire, saying, "I place thee in Prajâpati's world, which is called *vibhân* (shining everywere), to be joined to the sacrificer, Svâhâ!" But thus the sacrificial priest ought not to proceed. For the portion to be eaten by the sacrificer is the sacrificer himself. What priest, therefore, asserts this, burns the sacrificer in the fire. (If anyone should observe a priest doing so) he ought to tell him, "Thou hast singed the sacrificer in the fire. Agni will burn his breaths, and he will consequently die." Thus it always happens. Therefore he should not think of doing so.

FIFTH CHAPTER.

On the Sacrificial Drink which the King has to Taste instead of Soma, According to the Instruction given by Râma Mârgaveya to the King Viśvantara.)

27.

(Story of the Śyâparṇas. Râma Defends their Rights.)

Viśvantara, the son of *Suṣâdman*, deprived the *Śyâparṇas* of their right of serving as his sacrificial [482] priests, and interdicted any one of this family to take part in his sacrifice. Having learnt (that) they went to the place of his sacrifice and seated themselves within the precincts of the Vedi.[1] On observing them, Viśvantara said (to his attendants), "There sit those Śyâparṇas, the scoundrels, who endeavour to sully another's fame. Turn them out; let them not sit in the Vedi." The attendants obeyed and turned the Śyâparṇas out. They then cried aloud, "When *Janamejaya*, the son of *Parikṣit*, was performing a sacrifice without the *Kaśyapas* (who were his hereditary priests), then the *Asitamṛigas* from among the Kaśyapas turned the *Bhûtavîras* (who were officiating instead of the Kaśyapas) out, not allowing them to administer the Soma rites. They succeeded because they had brave men with them. "Well, what hero is now among us,[2] who might by force take away this Soma beverage (that we might administer it ourselves)?" "This your man am I," said *Râma Mârgaveya.*[3] This Râma belonged to the Śyâparnas, and had completed the sacred study. When the Śyâparṇas rose

---

[1] This place is to be occupied by the priests and the sacrificer only.

[2] In the text is *asmâka*, instead of *asmâkam*.

[3] Son of a woman *Mṛigavu* or *Mriganîyu* (both forms are used). *Sây.* He is quite different from Râma, the hero of the Râmyâna.

to leave, then he said to the king, " Will (thy servants), O king, turn out of the Vedi even a man (like me) who knows the sacred science ?" (The king answered), "O thou member of the vile Brahman brood,[4] whoever thou art, how hast thou any knowledge (of such matters)? "

28.

[483] (*Why Indra was Excluded from his Share in the Soma. The Kṣattriya Race Became also Excluded.*)

(Râma said) "I know it from the fact, that Indra had been excluded by the gods (from having any share in the sacrifices). For he had scorned[5] Viśvarûpa, the son of Tvaṣṭar, cast down Vṛitra (and killed him), thrown pious men (*yatis*) before the jackals (or wolves) and killed the *Arurmaghas*,[6] and rebuked **[484]** (his teacher) Bṛihaspati.

---

[4] Sây. explains *brahmabandhu* by *brâhmaṇa adhama, i.e.*, lowest Brahman. No doubt, there is something contemptible in this expression.

[5] In the original, *abhyamaṁsta.* This cannot mean (according to etymology), " he killed " as Sây. supposes, misguided by the story told in the Taittir. Saṁh. 2, 4, where Indra is said to have cut the three heads of Viśvarûpa, which were *somapânam* (drinking of Soma), *surâpânam* (drinking of spirituous liquor), and *annâdanam* (eating of food). The reason alleged for Indra's killing him is that he, as a relation of the Asuras, informed them about the secret portions of the sacrificial food, Soma, &c., whilst he told the Devas, whose associate he was, only the real and visible ones. Indra holding that he who knows the secret portions of Soma, &c., will come to know the real ones also, became afraid lest the Asuras might, strengthened by Soma, overthrow his rule, and killed the perpetralor of such a treason by cutting off his three heads, each of which was transformed into a particular kind of bird. Viśvarûpa being a Brahman, Indra thus became guilty of the horrible crime of Brahman-murder (*brahmahatyā*). All beings called him " murderer of a Brahman," so that he could not find rest anywhere. He requested the Earth to take off the third part of his guilt, who under certain conditions complied with his request. To be relieved from the two remaining thirds of his burden, he applied to the trees, and the women, who readily took under certain conditions a part of his guilt upon themselves. Tvaṣṭar, the father of Vairûpa, excluded Indra from any share in the Soma sacrifice ; but he took his share with force. The remaining portion of Indra's share was thrown into the sacrificial fire by Tvaṣṭar, with the words, " Grow (*vardhasva*) into an enemy of Indra." This became the terrible foe of Indra, known in the legends by the name of *Vṛitra.* Indra succeeded afterwards in killing him. See the same legend in the Kâuṣîtaki Upaniṣad. 3, 1.

[6] In the Kâuṣ. Up. 3, 1, we find the form *Arunmukha.* Sây. thinks them to be Asuras in the disguise of Brahmans. With this explanation agrees Śankarâchârya on the whole in his Commentary on the Kâuṣ. Up. (page 75, ed. Cowell). He divides the word into *rurmukha*, and the negative *a*. The first is to mean " the study of the Vedas," and the second " mouth." Therefore the whole means, according to him, in " whose mouth is not the study of the Vedas." This explanation is quite artificial and unsatisfactory. The Arurmaghas (this is propably the right form) were, no doubt, a kind of degraded Aryas, very likely a tribe of the ancient Iranians, in whose language (the Zend) the words *aurvo* and *magha* are frequently to be met with.

On account of these faults, Indra was forthwith excluded from participation in the Soma beverage. And after Indra had been excluded in this way from the Soma, all the Kṣattriyas (at whose head he is) were likewise excluded from it. But he was allowed a share in it afterwards, having stolen the Soma from Tvaṣṭar. But the Kṣattriya race remains excluded from the Soma beverage to this day. There is one here who knows the way in which the Kṣattriya, who is properly excluded from the Soma beverage, may relish in this juice. Why do thy men expel such a man from the Vedi?" The king asked then, "Dost thou, O Brâhmaṇa, know this way?" Râma answered, "Yes, I know it." The king then replied, "Let me know it, O Brâhmaṇa." Râma answered, "I will let thee know here, O king."

29.

(Which Portions of Sacrificial Drink the King has to Avoid.)

The priests may take any one of the three portions (which are to be left), either Soma, or curds, or water. When they take the Soma, which is the portion allotted to Brâhmaṇas, then thou wilt favour the Brâhmaṇas by it.[1] Thy progeny will be distinguished by the characteristics of the Brâhmaṇa; for they will be ready to take gifts, thirsty after drinking (Soma), and hungry of eating food, and ready to roam about everywhere according to their pleasure. **[485]** When there is any fault on the Kṣattriya (who, when sacrificing, eats the Brâhmaṇa portion), then his progeny has the characteristics of a Brâhmaṇa; but in the second or third generation he is then capable of entering completely the Brâhmaṇaship, and he will have the desire of living with the Brahmâṇic fraternity.

When they take the curds, which is the share of the Vaiśyas, then thou wilt favour the Vaiśyas by it (and consequently be brought near them). Thy offspring will be born with the characteristics of the Vaiśyas, paying taxes to another king, to be enjoyed by another; they will be oppressed according to the pleasure of the king. When there is any fault on the Kṣattriya (who, when sacrificing, eats the Vaiśya portion), then his progeny is born with the characteristics of a Vaiśya; and in the second or third degree, they are capable of entering the caste of the Vaiśyas, and are desirous of living in the condition of a Vaiśya (*i.e.*, they will have the nature of a Vaiśya).

[1] That is to say, thou wilt, when regenerated in thy son and grandson, be accepted by the Brâhmaṇas as a member of their caste.

When thou takest the water, which is the share of the Śûdras, then thou wilt please the Śûdras by it. Thy progeny will have the characteristics of the Śûdras, they are to serve another the three higher castes, to be expelled and beaten according to the pleasure (of their masters.) When there is any fault on the Kṣattriya (who, when sacrificing, eats the Śûdra portion), then his offspring will be born with the characteristics of the Śûdras; and in the second or third degree, he is capable of entering the condition of the Śûdras, and will be desirous of passing his life in that condition.

30.

(*Which Portion the King should Choose at the Sacrifice. The Origin and Meaning of Nyagrodha.*)

These are the three portions (*bhakṣas,*) O King, of which the Kṣattriya, when performing a sacrifice, **[486]** must choose none. But the following is his own portion, which he is to enjoy. He must squeeze the airy descending roots of the *Nyagrodha* tree, together with the fruits of the *Udumbara, Aśvattha,* and *Plakṣa* trees, and drink the juice of them. This is his own portion.

(For the origin of the Nyagrodha tree is as follows): When the gods, after the (successful) performance of their sacrifice, went up to heaven, they tilted over (*ny-ubjan*) the Soma cups, whence the Nyagrodha trees grew up. And by the name of *Nyubja, i.e.*, tilted over, they are now called in Kurukṣetra, where they grew first; from them all the others originated. They grew descending the roots (*nyañcho rohanti*). Therefore what grows downwards, is a downward growth (*nyagroha*); and for this name, signifying "downward growth," they called the tree "*Nyagrodha*."[*] It is called by the name *Nyagrodha,* whose meaning is hidden (to men), and not by the more intelligible name *Nyagroha,* for the gods like to conceal the very names of objects from men, and call them by names unintelligible to them.

31.

(*On the Meaning of the King's Drinking the Juice of the Nyagrodha Tree instead of Soma.*)

That portion of the juice in these Soma cups which went downwards became the descending roots, and of the other which went up, the fruits were produced. That Kṣattriya, therefore, who enjoys the juice of

[*] The word is traced to the root *ruh,* to grow, the older form of which is *rudh*; compare *avoradha,* "the descending roots."

the descending roots of the Nyagrodha tree, and that of its fruits, is not debarred from his own share (*bhakṣa*). Further, he thus obtains the Soma beverage by means of a substitute, though he does not enjoy [**487**] the real Soma, but only in the form of a substitute; for the Nyagrodha is just this substitute of the Soma. The Kṣattriya (when drinking the juice of the Nyagrodha) enters the form of the Brahma by the medium of another (not direct), *viz.*, through the relationship of his purohita (with the Brahmans), his own Dîkṣâ (at which the king himself was made a Brâhmaṇa for a little while), and the Pravara of his Purohita. The Kṣattra (ruling power) occupies (among men- the same place as) the Nyagrodha among the trees; for the Kṣattra are the royal princes, whose power alone is spread here (on this earth), as being alone invested with sovereign power. The Nyagrodha is,[9] as it were, firmly established in the earth (and thus a sign of the duration of the royal power); and by means of its descending roots expanded (in all directions, and therefore a sign of the great extent of the power of the Kṣattriyas over the whole earth). When the Kṣattriya who performs a sacrifice enjoys (the juice squeezed out of the) descending roots of the Nyagrodha tree, and its fruits, then he places in himself royal power (exercised by the Nyagrodha) over the trees, and into the Kṣattra his own Self. He then is in the Kṣattra, and the royal power represented by the Nyagrodha over the trees, is then placed in him. Just as the Nyagrodha tree has, by means of its descending roots, a firm footing on the earth (for it is multiplied in this way), the royal power of a Kṣattriya who enjoys, when sacrificing, this portion (as food) has a firm footing, and his rule cannot be overthrown.

32.

[488] (*The Symbolical Meaning of the Fruits of the Udumbara, Aśvattha, and Plakṣa Trees. What Implements are Required for this quasi-Soma Feast of the King.*)

As to the fruits of the Udumbara tree, which originated from the vigour which is in food, and in which there is all the vigour of the trees, furnishing nourishments, the Kṣatriya (when drinking the juice prepared from its fruits) places in the Kṣattra food, and what yields nourishment from the trees.

---

[9] The tree (a kind of the *Ficus indica*) is very strong.

As to the fruits of the Aśvattha tree, which sprang out of lustre, and which has the sovereignty over the trees, the Kṣattriya (when drinking the juice prepared from its fruits) places in the Kṣattra lustre and the sovereignty over the trees.

As to the fruits of the Plakṣa tree, which sprang out of glory, and in which there is the independence and brilliancy of the trees represented, the Kṣattriya places in this way the independence and brilliancy which is in the trees in the Kshattra.

When all these things (the roots of the Nyagrodha tree, &c.) are in readiness for him, then the priests buy the Soma, and perform for the king the several ceremonies preceding the eve of the festival, just in the same way as the real Soma is treated. Then the day before the celebration (of the feast) the Adhvaryu should have all these things ready which are required for the preparation of the Soma juice, such as the (goat) skin (placed below), the two boards required for squeezing, the *Droṇakalaśa*, the cloth (for purifying), the stones, the *Pûtabhṛit*, the *Adhavanîya*, the *Sthâlî*, the *Udanehnam* and the *Chamasa*.[10] Then **[489]** they should make

[10] Here are the principal implements required for squeezing, preparing, keeping, sacrificing and drinking the Soma juice mentioned. A detailed knowledge of them constitutes one of the principal qualifications of an Adhvaryu. Their description is therefore to be found principally in the Sûtras of the Yajurveda (see the 9th and 10th Adhyáya of the Kâtiya sûtras, the 8th and 9th Praśna of the Hiraṇ yakeśi Sûtras, Sâyaṇa's Commentary on the 4th Prapâṭhaka of the 1st Kâṇḍa of the Taittirîya Saṁhitâ, founded on the Apastamba Śrauta Sûtras).

In order to make the use of these vessels intelligible to the reader, I subjoin here a short description of the preparation of the Soma juice, partially from what I myself have witnessed, partially from the ritual books and oral information.

The plant which is at present used by the sacrificial priests of the Dekkhan at the Soma feast, is not the Soma of the Vedas, but appears to belong to the same order. It grows on hills in the neighbourhood of Poona, to the height of about 4 to 5 feet, and forms a kind of bush, consisting of a certain number of shoots, all coming from the same root; their stem is solid like wood; the bark greyish; they are without leaves, the sap appears whitish, has a very stringent taste, is bitter, but not sour; it is a very nasty drink, and has some intoxicating effect. I tasted it several times, but it was impossible for me to drink more than some tea-spoonfulls.

The juice is obtaind in the following way: The Adhvaryu first spreads a skin (*charma*), and puts on it the Soma shoots which are called *aṁśu* or *vallí*. He now takes two boards, *adhiṣavaṇa*; the first is placed above the Soma. He beats the board with one of the so-called *grávaṇas, i.e.*, Soma squeezing stones, takes the shoots (as many as he requires for the particular Savana) from below the boards, ties them together, and places the other board above them. He then pours water from the Vasatîvarî pot (see page 114-115) on this board; this water is called *nigrâbhya*. He now takes certain number of shoots (there are, for instance, for the libation from the Upâṁśu Graha, which is the first of all, six required) out of the whole bunch which lies between the two boards,

two parts of what is squeezed for the king (the roots of the Nyagrodha, &c.); one is to [**490**] be made ready for the morning libation, the other to be left for the midday libation.

33.

(*The Drinking from the Traita Cups.*)

When the priests lift the *Traita* cups for [11] sacrificing, then they shall lift up the cup of the sacrificer [**491**] also, having thrown upon it

holds over them the Soma squeezing stone, and shakes them thrice in the Chamasa (cup) of the Hotar, towards the right side. This is the *Nigrâbha*. He wets them with the waters of the Vasatîvarî pot. Now he puts them on a large stone, places upon them some grass, and beats the shoots in order to extract the juice. The technical term for this beating is, *abhiṣuṇoti*. Each *abhiṣava*, or complete extracting of the Soma juice consists of three turns (*paryâyas*); in the first, the Adhvaryu beats the shoots eight times, and makes the *Nigrâbha* in the manner described above; in the second turn, he beats them eleven times, and in the third twelve times, making at the end of each the Nigrâbha. The juice which the Adhvaryu catches at the end of each turn with his hand, is thrown into a vessel (at the first *abhiṣava* in the Upâṁśu Graha).

After this first or preliminary *abhiṣava*, follows the *mahâbhiṣava* or the great squeezing ceremony, performed exactly in the same way as the first, with the only difference, that the Adhvaryu takes from between the two boards as many Soma shoots as are required for the rest of the Savanam (libation). If the juice is extracted, it is poured in the *Adhavanîya*, a kind of trough. Thence it is poured in a cloth, in order to strain it. This cloth is called *Pavitra* or *Daśâpavitra*. Below the cloth is another trough, called *Pûtâbhṛit* (*i.e.*, the bearer of what is strained, purified). The Udgâtar must hold the cloth when the juice is strained.

Single shoots of the Soma, and drops of its juice, are put in several *sthâlis* or small vessels generally used for keeping butter. The libations are poured from two kinds of vessels, from the Grahas (see page 118), and the Chamasas (cups). Each offering from a Graha consists of a certain number of *Dhârâs* or portions (of a liquid substance). So, for instance, the offering from the Agrayaṇa Graha, at the evening libation, consists of the following four *Dhârâs*: that one which is in the Agrayaṇa sthâlî (*not* the Graha) taken by the Adhvaryu; the two portions which remained in the Aditya Graha (the libation from which precedes that from the Agrayaṇa), and in the Ajya sthâlî (the pot with melted butter); these two are taken by the Pratipasthâtar; the fourth Dhârâ is taken from the Adhavanîya trough by the Unnetar. Each of the four Dhârâs is first strained by a cloth held over the Pûtâbhṛit vessel. The Unnetar takes his Dhârâ with a vessel, called *Udañchana*, or with a Chamasa. These four Dhârâs are then filled from the Pûtâbhṛit in the Agrayaṇa Graha, and sacrificed in the usual way. Certain offerings are filled in the Grahas from another very large trough, the so-called *Dronakalaśa* (one such vessel is in my possession). At certain occasions, there is not only the mouth of the Graha to be filled up to the brim, but the small cup, put in it (which alone was *originally* the Graha; but, after the latter term had become identical with Pâtra, the vessel itself, the small cup, was called *atigraha*), is also filled; this is called *atigrâhya*.

[11] They are called here *trâita chamasa*. There are, on the whole, ten such cups; therefore *traita* cannot be referred to *tri*, *i.e.*, three. In all likelihood, the word is

two young sprouts of Dharba grass; both are then (one after the other) to be thrown on the wooden sticks surrounding the fire, by the formula *Vauṣaṭ*! After having thrown the first, the priest repeats the verse, *dadhikrâvṇo akâriṣam* (4, 39, 6), concluding with *Svâhâ* and *Vausat.* After having thrown the second Dharba stalk, he repeats the verse, *â dadhikrâḥ śavasâ* (4, 38, 10.) When the priests then take the Soma cups to drink themselves, the sacrificer should take his cup also. When they lift them up (to drink), the sacrificer should do the same. When the Hotar then calls the Iḷâ (just before drinking) to the place, and drinks from his cup, then the sacrificer should drink his cup whilst repeating the following verse, "What has remained of the juicy Soma beverage whilst Indra drank with his hosts, this his remainder I enjoy with my happy mind, I drink the king Soma." This beverage prepared from the trees (above mentioned) promising fortune to him, becomes drunk with a happy mind. The royal power of a Kṣattriya who, when sacrificing, drinks only this portion described, becomes strong, and is not to be shaken.

[492] By the words, "Be a blessing to our heart thou who art drunk! prolong our life, O Soma, that we may live long!" he then cleans his mouth; for, if the juice (remaining on his lips) is not wiped off, then Soma, thinking, "an unworthy drinks me," is able to destroy the life of a man. But if the juice is wiped off in this way, then he prolongs the life. With the following two verses, which are appropriate for the sacrifice, *âpyâyasva sametu* (1, 91, 16) and *saṁ te payâṁsi samayantu* (1, 91, 18), he blesses the Chamasa (*i. e.*, what he has drunk from it) to bear fruit. What is appropriate in the sacrifice, that is successful.

---

connected with Trita, who was the first physician, and the Soma being the best of all medicines, supposed to have invented such cups. Sâyaṇa does not explain the term in his Commentary on the Aitareya Brâhmaṇam: but his attempt at an explanation in that on the Taittirîya Saṁhitâ (ii. page 253, ed. Cowell) shows that he had evidently no clear idea of what the original meaning was; for after having tried more than one explanation from the numeral *tri*, he exclaims, "but it is now enough; one should see that *traita* means 'good, excellent,' (*praśasta*)." But we need not despair of making out its meaning. If we compare the term, *trâita chamasa* with that of *narâśaṁsa chamasa* (in 7, 34), we can pretty clearly see what it must mean. As I have stated above (in note 24, on page 124-125), the Chamasa are *Narâśaṁsa*, that is to say, they belong to the deity Narâśaṁsa, after one has drunk out of them, sprinkled water over them, &c. Now, from a Chamasa, they generally drink twice. What is filled in for the first time is *Trâita*, *i. e*, belongs to *Trita*; afterwards, it is cleaned and filled again. This then is the Narâśaṁsa draught. [In Corrigenda the translator says "my opinion on the Traita cups rests on a doubtful reading." Again, in the Corrections to Vol, I,, he writes:—"The rare word *traita* appears to have been very early misunderstood."—Editor.]

34.

(The Drinking from the Narâśaṁsa cups. The List of Teachers of the Substitute for the Soma Juice, and the Rites Connected with it.)

When the priests put the Traita cups down, then the king should put down the sacrificer's cup also; when they incline their cups (after having put them down), then the king should do the same with his cup. Then he should take up the [Narâśaṁsa] cup, and by the recital of the verse, "O thou divine Soma, who knowest my mind, who art drunk by Narâśaṁsa, and enjoyed by the *Uma-Pitaras* [12] I enjoy thee!" In this way the king enjoys the Narâśaṁsa portion at the morning libation. At the midday libation, he repeats the same mantra, but says, "enjoyed by the *Urva-*(Pitaras)," and at the evening libation, he says, "enjoyed by the *Kâvya* [493] (Pitaras)." For the Pitaras (present) at the morning libation, are the Umas, those (present) at the midday libation, are the Urvas, and those at the evening libation, are the Kâvyas. In this way, he makes the immortal Pitaras enjoy the libations.

Priyavrata, the Soma drinker, said, "Whoever enjoys the Soma beverage, he certainly will be immortal." The ancestors of a king who enjoys, when sacrificing, this Narâśaṁsa portion, therefore, become immortal (*i. e.*, they never will perish), when they enjoy (in such a way) the Soma libation, and his royal power will be strong and is not to be shaken. The ceremony of wiping off from the mouth what of the juice remained, and the sprinking of the cup with water (*âpyâyanam*) is the same as above (when the Traita Chamasa are emptied). All the three libations of the juice prepared for the king, should be performed in the same way as the real Soma libation.

This way of enjoying the Soma juice (by means of a substitute), was told by Râma Mârgaveya to Viśvantara, the son of Suṣadman. The king then, after having been told it, said, "We give thee a thousand cows, O Brâhmaṇa. My sacrifice is to be attended by the Śyâparnas."

This portion (*bhakṣa*) was told by *Tura*, the son of *Kavaṣa*, to *Janamejaya*, the son of *Parikṣit;* then by *Parvata* and *Nârada* to *Somaka*, the son of *Sahadeva;* thence (this traditional knowledge) passed to *Sahadeva*

---

[12] A division of the Pitaras, or manes. It is the proper name of a certain class of the Pitaras. The original meaning of the word is uncertain. The root is, no doubt, *av*, but it has so many meanings that it is difficult to state satisfactorily the meaning. Another division of the Pitaras, see on page 226.

Sârjaya; thence to *Babhru Daivâvridha;* thence to *Bhîma Vaidarbha*, and *Nagnajit Gândhâra*.

This portion, further, was told by Agni to *Samaśruta Arindama;* thence it passed to *Kratuvid Jânaki*. This portion was further told by *Vasiṣṭha* to *Sudâs*, the son of *Pijavana*.

[**494**] All these became great, in consequence of their having drunk the Soma in this way (by means of a substitute), and were great kings. Just as the sun (placed on the sky) sends forth warmth, thus the king who, when sacrificing drinks the Soma in this way, is placed amidst fortune and shines everywhere, from all directions he exacts tribute, his kingdom becomes strong, and is not to be shaken.

[495] # EIGHTH BOOK.

FIRST CHAPTER.

(The Śastras and Stotras required at the Soma Day of the Râjasûya.)

1

(The Use of Both the Rathantaram and Bṛihat at the Midday Libation.)

Now, as regards the Stotras and Śastras (required at the king's libation), both the morning and the evening libations do not differ in this point from the rule of the Aikâhikas (Soma sacrifice of one day's duration); for both these libations at the Aikâhika sacrifices are indisturbable, well arranged, and firmly standing, and they produce quiet, good order, firm footing, and security.

(But there is a difference in the ceremonies of the midday libation.) The midday Pavamâna performance (of a sacrifice, which requires both Sâmans with the Bṛihat for the Pṛiṣṭha Stotra, has been told;[1]

[1] The expression *ukta*, "told," appears to refer to 4, 19, *ubhe bṛihad rathantare pâvamânayor bhavatas*. But the reference is not quite exact. The author wishes, doubtless, to advert to the peculiar circumstance, that both the principal Sâmans are used at one and the same day, *viz.*, on the Soma day of the Râjasûya. It is even against the general principles of the sacrificial theory to use both on the same day (see 4, 13), as the whole arrangement of the Dvâdaśâha sacrifice with its Rathantara and Bṛihat days clearly shows. There are only three exceptions to this rule, as far as my knowledge goes, *viz.*, on the *Abhijit* and *Viṣuvan* days, and on the *Abhiṣechanîya* day of the Râjasûya, which is performed according to the rites of an *aikâhika* Soma sacrifice (see 8, 4). The particulars of the ceremonies of the Abhijit day are not given in our Brâhmaṇam; but we learn them from the Aśval. Sûtras (8, 5). There it is said: *Abhijit Bṛihat-pṛiṣṭha ubhayasâmâ yadyapi Rathantaram yajñayajñîyasîthâne*, *i.e.*, the Abhijit sacrifice requires the Bṛihat as its Pṛiṣṭha Stotra (at the midday libation), and (thus) both (the principal) Sâmans, if the Rathantaram (is used at the evening libation) instead of the Yajñayajnîya Sâman (used at the evening libation of the Agniṣṭoma). The exceptional use of Bṛihat and Rathantaram on the Viṣuvan day has been stated by our author (4, 19, compare Aśval. 8, 6). On the use of both these Sâmans at the Râjasûya sacrifice, Aśval. (9, 3) makes the following remark: *ukthyo bṛihat pṛiṣṭha ubhayasâmâ abhishechanîyah*, *i.e.*, on the inauguration day, the Ukthya sacrifice takes place, with the modification that the Bṛihat is the Sâma of the Pṛiṣṭha Stotra, and that both (the principal) Sâmans (Bṛihat and Rathantaram) are required. Both are, as we learn distinctly from our Brâhmaṇam, required at the midday libation ; the Rathantaram being chanted

[496] for the chanting of both Sâmans (the Rathantara and Bṛihat) is performed. The verse, *â tvâ rathaṁ yathotaya* (8, 57, 1-3) is the beginning (required for the Śastra) belonging to the Rathantara Sâman; the verse *idam vaso sutam andha* (8, 53, 5-7), the sequel required for the same Śastra. This Pavamâna Uktham (the just-mentioned Shastra) is just the Marutvatîya Śastra, to which the Rathantara Sâman (at the Agniṣṭoma, for instance) belongs. They perform the Rathantara chant at the Pavamâna Stotra (of the midday libation) praised at this (sacrifice); the Bṛihat is the Pṛiṣṭha (Stotra), in order to give a prop (to the whole). For the Rathantara is Brahma; the Bṛihat is the Kṣattra.[2] The Brahma certainly precedes the Kṣattra. For the **[497]** king should think "when the Brahma is at the head, then my royal power would become strong and not be shaken." Further, the Rathantara is food; if placed first, it procures food to the king. The Rathantara further is the earth, which is a firm footing; if placed first, it therefore procures a firm footing to the king.

The Pragâtha for calling Indra[3] near remains the same without any modification (as in the Brahmanical sacrifices), this Pragâtha belonging to (all) Soma days. The Pragâtha addressed to Brahmaṇaspati,[4] which has the characteristic of *ut* (*utliṣtha*, rise!) is appropriate to both the Sâmans which are chanted. The Dhyâyyâs[5] are the same without any modification; they are those appropriate for the Ahîna sacrifices, whilst that Marutvatîya Pragâtha,[6] which is peculiar to the Aikâhikas, is chosen.

2.

(The Remainder of the Marutvatîya Shastra, and the Nishkevalya Śastra.)

The (Nivid) hymn (of the *Pavamâna uktham*) is *janiṣṭhâ ugraḥ* (10, 73).[7] It contains the terms, *ugra* strong, and *sahas* power, which

first, and the Bṛihat after it. The former forms here part of the Pavamâna Stotra (the first at the midday libation), the latter is the (principal) Pṛiṣṭha Stotra which follows the first. The Śastra belonging to the Pavamâna Stotra is the Marutvatîya (see 3, 12-20), that for the Pṛiṣṭha Stotra is the Niṣkevalya (see 3, 21-24). At the Râjasûya sacrifice, the first goes by the name of *Pavamâna-uktham*, the latter by that of *Graha-uktham*.

[2] The royal sacrifice differs from the Brahmanical here by the employment of both the principal Sâmans at the same time; whilst at the latter sacrifice, either is employed separately.

[3] See about it 3, 16. It is repeated on all Soma days, and forms always part of the first Śastra of the midday libation. Thence it is also necessary at the Râjasûya).

[4] See 3, 17 (page 184).

[5] See 3, 18.

[6] See 4, 19.

[7] See pages 188-89. It is the same as at the Marutvatîya Śastra.

are chracteristic of the Kṣattra. The word, *ojiṣṭha*, "the strongest," is also a characteristic of the Kṣattra. The words, *bahulâbhimânaḥ* (in the first verse) contain the term *abhi*, which means, "to overpower, defeat," (which is a characteristic of the Kṣattram **[498]** also). The hymn consists of eleven verses, for the Triṣṭubh comprises eleven syllables, and the Kṣattriyas share in the nature of the Triṣṭubh. *Ojas* (in *ojiṣṭha*) is Indra's power, *vîryam* (strength) is Triṣṭubh ; the Kṣattra is power (*ojas*), and the Kṣattriya race is the strength (as to progeny). Thus he (the priest) makes him (the Kṣattriya) successful in strength, royal power, and progeny. By this Gaurivîti hymn[8] the Marutvatîya Śastra becomes successful, on which a Brâhmaṇam[9] has been told.

(*Now Follows the Niṣkevalya Śastram.*)

The verse, *tvâm iddhi havâmahe* (6, 46, 1-2), forms the Bṛihat Pṛiṣṭha. For the Bṛihat Sâma is the Kṣattram ; by means of the Kṣattra, the king makes complete his royal power. If the Bṛihat is the Kṣattra, then the soul of the sacrificer is the Niṣkevalya Ṣastra (to which the Bṛihat Sâma belongs). That is what the Bṛihat Pṛiṣṭha becomes (for the sacrificer). The Bṛihat is the Kshattra ; by means of the Kṣattra, the Bṛihat makes him successful. The Bṛihat is further precedence, and in this respect it makes him successful also. The Bṛihat is further excellence, and in this respect it makes him successful also.

They make the Rathantara Sâma, *abhi tvâ śûra nonumaḥ* , the *Anurûpa*[10] to the Bṛihat. For the Rathantara is this world, and the Bṛihat is that world. That world corresponds to this one, and this **[499]** world to that one. Therefore, they make the Rathantara the Anurûpa to the Bṛihat, for thus they make the sacrificer enjoy both worlds.

Further, the Rathantara is the Brahma, and the Kṣattra the Bṛihat ; thus the Kṣattra is then placed in the Brahma, and the Brahma in the Kṣattra. There is then prepared for both the Sâmans the same place. The Dhâyyâ is *yad vâvâna* (10, 74, 6), of which a Brâhmaṇam[11] has been already told. The Sâma Pragâtha is, *ubhayam śriṇavachcha* (8, 50, 1-2) ; for it is a characteristic of both Sâmans which are sung (on account of its containing the word *ubhayam*, both.)

---

[8] *Janiṣṭâugraḥ* (See above). The Riṣi is supposed to be Gaurivîti.

[9] It begins, *tad vâ etad yajamâna jananam*. See 4, 19 (page 65 of the text).

[10] That is to say, the Hotar repeats as counterpart to the Stotriya of the Niṣkevalya Śastra, which is at this occasion the text of the Bṛihat Sâma, the text of the Rathantaram, which is quite unusual.

[11] This Brâhmaṇam is, *te devâ abruvan sarvaṁ vâ*. See 3, 22 (page 67 of the text).

3.

(*The Nivid Sûkta of the Niṣkevalya Śastra*).

The hymn, *tam ṣu ṭuhi yo abhibhûtyojâ* (6, 18), contains the characteristic *abhi* in the word *abhibhûti*. Its words, *aṣâḷham* (unconquerable), *ugram* (strong), *sahamânam* (being strong), contain characteristics of the Kṣattra also. It consists of fifteen verses; for the number fifteen is strength, sharpness of senses, and power, the Kṣattra is strength, the royal prince, is might (*vîryam*). The hymn thus makes the king successful in strength, royal power and might. It is a hymn of Bharadvâja. The Bṛihat Sâman was seen by Bharadvâja also (and) is in direct relationship with the ancestral fire.[12] The sacrifice of the Kṣattriya which has the Bṛihat for [**500**] (Stotra) becomes successful. Thence, wherever a Kṣattriya brings a sacrifice, there the Bṛihat Pṛiṣṭha is to be employed, for this makes it (the sacrifice) complete.

4.

(*The Śastras of the Minor Hotṛi-priests.*)

The performances of the minor Hotṛi-priests (Maitrâvaruṇa, Brâḥmaṇáchaṁsi, and Achhâvâka) required (at the sacrifice of a Kṣattriya) are those allotted to the Aikâhika sacrifices. For these Aikâhika performances are propitiatory, ready made, and placed on a footing, in order to make the sacrifice successful to accomplish it, and place it on a firm footing whence it cannot fall down. These (performances) contain all the forms (required), and are quite complete. (They are repeated) in order to accomplish the integrity and completeness (of the sacrifice). The Kṣattriyas who perform a sacrifice should think, "Let us obtain all desires by means of the all-perfect and complete performances of the minor Hotṛi-priests." Therefore, wherever the Ekâhas are not complete as to the number of Stomas and Pṛiṣṭhas, there are the Aikâhika perform-

[12] Sây. explains the expression, *ârṣeyena saloma*, in the following manner: *ârṣeyo bharadvâjamunisaṁbandhaḥ, lomaś abdena keśayukto mûrddhopalakṣyate, salomâ saśirskaḥ saṁpûrṇa ity arthaḥ*. The word *loma* means, according to him, "the head with the hair;" and to *salomâ* he attributes the meaning "having a helmet, or turban," that is, "complete." But this explanation is too artificial and far-fetched to meet with the approval of modern philologists. To arrive at the proper meaning of the obsolete term, *saloma*, we have to consult the cognate words, *anuloma* and *pratiloma*, both applied to deterioration of lineage by mixing with lower castes. In reference to these terms, I translated the passage.

ances of the minor Hotṛi-priests required,[13] then it (the sacrifice) becomes completed.

This sacrifice (performed by a Kṣattriya) should be the Ukthya, which has fifteen Stotras and Śastras. [501] Such is the opinion of some. Eor the sharpness of senses is a power (*ojas*), and the number fifteen is strength; (furtner) the Kṣattra is power, and the Kṣattriya is strength. Thus the priest makes him (the Kṣattriya) succeseful by means of power, Kṣattra, (and) strength. This sacrifice requires thirty Stotras and Śastras (*viz.*, fifteen each). For the Virâj consists of thirty syllables. The Virâj is food. When he places him (the sacrificer) in the Virâj, then he places him in food. Therefore the Ukthya, which is fifteen-fold, should be (employed for the king at this occasion). But the Agniṣṭoma, which forms part of the Jyotiṣṭoma, would more properly answer this purpose.[14] For, among the Stomas, the Trivṛit (nine-fold) is the Brahma, and the fifteen-fold Stoma is the Kṣattra. But the Brahma precedes the Kṣattra: (for the king should think) "If the Brahma is placed first, my kingdom will be strong and not to be shaken. The number seventeen represents the Vaiśyas, and twenty-one the Śûdras. If these two Stomas (the seventeen and twenty-one fold) are employed, then they make the Vaiśyas and Śûdras follow him (the king). Among the Stomas, the Trivṛit is splendour, the fifteen-fold is strength, the seventeen-fold is offspring, the twenty-one-fold is the footing. Thus the priest makes the king, who (thus) sacrifices, successful in gaining splendour, strength, offspring, and a firm footing. Therefore the Jyotiṣṭoma (Agniṣṭoma) is required. This requires twenty-four Stotras and Śastras (twelve each). For the year consists of twenty-four half months; in the year there are all (kinds of) nourishment. Thus he places him (the sacrificer) in all (kinds of) nourishment. Thence the Jyotiṣṭoma-Agniṣṭoma alone is required (and not the Ukthya).

---

[13] For the Ekâhas, which are *sarvastoma* and *sarvapṛiṣṭha*, the following six Stomas are required: *trivrit*, *pañchadaśa*, *saptadaśa ekaviṁśa*, *triṇava*, *trayastriṁśa*; and the following Pṛiṣṭhas: *Bṛihat*, *Rathantara*, *Vairûpa*, *Vâirâja*, *Sâkvara*, *Rairata*. In the Kṣattriya sacrifice, there are only the Bṛihat and Rathantara required. In is therefore incomplete; the defects are to be supplied by the minor Hotṛi-priests.

[14] In this sacrifice, there are the four Stomas, subsequently mentioned, required.

[502] SECOND CHAPTER.

(*Punarabhiṣeka, or Repetition of the Inauguration Ceremony.*)

5.

(*The Implements and Preparation for Punarabhiṣeka.*)

Now follows (the rule) of Punarabhiṣeka of the Kṣattriya who is inaugurated as a sacrificer, and whose Kṣattram is in (such a way) new born.[1] After having undergone the ceremonies of ablution[2] and performed the animal sacrifice (*anubandhya*), he performs the concluding Iṣṭi.

After this Iṣṭi is finished (and thus the Soma day of the Râjasûya concluded), they sprinkle him again with the holy water (they make *punarabhiṣeka*). Before it commences, all implements must be in readiness, *viz.*, a throne, made from Udumbara wood, with feet only as large as the span between the thumb and forefinger, and successive helmets of the length of half an arm, (besides there must be provided for) cords for binding made of Muñja grass, a tiger skin for covering the throne, a (large) ladle of Udumbara wood and a (small) branch of the Udumbara tree. In this ladle the following eight substances are thrown: curds, honey, clarified butter, rain-water fallen, during sunshine, young sprouts of grass and of green barley, liquor and Dûb grass (Dûrvâ). The throne is to be placed in the southern line,[3] drawn by a wooden sword (*sphya*) in the Vedi, the front part **[503]** turned eastwards. Two of its feet are to be within the Vedi and two outside. For this earth is (the goddess of) fortune; the little space within the Vedi is thus allotted to her, as well as the large (infinite) region outside. If thus two feet of the throne are inside and two outside the Vedi, both kinds of desires, those obtainable from the place within as well as from outside the Vedi, are to be gained.

6.

(*How the King has to Ascend hi Throne at the Inauguration Ceremony; what Mantras he has to Repeat at this Occasion.*)

He spreads the tiger skin on the throne in such a manner that the hairs come outside, and that part which covered the neck is turned eastward. For the tiger is the Kṣattra (royal power) of the beasts in the forest. The Kṣattra is the royal prince; by means of this Kṣattra, the

[1] The term is *sûyate*, containing an allusion to the name of the sacrifice, *râjasûya*.

[2] This is the so-called *avabhṛitha* ceremony which takes place at the end of the sacrifice before the concluding Iṣṭi.

[3] By means of a wooden sword, three lines are drawn in the Vedi, *viz.*, one towards the south, one towards the west, and one towards the east.

king makes his Kṣattra (royal power) prosper. The king, when taking his seat on the throne, approaches it from behind, turning his face eastwards, kneels down with crossed legs, so that his right knee touches the earth,[4] and (holding the throne with his hands) prays over it the following mantra :—

"May Agni ascend thee, O throne, with the Gâyatrî metre! May Savitar ascend (thee) with the Uṣṇiḥ, Soma with the Anuṣṭubh, Bṛihaspati with the Bṛihat, Mitra and Varuṇa with the Pañkti, Indra with the Tristubh, and the Viśve Devâḥ with the Jagatî metres. After them I ascend this throne, to be ruler, to be a great ruler, to be an universal ruler, to obtain all desires fulfilled, to be an indepen- [504]
dent and most distinguished ruler (on this earth), and to reach the world of Prajâpati, to be there a ruler, a great ruler, a supreme ruler, to be independent, and to live there for a long time!"

After having repeated this mantra, the king should ascend the throne, with his right knee first, and then with his left. This, this is done; so they say.

The gods joined with the metres, which were placed in such an order that the following exceeded the preceding one always by four syllables,[5] ascended this (throne,) which is fortune, and posted themselves on it, Agni with the Gâyatrî, Savitar with the Uṣṇih, Soma with the Anuṣṭubh, Bṛihaspati with the Bṛihati, Mitra and Varuna with the Pañkti, Indra with the Triṣṭubh, the Viśvedevâḥ with the Jagatî. The two verses (where the joining of the gods to their metres is mentioned) commencing, *Agner Gâyatrî abhavat* (10, 130, 4-5) are then recited.

The Kṣattriya, who, after these deities (after having previously invoked them in this manner) ascends his throne, obtains for himself the power not only of acquiring anything, but of keeping what he has acquired;[6] his prosperity increases from day to day, and he will rule supreme over all his subjects.

---

[4] This particular posture is called *jânvachya*. The Hotar, principally, must on many occasions take it; it is very awkward and troublesome; I could not imitate it well, though I tried.

[5] Gâyatrî with 24 syllables comes first; $24 + 4 = 28$ is Uṣṇih; $28+4=32$ is Anuṣṭubh; $32+4=36$ is Bṛihati; $36+4=40$ is Pañkti; $40+4=44$ is Triṣṭubh; $44+4=48$ is Jagatî.

[6] This is the translation of the word, *Yoga-kṣema*.

When the priest is about to sprinkle him (with water) then he makes the king invoke the waters for their blessing (by these words): "Look upon me, ye waters, with a favourable eye! touch my skin with your happy body! I invoke all the fires which reside in the waters to bestow on me splendour, strength, and vigour." For the waters, if not invoked for a blessing (by a mantra), take away the strength from **[505]** a Kṣattriya who is already consecrated; but not (if they have been duly invoked).

7.

(The Inauguration Mantra when the King is Sprinkled with the Holy Water. Whether the Sacred Words, "bhûr," &c., are to be Pronounced along with this Mantra or not. Different Opinions on this Point.)

They now put the branch of the Udumbara tree on the head of the Kṣattriya, and pour the liquids (which are in the large ladle) on it. (When doing so), the priest repeats the following mantras: "With these waters, which are most happy, which cure everything, increase the royal power, and hold up the royal power, the immortal Prajâpati sprinkled Indra, Soma the king, Varuna, Yama, Manu; with the same, sprinkle I thee! Be the ruler over kings in this world. Thy illustrious mother bore thee as the great universal ruler over great men; the blessed mother has borne thee! By command of the divine Savitar I sprinkle [7] (thee) with the arms of the Aśvins, with the hands of Pûṣan, with the lustre of Agni, the splendour of Sûrya, the power of Indra, that thou mayest obtain strength, happiness, fame, and food."

If the priest, who sprinkles the king, wishes him alone to enjoy good health,[8] then he shall pronounce (when sprinkling) the sacred word, *bhûr*. If he wishes that two men (son and grandson) should enjoy this benefit together with him, then he shall pronounce the two sacred words, *bhûr, bhuvaḥ*. If he wishes to benefit in this way three men (son, grandson, and great grandson), or to make (the king) un-**[506]** rivalled, then he ought to pronounce the three sacred words, *bhûr, bhuvaḥ, svar*.

---

[7] The arms of the Aśvins, &c., are here regarded as the instruments by which the ceremony is performed in a mystical way on the king.

[8] Lit., that he may eat food.

Some say, These sacred words having the power of bringing every thing within grasp, the Kṣattriya who has the mantra recited with the addition of these sacred words,[9] provides for another (not for himself); therefore, one should sprinkle him only under the recital of the mantra, "By command of the divine Savitar," &c. They, again, are of opinion that the Kṣattriya, when sprinkled, not under the recital of the whole mantra (*i.e.*, with omission of the sacred words), has power only over his former life.

Satyakâma, the son of *Jabalâ*, said, "If they do not sprinkle him under the recital of these sacred words (in addition to the mantra), then he is able to go through his whole life (as much as is apportioned to him)." But *Uddâlaka Aruṇiḥ* said, "He who is sprinkled under the recital of these sacred words obtains everything by conquest."

He (the priest) should sprinkle him under the recital of the whole mantra, "By the command of the divine Savitar," &c., and conclude by *bhûr*, *bhuvaḥ*, *svar*!

The Kṣattriya who has thus performed a sacrifice loses (in consequence of his sacrifice) all these things (which were in him), *viz.*, the Brahma which was placed in the Kṣattra, the sap, nourishment, the essence of water and herbs, the character of holiness (*brahmavarchasam*), the thriving consequent on food, the begetting of children, and the peculiar form of the Kṣattra (all that it comprises). And as further regards the sap for (producing) nourishing substances, the Kṣattra is the protection of the herbs (the fields of grain, &c., being protected by the Kṣattriyas, these things must be kept). If he therefore brings those two invocation offerings before the inaugur-**[507]** ation ceremony,[10] then he places the Brahma in this Kṣattra (and all those things will be consequently kept).

8.

(*The Symbolical Meaning of the Different Implements and Liquids required for the Inauguration Ceremony. The Drinking of Spirituous Liquor (surâ) by the King.*)

The reason that the throne-seat, the ladle, and the branch is of the Udumbara tree is because the Udumbara is vigour and a nourishing

Atisarveṇa, *i.e.*, by what is beyond the whole mantra, that is, the sacred words, *bhûr*, &c., which are added to it.

[10] See above 7, 22, one to the Brahma, the other to the Kṣattra: "I enter the Brahma," &c.

substance. The priest thus places vigour in him (the Kings) as his nourishing substance.

As to curds, honey, and melted butter, they represent the liquid (essence) in the waters and herbs. The priest, therefore, places the essence of the waters and the herbs in him.

The rain water fallen during sunshine, represents the splendour and lustre of sanctity, which are in this way placed in him.

The young grass and young barley represent provisions and the thriving by their means, which are thus placed in him for (producing) offspring, and consequently (provide him with) offspring.

The spirituous liquor represents the Kṣattra, and, further, the juice in the food; thus both the Kṣattra and the juice in the food, are placed in him.

The Dûrvâ grass is Kṣattra; for this is the ruler of the herbs. The Kṣattra, *viz.*, the princely race, is represented by it, as it were, spread everywhere; the Kṣattriya becomes residing here (on this earth), in his kingdom, he becomes established, as it were, his rule extended, as it were. This is represented by the sprouts of the Dûrvâ, which have, [508] as it were, a firm footing on the earth. In this way, the Kṣattra of the herbs is placed in him (the king) and a firm footing thus given him.

All those things (the Brahma, sap, &c.), which had gone from the king after having performed a sacrifice, are in this way placed in him (again). By their (of curds, honey, &c.) means he makes him thus successful.

Now he gives into his hand a goblet of spirituous liquor, under the recital of the verse, *svâdiṣṭhayâ madiṣṭhayâ*, &c. (9, 1, 1) *i.e.*, "Purify, O Soma! with thy sweetest, most exhilarating drops (the sacrificer), thou who art squeezed for Indra, to be drunk by him."[11] After having put the spirituous liquor into his hand, the priest repeats a propitiatory mantra[12] (which runs thus): "To either of you (spirituous liquor and Soma!) a separate residence has been prepared, and allotted by the gods. Do not mix with one another in the highest heaven; liquor! thou art powerful; Soma! thou art a king. Do not harm him (the king)! May either go to his own place." (Here is said), that the drinking of the Soma and that of liquor, exclude one another (they are not to be mixed).

---

[11] This interpretation is given by Sâyaṇa, which, no doubt, is suitable to the occasion at which this mantra is used; and thus it certainly was interpreted even in ancient times. However, it does not appear to be the original meaning of the verse.

[12] It is with some variations to be found in the Vâjasaneyi Saṁhitâ (19, 7).

After having drunk it, he should think, "the giver (the priest) of the goblet (to be his friend) and give him (the remainder of) this (liquor)." This is the characteristic of a friend. Thus he finally places the liquor in his friend (gives him a share in it). And thus has he who possesses such a knowledge, a place in his friend (they are mutually connected).

9.

[**509**] (*The Descent of the King from the Throne, after having been Inaugurated. The Mantras which he has to Repeat at this Occasion.*)

He now descends (from the throne-seat), facing the branch of the Udumbara tree (which was placed in the ground). The Udumbara being sap, and consequently a nourishing substance, the king goes thus (to receive) these gifts (hidden in the Udumbara tree). Being seated above, and having put both his feet on the ground, he announces his descent (facing the Udumbara), (by uttering the following words:) "I stand in the heavens, and on the earth; I stand in the air exhaled and inhaled; I stand on day and night; I stand on food and drink; I stand on Brahma, Kṣattra, and these three worlds." Finally, he stands firmly through the universal soul (*sarva-âtmâ*, which connects all the things just mentioned), and thence has a firm footing in the universe. He obtains continuous prosperity. The king who descends, after having been inaugurated by the ceremony of Punarabhiṣeka in this way (from the throne-seat), obtains supremacy over his subjects, and royal power.

After having descended,[13] he then stands, inclining his body (*upastham kṛitvâ*) with his face towards the east, and utters thrice the words, "Adoration to the Brahma!" Then he says aloud, "I present a gift for the attainment of victory (in general), of victory everywhere (*abhijiti*), of victory over strong and weak enemies (*vijiti*), and of complete victory (*saṁjiti*)." [**510**] By thus making thrice salutation to the Brahma, the Kṣattra comes under the sway of the Brahma, and consequently the rule of the king becomes prosperous, and he will have issue. As regards (the mantra), "I present a gift for the attainment of victory," &c., he emits Speech by it. For the words, "I give," imply that Speech is conquered, (recovered, after having been silent).

"When Speech is recovered, then (consequently) all this my per formance shall be completed," having (so thinking) emitted Speech, he approaches the Ahavanîya fire, and puts a stick into it, reciting, "Thou

[13] *Pratyavarûhya*, instead of *ruhya*; long *û*, instead of short *u*, being a Vedic form.

art a wooden stick, become joined to the sharpness of senses and strength of the body, Svâhâ!" Finally, he succeeds thus in making himself sharpness of senses and valiant. After having put the stick into the fire, he walks three steps towards the east and north, (and addresses the step he is taking thus): "Thou art the means of subduing the regions; ye (steps), make me capable of adoring (in the right manner) the gods; may I obtain my desires wished for and preserve what is granted to me, and safety." He now proceeds to the north-east, that is, to undo again a defeat. Such is the meaning (they say).

10.

(Magical Performance of a King for Defeating an Enemy.)

The Devas and Asuras were fighting in these worlds. They fought in the eastern direction, then the Asuras defeated them. They then fought in the southern direction, and the Asuras defeated them again; and, likewise, they were defeated by the Asuras when fighting in the western and northern directions. They were then fighting between the eastern and northern directions, and remained victors. The **[511]** Kṣattriya, therefore, standing amidst both armies arrayed in battle lines, shall proceed to the northeast, saying to him (to the house-priest), "do so [14] that I may conquer this army." After he (the house-priest) has consented, he should touch the upper part of the king's chariot and repeat the mantra, *vanaspate vîḍvângo hi* (6, 47, 26). Then he shall say to (the king), "Turn towards this (north-east) direction; thy chariot with all its implements should be turned thither (north-east); then to the north-west, south and east, and (lastly) towards the enemy." With the hymn, *abhivartena haviṣâ* (10, 174) shall he turn his chariot, and when reciting the *Apratiratha* (10, 103 *âśuh śiśâno) Śâsâ* (1, 152 *śâsa itthâ*), and *Sauparṇa* (*pra dhârâ yantu madhuna*) hymns, he shall look upon it (the chariot).

The Kṣattriya conquers (the hostile) army, when he, at the time of just being about fighting (with the enemy), takes thus his refuge (with the house-priest), saying, "Make me win this battle." He then shall let

[14] Sây. refers this address to the king who is sitting in his chariot. A Kṣattriya is speaking these words. He asks first the king's permission to perform the ceremony mentioned. The person to whom the Kṣattriya addresses his words, is only hinted at by the demonstrative pronoun, but never explicitly mentioned. I think it refers to the Purohita or house-priest, who has always to accompany the king when going to fight a battle, and give him his advice. Sâyaṇa's opinion is hardly correct,

him fight in the north-eastern direction, and he (the Kṣattriya) wins the battle. If he be turned out of his dominions, and thus takes his refuge with him (the house-priest), saying, "Make me return to my dominions," then he (the house-priest) shall let him, when going away, proceed to this (north-eastern) direction, (and) thus he recovers his dominions.

(The king, whose inauguration ceremony is performed) after having been standing (in northeastern direction) recites then, when going **[512]** to his palace, (the verse) calculated to drive away all enemies altogether. (This verse is), *apa prâcha* (10, 131 1.) Then he will be made rid of all his enemies and live in safety, and enjoy happiness increasing from day to day. He who returns to his palace whilst reciting the above-mentioned mantra (10, 131, 1) obtains sovereignty over his subjects, and supreme power. After having come home, he sits behind the household fire. His priest then, after having touched him, fills a goblet four times with melted butter, and makes thus three (each consisting of four spoonfuls) offerings addressed to Indra, the mantras being recited in the Prapada [15] form, in order that he might be protected from disease, injury from any loss, and enjoy perfect safety.

11.

(*The Repetition of Three Mantras, with Insertion of a certain Formula. Its Effect. Janmejaya's Opinion on the Effect of this Magical Performance.*)

(The verses to be recited in the Prapada way follow) *Paryû ṣu pradhanva* (9, 110, 1), *i.e.*, acquire everywhere riches, in order to grant them (to thy worshipper). In the midst of the word, *vṛitrâṇi* (of the just mentioned mantra), after *â*, and before *ṇi*, he inserts the words, "*bhûr, brahma, prâṇam* (breath), *amṛitam* (ambrosia) is such one (the name is required) **[513]** who seeks for shelter and safety, for welfare with his children and cattle." (Now follows the remaining part of the verse), *ṇi sakṣaṇir,*

---

[15] Sây. adduces for explaining this term a memorial verse (*kârikâ*) :

Pâdâ yasyâṁstu yâvanto yâvanâ akṣarasaṁmitaḥ,

Richy adayayanam eteṣâm prapadam tad vidur budhâḥ,

i. e., the wise call that recital of the (several) pâdas of a Rik verse *prapada*, when they all are measured by the syllables of which they consist. This means that each syllable of the pâda is to be pronounced quite distinctly, and that there should be a stop at the end of each pâda. This explanation appears, however, not to be quite correct. From the following paragraph, we learn that *prapada* is the insertion of a formula in a pâda of a verse.

&c. *i.e.*, being a conqueror of enemies, thou makest efforts of crossing the lines of our adversaries.

(Now follows the second verse), *Anu hi tvâ sutam*, &c. (9, 110, 2). In the midst of the word, *samarya*, in the second pâda, after the syllable "*ma*," the words, *bhuvo*, *brahma*, &c. (the remainder just as above) are inserted.

(Now follows the third verse), *ajîjano hi pavamâno*, &c. (9, 110, 3). In the midst of the word, *śakmanâ*, after *sa* and before *ma*, he inserts the words, *svar*, *brahma*, &c. (just as above). After the last word of the interpolation, *viz.*, "*paśubhir*," he then proceeds to finish the verse recommencing by *kmanâ*.

The Kṣattriya, for whose benefit the house-priest sacrifices three offerings of melted butter, each consisting of four spoonfuls, whilst reciting these Indra verses in the above-mentioned Prapada way, thus becomes free of disease, free of enemies, does not suffer any loss, and, screened by the form of the three-fold science (the three Vedas), walks in all directions, and becomes established (after his death) in Indra's world.

Finally, he prays for increase in cows, horses, and progeny, with the words, "Cows, may ye be born here! horses, may ye be born here! men, may ye be born here! may here sit a hero (my son), as protector (of the country), who presents the priests gifts, consisting of a thousand (cows)." He who thus prays, will be blessed with plenty of children and cattle.

The Kṣattriya, whom those (priests) who have this knowledge make sacrifice in such a way, will be raised to an exalted position. But those who make the king sacrifice in this way, without possessing this knowledge, they kill him, drag him away, and deprive **[514]** him of his property, as the most degraded of men (*niṣâdas*), robbers, murderers, seize a wealthy man (when travelling) in a forest, and, after having thrown him into a ditch, run away with his property.

Janamejaya, the son of *Parikṣit*, who possessed this knowledge, said, "My priests, who possess this knowledge, made me sacrifice, I who have the same knowledge (in such a manner). Therefore I am victorious; I conquer a hostile army eager for fighting;[16] neither the divine nor the human arrows coming from such an army can reach me. I shall attain the full age allotted to man (100 years), I shall become master of the whole earth. The same falls to the lot of him, who knowing this, is made to sacrifice (by priests) in this way.

[16] In the original, *abhîtvarî*. Sây. *abhito yuddhârtha-mudayuktâ parakiyâ senâ*

THIRD CHAPTER.

(The Mahâbhiseka or Grand Inauguration Ceremony of Indra.)

12.

(The Elevation of Indra to the Royalty over the Gods. His Throne-seat. By what Mantras he Ascended it. The Gods Proclaim him as King by mentioning all his Titles.)

Now follows the great inauguration (*mahâbhiṣeka*) of Indra. The gods, headed by Prajâpati, said to one another (pointing with their hands to Indra) : "This one is among the gods the most vigorous, most strong, most valiant, most perfect, who carries best out any work (to be done). Let us instal him (to the kingship over us)." They all consented to **[515]** perform just this ceremony (*mahâbhiṣeka*) on Indra. They brought for him that throne-seat, which is called the Rik-formed.[1] They made the Bṛihat and Rathantara verses its two forelegs, the Vairûpa and Vairâja verses its hind-legs, the Śâkvara and Raivata (verses) its top-boards, the Nâudhasa and Kâleya its side-boards. The Rik verses were made the threads of the texture which went lengthwise, the Sâmans were the threads which went crossways, the Yajus verses the intervals in the texture. They made (the goddess of) Glory its covering, and (the goddess of) Fortune its pillow, Savitar and Bṛihaspati were holding its two fore-legs, Vâyu and Pûṣan the two hind-legs, Mitra and Varuṇa the two top-boards, the Aśvins the two side-boards.

Indra then ascended the throne-seat, addressing it thus: "May the Vasus ascend thee with the Gâyatrî metre, with the Trivṛit Stoma, with the Rathantara Sâma. After them I then ascend for obtaining universal sovereignty. May the Rudras ascend thee with the Triṣṭubh metre, the fifteen-fold Stoma, and the Bṛihat Sâma. After them then I ascend for obtaining increase of enjoyment. May the Adityas ascend thee with the Jagatî metre, the seventeen-fold Stoma, and the Vairûpa Sâma. After them I ascend for obtaining independent rule. May the Viśve Devâḥ ascend thee with the Anuṣṭubh metre, the twenty-one-fold Stoma, and the Vairâja Sâma. After them I ascend for obtaining distinguished rule. May the divine *Sâdhyâs* and *Aptyas* ascend thee with the Paṅkti metre, the Tṛinava (twenty-seven-fold) Stoma, and the Śâkvara Sâma. After them I ascend for obtaining royal power. May the divine Marutas and

[1] It was composed of all the sacred mantras of the Rigveda. On the different Sâmans mentioned here, see the notes on page 282.

Aṅgiras ascend thee with the Atichandas metre, the thirty-three-fold Stoma, and the Raivata Sâma. After **[516]** them, then, I ascend for obtaining the fulfilment of the highest desires for becoming a great king, for supreme mastership, independence, and a long residence. By these words, one should ascend the throne-seat.

After Indra had seated himself on this throne-seat, the Viśve Devâḥ said to him, "Indra cannot achieve any feat if he is not everywhere publicly proclaimed [2] (as hero); but if he be thus proclaimed, he can do so." They then consented to do so, and consequently, turning towards Indra, cried aloud (calling him by all his titles.)

The gods bestowed on him (Indra), by proclaiming him as "universal ruler," universal rule; by proclaiming him as "enjoyer (of pleasures)," they made him father (of pleasures); by proclaiming him as "independent ruler," they granted him independence of rule; by proclaiming him as "distinguished king," they conferred on him royal distinction; by proclaiming him "king," they made him father of kings; by calling him "one who has attained the highest desires," they granted him fulfilment of the highest desires.

(The gods then continued proclaiming his heroic virtues in the following manner): "The Kṣattra is born; the Kṣattriya is born; the supreme master of the whole creation is born; the devourer of the (hostile) tribes is born; the destroyer of the hostile castles is born; the slayer of the Asuras is born; the protector of the Brahma is born; the protector of the religion is born."

After (his royal dignity) was thus proclaimed, Prajâpati, when being just about performing the inauguration ceremony, recited over him (consecrated him with) the following mantra:

13.

[517] (*The Mantras by which Indra was Consecrated. He was Installed by **Prajâpati**.*)

"Varuṇa, the faithful, sat down in his premises—for obtaining universal rule, enjoyment (of pleasures), independence, distinction as sovereign, fulfilment of the highest desires—he, the wise, &c.," (1, 25, 10). Prajâpati, standing in front of Indra who was sitting on the throne-seat, turned his face to the west, and, after having put on his head a gold leaf, sprinkled him with the moist branch of an Udumbara, together with that of a Palâśa tree, reciting the three Rik verses, *imâ âpaḥ śivatamâ*,

---

[2] The term is *anabhyutkruṣṭa*.

i.e., these most happy waters, &c. (Ait. Br. 8, 7); and the Yajus verse, *devasya tvâ* (Vâjasan. Saṁh. 1, 10. Ait Br. 8, 1); and the great words, *bhûr, bhuvaḥ, svar.*

14.

Indra Inaugurated by Various Deities in the Various Directions to the Kingship, becomes Universal Ruler.

The Vasavas then inaugurated him (Indra) in the eastern direction, during thirty-one days, by these three Rik verses, the Yajus verse, and the great words (all just mentioned), for the sake of obtaining universal sovereignty. Hence all kings of eastern nations, in the eastern regions, are inaugurated to universal sovereignty, and called *samrâj*, *i.e.*, universal sovereign, after this precedent made once by the gods.

Then the Rudras inaugurated Indra in the southern region, during thirty-one days, with the three Rik verses, the Yajus and the great words (just mentioned), for obtaining enjoyment (of pleasures). Hence all kings of living creatures (chiefly beasts) in the southern region are inaugurated for the enjoyment (of pleasures) and called *bhoja*, *i.e.*, enjoyer.

[518] Then the divine Adityas inaugurated him in the western region, during thirty-one days, with those three Rik verses, that Yajus verse, and those great words, for obtaining independent rule. Hence all kings of the *Nîchyas* and *Apâchyas* in the western countries, are inaugurated to independent rule, and called "independent rulers."

Then the Viśve Devâḥ inaugurated him during thirty-one days, in the northern region, by those three Rik verses, &c. for distinguished rule. Hence all people living in northern countries beyond the Himalaya, such as the *Uttarakurûs*, *Uttaramadras*, are inaugurated for living without a king (*vairâjyam*), and called Virâj,[3] *i.e.* without king.

Then the divine Sâdhyas and Aptyas inaugurated Indra, during thirty-one days, in the middle region, which is a firmly established footing (the immovable centre) to the kingship (*râjya*). Hence the kings of the *Kurûpañchâlas*, with the *Vaśas* and *Uśînaras*, are inaugurated to kingship, and called Kings (*râjâ*).

---

[3] To this word two meanings can be given: 1 (without king;) 2 a very distinguished king. In this passage, we must take it in the first meaning; for here are *janapadâḥ*, *i. e*, people in opposition to the king mentioned, as *abhiṣikta*, *i.e.*, inaugurated, whilst in all other passages of this chapter, we find instead of them, the *râjânaḥ* or kings.

Then the divine Marutas and Angiras inaugurated him, during thirty-one days, in the upper (*ûrdhva*) region, for attaining fulfilment of the highest wishes, the position of a great king, of a supreme ruler, of an independant king, and long duration of his rule.

Indra thus became, by means of this great inauguration ceremony, possessed of the power of obtaining anything wished for, as had been only the prerogative of Prajâpati.[4] He conquered in all the various ways **[519]** of possible conquest, [5] and won all people. He obtained the leadership, precedence, and supremacy over all gods. After having conquered the position of a *samrâj* (universal ruler), &c., he became in this world self-existing (*svayambhûḥ*), an independent ruler, immortal,[6] and, in the heaven-world, after having attained all desires wished for, he became immortal (also).

FOURTH CHAPTER.

(The Mahâbhiṣeka Ceremony Performed on a King. What Riṣis Performed it, and for what Kings they Performed it.)

15.

(The Consequences of the Mahâbhiṣeka. The Oath which the King must take Before the Priest Performs the Ceremony.)

The priest who, with this knowledge (about the Mahâbhiṣeka ceremony), wishes that a Kṣattriya should conquer in all the various ways of conquest, to subjugate all people, and that he should attain to leadership, precedence, and supremacy over all kings, and attain everywhere and at all times to universal sovereignty, enjoyment (of pleasures), independence, distinguished distinction as king, the fulfilment of the highest desires, the position of a king, of a great king, and supreme mastership, that he might cross (with his arms) the universe, and become the ruler of the whole earth during all his life, which may last for an infinitely long time, that he might be the sole king of the earth up to its **[520]** shores bordering on the ocean ; such a priest should inaugurate the Kṣattriya with Indra's great inauguration ceremony. But, before doing so, the priest must make the king take the following oath : " What-

---

[4] This whole sentence is only a translation of the full import implied in the words, *parameṣṭi prâjâpatya.*

[5] Lit., he conquered all the conquests (*jitis, i.e., abhijiti, vijiti, saṁjiti,* &c. See above.)

[6] Here Sâyaṇa explains it as " long-lived,"

ever pious works thou mightest have done during the time which may elapse from the day[1] of thy birth to the day of thy death, all these, together with the position, thy good deeds, thy life, thy children, I would wrest from thee, shouldest thou do me any harm."

The Kṣattriya, then, who wishes to attain to all this, should well consider and say in good faith all that is above-mentioned (thou mayest wrest from me, &c., &c.)

16.

(*The Woods and Grains Required for the Performance of Mahâbhiṣeka.*)

The priest then shall say (to his attendants), "Bring four kinds of wood: Nyagrodha, Udumbara, Aśvattha, and Plakṣa." Among the trees, the Nyagrodha is the Kṣattra. Thus by bringing Nyagrodha wood, he places in the king the Kṣattram, the Udumbara representing the enjoyment, the Aśvattha universal sovereignty, the Plakṣa independence and freedom of the rule of another king. The priest, by having these woods brought to the spot, thus makes the king participate in all these qualities (universal sovereignty, &c., &c.). Next he shall order to bring four kinds of grain from vegetables (*auṣadha tokmakṛita*), *viz.*, rice with small grains, rice with large grains, Priyaṅgu, and barley. For, amongst herbs, rice with small grains represents the Kṣattra. Thus, by bringing sprouts of such grains, he **[521]** places the Kṣattra in him. Rice with large grains represents universal sovereignty. Therefore, by bringing sprouts of such grains (to the spot), he places universal sovereignty in him. The Priyaṅgus, among herbs, represent enjoyment of pleasures, By bringing their sprouts, he places the enjoyment of pleasures in him. Barley represents the skill as military commander. By bringing their sprouts, he places such a skill in him (the king).

17.

(*The Implements for Making Mahâbhiṣeka.*)

Now they bring for him a throne-seat made of Udumbara wood, of which the Brâhmaṇam has been already told (see 8, 8). The ladle of Udumbara wood is here optional; instead of it, a vessel of the same wood (*pâtrî*) may be taken. Besides, they bring an Udumbara branch. Then they mix those four kinds of fruit and grain in a vessel, and, after having poured over them curds, honey, clarified butter, and rain-water fallen

[1] In the original, *râtrî*, night. The day commenced at evening, as it appears.

during sunshine, put it down. He (the priest) should then consecrate the throne-seat in the following way : " thy two forelegs are the Bṛihat and Rathantaram Sâmans, &c. (just as above, see 8, 12).

18=13, and 19=14.

20.

(*The Meaning and Effect of the Various Liquids Poured over the Head of the King. His Drinking of Spirituous Liquor. He drinks the Soma Mystically.*)

By sprinkling the king with curds, the priest makes his senses sharp ; for curds represent sharpness of senses in this world. By sprinkling him with honey, the priest makes him vigourous ; for honey is the vigour in herbs and trees. By sprinkling him with clarified butter, he bestows upon him splendour ; for **[522]** clarified butter is the brightness of cattle. By sprinkling him with water, he makes him free from death (immortal) ; for waters represent in this world the drinking of immortality (*amṛita*).

The king who is thus inagurated, should present to the Brahman who has inaugurated him gold, a thousand cows, and a field in form of a quadrangle. They say, however, that the amount of the reward is not limited and restricted to this (it may be much higher), for the Kṣattriya (*i.e.*, his power) has no limits, and to obtain unlimited (power, the reward should, as to its greatness, be unlimited also).

Then the priest gives into his hands a goblet filled with spirituous liquor, repeating the mantra, *svâdiṣṭhayâ*, &c. (see 8, 8). He then should drink the remainder (after previuos libation to the gods), when repeating the following two mantras : " Of what juicy, well-prepared beverage[2] Indra drank with his associates, just the same, *viz.*, the king Soma, I drink here, with my mind being devoted to him (Soma)." The second mantra (Rigveda, 8, 45, 22), " To thee who growest like a bullock (Indra), by drinking Soma, I send off (the Soma juice), which was squeezed, to drink it ; may it satiate thee and make thee well drunk."

The Soma beverage which is (in a mystical way) contained in the spirituous liquor, is thus drunk by the king, who is inaugurated by means of Indra's geat inauguration ceremony (the ceremony just described), and not the spirituous liquor.[3] (After having drunk this mystical Soma) he should

[2] The spirituous liquor is here a substitute for the Soma, which the Kṣattriyas were not allowed to drink.

[3] By means of mantras, the liquor was transformed into real Soma. We have here a sample of a supposed miraculous transformation of one matter into another.

repeat the [**523**] following mantras, *apâma Somam* (8, 48, 3), *i.e.*, we have drunk, Soma, and *śan no bhava* (10, 37, 10), *i.e.*, Be it propitious to us !

The drinking of spirituous liquor, or Soma, or the enjoyment of some other exquisite food, affects the body of the Kṣattriya who is inaugurated by means of Indra's great inauguration ceremony, just as pleasantly and agreeably till it falls down (on account of drunkenness), as the son feels such an excess of joy when embracing his father, or the wife when embracing her husband, as to lose all self-command.

21.

(*What Kings had the Mahâbhiṣeka Ceremony Performed ; their Conquest of the Whole Earth, and the Horse Sacrifices. Stanzas on Janamejaya, Viśvakarmâ and Marutta.*)

Tura, the son of *Kavaṣa*, inaugurated with this great inauguration ceremony of Indra, *Janamejaya*, the son of *Parikṣit*. Thence Janamejaya went everywhere conquering the earth, up to its ends, and sacrificed the sacrificial horse. To this fact refers the following Gâthâ (stanza), which is sung : " In the land where the throne-seat was erected, Janamejaya bound a horse, which was eating grain, adorned with a mark on its forehead (*rukmin*), and with yellow flower garlands, which was walking over the best (fields full of fodder), for the gods."

With this ceremony, *Śârayâta*, the son of *Manu*, was inaugurated by *Chyavana*, the son of *Bhṛigu*. Thence Śâryâta went conquering all over the earth, and sacrificed the sacrificial horse, and was even, at the sacrificial session held by the gods, the house-father.

With this ceremony, *Samaśuṣmâ*, the son of *Vâjaratna*, inaugurated *Śatânîka*, the son *Satrajît*. [**524**] Thence Śatânîka went conquering everywhere over the whole earth, up to its ends, and sacrificed the sacrificial horse.

With this ceremony, *Parvata* and *Nârada* inaugurated *Ambaṣṭya*. Thence Ambaṣṭya went conquering everywhere over the whole earth, up to its ends, and sacrificed the sacrificial horse.

With this ceremony *Parvata* and *Nârada* inaugurated *Yudhâṁśrauṣṭi*, the son of *Ugrasena*. Thence Yudhâṁśrauṣṭi went conquering everywhere over the whole earth, up to its ends, and sacrificed the sacrificial horse.

With this inauguration ceremony, *Kaśyapa* inaugurated *Viśvakarmâ*, the son of *Bhuvana*. Thence Viśvakarmâ went conquering everywhere over the whole earth, up to its ends, and sacrificed the sacrificial horse.

They say that the earth sang to Viśvakarmâ the following stanza: "No mortal is allowed to give me away (as donation),[4] O Viśvakarmâ, thou hast given me, (therefore) I shall plunge into the midst of the sea. In vain was thy promise made to Kaśyapa."

With this ceremony *Vasiṣtha* inaugurated *Sudâs*, the son of *Pijavana*. Thence Sudâs went conquering everywhere over the whole earth, up to its ends, and sacrificed the sacrificial horse.

With this inauguration ceremony *Saṁvarta*, the son of *Aṅgiras*, inaugurated *Marutta*, the son of *Avikshit*. Thence Marutta went conquering everywhere over the whole earth, up to its ends, and sacrificed the sacrificial horse.

Regarding this event, there is the following Stotra chanted: "The Maruts resided as distributors of [**525**] food in the house of Marutta, the son of Avikṣit, who had fulfilled all his desires; all the gods were present at the gathering."

22.

(*Continuation of the Preceding. Stanzas on the Liberality of Aṅga, Udamaya, and Virochana.*)

With this ceremony, *Udamaya*, the son of *Atri*, inaugurated *Aṅga*. Thence Aṅga went conquering everywhere over the whole earth, up to its ends, and sacrificed the sacrificial horse. This Aṅga, who was not defective in any respect (thence called *alopâṅga*), had once said, "I give thee, O Brahman, ten thousand elephants, and ten thousand slave girls, if you call me to this (thy) sacrifice."[5] Regarding them, the following (five) stanzas (*ślokas*) were sung:—

(1) "Whatever cows the sons of Priyamedhas had ordered (Udamaya to give (in the midst of the sacrifice at the midday libation), the Atri son (Udamaya) at each time presented two thousand Badvas.

(2) "The son of *Virochana* loosened eighty-eight thousand white horses from their strings, and presented those, which were fit for drawing a carriage, to the sacrificing Purohita."[7]

(3) "The son of Atri presented ten thousand girls, well endowed with ornaments on their necks, who had been gathered from all quarters."

---

[4] The king had promised the whole earth as gift to his officiating priest.

[5] Udamaya, the son of Atri, was at this time himself the sacrificer. The Priyamedhas were his officiating priests.

[6] A *Badva* is, according to Sâyaṇa, 100 kotis, *i.e.*, a billion. But I doubt very much whether this is the original meaning of *badva*. It is perhaps related to the Zend *baévare*, which means "ten thousand."

[7] This Śloka does not refer to king Aṅga.

(4) The son of Atri, having given ten thousand elephants in the country *Avachatnuka*, the Brahman [**526**] (Atri's son) being tired, desired his servants (to take charge) of Aṅga's gift."

(5) "(From saying) I give thee a hundred (only), I give thee a hundred, he got tired; (thence) he said, I give thee a thousand, and stopped often in order to breathe, for there were too many thousands to be given."

23.

(*Continuation. Stanzas on the Liberality of Bharata. Story of Satyahavya, who was Created out of his Reward by the King Atyarâti.*)

With this ceremony, *Dîrghatamas*, the son of an unmarried woman, inaugurated *Bharata*, the son of *Duṣyanta*. Thence Bharata went conquering everywhere over the whole earth, up to its ends, and sacrificed those horses which were fit for being sacrificed. Regarding this event, the following stanzas are sung:

(1) Bharata presented one hundred and seven Badvas (large flocks) of elephants,[8] of a dark complexion, with white teeth, all decked with gold, in the country *Maṣṇâra*.

(2) At the time when Bharata, the son of Duṣyanta constructed a sacred hearth in (the country of) *Sâchiguna*, the Brahmans got distributed flocks of cows by thousands.

(3) Bharata, the son of Duṣyanta, bound seventy-eight horses (for being sacrificed) on the banks of the Yamuná, and fifty-five on the Gangâ for Indra.[9]

(4) The son Duṣyanta, after having bound (for sacrificing) one hundred and thirty-three horses [**527**], overcame the stratagems of his royal enemy, by means of the superiority of his own stratagems.

(5) The great work achieved by Bharata, neither the forefathers achieved it, nor will future generations achieve it, (for it is as impossible to do it) as any mortal, belonging to the five divisions of mankind, [10] can touch with his hands the sky.

---

[8] *Mṛiga* in Sanscrit. Sây. says, that elephants are to be understood here. *Mṛiga* appears to be a general term for a wild beast.

[9] *Vṛitraghne*, Sây. takes it, however, as name of a country, for which I see, however, no reason.

[10] *Pañcha mânavâḥ*. Sây. explains the four castes, with the Niṣâdas as the fifth. But I am rather inclined to take the word in the sense of *pañchakṛiṣṭi*, or *pañchakṣiti*, *i. e.*, five tribes frequently mentioned in the Saṁahitâ. It then denotes the whole human race, including the superior beings. See page 214.

The Riṣi *Brihad Uktha* communicated this great inauguration ceremony to *Durmukha*, the Pañchâla. Thence Durmukha, who was no king, being possessed of this knowledge, went conquering everywhere over the whole earth, up to its ends, and sacrificed the sacrificial horse.

The son of *Satyahavya*, of the *Vasiṣṭha* Gotra, communicated this ceremony to *Atyarâti*, the son of *Janantapaya*. Thence Atyarâti, who was no king, being possessed of such a knowledge, went conquering everywhere over the whole earth, up to its end, and sacrificed the sacrificial horse.

The son of Satyahavya, of the Vasiṣṭha Gotra, then told (the king), "Thou hast (now) conquered the whole earth up to the shore of the sea; let me obtain now greatness (as reward for my services)." Atyarâti answered, "When, O Brahmana, I shall have conquered the Uttara Kurus,[11] then thou shalt be king of the earth, and I will be thy general." The son of Satyahavya said, "This is the land of the gods, no mortal can conquer it. Thou hast cheated me; therefore I take all this (from thee)." Atyarâti, after having been thus deprived of his powers and majesty, was slain by the victorious king *Śuṣmiṇa*, [**528**] the son of *Śibya*. Thence a Kṣattriya should not cheat a Brahman who has this knowledge and performed this (inauguration) ceremony, unless he wishes to be turned out of his dominions, and to lose his life.

FIFTH CHAPTER.

(On the Office of the Purohita, or House-priest. The Brahmaṇaḥ Parimara, i. e., Dying Around the Brahma.)

24.

(The Necessity for a King to Appoint a House-priest. In what Way the King Keeps the Sacred Fires. How to Appease the Five Destructive Powers of Agni).

Now, about the office of a Purohita (house-priest). The gods do not eat the food offered by a king who has no house-priest (Purohita). Thence the king even when (not) intending to bring a sacrifice, should appoint a Brahman to the office of house-priest.

The king who (wishes) that the gods might eat his food, has, after having appointed a Purohita, however, the use of the (sacred) fires (without having actually established them) which lead to heaven; for the Purohita is his Ahavanîya fire, his wife the Gârhapatya, and his son the

---

[11] In the north of the Himalaya.—*Sây.*

Dakṣiṇa fire. When he does (anything) for the Purohita, then he sacrifices in the Ahavanîya fire (for the Purohita represents this fire). When he does (anything) for his wife, then he verily sacrifices in the Gârhapatya fire. When he does (anything) for his son, then he verily sacrifices in the Dakṣiṇa fire. These fires (which are led by the Purohita) which are thus freed from their destructive power[1] (for the Kṣattriya, *i.e.*, **[529]** they do not burn him), carry, pleased by the wish for sacrificing,[2] the Kṣattriya to the heaven-world, and (make him obtain) the royal dignity, bravery, a kingdom, and subjects to rule over. But, if the Kṣattriya has no wish for sacrificing (by not appointing a Purohita), then the fires get displeased with him, and being not freed from their destructive power, throw him out of the heaven-world (and deprive him) of the royal dignity, bravery, his kingdom, and subjects over whom he rules.

This Agni Vaiśvanara, which is the Purohita, is possessed of five destructive powers;[3] one of them is in his speech, one in his feet, onein his skin, one in his heart, and one in the organ of generation. With these (five) powers, which are burning and blazing, he (Agni) attacks the king.

By saying, "Where,[4] O master, hast thou been residing (for so long a time)? Servants, bring (kuśa) grass for him," the king propitiates the destructive power which is in Agni's speech. When they bring water for washing the feet, then the king propitiates the destructive power which is in Agni's feet. When they adorn him, then he propitiates by it the destructive power which is in Agni's skin. When they satiate him (with food), then the king propitiates the destructive power which is in Agni's heart. When Agni lives unrestrained (at ease) in the king's premises, then he propitiates the destructive power which is in Agni's organ of generation. Agni, then, if all the destructive powers which are in his body have been propitiated, and he is pleased by the king's wish **[530]** for sacrificing, conveys him to the heaven-worlds and (grants him) royal dignity, bravery, a kingdom, and subjects over whom he might rule. But should the king not do so, he will be deprived of all these gifts.

25.

(*Agni Protects the King who Appoints a House-priest.*)

This Agni Vaiśvânara, who is the Purohita, is possessed of five destructive powers. With them he surrounds the king (for his defence), just

---

[1] Literally, the bodies of which are appeased.

[2] The king manifests his wish by appointing a Purohita.

[3] They are called *meni*. Sây. explains *paropadravakârinî krodharûpâ śaktir*.

Agni, or his representative, the Purohita, is here treated as a guest.

as the sea surrounds the earth. The empire of such a ruler (*ârya*) will be safe. Neither will he die before the expiration of the full life term (100 years); but live up to his old age, and enjoy the full term apportioned for his life. Nor will he die again (for he is free from being born again as a mortal), if he has a Brâhmaṇa who possesses such a knowledge as his Purohita, and guardian of his empire; for he obtains by means (of his own) royal dignity that (for another, his son), and by means of his bravery that (of another). The subjects of such a king obey him unanimously and undivided.

26.

(The Importance of the Office of a Purohita Proved from Three Verses of a Vedic Hymn).

To this power of the Purohita, a Riṣı alludes in the the followıng verses: *sa id râjâ pratijanyâni*, &c. (4, 50, 7), *i.e.*, the king defeated by his prowess and bravery all his adversaries. By *janyâni* are enemies and adversaries to be understood; he conquers them by means of his prowess and bravery. (The other half of this verse is as follows) *Biṛhaspatim yaḥ subhṛitam bibharti, i. e.*, "who (the king) supports Bṛihaspati who is well to be supported." For Bṛihaspati is the **[531]** Purohita of the gods and him follow the Purohitas of the human kings. The words, "who supports Bṛihaspati who is well to be supported," therefore mean, who (what king) supports the Purohita who is well to be supported. By the words (the last quarter of the verse above mentioned) *valgûyati vandate pûrvabhajam, i.e.*, he honours and salutes him who has the precedence of enjoyment (*i.e.*, the Purohita), he recommends his (the Purohita's) distinction.

(In the first half of the following verse), *sa ît kṣetti sudhita okasi sve* (4, 50, 8), the idea is expressed, that he (the Purohita) lives in his own premises; the word *okas* means *griha, i. e.*, house, and the word *sudhita* is the same as *suhita, i e.*, well-disposed, pleased. (The second half of the verse) *tasmâ iḷâ pinvate viśvadânîm, i. e.*, food grows for him (the king who keeps a Purohita) at all times. *Iḷâ* here means *anna, i.e.*, food; such one (such a king) is always possessed of essential juice (for keeping the life again); his subjects bow before him. The subjects (the tribes) form kingdoms; kingdoms by themselves bow before such a king who is preceded (*pûrva eti*) by a Brahma. Thus one calls him (such a Brâhmaṇa) a Purohita.

(The first quarter of the third verse 4, 50, 9 is as follows) *apratîto jayati saṁ dhanâni, i. e.*, he (such a king) conquers realms without being opposed by enemies. By *dhanâni* kingdoms are to be understood; he conquers them without meeting any opposition. The second quarter of the verse is as follows) *prati janyáni uta yâ sajanyâ*. By *janyâni* are enemies and adversaries to be understood; he conquers them without meeting any opposition. (In the third quarter) *avasyave yo varivaḥ karoti*, there is said, "who (what king) not being possessed of any wealth renders service (*varivaḥ*) to a very indigent (Purohita)." (In the last quarter of the verse) *brahmaṇe râjâ tam avanti devâḥ, i.e.*, "if the king is **[532]** for the Brahman (if he support him), then the gods protect him (the king)" he speaks about the Purohita.

27.

The Three Divine Purohitas. Who is Fit for the Office of a Purohita. By Repeating of What Mantra and Performance, of What Ceremony the King has to Engage him.)

The Brahman who knows the (following) three (divine) Purohitas, as well as the three appointers to this office, should be nominated to such a post. Agni is one of these (three) Purohitas; his appointer is the earth; the (other) Purohita is Vâyu, his appointer is the air; the (third) Purohita is Âditya, his appointer is the sky. Who knows this is (fit for the office of a) Purohita; but he who does not know it, is unworthy of holding such an office.

That king who appoints a Brâhmaṇa who has this knowledge to be his Purohita and protector of his kingdom, succeeds in making (another) king his friend, and conquers his enemy. The king who does so, obtains by means of (his own) royal dignity that (for another), and by means of (his) bravery that for another (*i. e.*, he defeats him). The subjects of such a king obey him unanimously and undivided.

(*Now Follows the Mantra for Appointing the Purohita*).

"*Bhûr, Bhuvaḥ, Svar, Om!* I am that one, thou art this one; thou art this one, I am that one; I am heaven, thou art the earth; I am the Sâman, thou art the Rik. Let us both find here our livelihood (support). Save us from great danger (just as was done) in former times; thou art (my) body, protect mine. All ye many herbs, of a hundred kinds, over which the king Soma rules, grant me (sitting) on this seat, uninterrupted hapiness. All ye herbs ruled by **[533]** Soma the king, which are spread over the earth, grant me (sitting) on this seat, uninterrupted hapiness. I cause to sit in the kingdom this goddess of fortune. Thence I look upon